Textile League Baseball

Textile League Baseball

Baseball

South Carolina's Mill Teams,
1880–1955

by
THOMAS K. PERRY

McFarland & Company, Inc., Publishers
Jefferson, North Carolina, and London

The present work is a reprint of the library bound edition of
Textile League Baseball: South Carolina's Mill Teams,
1880–1955, first published in 1993 by McFarland.

LIBRARY OF CONGRESS CATALOGUING-IN-PUBLICATION DATA

Perry, Thomas K., 1952–
  Textile league baseball : South Carolina's mill teams,
1880–1955 / by Thomas K. Perry.
    p.   cm.
  Includes bibliographical references and index.

  ISBN-13: 978-0-7864-1875-6
  (softcover : 50# alkaline paper) ∞

  1. Baseball—South Carolina—History. I. Title.
GV863.S6P47   2004
796.357'64'09757—dc20   92-56680

British Library cataloguing data are available

Cover photograph: The 1904 Monaghan Mill team
(Greenville Public Library)

Manufactured in the United States of America

McFarland & Company, Inc., Publishers
  Box 611, Jefferson, North Carolina 28640
   www.mcfarlandpub.com

To those who played

Table of Contents

Acknowledgments

Throughout the ten years encompassing this textile baseball research, players, players' families, and fans have graciously shared their stories with me. They all understood, as I did, that those of us raised on the "mill hill" shared a special heritage, and a large portion of that heritage was tied to baseball.

Folks wrote letters, placed telephone calls, spoke with me at old timers' reunions, and agreed to interviews, making certain that a composite snapshot of our grand old game would emerge. To each of you who shared such wonderful memories, I owe a special measure of gratitude.

Many friends gave unselfishly of their technical expertise. Bill Cunningham offered advice on the intricacies of WordPerfect, and also proofread the manuscript. Beth Bernhardt, of the Newberry College Library, patiently filled every request for microfilm, and made certain that I was never delayed in my research. Jesse Scott, professor of history at Newberry College, directed students Jeff Duncan and Scott Robinson in an independent study which furthered this research. Dick Shelton and Tommy Gortney, of Piedmont Technical College, helped develop the photos of the old teams.

Mac Kirkpatrick was not only a principal researcher in this project during the last three years, but also a good friend who proofread, served as a sounding board, and helped to keep everything in perspective when things got tough. And most of all, to my wife and daughter who rewrote the parameters for long suffering and patience, this book is for you.

Preface

Treasure hunting, that's really what it was about. Discovering — through ten years of research and writing, the precious glistening gems of stories, anecdotes, names and photographs which would validate all that textile baseball meant — was the only directive to be fulfilled.

Like treasure hunting, the search for information meant, more often than not, sifting through stacks of paper and microfilm to gather for the first time the history of baseball on the mill hills of South Carolina. Though the leagues had died in the mid- to late-1950s, folks held tightly to their memories and, like my family, passed them down at homecomings and reunions. With hundreds of teams and thousands of players, the question became how to include as many of the former participants as possible without creating a statistical monstrosity. So was born the idea of the "Records and Rosters" portion of this book.

With the help of Mac Kirkpatrick, trusted friend and researcher, I first concentrated on finding the truly unique games during the long history of mill ball. This factual material was available only in the microfilmed records of the upstate area's newspapers. With tedious exactness, we moved through the reels: 1900–1955 in the Greenville *News;* 1906–1955 in the Spartanburg *Herald;* 1929–1955 in the Anderson *Independent;* 1880–1916 in the Anderson *Intelligencer;* 1897–1915 in the Greenwood *Index;* 1895–1915 in the Greenwood *Journal;* and 1886–1925 in the Newberry *Observer.*

Not only did truly unusual and heroic accounts of the games emerge, but we were able to construct representative rosters of the teams which made textile baseball history from 1880 to 1955. Granted, many times the lineups revealed only the last names of the players, with sportswriters usually including these in their game summaries. Yet, there would be those glorious occasions when a first name, an initial, or a nickname would find its way into print. Double and triple checking the microfilm, we studied, culled, and catalogued.

Paralleling this research of secondary sources was the search for the players and fans who had been eyewitnesses to the mill hill excitement. Their stories — from Ed Brinson to Powerhouse Hawkins to Earl Wooten, all of whom you will meet a little later — were the centerpieces. These also yielded other previously unknown first names and initials.

Filling in some of the gaps came easily as more than two hundred people sat with us and shared their reminiscences. Hundreds of others heard, either by word of mouth or through my letter-to-the-editor campaign in almost every community newspaper in upstate South Carolina, and wrote to share what they had personally experienced or had been told by family members who were players and fans.

As the gaps were filled, the old warriors were given distinct identity. Many of the old photos that folks shared, which you will soon enjoy in these pages, had lineups scripted in fading ink or pencil on the back. With the use of a magnifying glass, a few more elusive appellations revealed themselves and were gathered. After all the interviews, letters, scrapbooks, photos, microfilm, and any other conceivably helpful piece of paper had been examined, the characters who shaped this upstate way of life were assembled.

Were all the names gathered? Did all the players escape anonymity? Both questions would have to be answered negatively, but such a lack is an inherent danger when the efforts at preservation begin more than 40 years after the end of an era. Though it was a way of life for three-quarters of a century, many games and titles and accomplishments have been long forgotten. What I do believe is that we "lintheads" now have a solid record, more than 90 percent complete, of our beloved mill hill baseball.

All the sharing, the believing, the encouragement through the ten years of this project saw to it that the legacy was preserved as completely as possible. The memories and the facts came together to form this effort at honoring those who played the game.

And it was our game, our wins and our losses. I hope the contents of the following pages are worthy recollections of that burning passion we all knew as textile league baseball.

Thomas K. Perry
Newberry, South Carolina
October 1992

Chapter 1

Beginnings

After the Civil War, the textile industry of the North began a sure migration into the southern states. Cheap land, the availability of swift rivers to generate power for the cotton mills, and cheaper labor were advantages that industrialists could not overlook.

Equipped by the machine shops of New England, both steam- and water-powered cotton mills flourished. The southern industry rivaled, for a while, its northern counterpart, and then surpassed it completely. Mill owners in both regions coped with the uncertainties of an evolving industrial climate, and while no single southern asset was individually decisive, the combination of advantages made the region irresistible.[1]

Hands for the cotton mills were attracted mostly from surrounding farms and rural crossroads communities. Many southerners, accustomed to the up-and-down existence of this agricultural economy and loving the freedom of the outdoors, still chose the mills as a place of steady employment. Suddenly they were placed indoors where the air was filled with lint and the noise was deafening. The factory whistle blew at 4:15 A.M. and the people readied themselves for a 6:00 A.M. starting time. It was the same every day, 6:00 A.M. to 6:00 P.M., day in and day out, 64 hours a week.

Locating the new cotton mills close to a source of water power meant that the towns were usually some distance away, so the southern owners adopted the long established custom of their northern business counterparts and developed a complete village system for the housing and accommodation of employees. Churches, schools, and the oft-despised company store were familiar sights. Ellison Smyth, for example, patterned the life of his new mill at Pelzer, South Carolina, after such establishments in Rhode Island and Massachusetts.

The mill village concept has been described as industrial totalitarianism at worst and paternalistic benevolence at best. Social workers saw squalid conditions, child labor, and shortages of meager necessities in almost every household. Mill owners and presidents pointed to improved conditions over the poor agrarian society of the post–Civil War South, and maintained that their workers were members of one big family. Like most absolutes, neither side was wholly the possessor of the truth.

Certainly there were dictatorial mill owners, whose demands for

1

profit *were* absolute, and who exploited any asset (including the workers) to maximize the return on their investment. There were also men who saw themselves as strong benefactors who could provide the necessities (and even occasional niceties) of life to people who, in all likelihood on the farms, had known neither. A classic example of the self-contained community, and at one time one of the largest textile concerns in the world, the Pelzer Manufacturing Company offers a portrait of the fabric of life within the mill village.

Chosen in 1881 by Captain Ellison Smyth (with his partners Francis J. Pelzer and William Lebby) because of its proximity to a branch of the Southern Railway and to the Saluda River, the site grew from three log cabins and 20 people to an astounding 700 dwellings and 4,000 people (2,800 employees) by 1895. There was no sewage system (except for the privy) and the water system consisted of wells. In swift succession, Mill One was completed in 1883, Mill Two in 1887, and Mill Three in 1890. Interconnected, these three became known as the Lower Plant, housing 52,000 spindles and 1,600 looms. Mill Four, the Upper Plant, was built in 1895 and began operation with 55,000 spindles and 1,600 looms.

A number of manufacturing innovations were associated with Smyth's enterprise. The first incandescent lighting system ever installed in a cotton mill was at Pelzer, greatly reducing the threat of fire that plagued earlier mills; original lighting had been supplied by kerosene lamps. The first 1,000 Draper automatic looms ever sold were installed in Mill One. The Lower Dam was the first built solely for the purpose of generating electricity to be used for manufacturing, and when electric turbines were installed in 1895, the company became the first to convey electric power from a distance for running a textile plant. Power was provided for the village dwellings as well.

Dissatisfied workers often wandered from place to place in search of a better life, either back to the farms or on to another cotton mill. Holding a trained and stable workforce became a unique problem for the owners, one demanding a quick and lasting solution. The Captain chose his answer well, and the village he founded was perhaps the most elaborate example of the paternalistic benevolence of earlier industrialism.

Smyth understood that the lives of Pelzer employees fell into the hands of his modern textile concern and sought to do what was possible (consistent with the preservation of profits) to provide an enlightened social atmosphere. If people chose to work at Pelzer, they signed an agreement listing the terms of employment. It is interesting that the first clause of this contract addressed education and mandated:

> That all children, members of my family, between the ages of five and twelve years, shall enter the school maintained by said company at

Pelzer, and shall attend every school day during the school session, unless prevented by sickness or other unavoidable causes.[2]

The second clause required all children over the age of 12 to take a job in the mill unless excused by the superintendent. An employee could be dismissed from the mill, and a family evicted from the village, for violating either of these rules.[3] Unfortunately, these two major clauses of the employment agreement often conflicted. The lax enforcement of the first (with the resulting strengthening of the second) showed a gap between Smyth's belief in providing an opportunity for advancement of mill children, and the execution of that policy by men whose livelihood depended on the profit margin.[4]

The first school was built in 1882, a second was added in 1896, and the first kindergarten in Anderson County began in 1899. Three years later, Pelzer was the only community in South Carolina to have compulsory education (ten months per year rather than the normal three months for the rest of the state). It was estimated that illiteracy fell from 75% of the adult population at the mill's inception to 20% in 1902. A lyceum was built, housing a well lighted library of five thousand volumes and an excellent reading room with subscriptions to twenty-five newspapers and magazines. The lyceum, night school, and lectures were made available after working hours.

Smyth, to his credit, made an effort to understand the problems of his workers. When the economy tightened early in the spring of 1917, he suspended rent payments at both his Pelzer and Belton, South Carolina, operations to help the village residents cut the high cost of living. Combined with their vegetable gardens, this was a mutual effort to make it through a tougher than usual year.

Much was done to provide recreational opportunities and family entertainment for the employees of the mill. Among the offerings were an opera house hosting plays and concerts, a roller skating rink, a pavilion for dancing, an outdoor swimming pool, a "Wheel Club" for bicycle enthusiasts, a park with benches and summer houses, an aviary, a menagerie (with badgers, deer, monkeys and brown bears), a brass band, and a military company known as the Smyth Rifles.

All of the amenities were provided for the employees and their families, but it was abundantly clear that everything belonged to the company. There was no concept of private property, though residents could rent houses for fifty cents per room per month, and they were free to cultivate a small plot of ground for growing needed vegetables. Even a few chickens or a cow could be kept. The Captain, though, was adamantly opposed to dogs, noting "the fact that dogs are in ninety nine cases out of one hundred worthless and troublesome property has been fully established."[5]

There were no municipal elections, since that would interfere with the control of the company. The bailiff was a mill employee appointed by the governor, so law and order were in corporate hands as well. No disreputable characters were tolerated or allowed to dwell within the settlement, and the company determined who fit the definition. Churches were largely supported by contributions from the mill, and ministers often echoed sentiments of management. The first sermon in Pelzer, given by the Reverend C.L. Stewart, used as a text "Stand fast in one spirit, with one mind, striving together...." The intent of the words was not wasted on either the operatives or their bosses.

Smyth disapproved of the "company store" concept, choosing to pay his employees in cash, but the retail stores in the village community paid rent to him. He also served as president of the oil mill, mattress factory, and bank, the only other business concerns in Pelzer.

The rural farmers and their families lost a great deal as they sacrificed their independence to work in the mill. What they found in exchange was a steady wage and, in many instances, decidedly better circumstances than those from which they came. But to prove the mill village system inherently good or evil was an exercise in futility. Hundreds of villages existed throughout upstate South Carolina and into neighboring North Carolina and Georgia, each with its own individual good and bad points. The simple words of one mill operative best summed up a way of life born of economic necessity but sustained solely by the spirit of its citizens:

> I knew practically all of them (village residents) from a kid up. It was kind of a cliché: You grew up here and you knew everybody. It had its good and bad points; we didn't make too much money, I know my father didn't. But like I said, it was kind of one big family, and we all hung together and survived...Everybody on this hill, we looked after one another.[6]

Whether North or South, it was a hard life for the mill operatives, softened only by precious moments of recreation, and those were usually confined to Saturday afternoons and Sundays. That interesting new game, base ball (it was two words until the 1920s), became the pride and passion of the "lintheads." Legend says the game migrated south during the Civil War, when captured Union soldiers introduced it to their Confederate captors, who proved insatiable students.

Even though the mill people shared the same profession, fierce competition developed. The Amoskeag Manufacturing Company of Manchester, New Hampshire, maintained a Textile Club to sponsor social events, correspondence courses and classes promoting domestic skills. Most important, the club also cared for the newly built ball field, where capacity crowds observed company sponsored athletics.[7]

For the workers of Grosvenordale Mill in Connecticut, sports and outings afforded interaction among diverse immigrant groups.[8] The operatives in the mills of Lawrence, Massachusetts and the surrounding Merrimack Valley embraced cricket and baseball, respective symbols of the old world and the new, as their most popular sports.[9]

And in Pelzer, the preoccupation was duly noted as well:

> Attention is directed to the training of the body also in the provision of opportunities for wholesome forms of athletic exercises and recreation. A base ball field is found on the edge of the settlement, and base ball seems to be the favorite sport.[10]

Young men played on, honing their skills. The mill operatives watched from the sidelines or the grandstands on warm Saturday afternoons, sipping ice water or, if an extra nickel could be had, a Coca-Cola. They became the mill's boys of summer, whose exploits on rough fields of baked clay waxed legendary when passed from father to son.

Chapter 2

Fun and Games

Baseball quickly became an integral part of the village life, with the ball clubs getting started almost as soon as the big machines in the mills started humming. "Cow pasture ball" was fun for the farm youths who came to the mills, but there was no effort made to go by the rules. Systematic recreation, and baseball was certainly that, meant a clear distinction between winners and losers, something that games on the farms seldom did. Rules demanded bending to authority, and young boys learned the importance of striving for both good performances and the necessary self-control. It was preparation for the discipline and close attention to detail required in their manufacturing jobs.[1]

The game provided recreation, competition, and community pride for players and spectators alike. Nowhere was the level of skill and intensity to win greater than in midland and upstate South Carolina. Big, strapping country boys, who swapped open fields for a steady wage, regained a measure of freedom with their exploits on the diamond. They were eager to join the mill team and participate in the textile leagues. Scheduled games gave players time away from work and, just as importantly, gave neighbors an opportunity to visit. Such events even provided young folks, with stars in their eyes and love in their hearts, a place to court.[2] Winning programs provided tremendous boosts to employee morale, a major productivity tool deftly used by the new mill owners.

The small towns and villages of South Carolina and the rest of the country heartily embraced this new pastime. It is believed that one of the earliest games was played in Cokesbury, near Greenwood, in 1873. A Prosperity club, near Newberry, was organized the following year.

By the 1880s, the mill villages and nearby towns were enthusiastically supporting their teams. Belton played regularly scheduled games with Anderson, Honea Path, Due West, Piedmont, Pelzer, Williamston and Calhoun Falls. Anderson Cotton Mill and Newberry Cotton Mill met in a contest at New Brooklyn (near Spartanburg) on September 4, 1895, with Anderson winning 2–1 in a game called after five innings by agreement. The premier event in the summer of 1886 was a tournament arranged by the people of Greenville and Honea Path. It included teams from those respective towns, Greenwood, Laurens and Columbia. Though the hometown Honea Path boys played well, they finished second to the powerful Columbia club.

Most of the attention given to amateur baseball in South Carolina focused upon teams sponsored by the towns and crossroad communities rather than by the mills. By 1893, teams from such locations as Beth Eden, Monticello, Cannon's Creek, Prosperity, Jalapa, Newberry, Newberry College, Clinton, Whitmire, Stony Battery, Laurens, Union, Honea Path, Helena, Spartanburg, Chappells, Higgins Ferry and Abbeville regularly competed against one another. And as early as 1896, professional batteries (pitcher and catcher) were used by local teams; both Newberry and Prosperity employed such players for a game on June 17th. The Greenville area added teams such as Yorkville, Piedmont, Anderson, Greenwood, Ninety Six, Blacksburg, Pelham, Pelzer and Belton.

Occasionally, some newspaper might suggest combining the local town and mill teams to form one powerful unit. On September 4, 1901, Newberry and Newberry Mill (West End) did just that, pounding Clinton 11-4. A sportswriter duly noted that, "With the combination of the two teams, we feel safe in saying that no amateur team in the state can lick them."[3] Such unions were not widespread, however, and the mill village folks were left to themselves by the local citizenry.

There was little socializing between the "lintheads" and the "townies" during the textile boom in the latter years of the nineteenth and the first few years of the twentieth centuries. Correspondingly, little attention was paid to the mill baseball teams and players. It took a performance like that of Newberry's Carlton Beusse on June 18, 1900, to gain a bit of attention. Slamming three consecutive home runs in three consecutive innings, Beusse led his team to a 7-4 upset of the powerful Piedmont club, captained by Champ Osteen. In fact, newspaper accounts in these early years were devoted almost exclusively to "town ball." But all that changed during one glorious day each year, because when it came to sponsoring celebrations on the Fourth of July, mill owners and their operatives did not take a back seat to anyone. Newspapers were filled with accounts of the day's festivities. In 1901, Pelzer Mill sponsored bag races, bicycle races, a mile run, a Shetland pony race, clay pigeon shooting, a farmers' hitch up-get ready-go race, and a 21-gun salute from cannons furnished by the city of Greenville. And yes, there was a baseball game, with Pelzer defeating arch rival Piedmont 6-3 that afternoon.

The next year 735 folks from Newberry Mill filled up 17 passenger coaches on the Southern Railroad Line for a trip to Columbia. They didn't want to miss a chance to see their boys meet a team composed of players from Olympia-Granby-Richland mills. In the first two games of the three game series the teams split the contests held on Thursday (July 3rd) and Friday (July 4th). Saturday's hard fought game was called after

11 innings due to darkness, with the score tied 5–5. There was no mention of fan reaction during the long return trip from Columbia's Hyatt Park.

While the tightly organized affairs encompassed the whole day, the featured events were the doubleheader games between traditional rivals. In 1907, Newberry Mill added a concert by the West End Band to begin the celebration. Amid all the sprints and hurdle races, the first ballgame with Clinton Mill began at 10:00 A.M. After a barbecue dinner, and adequate time to recover from the ritual of "stuffing oneself 'til sick," after more races and a second concert were completed, the teams squared away again at 4:00 P.M. Newberry swept both ends of the doubleheader that year, 12–0 and 9–1.

Parades and oratorical contests eventually became a part of the Independence Day festivities, and there was truly something for everyone. These were great occasions, very well attended, as evidenced by the 4,000 fans who saw Pelzer edge Piedmont 3–1 in 1915. More than anything else, the Fourth of July games formed the base of popularity that textile baseball would enjoy in the coming years.

At other times, specialty games were organized. These were not the exclusive property of the cotton mills, however. The Greenville *Mountaineer and Enterprise* mentioned that "One of the advertised sensational novelties in this conservative section of our country is that of a match game of base ball between a young ladies' club and the Greenville club."[4] Sadly, the outcome of the game was not reported.

Though not as popular as the Fourth of July contests, such tests of skill did serve to keep the mill teams in the news. One of the most interesting of these involved a game in Biddeford, Maine. Young men from South Carolina were sent by the mill owners to learn the machinist's trade in the Saco and Platt cotton mills, but they found time on Saturday afternoons to organize a baseball team and take on all comers. The local citizens noted, "The team cleans up everything that goes against them, and the Southerners are a heady lot of ballplayers."[5]

The occasions for such games were widely varied, and the local press often noted such contests with lavish write-ups. On July 22, 1901, at a lawn party of the Ladies' Aid Society, the boss men (superintendents) of Piedmont Mill played the second hands (supervisors). The result was a truly remarkable score of 117–114 in favor of the bosses. Colonel Orr, one of the founding fathers of Southern textiles (and who gave his name to the mill in Anderson), played in the game, as did Dave Tice, a former pitcher in the Southern League and a member of the slick Piedmont Mill team of 1898–1899.

The local Cotton Men of Greenville defeated the Pythian team on May 27, 1903, in "a game all in fun." The Greenville Uptown Clerks bound together to defeat the Hugenot Mill team 4–3 on the Furman

The 1904 Monaghan Mill (Greenville, SC) team. *Photo courtesy of Greenville Public Library.*

College campus June 17, 1903. Boss men from Poe Mill played their counterparts from American Spinning (Sampson Mill) on July 4, 1907, winning 20–19 in six innings.

The most interesting of these specialty games involved teams of American Indians. Two took place in June of 1904. The Carlisle, Minnesota, team, represented by six full-blooded Native Americans and three white players, traveled from their home state for games with Piedmont Mill and the Greenville town team. Piedmont took a 3–1 win on the June 18th as Laval, the mill's pitcher, had the visitors guessing at his offerings and the large contingent of home folks roaring with approval. The victory march, though, was of short duration.

Moving to Greenville for a doubleheader on June 20th, the Carlisle team, behind the fine play of Coates and Weaver, took a ten inning 11–10 thriller. In the losing cause Hugenot Mill's Hughes hit four home runs. The second game, though, probably represented the first game in South Carolina played under the glare of electric lights. The local boys were not able to see the ball, and the Carlisle team, who traveled with the lights, seats, and tent enclosures and were used to night baseball, won handily. The score was so onesided that no one remembered to count.

On April 17, 1911, a Cherokee Indian club played and defeated Seneca 5–4; they were led by the fine play of Brown Bear and Bear Chief. Three days later the same team, sporting a lineup that also included Tall

The 1915 Inman Mill team. *Front row (l-r):* **Monroe Teague, Jennings Waldrop, Alex Cothran, Bass Waters, Bill Gowan.** *Back row (l-r):* **Luther Mabry, Bob Nichols, Earl Buice (manager), Johnny Lawrence, Ellard Nix, Grady Stone.** *Photo courtesy of Jim Everhart.*

Chief and Tooshkenig, defeated Greenville's Carolina Association team 7–1 in what was called an exciting game.

At the Woodside YMCA there was an indoor baseball game April 11, 1912. More than 200 fans watched the Monaghan Mill (Greenville) Scout Troop defeat their rivals from Mills Mill (Greenville) 3–2 on August 1, 1914. And on August 22nd, Pendleton Street Baptist Church Sunday School lost to the team from Reedy River Mill 4–1.

Not to be outdone, Tucapau Mill defeated the Spartanburg team of the Carolina Association 2–0 on May 18, 1907, a nearly unimaginable defeat for the fans of a legitimate team to swallow. Tucapau also played the Chicago Bloomer Girls, starring the famous lady pitcher Maude Nelson, May 12, 1910, but no score was given. And sometimes the mill operatives got a chance to go against their bosses, as the Inman Mill Hornets (bosses) defeated the Inman Mill Tigers (operatives) 17–14 August 21, 1915.

Baseball yielded itself to the social controversies raging around the mill village way of life. Many writers chronicled this self-contained system in the early part of the twentieth century, either supporting management or condemning such paternalistic and exploitative ventures. Regardless of their leanings, such writings leave us with a great many facts concerning textile baseball.

August Kohn found from a survey that only one cotton mill was without a ballpark, noting that the "base ball fever extends from the mill president to the janitor, and the community that did not have its bunch of fans was indeed a rarity."[6]

W.H. Simpson noted that the athletic program was generally the most developed of all the activities offered by the mills. Most of the facilities in his study had baseball fields and some were even lighted for night play (one can only imagine the quality of the lighting). Well constructed grandstands were common and many of the diamonds were kept in splendid condition. There were intermill leagues, interdepartmental games at individual mills, and even leagues with teams representing different industrial groups and communities. Like Kohn, Simpson agreed that the games were well attended by ardent fans who cheered their teams to victory. Sometimes it was unsafe for a citizen of one mill village to venture into another, so heated were the rivalries.[7]

A.S. Rowell, editor of the *Mountaineer and Enterprise,* admonished local players and fans to compete in the best of sportsmanship, noting that baseball was a fine sport when kept in proper bounds. Frequently, "improper bounds" were introduced, and the game degenerated into a loudmouthed brawl populated by unseemly characters. He believed that a game played with the mouth, by disgusting and disreputable individuals rather than by mannerly men who could skillfully manipulate the ball, was of no enjoyment to anyone.[8]

Before the child labor laws were passed, Marjorie Potwin chronicled the often grim story of the sons and daughters of mill operatives working side by side with their parents during the arduous 64 hour weeks. Shut away from the outdoors, the children's collective imaginations provided a blessed diversion. A ball of tightly wound yarn and a pilfered picker stick from the weave room made for a few innings of an improvisational game in the alleys between the looms and spinning frames.[9]

In Newberry, the concern for social matters prompted the Reverend W.L. Seabrook of the Lutheran Church of the Redeemer to preach a sermon entitled "Baseball and Public Morals." The good reverend did not condemn baseball, calling it a good game, healthful in mind and body to college students. He did, however, speak against professionalism and the related custom of betting.[10] Paying players was indeed a part of textile baseball and betting on games would haunt more than a few players during their careers.

Still, for all practical purposes, there was little credence given to textile baseball except by those citizens of the mill hill. The Fourth of July celebrations offered baseball basically as a sidelight, and the specialty games strengthened the view of most people that such a sport was a good diversion now and then, a source of entertainment and nothing more. All that changed with the coming of a kid from Piedmont they called Champ.

Chapter 3

Champ Osteen

From such humble beginnings heroes emerged, and in each generation there were men whose abilities lifted them above the status of mere mortals. The ball park was the center of their activities. Players often took the time to help youngsters develop their skills, passing on an appreciation for the greatest game in the world. Champ Osteen, playing with the mill team from Piedmont, was the first great star of the mill leagues. From 1898 to 1900 he was a steadying force, playing either first base or shortstop for a team labeled "Champions of South Carolina"; in 1899 Piedmont posted a 19-6 record. Osteen made quite a name for himself, and it was often said that he made more money playing ball around the mill villages ($40 a month plus room and board while at Piedmont) than the governor of the state made doing whatever it was politicians did.

The team played in an independent league which included Union, Pelzer, Anderson, Greenwood, Abbeville and Asheville (NC). It was a powerful bunch managed by Will Hammett, with a line-up including Champ (1b), Davey Crockett (2b), Jack Frost (ss), Pat Callahan (3b), Sug Morris (lf), Bob Poole (cf), Luke Chandler (rf), and Victor Ackersino (c). Harry Cooper, M.M. Marsh, Walter Harrison and Claude Iler also made appearances. The pitching staff boasted lefty Rome Chambers and righties Arthur Smith and Dave Tice (remembered as the first in the area to throw a curve ball). Morris, Frost, Ackersino and Tice all played in the high minor leagues; Osteen, Crockett, and Chambers made it to the majors.

A three game series was arranged between that 1899 championship team and Augusta (GA) of the Southern League. There was tremendous fanfare and heavy betting, though the players did not indulge. Folks from Greenville got several thousand dollars together and sent representatives to Augusta to place their wagers. Most chose to do so in local taverns, feigning a good drunk, boasting loudly of the mill boys' prowess, and luring heavy bets into the hat.

It was a memorable series for the team from the small mill town. Arthur Smith pitched a gem of a first game, winning 3-1 as Osteen homered. Manager Will Hammett sent a wire from Augusta to Piedmont to notify Champ's father, "Uncle Dick, keep your eyes open. Champ hit a ball in that direction!" They continued their winning ways in the second game with a 12–4 victory, and won the third game for a complete sweep. The Augusta gamblers had been picked clean.

Champ was the undisputed star of the team, and in 1901 embarked on an odyssey that kept him away from home for quite a while. The first stop was Wilmington (NC) in the Virginia–North Carolina League, where he misjudged a fly ball and went hitless in his first game. Newport News (VA) manager Ed Ashenback, though, liked what he saw of Osteen in batting practice and arranged for a trade. So quickly was the transaction made that Champ and the other player went under the grandstand and exchanged uniforms. The day after the trade, he was at shortstop ("I can play anywhere in the infield," he was fond of saying) and went four for four. He wound up leading the league for the season with a .420 batting average.

His trek through organized baseball continued for more than a quarter of a century, and the list read like a man possessed of *wanderlust*: 1901, Newport News (VA) and Wilmington (DE); 1902, Charlotte (NC) and Shreveport (LA); 1903, Shreveport (LA), Birmingham (AL), Worcester (MA), Davenport (IA), Washington Senators, Atlanta (GA); 1904, New York Highlanders; 1905, Indianapolis (IN); 1906, coach for Furman College (Greenville, SC), Springfield (OH); 1907, Springfield (OH), Chicago White Sox; 1908–09, St. Louis Cardinals; 1911–1912, manager Dallas (TX); 1912–1913, manager Charlotte (NC); 1914, manager Columbia (SC), Montgomery (AL), Durham (NC); Chattanooga (TN); 1915, Chattanooga (TN), Columbia (SC); 1916, coach for Furman College (Greenville, SC); 1917, coach for Erskine College (Due West, SC); 1918, coach for Harmer Academy (Oxford, NC); 1919–1926, umpired in textile leagues, Florida State League, South Atlantic League, and Western Carolina Professional League.

It was his years in the major leagues, though, that meant the most. Champ was with Clark Griffith's Washington Senators in 1903 and was teammates with the likes of fiery "Tabasco Kid" Elberfield. In 1904 he was traded to the New York Highlanders (later the Yankees). While there he experienced one of his most disappointing moments as a ballplayer. The Highlanders lost a chance at the pennant in the last game of the season when pitching great Jack Chesbro uncorked a wild pitch in the seventh inning against the Boston club. The 2–1 New York lead evaporated as the runners on second and third scored. Osteen vividly remembered he and his mates crying like babies after the game, knowing that their chance at glory had slipped away. He moved back into the minors the next year, and then finished up his big league career with the St. Louis Cardinals in 1908–09.

While with the Highlanders, he notified his manager that come the Fourth of July, he would be taking off a few days to return to South

Carolina. When asked why, he answered simply, "Piedmont is playing Pelzer, and I'm needed." One's loyalty was never questioned when such bitter rivals met on the field, especially on days so dusty and hot that the crowd of five to ten thousand fans would pay ten cents a glass for sparkling spring water.

After his days in baseball, Osteen worked for the city of Greenville as a blacksmith and served as assistant jailer at the stockade on Hudson Street. In the glow of the furnace, he reminisced about his playing days and noted that it was a game where no quarter was asked nor given, where sharp spikes, open wounds and tobacco juice were items of the trade. Champ's favorite pastime was to debate anyone within earshot on the merits of the modern player when compared to the men against whom he competed. Commenting on Dizzy Dean's talent as a pitcher, Osteen always stopped short of putting "Ol' Diz" on the same level as hurlers he faced in that long ago era, the likes of Christy Mathewson, Eddie Plank, Chief Bender, Jack Chesbro, and Rube Waddell. Reflecting on the "eye for an eye" style of play at the turn of the century, he did not mince words, saying that the game of the 1940s and 1950s was for spoiled stars who, on the whole, cried and complained better than they played.

In his later years, Osteen organized a girls' team — Daughters of the American Baseball Revolution — starring seven of his daughters. They played regular games with other girls' teams from Lyman and Pelzer and formed the nucleus for a women's textile baseball league. That was Champ, always creating some sort of legacy for himself among the mill hill folks who loved him. He set the stage for so many who would follow and excel on the diamond, both with local teams and with major league clubs.

It was said that everyone in the village turned out for the ball games, with more baseball enthusiasm per square inch in the community than was probably found in some big league training camps. Team members were still legitimate employees of the mill and payment for play came only from "passing the hat," a tradition established in textile baseball. As the hat made its way through the grandstands, it was filled with coins when someone hit a home run, slapped out a winning hit, or pulled off a spectacular fielding play. Appreciation was also shown to the team at the end of the season, when a big meal was served and awards given to the players courtesy of the mill executives.

As baseball gave status to the textile men, so too, did it bring a measure of respectability to the citizens of the mill village. By the early 1920s, Olin D. Johnston, a future governor of South Carolina and U.S. Senator, and a textile baseball player from Honea Path, wrote:

> The attitudes of outsiders toward mill people have changed considerably during the last decade. Ten years ago the mill employees were looked

upon as a backward, low bred, and uneducated class of people. Today they are considered as an energetic, educated, law abiding and home loving people. It is true that this class of people has to struggle very hard for its existence. Therefore, taking everything into consideration in reference to their status, there is no reason why they should be looked down upon.[1]

To some degree, the "lintheads" were not so severely judged as second class citizens by the local farmers and townspeople. The success of the ball teams was partially responsible for this shift in attitude.

In 1909, the Greenville Mill League was supported by an impressive list of uptown merchants and businesses. Certainly getting the best for their advertising dollar, shrewd men were quick to realize the impact of a vast new market. The likes of America's Shoe Company, The Fourth National Bank, West Hardware Company, Coca-Cola, Symmes and Browning Furniture, Carolina Supply, Burns-McGee, Wood Drugs, Gordon Mercantile, and 40 other establishments sought to become familiar names with the mill village population.

It was difficult for townspeople to look down their collective noses at a group consistently sending ballplayers to the major leagues, especially when that group was capable of beating the "townies'" brains out any time they were willing to send a team onto the diamond. Folks sat up and took notice when Sampson's Fisher belted six hits and lifted his team to a 12-4 win over Monaghan (Greenville) on May 1, 1909. Beaumont's Mayberry awed the crowd on June 15, 1912, as he fanned 28 men in a 21-inning 1-0 win over Inman; his mound foe, Nix, whiffed 24 in a losing cause. And Whitney's Nashburn pitched no-hitters exactly four weeks apart in 1915, beating Drayton 2-1 on May 22 and Arkwright 12-0 on June 19.

Embraced with such loyalty by the mill hands, baseball did not remain an innocent sport populated by amateurs. As the 64 hour work week was scaled back to 55, there was more time for practice and warm Saturday afternoons were devoted almost exclusively to baseball. Mill owners were quick to realize, and to seize upon, the opportunity offered by the game: winning programs gave tremendous boosts to employee morale and community pride.

That textile baseball was increasing in popularity was evidenced by a special column running in the Greenville *News* in 1917. "Introducing A Leaguer" debuted in the Saturday, May 12 edition, spotlighting pitcher Ellis Blackstone of Judson, a talented athlete often compared to Joe Jackson. By the time the column ended on Saturday, July 14, with a profile of Judson's "Bad Eye" Guthrie, the careers of 55 players and managers in the six team Greenville Mill League had become public knowledge. This column presented a most concise snapshot of the *entire* league for the 1917 season. Players profiled were:

For *Judson*: Ellis Blackstone (May 12), pitcher; Paul "Chubby" Troutman (May 18), outfielder, comedian and Newberry College alumnus; Jim Weston (May 21), second baseman and Furman College football player; Pel Ballenger (May 31), shortstop who had played in the Virginia League; "Mutt" Rollins (June 3), scrappy infielder; Webb Cashion (June 8), first baseman and former player in the South Atlantic League; Bill Laval (June 10), manager and Furman College coach; Ernie Martin (June 22), infielder who started in the Central League in Dayton, OH; Millwood (June 27), catcher; Gault (July 6), second baseman from Erskine College; Tidwell (July 12), coach; and "Bad Eye" Guthrie (July 14), pitcher and veteran of the Spartanburg Mill League as well.

For *Victor (Greer)*: Tom Bray (May 13), third baseman who chose mill ball over pro ball; "Lefty" Gordon (May 22), star pitcher for the club; Lester Fisher (May 26), first baseman and good left handed hitter; Pete Newman (June 2), shortstop; "Red" Childers (June 5), utility player; "Honest" Ben Lark (June 9), comedian and right fielder; Bert Gardin (June 12), southpaw pitcher and former South Atlantic League hurler; "Shorty" Long (June 19), third baseman formerly with Raleigh of the North Carolina League; Robert Patrick (June 20), big veteran catcher; Ray Mabry (June 29), center fielder who once played on a team with eight of his brothers; Clarence "Chick" Galloway (July 9), shortstop and active student at Presbyterian College; and Jim Gilreath (July 13), manager.

For *Poe*: Dick Osteen (May 14), first baseman; Bill Osteen (May 25), pitcher and Davidson College man; "Speedy" Ballard (May 28), soon-to-retire pitcher known for taking time with the kids at the ballpark; Maurice McDonald (June 6), catcher from St. Louis, MO; Tommy Lewis (June 11), catcher still in his teens; Doc Miller (June 17), slick outfielder; "Pole" Jenkins (June 24), aging pitcher struggling to keep a place on the team; Bowen (June 26), second baseman and twelve year veteran; and Oscar Donaldson (July 4), third baseman and one of the best players in the league.

For *Brandon (Greenville)*: Kay Cashion (May 16), southpaw pitcher and captain of the team; "Pep" Friar (May 29), veteran second baseman; "G" Turner (June 13), catcher and manager; Jerry Jackson (June 25), pitcher and brother of Shoeless Joe; "Shorty" Campbell (July 1), second baseman; "Red" Sullivan (July 12), veteran shortstop; and Murphy Grumbles (July 7), big first baseman.

For *Dunean*: Ollie Springfield (May 19), first baseman; Laddy Anderson (May 27), shortstop; Alvin Granger (June 7) left handed pitcher from Bailey Military Institute in Greenwood; Bill Fisher (June 21), outfielder and Newberry College graduate; and Reuben Thompson (June 28), utility player.

For *Woodside*: Hovey Pruitt (May 20), outfielder; Frank Jamison (May 24), pitcher; Fred Cisson (May 30), second baseman who played his whole career with this club; Roland Cain (June 1), catcher and Furman College alumnus; Fred Ellis (June 4), shortstop still in his teens; Milton Melton (June 23), veteran catcher; Sam Mills (June 30), outfielder and Newberry College graduate; Charlie Verner (July 5), outfielder and a textile basketball player; and John Ross (July 11), manager.

In the late 1910s and early 1920s, the mills began bidding against each other for the best players and the true amateur ways were gone. By most accounts of the men who played, their skills were on par with the mid-level minor leagues. These talented mill workers were quite adept at the game and often had the opportunity to play against barnstorming teams starring Ty Cobb and other major leaguers. In a survey of southern mill villages conducted by Herbert Lahne, more than two thirds of the mills subsidized baseball teams by the mid 1920s.[2]

More than any other personality, Champ Osteen's success legitimized textile baseball. What people once viewed as mere entertainment (and it was *still* the best show in town) had now become hard fought contests between truly superb athletes. The random scheduling of games on Saturday afternoons gave way to a more structured league format. By 1906, the Piedmont Athletic Association was formed, with President Beatty of Piedmont Mill taking a personal interest in the baseball team. In 1907 a league was formed around the scheduled stops on the Interurban Streetcar Line; the villages of Riverside, Appleton, Orr, Gluck and Belton mills in Anderson County offered spectators a good brand of ball with the convenience of trolley travel.

Year by year, leagues seemed to multiply as every cotton mill wanted a piece of the baseball action. In 1908 the South Carolina Mill League was formed, including Grendel (Greenwood, SC), Williamston, Belton and Ware Shoals. In 1909, Watts Mill (Laurens), Newberry Mill, Lydia Mill (Clinton), and Laurens Mill made up an informal league offering sturdy competition.

The two most prominent and enduring of these organizations, however, were the Greenville and Spartanburg mill leagues. The Greenville Cotton Mill Base Ball League began in 1907 with teams from Monaghan (Greenville), Poe, Mills Mill (Greenville) and Sampson. Other teams featured in the earlier years were those from the villages of Brandon (Greenville), Southern Bleachery, Woodside, Camperdown, Dunean and Judson. Teams were free to move in and out of the league format and did so on a regular basis. The Spartanburg Mill Base Ball League, beginning some six years later, included at any one time Drayton, Saxon, Glendale, Whitney, Converse, Beaumont, Arkwright, Spartan Mill and Arcadia.

Other leagues would come into being, most for a short while, and then fade. The 1912 Piedmont League fielded teams from the mills of Pelzer, Easley, Piedmont and Victor (Greer). The Interurban League was still strong in 1913, boasting teams from Riverside, Williamston, Piedmont, Pelzer, Belton and Brogan (Anderson); Tucapau (Spartanburg) was a member in succeeding years. The Union County League offered strong teams from Buffalo, Lockhart, and Ottaray in 1915.

Not content with one representative team, the mill executives decided to sustain their flow of good players. The result was a minor league system on a limited scale. Second, or "B", teams were very much the norm in textile league baseball, allowing young men the time to develop their skills against equal competition before moving up with the regulars. There were even third teams involved in this farm system scheme.

A Class F league began in 1909 with players from Sampson, Poe, Woodside, and Monaghan (Greenville), and included boys under the age of eighteen who were employed in the mills. The binding rule was that no profanity would be used. Violators were banned from playing. YMCA leagues were also sponsored by the mills. In 1915 Mills Mill (Greenville), Central, Monaghan (Greenville) and Woodside completed a successful year. The Boy Scout Troops and RA's (Royal Ambassadors, a Christian boy's organization in the Baptist church) on the villages also put together talented teams, competing on a regular basis with their counterparts from the neighboring mill hills.

As textile baseball was more widely accepted, college players began showing up on mill team rosters. Companies soon followed the practice of hiring them in the double capacity of worker and ball player. Though their principal job involved being a baseball player, carrying tools in a back pocket and walking around the mill a few hours each day during the summer before heading off to practice avoided any challenge to their amateur status. In the lineup for Easley against Poe on May 23, 1903, was Furman graduate R.A. Gentry, whose home run helped propel Easley to a 10–6 victory. Montague Nichols, a lad who starred at the United States Naval Academy, began the 1914 season with Spartan Mill in the Spartanburg Mill League. Not to be outdone, Drayton Mill, also in that league, signed Arthur Hamilton, a former Wofford College player who had transferred to the University of Alabama.

It was another measure of respectabililty for textile baseball that teams not only signed college players to their rosters, but also competed regularly against the teams from a number of local institutions. Wofford College won over Tucapau of Spartanburg 4–3 April 5, 1906, Newberry College defeated Newberry Mill 8–6 March 27, 1909, and Clinton Mill edged Presbyterian College 3–2 April 19 of the same year. Even Shoeless Joe Jackson got into the act, pitching for Brandon (Greenville) and winning 4–0 against Wake Forest College (Wake Forest, NC) April 25, 1908. He tossed a four hitter, but oddly tallied no safeties of his own. The most active of the collegiate teams was Draughon's Business College of Greenville, whose first recorded game with the mill boys was on August 8, 1910, as they bested Pelzer 7–5, only the third loss for the homestanding team. The two teams met again in Greenville eight days later, and the revenge-minded Pelzerites lost again, 5–2.

The magnitude of Osteen's impact on textile baseball was felt in another area of play. What had primarily been a game of local interest soon became a commodity exported into neighboring states. As early as June 25, 1906, Tucapau played games in Spartanburg with Loray Mill of Gastonia, NC, losing Friday 11–6 and winning the Saturday contest 14–5. In September, 1911, Cowpens of Spartanburg County took two of three games from Rutherfordton (NC) to be crowned the unofficial champions of Western North Carolina. And in a somewhat backward sequence, they then swept the local championship as well by taking two games from Greer.

Inman Mill found it profitable enough to forego traditional local rivalries and journey to Tuxedo, North Carolina, and play in a Fourth of July doubleheader in 1912. The visitors swept both games, 3–1 and 3–2. A year later, Spartan Mill was invited to play its Independence Day game with a city team from Irwin, Tennessee, but since the day was one of the biggest of the mill league it was impossible for Manager Hancock, the players and the fans to make the trip. The winners of the 1914 Spartanburg Mill League, Beaumont Mill, traveled to Cliffside (NC) to answer the challenge of that mill team on September 12. The North Carolina group was no match for the upstate boys, losing 9–0 on a two hitter; they also made a whopping *nine* errors.

The simple game was slowly becoming more complicated. The pure local flavor of the mill hill became mixed with a new energy as college boys showed up on the team rosters. Competition moved from bitter intermill rivalries to include nearby college baseball squads. As mills in neighboring states sought to play the slick fielding, power hitting teams of upstate South Carolina, it was certain that textile baseball had come of age right along with its first true hero. Champ laid the groundwork, and the mill teams tagged along to bask in the glory.

The only thing to slow the growth of textile league baseball was World War I. Leagues faltered as hostilities heated up in 1917, though local newspapers mentioned the resilience of the textile organizations, as they outlasted the North Carolina, Virginia, Dixie and Georgia/Alabama professional leagues and attracted players from them.

But slowly players began enlisting in various branches of the service, and the leagues closed shop early. Alvin Granger, an exceptional pitcher for Dunean, went to the ambulance corps; Brum Mobley of Judson joined the Butler Guards; Walter Turner of Brandon (Greenville) and Bowen of Poe signed on with the Smyth Rifles of Pelzer, stationed at Greenville City Park.

On July 15, 1917, the Spartanburg *Herald* mentioned baseball for the last time that year, and nothing was said about a league championship. In the Greenville Mill League, Dunean and Poe withdrew in early July, leading the directors to establish a split season format; Victor (Greer) was declared the first half winner. By the end of July, however, the Woodside team folded and Judson was declared the second half winner. Victor took the best two of three games in the mid–August championship series.

The next year proved even leaner. The Greenville *News* covered only four games between mill teams, but noted that many were played during the summer between companies at Camp Sevier or between different military camps. Brandon (Greenville) played the Quartermaster Corps at Camp Sevier on March 23 (losing 5-1), Company C on June 23 (winning 1-0), and the 321st Infantry Division June 30 (losing 17-1). The Spartanburg *Herald* gave accounts of only three mill games that year. A fourth account detailed Victor's 7-0 loss to the 31st Pioneer Division on April 2.

Though 1917 and 1918 were seasons of struggle, the game endured. Succeeding years would prove favorable for textile baseball as the quality of the players and the teams continued to improve. It was a way of life come of age.

Chapter 4

Fields, Trains, Bands and Such

Sometimes just getting to the games provided stories worth remembering. It was a time when the Saturday excursion from Newberry to Whitmire by horse and wagon took the better part of the morning, and the journey from Pelzer to Liberty took all night. Streetcars provided comfortable transportation for the teams and fans in or near the larger towns, but they were a rare luxury for most of the mill villages.

The Piedmont and Northern Railroad ran through Spartanburg and vicinity, the Seaboard through Anderson and Greenville counties, and the Southern in the midstate region. Teams and spectators used this method of speedy travel to move across the state and challenge one another. It was not unusual for a game to be called in one of the late innings to allow the visiting club time to catch the scheduled run back home. Later, tin lizzies and flatbed trucks offered the quickest way to a rival's baseball field, though in case of rain the players had to be prepared to get out and push after the vehicle invariably slid into a nearby ditch.

Everyone waited for that magical Saturday when the mill shut down at noon. Operatives made plans for a big afternoon. Players went home to eat before reporting for the game. Though transportation offered adequate adventures, they sometimes paled before those experienced on the diamond.

The fields were endowed, it seemed, with personalities all their own. Some were located at the end of a street car route; on June 21, 1903, Pelzer defeated Mills Mill (Greenville) 13–3 in a game played at the end of the Augusta line. Some, on the other hand, were plagued by the steel rails; the Woodside team of Greenville found it difficult to practice, since the Interurban line bisected their facility. The truly unfortunate teams were handicapped by having no regular place to play at all.

Around the field, a wire fence often ran with a set of steps that went up and over it. At this unique turnstile, the fans entered, paying their admission fees for an afternoon's worth of entertainment. There were always those, however, who preferred to be "fence hangers" or "tree climbers" rather than legitimate clientele. Some parks were actually part of a pasture used by the company, and the game often had to be stopped

21

when cows wandered across the playing area (undoubtedly, there would be some extra clean-up after such visits). After all, it was *their* home during the week.

Sun glinted off mica-flecked infields, the rough surfaces contributing to errors as much as a bonehead play or less-than-adequate ability. Stack, shortstop for Poe Mill, was the talk of the mill league on May 28, 1916, after a ground ball struck a pebble, rolled up his arm and into his large shirt sleeve, lodged somewhere in the voluminous material, and allowed the batter to reach first base safely. The official scorer must have chuckled and labeled the play a special sort of error.

The outfields sometimes had to be seen to be believed. Games could be won or lost depending on how certain obstacles came into play. On May 31, 1913, Converse defeated Saxon 8-7, scoring two runs in the bottom of the tenth inning on a long fly in the direction of the left fielder that hit a telegraph wire and bounded away. A favorite target for Bill Osteen and his teammates in 1916 was an oak tree in center field at Poe Mill Park *inside* the fence. The ground rule was that "a person cannot take more than two bases on a ball hit to a field ornament."[1]

There were, however, greater adventures than these, as a 1914 game in Spartanburg between Arkwright and Saxon mills showed. Although his team lost, right fielder O'Dell's amazing catch for Arkwright was the highlight of the game. One witness noted, "He ran back on a ball that looked impossible to catch, ran down into a cornfield, and caught the fly just off the silk of a big roasting ear."[2] Saxon center fielder Johnson had his own show April 25 of the next year in a 2-1 win over Spartan Mill, making two brilliant barehanded catches while running in a plowed portion of the field.

With grounds that sometimes could be called primitive at best, and absolutely unplayable at worst, the weather could wreak havoc at a moment's notice. When it rained infields became quagmires and outfields veritable marshlands. A game was called, however, only as a last resort, and teams played both through drizzles and copious downpours on dreary days. Nor were fans immune from the discomfort, as rain often dripped through the roof of the grandstand, onto the heads and down the necks of the faithful.

The 1916 season became "the summer of the washout." Eight inches of rain fell Friday, July 14. The North Pacolet River crested at seventeen feet. Mill teams throughout the area had not played in three weeks due to severe flooding, and several deaths were attributed to these conditions. Nevertheless, the teams tried to play on Saturday, July 22, and Brandon (Greenville) defeated Monaghan (Greenville) 5-0 as Miller tossed a shutout in steadily falling rain. All other games, though, were called before they became official.

There were other conditions to fear as well. Cold weather early in the season could make rough infields rock hard, and bad bounces became the rule. The dry weather of summer, too, could play as much devilment with the games as did the rain. High winds and dust made these outings most disagreeable for players and fans. With gusts blowing into the pitcher's face, control and speed were almost impossible to manage, and hitters would have a banquet from such offerings. Games were often delayed until the flying debris settled or called off if the bad winds persisted.

At many of the fields, the distant border always seemed to be defined by the railroad tracks skirting the edges of the playing area, giving rise to stories of tape measure shots landing far beyond the steel rails. Better yet were the stories of the longest home runs, when a ball would land in an open boxcar or on a flatbed and chug on to some distant city.

Though often accused of harboring cow pasture baseball, many mill owners attempted to upgrade their facilities. Bleachers and grandstands were eventually erected on the grounds of most clubs. President John A. Law of Saxon Mill provided a club house, showers, and other modern conveniences for his players. Fans were afforded the opportunity to sit and sip a Coca-Cola or glass of ice water in the relative comfort of the park.

In the summer of 1938, Piedmont dedicated its new facility, Buchanan Field. Boasting a seating capacity of 1,200, there were dressing rooms, rest rooms, and a concession stand. The bleacher section, known as the "peanut gallery," extended along the third base line; there was one down the first base line for the Negro fans of the team. The park was built at a cost of $3,000, and WPA funds were secured to complete the stadium.

For those few precious moments of involvement in the ball game, players and fans forgot about the long, arduous hours in the mill. When the contest finally ended, the players packed up their spikes and gloves, and everyone headed home. Tomorrow would be another day spent making cloth.

Game day became an occasion for noise and excitement. Cheers and boos filled the air as the fortunes of the team flowed and ebbed, and joyful music filtered through it all. Bands for the local mills (and the mill-sponsored YMCAs) seemed to increase the home field advantage with their robust clamor for the heroes of the summer game and had a way of making forays into enemy territory a bit less intimidating. These musical organizations were formed right along with the teams.

As early as 1901, the Smyth Band from Pelzer provided excellent music during the big games with rival Piedmont Mill. The Piedmont Brass Band returned the favor with a number of lively selections adding to the pleasure of the afternoon. For the last game of the 1909 season, the Smyth

The 1920s Whitmire (Glenn-Lowry) Mill Concert Band, a regular feature at the ball park. *Photo courtesy of Steve Armfield.*

Band was part of several hundred fans making the trip to Easley. Even with such inspiration and support, Easley won both games.

On days when Poe played nearby Monaghan (Greenville), fans would come out in force. The mill bands would be with them, keeping their instruments going throughout the game. When the mills around Spartanburg did battle at Wofford Park, the band of W.A. McSwain not only rendered musical selections throughout the contests, but also marched in advance of the teams from the outfield to home plate in pregame festivities. This was a common occurrence with major league teams at that time, so the mill owners decided to include a pep rally of their own. The bands were often called upon to lead the traditional Fourth of July parade as well. It was a dandy way to get the excitement flowing for the events of the big day.

There were other forms of entertainment associated with the baseball games. R.W. Lewis, manager of Tucapau in 1910, performed stunts during games and the fans were always happy to see him come to town.[3]

Another welcomed face was Paul "Chubby" Troutman, a Newberry College graduate who played ball for several mills in the upstate area over the years. While with Judson Mill in 1917, "Chubby" was lauded by one sportswriter for the joy he brought as the greatest comedian in the circuit, unsurpassed by major leaguers Germany Schaefer (fun loving catcher for the Detroit Tigers and Washington Senators who once stole *first base*) or Rube Waddell (Connie Mack's "forever child" with the Philadelphia

Athletics). A popular player and a good outfielder with speed despite his two hundred plus pounds, he was a character likened to Charlie Chaplin. His antics enabled fans to return home from the game with a brighter outlook. It was to "Chubby's" credit that fans said the game was made better by his presence, because he gave smiles as well as thrills with his athletic prowess.[4] "Speedy" Ballard of Poe and "Honest" Ben Lark of Victor (Greer), an Irish lover of life in all its fine forms, also entertained fans with antics both on and off the field.

The ball teams often arranged for parties and gatherings, inviting their fans to participate. At-large invitations were made for parties and ice cream socials. It was family, after all, with folks looking after their own. Loyalty was the key word, and fans responded to their teams with pride and enthusiasm.

Big crowds were not at all uncommon, especially when the mill shut down at noon and there was no reason for a person not to be part of the big celebration. Crowds of 1,000 or more were present on several occasions: 1,000 on Saturday, May 8, 1909, as Union defeated Victor (Greer) 2-1 in Union; the same on Saturday, May 21, 1910, when homestanding Woodside defeated Monaghan (Greenville) 5-2; 1,500 when Monaghan (Greenville) and Mills Mill (Greenville) split a Saturday doubleheader on July 4, 1914; the same number for a game between the *second* teams of Pelzer and Piedmont May 22, 1915; 1,800 as Brandon (Greenville) clinched the Greenville Mill League pennant Saturday, August 14, 1915, with a 2-0 win over Dunean; 1,500 at a Saturday, July 1, 1916, doubleheader to watch Poe win the first game 4-3 and Victor (Greer) the second 2-1; and 1,000 to see Judson defeat Victor 3-1 on Saturday July 4, 1917.

On special occasions, huge numbers of people would pack the bleachers or stand along the foul lines to watch. A crowd of 10,000 people was at Pelzer on Saturday, August 21, 1915, to see the home team cop the Interurban League title with a doubleheader sweep of Tucapau, 13-2 and 3-0. Approximately 4,000 had attended a few Saturdays earlier as Pelzer edged Piedmont in their traditional Independence Day battle. At the Pelzer Homecoming on Saturday, August 21, 1920, visiting Whitmire may have been intimidated by the 5,000 hearty souls who cheered the home team to a doubleheader sweep, 4-3 and 3-2.

In the Spartanburg area a Monday-Tuesday series (July 7 and 8, 1913) between Buffalo Mill and Whitmire drew 2,000 people; the home Buffalo squad dropped the first game 7-1, but came back to take the second 9-7. Victor (Greer) and Tucapau brought 1,000 fans together for the Saturday, July 3 doubleheader in 1915, and after a 2-2 tie in the opener, Tucapau fans must have groaned as shortstop Newman made five errors to give Victor a win in the second contest. Clifton, which had a small park, had the place overflowing in a Saturday tilt against Pacolet

The 1920s Piedmont Mill team. *Photo courtesy of Donna Roper, Pendleton Historical Society.*

May 22, 1920. Pacolet won 5-1, but the 2,000 folks ringing the field necessitated a ground rule that any fair ball hit into the crowd was only a double.

The love affair with baseball was so passionate that the game could not be confined to the warm months of spring, summer, and early autumn. In the mill villages with a gymnasium (often called the "Game Shack" or "Playhouse"), many activities filled the winter days, but none was more popular than indoor baseball. At Piedmont on September 10, 1920, the Owls bested the Bats 13-12 in a game played on skates in the local gym. It was amusing and required deft balance for the players to stay afoot.

With all of the attention given to textile baseball, sportswriters battled to outdo one another in their accounts of the games. After all, they had new readers to impress every week. One such gentleman from the Greenville *News* lamented the redundancy of choosing team nicknames. Titled "Must Be Sluggers or 'Tis No Team," his story concludes with:

> A reward of one switzer sandwich is offered to the first team that organizes in 1916 for the sole and only purpose of playing baseball, and leaves off the word "Sluggers". At present count is found 1,123 teams in Greenville County all labeled Wooftown Sluggers, Pankville Sluggers, Terrible Sluggers, and of course all the other 1,120. Why can't some teams brand themselves the Culleyville Bat Smashers, Horsehide Split-

ters, Circuit Drivers, Fadeaway Bangers, or some other name equally as euphoneous or compatible with the manly art of baseball? Invariably it is the "Sluggers," and that most of them fail to do.[5]

Given the fact that textile league pitchers normally overshadowed the hitters, attaching "Sluggers" to the team name did border on the oxy-moronic.

The epic language, though, was usually reserved for the games themselves, and the writers did wax poetic. One unknown Milton described a 17-inning affair between Poe and Greer, a 1–1 tie not resolved "until the sun began to disappear in the evening sky, and until the official scorer had to utilize every bare space on the margin of his book."[6]

Two weeks later he (or someone in a like voice), returned, heaping disgust upon league-leading Brandon (Greenville) as they dropped a 7–5 decision to second place Dunean in the Greenville Mill League pennant race.

Brandon used every science in trying to make their cudgels proclaim resounding joy. But to every action there is an equal reaction, and when Dunean saw the victory only a pace ahead, they put on the battle girds and gave the opponents a big show performance in the remaining innings. Both teams played wretched ball in the field after the sixth inning, and the victory was composed as much of gratis as of dessert.[7]

Aspiring to equal heights, the Spartanburg *Herald* indulged in like verbal pomposity. Describing one team in the local mill league in 1913, the writer noted:

Henderson and his able corps of accomplices trim their rivals with such regularity that there now seems little doubt that the gonfalon has embroidered in some conspicuous portion of its anatomy "Beaumont."[8]

Another time he chose to wax satirical, calling a 24–17 Saxon defeat of Whitney "a game that would have done credit to the Boston Bloomer Girls and Miss Pankhurst's Militants."[9]

Folks enjoyed the accounts of the games because reading them was almost as much fun as witnessing the contests in person. More people than ever were noticing the caliber of baseball being played in the textile leagues, and in Greenville, there was a quiet barefoot kid whose incredible talents caught the imaginations of folks from every mill village.

Chapter 5

Shoeless Joe

His beginnings were no different from hundreds of other children on the mill hill in the last years of the 19th century. Born of parents who moved from the rural farm life to the mill, and then from mill to mill, his childhood was short and formal schooling was sporadic at best. As boys and girls of the operatives "came of age" (in most cases, no later than six or seven years old), they went with their parents to face the long hours surrounded by the noise and lint from spinning frames and looms.

At age six, Joseph Jefferson Jackson walked with his father, brothers, and sisters to Brandon Mill (Greenville), where his job was to sweep the floors. He worked the long, boring hours, but played pick-up baseball games with other children during the scheduled work breaks. Occasionally, he and other boys would sneak away from their tasks to play a few innings. The older workers may not have approved of these antics, but there was no denying his extraordinary grace and coordination as he galloped after fly balls and swung full and fluid from the left side of the plate.

As a 13-year-old boy he was a regular on the men's team at Brandon, possessed of a talent so uncommon that legends grew from his deeds. He could throw harder, run faster, and hit with more power than anyone that folks could remember. His home runs were "Saturday Specials," since most textile games were scheduled after the half day of work was completed. Joe's brothers used to "pass the hat" after one of his round trippers, and Jackson seldom wanted for spending money. Years later, he remembered that $25 was not an uncommon haul. The line drives he hit were labeled "blue darters," which *spectators* (and some fielders, no doubt) swore crackled and smoked as they went by. The phrase was a favorite of Dizzy Dean's in the early 1960s as he announced the "Game of the Week" on television.

Under Joe's supervision, his bat was made by a local lumberman. It weighed 48 ounces and was lacquered with uncounted coats of tobacco juice. "Black Betsy" and one or two "sisters" accompanied him for most of his baseball career, and a favorite cheer of the fans became "Give 'em Black Betsy, Joe!" His fielding prowess made his glove "a place where triples go to die." Occasionally he tried his luck at pitching, but one day he broke a batter's arm with an errant throw; that discouraged the young man from pursuing a mound career. It was his hitting that turned heads. On May 28, 1904, he led his Brandon mates to a 21–0 shellacking of Anderson Mill. On April 11, 1908, he pitched a two hitter and, for good measure, tripled, doubled, and homered as Brandon defeated Sampson 9–3.

It was during this time that the legend was pronounced immortal. His nickname was often credited to Scoop Latimer, a Greenville *News* sportswriter, and occurred while he was still playing textile ball. Breaking in a new pair of cleats in a game against the Anderson Electricians, his feet became blistered. The manager, however, refused his request to be removed from the game. Who in his right mind would bench Joe Jackson? Joe opted to finish the game in his stocking feet. None of the boisterous Anderson fans noticed until he cracked a homer over the right fielder's head in the late innings. As Jackson rounded third, one observant fan bolted from his seat, screaming, "Oh, you shoeless son of a bitch!" Scoop overheard, modified the vile phrase to Shoeless Joe to better fit his Bible belt audience, and baseball was never the same.

By age 19, Jackson was a legend in the upstate area. He went from Brandon to Victor Mill in Greer, accepting a better offer to play baseball. While there, he was spotted by members of the semi-professional Greenville Near Leaguers, was signed by the team, and stayed with them for awhile. His first professional stint came with manager Tommy Stouch and the Greenville Spinners of the South Atlantic League. Though respectable middle class society marveled at his athletic ability, they hatefully ridiculed his illiteracy. In their eyes, he remained a good-for-nothing mill worker making the extraordinary salary of $75 per month. Still, the legend grew.

Joe always had a bit of the showman in him and, beginning in his textile days, wanted to please the folks who came to watch him. After making a catch for the final out of a game, he would run to the deepest part of the outfield, turn at the fence, and throw the ball on a line over the backstop. Fans called such demonstrations "showouts" and loved him for it. The strong arm was just another weapon in the arsenal of a wonderfully gifted athlete. Much later in his career (1917), he defeated Babe Ruth, Ty Cobb, Tris Speaker and Duffy Lewis — the premier outfielders of the day — in a throwing contest with an effort of 396 feet in the air.

Such talent could not remain local knowledge. Soon big league scouts were showing up at his games, determining for themselves whether this mill hill kid could live up to all they had heard about him. Jackson lived up to his advanced billing. Piedmont's Rome Chambers, Davey Crockett, and Champ Osteen, and Greenville's Sydney Smith had made it to the majors, so the area was not unknown to baseball's premier teams. Connie Mack signed Jackson to play for his Athletics for $900 and arranged for

Spinner's manager Tommy Stouch to accompany Joe on the train to Philadelphia. To say that Jackson was eager to report would be a lie; he gave his friend the slip in the Charlotte, North Carolina, station, boarded another train, and returned home to Greenville. Mack was a man of patience and a few weeks later sent veteran scout "Socks" Seybold to escort the reticent rookie to the city of brotherly love. Just imagine, sending "Socks" to fetch "Shoeless."

He was traded to the Cleveland Indians after spending the 1908–09 seasons with the Athletics and their minor league affiliates. Joe left behind both his brutal hazing by Philadelphia veterans and the ridicule by fans and players regarding his inability to read and write. What he found in Cleveland was a much more congenial atmosphere, good rapport with teammates and fans, and appreciation for his considerable talents. A member of the Naps from 1910 to 1915, his shining moment occurred in 1911, when he hit .408 for the season but still lost the batting title to Ty Cobb's .420. That remains the highest season average in the history of baseball *not* to win the batting title.

Best of all, he was recognized as a true professional by his peers. Ty Cobb called Jackson the finest natural hitter the game had ever seen. The Yankee's Babe Ruth molded his swing after Joe's, maintaining that he took the best swing he could find for that purpose. Washington's Walter Johnson said that Shoeless was the greatest natural ballplayer he ever competed against.

Toward the end of the 1915 season, Jackson was traded to Charles Comiskey's Chicago White Sox, setting the stage for the drama which baseball fans refer to as "The Scandal." Joe had good years with the Sox and played on their World Series championship team of 1917. It is, however, for the part he played, or did not play, in throwing the 1919 Series against the Cincinnati Reds that he is best remembered. The story is familiar: he and seven teammates, found innocent in a trial by jury in 1921, were nevertheless banished from organized baseball for life by the newly appointed commissioner, Judge Kenesaw Mountain Landis.

Joe's statistics for the Series served to underscore his greatness, without a hint of playing to lose: a leading batting average of .375; a record twelve hits (a mark that stood for more than 40 years); leader in both total bases and slugging percentage; the leading outfielder, with no errors and five runners gunned down on the base paths; and possessor of the only home run. In the face of such charges, Robert Ripley felt it only fair to include Jackson's incredible performance in his *Believe It or Not* collection. Surely no one with such numbers could be accused of playing to lose.

Despite his performance and the finding of the jury, Landis's words rang like a death sentence in the ears of Shoeless Joe: "throws a ball game...sits in conference with crooked players and gamblers...ways of throwing games are planned...will never play professional baseball." There was no appeal. For the rest of his life, perhaps the greatest of them all was banned from playing the game on the professional level. After the scandal, Jackson played under pseudonyms in New York and New Jersey and barnstormed with fellow Black Sox teammates Eddie Cicotte and Lefty Williams through small towns and rural communities.

When Jackson returned to Greenville in the autumn of 1920 for a visit in the company of Williams, there were hearty demonstrations of cordiality toward Shoeless Joe. There was also an announcement that a series of all star games would be played. The All Stars included: Jackson; Williams; Melton (catcher from the Million Dollar League); Cashion and Jamison (pitchers in the Florida State League); Webb Cashion (1b of the minor league Bradenton, Florida, team); Pel Ballenger (shortstop of the minor league Louisville, Kentucky, team); Paul Troutman (outfielder of the Lakeland, Florida, team in the Florida State League); Cisson (2b), and Mutt Rollins (3b), both current players in the Greenville Mill League.

The opposing Monaghan team consisted of: Walt Barbare (shortstop of the Pittsburgh Pirates); Thompson (pitcher from the Greenville Mill League); Jenkins (pitcher from the Million Dollar League); G. Barber and Hunnicutt (shortstop and 2b, respectively, from the Million Dollar League); Maumon (1b from the Whitmire team); and Shorty Long (3b), Kelly, Whitener, Camp, "Jenny" Long, Dalton, Henson, Tipton, and Heath, all current participants in the Greenville Mill League. In fact, everyone from both teams, with the exception of Lefty Williams, was a past or current player in the league. It was disappointing that no accounts of the games (if they were played) appeared.

Traveling on to Savannah, Georgia, with Williams, Jackson opened a successful dry cleaning business, but baseball would not let him alone. The March 22, 1924 Greenville *News* mentioned that Jackson, Williams, Cicotte, "Shufflin'" Phil Douglas (a man banished from organized ball on the word of New York Giants' manager John McGraw), and other outlawed major leaguers played in the South Georgia League. The same year, Jackson sued White Sox owner Charles Comiskey for back pay in the amount of $16,000. Again, the jury found in his favor, affirming that Jackson did not unlawfully conspire with Gandhil, Williams and other members of the White Sox to throw any of the 1919 Series with Cincinnati. Remarkably, the presiding judge overturned the verdict, and even had Jackson jailed for one night for perjury when his testimony did not agree with his earlier Chicago Grand Jury "confession." Joe was eventually awarded only a small amount of his earnings.

Home was beckoning, and in 1929 he and wife Katie returned to Greenville to open another dry cleaning establishment. Later, a liquor store was added to his list of successful entrepreneurial ventures. For the folks on the mill hill, the hero had returned. He may have been bloodied, his armor dented by a vindictive commissioner of baseball and a selfish owner, but Jackson was home, and village citizens looked after their own.

Joe's ties with textile baseball were never really broken. He was available to the players, working with and encouraging them. Murphy Grumbles of Brandon was so favored, as his mentor noted, "Murph, you have the makings of a great first baseman; keep it up and you'll shine yet."[1] Determined to prove him right, Grumbles did, in fact, become a very good player during his years in the mill leagues. Jackson was also the yardstick against whom all players were judged. Pel Ballenger of Judson, who had a brief stay in the majors with the Washington Senators, knew the burden of such a comparison. Brother Jerry Jackson, a long-armed fireballer for Brandon, understood the hardships of living up to the legend of his older brother.

In the mid–1930s, Joe managed the Winnsboro team. He moved on to Woodside in Greenville in 1938, reuniting with brother Jerry. He also regularly played well into his forties. Joe Anders of Easley, a textile player who later moved into Triple A baseball, remembered seeing Jackson pinch hit in a mill league game at the age of 56. Already weakened by the first of several heart attacks, he nevertheless smashed the ball off the centerfield fence, 415 feet from home plate.

When Greenville finally regained a minor league franchise, Jackson was offered the job of player-manager, but Commissioner Landis reared his ugly head, standing by his verdict of guilty and the sentence of lifetime banishment from organized baseball. Yet, after Landis's death, Joe was made a Minor League Board of Protest official. Former commissioner Happy Chandler (1946–1951) was involved in efforts to clear Jackson, believing he did not take part in the scandal.

Denied official entrance into the Baseball Hall of Fame, Shoeless Joe is nevertheless represented there—by a pair of his cleats. When nominees were being gathered for the Cleveland Baseball Hall of Fame, he was not even included on the ballot. Such a furor erupted, however, that his name *was* placed in nomination, and he was ultimately elected and enshrined with the other legendary players of that city.

Death came calling December 5, 1951, ten days before he was to be a guest on Ed Sullivan's *Toast of the Town*. The appearance was crucial in a movement to clear his name, a movement begun on February 27 of that year when the South Carolina Legislature adopted a formal resolution calling for his reinstatement into baseball's good graces. When he died, so did the efforts toward vindication. In retrospect, his whole life was shadowed by such paradoxes.

Perhaps he was innocence personified, swept away by forces he could

Shoeless Joe Jackson, 1937. Fifty and overweight, he was managing the Woodside team of Brandon. *Photo courtesy of Fred McAbee.*

neither understand nor fight. Whatever the reasons, the legend of Shoeless Joe grew to near mythic proportions. Jackson always denied any truth to the story of the little boy clutching at his sleeve and pleading, "Say it ain't so, Joe! Say it ain't!" as players were leaving the courtroom in 1921. For those who knew him from his days on the mill village teams, from his "Saturday Specials" to his "showouts," this was a moot point. He never had to say it wasn't so. Intrinsically, the folks who knew him best never questioned his integrity.

As Champ Osteen legitimized textile baseball, Shoeless Joe ushered in the growth years of the late 1910s and 1920s. The dominant Greenville

and Spartanburg Mill leagues had given way to a host of others. The
Anderson County, Reedy River, Greer, Piedmont, G.W.P. (Greenwood,
Whitmire, Pelzer, Piedmont), Saluda, Victor-Monaghan, Western Carolina, Carolina, Interurban, Greenville City, Oconee County, Pickens
County, Laurens County, Eastern Carolina, Central Carolina, Greenwood, Spartanburg/Laurens, Palmetto, Tri-County, Parker, Independent, Big Four, Big Six, Georgia/South Carolina, Paris Mountain and
King Cotton leagues offered entertainment galore for the baseball hungry
citizens of mill villages. Johnny Burton, scorekeeper and publicity man
for Calhoun Falls, remembered his beloved Clippers playing against
Abbeville, Iva, McCormick, and Antreville (all South Carolina towns),
and then journeying into Georgia to play Elberton, Fort Sonia, Sweet
City, Bowman, and Hartwell. Both the numbers of games and leagues,
(and the level of competition) increased during the 1920s.

The result of this heightened competitive spirit was often a win-at-all-
cost confrontation. The editor of one mill publication, the Piedmont
Bridge, chose to admonish the village players and fans for such disagreeable tendencies, noting that gambling, brawling, cursing and loud mouth
bragging became contemptible habits easily acquired when the wrong
kinds of people were involved in the game.

"To be a gentleman," he continued, "should be the first requisite of
any person who bids for public favor. And inasmuch as baseball and the
movies are the most prominent sources of entertainment and education
these days, they should be kept pure and clean."

Though the local team prepared to be the best team in the league,
they should do so by engaging in clean sportmanship. Players and
spectators were encouraged to conduct themselves in a mannerly way
upon entrance into the ball park.[2] After all, children and ladies were
among the growing number of fans who intently followed textile baseball.

For many, it was still a family affair. Gene Snipes, pitcher and
outfielder for Belton Mill, followed brothers Dewitt, Clyde and Ray into
the limelight. And Mrs. Mildred Hughey recalled how textile baseball
included her whole family: "My father was 'Dutch' Vaughn, catcher and
manager for Arial (Easley, SC) and Pelzer Mill, and in 1927 he led the
Pelzer team to the Tri-County League championship. He used to take me
to those games when I was just a little girl, and made sure that I sat *very*
still so he didn't have to worry about me and the action on the field at the
same time.

"Dad's brother, Bill, played mill ball sometime before 1915, and my
brothers, Foster and Charles, played for Arial around 1939 to 1940. It
was quite a thrill being part of a baseball family, and it was something we
were very proud of."[3]

For most, though, it was a highly competitive game involving men who loved to win. Dominant teams began to emerge. Brandon (Greenville), Jackson's old stomping grounds, ruled the baseball scene in the Greenville area.

The team copped the Greenville Mill League pennants in 1912, 1913, 1914; the Piedmont Textile League championships in 1920, 1921, 1923, 1924; and the Western Carolina top spot in 1927. When Pelzer stopped the juggernaut to win the 1928 Western Carolina League, it was the first time since 1922 that Brandon had missed a league pennant. Of all their championships, however, perhaps none epitomized the fierce competition more than the 1924 season.

Judson, Camperdown, Dunean, Monaghan, Union Bleachery, Victor, Greer and Brandon came to play in that fifth year of the Piedmont Textile League. Entering the last day of the season, Saturday, August 16, the defending champions led Judson by the narrowest of margins. Judson defeated Camperdown 3–2 in a five inning game that day, called so fans could leave to see Brandon play Dunean in a climactic doubleheader. In front of 2,000 vocal fans Dunean won the first, a 5–4 ten-inning thriller as first baseman Medlock homered to seal the victory. Brandon came back for a 1–0 squeaker that clinched a tie for the league lead. The August 17, 1924 Greenville *News* carried on its sports page the headline: BRANDON AND JUDSON TIE FOR PENNANT. Under this was the less important *"Yankees Win!"*

This was the beginning of a classic confrontation. The two teams met again on August 30, battling to a 4–4 tie as darkness fell over Perry Avenue Park. September 13, Brandon defeated Judson 9–6 before 1,500 fans and evened the series (there was an unreported Judson win between August 30 and September 14). Again, after a two week postponement due to bad weather, the clubs battled to another 4–4 tie on October 4, called due to darkness.

The marathon season was finally decided on Saturday, October 11, the latest date a champion had been crowned. Brandon won in a rout, 12–2, and the Sunday *News* proclaimed: BRANDON DEFEATS JUDSON FOR TEXTILE LEAGUE CHAMPIONSHIP. The most interesting aspect of this final game shows up in a careful perusal of the box scores. The players of the previous four games were, by and large, conspicuously absent. In their places for Judson were the likes of shortstop Walt Barbare (late of the Pittsburgh Pirates) and first baseman Emerson Cashion (of the Greenville Spinners of the South Atlantic League). Flint Rhem was on the mound for the winners (after completing his first year with the St. Louis Cardinals) and Pel Ballenger was at shortstop (a Class B minor leaguer four years away from his stint with the Washington Senators). The newspaper, in fact, referred to the Brandon and Judson professionals. For the players and fans, it was quite a season.

Something, though, was changing about textile baseball, perhaps reflected in the 1924 Piedmont League championship series. To be sure, there were still the brass bands to serenade the fans at games and give encouragement to the players on the field. And the Fourth of July still held some very special moments, as when the Victor team of 1906 met the current edition of the Greer team, but lost. It was a treat to see the Chicago Bloomer Girls perform during their 1922 tour, though they lost to Victor 18–1 on June 14, to Belton 9–3 on June 15, to Fountain Inn 7–3 on June 17, and to Laurens 11–5 on June 19.

In these growing years, however, much of the innocence was lost as winning became foremost in the minds of players, fans, and owners. Teams came, saw, conquered, and were conquered, in turn, a thousand times over on hot, dusty summer afternoons. The Pelzer Pelicans, Easley Eagles, Lyceum Sluggers, Lightning Sluggers, Easley Giants, Brandon Braves, Poe Ravens, Fairmont Tigers, Victor Wildcats, Equinox Hornets, Orr Rifles, Beaumont Mountaineers and the second team Overalls, Glendale Tigers, Spartan Red Sox and the second team Red Roosters, Monaghan Speedsters, Piedmont Doffers, Riverside Giants, Mills Mill Millers, Beattie Sluggers, Smyth Sluggers, Pelzer Blue Hose, Williamston Spinners, Belton Blue Stockings, Judson Tigers, Woodside Boll Weevils, Anderson Tigers, Poinsett Sluggers, and a hundred other organizations vied for league championships, defended community pride, and, more and more, played as much for the money as for the glory.

There were memorable performances. Bolt of Clifton had a strong pitching streak in May of 1920, no-hitting Glendale 9–0 on the first and Saxon 4–0 on the eighth, and then one hitting Whitney 6–0 on the fifteenth. Horace Long of Monaghan (Greenville) owned the mound in 1920, boasting a 19–5 record which included two no-hitters. When Camperdown defeated Poe 8–7 on May 24, 1921, Jenkins stole six bases, including thefts of second, third and home for the winning tally in the ninth.

White of Tucapau had three home runs to lead his team to a 10–8 decision over Inman on June 25, 1921. A week later teammate Waldrop had 3 homers in an 18–0 shutout of Greer. Both Ellis and Henson had six hits as Monaghan (Greenville) blasted Union Bleachery 16–4 on June 10, 1922. Henderson of Arkwright pitched a no-hitter against Clifton on July 15, 1922, while his counterpart, Vaughn, allowed only one hit.

Al Shealy stroked five extra base hits, including four triples, as Mollohon of Newberry defeated the Winnsboro Royal Cords 16–3 on July 6, 1923. Simpsonville's Yeargin hit three homers, leading that team to a 14–5 win over Williamston July 7, 1923. When visiting Judson defeated Victor 4–3 June 21, 1924, Chandler saved the game when he threw out Clark at first base on a clean hit to right field with the bases loaded. Perhaps the all time blowout occurred July 17, 1926, when Judson beat Poe 39–2 in a Parker League tilt.

Jim Blackwell, a longtime textile league great, recalled his 1927 Lonsdale team journeying to Carnesville, Georgia, for a game with the local aggregation. The man they faced on the mound that day was Spud Chandler, later a star pitcher for the New York Yankees and arguably the best pitcher not included in the Hall of Fame. The mill boys beat Chandler and his Georgia teammates 2–1 that day.

Toward the decade's end, excitement skyrocketed. Smith for Piedmont (he was actually "on loan" from Lyman of Spartanburg's Independent Mill League) hurled a no-hitter and fanned 23 Chiquola batters in a 4–0 win on July 14, 1928. A week later, Poole stole 9 bases, "taking the umpire's chest protector for good measure," as Piedmont won over Ware Shoals. In a May 4, 1929, slugfest, Godfrey of Ware Shoals hit three homers, teammate Dowis two, and opponent Clark two as Ninety Six prevailed 14–9. In a five game stretch that year, Belton's Vance Escoe allowed only two runs, pitched three consecutive shutouts, and gave up only 17 hits.

But perhaps *the* stellar performance in the history of textile baseball to that point in time occurred June 23, 1928, when Brandon (Greenville) defeated Mills Mill (Greenville) 17–2 in the Section B portion of the Piedmont Textile League. Pitcher Granger hit two grand slams *in one inning,* and fanned 15 of the Millers. The hot times on the village diamonds burned more intensely than ever.

The outstanding feats accomplished on game day, however, were only a small measure of how much the skill level had increased in textile baseball. Jim Blackwell also noted that the professional teams went to the colleges to choose players. "But, hell," he laughed, "those boys couldn't make the textile league rosters half the time. They came and tried out with us, but most of them couldn't cut it!"[4] For the mill leagues, the true yardstick was the number of players making their way from semi-professional baseball to the major leagues. What had begun as a trickle with the 1899 Piedmont team, as Champ Osteen, Davey Crockett and Rome Chambers made it to the "big time", became a regular flow of talent north to the cities rich in baseball history.

Some knew only limited success, and their careers were correspondingly short. Al Shealy (Mollohon, Newberry Mill, New York Yankees), Pete Fowler (Converse, Clifton Mill, St. Louis Cardinals), Pel Ballenger (Judson Mill, Washington Senators), and Cy Pieh (Brandon Mill, New York Yankees), lived the dream only briefly. Johnny Wertz (Newberry, Ware Shoals mills, Boston Braves) showed great promise as he ended the 1926 season with an 11–9 record and a 3.28 ERA. Arm trouble, though, cut short the career of the "Giant Killer."

The 1928 Piedmont Textile League trophy, won by Brandon Mill of Greenville.
Photo courtesy of Fred McAbee.

Others managed to find respectable careers. Walt Barbare (Brandon Mill, Cleveland Indians, Pittsburgh Pirates) was good enough at shortstop to be involved in a trade for future Hall of Famer "Rabbit" Maranville. Leroy Mahaffey (Appleton, Anderson, Belton mills, Philadelphia Athletics) rubbed shoulders with greatness, playing several years with Connie Mack and posting a 15–4 record in 1931 to lead the A's into the World Series; he also was the victim of Lou Gehrig's fourth homer when the Iron Horse hit four in one game in 1932. Carlisle Smith (Greenville area mills, Brooklyn Dodgers, Boston Braves), Sydney Smith (Greenville area mills, Cleveland Indians, Pittsburgh Pirates), Flint Rhem (Belton,

Westminster mills, St. Louis Cardinals) and Chick Galloway (Judson Mill, Philadelphia Athletics) could all boast of solid performances over the years.

Mill villages buzzed with excitement over the exploits of their heroes. With the influences of Osteen and Jackson to pave the way, action on the village diamonds became the talk of the towns. Wherever a game was played, it was the right and respectable place to be, cheering on the local boys and getting in some good natured ragging of the opponents. There were times, though, when the play was intense, the outcome of the game hung in the balance, and the stakes were high. The overwrought pride and good natured hazing were stirred into a mixture that was not sporting, not pretty to watch, and not safe for the visiting teams and spectators.

Chapter 6

Fussin' and Fightin'

For the most part, textile baseball was good sport, a diversion for the spectators who worked hard all week and had precious little time for recreation. Mill employees came out to enjoy the game, to get away from tedious jobs in the midst of roaring machinery, to bask in the sunshine, to visit with neighbors and catch up on the latest village gossip. Of course, there would always be the good natured kidding of opposing players and fans. Would it even be a decent baseball game if a loyal supporter did not defend the honor of the home team and lambast the umpire now and then?

In the early days, when one umpire stood behind the pitcher's mound and was responsible for calling balls and strikes as well as the plays at the bases, there was a pronounced tendency to take shortcuts. Pulling up short at one base to head for the next on a hit to the outfield was a common enough occurrence when the arbiter's back was turned. Beefing about the location of pitches was almost a given when the determining pair of eyes was more than sixty feet from the target. Sportswriters, though, sometimes moved to defend the work of the men who controlled the games, one Spartanburg writer noting, "The umpiring of Wright was the best ever seen on the local grounds," in a game between Beaumont and Spartan mills.[1]

In 1915, the writer of the column "Mill League Whoops" in the Spartanburg *Herald* took the fans to task for their behavior.

> Why rag the umpire? It's about time to get rid of this idea that the umpires lean toward one team or another. It would be too open a thing to do. The umpires of the mill leagues are good men, and are giving the teams all that's within their power fairly."[2]

By this time, the Spartanburg Mill League paid their umpires a regular salary for their jobs and backed their decisions from the office of the league president.

> These are the only salaried officials of the Association, and are vested with the authorities of major league umpires, having the right to impose fines or suspend a player for his conduct on the field. They will be upheld by President Herron. The Board of Directors has voted to furnish clean

40

baseball to the public. Rowdyism will not be tolerated; dilatory tactics, such as arguing with the umpire, will not be permitted...?[3]

It was an impressive declaration, but the necessity for its existence pointed to the fact that trouble did exist.

Those men who commanded the most respect were former players whose reputations were made on the village diamonds and beyond. Champ Osteen's mill career encompassed the beginnings of baseball in the South, and his major league days were spent in the infancy of the American League. They were rough-and-tumble days when players were undaunted by rules, and fisticuffs remained the preferred way to settle differences of opinion. As much as he was a fighter and scrapper during his playing days, Champ expected — and was accorded — a clean and orderly game when he umpired. No one, it seemed, cared to challenge the supremacy of his decisions between the foul lines.

Mac Bannister was another man whose playing reputation won him the respect of his peers. Though he did not play major league baseball, Mac was a fine all around player in the mill leagues for a number of years. Always a good hitter, he filled in ably at a number of positions. He was best remembered as a superb control pitcher, a master of the spitball when it was still a legal pitch. Like Champ, Mac's decisions commanded respect, but there was a particular incident early in his textile baseball career which showed him the need to maintain control over the game.

"When he pitched for Pelzer in the 1920s," Bannister's wife related, "the big rivalry was always with Piedmont, and those games were taken seriously, let me tell you. We played up there one time, and Mac pitched an especially good game and got the win. As we were leaving the ballpark after the game, two men followed us out. These roughnecks cursed us, and then they pulled knives and threatened to cut us up. Fortunately, another young Pelzer player had come out *behind* these Piedmont boys. It was the Reverend George Belk, a Presbyterian minister and a good player as well, who came to our rescue by threatening the two men with a baseball bat! I don't think I ever felt comfortable again when Pelzer went up to play Piedmont. That memory was just always too keen."[4]

Rivalries heated up between the teams and the villages they represented and were often inflamed by mill personnel who reported the games. In the *Gauzette*, a newsletter published by The Kendall Company, the writer chastised the Winnsboro Mill team after they lost to the company's Wateree nine 17–1 on June 25, 1927. "If Winnsboro can't get together a better team than the one which was on the field against Wateree, they'd better hang up their baseball togs and try tiddle-de-winks or ping pong." Relations between the two villages were at best strained during subsequent contests.

Loyalties ran deep, so when fans and sportswriters saw their favorite teams on the short end of the score, it was natural to assume the fault must be the bad and prejudiced calls made by the umpire. When visiting Belton edged Piedmont 5–4 in 14 innings July 28, 1905, it was noted that the umpire had much to learn about the rules governing the game. One of his decisions "was such to disgust everyone present who believe that fair play and strict impartiality should govern decisions."[5] Brandon (Greenville) lost to Pelzer 6–5 in 12 innings on August 7, 1915, and umpire James was said "to be off on his decisions, especially in the eighth when he donated a run to Pelzer by calling a play safe which could be seen to be out a block away."[6] Poor vision associated with the men in blue, it would seem, is not a modern phenomenon. But Brandon's setback was only temporary, since the next week they captured the 1915 Greenville Mill League pennant. When the fussing got out of control, discretion could be the better part of valor. Mr. Turner began umpiring a July 4, 1919, game won by Greer over Woodside of Greenville 8–7, but he chose to leave in the third inning as the more than 2,000 fans voiced displeasure with his decisions. It was left to two players, Patrick and Jones, to finish the game.[7]

Not to be outdone, Spartanburg fans tossed their own vindictive opinions at that lone figure of authority on the field. After Woodruff had defeated Drayton 6–4 on May 31, 1919, the Drayton manager filed a protest with Spartanburg Mill League president Thomas, charging discrimination because the umpire's rank decisions went against his team. Two months later, on August 20, Spartan Mill defeated Converse 9–6 and fingers were pointed at umpire Lane because of prejudiced calls. Criticism was only a step away from formal protests, a frequent happening when the faithful were wounded by the uncaring gods of baseball.

One of the most commonly voiced rules of the mill leagues was that a player must be a *bona fide* employee of the mill, but to enforce such a seemingly innocent rule was difficult at best. Binding contracts were nonexistent, and what constituted a *bona fide* mill employee was ambiguous. Players would report for work and go about with the village crew, doing repairs on mill houses or other property. Often a paint brush or screwdriver in the back pocket and an hour or two walking around sufficed. Then it was off to the ballpark for practice.

A rule so loosely interpreted invited protests from teams, always couched in the correct, precise terminology required by the league office: the protest is lodged, insisting that alias Smith and Jones are not *bona fide* mill employees, as required in the by-laws of the league. To their credit, league officials dutifully investigated the complaints and occasionally ordered games to be replayed after announcing that a player was not a worker at the mill.

In the May 21, 1921, doubleheader between Greer and visiting Tucapau, the home team took the opening game 7-2, but was nosed out 1-0 in the second contest. The locals took great exception to their loss and protested that a player for Tucapau was not that rare and elusive *bona fide* mill employee. Their case, though, was well made. Tucapau used a player from Apalache Mill who chose to wear his own uniform, with the embroidered "A" on the jersey, rather than try to find a nice fitting Tucapau shirt. The protest, quite logically, was upheld.

Another frequent complaint among the mill teams was that certain other clubs used professional players, those men who had participated at some level of organized baseball. In an April 26, 1915, game between Beaumont and Drayton, *both* teams lodged formal protests; Beaumont because Gowans signed to play with them but showed up that day to play with the opposition and Drayton because they contested that Simmons of Beaumont was a professional player. The Spartanburg Mill League president, Charles Herron, was concerned enough to call a special meeting of the league directors. On his recommendation, the by-laws were amended so that any individual who had played as a professional in organized baseball was ineligible to play in the league. Oddly enough, the team most affected was Beaumont, who lost the services of both Simmons and "Bad Eye" Guthrie, a fine pitcher recently signed by the team. Brandon, the 1923 champions of the Piedmont Textile League of Greenville, defeated Dunean 5-2 on July 21st as the losers protested. Emerson Cashion, the Brandon catcher, had been playing with the Greenville Spinners of the South Atlantic League. There was no mention of the protest being upheld, though it was remarkable that league officials could overlook such obvious evidence as a man playing for two teams in the same town.

There were even instances of league championships being disputed. Judson, which finished one game behind Dunean in the 1916 Greenville Mill League, accused an umpire of leaning blatantly toward the winners in an early season doubleheader. In that May 27th contest, there were no ropes to hold the home crowd off the field, and the umpire supposedly stated that if Dunean had not won that second game, he would not have "gotten out of there alive."[8]

The Duncan-Judson game was officially protested, and the protest was upheld by the league office. However, the Dunean win was never stricken from the record, and they remained pennant winners.

Three years later, almost to the day, Pacolet disputed the Spartanburg Mill League pennant awarded to Whitney. The sore point was a five inning game the winners played with Arkwright. Though not a regularly scheduled league game, it somehow was allowed to count in the final standings. Pacolet offered to play Whitney in a three game series on neutral grounds to decide the true league champion, but the challenge fell upon deaf ears.

Though most of the protests were straightforward, some were truly unusual, certainly worthy of enshrinement in the "mill village hall of memories." An incensed Belton team protested a 5–3 loss to Anderson Mill in the 1921 Anderson County League, claiming a bit too much "home field" advantage for the winners. Three fly balls to right field went for hits on August 20th (two for home runs) when the Belton player fell into a ditch attempting to make the catches. Eyewitnesses intimated that he disappeared from sight during these efforts.[9] Whether he should have remembered the location of the ditch was not in question for Belton fans, since the rough territory contributed significantly to the visitors' defeat.

A little sleight of hand would have been to blame in Conestee's protest of a loss to Simpsonville Mill in a May 31, 1924, Eastern Carolina League game. The losers accused their host's pitchers of using "dead" baseballs. The balls would either be old, with a little starch and sizing from the mill's slasher room used to whiten them back up, or new balls that had been wrapped in towels and placed in a local ice house until just before game time. Regardless of the method, some quick-witted bench warmer had to get the doctored balls to the umpire in an innocent fashion at the end of each inning so the Simpsonville pitchers could use them effectively.

Since second ("B") team leagues were commonplace, it was always ripe for a disgruntled group to maintain that first ("A") team players were used in a "B" team game. Judson charged Poe with such an offense in an April 16, 1927, Parker League game. Even those protests which brought a chuckle to the interested citizenry possessed a darker side. Lurking not far behind the accusations of unfairness and favoritism was the reality that teams would forfeit and walk away from the game before accepting the loss.

It was a ploy which had been around since the beginnings of textile baseball. In a June 4, 1904, battle between homestanding Piedmont and Pelzer, the visitors had fallen behind 11–0 by the third inning, so they simply left the field and abandoned the game. Obviously, the large crowd in attendance was not happy with this outcome. Thankfully few and far between, such occurrences nevertheless cropped up though the years, especially as the level of competition led to an almost insatiable desire to win.

Discreetly sizing up the situation in a July 23, 1914, game against Tucapau, the Pelzer manager called his team off the field, saying the umpire was not treating his team fairly. That the Tucapau pitcher was hurling a no-hitter at the time must simply have been a coincidence. Much the same circumstance occurred as manager McClure of Poe gave notice of protest over a decision at the plate when the umpire called left fielder Welch out in a July 10, 1915, game. It was the eighth inning, with Poe trailing Brandon (Greenville) 8-0, but perhaps that did not figure at all in the field general's decision.

Sometimes the protests were hard to figure. On August 28, 1915, visiting Brandon led Fountain Inn 2-1 in the late innings. Incensed over a decision on a close play at third base, the Greenville team walked off the field, got into their automobiles, and returned home. The league office must have wondered when the Poe team forfeited to Belton in a scheduled Interurban League tussle on July 22, 1916. The manager had to explain that most of his players had journeyed north to Fountain Inn to temporarily join that team in its battle with Gaffney, and there were simply not enough Ravens available to take the field.

There were numerous times when teams did not even bother to show up, leaving opponents and fans to wonder what had happened. Even when a phone call was made to discuss why an opponent did not show up, as Dunean representatives did to the Brandon (Greenville) team on April 19, 1919, no one was available to answer the summons.

When protests began to plague the leagues, sportswriters became involved in admonishing both teams and their fans. The Spartanburg *Herald*'s "Mill League Notes" of 1913 stated that

> Something should be done to stop the infernal fussing between spectators at Wofford Park. At every game, someone feels that it is his duty to start a row with someone else. If the persons who are guilty could be arrested and subjected to the payment of a neat little sum, rowdyism would soon cease. If it doesn't cease, ladies are sure to stop attending games.
>
> When a man is convicted of a crime in this county, he ought to be compelled to act as umpire in the mill league. When he completed the term imposed upon him, it is a 10-1 bet he'd always be a law abiding citizen![10]

Admonitions were sometimes not enough, and league officials resorted to a drastic measure to solve problems. The headline on the sports page of the Friday, July 30, 1915 Spartanburg *Herald* announced "Spartanburg Mill League Disbanded." League directors came to such an extreme decision after long hours attempting to settle various protests. They saw, unfortunately, many more incidents requiring the same attention. The executives unanimously voted it was better for the mill league to disband than to continue operating under the present conditions.

It was most bothersome when the fans became emotionally involved in the contests they watched, since it was outside interference, rather than individual talent and team play, which had the most bearing on the outcome. The popularity of textile baseball meant that playing fields often had to be roped off, and only participants and officials were allowed inside. During a closely contested game, however, order could be lost quickly as spectators surged onto the playing area. Police protection was often the only solution when the big rivalries or league playoffs got underway.

When Camperdown forfeited a June 10, 1922, game, they accused the home Judson team of failing to provide this necessary police protection, maintaining that the fans swarmed around them and made playing the close game (it was 5–4 at the time) impossible.

More amazing was the deciding game of the 1938 Mid State League semifinals. With the home Monarch team leading the August 20th game 3–2 in the eighth inning, a close play at second went against Lockhart. The visiting fans rushed onto the field, refusing to leave even after being given a ten minute deadline. When those agonizing moments had passed and the fans still swarmed between the foul lines, the umpire, true to his word, awarded the game to Monarch, sending them into the league championship series while Lockhart went home the loser.

Once the rowdyism moved to the point of spectators ruling the field, a down-to-earth brawl could not be that far away. When Union Bleachery defeated Dunean 3–2 June 12, 1923, a fight started in the ninth inning after a close play at the plate. Several Bleachery players were badly bruised and cut about the the face in the encounter. J.M. Clements, a journeyman infielder from 1917 to 1930, noted with a chuckle, "If there wasn't a fight, then the game just didn't seem complete. As a player, I knew how to hit, throw, run and fight. Why, I even recall seeing women fighting in the grandstands, hitting one another with umbrellas!"[11]

Leo Tober, a fine pitcher for Ware Shoals, remembered a game in the mid-1930s, when he hooked up with Jean Belue of Ninety Six in a classic mound duel. "Umpires were known to carry guns just in case things got too much out of hand," he said. "We had a lead when one of the Indians lined a ball over the left field fence, clearly foul, but only by a couple of feet. The batter never argued, but the fans came out of the stands after the umpire. The man in blue fired his gun into the ground, momentarily stopping the surge of angry people. This gave him a chance to run into a house near the ball field, where he stayed until the police arrived and quelled the riot.

"And me? I was nestled down on one end of the bench, real close to the bats, hoping and praying all that anger would go away. I'm thankful things got back to normal, and we continued with the game."[12] The score, though, was something he could not recall. Mr. Eddie Hall witnessed the game, and the ugly drama as well. His one comment on the situation was, "Thank God they didn't catch the ump."[13]

Bill "Lightning" Webb was locked in a pitching duel with Bob Bowman of Orr Mill in a May 29, 1937, game. The lanky Equinox Mill hurler, who had a brief stay with the Philadelphia Phillies in 1943, and Bowman, a St. Louis Cardinals rookie in 1939, were the contest's featured stars, but that distinction soon belonged to a violent fourth inning brawl.

"With the score tied, left fielder Dumb Price was called out on a close play at first base by lone umpire Henson, who presided over the game from behind the pitcher's mound," Webb recounted. "Price attacked Henson, the two men exchanged blows, and the player was ejected from the game. At the end of the inning, Price attempted to take his position in left field, but the umpire refused to allow the game to proceed until the banished player was removed. It was the only time I ever saw police being used to restore order at a game."[14]

During the late 1920s and far into the 1930s, there was an outside influence which touched not only baseball, but every aspect of mill village life. Labor unrest had begun. Union organizing efforts were underway at nearly every mill as Workers of the World and the United Textile Workers made their pleas for solidarity. At issue were higher wages, better working conditions, and an end to the hated "stretch out" where workers were given more and more machinery to tend, with less and less rest time, and with no increase in their pay.

Ominous signs began as early as 1929, when the local press reported that "Brandon's failure to quit Piedmont A baseball was a source of joy to a lot of textile followers. The strike settlement couldn't have come at a more opportune moment."[15] Settlements of a different nature occurred as well.

"Tough" Embler played most of his career around Anderson and Laurens, and came from a baseball family; brothers Ezra and Jimmy also played on a number of mill teams. During the 1934 season, with labor unrest growing stronger, "Tough" witnessed one of the real tragedies in textile baseball history:

"That year, Anderson Mill played a game at Appleton, and the two teams were longstanding rivals. A foul ball went into the stands and was caught by an ardent Anderson supporter. Appleton manager Bill Tidwell went up to retrieve the ball, a necessary task for the home team during the days of real tight money. A heated argument started between the two, and before anyone really knew what had happened, the man had plunged a big knife deep into Tidwell's chest. Mr. Bill died later that night. I guess that moment was one part of textile baseball most of us who were there would like to forget."[16]

The heated arguments and accompanying threats of violence between management and labor reached fever pitch. In the small Anderson County community of Honea Path, the confrontation everyone had long feared finally happened. The night shift employees at Chiquola Manufacturing Company completed their work and left the mill quietly. As members of the day shift began arriving, Superintendent Beacham gave orders that the doors be kept closed until adequate police protection could be arranged. The order created a volatile situation as people milled around with picker sticks and green oak boughs. Angry words were exchanged between company supporters and labor activists.

Shortly before 8:00 A.M. on September 6, 1934, taunts and fist fights were intermingled as 300 picketers, employees, and law officers crowded around the main entrance of the mill. A "flying squadron" (armed union supporters on flatbed trucks who traveled from location to location) and strikers from closed mills in nearby Belton and Greenwood swelled the ranks of the labor loyalists. After one prolonged altercation, shots were fired, and for three minutes a bloody battle raged. Both sides always denied firing the opening salvo.

When quiet descended, six men lay dead and 13 were wounded (one a woman) as a National Guard Machine Gun unit from Orangeburg was called in to maintain order. There was no further violence as the strikers fled, and the remaining employees and officers ministered as best they could to the wounded. Bloody Thursday was over.

The championship series of the Anderson County League, a best three-of-five format between Gluck and Chiquola mills, had begun Saturday, September 1st at Gluck. The Saturday, September 8th game was scheduled at the Chiquola field in Honea Path but, because of the bloody and tense labor situation, was not played. The series was forfeited to Gluck and became known as the championship series that never was.

Perhaps it was the death of innocence, perhaps only a recognition that even the best things have a dark side. Textile baseball confronted itself with the protests, illegal players, rowdyism, labor unrest, and even death, and it survived. No, more than that. It grew stronger in the decade of the 1930s and, in many instances, served as an unofficial farm system for both the National and American Leagues. In the Depression years, folks crowded to the edges of the fields, watching the only entertainment affordable to most of the mill village inhabitants. It was stiff competition and spirited pennant races, but it was no longer an innocent game. That part of textile baseball was gone forever.

Chapter 7

The Maturing Years

The 1930s became the true glory days of textile baseball, both in the quality of play and in spectator interest. The game's innocence may have suffered in the labor violence spanning the late 1920s to mid–1930s and in the bleak economic times of the Great Depression, but its popularity could not be denied. Though some mills were forced to disband teams for a year or two, most owners kept the game going because it was such an established part of mill life, to be counted on as much as the arrival of spring itself. Folks seemed to live from one season to the next just to root for the home team. Who could resist the charms of such a time-honored tradition? Watching the game from a splintery bleacher seat on a warm Saturday afternoon could cure many of the world's ills, at least for a time.

Jim Blackwell, a scrappy shortstop who moved from Walhalla to Gossett Mill in 1935 and on to Appleton Mill in 1936, spoke of the level of play by major league standards. "If you weren't good enough to play big league ball," he said "you didn't play around the Anderson area! Many a man tried out, was given his supper, and sent on his way."[1]

A desire to excel was the hallmark of the players of this era. The very fabric of their lives was built around baseball since there was little else open to them except working in the mill, practicing, and playing the game. If a man was good enough, the money was there. Players like Leroy Mahaffey (Appleton, Lyman and Gossett mills) finished careers in the majors and came back to play. College players like Bo Dotherow (Inman Mill), an All-American end in football at Alabama, came to share a piece of the action.

Throughout the years of textile baseball, mill management skillfully bent the rules for players in order to justify them as employees, and the 1930s were no different. A man might push empty boxes for a while or walk through the mill early in the morning, carrying a hammer or screwdriver before going out to practice. Owners wanted to protect their investments and avoid injuries that did befall players like Hinkie Allen, an Anderson County League mainstay who was hurt on the job in mid–1937 and missed several crucial games down the stretch. What a player could make depended most often upon the size of the mill and where it was located. At a time when the average mill worker might earn $7 to $10 a week, a good player in a city mill, where competition to retain talent was fierce, could earn as much as $100 to $200 a week. In the smaller mills of more rural areas, though, he might work 55 hours a week in a legitimate job and then make $5 to $15 a game. In either case, it was more than most people made, but it seemed to spawn little jealousy. To the contrary, folks always got to the ballpark early in order to get good seats.

Though owners controlled the game, there were times when players got the upper hand. Mr. James C. Self, owner of Greenwood Mills Company, was outmaneuvered on at least one occasion in a financial transaction. One rainy spring afternoon, a member of the team arrived at "Mister Jim's" office, always open to employees who wanted to talk, to request a contribution for the mill's baseball club.

"When I asked him how much," Mr. Self said, "he responded with a request for $500. I hit the ceiling! I lectured him about money not growing on trees and such, and wound up giving him a check for $250. But the joke was on me. I found out later that he had been sent to get $150!"[2]

As the Depression continued to hammer at the mill villages in the early 1930s, ballplayers were among the fortunate few who had a relative sense of job security and a chance at decent money. It quickly became obvious, though, that only the talented few were guaranteed a roster spot, so keen was the competition. Virgil Lavender, a native of Greenville who played textile baseball from the late–1920s to the early–1950s, made the team at Poinsett Mill while still a student in high school.

"Baseball had become a big part of mill life," he remembers, "as management continued to give strong support to the teams even though the Depression was deepening. After high school, I got my first job at Mills Mill in Greenville."[3]

By 1934, the mills which had suspended baseball due to the economy fielded teams once more. A recruiting war of sorts started. If the grass was a little bit greener, a player could be induced by a better offer to jump from team to team. Virgil took advantage of his talents and moved on to other Greenville area mills like Poe, Brandon, and Woodside (where he was a member of the 1936 Western Carolina League championship team) before settling in Pelzer and finishing his career. Playing for more than one team was not all that uncommon and was not frowned upon by mill management, so long as such an endeavor was discreetly handled and teams were not competing in the same general vicinity. It was a great way to make extra money.

Leagues grew in the 1930s at a rate which must have seemed astounding. It was a time for expansion, so when established organizations acted to protect their own identities and exclude additional teams, new leagues came into being. When the managers of the teams in the Anderson County League met in the back of Fant's Book Store to draw up the 1933 schedule, there was other business at hand. Representatives from Calhoun Falls, Central, Abbeville and several northeast Georgia communities asked for their teams to be admitted. League officials were not enthusiastic about expanding their compact league to accommodate all who wanted to join. The petitioners reconvened later and formed the Georgia-Carolina League, electing "Red" Canup president. As sports editor of the Anderson *Independent,* his position lent immediate credibility to the new league and guaranteed excellent coverage on the sports pages.

It was not unusual for fifteen or more leagues to operate simultaneously in the upstate towns and communities, but there was no shortage of spectators as large crowds continued to pack the ballparks in the mill villages. The folks came to enjoy each other's fellowship, to share their fears, to forget the hard times for awhile, and cheer the local boys on. A crowd of 3,000 saw Gossett beat Anderson during the 1930 Independence Day celebration, and 3,500 watched as Appleton beat Gluck 8-3 on August 30th to finish the year. Over 3,000 people witnessed plenty of action as Orr beat Anderson 22-15 on June 4, 1932, and a month later 5,000 hearty souls cheered LaFrance to an 8-7 July 4th win over Appleton. On a hot August 24, 1934, 3,000 watched as Chiquola beat Orr 11-5 and captured the second half Anderson County League championship. A little more than one week later, labor violence would erupt at Chiquola Mill, leaving six dead and the town of Honea Path in the grip of terror. Interestingly, the total population of the mill village did not exceed the attendance at the park. When folks said, "Everyone went to the ballgame, 'cause it was the best thing around," they did not speak idly.

With unerring judgment, the owners instituted a change in the league playoff system during these years. The 1920s leagues had a split season, with the first and second half winners meeting for the championship. The 1930s teams, though, used the Shaughnessy playoff system, where the first and fourth place teams would play in one semifinal and the second and third place teams in the other. The winners of these series would then meet for the title in the same three-of-five or four-of-seven game format used in the semis. The extra playoff series brought more people to the park and sustained the intense championship fever for another week or two. It was a solid big bucks decision.

Crowds were treated to memorable games, sharing the heartbreak with Badger of Sampson Mill as he tossed a no-hitter against Renfrew, but still lost a June 21, 1930, contest 3-1. The same day, Hendrix of neighboring Monaghan (Greenville) blasted six hits in an 18-5 win over Woodside. Fans long remembered Appleton's 14-game winning streak in 1931, halted by a 6-5 loss to Gluck on July 12th. How they enjoyed watching R.B. Speares, with his 100 m.p.h. fastball, garner the major portion of the wins during that run. Hopkins of LaFrance amassed 21 strikeouts in a 4–3, 12-inning thriller over Gluck on April 30, 1932, and future major leaguer Kirby Higbe pitched Anderson to a 14–0 win over Gossett on August 27th of that year. The 1934 Palmetto League final series was all that anyone could have hoped for, as Ninety Six bested Greenwood 3–2 in an 11-inning squeaker to capture the championship. One added attraction to the 1934 season was the Most Popular Player contest, voted on by the readers of the Anderson *Independent*. At the end of the season, one player from each of the twelve teams in the county was chosen for the honor and presented with an engraved bronze medallion.*

When the bidding wars began in the mid–1930s, rivalries heated up and fierce loyalties were born. A crowd of 3,000 saw Newberry lose to Buffalo 8–1 on June 22, 1935. Over 3,500 fans sat through August 3rd heat in Spartanburg two years later as the Eastern Carolina and Western Carolina League All-Stars battled to a 3–3 tie, and 4,500 enjoyed a sun drenched September 14th afternoon in 1938 as Brandon (Greenville) beat Lyman 4–2 for the King Cotton League championship.

Fans were treated to Johnny Wertz, a Newberry Mill pitcher and former Boston Brave, and his 31-win season in the 1935 Mid-State League; his total broke the record of Whitmire pitcher Rhem, who had carded 28 wins only a year earlier. They cheered later in the year when Watts Mill played in the Southern Textile Athletic Association Baseball Tournament (a mirror image of the basketball competition held each March), open only to winners and runners-up of the leagues, and brought the championship home to Laurens County on September 20th.

Brown of Slater aptly christened the 1936 season with a 1–0 no-hit, 18-strikeout performance against Camperdown on April 4th. Wertz continued his magic with 163 strikeouts of Mid-State opponents that same year. Fans whooped it up for youngsters like the Spartanburg American Legion team, a familiar entry in the Spartanburg County League, who used the experience gleaned from stiff competition with the mill teams to capture the year's National American Legion Championship.

It was the 1937 season which offered perhaps the keenest competition and best performances. Buster Hair was a hot topic, fanning 20 for Glendale in a 7–0 win over Clifton on April 17th, then claiming 17 on April 27th (a 2–0 win over Fingerville) and 23 on April 30th (4–0 over Spartan Mill). Brandon (Woodruff) scored 12 runs in the ninth inning to secure a July 2nd win from Monarch 15–5, and the fireworks continued 10 days later as the Drayton club slammed four homers in the sixth inning of

---

* The recipients of the Most Popular Player, in order of votes cast, were: Dick Smith (Gossett), Buck Moore (Gluck), C.R. Williams (Anderson), Jerry Whitten (Orr), Guy Powell (Appleton), Larry Harbin (Equinox), Cunningham (Chiquola), Ira Thompson (Belton), J.L. Green (Iva), Lefty Helms (Pelzer), Raymond Garner (Williamston), and Clement Duncan (Pendleton).

a 9–2 win over Whitney. Not to be outdone, Whitney ran wild over Brandon (Woodruff) on July 27th, stealing twelve bases against the loser's frustrated catcher.

Soon-to-be St. Louis Cardinal Ernie White garnered 155 strikeouts in only 126 innings as a Pacolet hurler. Whitney Mill clamored for headlines of its own, winning the state's semi-pro tourney and heading on to Wichita, Kansas, for a shot at the National Semi-Pro Baseball Championship. Orr's victory in the opener of the Anderson County League playoffs on April 28th epitomized excitement; the Rifles executed a 7th inning hit-and-run with runners on second and third, with both runners breaking on the pitch and scoring on a perfect bunt up the third base line, triggering a 5–2 win and an eventual sweep of Equinox.

The 1938 season reflected an ever increasing enthusiasm for the game. The bad economic times were finally easing, the rumblings of global war were still confined to Europe and the Far East, and fans were content with a bit more job security and a seat in the grandstands. Some of the ballparks, interestingly, had moved away from the cozy fields to those of truly monstrous dimensions. Deep center field in Pelzer was nearly unreachable, and well-to-do fans parked their cars on the outer perimeter (formed by a harness racing track), since there was little danger of a dented fender, though a long drive might roll that far. The old park saw many crowds like the 5,000 for July 4th doubleheader between Pelzer and Appleton. The *whole* outfield at Riegel Stadium in Ware Shoals was expansive enough to allow for the storage of cotton bales there, with 600 or more feet of playing area still available. Home runs were inside-the-park, and it often took three men to peg the ball back in from the fence. There are legends of sluggers who supposedly hit one out of the original boundaries, but no documented proof.

Wonderful performances were abundant and reflected excellence in all phases of the game. Orr of Liberty blasted 3 homers on June 4th, but his team still lost to Pickens 14–13. Green of Clifton duplicated the feat on August 5th in an 8–7 win over Glendale. Defying all the odds, both Casey Jones of Jackson and Don Jackson of Greer hurled no hitters on June 4th, Jones in a 6–0 masterpiece against Jonesville and Jackson a 7–0 beauty over Piedmont. Strickland of Mills Mill (Greenville) had seven RBI's in a 13–7 walk over Pelzer on July 9th, and Lee collected the lucky seven hits in a 16–5 Pacolet win over Converse on August 5th.

The Union team set some sort of record eight days later when they stroked eight straight doubles in a fifth inning uprising and defeated Jonesville 11–4. Appleton's Larry Harbin, in a 6–3 loss on August 13th, launched a homer against Pelzer which carried 450 feet, one of the very few tape measure shots recorded. Stove Taylor, who had chased foul balls at Pelzer for more than 25 years, declared Harbin's drive the longest he

Johnny Wertz of the Boston Braves. *Photo courtesy of Emily Clements.*

had ever seen. Such feats could bring additional rewards, as "Rags" Suddeth of Southern Bleachery discovered when he homered to win an April 15th game against Piedmont. He earned five dollars, five gallons of gas, a carton of cigarettes, and a 24-pound sack of flour. Seasonal records of note were Stribbling's streak of one earned run in 41 innings for Southern Bleachery, and "Wild Bill" Broome's 173 strikeouts for the season, moving the Lockhart hurler past Johnny Wertz's Mid–State League mark.

The final year of textile baseball's boom decade possessed its own share of the great and the interesting. Pacolet of the Eastern Carolina League won 18 games in a row, but that mark paled beside Rock Hill

Bleachery's achievement. Bringing up the rear of the Mid-State League in mid–July, they launched a drive which culminated in the championship and became the local version of the 1914 Miracle Braves. In the big Piedmont-Pelzer rivalry, odd things usually found a way to happen, like a freak play allowing the Piedmont boys to claim an extra inning 8–7 win on July 14th; a pop up landed three feet in front of the plate, but spun crazily *back into* the infield as the winning run raced home.

In addition to the exhibitions and regular league games, there were always special events going on at the ballpark. Fans attending an August 10, 1935, game between Orr and Equinox witnessed perhaps the youngest performer ever in the textile leagues as Crate Herring substituted his twelve-year-old son, Cotton, into Orr's line-up. The young man drew a walk and played a credible right field. Later that month, the people of Belton and Judson mills were treated to visits by the New York Bloomer Girls, featuring the keystone combination of Hattie Michaels and Ginger Robinson. The team was the self-proclaimed undefeated female baseball champions of the East since 1910.

Donkey baseball popped up now and then on the village diamond, always drawing a big crowd and becoming quite a social occasion when the local team played the overseers of the mill. It was a sight watching riders trying to persuade recalcitrant animals to try a game the poor beasts had no intentions of enjoying.

One event long anticipated was the 1937 visit to Orr Mill Park of Al Schacht, the "Clown Prince of Baseball." His three-year major league career may not have amounted to much, but folks didn't care about that. On August 13, 1937, they were treated to an hour of hilarity and belly laughs long remembered and cherished.

Occasionally, the greatest of them all would put in an appearance. Shoeless Joe Jackson, well past his prime but still possessor of Black Betsy and the fluid swing, hit for both the Eastern and Western Carolina All-Stars in the third inning of an August 1, 1939, affair. So that favoritism could not be claimed, the Shoeless one rifled out doubles in each of his plate appearances. He gave the 3,000 in attendance a wonderful performance, and to him they gave back the assurance that, for the people of the mill villages, the legend would never die.

The popularity of the game led to some interesting innovations. Womens' baseball had been a novelty in the South for years. As early as March, 1899, the ladies' champion Boston Bloomers traveled in their special Pullman car, destined for Newberry to play the local team on a vacant lot near an old dairy farm. Not only did proper society disallow the use of a regular field, but evidently discouraged the game from occurring at all. The Boston lasses did not even stop, choosing to travel on to Greenwood.

There were many games between the Chicago Bloomer Girls and the mill teams, and at least one with the American Athletic Baseball Club (five women and four men), who lost to Whitmire's Glen Lowery Mill 7-2 June 23, 1922. There was a July 4th battle at the Piedmont festivities the same year, when the team coached by T.B. Gresham beat one directed by Joe Patterson 30-9. And, of course, Champ Osteen's daughters formed the Daughters of the American Baseball Revolution. In 1934, there was the beginning of the Anderson County Textile Girls Baseball League, the first systematic attempt to develop local women's competition. Appleton Mill showed the most enthusiasm, with 30 girls trying out and choosing up sides for several innings in the cool of the late afternoon. They were the driving force, the first to be given coverage by the local media and the first to schedule competition with other teams. Games were solicited through the newspaper, and requests dropped off (or called in by phone) at the company store.

Records show that Appleton was undefeated in six games during July and August, beating Gossett Mill of Williamston five times and Anderson Mill once. Complimented on their colorful uniforms, Appleton players included Margaret Humphries, Maggie Whitworth, Ruth Watkins, Vickery, Hawkins and Powell. Other players mentioned in newspaper coverage were Anderson's Honea and Fredricks, and Gossett's Owens and Singer. In neighboring Greenville, the Poe Mill Red Pants held center stage briefly on August 4th, besting a team of "elderly men" 7-6 behind the performances of star players Hutchinson and Cleveland. Though plans were made for a 1935 season, there were no indications the league materialized. Instead, softball became the game of the lassies of the village. Still, for a few games in the late summer of 1934, the women shared the spotlight with the men in textile baseball.

Better able to weather the years was the coming of night baseball to the leagues. Like their counterparts in the majors, mill owners reasoned that scheduling games after people had a chance to get home from work, rest, clean up and eat would draw larger crowds to the park than traditional afternoon games. Friday, May 7, 1937, was the date set for the first night baseball game in Spartanburg County, and 2,000 fans witnessed history being made when Lyman defeated Hickory (NC) 4-1 "under the floodlights." The next evening 2,500 turned out as the Pacifics edged Pacolet 3-2 in an Eastern Carolina League tilt. A week later the team remained perfect evening gentlemen with a 10-3 win over the King Cotton League-leading Judson Redcoats.

Lyman remained the foremost supporters of night baseball and two years later introduced the twi-night doubleheader to the Western Carolina League. They defeated league foe Appleton 15-2 and 20-0 on July 29th, the evening game mercifully called after seven innings. The Mid-Carolina

League also offered its first night game on July 22, 1939, as Newberry beat Clinton 6-0 on George Hiller's dim lit two-hitter. Teammate Bob Creekmore's fluke inside-the-park two run homer proved to be the winning hit of the game. The true features of many "owl" contests, however, were the odd bounces of the ball betwixt and between crazily angled shadows created by the early lighting systems.

If baseball under the lights was the first concession to surging popularity, then certainly a second was carrying the games over the radio. As early as May 5, 1935, Harold Lyle and H.E. Bunge did the play-by-play for Joanna during the home club's 9-6 win over Mathews in the Central Carolina League, and it was a logical progression from the public address system to the airwaves. Fans thirsted for more coverage, to keep up with both the home team and the rivals of their local heroes. During the 1937 playoffs for the King Cotton League pennant, station WFBC in Greenville broadcast Judson's 11-3 triumph over Piedmont on September 2nd. In addition to the radio audience, there were 3,000 fans attending the game, a truly extraordinary event for textile baseball.

The broadcasts were sufficiently popular that WFBC opted to begin carrying games the opening week of the 1938 season, when Southern Bleachery bested Piedmont 6-2 on April 15th. The popularity of the game seemed to know few limits, and mill owners gave both employees and the surrounding communities a way to enjoy the action even when they could not spend the day in the grandstands.

For all the excitement, rivalries, and trappings of a big time show, there was something wistful about the game as the 1930s came to a close. For the first time, Old Timers' games became popular, as if players, fans, and owners all attempted to grab a tattered piece of bygone days before the magic was gone. The opening day festivities of the 1937 King Cotton League revolved more around former players than it depended upon Pelzer's 12-5 blowout of Greer that April 17th. The 1,200 spectators had come to see the Victor Mill club of 1908-09, remembered as one of the greatest amateur/semi-pro teams ever assembled in the South (once posting a 19-game winning streak over stiff competition). The first pitch was made by Greer mayor J.H. Lanford to the legendary Shoeless Joe Jackson (who missed the easy offering and laughed about it) and caught by Bob Patrick; Jackson and Patrick were the only members of the old team to actively participate in the ceremonies that day.

Sometimes it was just a matter of a team playing men from the same community only old enough to be big brothers. The 1939 Pacolet team of the Eastern Carolina League took on the Pacolet championship team of 1927-28, and the youngsters shut out the old guys 7-0 on July 27th. It was fun, though, and doubled the memories for folks who did not yet fully realize how quickly the days of textile baseball would pass.

By the middle years of the decade, the textile leagues were constitut-
ing an unofficial farm system for major league teams, particularly the St.
Louis Cardinals, Brooklyn Dodgers, Philadelphia Athletics, and Washington Senators. Of the fifteen players of the decade who made it to the
big time, Washington claimed six: Joe Haynes (Appleton), Al Evans
(Chiquola), Buddy Lewis (Joanna), Mickey Livingston (Newberry), Red
Marion (Joanna), and Taft Wright (York). The Senators were followed
by Brooklyn with three: Jake Daniel (Joanna), Kirby Higbe (Anderson),
and George Jeffcoat (Anderson). Philadelphia nabbed two: Sam Page
(Mills Mill of Woodruff) and Al Veach (Lancaster). St Louis also claimed
two players: Clyde Shoun (Baldwin) and Bob Bowman (Orr). It was never
by chance that major league scouts sat inconspicuously in the grandstands
to watch the mill boys. Bill Laval, former University of South Carolina
coach and later a scout for the Boston Red Sox, made a special trip to
catch the 1935 Anderson County League championship battle between
Chiquola and Equinox.

Bob Bowman was of special interest. Former players maintain that
an agreement between Branch Rickey, St. Louis Cardinal general manager, and Joe Lyons, general manager at Orr Mill, allowed Cardinal
players not quite ready for the majors to compete on Mr. Joe's team in the
Anderson County League for a year or so. Field manager Crate Herring
had not only the luxury of Bowman's talents, but also those of Ike
Pearson and Alf Anderson, both future major leaguers. In the off-season,
the star pitcher was known on occasion to grant the request of Orr
basketball coach Fred Whitten, grab his guitar, and perform a few lively
numbers prior to tipoff. He was an irrepressible character, truly adored by
his fans.

If the 1937 Anderson County League championship series was any
indication, Bowman had progressed quite nicely. In the four game sweep
of Equinox Mill, he was credited with all four wins (three complete games
and one in relief), worked 30 innings, fanned 25 and allowed only 16 hits.
His tenure in the area was understood to be temporary as the local media
mentioned his textile career ending in a blaze of glory, citing him as a
member of the "far flung St. Louis Cardinal chain," and even predicting
his 1938 destination to either Class A or AA ball. By 1939 Bowman was a
hotshot Cardinal rookie, posting a 13-5 record and a 2.60 ERA; they
were, incidentally, the best numbers of his career. He had seasoned well
amid the stiff competition of the textile leagues.

Against a background of heartbreak from the Depression and labor
violence, and faced with the reality that the game so long loved had
changed into a serious business, fans were occasionally treated to diver-
sions from these do-or-die attitudes by the pranks of fun-loving players.
Such moments brought laughter from deep down in the soul. Frank

Howard, former football coach at Clemson University and a genuine sports legend in South Carolina, recounted a game in the mid-1930s, whose outcome depended on his success as a hitter in the last of the ninth inning. With a man on base and two outs, Howard, playing for the mill in Central, managed only a grounder to the opposing second baseman, who promptly booted the easy chance for an error.

"Our man scored the winning run," Coach Howard remembered, "and the fans took up a six-dollar collection for me. I marched right out to that second baseman and gave him three dollars. I was crazy as hell then, too."[4]

Bill Womack, a pitcher with Chiquola Mill, talked of another game with an equally interesting prank. "We played Equinox that day, and they hit us pretty hard, having baserunners nearly every inning. Al Evans, our fine catcher (and future major leaguer), sat on the bench between innings and peeled a potato; it had been a long game and I thought he was hungry. But as we took the field again, he put that potato in his mitt."[5]

That inning, Equinox runners perched on 2nd and 3rd with only one out. On the next pitch, Evans attempted to pick off the lead man, but threw the ball into left field. "The 'ball,' of course, was that potato," Womack laughed, "and as both runners approached the plate, Al tagged them out with the real horsehide, which was in his mitt all the time. That whole Equinox team chased the umpire, protesting the whole play, start to finish." The umpire, though sympathetic, maintained there was nothing he could do, since there was no rule prohibiting throwing a potato on the field.

There were stories that touched the heart and served to remind us that baseball was, after all, only a game, only a part of life, and most often not the most important part at all. Fred "Shag" Knox had played well enough at Renfrew Bleachery to attract the attention of Pittsburgh scout Carlton Molesworth, who called the lanky shortstop the best pro prospect he had seen in 30 years of beating the bushes. Knox signed a contract, and agreed to report to the Buc's farm club in Hutchinson, Kansas.

Before leaving for the Midwest, he intended to fulfill an obligation he had made to play one game with Chiquola Manufacturing Company in the Anderson County League. True love, though, affected the best of his plans. Shag was introduced to Miss Mae, a young lady who was to become his wife. The Pittsburgh Pirates organization lost an outstanding baseball player, but the Honea Path community gained a fine gentleman whose actions influenced both the caliber of baseball and its integrity for more than 40 years.[6]

Tragedy was no stranger to textile baseball, either. The Appleton Mill team had lost its own manager, Bill Tidwell, in a violent confrontation during a game in 1934. Later that year, they were the opponent the day Greene, the Dunean manager, died of a heart attack while directing his team from the coach's box. Wanting to help as much as possible, both Appleton and Dunean players arranged an August 20th memorial game, with proceeds going to Greene's widow. And on May 22, 1937, in the midst of visiting Lyman's 10–3 win, the ballpark at Whitney became a place of mourning. Second baseman Mud Owens of the home team had singled and was standing on first base when he received word of the death of his infant daughter. The crowd on that spring afternoon offered what condolences they could to a heartbroken young father making his way home to a grief-stricken family. Mill folks could always be counted on to share in both the good and bad times.

As the decade closed, there were indications that textile baseball, which had weathered so much external pressure the past several years, was subtly changing from the inside out. For years the game had been so prolific and so good that even professional minor leagues stood little chance of prospering in the state. People often joked that South Carolinians would go for pro ball like the South went for Alf Landon, the 1936 Republican presidential candidate. But now, mill officials were openly questioning whether they would continue to spend as much on their teams as in the past, or whether they would continue at all.

Sportswriters like "Red" Canup and Scoop Latimer might pass this off as sour grapes for teams which had paid much for the talent but still failed to win with it. Players like Bob Creekmore, however, saw the heart of the matter. "The leagues started downhill in the late 1930s for one reason," he said. "They simply outpriced themselves by trying to obtain highly paid ballplayers."[7] And that fundamental change became apparent in the war-torn decade of the 1940s.

Chapter 8

The Negro Textile Leagues

Theirs was a legacy built in the shadows of a white society, mirroring the same facets of that culture, but confined behind a web-thin boundary which may as well have been an ocean. It was Jim Crow law, separate but equal, with an emphasis upon the former, and it touched every part of life. Work, home, church, school, business, everything was carefully segregated so that the fragile separation remained intact. Blacks held menial jobs in the mill from the early days of the industry, mostly as janitors or laborers on the village crews, and, though not strongly supported in their recreational efforts, they did manage to field baseball teams alongside their white counterparts.

The first game mentioned in local papers was a September 4, 1895, Newberry Mill 9–7 victory over Anderson Mill. Played near the Helena community in Newberry County, it occurred the same day the mills' white teams met at New Brooklyn, near Spartanburg. A second game was covered during the 1900 Independence Day festivities at Pacolet, when the Jonesville team defeated The Quarry, though no details were made available. Like the white mill teams, the Independence Day holiday became their moment in the sun, but during the season the black teams found not only "linthead" mockery, but also racial discrimination. Scant sports page coverage was attributed to both reasons, but it was more cultural this time.

No mill team gained much notoriety during these early years when town teams, both black and white, were considered the finer, more serious purveyors of the game. And with the likes of the Greenville Stars, no other Negro League team would be a threat to overshadow their excellent talent.

The Stars were front page news, claiming the state title among the Negro League teams. Their game with the Due West club July 9, 1901, a 5–3 Greenville victory, was the first reference of a substantial crowd in attendance. On July 31st of the same year, there was bigger news stirring. E.B. Lamar, Jr., manager of the Cuban X Giants, contacted manager Johnson of the local club about the possibility of a two game series in the early autumn. Crowned Negro League champions of both the United States and Cuba, the X Giants had just completed a three season stretch of averaging more than 120 wins a season: 120 in 1898, 126 in 1899, and

129 in 1900. There were no further records, however, to substantiate whether the series was played.

Black or white, baseball in those early days was anything but a gentlemen's game. The Stars were subjected to this negative publicity as well. Returning home by mule and wagon after a win over Anderson on August 26, 1901, members of the team engaged in a brawl with employees of Fowler's Livery Stable. The victors, it seemed, had celebrated a bit too much with some alcoholic brew, and the Anderson men were likewise drowning their sorrows to ease the pain of defeat. The Anderson police were called in to break up the altercation. The Stars were good fighters as well as adroit ballplayers, since they also won the fisticuffs.

By 1909, a significant rivalry heated up between the cities of Greenville and Spartanburg, and baseball always fit nicely into such a competitive scene. That year the Spartan team gained the upper hand, a 4–3 win in front of 1,500 fans on July 5th, and they followed that up with a 16–0 shutout the next day before another overflow crowd. Ten days later, the red hot Spartans swept Newberry, 9–0 and 6–1 at Wofford Park, and then topped off a perfect 8–0 season by edging Greenwood 4–3.

Greenville, though, began a measure of revenge the next season, as the newly named Giants beat their guests 4–0 on June 3rd at League Park (a field available to them and local mill teams only when the semi-pro Carolina League club was on the road). More than 100 white fans, including Mayor Marshall, were in attendance, as were more than 100 ladies (a goodly number in the years just after the turn of the century). The Giants pulled off four double plays to back the superb three-hit pitching of Lefty Bates, and also smacked three homers.

Succeeding years saw attendance remain at high levels. The Giants defeated Anderson 7–2 on April 8, 1912, as 1,400 witnessed the good performances of Donalds, the winning pitcher who tossed a four-hitter while fanning ten, and Hardin, who doubled twice. On May 13th it was a battle of Giants in name only, as Greenville beat New Brooklyn 11–0. This time Tigue allowed but three hits (he carried a one-hitter into the ninth) and the locals were gaining quite a reputation as the best black team in the Piedmont.

Interest continued to build, and on April 20, 1914, the Carolina Colored League began operation. A carbon copy of the white semi-pro league operating at that time, the league included Greenville, Spartanburg, Anderson and Greenwood. The few existing details point to a successful season. The Jenkins Orphanage Band filled League Park with music on April 27th and serenaded 1,000 fans throughout Greenville's 4–1 win over Spartanburg. Sportswriters not only noticed that second baseman Brown possessed the adroit base stealing skills of Ty Cobb, but took time to comment on the gorgeous attire worn by the belles who came to cheer their heroes on. By May 25th, when the Giants edged the Anderson White Sox 10–9 in 11 innings (not a pretty game by any means, since the winners committed five errors, the losers six), the league was well underway. The first standings were issued, showing Greenville at 5-0, followed by Greenwood at 4-3, Anderson at 3-3 and Spartanburg at 2-4. As successful as 1914 proved to be, it was a mere prelude to the growing demand for baseball, and for the next eight years (1915-1922), the local Negro League outfits were as good as any teams fielded in the area.

Kicking off the 1915 season, Greenville continued its domination with a 13-1 win over Greer on April 13th. This heady ball club, blessed with incredible speed, was now looked upon as a credit to the local community. In return, the team solicited the support of the townspeople and extended a special invitation to white fans to attend Giant games. This growing interest was evident in all the pregame glitz for a July 15th contest with the Spartanburg Negro YMCA. More than 800 visiting fans were to come by train and diminish the Giants' home field advantage at Riverdale Park. The local press trumpeted the comparative records of the teams (but ultimately failed to give results of the game!), and emphasized what became a common marketing ploy, reserved seats for white fans.

On May 27, 1916, Negro teams at two local mills showcased their talents when the visiting Dunean Giants defeated the Piedmont Black Sox 4-2 behind Milam's no-hitter. The last two games documented before the U.S. entry into World War I underscored how popular the game had become. When the home Giants beat Anderson 4-3 on May 1, 1917, rail excursions came from both Greenwood and Anderson, bringing several hundred fans to watch the game held behind Greenville's Southern Depot. On June 25th, the local team played Greer in a game to benefit the Red Cross Fund, and a big crowd was on hand to support the worthy cause, including the white fans in their reserved section.

Following the close of World War I, the popularity of baseball rose astronomically, and the area's Negro League teams moved right along with the trend. The 1919 season was a huge success. On May 10th, the Greenville Stars (reverting to their old name) and a team of ex-soldiers played to a fast and snappy 3-3 tie at Poe Mill Park; to draw more people, both teams staged an impromptu parade through the mill village and surrounding area. The brightest of the Stars was Archer, holder of the state's Negro League strikeout record, who kept the hard hitting soldiers off balance.

Any time there was a big game on the schedule, like the Greenwood game on June 2nd, the team's management would begin drumming up the support of both black and white local fans. Since the Buncombe Streetcar Line passed Poe's field, it was easy for fans to get there and make certain the visitor's contingent would not outnumber them.

The team also used the monicker Colored Spinners for a trip to Atlanta's Ponce de Leon Park for a June 7th doubleheader. Archer fanned 13 in the opener and shut out the Colored Crackers 1-0, and Harper breezed through the second game to a 9-1 decision. An international flavor was apt to occur now and then at Poe Mill Park, like the 3-2 Greenville win June 13th over the Havana, Cuba team behind the good hitting of Earl and Minus.

The 1919 season climaxed with the Stars' 8-2 win over Greenwood at the Augusta Street Park on July 28th. The two teams sported excellent records (Greenville was 18-5 and Greenwood 10-2), and the Stars continued to draw much praise from Atlanta sportswriters as a top notch team. In the large crowd that day were more than 200 white patrons; advertisements proclaimed that half the grandstand would be reserved for them, and they would be afforded every courtesy. The good attendance was evidence that management's efforts to heighten the interest of the general public in the Stars' superb play was successful.

The early years of the 1920s not only continued the popularity of the game, but proved to be a high water mark in the recognition given to the local Negro Leagues in the segregated South. The Stars lent their good name to games with all black institutions like Allen University, edging the college men 4-3 at Poe's field on May 14, 1920. Greenville was also the anchor of the Piedmont Colored League that year, beating the circuit's Greenwood team 6-3 on May 31st as Robertson chalked up the win, slipping by the Spartanburg Sluggers 5-4 June 21st as shortstop Jackson's timely hitting earned Benton the victory, and finally sweeping Spartanburg 10-5 and 9-2 during the Fourth of July celebration.

By 1921, the Stars/Spinners were expanding their competitive clientele. Though losing to the power-laden All-Cuban Team 11-6 on April 25th, Jackson still had a stellar game. On May 9th the team lost to the Athens Red Sox, but avenged the defeat two weeks later in an exciting 5-4 win and followed it up with a 15-2 rout of the Sox the next day before a big crowd. Fame took its toll, but in a good way: shortstop Jackson proved himself worthy to join the Bacharach Giants, one of the nation's premiere Negro League teams.

Considered by many fans as the best of the local teams — either black or white — the Stars/Spinners served as a catalyst for the formation of a Negro mill league that year. Though his men were too talented to join the circuit, manager Jim Kennedy conducted a meeting at Jones Hardware Company on a steamy June 17th, and the fruit of his labor was the formation of the Piedmont Negro League. Easley, Fountain Inn, Greenville, and Piedmont were member teams, but the only competition recorded was a July 23rd Piedmont win. Even with the new league, it was the Stars' July 4th battle with the Spartanburg Sluggers at League Park that stirred the most interest. The Greenville Concert Band added a classy touch for those fans city-bound during the mid–summer holiday. Kennedy's strong contingent finished the year 23-7.

One other 1921 game earned notoriety because it demonstrated how brightly competitive fires glowed within the local Negro League teams. When the Rock Hill ABC's nailed the Spartanburg Quick Steps 10-2 on September 5th, the victory was so complete that the Spartanburg owners fired both the manager and his coaches on the spot. Some things, like managerial job security, never change.

From the mid–1920s through the 1930s Negro baseball was afforded less coverage. The July 4th festivities at Piedmont in 1924 offered a "round robin" tournament for the local mill teams. The home Champions defeated the Belton Tigers 14-5 and topped off a successful day by outlasting Honea Path 13-9 to claim the championship. On April 21, 1928, the Greenville Black Spinners lost to the Anderson Hard Hitters 6-5 in a Negro Business League game. The crowd was a large one, with special trains running between the two cities and shuttling fans to the park.

With the approach of World War II, details of games remained sketchy at best. There was some coverage afforded the 1939 and 1940 Spartanburg County Colored League; Converse was crowned the 1939 champions with an 11-3 record and had the best record (5-1) of the eight team league the next year. In 1941, Arcadia was declared the first half winner and Pacolet claimed the second half flag, though there was no series played to determine the season's champs.

Barnstorming teams offered the premiere event in 1942 when the Ethiopian Clowns, Negro National semi-pro champions, met the Chicago Brown Bombers at Greenville's League Park April 22nd. The great Elwood "Bingo" De Moss managed and played second base for the Bombers, and the legendary player was afforded the respect of the crowd that April day. That was also a good year for the five team Spartanburg County Colored League, with Pacolet's Black Trojans taking the championship. The season was made special with the first-ever listing of a Negro League All Star team. T.C. Garner, R. Gleen, W. Foster, T.J. Gleen, B. Bryson, G.T. Stewart, L. Tracy, T.B. Stewart, and R. Evans were honored for their excellent efforts. And at Pelzer on July 4th, the teams from Williamston and Belton clashed at 9:00 A.M. to begin the day's festivities.

Like their white textile league counterparts, the Negro teams also flourished in the postwar rededication of an old tradition. At Pacolet during the 1946 Independence Day celebration, the morning baseball game featured the homestanding Black Trojans and the Lyman Negro team, with the afternoon clash pitting the White Trojans against the Greenville Air Base. Such a schedule was an unusual blurring of the

The 1950 Joanna Mill Negro League team. *Front row (l-r):* **Tot Sanders, Villian Crawfield, Odell Suber, Arthur Davis, Odell Wilson.** *Back row (l-r):* **William McCracklin (secretary), Leroy Higgins, Eugene McCracklin, Henry Higgins, Colie McCracklin (batboy), John A. Burton, Eddie Burton.** *Photo courtesy of Naomi Wier.*

segregated holiday festivities, much like the Pelzer festivities four years earlier. With Jackie Robinson's emergence as a genuine star for Brooklyn in 1947, the Negro teams of the textile mills had their games covered more extensively, with local newspapers paying closer attention to lineups, standings, and game details.

Stellar individual performances were given their rightful accolades. When the Pacolet Black Trojans beat Hayne Shops 16-5 on April 26, 1947, six starters (W. Bailey, D. Bailey, J. Johnson, S. Shippey, R. Hardy, and C. Norris) had two or more hits.

A team of soldiers trained at Sterling High in Greenville for a game with the Charlotte, North Carolina, Black Hornets on June 25, 1948. The undefeated Veterans entertained their guests at Meadowbrook Park, home of the minor league Greenville Spinners.

On July 9, 1948, Willie Dawkins of the Gaffney Black Tigers fashioned a 5-0 no-hit victory over Lowenstein. Later, on August 7th, Pacolet beat Converse 7-3 in a Spartanburg County Colored League game, then traveled 30 miles to Caroleen, North Carolina, and handily defeated that mill team 16-5. On August 21st, Haynes Shop's Ralph Russell blasted three triples, as he and his mates blanked Converse 9-0.

With the arrival of the 1950s, the fortunes of the black teams again mirrored those of the white teams. Joanna fielded a strong contingent for the 1950 season, and played teams from Chappells, Greenwood, Whitmire, Clinton, Tryon (NC), and Charlotte (NC). As the schedule shows, they were having to travel further to get the same number of games as local mill-sponsored teams. These years of fading fortunes, though, produced some moments to remember. On August 1, 1950, Willie Bailey of Pacolet hit for the cycle and led the Black Trojans to a win over the Lyman Blues. The next year John Wesley Gossett, of the Drayton Black Dragons, provided his own Fourth of July fireworks in hurling a no-hitter as he blanked the Jonesville Black Tigers 3–0.

The Negro American League made a barnstorming stop at Spartanburg's Duncan Park on May 3, 1952, scheduling a game between the Philadelphia Stars and Indianapolis Clowns. In addition to fine baseball, King Tut, clown prince of Negro League baseball, performed for the crowd. The old city rivalry still managed to stir the local folks, and they witnessed a 1–1 tie between the Spartanburg Sluggers and Greenville Black Spinners on June 25th as 17-year-old Bobby Anderson of the Sluggers fashioned a nifty two-hitter.

The leagues were winding down in 1954. Two last stories were told. Joe Free of Draper put on a hitting clinic May 9th, blasting three triples and a double to set the pace for his team's 8–5 win over Fairforest. The Georgia-Carolina Negro League operated that summer, and drew teams from Calhoun Falls, the local Anderson VFW, Belton, Chiquola, Fiberglass, Center Rock, and Flat Rock, Georgia. Unfortunately, the league remained an obscure operation and details of the competition were unavailable.

Then, like all of mill baseball, it was gone. The game spanned times which seemed incapable of finding any mutual ground. Beginning only a generation removed from slavery and ending near the passage of the first major civil rights legislation, Negro League baseball may have existed separately, but the fine teams and dazzling performances served to claim a rightful portion of greatness. Its lot may have been relative obscurity, but the legacy burned long and hot enough to be cherished for the keen competition and absolute joy so freely given through the years. To have been a part of life, to have persevered, to have been remembered—in all these, the black textile teams were successful.

Chapter 9

War and Renaissance

The popularity of textile baseball remained strong entering the early years of the new decade, and children on the mill village seemed to grow up at the ball park. Small boys dragged bats to and from the dugout during the lengthy practices and made their own baseballs, wrapping yards of filling yarn around a small rubber ball before encasing it all in a roll of electrician's tape. Broken bats were taken home and nailed back together, or a discarded picker stick from the weave room found its way into "choose up" games in the late afternoon.

When the field was in use by the big teams, inventive kids created their own versions of the game. Richard Thorpe, whose *Cotton Mill Cowboys* offers a perspective of growing up on the mill village, recalls one such effort: "Stopper ball was played much like baseball, but the only active players at any one time were the batter and pitcher. Everyone else helped retrieve the soft drink bottle caps. Using a broom handle, the batter would attempt to hit the cap as far as possible. At various distances from home plate, areas were designated as singles, doubles, triples and home runs. A batter could be called out on three strikes or on a hit cap caught in the air, and hits were registered when a cap fell in the marked areas." Dreams grew big during endless hours of play.[1]

On game day, there were ways to get into the ballpark, even when the price of a ticket was hard to come by. It was first come, first serve, and the jobs were always at a premium. Ball boys furnished the umpire with new horsehide and were responsible for cleaning up the foul balls retrieved for future use. Balls hit over the fence or fouled out of play were chased down and presented at the gate for free admission. Kids could also bring their own gloves and retrieve the long drives banged out during batting practice, hopefully showing off a little talent for future consideration, and getting a free seat for the game.

Working the concession, though, was the way to make some money. Circulating through the bleachers with the heavy metal box held by a strap around the neck, hawking Double Cola or Chero Cola, peanuts, candy and hot dogs, brought forth some hard cash at the end of the evening. Good salespeople also offered one other item of convenience: seat cushions, which could be rented for the duration of the game. Nurtured lovingly in the minds of youngsters working the games was the desire to play, to excel, to make the big show. They understood that major league scouts were no strangers to textile league ball parks, having found the way there to observe both the bona fide legends and the hot shot prospects of the 1920s and 1930s. It had happened before, and there was always the chance that next time...

It was still the best thing in town, the place to be when game time rolled around. They watched players with nicknames like Shag, Powerhouse, Splat, Country, Shine, Mutt, and Rube, though none could match the colorful John "The Gorgeous" Mosteller of Clifton. Fans witnessed the bearded House of David team in exhibitions with Inman, Mills Mill of Woodruff, and Pacolet, and watched on April 25, 1940, as Converse devoured the Washington, DC, Ambassadors 11-2 on that team's tour through the south. The younger edition was also available for viewing, as the mills continued to sponsor the American Legion teams.

There was always something different going on. Once a novelty, night baseball became almost a way of life. The Anderson County League offered Family Night on June 21, 1940, when husband, wife, and all the children got into the game for 40 cents; they cheered for twelve innings before Orr bested Gossett 5-4. A week later the same league sponsored Children's Night, when the kids got in free; the affair was a lopsided 12-0 Gossett shellacking of Equinox. Donkey baseball was still around, and the 1941 Lyman Pacifics battled the mill's overseers during a steamy July 22nd evening. Radio coverage kept expanding as WAIM in Anderson joined Greenville's WFBC to carry more games over the airwaves.

Opening Day was like Christmas for the fans of textile ball, who loved the glitz and splendor of their game. As Drayton played Lyman in its Western Carolina League home inaugural on April 19, 1941, superintendent Smith Crow urged all hometown Draytonites to back the team. As a gesture of support and good luck, and with the local band blaring hearty tunes, he placed a horseshoe-shaped flower arrangement around the neck of manager Dick Corbin. All the hoopla was to no avail as Lyman won going away, 8-4.

For all the trappings and promotions, though, it was rawboned baseball the fans came to see during the prewar years. Good players could still lead a journeyman's life playing for a team in one league during the day and take advantage of the explosion of night baseball to play for a second team in a different league. There never seemed to be a shortage of teams to demand the talents of good players or of fans who gladly paid to see their heroes perform.

A crowd of 3,000 packed the lighted stadium to see Ware Shoals take a 4-0 West State win over Mathews June 1, 1940. On successive September nights that same year, Eastern Carolina League powers Pacolet and Drayton drew 1,500 (on the 6th) and 2,000 (on the 7th); the Trojans swept the Dragons of Drayton 5–3 and 7–4. From all corners of the upstate area there were records being made.

Former major leaguer Leroy Mahaffey fanned 21 Oconee batters and led his Gossett mates to a 14–1 win May 18, 1940. Later, on August 3rd, Apalache first baseman Ballenger had four hits and scored five times as the home boys skunked Glendale 14–0. The talk, though, focused on a freak hit and a wild pennant race. Those who watched Pacolet's 1–0 win over Avondale, North Carolina, in a classic Eastern Carolina League battle on May 5, 1940 would never forget the game winning RBI. As Tee Fleming dodged one of Jake Cantrell's heated offerings, the ball struck the bat and blooped lazily over third base for his only hit of the night. Folks who followed the Anderson County League that year had their hands full separating first and second half winners and losers. Seven games had been played in the *second half of the season* before Williamston won the *first half* after an extended three-way playoff.

The 1941 season offered excitement as well. Dunean's Cox and Cantrell together produced a baseball rarity, a shared no-hitter, as they blanked Fork Shoals 2–0 in a May 21st Greenville County League tilt. August brought tight pennant races, yet even Lando's 18-game winning streak could not produce a *Mid-State* League pennant for the club. Nothing, though, could prepare folks for the September 20th heroics of Joanna's Earl Morse, whose *three* two run homers and 9 RBI's sparked a 14–1 rout of Newberry in the Mid Carolina League championship game.

Even with all the excitement, there was the realization that war was close at hand. In Anderson, the County League All Stars beat the City League Stars 7–4 on June 6, 1940; tickets went for 25 cents, and the $300 in gate receipts benefitted the Red Cross. Later, on July 26th, the 178th Field Artillery of Fort Jackson beat Lyman 6–4, a glimpse of what would become a common sight during the war years. After Pearl Harbor was bombed and the nation mobilized for war, several teams and leagues cancelled the upcoming seasons. There would still be activity in textile baseball, but the magnitude and intensity were lessened.

From 1942 to 1945, many of the ball parks were idle except for fast pitch softball, both in leagues and inter-departmental competition within the same mill, and both for men and women. The Greenville area boasted of the Barefoot League, which offered girls' softball, adult (over 30) softball, and boys' (under 16) baseball. War blackouts and curfews affected night baseball and softball in the area and, with mills running at capacity to produce needed goods for the armed forces, the games were relegated to the precious few recreational hours available.

Much of the competition on the diamond involved mill clubs and military units, and it was a decent brand of baseball. The 25th Service Group was a part of the 1943 Greenville Textile League, but withdrew late in the year. In addition, Donaldson Air Base sponsored several other teams, including the 334th and 342nd Bomber Groups, and Camp Croft in Spartanburg offered competition by backing several clubs.

Fans still came to the parks, much as they had during the Depression, to share their fears and dark anxieties, to forget for a moment the horrors of war, to cheer, and to laugh for a while before reality claimed them once more. July 4, 1942, saw two big crowds gather for the festivities: 3,500 watched as Union edged Clifton 1-0, and 4,000 cheered as Pacolet slipped past Limestone 4-3. On September 22nd, Lyman defeated Mills Mill (Greenville) 10-6 before 3,000 fans to take the Western Carolina League title. One championship series in late August 1943 drew successive crowds of 2,000 (19th), 3,000 (21st) and 2,000 (25th) as the powerful Pacolet team swept the series four games to one over Gaffney in the Spartanburg County League finals.

What the fans saw was a good brand of baseball seasoned with the sublime and the incredulous. Simpsonville's 22-5 blowout of Camperdown made few heads turn even though O'dell Barbery had five doubles for the winners in that May 10, 1942, afternoon game. That the Little Yankees remained at bat for one hour and five minutes in the top of the ninth, scoring 13 runs, was a feat worth remembering. When Piedmont and Pelzer met on July 4th a couple of months later, there was the usual excitement running through the 4,000 who came to partake of this keen old rivalry. After Pelzer's lopsided 14-2 win in the morning game, the teams drove the few miles from Piedmont back to the winner's home field. A doubleheader sweep seemed a real possibility, but no one in that huge audience could have imagined the coming heroics of one John Emery. With his team trailing 1-0 in the top of the ninth of the evening tilt, the Piedmont slugger homered to tie the game. One inning later he came to bat with three mates on board and launched a titanic shot over the wall to earn a split with their bitter rivals.

There were other strong performances that year. Two notable achievements were Harry Sullivan's six-hit performance in leading Limestone to a 24-4 lambasting of Clifton on May 30th, and Strickland's duplication of the feat a few weeks later on July 30th as his Mills Mill (Woodruff) team bested Union 9-4. More than individual records, though, 1942 was the year of the streak. Clifton celebrated big time on July 18th, beating Converse 7-5 to bring a 20-game losing streak to a close in the Spartanburg County League. On August 11th, Lyman's Denny Smith hit safely in his 35th consecutive game, leading his team to an 8-7 Western Carolina League win over Dunean. The next day Rube Morgan won his 14th straight complete game in the Central Carolina League as he and his Mathews mates slaughtered Ninety Six 11-1.

It was also a year of charity. Mill folks made it a practice to take care

The 1942 Dunean Mill team. *Photo courtesy of John T. Hannon.*

of their own, especially during hard times. Two All Star games were staged between the Eastern Carolina and Western Carolina leagues, and the Spartanburg-based Eastern organization swept both, 2–0 on May 18th and 8–2 on June 16th. What made the games special was that both were played to raise money for "Rags" Suddeth, a long time textile league player who was stricken with paralysis. When Gaffney beat Lyman 4–3 in an 11-inning thriller on July 7th, all proceeds went to benefit a local charity.

It was hard to match such achievements in the succeeding years of wartime baseball, but there were special moments waiting around the corner. When Monaghan (Greenville) blasted Woodside 31-7 on August 27, 1943, they did so with the long ball and one big inning; they scored 11 runs in the seventh on five homers, two triples and a double, and amassed 10 round trippers for the game. Spartan Mill fans wondered if the hands of their beloved catcher, Stone, were carved from solid rock; he made five errors as Brandon (Woodruff) captured a less-than-spectacular 13–10 victory on July 15th of the following year.

What 1944 was best remembered for was perhaps the finest combined pitching performance in the history of textile baseball. Monaghan (Greenville) featured pitcher Lou Brissie of Ware Shoals, stationed at Fort Jackson and the property of Connie Mack's Philadelphia Athletics. Easley countered with Greenville native Wayne Johnson, a hurler in the Brooklyn Dodger system and home on furlough from Europe. The classic duel on the evening of June 10th was won by Easley 1–0, with Brissie fanning 22 and Johnson 18.

With the end of World War II, players returned from the service and went back to the mills. Others, who had played major league baseball during the war, came back down. Some AA and AAA players left their teams to return to textile baseball. The years 1946 to 1949 were a renaissance of sorts, in many ways the best of times on the mill diamonds.

Great performers graced the leagues in the upstate. Harry Potts, a crafty pitcher for Watts Mill, was chosen Most Valuable Player in the 1948 Central Carolina League after posting an 18–4 record. An all star in the league, he homered in one game against the Mid State stars and always talked more of that than his pitching.

Another pitcher residing in the near vicinity drew attention as well. Clinton star Claude Crocker was signed by Branch Rickey of the Dodgers in 1944, receiving a no-cut $3,500 contract. By 1949, though, nerve damage to his pitching arm cut short a promising career, and he accepted a job as athletic director at Clinton Mill, where he continued playing, becoming manager of the Cavaliers. After a 32-year career, he retired as vice president of human resources with the company.

Just down the road in Joanna, Dodger scout Blackie Carter found power-hitting Guy Prater and convinced Rickey to sign him to a $5,000 contract. The young man had played ball at the army bases where he was stationed during the war years, and his experience served him well as he was invited to 1947 spring training with the Dodgers. He showed enough talent to be assigned to the Class B Newport News team, but soon returned to play with the mill team, where the money was as good and the competition better.

Another promising youngster found his way to Joanna and the Central Carolina League through the army connection. Pitching for Fort Jackson in an exhibition game against Erskine College in Due West, Tommy Lasorda struck out the side in the 7th, 8th, and 9th innings. One of his victims was Guy Prater, the hurler for the collegiate team, who was impressed enough to return the next day with his brother Snow and Wheeze Farmer to work out arrangements for Lasorda to come to Joanna as soon as he was discharged from the service. The offer was $25 per game, but the lad asked for $50 and got it. He also managed to get in a little work with the Camden, South Carolina, team. Major Smalley made the trip up to Joanna to talk business, and Lasorda asked for $100 a game, offering to pitch that night as a tryout. All he could accomplish was to fan 18 and hit a grand slam. After the hat was passed, he had an additional $65 to go with his new salary. Lasorda did some time with the minor league Spinners and made lasting ties with the state when he married a local Greenville girl.

Tommy had played one year of Class D ball with the Phillies organization in Concord, North Carolina, before entering the service. He did well enough in Camden and Joanna, like the seven-hit 4–3 complete game win over Newberry on July 7, 1947, to attract the eye of Blackie Carter and convince the old scout to buy out his Phillie contract. He and Guy Prater both earned spring training invitations. Lasorda's, though, turned into a lifetime commitment to the Dodger blue.

For many years, it was the pitchers who usually made the better showing in competition, especially when major league scouts sat gazing from the bleachers. Lou Brissie had been good enough to pitch with the Ware Shoals club in his early teens and was signed to a contract by the Philadelphia Athletics. Before he could report, there was the matter of honoring a draft notice. Brissie's years in the army, however, were anything but routine, spent far from the baseball diamond.

Brissie's legs were severely wounded in the Apennine campaign in Italy during the Battle of the Bulge; afterwards, his right leg required twenty-three operations. He recovered enough to become, according to Connie Mack, "potentially a greater pitcher than Lefty Grove." Lou was a true war hero, pitching in the majors for seven years with the help of a steel brace. He was honored by the Christian Athletic Foundation in 1948 for his wholesome influence on youth and compiled enough impressive stastics in 1949 to be named to the American League All Star team. The same unwavering loyalty which Lou gave to the Riegels of Ware Shoals during his early baseball career, to his country during World War II, and to Mr. Mack and the Philadelphia Athletics after his tour of duty, was returned by the fans of textile league baseball. Like many of the players before him who made it to the majors, he was the hometown kid who made good, but because of the adversity he overcame due to his war wounds, he held a special place in the hearts of the mill village folks.

The town of Ninety Six boasted another big pitcher to move into the majors during wartime baseball. The support of the fans was not lost on Bill Voiselle; he became the only player in the history of major league baseball whose uniform number matched the name of his home town. "Old Ninety Six" pitched with the Boston Braves, and the team had to get special permission from the National League for him to wear such a high number. His eight-year career with the Braves and New York Giants allowed for friendships with some of the game's great personalities. While with the Giants, he roomed with future Hall of Fame catcher Ernie Lombardi, and with the Braves he shared quarters with another future resident of the Hall, Warren Spahn. He chose his company well.

Bill was from a baseball family, and brothers Jim and Claude played for years in the mill leagues, all of them primarily with the Ninety Six club in the Central Carolina League. It was Bill, though, who made his mark,

The 1947 Ninety Six Mill team. *Batboys (l-r):* Dewey Lowery, Sam Corley, John Dowis, Milton Harter. *Front row (l-r):* Gracie Allen, Carl Alexander, Bill Corley, Blackie Drummond, Frank Edwards, Willie Sanders. *Back row (l-r):* Ralph Spires, Hoss McBride, Buna Wells, Granny Hightower, Jim Voiselle, Glenn Forrester, Fred Dowis, Shorty Harris. *Photo courtesy of Cambridge United Methodist Church.*

especially in 1944 when he was still considered a New York Giant rookie. He had 21 wins and 25 complete games; a National League–leading 161 strikeouts and 313 innings pitched; and a 3.02 earned run average. Like Brissie, he was a hard working, grinding performer whose wit and determination kept him with the game's best for several years.

College players made a significant contribution to the level of competition during the later years of the 1940s. Carl Adams returned from the war after serving as a tail gunner on a B-24 bomber with fifty missions over North Africa and Italy, and he enrolled at the University of Georgia. A student-athlete in 1946 and 1947, he remembered his summers playing ball for Greenwood Mill in the Central Carolina League: "Those years in textile baseball made it a lot easier playing at both the college and minor league levels for me. After playing with and against the likes of Brissie, the Voiselle brothers, Doodie Franklin, Lonnie Holbrook and Earl Wooten, the jump to professional baseball wasn't bad at all." [2]

Johnny Moore stayed close to his home in Joanna and attended Presbyterian College, where his talents were good enough to land a contract in the New York Yankee organization. Beginning with the Class D Gainesville, Florida, team (where he pitched a no-hitter), Johnny moved through the ranks and eventually played at the Triple A level in Kansas City, Portland, Oregon, and Newark, New Jersey. He chose to make 1948 his last year in professional baseball, returned home to marry his childhood sweetheart, and accepted a job as the mill's athletic director. Like his father, Moore hurled for the Joanna Hornets, becoming a vital part of that team into the 1950s.

The great teams during this baseball renaissance were sights to behold. The Lyman Pacifics, sponsored by the Lyman Printing and Finishing Company, were longstanding members of the Western Carolina League. Led by the pitching duo of Jack Anderson and Johnny Wahonic, the team swept league titles from 1947 through 1949.

The Calhoun Falls Clippers, managed by former Cleveland Indian Russ Lyon, powered their way to Anderson County League championships from 1948 through 1951. During the same years, skipper Lyon, who doubled as the team's catcher, led the league in home runs. The whole town, remembered team publicist Johnny Burton, supported their Clippers. "The mill provided the field, but the bleachers, dugouts, concession stand and press box were paid for by the Calhoun Falls Community Club. All the gate receipts went back into the treasury and were used to operate the ball club, as well as other programs beneficial to the town in general." [3]

The team from Watts Mill, champions of the Mid State League in 1947, moved into the faster company of the Central Carolina League the following year. Playing three night games each week, these players, with a Gas House Gang love for the game, clawed and scrapped their way to the title in 1948 in a most impressive fashion. They were cocky and aggressive, posted a 46–18 record, and swept Ware Shoals four straight in the championship series on the strength of the pitching tandem of Roy Peeler and Harry Potts. Both sported fine minor league credentials before coming to play ball in Laurens.

They were strongly backed by the mill company. Where the Clifton team, of the Spartanburg area, received $600 in equipment and $237 in operating expenses from the mill,[4] the Watts team received more than $8000. Gate and concession receipts from Clifton totaled just under $435 (including a $10 donation from the Hubba Hubba Ice Cream Company), while the same two items totaled a bit less than $20,000 for Watts. No mention was made of payment to the Clifton players, but 13 Watts men split $800 per week for 18 weeks, and the manager was paid $100 a week for 21 weeks.[5] The only thing the two bookkeeping ledgers had in common was that credits and debits balanced to zero at season's end. Good players, well paid, produced championship teams, and it was a lesson in free agency thirty years ahead of the major leagues.

Fans poured into the parks to take in the night games, and gazed at outfield fences covered with advertising from businesses all over town.

There was always the "free block" with some reward promised for a home run over this sign. They watched the scoreboard as two men handed the numbers lying on the ground to a third gentleman on a platform, who with a sliding arm device similar to a shuffleboard cue made the necessary changes for balls, strikes, and outs. They listened to music before the games and between innings as the old 78s were played over the public address system. In the parks they sat shoulder to shoulder, cheering until they could not talk above a whisper the next day. There were 3,500 August 13, 1948, as Woodside beat Brandon (Greenville) 5-1 in the tight Western Carolina League race, and 3,000 on September 14th when Watts edged Ware Shoals 7-5 in the opening game of the Central Carolina League finals. On September 17, 1949, 3,500 at Excelsior watched the home boys beat Pacolet 7-4 in the Eastern Carolina League finals. However, a week later 3,000 Pacolet faithful celebrated the Trojans' 3-2 squeaker to clinch the championship.

All over the Upstate, folks kept coming back for more. Fans yawned through most of Riverdale's 25-6 pounding of Joanna on May 1, 1947, and it didn't help that the game ended long after midnight. They were certainly awake as Johnny Wahonic, Lyman's superb pitcher, fashioned a 5-0 no-hit gem against Brandon (Greenville) six days later. Two July evenings in 1948 provided a taste of the truly unusual. In the Mid State League on July 22nd, Claudell Smith of Brandon (Woodruff) hit an inside-the-park grand slam that was the game winning hit in a 7-3 victory over Riverdale. Two days later Chesnee turned two triple plays in a 5-0 Spartanburg County League shutout over Arkwright. Stellar individual performances also highlighted the 1948 season. Two notable achievements were Guy Prater's 33 home runs for the Joanna Hornets of the Mid State League and Tip Massey's 27-game hitting streak as a member of Clifton's Spartanburg County League team.

There were always the humorous misadventures which could only happen in textile baseball. Fans were left in the dark when a foul ball hit and exploded a transformer in the third inning of the Union-Inman semifinal clash in the Eastern Carolina League; it was just one of the perils of night baseball. Clifton fans recalled Sike Melton's antics as an ice cream vendor (perhaps working for the Hubba Hubba Company) and the evening in 1949 when he helped out the local boys. Joe McDowell hit a ball into the trees in deep center, near where Sike was selling his ice cream to the fans. He calmly picked up the ball and hid it in his churn before the visiting centerfielder could arrive. Amid the commotion that followed, McDowell blissfully trotted home.[6]

All Star games became a huge business in the late 1940s as the fans displayed a nearly insatiable appetite for mill hill baseball. When the Central Carolina League representatives blew away their Mid State League rivals 14–5 on July 7, 1948, 5,000 people saw the winners unleash a 20-hit attack which featured homers by Watts' Harry Potts, Ware Shoals' O'dell Barbery, and Greenwood's Earl Morse. The formidable collection of brash CCL all stars issued a challenge to any of the South Atlantic or Tri-State minor league teams to determine whether textile baseball was superior to any other brand elsewhere in the state. Sadly, there seemed to have been no takers of the proffered gauntlet.

The last day of that July found the Anderson City League stars edging the Anderson County League boys in an 11–10 slugfest. An overflow crowd of more than 2,000 crammed Honea Path's Hammett Field for the game. The undisputed star of the game for the City Leaguers was shortstop Ezra Embler of Abney, who went five for five with two homers, four RBI's, and a stolen base for good measure. After expenses were deducted, the individual players' share was $12.20, not a bad night's work at all.

The frenzy carried over into the next year, and on July 16, 1949, the Anderson County League textile stars gathered a measure of revenge in front of 5,000 baseball afficionados as they bested their City League brethren 5–2. Never ones to rest on their laurels, the Central Carolina League bunch came back for more on August 7th, smashing 23 hits to blow away the King Cotton League All Stars 18–2 before 2,000 rather bored fans. But there were new heroes, as Watts' Lloyd Moore, Clinton's Louie Lyles and Joanna's Guy Prater each collected 3 hits.

Those special games, and others, like Pelzer's 1947 victory in the state's semipro championship and a trip to Wichita, Kansas, for the nationals, and Woodside's 1948 win in the Southern Textile Athletic Association Baseball Tournament, became part of the lore of textile ball. Yet, there were times when games were held simply because someone needed help. When Jackson (Wellford) beat Jonesville 6–4 on May 25, 1946, few people cared about the score; that $126.18 and $75 in canned goods were raised to benefit the hungry of postwar Europe was the only thing that mattered. On August 27, 1948, the Spartanburg County League All Stars met their Tri-County League counterparts and raised money for Fred Moss, a bad luck Arkwright pitcher who broke his arm during a game. Interestingly, there was only one price charged, since no children were allowed at the park because of health restrictions due to an outbreak of polio. A few weeks later, on September 18th, Brandon edged Mills Mill 7–6 in a game of Woodruff neighbors, and the teams presented the $525 in gate receipts to defray the medical costs of Kenny Jones, a seriously ill 15-year-old.

Perhaps the most elaborate planning involved Bill Voiselle's efforts to stage "Jackie Spearman Day" in Ninety Six. Moved by the courage of the teenage girl who had an arm amputated below the elbow because of a malignant tumor, the classy Boston Braves hurler acted in dramatic fashion. After securing commitments from both textile and major league players, Voiselle's all star game came off without a hitch (except for Lou Brissie's unavoidable absence) on Saturday, October 15, 1949. Textile heroes-turned major leaguers Earl Wooten (Senators), Sammy Meeks (Reds), Marvin Rackley (Dodgers), and Virgil Stallcup (Reds) joined Voiselle and lent their considerable talents to make the day a success. An overflow crowd of more than 2,700 joined in the cheers for the players as well as for Miss Spearman. The gate receipts exceeded $1,000, more than enough to allow the girl to pay for a prosthesis. When mill folks opened their hearts and pocketbooks, their generosity seemed boundless.

During the renaissance, everything pointed to bigger and better. In 1947, Joanna added a 150,000 watt lighting system at their park, twice the wattage of an average South Atlantic League stadium. On April 30, 1949, Kendall's Mollohon plant installed lights for their Mid State League games. No expense was spared by the Newberry people in their welcome to guests Governor Strom Thurmond, Commissioner of Labor Frank Ponde, and Kendall Company president Alex Savage. Later that year, on July 14th, at a dedication ceremony, the employees of Easley Mill were honored with an Appreciation Day for their donation of a day's work (or pay) toward the cost of the new lighting system at the local field. The best of times looked to go on forever.

Cracks, though, were beginning to show in the once solid foundation. "Ivory hunting," that widely practiced art of picking up good players from other teams and leagues to augment local talent for a realistic run at the championship, had finally gone too far. This early form of free agency had driven up the cost of doing business, and several mills no longer tried to match the larger player payrolls of their competitors.

Before World War II and for a few years after, mill management left it up to the player to decide if he wanted a job in addition to playing baseball. But by the close of the decade, it was work first and baseball second. One of the few concessions to players was to be let off a little early for out-of-town games.

"I worked from 6:00 A.M. to 2:00 P.M. as a loom fixer," remembered Earl Morton of Greenwood Mill. "They would let us off to get to afternoon games, and that was about it. It certainly wasn't like the earlier days."[7] No one could ever imagine that the decline and fall of textile baseball was at hand.

Chapter 10

Decline and Fall

The renaissance peaked in 1949, and there were estimates that two million fans had watched textile league baseball that season. At first glance 1950 promised much the same, with 20 leagues, 120 teams and 2,000 players filling the warm afternoons of spring and summer with excitement. And yet, changes occurred which altered the very fabric of this game so long cherished by the local citizens.

One by one, the owners began to sell the houses in the mill villages and that fierce community pride was lost. For the first time, there were folks living in the village whose personal welfare was not tied to the fortunes of the company, and the sense of family quietly died. With postwar prosperity, more people bought automobiles, and a trip to the lake or some other destination away from the village became preferable to the short walk to the ballfield. That new technological marvel, the television, made its way into homes, and it brought the whole world to our doorsteps. With this new found freedom, folks had less and less time to cheer the boys on to victory as the decade wore on.

There were still good sized crowds at some league games. Over 2,500 customers saw visiting Riverdale win their 12th straight Eastern Carolina League game, an 11–5 blowout of Union on May 27, 1950. Exactly one month later 2,000 Union faithful watched the home boys lose a titanic 19–17 slugfest to Mills Mill of Woodruff, thanks primarily to the 6 RBIs of Bert Sumner. That season, teams in the Central Carolina League routinely drew more than 2,500 fans. On April 22nd, 4,000 cheered Joanna to an 11–2 victory over rival Clinton, and in a May 9th squeaker, Clinton slipped by Ware Shoals 6–5 as 3,000 home folk roared approval. What began to show in these years, however, was a growing disparity which caused more and more mills to cease sponsoring teams.

In earlier years, championship series guaranteed a huge gathering, yet the September 19, 1951, Anderson County League final game drew only 300 to witness Calhoun Falls' 6–3 victory over Abney, their fourth straight league championship. It was a game replete with heroics: manager Russ Lyon's three run homer in the sixth inning, third baseman Tommy Ivey's four-for-four performance, and Pick Riser's complete game five hitter were gems to remember. In fact, fan Emmett Manning flew his plane to Newberry College to get Riser, a student there, and return him to Calhoun Falls in time for the game.

Still, the teams lost money on the game, an event unheard of in the earlier years of textile baseball. It seemed a vicious cycle. With the tight knit community gone, there were smaller crowds; the mill management reacted to the lack of interest and allocated less money; and finally, the lack of financial backing meant the good players sought out the owners who were still willing to pay good salaries to assemble a winning team on the field.

Walter Regnery, chief executive officer at Joanna Mill, had a payroll of $1,000 a week for his Central Carolina League team. This was in addition to paying players for their work in the mill and allocating free housing in the village for his boys. The shrewd businessman had learned a lesson. In 1949, his Joanna club participated in the King Cotton League, used mostly homegrown talent, finished last in the league, and drew no more than fifteen to twenty paying customers per game. The next year, he returned his men to the CCL, upped his player payroll to bring in outside talent to supplement his good local players, improved to 34-27 and a second place league finish, and drew over 2,000 fans several times. The other Central Carolina League teams did likewise, and the loop became perhaps the hottest ticket in the Upstate. The gap between the "haves" and the "have nots" had finally widened to a point of no return.

Textile player Claude Center commented on the state of affairs: "The outside talent cost owners a lot of money, since they paid these players more than the fellows who lived in their own back yards, and who may have been just as good. Guess there may have been some jealousy, too. But, you know, despite all the reasons given about the demise of textile baseball, it was just a great heritage whose time had passed. All these other things were symptoms of the painful death of a wonderful game."[1]

Fans were still in for a treat when they found time to head to the park. The Optimist Club sponsored the biggest drawing card in the early-to mid–1950s, the Greenville Textile All Star Game featuring players from the Western Carolina and Greenville Textile leagues.

The 1950 game was a 4-2 WCL win, and the winning manager was Woodside's Floyd Giebell, a former Detroit Tiger pitcher. The Westerners made it two straight with a 4–3 victory in 1951, though George Blackwell was the game's Most Valuable Player in a losing cause. Dewey Quinn was all the Greenville Textile League needed to break into the winner's circle the next year, belting a two-run, inside-the-park homer and a game winning RBI single in the ninth to nail down a 4–3 verdict. The Western loop returned to form in 1953 with an 8–5 victory as Woodside's Cy Faircloth was the winning pitcher and Dunean's Mel Galliard had 5 RBIs. The 1954 contest was certainly the most exciting and unusual, a 4–3 14-inning Greenville league win behind the last inning relief work of Simpsonville's O'dell "Red" Barbery, who was credited with the win. The regular catcher, he filled in on the mound since all the pitchers had been used. With the folding of the Greenville Textile League in 1955, the Cottonwood League All Stars took over and won 4-0 from the WCL as Easley's Joe Anders had three hits.

More than a few sensed that such performances were becoming the last additions to the memories of textile baseball. In a Western Carolina League battle on May 27, 1950, Dunean's Bob Stowe bested Southern Bleachery's George Blackwell 1-0 as *both* men pitched one-hitters. June 1st in the Eastern Carolina League found Inman's A.L. Curtis chalking up 21 strikeouts against Riverdale, but still losing a 5-4 heartbreaker. Chesnee wasted no time in claiming a July 15th Spartanburg County League contest against Jackson, scoring 13 runs in the first inning and coasting to a 15-5 win. Former major leaguer Red Marion hustled a tenth inning, inside-the-park homer to lead Joanna to a victory over Ware Shoals in a May 3, 1950, Central Carolina League contest.

The next season's stellar performance, however, belonged to Bob Stowe. Though Dunean eventually lost the Western Carolina League pennant to the Woodside Wolves, the crafty hurler won more than twenty games. A remarkable athlete (he was a five time All Southern Textile League basketball player in 1947, 1948, 1952, 1954, and 1955), Stowe earned an invitation from Branch Rickey to the Dodgers' 1948 spring training camp in Vero Beach, Florida, but skipped camp and returned home to finish his baseball career in the textile leagues.

The big stories of 1952 were team related: Abney's 14-game win streak in Spartanburg's Textile Industrial League, and Buffalo's 16-game victory march in the Mid Carolina League. In 1955, Joe Anders of Easley was the Cottonwood League's Most Valuable Player, hitting .505 and compiling a thirty-game hitting streak, and teammate Juber Hairston completed his twenty-ninth season as an active player. LaFrance's Alvin Clark compiled the most impressive pitching statistics that year: his 12-1 mark was tops for the Palmetto League. Since the team recorded fourteen wins on the way to a first place finish, his contribution was significant.

Lurking just below the surface, though, was that ever growing problem of disparity, now being addressed by sportswriters in their daily columns. The scenario had become all too familiar to the perceptive fan. Large mills provided better jobs and more financial support to draw the best athletes. Since these players were the "outsiders" rather than employees, they hampered the neighborhood youngsters' efforts to make the teams. But what manager would put his local talent on the field and subject them to a beating by an opposing team loaded with veterans? It was a dilemma which proved to have no solution.

Making a few last memories was certainly the goal of the Old Timers' games which were held during those quickly fading years. The Mills Mill

(Woodruff) team of former players defeated the local Pony League team 6-1 on August 21, 1953, proving that experience still could best youth when properly applied. One of the best organized games was the April 13, 1955, contest pitting the old guys from the Anderson County League teams of the 1920s and 1930s, and the reigning league champs, Abney Mill. A crowd of 1,500 saw the new edition take a 13-6 win, but the names of the former players were spoken quietly and intensely, in deference to past deeds which had become legend.*

While the final memories were made, kids still dreamed and played so late on summer evenings that darkness was the only force strong enough to end their epic struggles. When there were not enough players for full nines at the ball field, which was seldom, small groups of children played makeshift games in back yards. A broom handle, any sphere nearly round, and designated areas for hits and outs were the only required tools. These sandlot quests for glory took them to the heights of baseball lore, where dreams were limited only by imagination, twilight, and the embankment over which home runs disappeared.

What kept the magic alive was the continued parade of textile players into the major leagues even during the years of decline. From the Spartanburg area came Sammy Taylor (Mills Mill of Woodruff), who went on to play for the Chicago Cubs and San Francisco Giants, and George Banks (Pacolet Mill), a member of the Cleveland Indians and Minnesota Twins. Prosperity's Johnny Buzhardt was a good pitcher with both the Cubs and Philadelphia Phillies. Don Dillard (Victor Mill of Greer) well represented that portion of the upstate in his years with the Indians and Milwaukee Braves.

There were also men whose position in baseball lore was underscored by their particular feats. Bob Hazle (Mills Mill of Woodruff and Watts Mill) gained notoriety for hitting at a .403 clip in a 41 game stretch for the 1957 Braves, propelling them into the World Series and an eventual seven-game win over the Yankees. Billy O'Dell (Newberry Mill) was a true mound artist with the Baltimore Orioles and San Francisco Giants. In the 1958 All Star Game, he was the pitcher of record in the American League's 4-3 win. Neil Chrisley (Calhoun Falls Mill) went first to the Washington Senators, but after being traded to the Detroit Tigers, roomed with Norm Cash and designed the bat which carried the big first baseman to a batting average of .361 in 1961 and the American League

* The Old Timers included Dick Sweetenburg, Berry McElrath, Lefty Robertson, Fred Powell, Sid Bailey, Punchy Williams, Larry Harbin, Leroy Mahaffey, Bill Webb, Jean Belue, Bill Womack, Ervin Sexton, Sam Jordan, Reid Blackstone, Clay Moore, Robert Dawson, J.B. Kelly, Lefty Walker, R.B. Speares, Hinkle Allen, Frank Lombardi, Furman Beck, Guy Willie Powell, Snag McAllister, Roy Jordan, Frank Keaton, Mule Shirley, Shag Knox, J.B. Spearman, Dude Buchanan, S.T. Gunter, Pop Allen, Crate Herring, Johnny Altrock, Carl Ripley, and Frank Morrison.

The 1950s Anderson County Old Timers' Game. *Front row (l-r):* **Jean Belue, Shag Knox.** *Back row (l-r):* **Frank Keaton, Berry McElrath, Lefty Robertson, Snag McAllister, Guy Willie Powell, Ervin Sexton, Sid Bailey.** *Photo courtesy of Mrs. Shag Knox.*

batting title. Art Fowler (Pacolet Mill, Clifton Mill) made it with the Cincinnati Reds and Los Angeles Angels, but is best remembered as the long suffering pitching coach of the New York Yankees and other teams where fiery manager Billy Martin landed. Dickie Dietz (Monaghan Mill of Greenville) was a youngster in this late era of textile baseball, but learned well enough to become a catcher for the Giants. He hit the only homer in the 1970 All Star Game, moving the contest into extra innings; his National League teammates finished off a fine 5–4 win in the twelfth. After all those years, the kids could still play.

But for all the efforts, the hero worship, and the dreaming, events already set in motion would not cease. In 1951, Inman stopped paying their players, though the mill picked up expenses for running the team as long as player and fan interest remained strong. The 1950s also witnessed an unimaginable break with the most treasured of all textile baseball traditions: the Fourth of July holiday games ceased to exist. Teams began to observe the "shutdown" week just like all other mill employees. The ball fields, home to so much of the Independence Day excitement since before the turn of the century, now stood strangely silent.

In July of 1953, officials of the Anderson area Palmetto League voted to stop the season. Due to drastically declining attendance, there was no longer any way to meet expenses. By 1955, many of the Belton Mill players were high school boys who had summer jobs there. Though the Anderson County League allowed three "outsiders," few teams exercised the option, and Belton and Anderson Mill were strictly amateur. If the sunset had been swift, the approach of midnight was even more accelerated.

Many of the former leagues ceased operations altogether. The Pickens County League, after years of participation, folded before the beginning of the 1959 season. Of the 1958 teams (Arial, Alice, Central, Easley, Glenwood and Pickens) only Central, Easley and prospective newcomer Pelzer expressed any interest in fielding teams. League officials, in an odd twist, cited a lack of *player* (rather than *spectator*) interest as the reason for the loop's demise.

Other organizations still existed precariously, revamping schedules time and again as teams dropped out. The Western Carolina League, an organization which spanned virtually the entire life of textile baseball, went from eight to five teams before opening day in 1959, as Monaghan (Greenville), Poe and Victor (Greer) declined to participate. Attendance and fan interest had declined dramatically over the last several years. People cited television and automobiles as two of the culprits. However, a growing interest in national sports, and participation in tennis and golf (there were textile golf leagues during the late 1950s) were given as additional reasons for mill ball's lingering illness and subsequent death.

There was one final nail to be driven loudly into the coffin. Prior to 1959, both textile baseball and basketball enjoyed a special exemption from the South Carolina Admissions Tax, much like high school and college teams. But now the exemption was withdrawn and the tax applied to both sports; since payment to the players was made from gate receipts, the money was considered taxable.

During the last years, all teams reverted to strictly amateur status and relied heavily on local high school talent to fill out their rosters. Leagues, which for years could field enough teams from a narrowly restricted geographical area, now had to extend their boundaries in order to discover enough willing participants. Some tenacious organizations, like the Western Carolina, Eastern Carolina, Spartanburg County and Twin County leagues, managed to hold on into the early 1960s, when crowds of 200 constituted a big night. It was fitting in such an atmosphere that one of the noteworthy "achievements" was the Apalache team's losing streak. They beat Dunean 7–6 in 12 innings on July 26, 1958, and did not win again until they beat the same team 11–5 515 days later. With a whimper the game finally died, the last mention of active textile baseball being Clifton's 1971 team.

The game so long loved was gone. What had thrilled fans through three generations and 75 years became only a memory. Thousands of players and teams faded into obscurity, remembered only by family and dedicated fans who flock to old timers' gatherings. Those good enough to make it to the major leagues, and a few select others whose careers remained in the public eye (U.S. Senator Olin D. Johnston, U.S. Congressman Dick Richards, batboy-turned-Newberry College president Hubert Setzler, Clemson University football legend Frank Howard, Furman University sports fixture Lyles Alley, and University of South Carolina baseball coach June Raines) seemed the only concrete evidence of a lost time.

But textile baseball was a way of life. It gave mill people a sense of legitimacy in a society content to see the "lintheads" remain invisible citizens dwelling somewhere far away on the wrong side of the tracks. It nursed its players and fans through three wars, the Great Depression, labor strife, and a host of other harsh times of lesser magnitude. Baseball was the equalizer, and those who possessed that wondrous talent for the game made it the best ticket in town on long spring and summer days and evenings. It was big league pride in a small town setting. Most of all, it existed not as a sport, but as a legacy. It was a remembrance of more than a game; indeed, it was a remembrance of a way of life whose time will not come again. It was family, community, togetherness, love, all those words which would be maudlin were they not true. Textile baseball belonged to the fans and they still cherish it.

Chapter 11

Profiles

Ed Brinson: A Time to Remember

Those days have faded into red-burning sunsets, a time when thoughts and deeds have collided and formed a pleasant reality. The dust of the infield has settled for the last time; no spikes crunch hard into the baked clay. Outfield grass is knee-high; swift antelopes make no backhand catches in the alleys of right and left center. The grandstand and the fences are gone, not bothering to witness this final passage.

But the old men remember, with minds as sharp as 50 years before. The spirited nature is still there, but locked within a body refusing to manufacture quick reflexes any longer. When you reach the age of 96 and the mind is quick, the old days, the wonderful, great, baseball days are just a thought away.

Ed Brinson remembers Pelzer at the turn of the century, when Cap-tain Ellison Smyth formed his community around the two huge cotton mills he had built: "He was something when he walked the village, straight-backed and well dressed. With his help, we had our opera house for plays and concerts, a skating rink and swimming pool, a zoo in the park complete with monkeys and lions, even a track around the ballfield for harness racing."

The voice drops momentarily to a whisper, and a big grin spreads across the kind face, preceding by just a few seconds the laughter, the kind that comes with a special remembrance.

"The Fourth of July, now that was some day when the Captain was still around. The picnic and the parade, games for the kids and horse races for the older folks to watch. But," and he smiles knowingly, "in those days people waited for mid–afternoon, because it would be baseball then. Us and Piedmont, and let me tell you we had some games."

It was the day of the contact hitter with a split grip on the bat, of speed on the base paths, and playing for one run. And how easily the names are recalled, as if just yesterday the game had been finished rather than 60 years lapsing in the blink of an eye. There were men like Walt Barnett and the Mahaffey brothers, Grady Davenport and Ben Lark (the night boss in the Pelzer card room), pitchers Wade Spencer and Ken Calvert, Coof Henderson and Oscar Donaldson (the versatile one who played at both Piedmont and Pelzer). In a special place stands pitcher Red Woods, who once twirled four straight shutouts. All this occurred before 1910.

"And I remember Joe Jackson, too." Mr. Brinson's eyes betray a sadness, a knowledge that so marvelous a player was trapped in the game's greatest scandal. "He and his family lived here in Pelzer a short time before moving on to Brandon Mill in Greenville, where his special abilities really attracted attention. Those wonderful talents sharpened when Jackson roamed the outfield for Nap Lajoie's Cleveland club and starred for Comiskey's White Sox until nineteen-twenty. Him banned for life, it was a terrible thing." Brinson's voice trailed off for a brief time, but then the old fire returned.

"Sixty games a year, that's what we played, and we were paid an unbelievable seven dollars a week. Going from Pelzer to Liberty was an overnight trip by horse and wagon, and I mean we rode *all* night. On toward nineteen-twenty, we could take the trolley to play some of our games over near Greenville against Poe, Monaghan, Mills Mill, Judson and Dunean. Keep in mind that we worked all week, up until three P.M. on Saturday. Then we'd get to play ball. We were workers first and then ballplayers. All that changed later, you know."

How different it was. The loosely webbed gloves were leather coverings, not much bigger than the hand. Thick handled bats seemed heavy as lead, and a wire mask and mitt were the only protection afforded the catcher. Thick woolen or flannel uniforms were buttoned tight at the neck. And all the tricky pitches, the spitter, mud ball and shine ball, served as a steady diet for the hitters.

The best he ever saw? "Tom Bray, fellow who played shortstop for Woodside over in Greenville. He was a high average hitter, and could have played pro ball but...well, he got the marrying urge and settled down over there. He was a fine ball player, just so good."

Take time to place these events in history. Ed Brinson was almost 13 years old when the Wright Brothers broke free of earth for those blessed seconds in 1903. He knew Ellison Smyth, one of the prime movers in establishing the textile industry in South Carolina in the late 19th century. He stopped playing ball in the late 1920s, moving from Pelzer to Belton and never picking up the mitt again. "Those were fine times out there on the field with those fine men. All of them gone now, I would guess."

The men passed on, and the game they loved, the fiercely loyal mill brand of baseball, followed a few short decades later. There still remain a few fragile tendrils connecting us to that time when summer seemed forever, when red infield dust showered over the players and streaked with sweat to form some secret tribe's war paint, and baseball was still a game for men who kept the exuberance of little boys in their veins for a lifetime.

Alvin Danielson: Let the Memories Linger

His eyes were always the giveaway, especially when he would squint, just like a third baseman peering toward the plate over flaked mica littering the infield. He'd be thinking hard then, remembering back more than 70 years to games and the exploits of the folks who played textile baseball. Propped up in his bed, Alvin Danielson prepared to relive a few glory days of baseball in South Carolina just after the turn of the century.

At West End, later Newberry Mill, it was a one shift operation, endless hours of work from Monday to Friday, But there was always Saturday waiting out there, never far away. A wonderful half day of work and all afternoon to play baseball.

"I never got paid," he would say, "but that didn't matter to me at all. It was all for the love of the game, and that was enough. How I did love to play."

Smoothing the blanket with his big hands and squinting a bit harder for a moment, he continued. "Those guys I played with, they were some fine players. Rip Simpson, quite a pitcher; Dave Bouknight at first base and Edgar Hiller at second. And Bob McCall catching, now he was one of the best. Back then his only fancy equipment was a wire mask, and heck, some of the catchers didn't even wear that! I really enjoyed watching that fellow play ball."

Those lost summer afternoons provided the backdrop for the only show in town, and a crowd of 1,500 was an average gathering for the Saturday festivities. This in a time when the trip from Newberry to Whitmire took a few hours by horse and wagon. Greenwood, Joanna, Saluda and a hundred other crossroads communities fielded teams whose fans displayed fierce loyalty to the local boys.

Scraps between the zealous followers were not uncommon, especially when Newberry played Mollohon or Whitmire, but few of the folks ever suffered any injuries. It was a fast, slick brand of baseball, certainly attracting most of the mill people, and though they would probably never admit it, even the townies and the farmers wandered in to see the lintheads sparkle in the field and at bat. And some sparkled like rough diamonds, just waiting to be noticed.

"Some of our folks made it on up to the majors. Mickey Livingston signed with Clark Griffith's Senators, and before he was through he played in the World Series as a member of the Chicago Cubs. Johnny Wertz pitched for the Boston Braves for three years, and Al Shealy made it to the Yankees. Others could have made it, too," the voice saddened, "but they enjoyed liquor a bit more than they enjoyed the game. Yes, we had some good players."

From 1910 to 1920 Alvin Danielson played the game he loved, forming close friendships with teammates and opponents alike. When he walked away from the diamond, he declined to return as a fan, choosing his memories over the changes in mill ball. With the demand for more and more cloth, the mills added second and third shifts. This competition carried over into the sport, and when the mills began paying their players, the sense of community suffered.

Players would be induced to leave one team and join another for a few dollars more, and the really good ones used assumed names to compete for two or more teams. "If you were good, the money was there," but his squint betrayed a little hurt for an innocent game grown suddenly complicated.

"When we got away from playing baseball for the pure love of it, we lost a bit of ourselves in the process. And what we lost was the best part, the joy of doing something well. Money couldn't make that up to me. Guess that's the reason I never wanted to play in the majors. All the joy would have been gone."

For an hour, Mr. Danielson recreated a world long since forgotten by most of us. In this reverie, he perhaps replayed hundreds of ball games in his mind. Once more he was the happy young man guarding the line at third, looking homeward across the mica-specked infield, daring the batter to pull the ball toward him. His rough hands smoothed the covers one more time. There was silence in the room. It was getting late.

Johnny Wertz: A Touch of Class

"Three years in the big leagues was fun, but I never regretted coming back home to work and play ball with Newberry Mill," Johnny Wertz recalled. Even at 90, the hands look as if they could throw baseballs through a brick wall. "Got to play against Ruth and Gehrig in exhibitions when the Boston Braves played the Yankees, and I competed all year against Rogers Hornsby, Hack Wilson, Bill Terry and them fellows." The memories he chooses to share flow smoothly, like the easy pitching delivery of his playing days.

The career was a long and memorable one, starting in the Jolly Street community when he was a boy. There was a Saturday in 1923 when Wertz pitched and won against a fine Newberry Mill team. The mill folks were so impressed they gave him a job and a place on the team. From then on, things were never quite the same. The next year (1924) he was with the Ware Shoals mill team. While there he caught the eye of the scout for the Greenville Spinners of the South Atlantic League.

Oddly, he never played for Greenville, since his contract was sold to the Winston-Salem, North Carolina, Braves of the Piedmont League. The parent club in Boston purchased his contract in 1925, invited him to spring training, and eventually assigned him to Worcester, Massachusetts, for the season. From 1926 to 1928, he was in the majors, living out a dream longed for by countless young men across the nation.

"That Boston club was good, but we didn't win no pennants," he said. "All them cities we visited, though, they were really something. And I did enjoy pitching against McGraw and the New York Giants." A big grin comes across his face when he remembers his nickname, "Giant Killer." Somebody once said that manager McGraw cursed and declared that all Wertz had to do was "throw his glove at the mound and he'd beat us!" But Johnny's major league career was destined to be short in spite of this success. Arm trouble set in in 1927, and he never recovered enough to compete at that level again.

Five years of kicking around in the minors followed : Buffalo, New York, in 1929–30, Wilkes-Barre, Pennsylvania, in 1931, Baltimore, Maryland, in 1932, and Nashville, Tennessee, in 1933. Finally, in 1934, he came on back home and started to work in the machine shop at Newberry Mill, and they paid him ten dollars or so a week to play ball. "I enjoyed coming down from the majors and playing textile ball," he says. "It was good to see some familiar faces for a change."

That Newberry team boasted some pretty good talent. Wertz and Al Shealy, who pitched for the 1928 Yankees and the 1930 Cubs, had completed careers in the big leagues. Mickey Livingston later played with the Chicago Cubs in the 1940s, and a few years later a kid by the name of Billy O'Dell played with the Baltimore Orioles and San Francisco Giants.

"We played mostly in the Mid State League, against Mollohon, Oakland, Goldville (now Joanna), Whitmire, Union, Buffalo and Lockhart. All were mill teams, and I think our biggest rival was Buffalo. The competition was fierce and the teams were good. We had fun, but danged if we didn't want to win bad. Lordy, them was *hot times!*" he says with a laugh.

"Everybody always asks me about the people I played against in the majors. And that's fine, but I want folks to remember we had some very good players close to home. Al Danielson, Paul Troutman, Bob Creekmore, Doodie Franklin, Harry Hedgepath—they could have held their own against the big league boys.

"We had good attendance at the games, too. Five hundred to one thousand people wasn't all that uncommon, but then the ballgame was the only entertainment in town. When cars and television came along, mill ball just died quietly. The last fifteen years I worked [he retired in 1968], there just wasn't much ball. When the game died, didn't too many folks seem to care at all." Johnny sat quietly for a few moments, perhaps letting a thousand memories of game day ease into his thoughts. "Lots of good people associated with textile ball," he added, "lots of good people."

Folks say Johnny was always the same, whether playing for Jolly Street, Newberry Mill or the Boston Braves. He played the game he loved with everything he had. When it was time to move on, he did so without any regrets. His career spanned the heyday of baseball, when it truly was the national pastime. Johnny Wertz was a worthy representative of textile baseball, a touch of class.

Harry Hedgepath: Special Man, Special Time

Some talents just seem to have always been there, waiting for the right time to blossom. By the time Harry Hedgepath reached Newberry College, he was already a superb player, lettering in each of his years at Columbia High. Small for a catcher, he played with a fire and tenacity uncommon even in those blood and guts days of baseball.

"There was always a team needing a good player, and right out of high school I played textile baseball with Columbia Mill, picking up three or four dollars a game. Not bad money in the late nineteen-tens and early nineteen-twenties, when folks would come to the games in wagons and on horseback. When I came to college, some of us guys would play in the Palmetto League [featuring teams from Newberry, Rock Hill, Union and York] in the summer and earn some extra spending cash. We could pick up a hefty weekly salary, I can tell you that."

Though he played several sports at Newberry College, it was baseball where his talents were the most accomplished. Hedgepath was captain of the freshman team in 1923, a letterman in each of his three varsity seasons, captain of the team as a senior in 1926, and an all state selection in both 1925 and 1926.

For 12 years after graduation, Harry pulled double duty by playing textile ball in the spring and summer for Oakland, Mollohon, and Mathews mills. "Those crowds were big at the mill league games, especially over at Oakland. It was good entertainment for the fans, and it was a game that made men out of boys. Those infields," he said with a laugh, "were hard red clay, and the outfields were bumpy and bare. But it was baseball, and it was fun."

There were plenty of personalities in the mill leagues, and Harry associated with some of the best. Johnny Wertz had already completed his major league career before returning to play for Newberry Mill. Al Shealy was another good pitcher who had one year with the New York Yankees before finishing up with the mill teams. And George Summer, when he was a mill executive at Mollohon, really put out the money to sign good prospects. The mill leagues, according to Hedgepath, were on par with the top minor league clubs of the era.

The comparison of textile and minor league baseball was one that he was qualified to make. During his career, Harry was signed by the Pittsburgh Pirates, playing with their Class A affiliate (Columbia, South Carolina) in the South Atlantic League. A teammate was Lloyd Waner, brother to Hall of Famer Paul Waner. After Lloyd made it to the majors, Hedgepath chanced to meet him years later; "Little Poison" never even spoke to him. "Such is the price of fame, I guess," he mused.

"I was fortunate enough to catch two major league pitchers during my years in baseball. During the fall All Star Game at Newberry Mill, I caught Johnny Wertz a number of times, and while I was in the Navy I warmed up Bob Feller before a game. Both were good, but Feller was really something."

Harry was at the helm of Newberry High School athletics for 38 years, leaving only for a three-year stint in the Navy during World War II. During those years, his teams won five state baseball championships, two state football championships, and six consecutive district basketball titles. Harry was also a pioneer in establishing American Legion baseball in South Carolina, and served as the first secretary/treasurer of the South Carolina Coaches Association.

For 63 years he was involved in sports as a student, player, coach and administrator. In honor of his service to the youth of the community, the old high school field was renamed Hedgepath Stadium in 1947. All the honors, the trophies and the records paled before the one important fact: he touched the lives of thousands of youngsters in his community.

His friends said Hedgepath never really retired. There was always somebody ready to talk about the glory days of the grand old game, and Harry relived every play of every game during the conversation. He loved every minute of it.

Mrs. Harry Potts, Mrs. "Shag" Knox: Through Other Eyes

The 1930s dawned a somber era. It was a time of the Great Depression. In the South, the mills were struggling to remain competitive in a business world suddenly turned upside down. Industries failed, there was labor unrest, and folks in general were having a hard time of it. But there was baseball in the mill village that somehow lifted the spirit and gave back the heroes, the boys of summer.

The focus was on the men who played. They were in the limelight, their deeds the topic of streetcorner conversation, their examples cited by fathers to sons in backyard games of catch. Always the men commanded the respect and awed with their skills. It was easy to forget the wives who stood behind the players, who listened patiently to complaints, who comforted when necessary, who encouraged more often than anyone might ever suspect. Mrs. Harry Potts and Mrs. "Shag" Knox remember, though, and recall the days of textile baseball as fondly as did their husbands.

"I followed Harry from Logan, West Virginia, in nineteen-thirty-nine, to Portsmouth, Virginia, after World War Two when he played for former Yankee great Tony Lazzeri, to Rome, New York. After the nineteen-forty-eight season in Rome," Mrs. Potts says, "we moved to Laurens, where Harry was to pitch for Watts Mill and manager Lloyd Moore."

She smiled, remembering the days in the mill village. "There were folks who signed a waiting list to be eligible for company housing, but because baseball was so important to the mills, we moved right in to one of the little bungalows. And you know, there was a nice chair, a table, and a few odds and ends in the house already, given by some of the local merchants." She points across the room. "I still have the chair, and you can see it has been a good one. Still in great shape, too."

There were very few games she missed, if any, sitting under a hot sun while her Harry labored on the mound, huddling beneath an umbrella waiting out a rain delay, always on the edge of her seat cheering hard for the Watts team. "To show you how big baseball was in Laurens, the birth of our first child was announced on the sports page! Now, can you believe that!"

The memories are of good times shared by two people, of days when things seemed a bit simpler and her husband was the idol of the mill village because of his skill and his gentlemanly manner. "Harry could make $110 a week playing baseball, and that was awfully good money in those days. But even if the pay had not been high, we wouldn't have changed places with anyone. He was doing what he loved, and we shared that just like we did everything else."

Up the road a ways, in the small town of Honea Path, Mrs. "Shag" Knox recalls the days of mill ball with the same fondness. "'Shag' was recruited by Chiquola Mill in the nineteen-thirties to play one game against Orr Mill over in Anderson. That was a pretty big rivalry, so he was given the royal treatment around town. McDavid Carr had him over for supper, and after the meal they sat on the porch. All the single girls walked by the house to have a look at the new players. One glance at 'Shag' and I knew he'd never get out of my sight again!"

That one game turned into a lifetime since "Shag" never left Honea Path. Originally, he was on his way to Hutchinson, Kansas, to play for the Pirates' AA team. The prediction made by Mrs. Knox proved true, however, and the two were married. He settled down to play baseball for the Chiquola team, maintaining throughout his life that "once you find a little parcel of heaven, a man would be foolish to leave."

The 1949 season. "Shag" Knox is about to be congratulated after belting a homer.
Photo courtesy of Mrs. "Shag" Knox.

Old time fans in the upstate area will tell you that "Shag" was one of the best shortstops to ever grace the diamond. He could hit for power and high average, field his position, and run like a rabbit. "We both loved baseball, and after a game the players and their wives came over to our house for supper. Lord, we used to replay the entire game around the table!" Her eyes sparkle as she remembers, "Those were good times and good friends."

Mrs. Knox acted as the family physician on those occasions when nagging injuries set in. "Shag" loved to steal, barreling into second or third and sliding in a cloud of dust. "Because of those rocky infields, I did my share of doctoring strawberries, cuts and bruises on his side. But he never missed a game. Both of us loved it too much to ever have let that happen," she says proudly.

Two men, two genuine heroes in the towns where folks witnessed their extraordinary skills; two consummate gentlemen and sportsmen who were fortunate enough to have very special ladies pulling for them. "When the mills finally gave up sponsoring the baseball teams, it made a difference in our lives," both women agreed. But just as strongly both affirm, "We still had our deep love for one another, so there was never any emptiness or bitterness because one part of our lives had changed."

After the crowds left the ballpark, even after the textile league games were no more and darkness settled over the abandoned playing fields, the

The 1950 season. Ben Day pulls up at third, as instructed by manager "Shag" Knox. *Photo courtesy of Mrs. "Shag" Knox.*

Potts and Knoxes still had one another. And that love, after all the years, makes the difference even now.

George Blackwell: The Greatest

His was the consummate legend, the Babe Ruth of the textile leagues, the man who could pulverize horsehide like no one before or after. He may have been the only player to hit a ball over the right field fence at Pelzer, a distance of more than 500 feet, but folks came to expect such feats. For Big George Blackwell, slugger extraordinaire, it was a devastating hit on the gridiron that landed him in baseball, and mill folks were always glad the blow brought him to his senses.

During Blackwell's senior year at Duncan High, the talented young man was offered seven football scholarships. He chose North Carolina State, and it was arranged for him to attend the Blue Ridge Preparatory School for one year to earn the two credits necessary to enter college. In his first full scrimmage at the Ridge, Big George did well until he met up with Charlie "Choo Choo" Justice in an open field confrontation. Charlie chugged on to a touchdown and greatness at the University of North Carolina; Blackwell was carried off the field, his shoulder broken in two places. Lots of folks, he concluded, were bigger than one South Carolina farmboy, so he went back to Southern Bleachery and Print Works, got a job, and played baseball.

He may have been a legend in the making, but his first tryout certainly gave little indication. Bleachery manager Lyles Alley felt that George was too wild on the mound and judged that he was not good enough to make the team. So it was on to Simpsonville Mill, working in the machine shop and pitching on the local team. Blackwell won his last 11 games, including the clincher in the finals, a three-hit, 12 strikeout performance against Brandon (Greenville), considered one of the best mill teams of the 1930s. After the game, a scout for the Boston Red Sox offered him $750 to sign with the club, but the big kid refused. He was about to get married and he wanted to stay at home.

Against stiff competition his performance continued to improve. In 1937 the St. Louis Cardinals invited him to a local tryout in Charlotte, North Carolina. One of his hits cleared the right field fence and a row of box cars behind it. Local folks said it was the longest shot ever hit there. The Cardinals offered him a contract as an outfielder but not as a pitcher. Again George turned down a major league opportunity. He returned to Southern Bleachery in 1938 and called it home for the next 21 years. Planted in the correct plot of ground, the legend grew and magnified year by year.

Though the Bleachery was his base of operations, Blackwell's considerable talents landed him offers to play ball at several mills, and since his job in the shop ended at noon, he readily accepted. Five teams in 1946, seven in 1947, and seven in 1948. At home, his wife prepared a bag lunch and packed the correct uniform for that particular game. "She always pointed me to the park I was supposed to go to," he said. Legend says that he once played nine games in one week and went 26 for 28 at the plate. Teams like Monaghan (Greenville), Brandon (Greenville), Mills Mill (Woodruff), Laurens, Easley, Woodside, Simpsonville, Lyman, Greenwood, Watts, Victor (Greer), Brandon (Woodruff), Pacolet, Fairmont, Pelham and Apalache frequently called for his services. George obliged them all.

He obliged well enough to finish third in the Western Carolina

League balloting for Most Valuable Player in 1945 and 1946, then captured the coveted award in 1947 and 1948, the only man ever to win twice. His most memorable performance also happened in 1947 as he pitched Southern Bleachery to an 11-inning 3-2 win over Brandon (Greenville) to capture the Western Carolina pennant. Unlike his pennant clinching victory over the same team a decade before, this one seemed anything but classic in the early going. Big George allowed three hits and two runs in the first inning, but then retired the last 29 hitters he faced. He won MVP honors twice (again, the only man to do so) in the Greenville Textile All Star Game, sponsored by the Optimist Club, and oddly both were in a losing cause: in 1949, when the Western Carolina League defeated the Greenville Textile League 7-3, and again in 1951 when the Western boys eked out a 4-3 win.

The legend grew to keep pace with his achievements. Catcher Claude Center enjoyed being behind the plate when Blackwell was on the mound. "When he was pitching, he would halt the game, take off his shoe and pretend to spit in it for good luck," Mr. Center recalled. "But I played with Southern Bleachery for a couple of years, and watched George closely. Though some people still say he used this bit of voodoo, I know he didn't."

There was a game when he opposed his good friend Juber Hairston on the mound. During Blackwell's first at bat, Juber tossed a couple of slow ones for strikes, then tried to sneak a fast ball down and in. The result was a monstrous home run. Later, with Hairston at the plate, Big George served up his best, and was accorded a duplicate of his own long blast. Juber wore a wide grin as he circled the bases, and even laughed out loud as Blackwell followed, yelling at him every step of the way.

The big man was a fearsome hitter. Sportswriter Dan Foster of the Greenville *News* described Blackwell at the plate, "the bat resting lazily on his shoulder like a broomstick in a lion's paw." Fielding, though, was an entirely different matter. "I was just as likely to get hit in the head as to catch a fly ball, and if there was any doubt on a grounder, I'd lay down in front of the ball," he said. One evening an opposing batter lofted a high infield fly just behind the mound, and George called for it. He tripped on the rubber and was lucky that the ball missed his head by a few inches as he lay on the ground. His manager sprinted out, but was relieved to find his star okay. "Thought the ball hit you in the head, George," he said, "it sounded so hollow when it landed."

He retired in 1956, at age 43, going out at the top of his game as textile baseball entered its twilight years. But the mill hill pastime refused to accept death gracefully, and called the big man from his leisure. George returned to the Greenville Textile League in 1959, getting a single and double in his first game back. The next year he was with Apalache, led the

Western Carolina League in hitting, and helped to make the former doormat of the circuit a solid team.

Big George was the tie that bound those last days to the glory days. He was the lover of the game, the idol of the fans, the man with the easy laugh and the burning competitive spirit, the extraordinary talent who stayed home and gave of himself for 30 years. He was legend, and the fans loved him in return.

Powerhouse Hawkins: A Thrill a Minute

He is the consummate storyteller, the oral traditionalist of the textile leagues unashamed to tell you how great the old times really were. "My whole life's been spent on the mill village, from being born at Jackson Mill in Wellford to enjoying my retirement here at Arkwright. Just a stone's throw from my porch is where the old ballfield used to be," he says wistfully, "but things have changed a lot."

In 1928, at age 14, he began playing on the Jackson team, and though his playing weight never got above 150 pounds, he earned the nickname "Powerhouse" because of his stinging hits and rifle arm. "And besides, it sounded better than Ernest." The talented performer became a journeyman player, an "outsider" who, by the rules, could legally play with several mill teams even though he was not employed by them. He moved among the Central Carolina League, Eastern Carolina League, Spartanburg County League, and Tri-County League, but the best baseball, by his recollections, was in the Central and Eastern circuits. By 1934, Hawkins commanded $100 a game when he pitched, a little less when roaming the outfield.

When he talks baseball, the names of the old guys seem a recitation of those honored for glorious deeds. "Pete Fowler from Converse, a good pitcher who went up with the Cardinals; Shuf Finley, another fine hurler with Spartan and Drayton; Sam Page, from Enoree and Mills Mill; Ox Taylor and son Sammy, fine players from over in Woodruff; Slim Smith, submarine pitcher from Tucapau; Mendel Ramsey, a Gaffney boy who played some pro ball; and, of course, me," he says with a grin. "But our close knit fraternity only gets smaller, since no new members have been admitted since mill ball died out in the late 1950s."

To preserve a bit of the glory that was textile baseball, he joined former players Manning Bagwell, Ty Wood, Pete Brown, Pete Kleitches, Ox Taylor, and Red Ellison, and radio personality Bill Drake in organizing the Spartanburg area Old Timers Reunion in the 1970s. A recognized tradition in the area, the August gathering consistently draws 400 dedicated followers of the game.

Hawkins hit well over .300 during his years as a player (registering a whopping .391 in 1938), but with his stories he's a perfect 1.000. His most memorable hit brings knowing chuckles from those who remember some of the mill village fields.

"It was in nineteen-thirty-six, and I didn't hit the ball very far out of the infield, so I figured it was just a single. I got to first base and stopped, but no one came up with the ball, so I ran on to second and made it easy. Still no ball, and I ended up with a homer on that puny hit. What happened? The outfielders couldn't find the ball because it landed in an empty tomato can."

What about the legend that he once hit a ball so hard that he knocked the cover off? He laughs and confesses that the cover was probably loose anyway and concludes the bat just happened to pop the seams perfectly. "Still, truth is truth," he said.

Game day was a festival atmosphere, especially when Harold Sullivan and the Spartan Mill Band used the company's flatbed truck to go through the mill village, playing loudly, and announcing the game at the park located just off Preston Street. "You met some interesting folks going over there, because nearby was the Cleveland pasture, with an artesian well shaded by crabapple trees, a hobo's paradise! But that old park was fun to hit in. Long home runs, and I hit a few there, carried the fence, the road, and even the red-topped Seay house."

World War II rolled around, and players exchanged ballfields for battlefields. Powerhouse enlisted as a member of the 101st Airborne Division, and often joked that he wouldn't have been so impulsive in his patriotism if he had known how rough it was going to be. As the war drew to a close, there was time for baseball, army style, and he played on the same team as Spud Chandler of the New York Yankees. "Best as I can remember, I was the only non-major leaguer on that team managed by Harry 'The Hat' Walker," he said. After his honorable discharge ("I did earn that, honest"), Powerhouse came back home and picked up his mill career again, having fun, playing hard and making memories.

"The roughest place I ever played was up at Cherokee Falls, and when Arkwright went up there for a game one hot summer afternoon, their fans were there, armed with shotguns and toting bootleg liquor. Our coach insisted on outfield practice, though most of us were scared to death and wanted to huddle in some out-of-the-way place. He fungoed the first ball out toward center, and in midflight about fifteen shotguns opened up and blew the ball out of the air. A second ball met the same fate, so he called out 'That's enough practice,' and waved us in. He didn't have to bother, since we were already running at full speed toward the vehicles we'd arrived in," he recalled.

"And that was only pregame warm-ups. As the game started and

WITH HIS TEAM BEHIND 1-0, THE BASES LOADED AND THE COUNT 3-0, POWERHOUSE HAWKINS CONCENTRATES ON THE NEXT PITCH!!

moved along, we were winning, and that only got those folks more riled up. When we took the field they started throwing rocks at us and kept it up until the game ended. Then the fans started chasing after us, if you can believe that," he said with a grin. Powerhouse made it safely to the back seat of a teammate's car, hiding there until the melee was over. "One of our other guys wasn't so lucky. Running through the woods to escape that mob, he ran right into a tree and knocked himself cold. Some of the guys did manage to find him and get everybody back home safe. Don't think I ever went back up there again."

"POWERHOUSE" HAWKINS
ON A
3-0 PITCH!!

There were great characters of the game, like his good friend Scoobyduck Powell, all 5 feet 2 inches, 120 pounds and size 15 feet of him.
"Scoob had never hit a home run in his life, but one day at Laurens he
lined a ball over third and took off running. All you could hear was the
plop-plop, plop-plop of his tennis shoes, since Scoob couldn't ever find
spikes big enough to fit. Around the bases he chugged, the umpire step for
step with him, and the left fielder nonchalantly running the ball down.
Scoobyduck just fell down tired when he reached the plate, and that old
ump leaned over him and said, 'That's a foul ball.' I laughed so hard..."
but that figured, since Powerhouse was doing the same thing again.

POWERHOUSE HAWKINS

"Then, in nineteen-forty-nine the superintendent of Arkwright Mill sent our whole team to New York for a World Series game," said Hawkins, laughing again as he remembered, "We had a fellow named Arthema, who really didn't want to go. So to keep in touch with home, he dropped his mother a telegram at every one of the fifty-six stops that bus made. I don't think any of us believed he'd keep it up."

He was a great player and remains a great storyteller, but Powerhouse is most proud of his efforts to keep the Old Timers Reunion going every year. "You know, in nineteen-thirty-two, Arkwright beat Valley Falls one to nothing in eleven innings. I bested a real good pitcher that day, Boyd Hughes, but do you know that after that game we didn't see each other again for forty-five years, not until the nineteen-seventy-seven reunion? Talking with him again, swapping tales that just got better with the passing of years, that's what makes good memories." To everything there is a season, and for Powerhouse, textile baseball's is forever.

Earl Wooten: The Reign of the Earl

Only once in a lifetime does there appear an athlete as good as Earl Wooten. Starring in both baseball and basketball for Pelzer and Piedmont from 1941 to 1961, he dominated both games with a flair that awed spectators, opponents and teammates alike.

At 5 feet 10, he was adept at playing either guard or forward. From the start of his career, he knew no equal; from the set shot to the "left hand driving out hook," he could do it all. His shooting, ball hawking, and all-around hustle made Wooten the favorite of fans wherever he played, and made the mill communities of Pelzer and Piedmont a byword in the annals of the Southern Textile League basketball tournament.

The laurels given to the victorious Earl were many, and his achievements in the textile tourney withstood the challenges throughout the course of the years. In one game, he was 21 of 21 from the free throw line. He scored 100 or more points in five different tournaments (1947, 1949, 1950, 1954, 1956). He played the most years (21) and games (45), scored the most points (1262) for the highest average (28 points per game), and was honored the most times for All Tournament and All Southern League (12).

The Earl of Pelzer once scored 60, 52, and 40 points in three consecutive games, even though he was limited to an average of three quarters of action in each. It was a matter of course that he was compared to basketball's best, Bob Cousy and George Mikan. Regarding Cousy, one college coach exclaimed, "If Wooten isn't in Cousy's class, then Cousy isn't human." A professional colleague went him one better. "If he had the height George Mikan had, Mikan wouldn't be in his class." Even during his major league baseball career, the Washington Capitols, (1948 runner up for the National Professional Basketball Championship) offered him a handsome salary to play for them. It may have been the only basketball offer he ever declined. No one could step onto the court and compete with him, and yet, it was this remarkable ability that prevented him from achieving an even greater glory. The conflict of Wooten's two great loves in athletics, basketball and baseball, finally occurred.

The two games existed side-by-side in peaceful harmony for many years. When basketball ended it was natural for Earl to move from the hardwood to the diamond. He played high school and American Legion baseball and found a home on the Western Carolina League Pelzer Bears beginning in 1941. Professional baseball, though, snapped him up, and he went off to play with the Chattanooga Lookouts and Atlanta Crackers of the Southern League.

Throughout his professional baseball career, Wooten continued to play basketball during the winter months, exciting crowds at the Southern Textile League tournament every March. But the two loves finally clashed, and, as Earl said, "I probably made my biggest mistake in nineteen-forty-eight." He ignored a stipulation in his Washington Senators' contract and played basketball in the offseason. The game at which he was so magnificent caused him to miss his calling in the major leagues.

He had played in 86 games with the Senators in 1948 as an outfielder, first baseman, and pitcher; he was even listed as the third string catcher, though he was left-handed. Wooten had signed a 1949 contract calling for a raise, but Senators' president Clark Griffith and Earl had reached agreement regarding his offseason occupation. Wooten was to abandon the Pelzer Bears during the winter of 1948-49 and instead work to stay in shape for the big leagues. Too much running during the winter months took a lot out of his legs and caused him to start slowly in the spring and early summer. In return for following the wishes of Mr. Griffith, disregarding basketball and his countles number of loyal fans at home, Wooten was to receive a payment each month from the Washington team. Earl accepted the money graciously, but he also played basketball as much as ever, often under an alias. He even said it was his brother pouring in all the points in those textile league games. When Mr. Griffith was informed of what was going on, he did not even bother to contact Wooten again, except to inform him that his contract had been sold to Chattanooga. Earl Wooten never got another shot at the major leagues.

So he simply switched one sports arena for another and came back home to the textile leagues, playing primarily in Pelzer and Piedmont. After one last stint in pro ball as manager of the Greenville Spinners in the Tri-State League in 1955, Wooten was a mainstay in textile's Western Carolina League. With the Piedmont Rangers, he was the league MVP in 1956 (tossing a no-hitter against Victor Mill of Greer in July of that year). He repeated the honor in 1957 on the strength of a .354 batting average and an 8-3 pitching record. In a game on July 11th, he spotted the Berkeley, North Carolina, Spinners four runs in the first, then hung up 13 scoreless innings before the Rangers claimed the win.

There was one last effort by organized baseball to lure him away from the mill village. The Milwaukee Braves asked him to manage their Waycross, Georgia, team in the Class D Georgia-Florida League in 1957. "Right now, I wouldn't leave Piedmont for anything," said the mill's athletic director. "The youngsters and veterans are hustling and playing heads up baseball, and I wouldn't leave them for any amount. And most important," continued Wooten, "I've learned what it feels like to be a family man again, to put my children to bed at night, and you don't put a price on such things."

Earl's finest textile athletic achievement occurred in 1958. As a player/coach for the basketball Rangers, he led them to championships in the Peach Blossom, Textile, and Southern Textile Class A tournaments; the team sported a neat 32-7 record. As player/manager for the baseball version of the Rangers, Piedmont won the Western Carolina League championship with a 23-5 record. Even as textile baseball and basketball began to die, Earl gave them both one last spark of greatness.

It seems almost a cliché, but the records didn't matter to Wooten. He was the local boy who made good, the hero who came back home and entertained the fans he knew and loved with unmatched skill, the gentleman who repaid loyalty with a like measure of the same. But even if there were no mention of the Earl of Pelzer, the Wonder Boy, or Mr. Basketball, there would still be Earl Wooten, the man, and that would be enough.

Chapter Notes

Chapter 1: Beginnings

1. Steve Dunwell, *The Run of the Mill* (Boston: David R. Godine, Publisher, 1978), 144.
2. Richard T. Ely, "An American Industrial Experiment," *Harper's Monthly,* CV, No. 625 (1902), 42.
3. David L. Carlton, *Mill and Town in South Carolina: 1880–1920* (Baton Rouge, LA: Louisiana State University Press, 1982), 70.
4. Ibid., 108.
5. Ibid., 70.
6. Jacquelyn Dowd Hall, et al., *Like a Family: The Making of a Southern Cotton Mill World* (Chapel Hill, NC: University of North Carolina Press, 1987), 146.
7. Dunwell, 128.
8. Ibid., 130–132.
9. Donald B. Cole, Immigrant City: Lawrence, Massachusetts 1845–1921 (Chapel Hill, NC: University of North Carolina Press, 1963), 65.
10. Ely, 42.

Chapter 2: Fun and Games

1. Jacquelyn Dowd Hall, et al., *Like a Family: The Making of a Southern Cotton Mill World* (Chapel Hill, NC: University of North Carolina Press, 1987), 137, 139.
2. Ibid., 139.
3. Newberry (SC) *Observer,* September 5, 1901.
4. Greenville (SC) *Mountaineer and Enterprise,* September 6, 1893. Courtesy of the Pendleton Historical Society.
5. Newberry (SC) *Observer,* June 16, 1903.
6. August Kohn, *The Cotton Mills of South Carolina* (Charleston, SC: Daggett Printing Co., 1907), 131.
7. William Hayes Simpson. *Life in Mill Communities* (Clinton, SC: Presbyterian College Press, 1941), 65–66.
8. Greenville (SC) *Mountaineer and Enterprise,* April 19, 1889. Courtesy the Pendleton Historical Society.
9. Marjorie Potwin, *Cotton Mill People of the Piedmont* (New York: Columbia University Press, 1927), 143.
10. Newberry (SC) *Observer,* May 5 and 9, 1905.

Chapter 3: Champ Osteen

    1. Olin D. Johnston, et al., *Anderson County, SC: Economic and Social* (Columbia, SC: University of South Carolina Press, 1923), 53.
    2. Herbert J. Lahne, *The Cotton Mill Worker* (New York: Farrar and Rinehart, Inc., 1944), 52.

Chapter 4: Fields, Trains, Bands and Such

    1. Greenville (SC) *News,* May 28, 1916.
    2. Spartanburg (SC) *Herald,* August 23, 1914.
    3. Spartanburg (SC) *Herald,* May 31, 1910.
    4. Greenville (SC) *News,* May 18, 1917.
    5. Greenville (SC) *News,* June 5, 1915.
    6. Greenville (SC) *News,* June 4, 1916.
    7. Greenville (SC) *News,* June 18, 1916.
    8. Spartanburg (SC) *Herald,* July 15, 1913.
    9. Spartanburg (SC) *Herald,* May 10, 1914.

Chapter 5: Shoeless Joe

    1. Greenville (SC) *News,* July 7, 1917.
    2. The Piedmont (SC) *Bridge,* Volume II, No. 8, August 1920. Courtesy of the Pendleton Historical Society.
    3. Interview with Mrs. Mildred Hughey, June 1987.
    4. Interview with Jim Blackwell, June 1986.

Chapter 6: Fussin' and Fightin'

    1. Spartanburg (SC) *Herald,* August 20, 1911.
    2. Spartanburg (SC) *Herald,* May 21, 1915.
    3. Spartanburg (SC) *Herald,* May 10, 1915.
    4. Interview with Mrs. Mac Bannister, June 1986.
    5. Greenville (SC) *News,* July 29, 1905.
    6. Greenville (SC) *News,* August 8, 1915.
    7. Greenville (SC) *News,* July 5, 1919.
    8. Greenville (SC) *News,* August 27, 1916.
    9. Greenville (SC) *News,* August 21, 1921.
    10. Spartanburg (SC) *Herald,* July 22, 1913.
    11. Taped interviews of the 1982 Anderson County Textile Baseball reunion. Courtesy of the Pendleton Historical Society.

12. Interview with Leo Tober, May 1986.
13. Letter from Eddie Hall, June 1987.
14. Letter from Bill Webb, June 1987.
15. Greenville (SC) *News,* July 29, 1929.
16. Interview with Tough Embler, July 1987.

Chapter 7: The Maturing Years

1. Jim Blackwell interview, June 1986.
2. George O. Robinson, *The Character of Quality* (Columbia, SC: The R.L. Bryan Co., 1964), 41.
3. Letter from Virgil Lavender, August 1985.
4. Letter from Coach Frank Howard, March 11, 1986.
5. Interview with Bill Womack, May 1986.
6. Interview with Mrs. "Shag" Knox, May 1986.
7. Interview with Bob Creekmore, May 1986.

Chapter 9: War and Renaissance

1. Richard Thorpe, *Cotton Mill Cowboys* (Greenville, SC: Richwood Press, 1984), 107.
2. Letter from Carl Adams, September 30, 1986.
3. Calhoun Falls (SC) *News,* May 2, 1947.
4. Michael Hembree and David Moore, *Clifton: A River of Memories* (Clinton, SC: Jacobs Press, 1988), 53.
5. Letter from Mrs. Harry Potts, May 1986.
6. Michael Hembree and David Moore, *A Place Called Clifton* (Clinton, SC: Jacobs Press, 1987), 143.
7. Letter from Earl Morton, August 1985.

Chapter 10: Decline and Fall

1. Letter from Claude Center, September 1986.

Appendix 1

From the Mills to the Majors

Only those players whose textile league careers were verified through box scores and game accounts have been included.

Alfred "Alf" Anderson
Mills: Orr (1936–1937).
Majors: Pittsburgh NL (1941–1942, 1946).

Woodrow Abernathy
Mills: Chesnee; Mills Mill of Woodruff (1939–1941; 1948).
Majors: New York NL (1946–1947).

Pelham "Pel" Ballenger
Mills: Judson (1917); Brandon of Greenville (1915–1916, 1924, 1936); Poinsett (1948).
Majors: Washington AL (1928).

George Banks
Mills: Pacolet (1961); Clifton (1969).
Majors: Minnesota AL (1962–1964); Cleveland AL (1964–1966).

Walter "Walt" Barbare
Mills: Judson (1924); Lyman (1926); Brandon of Greenville (1911, 1928).
Majors: Cleveland AL (1914–1916); Boston AL (1918); Pittsburgh NL (1919–1920); Boston NL (1921–1922).

O'dell "Red" Barbery
Mills: Simpsonville (1937, 1943–1945, 1947, 1949, 1952–1954); Ware Shoals (1941, 1946–1951); Southern Bleachery (1940–1942, 1945, 1948, 1951).
Majors: Washington AL (1943).

Bob Bowman
Mills: Orr (1937).

Majors: St. Louis NL (1939–1940); New York NL (1941); Chicago NL (1942).

Leland "Lou" Brissie
Mills: Ware Shoals (1938, 1940–1942, 1946); Monaghan of Greenville (1944).
Majors: Philadelphia AL (1947–1951); Cleveland AL (1951–1953).

Johnny Buzhardt
Mills: Dutch Fork League (1952–1954).
Majors: Chicago NL (1958–1959); Philadelphia NL (1960–1961); Chicago AL (1962–1967); Baltimore AL (1967); Houston NL (1967–1968).

Paul Campbell
Mills: Arcadia; Pacolet.
Majors: Boston AL (1941–1942, 1946); Detroit AL (1948–1950).

Rome Chambers
Mills: Piedmont (1899).
Majors: Boston NL (1900).

Neil Chrisley
Mills: Calhoun Falls (1934, 1936, 1938, 1940, 1948–1950, 1954).
Majors: Washington AL (1957–1958); Detroit AL (1959–1960); Milwaukee NL (1961).

Tom Clyde
Mills: Oakland; Joanna (1941); Greenwood (1942).
Majors: Philadelphia AL (1943).

Calvin Cooper
Mills: Ware Shoals (1939, 1943, 1947–
  1949); Clinton (1949–1950, 1952–
  1954); Ninety Six (1942, 1946).
Majors: Washington AL (1948).

Claude Crocker
Mills: Lydia (1937, 1938); Clinton
  (1949–1950).
Majors: Brooklyn NL (1944–1945).

Davey Crockett
Mills: Piedmont (1899).
Majors: Detroit AL (1901).

Jake Daniel
Mills: Joanna (1950).
Majors: Brooklyn NL (1937).

Richard "Dickie" Dietz
Mills: Monaghan of Greenville (1960).
Majors: San Francisco NL (1966–
  1971); Los Angeles NL (1972);
  Atlanta (1973).

Don Dillard
Mills: Victor (1955).
Majors: Cleveland AL (1959–1962);
  Milwaukee NL (1963, 1965).

Cal Drummond
Mills: Ninety Six (1937, 1938); Green-
  wood (1946–1947).
Majors: American League umpire.

Clise Dudley
Mills: Monarch (1932); Lyman (1940).
Majors: Brooklyn NL (1929–1930);
  Philadelphia NL (1931–1932); Pitts-
  burgh NL (1933).

Ed Durham
Mills: Chester (1934, 1937, 1942); Eureka (1944).
Majors: Boston AL (1929–1932); Chicago AL (1933).

Zebulon "Zeb" Eaton
Mills: Clinton (1950); Joanna.
Majors: Detroit AL (1944–1945).

Al Evans
Mills: Chiquola (1936), Equinox
  (1937).
Majors: Washington AL (1939–1950);
  Boston AL (1951).

Art Fowler (Brother of Pete Fowler)
Mills: Pacolet (1942–1943); Clifton
  (1941, 1943); Converse (1942,
  1945).
Majors: Cincinnati NL (1954–1957);
  Los Angeles NL (1959); Los Angeles AL (1961–1964).

Jesse "Pete" Fowler (Brother of Art
  Fowler)
Mills: Converse (1922, 1934, 1937–
  1940, 1942–1943, 1945–1946); Ches-
  ter; Clifton (1920–1921).
Majors: St. Louis NL (1924).

Chick Galloway
Mills: Victor (1917); Clinton (1928).
Majors: Philadelphia AL (1919–
  1927); Detroit AL (1928).

Ford Garrison
Mills: Judson (1933); Dixie Stores
  (1934); Woodside; Poe.
Majors: Boston AL (1943–1944); Philadelphia AL (1944–1946).

Floyd Giebell
Mills: Woodside (1949–1951).
Majors: Detroit AL (1939–1941).

Claral Gillenwater
Mills: Easley (1923).
Majors: Chicago AL (1923).

Raymond Goolsby
Mills: Ware Shoals (1947–1950).
Majors: Washington AL (1946).

Ned Harris
Mills: Chiquola (1936–1937).
Majors: Detroit AL (1941–1943, 1946).

Joe Haynes
Mills: Appleton; Laurens; Anderson
  (1935).
Majors: Washington AL (1939–1940,
  1949–1952); Chicago AL (1941–
  1948).

Bob Hazle
Mills: Mills Mill of Woodruff (1947);
  Watts (1946–1949).
Majors: Cincinnati NL (1955); Mil-
  waukee NL (1957–1958); Detroit
  AL (1958).

Ⅴ **Kirby Higbe**
Mills: Anderson (1930, 1932);
  Laurens (1933–1934, 1940); Apple-
  ton (1937).
Majors: Chicago NL (1937–1939);
  Philadelphia NL (1940); Brooklyn
  NL (1941–1947); Pittsburgh NL
  (1947–1949); New York NL (1949–
  1950).

Ken Holcombe
Mills: Mathews (1940).
Majors: New York AL (1945); Cincin-
  nati NL (1948); Chicago AL (1950–
  1952); St. Louis AL (1952); Boston
  AL (1953).

ⵗ **Joseph Jefferson "Shoeless Joe" Jack-
son**
Mills: Brandon of Greenville (1905–
  1906, 1908); Victor (1907–1908);
  Woodside (1937); Winnsboro (1934).
Majors: Philadelphia AL (1908–
  1909); Cleveland AL (1910–1915);
  Chicago AL (1915–1920).

George Jeffcoat
Mills: Anderson (1930–1932);
  Mathews (1937–1939); Pelzer
  (1938).
Majors: Brooklyn NL (1936–1939);
  Boston NL (1943).

Ben Johnson
Mills: Panola (1952).
Majors: Chicago NL (1959–1960).

Jimmy Jordan
Mills: Tucapau.
Majors: Brooklyn NL (1933–1936).

ⵗ **Joe Landrum**
Mills: Clinton (1945); Dunean (1949);
  Brandon of Greenville (1951).
Majors: Brooklyn NL (1950, 1952).

ⵗ **Tommy Lasorda**
Mills: Joanna (1947).
Majors: Brooklyn NL (1954–1955);
  Kansas City AL (1956).

John "Buddy" Lewis
Mills: Ware Shoals (1935); Joanna (1950).
Majors: Washington AL (1935–1949).

Eddy Levy
Mills: Poe (1935); Union Bleachery
  (1935).
Majors: Philadelphia NL (1940); New
  York (1942, 1944).

Mickey Livingston
Mills: Newberry (1935, 1938); Clinton
  (1950).
Majors: Washington AL (1938); Phil-
  adelphia NL (1941–1943); Chicago
  NL (1943, 1945–1947); New York
  NL (1947–1949); Boston NL (1949);
  Brooklyn NL (1951).

Russ Lyon
Mills: Calhoun Falls (1948–1952);
  Greenwood (1946–1948); Mills Mill
  of Woodruff (1948).
Majors: Cleveland AL (1944).

Leroy Mahaffey
Mills: Belton (1923); Appleton (1933,
  1936–1938); Gossett (1940–1941);
  Piedmont (1941); Lyman (1941).
Majors: Pittsburgh NL (1926–1927);
  Philadelphia AL (1930–1935); St.
  Louis AL (1936).

John "Red" Marion
Mills: Joanna (1950).
Majors: Washington AL (1935, 1943).

Sammy Meeks
Mills: Orr (1943, 1946, 1948, 1950).
Majors: Washington AL (1948); Cin-
  cinnati NL (1949–1951).

Reuben "Rube" Melton
Mills: Greenwood (1940); Joanna (1950).
Majors: Philadelphia NL (1941–
  1942); Brooklyn NL (1943–1944;
  1946–1947).

ⵗ **Billy O'Dell**
Mills: Newberry (1949); Mollohon
  (1950); Liberty (1951–1953).
Majors: Baltimore AL (1954–1959);
  San Francisco NL (1960–1964); Milwaukee NL (1965); Atlanta NL
  (1966); Pittsburgh NL (1966–1967).

James "Champ" Osteen
Mills: Piedmont (1899–1900, 1922);
  Poe (1916).

Majors: Washington AL (1901); New
  York AL (1904); St. Louis AL
  (1908–1909).

Sam Page
Mills: Enoree (1935); Mills Mill of
  Woodruff (1935, 1937–1941, 1950);
  Riverdale (1947–1948); Brandon of
  Woodruff (1948); Excelsior (1949).
Majors: Philadelphia AL (1939).

Isaac "Ike" Pearson
Mills: Orr (1937); Whitney (1937).
Majors: Philadelphia NL (1939–1942;
  1946); Chicago AL (1948).

Cy Pieh
Mills: Brandon of Greenville (1920).
Majors: New York AL (1913–1915).

Marvin Rackley
Mills: Walhalla (1938); Oconee (1939–
  1940).
Majors: Brooklyn NL (1947–1949);
  Pittsburgh NL (1949); Cincinnati
  NL (1950).

Flint Rhem
Mills: Westminster (1922); Belton
  (1923); Brandon of Greenville
  (1924).
Majors: St. Louis NL (1924–1932,
  1934, 1936); Philadelphia NL
  (1932–1933); Boston NL (1934–
  1935).

Billy Rhiel
Mills: Newberry (1929).
Majors: Brooklyn NL (1929); Boston
  NL (1930); Detroit AL (1932–1933).

Johnny Riddle
Mills: Clinton (1923); Laurens (1926–
  1927).
Majors: Chicago AL (1930); Boston
  NL (1937–1938); Cincinnati NL
  (1941, 1944–1945); Pittsburgh NL
  (1948).

Aaron Robinson
Mills: Lancaster; Chester.
Majors: New York AL (1943, 1945–
  1947); Chicago AL (1948);
  Detroit AL (1949–1951); Boston
  AL (1951).

Ralph Rowe
Mills: Newberry (1940–1941, 1946);
  Clinton (1945).
Majors: Hitting Instructor, Baltimore
  AL, Atlanta NL.

Al Shealy
Mills: Mollohon (1922–1923); Newberry (1934–1936).
Majors: New York AL (1928); Chicago NL (1930).

Ben Shields
Mills: Tucapau (1934); Drayton.
Majors: New York AL (1924–1925);
  Boston AL (1930); Philadelphia NL
  (1931).

Clyde Shoun
Mills: Baldwin (1934).
Majors: Chicago NL (1935–1937); St.
  Louis NL (1938–1942); Cincinnati
  NL (1942–1944, 1946–1947); Bos-
  ton NL (1947–1949); Chicago AL
  (1949).

Carlisle "Red" Smith
Mills: Poe (1908–1909).
Majors: Brooklyn NL (1911–1914);
  Boston NL (1914–1918).

Sydney Smith
Mills: Poe (1909–1910); Brandon of
  Greenville (1910); Mills Mill of
  Greenville (1912).
Majors: Philadelphia AL (1908); St.
  Louis AL (1908); Cleveland AL
  (1910–1911); Pittsburgh NL (1914–
  1915).

Virgil Stallcup
Mills: Chiquola; Mathews; Ware
  Shoals (1938, 1941).
Majors: Cincinnati NL (1947–1952);
  St. Louis NL (1952–1953).

Hal Stowe
Mills: Liberty.
Majors: New York AL (1960).

Sammy Taylor
Mills: Mills Mill of Woodruff (1949,
  1951).
Majors: Chicago NL (1958–1962);

New York NL (1962 -1963); Cincinnati NL (1963); Cleveland AL (1963).

Al Veach
Mills: Lancaster (1932); York; Greenwood (1935); Brandon of Greenville (1935).
Majors: Philadelphia AL (1935).

Bill Voiselle
Mills: Ninety Six (1937, 1938, 1941, 1946-1949); Ware Shoals (1950).
Majors: New York NL (1942-1947); Boston NL (1947-1949); Chicago NL (1950).

Frank Walker
Mills: Enoree (1912).
Majors: Detroit AL (1917-1918); Philadelphia AL (1920-1921); New York NL (1925).

Bill "Lightning" Webb
Mills: Equinox (1934-1938).
Majors: Philadelphia NL (1943).

Henry Levi "Johnny" Wertz
Mills: Newberry (1920-1923, 1934-1938); Ware Shoals (1923).
Majors: Boston NL (1926-1929).

Ernie White
Mills: Pacolet (1934, 1936-1937).
Majors: St. Louis NL (1940-1943); Boston NL (1946-1948).

Charlie Wilson
Mills: Clinton (1920, 1928); Laurens (1922).
Majors: Boston NL (1931); St. Louis NL (1932-1933; 1935).

Charlie Wood
Mills: Glendale (1932).
Majors: Pittsburgh NL (1930-1931).

Earl Wooten
Mills: Pelzer (1940-1945, 1950, 1953, 1955); Piedmont (1956-1961); Ware Shoals (1943); Bahan (1941).
Majors: Washington AL (1947-1948).

Taft Wright
Mills: York (1931, 1933); Lancaster (1932).
Majors: Washington AL (1938-1939); Chicago AL (1940-1942, 1946-1948); Philadelphia AL (1949).

Jim Yeargin
Mills: Simpsonville (1921, 1923, 1928); Laurens (1926, 1927).
Majors: Boston NL (1922, 1924).

Appendix 2

Records and Rosters
1888–1955

The following records and rosters were compiled primarily from old newspapers, photographs and interviews with former players and fans. This representative listing in no way claims to be all inclusive. No information was available for the period 1880–1887.

1888

Williamston (1-0)
Piedmont (0-1)

1889

Piedmont #1 (no records): Charles B. Iler, Wallace Norris, John Iler, William Clifford, Sam Buchanan, B.W. Rowell, James Tice, Samuel Owens, Henry Humphries.
Piedmont #2 (no records): John Rogers, Bert Summey, George Young, Oscar Roberts, James McClellion, Henry Hamby, Clayton Roberts, W.C. Cobb, John Deal.

1895

Anderson (1-0)
Newberry (0-1)

1898

Newberry (1-0)

1899

Piedmont (19-6): Ryan, Holliday, Luke Chandler, Rankin, Tarrant,

W.H. Hammett (manager), Bob Poole, Pat Callahan, Champ Osteen, Davey Crockett, Sug Morris, Jack Frost, Victor Ackersino, Harry Cooper, M.M. Marsh, Walter Harrison, Rome Chambers, Claude Iler, Arthur Smith, Dave Tice.
Newberry (2-0): Dave Rhoden, Elkins, Jones, Gibson, Rube Boozer, Owens.

1900

Newberry 2nd Team (3-2): Rhoden, Senn, Boozer, Pitts, King.
Newberry (2-1): Billy Weddington, Carlton Beusse, Case, Caldwell.
Jonesville (1-0)
Piedmont (1-2): Champ Osteen, White, Crockett, Malcolm, Barker, Marsh.

1901

Newberry (3-0): Makepeace, Freeman, Caldwell, Rufus Senn, King.
Piedmont (3-1): Frost, Ragan, Cooper, McTier, Fehl, Turner, Marsh, Everett, Whistler, Stuckey.
Pelzer (2-4): Bradley, Burbank,

117

Loudenslager, Pritchett, Ottman, Dougherty, Warner, Bankston, Quick, Pelzer, Darby, Crawley, Sullivan, Fay.
Anderson (0-1)
Orr (no records): Nelson Buchanan, T.C. Kay, Jim McAllister, Grover Gilliard, Charlie Buchanan, Ben Ellison (manager)

1902

Piedmont (2-0): Everett.
Mills Mill of Greenville (2-0)
St. Albans (1-1): Tim Griffin.
Newberry (1-1)
Poe (0-2): Jack Hayden, Hub Fleming, Jim Jones, Doyle Westmoreland, Clarence Coleman, Bob Griffith, Walter Jackson, Monroe Samples, Oscar Richey, J.V. Jones.

1903

Tucapau (2-0): Harrison, Olden.
Pelzer (2-0): Lyles, Spearman, Pelzer, Crenshaw, Daniels, H. Sullivan, Henderson, Williamson, E. Sullivan.
Hugenot (2-2): Murphy, Corsey, Kemp, Brown, Floyd, Mitch, O'Neil, Lane, Powell, Collins, Coach.
Brandon of Greenville (1-0)
Reedy River (1-0)
Easley (1-0): R.A. Gentry.
Sampson (1-1): Shippey, Pruitt.
Poe (0-1)
Piedmont (0-1): Cleveland, McCall.
Newberry (0-1): Taylor, Stone.
Mills Mill of Greenville (0-4)

1904

Monaghan of Greenville (4-0): Mills, Melton, Bennett, Clippard.
Piedmont (3-0): Dendy, R.H. Shaver, McClase, Laval, McCall.
Brandon of Greenville (3-0): Roddy, Childress, Ferguson.

Tucapau (2-0): Jordan, Oldham, Laval.
Mills Mill of Greenville (1-0): Trammell.
Hugenot (0-1) Laval, Rogers, Hughes.
Orr (0-1)
Reedy River (0-1): Tucker, Garrett.
Williamston (0-1): Pelzer, Kelly.
Sampson (0-2): Snipes, Long.
Pelzer (0-2)
Easley (0-4): Melcher, Fletcher, Keller.

1905

Piedmont (3-1): Secrist, McCall, Laval.
Brandon of Greenville (2-0): Shoeless Joe Jackson.
Mills Mill of Greenville (1-0): Trammell.
Belton (1-0)
Pelham (1-0)
Hugenot/Camperdown (1-1): Causey, Floyd, C. Blair, Brown, Tassiter, Hall, Coursey, T. Blair, Davis, Stewart.
Woodside (1-2): Tabor, Emory, Roddy, Jackson.
Reedy River (0-1): Tucker.
Sampson (0-1): Ellison.
Williamston (0-1): Secrist, Kelly.
Mollohon (0-1)
Jackson of Iva (no records): Ernest Gailey, Sloan Evans, Eddie Adkins, John Davis, Jim Sullivan, J.R. McBride, Will Stewart, Frank Brown, Sam Patterson (manager), George Vaughn, Jim Keller.
Greenwood (no records): Wilcox, Ellis, Kelly.
Whitmire (no records): Meg, Moss.
Grendel (no records)

1906

Newberry (4-1): Williams, Waldrop, Cabiness.
Victor of Greer (2-0)
Mollohon (2-1): Crouch, Moore, Boozer.
Fairmont (1-0): Bright, Baxter.

Valley Falls (1-0)
Grendel (1-0)
Laurens (1-0)
Saxon (1-1): Lee, Bryant.
Inman (1-1)
Whitney (1-1)
Tucapau (1-3): Jackson, Rogers, Wilcox, Johnson, Davis, Davis, Jordan, R.W. Lewis (manager), Swink.
Pacolet (0-1): Horn, Motts.
Arcadia (0-1): Barnett, Caldwell.
Lydia (0-3)

1907

Whitney (6-2): Jordan, Davis.
Newberry (4-0): Simpson, Shealy.
Mollohon (2-0): Scurry, Benton, Morse.
Reedy River (1-0): Bannister, Smith.
Enoree (1-0): Horn, Taylor.
Spartan (1-0)
Pacolet (1-1): Brown, Motts, A.J. Lee.
Tucapau (1-3): James, Williams, Fanderberg, Prior, Jackson, Horn, Williams, West, Gresham, Linder, Suttles, Davis, Taylor, Plyler.
Brandon of Greenville (0-1): Wilson, Turner.
Clifton (0-1)
Drayton (0-1)
Whitmire (0-1)
Clinton (0-4): Bailey, Chandler, Robertson, Young.
Gluck (no records): Claude Ripley, Lee Allen, Charlie Keller, Ernest Hanks, Rip Major, Dick Keller, John Perry, Grover Heaton, June Ellison, Ode Ellison, Charles Plier.

1908

South Carolina Mill League

Ware Shoals (9-2): Horn, Castleberry, Fletcher.
Grendel (7-4): Wells Riley (manager)
Williamston (4-7): Bannister, McCall.
Belton (2-9): Bannister, Lyles.

Greenville Mill League: Dr. Hollis (president), Sims (vice president)

Monaghan of Greenville, champions (10-2): Charlie Waldrop, Tipton, Ellis Blackstone, Oscar Gregory, A. Bradley, Campbell, Hunnicutt, M. McWhite, Bradley, Barnum, Arthur, Roy McWhite, Corn, Shelton, Litterfield, Cherry, Lipton.
Poe (3-3): Ludwig, Kilpatrick, Newman, Spearman, Carlisle Smith, Harris, Pettit, Mims, Turner, Garrett, Estep, Hamby, Bill Osteen.
Mills Mill of Greenville (1-3): Leslie, Simmons, Putnam, Finley, Arker.
Brandon of Greenville (1-0): G.M. Thackston (manager), Abercrombie, Hunt, Hale, H. Epting, Garrett, Wheat, Joe Jackson.
Sampson (1-2): Jenkins, Leslie, Findelay, Putman, Fisher, Allison, Simonds, Barton, Davis, Coward, Pike, Lesby, Ballew, Springfield, Hughes.

Independent Teams

Victor of Greer (19-0): Percy Trammell, Walter Trammell, Red Childers, Ras Poole, Roy Cottingham, Shoeless Joe Jackson, Joe Wofford, Bob Patrick, Sim Cleary, Suttles.
Newberry (4-1): Simpson, McCall.
Gaffney (3-0): Ward, Little, Byrd, Corey, Lipscomb, Ballew, Harris, Maxwell, Wood, Curry, Richardson, Bell, McFadden, Robins, Prior, Martin, Hamrick.
Pacolet (3-1): Holmes, Ballard, Gossett, Crocker, Mott, A.J. Lee.
Converse (1-0): McGraw, Bergen.
Campobello (1-0): Nix, Benson.
Arkwright (1-0): Holt, Brown.
Beaumont (1-0)
Spartan (1-2): Posey, Grant, Burrell, Crocker, Rickman.
Tucapau (0-1): Jackson, Suttles, Turner, Irby, Childers, West, Linder, Trammell.

Pacolet Station (0-1): Sanders, Coleman, Brown, Littlejohn, Scott, Redd, Harvey, Mabry, Hanes, Miller.

Cowpens (0-1): Oglesby, Henry.

Landrum (0-1): Irvin, Doral, Neeton.

Clifton (0-1): Tom Burns.

Buffalo (0-1): Rickard, Dobson, Watson, G. Justus, W. Justus, Gresham, Garden, Burns, Padgett.

Whitney (0-1)

Whitmire (0-1)

Watts (0-1)

Clinton (0-2): Bailey, Young.

Monarch (no records): Paul West, Wes Carter, Will Brown, Sanford Hart, Walt West, Judson Long, Will Sparks, Robert Eubanks, Walter Hewitt, Clarence Webb, Derieux Nabors.

Inman (no records): A.J. Lee.

1909

Greenville Mill League

Monaghan of Greenville, champions (7-2): Gregory, Putnam, Kilpatrick, Barbery, Lucas, King, Bowden, Scroggins, Ballard, Jones, Waldrop, Hughes, Tipton, Putnam, Hastings, Poole.

Sampson (4-3): Miller, Davis, Fisher, Jenkins, Jordan, Simmons, Turner, Turner, Coker, Key.

Poe (4-3): Hamilton, Carlisle Smith, R. Osteen, Ludwig, Spearman, Jackson, Hamby, P. Garrett, Hamilton, Sydney Smith, W. Osteen, Harris, E. Garrett, Harris.

Brandon of Greenville (3-4): Campbell, Epting, Richardson, Roddy, Childress, Hatch, Childress, B. Turner, G. Turner, Reynolds, Hill, Coker, Davis, Smith.

Mills Mill of Greenville (2-5): Fellows, Finley, Barrett, Putnam, Smith, Goss, Hawkins, Johnson, Dross, Davis.

Camperdown (3-4): Gillespie, Melton, Spain, Graham, Tucker, Brown, Hatcher, Jenkins, Rose, Tipton.

Independent Teams

Watts (5-1)

Drayton (5-2): Mahaffey, Lavender, Lavender.

Newberry (3-1)

Glendale (3-1): Reeves, Branch, Guthrie, Easler, Gosnell.

Lydia (3-3)

Easley (2-0)

Pacolet (2-1): Holmes, Kirby.

Spartan (2-1): Cudd, Rush, Burrell, Foster, Rickman, B. Ballard, Rogers, Hammett, Grant, Bobo, Ingle, J. Ballard.

Union (1-0): Gilliam.

Clinton (1-0): Benton.

Greer (1-0): Suttles, W. Trammell, Patrick.

Enoree (1-0)

Whitmire (1-0)

Victor of Greer (1-1): Trammell, Shoeless Joe Jackson, Bob Patrick.

Arkwright (1-1): Brown, Brown, Bailey.

Whitney (1-1): Brown, Rush, Posey, Stone, Foster.

Tucapau (1-1): Miller, West.

Clifton (1-2): McMahon, Cannon, McDowell.

Cowpens (0-1): L. Moore, Bradley, B. Moore, Thomas, F. Bailey, Henry, Clary, Moore, Barton.

Lockhart (0-1)

Converse (0-1): Blackwell, Martin.

Inman (0-2): Garner, Goings.

Valley Falls (0-2): Petty, Seay.

Laurens (0-2)

Gluck (no records): "Nancy" Hanks.

1910

Greenville Mill League: R.M. Dacus (president), Burnett (secretary)

Poe, champions (16-2): Foster, Jones, W. Harris, McAby, Jackson, Hamilton, W. Osteen, Whitener,

R. Osteen, Ingle, J. Whitener,
Whitney, Bridwell.

Sampson (10-6): Ballew, Springfield,
Coker, Simpson, Simmons, Davis,
Mason, Lyle, Posey, Lowe, Bell,
Belk, Summey, Painter.

Monaghan of Greenville (8-8):
Waldrop, Gibson, Newman,
Tipton, H. Campbell, Gregory,
Reed, J. Campbell, Sheppard, Bell,
Kilpatrick, Shelton, Tipton,
Jenkins.

Brandon of Greenville (8-8): H. Epting, Campbell, Sydney Smith, Hawkins, R. Epting, Mace, Jackson,
Tipton, Turner, Henderson, Turner,
Christopher.

Mills Mill of Greenville (6-12): J. Put-
nam, Davis, B. Putnam, Goss,
Hawkins, Williamson, Finley,
Brothers, Wood, Green, Harris,
Ballenger, Westmoreland.

Woodside (5-13): Donaldson, G.
Brown, Dodgin, Wiley, Henson,
Fryar, Craigo, Sullivan, Gossett,
Millwood, Handcock, Henderson,
Hudson, T. Jones, E. Jones,
Mason, H. Painter.

Independent Teams

Pelzer (5-4): Ben Lark, Wade Spen-
cer, Castleberry, Mac Bannister,
Lawrence, Vaughn, Watson, Cox,
Berry.

Camperdown (3-0): Whitaker, De-
Long, Edwards, Cooksey,
Marchbanks, Hatcher.

Newberry (3-0): Scurry, Johnson,
Wicker, Boozer, Jones, Smith,
Bouknight, Garlington, McCall,
Harper, Havird.

Tucapau (2-1): John Cleveland (president), E.A. Hill (manager), R.W.
Lewis (ass't manager), John Jordan
(secretary), H.A. Johnson (trea-
surer), Lanford, Justice, Miller,
Swink, Will Ballenger.

Williamston (1-0): Williams, McAllister.

Glendale (1-0)

Whitney (1-0): Cudd, Cantrell,
Brown, Rush.

Converse (1-1): McGraw, Cavins,
Cooksey, Cabiness.

Clifton (1-1): McMahon, Connor, H.
Lark, Lark, Adam Massey.

Southern Bleachery (1-1): Keeler, Holland.

Spartan (1-1): Posey, Grant, Burrell.

Easley (0-1): Melton, Gordon.

Vardry (0-1)

Victor of Greer (0-1): Trammell, Patrick.

Gaffney (0-1): F. Seagall, E. Parks.

Drayton (0-1)

Laurens (0-1): Prince, Nesbitt, Fisher,
Hawkins, Irby.

Poe 2nd Team (0-2): Watts, Fortner,
Manns, Barton.

Watts (0-2): Prince, Swygert.

Piedmont (0-4): McCall, Lucas, Doug
James, Morgan, Robinson, Joe
Draughn, Painter.

Pelzer 2nd Team (no records): Harley
Heath, Lefty Crymes, Fidge
Wooten, Truman Crymes, Jim
Westmoreland, Nig Haney,
Fronnie Golden, John Earl Can-
non, Charlie Hopkins.

Greenwood (no records): Baynes,
Stephens, Summey, Terrell Jones,
Castleberry.

1911

Independent Teams

Cowpens (10-0): Oglesby, Sims,
L. Moore, Davis, Mabry, E. Mar-
tin, B. Moore, B. Martin, Ezell,
Gregory, Henry.

Beaumont (8-6): Matthews, Gosnell
(manager), Matthis, Tom Brown,
Sowers, Lindsay, Walters, Williams,
Grant.

Clifton (6-3): Guthrie, A. Holcombe,
Hawkins, Quiller, Greg, Massey,
McGraw, Martin, Wyatt, Hatchett,
Cannon.

Inman (5-1): Gowan, Cook, Lowe,
Smith, Tate, Whitson.

Pacolet (4-0): Worthy, Holmes,
L. Kirby, Hopper, Gossett, Kitchen,
Mills.

Saxon (4-3): H. Rogers, J. Rogers,
Walker, Holt, Walden, Charlie
Vaughn, Hawkins.

Spartan (4-3): T. Burrell, W. Grant,
J. Crocker, F. Burrell, Rickman,
Lowe, Black, Gilmer, C. Grant,
C. Thomas, McAbee, Rusk, Guy,
Posey, Fleming, Garner.

Pelzer Pelicans (3-0): Spencer, Burns,
Donaldson, Hooper.

Monaghan of Greenville (2-0): Tipton,
Waldrop, Walt Barbare, Campbell,
Ballard, Tipton, Jenkins.

Enoree (2-0): Bobo, Moore, Byrd,
Betsil, Stevens, Yeargin.

Piedmont Pipers (2-1): Robinson,
Watson, Castleberry, Long, Hicks.

Whitney (2-4): Guthrie, Cudd, Bailey,
Grant, Walls, Brown, Somers, Burnett, Sarsey, Thomas.

Union Bleachery (1-0): Runion,
Kneece.

Easley Eagles (1-0): McCoy, Milton.

Tucapau 2nd Team (1-0): Blackwell,
Calheron, Jackson.

Spartan 2nd Team (1-0): Clement,
Harrison.

Arcadia (1-1): Fray, Bridgman, Frye,
Bradley.

Tucapau (1-1): Miller, E. Davis,
B. Mason, N. Mason, Lockman,
Wood, Williams, C. Davis,
McAbee.

Crescent (1-3): Kelly, Mabry, Brown,
J.M. Mitchell, Whitlock.

Drayton (1-4): Prince, Belcher, Lark,
Rogers, Lynch, Miller, Nesbitt.

Brandon of Greenville (0-1): Turner,
Turner.

Sampson (0-1): Henson, Manns.

Westminster (0-1): Goss, Clark.

Campobello (0-1): Dugeness, Nix.

Powell (0-1): May, Gilliam, Holcombe,
Walker.

Saxon 2nd Team (0-2): Walker, Holt.

Greer (0-2): Rogers, Sellers, Patrick.

Belton (0-2): McAllister, Lowry,
Lyles.

Buffalo (0-3): Malone, Crocker, Bolling, Burns, Millwood.

Monarch (0-3): F. Burrell, Nabors,
Brown, C. Grant, Hart, Hames,
Darby.

Glendale (0-4): Gossett, Easler, Lockman, Guthrie, Smith, West, Black,
Brown, Parr, Land, Black.

1912

Greenville Mill League

Woodside, champions (10-7): Laven-
der, Cisson, Spearman, Ed Barrett,
Mason, Craigo, Harrison, Reed,
Ballard, Case.

Mills Mill of Greenville (8-8): R.
Smith, Jess Putnam, J. Davis, Sydney Smith, Finley, Hawkins, Anderson.

Brandon of Greenville (7-4): G.
Turner, Turner, Epting, Hawkins,
Paul Campbell, Kay Cashion,
Mahan, McCaslin, Ballard.

Monaghan of Greenville (7-10):
Jenkins, Tipton, H. Campbell,
Kelly, Ernest Jones, Sheppard,
Waldrop, J. Campbell, Simmons,
Hamby, Fred Ellis, Moman,
Speedy Howard, Ralph Cureton.

Sampson (6-6); withdrew. Robertson,
Mann, Timms, Henderson,
Springfield, Ballew, Keys.

Union Bleachery (2-10); withdrew.
Meisenheimer, Phillips, Garrison,
Keeler, Miller, Perry, Langston,
Watson.

Piedmont League

Pelzer (20-4): Donaldson, Bill
Vaughn, Dollan, Bridgman,
Brewer, Cox, Jordan, Doug Spen-
cer, Randall, Clark, L. Hooper,
Mac Bannister, Ben Lark, Hayes,
Tom Bray, Bud Burns, Rink Boyce,
Doe, Long, E. Godfrey, Ernest

Jenkins, Olin Millwood, Bob Heyward (manager), Ed Brinson.

Victor of Greer (3-1): P. Trammell, Miller, Patrick, Wood, Morgan, Justus, Clary, Childers, Tipton, W. Trammell.

Piedmont (1-5): Ballard, Foster, Timmons, Castleberry, Jamison, Watson, Newman, Poole, Boyce, Fisher, Ellison, Hooper.

Easley Giants (1-1): Dunn, McCoy, Baldwin, Drake.

Independent Teams

Inman (9-5): Seay, Nix, Fike, Rogers, Smith, Wofford, Whitener, Rogers.

Beaumont (7-2): Mayberry, Matthews, Wells, Matthis, Jackson.

Spartan (5-1): Love, McAbee, Kennett, DeShields, Towry, Danner.

Enoree (5-1): E. Betsil, Lynch, Burch, Hollie, Gresham, Frank, Walker.

Cowpens (4-0): Ezell, Martin, Davis, Vassey, Moore, Black, Oglesby.

Whitney (4-2): Cudd, Brown, Suttles, Kirby.

Spartan 2nd Team (4-2): Love, Garner, Maddox, Lowe, McAbee, Raymond.

Piedmont Lyceum Sluggers (3-1): Ashmore, Heston, Key, Henson, King.

Clifton (3-1): Dearberry, Hawkins, Mooney, Gossett, Holcombe.

Crescent (3-3): Mabry, Brown, Bishop, Turner, Howard, Brown, Bishop.

Saxon (3-8): Vaughn, Walker, Bryant, Kennett, Bobo, Waldrop, Hawkins.

Westervelt (2-0): Farmer, Putman.

Arcadia (2-1): Benson, Frey, Prior.

Williamston (2-1): Livingston, Williams, McAllister, Donaldson.

Tucapau (2-2): Trammell, Beatty, Bright, Caughman, Williams, Lowe, McMillan.

St. Albans (1-0): Black, Ashmore.

Sampson 2nd Team (1-0): Grant, Miller.

Camperdown (1-0): Owens, Owens.

Drayton 2nd Team (1-0): Seay, Seay.

Inman 2nd Team (1-0): Smith.

Watts (1-0): Mayberry, Yeargin.

Arkwright (1-1): Brown, Mayberry.

Poe (1-1): Bill Osteen, Gosnell.

Clifton 2nd Team (1-1): Dearberry, Smith.

Valley Falls (1-1): Ezell, Young, Small.

Converse (1-3): McGraw, Hopper, Lark.

Drayton (1-5): Eddies, Johnson, Ezell, Grant, Seay, Callahan, Prince, Lark, Wyatt, Belcher, Burrell.

Camperdown 2nd Team (0-1): Wilson, Chandler.

Brandon of Greenville 2nd Team (0-1): Sullivan, Sizemore.

Lydia (0-1): Barnett, Barksdale.

Woodruff (0-1): Swink, Irby.

Mollohon (0-1): Epting, Neal.

Fairmont (0-1)

Landrum (0-1)

Pacolet (0-1)

Belton (0-2): Summey, Lowe.

Clinton (0-2): Smith, Campbell, Eubanks.

Chesnee (0-2): Bonner, Turner, McClure.

Fairforest (0-2): Frey, Benson, Taylor.

Glendale (0-3): Gossett, Easler, Gosnell, Allen.

Alice (0-4): Christopher, Smith, Gregory, Tillison.

1913

Greenville Mill League

Brandon of Greenville (15-3): Lavender, Turner, Turner, Kay Cashion, Rollins, Cy Young.

Mills Mill of Greenville (16-4): Railroad Smith, Jess Putman, Dill, Anderson, Langston, Dewey Young, Mahaffey, Clayton Blackstone, Bill

Fletcher, Jess Davis, Fred Bruthers, Mack Turner, W.W. Bruthers, Metcalf.

Woodside (10-4): Ewell Craigo, Barrett, Nesbitt, Mahon, Coward, Freeman, Porter, Long, Mathis.

Monaghan of Greenville (7-9): Ellis, Campbell, Tipton, Robertson, B. Simpson, Needham, Shelton.

Sampson (6-11): Timms, Drake, Springfield, Bradley, Kirke, Jenkins, Pike, J. Barton, Tillison, Parris.

Dunean (no records)

Interurban League

Piedmont, champions (12-2): McCall, Robertson, Mann, Childers, Kelly, Hooper, Watson, Fisher, Cureton, Donaldson, Henson.

Pelzer (4-2) Wade Spencer, Jenkins, Leach, Dutch Vaughn, Ballard, Snipes, Ben Lark, Bill Vaughn, Cooley, McAllister, Mac Bannister, Hooper.

Williamston (0-1); withdrew. McAllister, Stone.

Brogan (0-2): Patterson, Hillford, English.

Belton (0-3): Graham, Hooper, Summey, Mahon, Suites.

Riverdale (no records); withdrew.

Spartanburg Mill League

Beaumont Mountaineers, champions (15-6): Guthrie, Matthews, Wall, Andy Gosnell, Worthy, James, Jackson, Pack, Soard, Mathis, Villen, Quillen, Hawkins, Williams, Holcombe, Owensby, Calvin, P. Pack, Gowan, Potter, Lawton, Holcombe, Henderson.

Whitney (14-7): Searcy, Kirby, O. Brown, T.J. Brown, Williams, Duncan, T.M. Brown, Cox, Thomason, Phillips, Welch, Wells, Cudd, Bridgman, Leonard, Darnell, Donaldson, Thomason, Guthrie, Laughlin.

Converse (12-7): Calvert, Brown, Hawkins, Lavender, Carswell, Cannon, Cooksey, Maynor, McGraw, Aker, Kirby, Lark, Davis, Dearberry, Vassey, Frady, Sims, Moore, B. Martin, Gossett, E. Martin, Donaldson, Lawson, Black, Hart, Hart, Eaker.

Drayton (11-9): Laughlin, H. Seay, Sanders, Nesbitt, Belcher, Prince, Stevens, Wyatt, W. Belcher, Seay, Lockabee, Mitchell, Lark, Jake Frey, Deagerhart, Earl Wofford, Mormon, Stevens.

Glendale Tigers (10-10): Gosnell, Mulligan, Allen, Smith, Sanders, Gilmer, Tindall, McGraw, Bagwell, Lowe, Coleman, Gilmore, Holmes, Gault (manager), Mulligan, Lockman, Reaves, Brown, Murray, Gossett, Guy, Scruggs, Bridgman.

Saxon (9-11): Bryant, Bobo, Johnson, Walton, Brooks, Vaughn, L. Vaughn, Morrow, Walker, J. Walden, Rogers, Lowe, Brown, C. Vaughn, L. Walden. Sibley, Teague, Martin, Kay, Keys, Lockabee, Long, Long.

Spartan Red Sox (9-11): Thomas, McAbee, Parris, Grant, Garner, Ballard, Harley, Lockman, Posey, Jackson, Gowan, Guy, Hancock (manager), Koon, Brooks, Burns, Duncan, Black, Shores, Rickman, Reed, Burrell, Hyde, Hyatt, Justus.

Arkwright (1-19): T. Shook, J. Brown, C. Shook, Earl Wofford, Braughn, C. Holt, Abonaha, Coker, Brum, A. Holt, Nix, Abernathey, Limbaugh, Whitener, Worthy, Howard, Cox, E. Brown, Mitchell, Williams (manager), Kelly, Mabry, Bishop, Lanhan, Cromer, Mahaffey, Wallicks, Leonard, Bryant, Searcy.

Union County League

Buffalo, champions (9-2): Malone, Burns, Banks, Gilliam.

Independent Teams

Spartan 2nd Team (8-2): Thomas, McAbee, Birchfield, Parris, Ballenger, Lindsay, Rinehart, Smith, Reed, Guy, Clark, Solesby, Ballenger, Fowler, Sanders, Lowry.

Saxon 2nd Team (6-4): Dixon, Chapman, Baldwin, Walker, Holt, Walden, Henderson, West, Sisk, Robinson, Wright, Ross, Pettus.

Tucapau (4-3): Williams, Jackson, Miller, Gresham, Oshields, N. Mason, Bridgman.

Arcadia (4-4): Robinson, Clark, Bridges, Broome, Robinson, Gosnell, Petty, Hunnicutt, Taylor, Bridgman, Ford, Walker.

Westervelt (3-0): Vardry, Ivester, Talbert, McGill, Burdette.

Valley Falls (3-4): Thomas, Howell, Sanders, Snell, Covil, Sisk, West, Carter, Clark.

Drayton 2nd Team (2-0): Wyatt, Adams.

Inman (2-1): Rogers, Nix, Lowe, Duncan, Whitener.

Clifton 2nd Team (2-1): Connor, Hawkins, Tindall, Dearyberry, Waldrop, Davis.

Liberty (1-0): Barrett, Medlock.

Poe (1-0): Pole Jenkins, Osteen, Cabiness.

Spartan 3rd Team (1-0): Solesby, Knipp.

Tucapau 2nd Team (1-0): Oshields, Cothran.

Piedmont Lyceum Sluggers (1-1): Bailey, McGee, Evans, Murphy.

Whitmire (1-1): Gilliam, Millwood, Aughtry.

Excelsior (1-1): Hart, Thomas, Allen, Cane, Donaldson, Whitener, Kirby, Beatenbaugh, Clowney, Hames, Johnson, Thompson, Burns.

Greer (0-1): Wood, Thomas.

Victor of Greer (0-1): Suttles, Patrick.

Glenwood (0-1):

Whitney 2nd Team (0-1): Davis, Gibson.

Beaumont 2nd Team (0-1): Dixon, Laughter.

Glendale 2nd Team (0-1): Bogan, Robertson, Mabry, Lands.

Pacolet (0-1): Smith, Mabry.

Enoree 2nd Team (0-1): Parham, Cogdill.

Jonesville (0-1): Holden, Spencer, Lewis Lamb, Lamb, Lybrand, Mitchell, Porter, Kitchens, Lee, Harris, McWhorter, Johnson, Moss, Smith, Oshields, Bolden.

Monarch (0-1): Gault, Hutt, Crocker, Lowe, Hames, Howell, Kirby, Allen, Corn.

Watts 2nd Team (0-1)

Lockhart (0-1)

Clifton (0-1)

Newberry (0-2): Alvin Danielson.

Fairmont (0-3): Morrow, Hill, J. Jones, C. Walker, Griffin, Case, Lydia, Jones, Wood, Justus.

1914

Greenville Textile League: Alonzo Eiler (president)

Brandon of Greenville, champions (12-8): B. Turner, Mahon, Rollins, W. Cashion, Young, G. Turner, Christopher, Brown, W. Turner, Frier, Chasteen, Black, Brown, McGill, Burdette, R. Turner, Kay Cashion, Woods, Jeffries.

Monaghan of Greenville (9-6): Jenkins, Springfield, Campbell, Tipton, Mann, Sheppard, Mason, Foster, Gourley, Anderson, Robertson, Ellis.

Woodside (8-7): Needham, Jackson, Ballard, Allen, Cisson, Whitmire, Burdette, Redmon, Jordan, Assam, Gosnell, Freeman, Mahon, Manos.

Dunean (8-7): Barrett, Putnam, Ivester, Gilmore, Abbott, J. Allen, Frank, Biddle, Chasteen, Thompson, Pittman, Wells, League.

Mills Mill of Greenville (8-8): Smith,

Medlock, Putnam, Langston, Davis,
W. Hawkins, Nichols, L. Anderson.
Judson (1-11): Mason, Tallant,
B. Burdette, Lindsay, G. Brown,
Robertson, Ivester, Brown, Bell,
McCarter, Fratt, Birdhead,
McAllister, C. Seay, H. Seay,
L. Burdette, Looper, Landers.

Interurban League: John Hudgens
(president), H.H. Moody (vice president), W.E. Hammonds (secre-
tary/treasurer)

Piedmont, champions (8-4): Lester
Fisher, Pete Robinson, McCabe,
J.C. McCall, T. Henson, Freeman,
E.R. Poole, Charles Thompson,
Mark Timmons, Brookshire, H. As-
hmore, Ben Lark, W.H. Cobb
(manager), Livingston, Malcomb,
Jameson, Hampton, Robertson,
Gilreath, W. Sealy, Lowe, Gilliard,
Graham, F. Sealy, Sullivan.
Pelzer (7-5): Boyce, Wade Spencer,
Dutch Vaughn, G.H. Hammonds
(manager), Hooper, Hooper,
Burns, Harper, Fisher, Watson,
Thompson, Poole, Hinson,
Gilreath, Singleton, Timmons, Mac
Bannister, Millwood, Jenkins,
York.
Tucapau (7-5): West, Miller, Melton,
E.H. Hill (manager), Miller,
N. Mason, Ellison, Newman, Wil-
liams, B. Mason, Lyle, Oshields,
Ballenger, McAbee, Watson,
Summie, Hamilton, McMahan,
Dagenhart, Clay, Keller.
Victor of Greer (4-8): McAllister, Pat-
rick, D.R. Harriman (manager),
F. Wood, Trammell, Cabiness,
Few, J. Wilson, J. Wood, Tipton,
R. Harris, W. Harris, S. Wilson,
Thomas, Poole, Suttles, Childers,
Ripley, Clary, Morgan.

Spartanburg Mill League: Charles
Hearon (president)

Beaumont Mountaineers, champions

(17-5): Walls, Jackson, Guthrie,
Holcombe, Reeves, Gowan, Eaker,
Gosnell, Pack, Swink, Rivers,
Groves, Erhu, Soard, Taylor,
Reeves, Lockman, Owensby,
Champion.
Drayton (12-8): Belcher, Sanders,
Leonard, C. Belcher, Jordan,
Owensby, C. Seay, H. Seay, Byce,
Langston (manager), Spencer,
Camp, Hamilton, W. Belcher,
L. Belcher, Dean, Hyde, Soard,
Cook, Prince, Adams, Stevens,
Halford.
Spartan Red Sox (11-8): Montague
Nichols, Posey, Loyless, Grant,
Hyde, Brooks, Moore, Garner,
Thomas, Cely, Garner, Roy Bridg-
man, Gilmer, R. Ballard, Bryant,
Gilmore, Sutton, Smith, B. Ballard,
McAbee.
Saxon (7-12): Walker, Brooks, Bry-
ant, Bobo, J. Martin, Case, Rick-
man, W. Martin, Hosea Rogers,
Mathis, Keller, Johnson, Vaughn,
Smith, Kennett, White, Garner,
McCravey, Caldwell, Brown,
Dearyberry, Davis, Robertson,
Bulman, Snell, Goslin, Taylor,
Sanders, Gosnell.
Whitney (7-12): Cudd, Kirby, Searcy,
D. Thomason, Mabry, Lowe, Dun-
can, Painter, C. Thomason,
Hughes, Burnett (manager), Kirby
(manager), Brown, Cox, Leonard,
Millwood, Henry, Wyatt, Sanders,
Welch, Murphy, Arnold.
Arkwright (5-14): John Brown,
Mabry, Bishop, Culbreth,
Wofford, Childers, C. Brown, Cal-
vert, Holt, Dearberry, P. Calvert,
Massey, Tindall, Kelly, Quillen,
Coleman, Cogswell, Carswell, Gos-
sett, Mathis, Teague, Shuck,
O'dell, Davenport.

Independent Teams

North Pacolet (10-2): Swain, Blackwell.

Buffalo (8-1): Johnson, Morgan, Allen, H. Branks, P. Smith, Martin, B. Branks, E. Smith, Melton, H. Malone, Bates (manager), W. Malone, Bolling.

Spartan 2nd Team (8-3): Sanders, C. Posey, S. Guy, Dixon, M. Guy, F. Guy, Solesbee, Rinehart, Parris, Lawson, Taylor, R. Ballard, W. Posey, Jackson.

Camperdown (3-0): Wilson, Wilson, Whitaker, Carter.

Watts (3-2): Christopher, Hooper, Fisher, Robinson, Clark, Justus, Mills, Sealy, Millwood, Nix, Lark, Vaughn, Williamson, Hill.

Clifton (3-3): Cook, Walker, Pryor, Harris, Carswell, Belcher, Mosely, Carter, Vassel, Etters, Hogan, Lantzy, Goforth, Beheler.

Glendale (3-3): Nicholls, Gossett, Sutton, Kirby, Parr, Black, T. Mabry, Cudd, Gilmer, Sanders, Miller, Arrowood.

Cowpens 2nd Team (2-0): S. Mosely, Vassey, Swofford.

Beaumont 2nd Team (2-0): Dixon, Bogan, Pack, Rinehart, Hammett, Lawrence, Wolf, Lindsay, Lauter, Adams.

Reedy River (2-0)

Arcadia (2-1): Robertson, Clark, Wyatt.

Whitney 2nd Team (1-0): Claude, Crowe, Sawer, Roberts, T. Sawer, M. Dan, Hollins, Woodell, Duncan.

Piedmont Lyceum Sluggers (1-0): Gilreath, Howard, Roland, Key, Browning.

Clifton #2 (1-0): Morrow, E. Davis, C. Davis, Dearyberry, Hatchett, Holcombe, Tindall, Quillen, Kirby.

Chesnee (1-1): Guthrie, Turner, A. McClure, L. McClure, Hodges, Cudd, W. Garrett, L. Garrett, Bomar, C. Cudd.

Union (1-1): Hanson, Sullivan, Sullivan, Matheny, Fowler, Hart, Lamb, Lamb, Lee, Kirby, Beatenbaugh, Horn.

Jonesville (1-1): Moss, Addis, Whitlock, Brown, Mulligan, Long, Coleman, Parks, Mabry, Spencer, Cudd, Allen.

Enoree (1-1): Moore, Parham, Waldrop.

Converse (1-1): Cooksey, Holden, Holland, Cannon, Pryor, Mayfield, Tindall, Cooksey.

Saxon 2nd Team (1-2): Hawkins, West, A. Patterson, Patterson, Turner, W. West, Hunter, Holt, Lamb.

Cowpens (1-2): Henry, E. Martin, Vassey, Sims, B. Moore, R. Moore, V. Martin, C. Martin, L. Moore, Oglesby, T. Martin.

Inman (1-2): Love, C. Blanton, McTiegel, Hinson, Smith, Mabry, N. Blanton, Cook, Thompson, Gowan.

Converse 2nd Team (1-3): Cannon, Cannon, Holland, Pryor, Mayfield, Cooksey, Cooksey, Mann, Holland.

Pacolet (1-9): Worthy, Gossett, Sparks, Millwood, Kirby, Sutton, Holmes, Guyton, Mabry, Brown, Martin, Metz, Coleman, Wells, Fowler, Cook, Petty, Tranham, Whitening, Jones, Wells, Williams, Porter, Bishop, Valentine, Sawyer, Duncan, Kirby, Spencer.

Sampson (0-1): Bradley, Miller, Miller.

Fingerville (0-1): Porter, Henderson.

Landrum (0-1): Jones.

Excelsior (0-1): Matheny, Hart, J. Sullivan, H. Harris, Betenbaugh, Fowler, H. Sullivan, Kirby, E. Harris.

Valley Falls (0-1): Burnett, Thomas.

Poe (0-1)

Mills Mill of Greenville 2nd Team (0-2): Nichols, Foster, Osborne.

Lockhart (0-2): Wylie, Allen, Inman.

Cohannet (0-2): Porter, Johnson.

Laurens (0-3): Bennett, Burgess, Rogers

Rock Hill (0-3): Brown, Thackum.

Glendale 2nd Team (0-3): Miller, Mabry, Black, Kirby, Gilmore, Smith, Nicholls, Sutton, Sanders, Gossett.

Newberry (no records): Alvin Danielson.

Chiquola (no records): James Monroe, R.A. Monroe, Rob Callahan, Johnnie Donald, Hop Tice, T.C. Cannon.

Greenwood (no records): Livingston, Gilliam, Clark, McPherson.

1915

Greenville Mill League

Brandon of Greenville, champions (16-5): W. Cashion, Brown, Turner, Frier, Rollins, McGill, Christopher, Mahon, Kay Cashion, Young, Grumbles, Jerry Jackson, O'shields, Verner, Pel Ballenger, Fisher, Osteen.

Dunean (15-5): Hill, Finley, Sam Anderson, Putman, Langston, Smith, K. Medlock, Springfield, L. Anderson, Granger, Ingle, Garner, Johnston, Frier, Childress, Childers.

Woodside (10-8): Epting, Verner, Moon, Whitener, Reed, B. Cisson, S. Ballard, R. Cisson, Crawford, H.F. Ross, F. Cisson, H. Ballard, Freeman, Pruitt, R. Jamison, Craigo, Case, Nainn, P. Neely, Barton.

Monaghan of Greenville (8-10): A. Turner, Kelly, Ellis, C. Waldrop, J. Campbell, Odom, Tipton, Jordan, Sullivan, Jenkins, B. Case, Harris, Sheppard, Steward, Gosnell, P. Campbell, Ellis, F. Waldrop, Needham, Simmons, Jones, Ben Turner, P. Waldrop, Burns.

Poe (6-10): Osteen, Richardson, W. Harris, S. Ballard, Adams, Welch,

Jackson, Rogers, W. Turner, Barrett, Trammell, Gosnell, Adams, Wilbanks, Ballew, Burdette, R. Harris, Frady, Drake, McClure (manager)

Sampson (3-11): C. Miller, Fisher, Bradley, D. Miller, Roberts, Nealy, Fowler, Brady, Hardin, Barton, Timms, Pike, Hardin, Pitts, Scott, Tollison, Fuller, Sims, Bolt, Littleson, Drake, Simmons.

Interurban League

Pelzer, champions (6-2): J. Burns, J. Hooper, Dutch Vaughn, Mac Bannister, Tom Bray, Carl Boyce, L. Hooper, Stack, E. Godfrey, Spencer, Hill, O. Millwood, Paul Troutman, Mills, Fisher, Robertson, Hammonds (manager), Flemmings (manager), Pearman (manager), Bill Vaughn.

Victor of Greer (7-3): Miller, Dagenhart, Patrick, Ferabee, Cunningham.

Tucapau (2-6): Miller, Newman, Miller, Linton, Melton, Blackstone, Pickett, Lindsay, Lark, Bowen, Mason, Cashion, Dagenhart, Welch, Hooper, Guthrie, Osteen, Ripley.

Piedmont (4-5): G. Turner, Osteen, Burdette, Robertson, Fisher, Poole, Troutman, Mills, Childers, Millwood, Henson, Evans, Robinson, Aughtry, Ballenger.

Spartanburg Mill League

Beaumont (9-8): Owensby, Loyless, Park, Taylor, Simmons, Lynch, Lockman, Eaker, Wood, Posey, Fletcher, Wyatt, W. Martin, Lattimore, S. Jackson, C. Jackson, Bridgman, Johnson, Rogers, Maynor, Champion, Patterson, Wooten, Bad Eye Guthrie.

Drayton (8-9): L. Belcher, Jackson, C. Belcher, C. Seay, Byce, Leonard, Gowans, H. Seay, W. Belcher,

Walls, Owensby, Spencer, Frady,
Sanders, James, Powell, C. Prince,
Mayfield, Grant, Henry, Vassey,
Gault, Kirby, Cook, Mahaffey, Al-
ford, Cannon, Sullivan, Adams.

Spartan (11-4): Thomas, R. Ballard,
Hyde, Grant, Wofford, Carswell,
Taylor, Bridgman, Cely, Moore,
J. Martin, Duncan, B. Ballard,
Dean, Kirby, Jones, Posey.

Saxon (5-13): Rogers, Kirby, Koon,
Searcy, Johnson, A. Patterson,
Robertson, M. Sanders, Hughes,
Mabry, H. Sanders, Walker, Haw-
kins, Allen, C. Patterson, Quillen,
Smith, Dearyberry, Bridgman, El-
liott, Vassey, Mosely, Henderson,
Tindall, Bishop, Davis, Atwater,
Reed, Brown, Lawson, Watson,
Brooks, Moore, Painter, Guy, Cal-
vert, Millwood.

Independent Teams

Union Bleachery (5-1): R. Owens,
Arrington, S. Owens, H. Owens,
Neely, Harrison.

Whitney (5-2): N. Sawyer, C. Thoma-
son, Duncan, Crowe, Hughes, W.
Sawyer, Holland, Arnold,
Nashburn, Searcy, Kirby, B.
Thomason, Farrow, Garner.

Inman (3-0): Love, Bass Waters,
Luther Mabry, Ellard Nix, Jen-
nings Waldrop, Monroe Teague,
Alex Cothran, Bill Gowan, Bob
Nichols, Johnny Lawrence, Grady
Stone, Earl Bice (manager)

Spartan 2nd Team (3-1): Dye,
McAbee, Henry Sanders, Harrison.

Carolina (3-2): Harrison, Lavender,
Mann, Williams, Champion, Burdette, Mitchell, Lauder.

Drayton 2nd Team (2-1): Halford,
Jesse Adams.

Arkwright (2-1): Henderson, Bishop,
Holt, Henson, Brown, Hawkins,
Mabry, Wofford, Holland, R. Gib-
son, L. Gibson, Dale.

Jonesville (2-1): Spencer, Gault,

Mabry, Osment, McWhorter,
Mathis, Morgan, McWhorter,
Littlejohn, Wyatt

Drayton 3rd Team (1-0)

Monaghan of Greenville 2nd Team
(1-0): Hall, B. Simpson, Compton.

West Piedmont (1-0): Vaughn, Jones.

Lydia (1-0): Davis, Porter, Jacks,
Matthews.

Mills Mill of Woodruff (1-0): Sam Anderson, Lamb, Mahaffey.

Excelsior (1-0): Lou Lamb, C. Lamb.

Clifton #2 (1-0): Calvert, Dearyberry.

Gaffney (1-0): Smith, Leopard.

Valley Falls (1-1): Kirby, Mabry.

Judson (1-1): Landers, Suddeth,
Horton, Landreth.

Piedmont Lyceum Sluggers (1-1):
Charles Thompson.

Fountain Inn (1-2): Lanford, Taylor,
Nix, Nelson, Woods, Gault, White,
Drummonds, Adams, Armstrong.

Union (0-1): Kirby, Harris.

Beaumont 3rd Team (0-1)

Central (0-1): Hatcher, Wilson.

Laurens (0-1): Burgess, Hill.

Cohannet (0-1): Johnson, Porter.

Landrum (0-1): Fox, Wolfe.

Converse (0-1): Cannon, Crosswell.

Pacolet (0-1): Gossett, Holt, Sutton.

Buffalo (0-1): Morgan, Mitchell,
Smith, Young, Sumner, Bryant,
Gilmer, Rinehart, Milner.

Chesnee (0-1): Fike, Garrett.

Lawrence (0-1): Burgess, Couch.

Glendale (0-2): Gossett, Nichols.

Clifton #1 (0-2): Cook, Lane.

Pelzer 2nd Team (0-2): Nichols,
Spearman.

Arcadia (0-4): Roberts, Petit, Bridgman, Biggs, Clark, Gosnell, Simpson, Gowan.

Newberry (no records): Hiller, Harde-
man, Alvin Danielson, Johnny
Wertz, Corley, Caldwell, Franklin,
Taylor, Vaughn, E. Bouknight,
Ammons, D. Bouknight, Cromer.

Joanna (no records): Bud Moseley,
Talmadge Hamm, Boggy O'dell,

James Browning, Charles Martin,
Will O'Shields, Archie Sheenan,
Roy Hickman, Will Hamm,
Charlie O'Shields.

1916

Greenville Mill League: John L. Harrison (secretary)

Dunean, champions (13-5): Barrett,
Turner, Langston, Friar, Putnam,
Springfield, Johnson, L. Anderson,
Medlock, Crouch, Ingle, Brooks,
Doggins, Hamrick, Livingston,
Granger, Granger, Ward, S. Anderson, Bridgman, Davis, Guthrie,
Patterson, Meredith.
Brandon of Greenville (15-5): Rollins,
G. Turner, McGill, Meisenheimer,
Mahon, Jones, Grumbles,
O'shields, Cashion, Thackston, Pel
Ballenger, W. Turner, Young,
Miller, Friar, Ellis Blackstone, Patrick, Christopher.
Judson (13-5): O.W. Donaldson, Hilton, Belcher, Godfrey, Sullivan,
F. McGill, Seay, Mulligan, Cely,
Pell, Calvert, Case, Burdette, Rickman, Cathcart, Laughlin, Hooper,
Rogers, Hooper, Boylin, Doran,
Bannister, Stack, Gault, White,
Ellis, Whitener.
Woodside (9-9): Barton, Verner,
F. Cisson, Jamison, Milton,
Timmons, Kay, Freeman, B. Cisson, Reed, Porter, J. Allison,
E. Epting, Pruitt, Lavender,
A. Epting, Parrott, Morely, Craigo,
Mann, Christopher, Melton, Vernon, Epting, Dodgins, D. Jackson.
Monaghan of Greenville (5-14):
Claude Whitener, J.R. Federline,
Jenkins, Ballentine, Kelly, Tipton,
Waldrop, Campbell, Christopher,
Mann, Compton, J. Tipton, Ellis,
Whitman, Crumpton, Hull, Barber, Grumbles, Odam, Barbare.
Sampson (1-15): Don Leonard,
Charles Ross, Lee Timms, P.L.

Campbell, Pike, Fowler, C. Miller,
Neely, D. Miller, Barton, Parris,
Tilloson, L. Miller, Simms, Spake,
Pitts, Bass, Roberts, Adkins,
Hunnicutt, Cross, Belue, R. Cantrell, Burdette, Epps, Ayers.

Interurban League: W.E. Hammond (secretary)

Victor of Greer, champions (11-4):
Robertson, Fisher, Newman, Lindsay, Stone, Long, Grubbs, Patrick,
Ben Lark, Lefty Gordon, Blackstone, Robinson, Millwood, Sealy,
James, Childers, Lanford, Causley,
Costner, Dixon, Federline, Tipton.
Poe (10-6): Smith, Dagenhart,
Owens, Evans, Bray, Long, Bill Osteen, Mason, Ripley, Ballard,
Welch, R. Osteen, Allen, Wingo,
Champ Osteen, Medlock, Pole
Jenkins, Troutman, Williams, Millwood, Thompson.
Pelzer (5-9): Mac Bannister, Campbell, Burns, Oscar Donaldson,
Dutch Vaughn, Livingston, Stack,
Hill, Boyce, Nig Haney, Hinson,
Hooper, Banks, Bowen, Godfrey,
Cameron, McLellan, Wade Spencer, Lyle, Miller.
Belton (1-11): Ward, Snipes, Evans,
Livingston, Summey, Campbell,
Garrett, Bowen, Herndon, Fisher,
Taylor, Hinson, Guy, Lyles, Hammonds, Hartley.

Spartanburg Mill League

Arkwright, champions (9-1): Brown,
Mabry, Shook, Thompson, Wilson, Hudson, J. Holt, Fleming,
Henderson, Harrison, R. Holt,
Camp, B. Holt, Lybrand, Sullivan.
Spartan (9-2): J. Martin, Vaughn,
Ballard, Posey, J. Taylor, Moore,
C. Taylor, Lawson, O'dell, Loyless, J.L. Martin, Thomas, Sealy.
Drayton (7-3): Mosely, Sanders,
Worthy, J. Vassey, Justice, Seay,
Martin, W. Belcher, W. Vassey,

C. Belcher, Gaston, Sullivan,
E. Vassey, Shetley, Splawn, Jenkins, Green, Buckman, Kirby.
Glendale (5-8): Dearyberry, Gossett, Brown, Pridmore, Gilmer, Smith, Guy, Sutton, Gosnell, Goodwin, Allen, E. Allen, Jones, Goodman.
Beaumont (4-7): Walls, Wood, Pack, Swink, Eaker, Wilson, Waldrop, Smith, Dickson, Frey, Lawrence, Rogers.
Arcadia (3-5): G. Turner, Waldrop, Johnson, W. Martin, J. Martin, Lawrence, Gowan, Pettus, Waters, Gosnell, Rhinehart, Easler, Otto Turner, Shockley.
Whitney (3-7): Searcy, Arnold, D. Thomason, R. Duncan, Cox, C. Thomason, Rogers, Hughes, Duncan, Cudd, Bogan.
Saxon (1-9): Solesbee, C. Walker, Brown, Howell, Quillen, Thomas, Walker, McBee, Kirby.

Union County League

Ottaray, champions (0-1): Pope, J. Sullivan.

Independent Teams

Fountain Inn (3-1): Lanford, Taylor, Gault, Wilson, Thomas, Woods, Troutman, Smith, Swink, Donaldson.
Gaffney (3-2): Guthrie, Wilson, Patterson, Ellis.
Monaghan of Greenville 2nd Team (1-0): Federline, Anderson, Olsen.
Greer (1-0): Clark, Bergen.
Dunean Black Giants (1-0): Milam
Poinsett (1-0): Lavender, Compton.
Cowpens (1-0): Inman.
Watts (1-0): Hill, Barrett.
Converse (1-0)
Piedmont (1-1): Vaughn, Shirley.
Easley (1-3): E. Dunn, Tilloson, J. Dunn, Simmons, Fletcher, Looper, Owens, Drake, McCall, Baldwin, Mann.
Sampson 2nd Team (0-1): Gregory, Pitts.

Franklin (0-1): Tucker, Rinehart.
Belton 2nd Team (0-1): Barnett, Shirley.
Piedmont Black Sox (0-1)
Conestee (0-1): Tucker, Mathis.
Clinton (0-1): Eubanks, Cunningham.
Clifton (0-1)
Pacolet (0-1): Gossett, Hawkins.
Riverside/Toxaway (no records): Lee Allen (manager), Jim Green, Tom Gunter, Walt Williams, Olin D. Johnston, Doc Ivester, Tommy Allen, English Beasley, Tom Ivester, John Thomas.

1917

Greenville Mill League: J.C. Lattimer (president), C.H. Garrison (secretary/treasurer)

Victor of Greer, champions (11-3): Robert Patrick, Lefty Gordon, Lester Fisher, Boyce, Pete Newman, Tom Bray, Ray Mabry, Tipton, Hudson, Red Childers, McCullom, Dagenhart, Vaughn, Pierotty, Raftry, Mills, Ben Lark, Shorty Long, Bert Gardin, Clarence "Chick" Galloway, Jim Gilreath.
Judson (9-7): Vaughn, Wofford, Boling, Ellis Blackstone, Mac Bannister, Mutt Rollins, Christopher, Paul Troutman, Speer, Belcher, Sullivan, Jim Weston, Brum Mobley, Miller, Pel Ballenger, Livingston, Bill Laval, Bannister, Webb Cashion, Ernie Martin, Kay Cashion, Millwood, Gault, Tidwell, "Bad Eye" Guthrie.
Woodside (7-5): Milton Melton, Frank Jamison, Jones, Reed, Epting, Fred Cisson, Fred Ellis, C.D. Whitener, Hovey Pruitt, Duncan, Ballenger, Craigo, Turner, Hooper, Roland Cain, Evans, Sam Mills, Osteen, Charlie Verner, John Ross (manager)
Dunean (4-6): Robert Putnam, Guthrie, Ram Smith, Ollie Springfield,

Frank Lybrand, John Langston, P.
Johnson, Sam Anderson, C. John-
son, R.B. Thompson, Medlock,
Reuben Medlock, Alvin Granger,
Nathan Doggans,
Mitchell, Laddy Anderson, Cain,
Bill Fisher.
Poe (4-7): Dick Osteen, Bill Osteen,
Speedy Ballard, White, P. Whatley,
Kelly, Doc Miller, Welch, McDan-
iel, J. Whatley, Spake, Fowler,
White, Tommy Lewis, Jones, Pole
Jenkins, McLintock, Tom Bray,
Maurice McDonald, Blackstone,
Oscar Donaldson, Bowen.
Brandon of Greenville (2-9): Kay
Cashion, Jerry Jackson, E. Cash-
ion, R. McGill, Murphy Grumbles,
Thackston, Morrow, G. Turner, E.
McGill, Brown, Goodenough, Pep
Friar, Varnadore, Rhame, Pitts, S.
Turner, Gilliard, Roland, Shorty
Campbell, Barrett, Red Sullivan,
Walter Turner.

Independent Teams

Dunean 2nd Team (3-1): Dodgens,
Burrell, Floyd, Duggins.
Mills Mill of Greenville (2-1): Black-
stone, Davis, Fletcher, Fisher.
Pelzer (1-0): Vaughn, McClelland,
Kay.
Poinsett (1-0): Ligon Compton.
Judson 2nd Team (1-0): Slim Rollins,
Trammell, McGill, Mahaffey,
Moore.
Beaumont (1-0): Walls, Maynor, Law-
rence, Pack.
Arcadia (1-0): Pettus, Bridgman, Wil-
liams.
Whitney (1-0): Tom Brown, Arnold.
Clifton (1-0)
Woodruff (1-0)
Conestee (1-1): Favor, Cusker,
Shaver, Beamer.
Gaffney (1-2): Donaldson, Patterson,
Robinson, Hamrick.
Easley (0-1): Tatten, Sanders.
Brandon of Greenville 2nd Team

(0-1): Anderson, Douglas, Jerry
Jackson.
Greenwood (0-1): Hill, Hooper.
Glendale (0-1): Gilmer, Dearyberry.
Pacolet (0-1): Kirby, Pettit.
Carolina (0-1)
Monaghan of Greenville (0-2), Hull,
Corn, Hunnicutt, Odam.
Enoree (0-2): Betsil, Swink, Gallo-
way, Guthrie, Sweeney.

1918

Interurban League

Dunean Bulldogs (3-0): Langston,
Dockery, Dodgin, Floyd, Burrell,
Rice, Davison, Hall, Floyd,
Springfield.
Easley (0-1): Tatham, Sanders.
Piedmont Sluggers (0-2)
Pelzer (no records): Gene Snipes.

Independent Teams

Monaghan of Greenville (1-0): Jones,
Heath, Hunnicutt, Henson, Wig-
gins, Glasco, Bagwell, Orr, Dalton.
Pacolet YMCA (1-0): Sullivan, Gar-
vey, Worthy, Kirby, Petty, Kirby,
Guyton, Nichols, Kirby.
Glendale (1-0): Pridmore, Tiddy, Mul-
ligan, Reaves, Poteat, Mabry, R.
Hunter, Gossett, H. Hunter.
Judson (0-1): Burdette, Tallant.
Arkwright (0-1): Terry, Windom,
Christopher, Brooks, Lamar,
Bouie, M. Paul, R. Paul, C. Brown.
Brandon of Greenville (0-2): Rollins,
Cisson, Turner, Osteen, Melton,
Cashion, Pitts, Thackston, McGill,
Gilliard.
Victor of Greer (0-2): Bailey, Bray,
McClure, Hooper, Miller, Taylor,
Davis, Hudson, Cagle, Gordon, Os-
teen, Ballenger.
Saxon (0-2): Arnold, Morgan, Wat-
son, Hogan, Loyless, Christopher,
Holt, Adams, Revan, Lamb,
Walden.

1919

Greenville Mill League

Monaghan of Greenville, champions (9-4): Campbell, Pole Jenkins, Tipton, Whitener, Trammell, Long, Jamison, Bagwell, Ellis, Kelly, Heath, Henson, Davis.

Dunean (8-6): Granger, O'Donnell, Putnam, Langston, Floyd, Burdette, Hawkins, Cox, Wood, Dockery, Burrell, Springfield, Burrell, Thompson.

Sampson (7-6): Spake, Pim, Penland, Barton, Carnes, Tillison, Owens, Batson, Ballew, Fowler, Black, Timms, Smith, Richardson, A. Bridwell, Sullivan, J. Bridwell, Miller, Pike, Neese.

Judson (4-6): McCloud, Meadors, Medlock, Bishop, Trammell, Belcher, Jones, Styles, Alexander, Baldwin, Davis, Landers, Leach, Talbert.

Piedmont Baseball League

Woodside, champions (9-5): Cisson, Hamrick, Klapp, Betsil, Whatley, Epting, Jamison, Cook, Pruitt, Jackson, Turner, Cox, Justus, Haggerty, Doyle, White, Eskew, Marion, Verner, Hooper, Owens, Ragan, Cooper, McMillan, Mooney.

Victor of Greer (9-6): Lindsay, Littlejohn, V. Martin, Newman, Cox, Mosely, Johnson, Milton, Hulbertson, Gordon, Mabry, Marrifino, Robertson, Brown, Martin, Donaldson, Van Pelt, Stone, Hunnicutt, Canfield, Smith, Jenkins, Tipton.

Poe (8-5): R. Osteen, Smith, Achinger, Troutman, Bannister, Ballenger, Smith, Williams, Kay, W. Osteen, Sullivan, Wingo, Camp, McMillan, Heck, Bray, Doyle, Jule Doyle, Bowen, McDonald, Cox, Rhame, Spear, Boyce, Godfrey, Marrifino.

Piedmont (1-11): E.B. Alexander, C. Cashion, Lester Hooper, J.C. Osteen, Alonzo Haney, J.L. Fisher, Robert Poole, Ben Lark, Charlie Verner, T.J. Henson, Judge Singleton, T. Hooper, Adkins, Duncan, Atkinson, Wofford, Lambright, Rhame, Swink, B. Chapman, Francis, Boyce, Rambo, Wright, Vassey, Inman.

Mills Baseball League: Charles Henna (president), W.A. Gibson (vice president), R.W. Phillips (secretary)

Whitmire (2-0): Watson, Aughtry, Betsil.

Mollohon (2-2): Luther.

Clinton (0-1)

Union (0-1)

Greer Mill League

Apalache (1-0)

Tucapau (1-0)

Greer (0-1)

Victor of Greer (0-1)

Spartanburg Mill League

Whitney, champions (9-4): Sumter, Ben Turner, C. Thomas, Searcy, Brown, Loyless, Hughes, Cox, Williams, Miller, Hooper, Gordon, Childers, Martin, Harley, Jordan.

Glendale (9-7): Guthrie, Gossett, Reeves, Ammons, Edwards, Gosnell, Holt, Sidder, Hunter, Lowe, G. Fleming, Allen, Tiddy, Almond, Lamb, Taylor, Robinson, Farr, O'Connor, Camp.

Pacolet (8-4): Sullivan, Harvey, Petty, Arnold, Guyton, Roney, Millwood, Lester, W. Kirby, J. Kirby, Fleming, Vassey, Worthy, Drayton (4-9): Belcher, Hagood, Seay, Federline, O'Sullivan, McAbee, Robertson, Young, Fleming, Turner, Marvin, Blecker, Camp, Sanders, Mabry, Sparks, Cashion, Marrifino, Halford,

Waldrop, Rogers, Taylor, Brooks,
Pack, Parks, Franks, Connor.
Clifton #2 (7-6): Tindall, Calvert,
Jackson, B. Dearyberry, Bowman,
W. Dearyberry, Quillen, McDow-
ell, Bragg, Bowen, Wyatt, Inman,
Mosely, B. Martin, Verner,
Cooksey, Holcombe, Jake Frey,
Sims, Moore, Christopher,
Vaughn, Leid, Smels.
Woodruff (4-4); withdrew. Matthis,
Godfrey, Vassey.
Arkwright (4-7); withdrew. Holt,
Brown, Shook, Bridgman, Frey,
Camp, Gosnell, H. Reeves, Rogers,
Hunter, C. Reeves, Meadows,
Thomas, Varner, Tiddy.
Beaumont (0-4), withdrew. Halford,
Waldrop, Walls, Larkin, Pack,
Rogers, Dickens, Powell, Wynn.

Independent Teams

Landrum (14-1): Capps.
Spartan (12-6): Berry, Moore, Bain,
Posey, Stepp, McBee, James,
Federline.
Cohannet (6-2): Hoots, Henderson,
Ruth, Prince, Porter, Cook.
Conestee (5-5): Black, Wilson,
Shaver, Clyde White, Surratt,
Tucker, Mills, Jones, Whatley.
Inman (4-0): Halford, Teague,
Waldrop.
Liberty (3-1): Osteen, Crane, Medl-
ock, Durham.
Union Bleachery (2-3): Turner, Kee-
ler, Weatherford, R. Belcher, Er-
nest, G. Turner, Bishop.
Poe 2nd Team (2-3): Clayton, Hill,
Raymer, Erwin, Guinn, McClure,
McAbee, Ewings, Long, Wiggins.
Piedmont Doffers (2-4): Poole,
Shaldeford, Shirley, Evans,
Breazeale, McGuffie.
Pelzer (2-4): Burns, Kelly, Bradley,
Hopkins, Burnette, McDuffie,
Burns, Bryson.
Sampson 2nd Team (1-0): Aymonds,
Tillison.

Cowpens (1-0): Whitestein,
Holcombe, Guy.
Arcadia (1-0): Patton, Black.
Vardry (1-0): Wilson, Jenkins, Wil-
liams.
Jonesville (1-0): Spencer.
Saxon (1-2): Black, Walker, Brooks,
Beach.
Franklin (1-2)
Brandon of Greenville (0-1)
Converse (0-1)
Buffalo (0-1)
Valley Falls (0-2): Floyd, Smith,
Mayer.
Monaghan of Greenville 2nd Team
(0-2): Ernest, Gregory, Pittman,
Stokes, Long.
Conestee 2nd Team (no records):
Owens, Clyde.
Simpsonville (no record): Wilson, Ow-
ings.

1920

Piedmont Textile League

Brandon of Greenville, champions
(12-7): Pendleton, Whitener, Jerry
Jackson, Floyd, Penland, Raw-
lings, Turner, Thackston, Moore,
McAbee, Ewings, Murphy Grum-
bles, Waldrop, Rollins, Good-
enough, Stokely, Cisson, Mel-
ton.
Liberty (17-5): Crane, C. Landreth,
G. Medlock, Finney, Landers, Jus-
tus, Osteen, Medlock.
Dunean (11-6): Floyd, Kay Cashion,
Springfield, Putnam, Mann,
Granger, Alexander.
Easley (8-11): Dunn, Tilson, McCoy,
Epps, Drake, Owens, Wilson,
Crawford, Duncan, Stewart.
Union Bleachery (7-9): Stancil, Spear-
man, G. Turner, Jamison, Dix,
Melton, P. Hunter, Milton, Harris,
Whitney, Neely, Lewis, McManus,
Bishop, Laval, Robertson.
Glenwood (7-9): P. Turner, Belue,
Spearman, Duncan, S. Stancil,

J. Stancil, Reese, Medlock, Cantrell, Sneed, Steanian.
Sampson (3-4): Owens, Smith, Owens, Spake, Landreth, Timms, Neely, Shaver.
Monaghan of Greenville (2-0): McCartney, Horace Long.
Poe Ravens (1-4): McAbee, Ewings, Ernest, H. Wallace.
Greer (0-1)

Saluda League

Belton (no records): Gene Snipes, Dewitt Snipes, Clyde Snipes, Ray Snipes.
Pelzer (no records)
Williamston (no records)
Piedmont (no records)

GWP (Greenwood-Whitmire-Piedmont-Pelzer League)

Whitmire (9-3): Atkins, Williams, Donaldson, Jenkins, Millwood, Gilliam, Laskey, Finney.
Piedmont (8-5): Henry, Stockley, Chapman, Foster, Padgett, Owens, Godfrey, Rhame, Millwood, Meeker, Vassey, Smith, Fisher.
Pelzer (5-7): Mac Bannister, Dutch Vaughn, Osteen, Hunnicutt, Spear, Kelly, Hooper, Baines, Arnold.
Greenwood (2-9): Bobo, Livingston, Parnell, Thomas.

Reedy River League

Simpsonville (11-6): Pruitt, Godfrey, Jones, Green, Carl Wilson, Lynch, Richardson, Joe Young, Sullivan.
Conestee (10-4): Surratt, F. Bain, Bramlett, Shaver, Tremlet, Cobb, Hane, Bain, Tucker.
Pelham (6-4): Moody, Gotshaw, Yeargin, Sullivan, Richardson.
Mills Mill of Greenville (5-9): Davis, Ballew, Hammond, Mahaffey, Fulbright, R. Smith, Saxton, Revis, G. Belue, H. Belue, Trammell, Putnam.

Poinsett (3-7): Pittman, Harris, Lavender, Lynch, Gray, Monroe, Henry, McAllister, Osborne.
Camperdown (3-4): Wilson, Chandler, Ballard, Tucker, Charles, Gosnell, Pittman, Gosnell, Bullard, Thompson.

Victor-Monaghan League

Apalache, champions (2-1): Stevenson, Davis.
Greer (3-1): Styles, Miller, Timmons, Woods, Williams.
Monaghan of Greer (4-5): McCartney, Hinson, Campbell, Long.
Victor of Greer (1-3): Brady, Brown, Smith, Brady, Hutchings, Luckshaw, Patrick.

Anderson Mill League

Riverside Giants (2-0): Jenkins, J. Stafford.
Orr (no records)
Toxaway (no records)
Anderson (no records)

Western Carolina League

Judson (8-1): Leach, Bishop, Tallent, Trammell, Leavin.
Alice (1-2): King, Aiken, D. Kirby.
Franklin (1-3): Pitts, Styles, Lindsay.
Beaver Duck (0-2)

Spartanburg Mill League: A.S. Thomas (president), Bagwell (vice president), L.A. Ramsey (secretary/treasurer)

Pacolet (8-2): Vassey, Claude Arnold, Federline, Holt, Patterson, Millwood, Sullivan, Patterson, Mosely, Martin, Holt, Worley, Kirby.
Clifton (9-6): Bolt, Shook, Boseman, Turnipseed, McDaniel, Lucas, Harris, Shook, McDowell, Bolt, Vaughn, Lattimore, D. Dearyberry, W. Dearyberry, Gossett, Potter, Patterson, Martin, Mabry, B. Martin, Camp, Crowell,

Pete Fowler, Bridges, Tatham, Koenigsmark, Drake.

Whitney (6-3): Ben Turner, Sumter, Thomas, Martin, Quillen, Epting, Carmichael, Porter, Cisson, Loyless, Jenkins, Stewart, Osteen, Simpson, Dort, Casey.

Woodruff (4-4): Godfrey, Mathis, Emory, Swink, Harbin, Little, Cook, Matthews, Phillips, Joe Wofford, Rogers.

Glendale (1-4): Guthrie, Lowe, Fleming, Williams, Frey, Potter, Gossett, Ammons, Allen, Gilmore.

Saxon (0-3): Bogan, Brooks, Bearden, Weir, Jamison, Black, Stewart, Littlejohn, Johnston, Bush, Christopher, Solesbee, Patterson, Hay, Parlor, Rogers.

Semi-Pro League

Cohannet (6-1): Hoots, Warden, Fox, Grant, Henderson.

Spartan (6-2): Bain, Posey, Posey, Davis, Petty, L. McAbee, J. McAbee, Rollins, Petit, Roland, Arrington, Mosely.

Chesnee (1-2): McMillan, Scruggs, Scruggs.

Inman (1-5): Morrow, Cunningham, Hunter, Waldrop, Gilmore, Holden, Warren.

Laurens County League

Clinton (5-0): Clim, Cunningham, Beckman, Charlie Wilson, Austin, Burgess, Adair, Brice.

Cross Hill (1-1):

Owings (0-2):

Laurens (0-2): Bobo, Cox, Barrett.

Another Mill League: J.C. Day (president), W.T. Swink (secretary/treasurer)

Woodruff (7-3): Cook, Matthews.

Cowpens (7-3): G. Martin, Gilbert, Mabry, Barnett, Jackson, E. Martin, Inman, Vassey.

Tucapau (3-7): Barnett, Jackson,

Love, Warden, Gilmer, Martin, Vassey, Perry.

Gray Mill (3-7): Guinn, Hostetler, Stewart.

Union County League

Buffalo Scrappers, champions (no records): Dan Sheatley, Carlton Thompson, Furman Quinn, Raymond Clark, Clay Liner, J.D. Lamb, Doss Allen, Amos Smith, Shorty Gilliam, Hobart Inman, Broadus Simmons, John D. Jones (manager).

Independent Teams

Arkwright (2-0): B. Holt, A. Varner, C. Varner, J. Henderson, Pittman, Casey, Meadows, Groom, Grange, Reeves.

Enoree (2-0): Cothran.

Newberry (2-1): E. Long, Roddy, Johnny Wertz, Roland, Boozer, Alvin Danielson.

Beaumont (2-1): Powell, Edgins, Smith, Putnam, Edgins.

Fountain Inn (1-1): Drummond, Lanford, McCloud.

Landrum (1-1): Poots, Morrow, Sheehan, Phillips, Morrow.

Union (0-1): Sullivan, Sullivan.

Drayton (0-1): Kirby, Wise.

Arcadia (0-1): T. McAbee, Sims.

Whitney 2nd Team (0-1)

Watts (0-2)

Mollohon (0-2): Derrick, Neel, Long, Scurry.

Franklin (0-2): Lindsay.

Glendale 2nd Team (0-2): Crocker, Rogers, Andrews, Poteat, Bradley, Reeves, Vernon, Pridmore, Antels.

1921

Piedmont Textile League: Charles Garrison (president), S.R. Buchanan (vice president), Harold McCarter (secretary/treasurer).

Brandon of Greenville, champions (18-9): Jerry Jackson, Rollins, Cashion, Taylor, Murphy Grumbles, Sullivan, Robins, Shelton, G. Turner, Cashion, Carnes, Morrow, Goodenough, Cisson, Scruggs, Friar, Dill, Duncan, Brown, Dick Owens, Jenkins, Floyd.

Monaghan of Greenville (19-7): Mormon, Hunnicutt, Tipton, Gus Barbare, Horace Long, Brown, Norman, Whitener, Heath, Dalton, Wiggins, Claude Whitener, Henson, Campbell, Bagwell, McCartney, Ansel, League, Summey, Reid, Anderson, Coleman, Ellis.

Dunean (17-4): Cothran, Landreth, Bob Putnam, Dave McAllister, Kay Cashion, Thomas, Floyd, Al Granger, McClure, Wyatt, Waldrop, Springfield.

Liberty (15-10): Thompson, Alexander, Smith, E. Medlock, Rube Medlock, Stewart, Crane, Finney, Gaines, Calvert, D. Medlock, Scott, Sweetenburg, Osteen, G. Medlock, Tatham, Waldrop.

Glenwood (9-11): Lathem, Charlie Alexander, J. Stancil, Smith, Spearman, Wood, Mace, Tatham, Tanner, Jasper, F. Stancil.

Piedmont (9-14): Vaughn, Shirley, McDuffie, McGuffey, Jones, Beamer, Fisher, Verner, Hendrix, Cargill, Shealy, Evans, Stewart, Fletcher, Reeves, Hall, League, Powell, Knight, Breazeale.

Easley (8-10): Dunn, McCoy, Crawford, Tillson, Wofford, Wiggins, Duncan, Owens, Galloway, Pace, Burns.

Interurban League

Pelzer (13-11): Lester Hooper, John Burns, Surratt, Kelly, Jordan, Dutch Vaughn, Toby, Hooper, Rogers, Bradley, Fennell, Nig Haney, Cannon, Wood, Sexton, Reeves, Hayward, Granger, Saxon, Westmoreland, Golden, Beards, Doug Spencer.

Woodside (2-0): Moody, Moody, Brookshire, Floyd.

Williamston (0-4): Brazenton, Lance, Stephenson, Brown, Worthy, Jenkins.

Monaghan of Greer (no records): Long, McCartney, Campbell, Wiggins.

Victor-Monaghan League

Apalache (5-2): Jones, Duncan, Stevenson, Smith, Davis, Tapp, Morgan of Greer.

Victor of Greer (3-1): E. Campbell, Lindsay, Moore, Greer.

Greer (2-3): Moore, Greer, Lindsay, Watson.

Monaghan of Greer (2-2): Christopher, Campbell, Brown.

Wallace (0-4): Addis, Rector, Spencer, Jones.

Ottaray (1-3): Mose, Whitlock.

Carolina Textile League

Enoree, champions (5-2): Mosely, Nelson, M.S. Bond (manager), Walden, Lynch, Emery, Troup, Betsill, Simmons, Waldrop, Boyd, Culbertson.

Woodruff (7-4): Lanford, Parrish, Swink, Rogers.

Tucapau (8-6): L.R. Boiter (manager), Gordon, West, Dobbins, Warden, Robins, Ward, Cunningham, Waldrop, Tillison, Davis, Barrett, Clark, Barnett, Southern, White, Walden, Love.

Greer (10-13): J.L. Woodward (manager), Bennett, Wood, Sam Williams, Grier, Poole, Green, Timmons, Putnam, Miller, Malone, Adams, Lefty Gardner, Morely, Brady, Cashion, Timmerman, Leatherwood.

Victor of Greer (5-7): Will Jenkins (manager), Pitton, Hudson,

Gotshaw, Brady, Patrick, Davis, Guinn, Mathis, Childers, Garrett, Steadman.

Gray Mill (3-5): Phillips, Mathis, Gotshaw, Davis, W.T. Swink (manager), Matthews, Miller, Richbourg, Westmoreland, Adams.

The Textile League

Arcadia, champions (8-5): Gosnell, A. Mabry, Pettus, Hunnicutt, Turner, Brooks, Corn, Boyd Bridgman, L. Mabry, O. Clark, Gillespie, Pettus, Barbery, Love, Taylor.

Glendale (4-2): Ed Allen, Rogers, W. Gossett, Ammons, John Tiddy, Messer, C. Gossett, Jim Harvey, Pridmore, Suttles, Vernon, Hunter, Montague Nicholls, Blackwell, Crocker, Reese, Bagwell, Ogler.

Clifton #1 (7-8): Ben Brown, Boyd Hughes, Haynes Pearson, Bill Holland, West, J.M. Oeland, G.L. Stepp, Jess Fowler, W.M. Price, Long, Dixon.

Spartan (5-9): Roland, Angel, C. Taylor, N. Clippard, R. Taylor, McAbee, Bowen, Sealand, B. Taylor, McMillan, Bright, Blane, Fine, Voiselle, Knepps, W. Clippard, Mason, Posey, Vaull.

Saxon (4-7): Henderson, Hoye, Champion, Paris, Bishop, Solesbee, R. Hawkins, O. Hawkins, Chapman, Mitchell, Smith, Corn, Bogan, Walden, Brannon.

Drayton (2-10): Cannon, Lawrence, Allen, O'Sullivan, D. Kirby, Franks, C. Kirby, Wyatt, Millwood, Davis, Byars, Vassey, Knight, Adams, Willis, Silvers, Cook, Lindsay.

Independent Mill League

Whitney, co-champions (8-4): Turner, Sumter, Cudd, C. Thomason, Hughes, Fortner, Fowler, Searcy, D. Thomason, Leery,

Ballard, Quillen, Loyless, Osteen, Young, Martin.

Landrum, co-champions (8-4): F. Morrow, Phillips, Capps, Culbreth, Shehan, Burns, Foster, Fox, Henderson, B. Morrow, Lambright, Forrester, Knox, Johns, Erwin, Gaines, Bridgman.

Clifton #2 (5-4): Gilbert, Calvert, Mabry, Waters, Potter, Martin, Tindall, Harris, McClure, Deberry, Whitsline, McDowell, C. Mathis, Swink.

Pacolet (6-8): Kirby, Sutton, Patterson, Harold, Millwood, Claude Arnold, Thompson, Holt, Vassey, Morgan, Guyton, Worthy, Lester, Mabry, Inman, Mosely, Gregory, Worthy, Gossett, Littlejohn, Mott.

Piedmont Negro Mill League

Piedmont (1-0)
Easley (no records)
Fountain Inn (no records)
Greenville (no records)

Anderson County League

Belton, 1st half champions (3-3): Barnett, M. Erwin, Davis, Strickland, Bailey, Revis.

Independent Teams

Fountain Inn (18-10): Powell, Weese, Sexton, Crawford, Ezell, Taylor, Drummond, Phillips, Woods, Cannon, Parker, Thackston, Barbare, Langford, Sam Kellett, Surratt, Dillard, Rogers, Peller, Betsil, Woods, Owings, Fair, Hendrix, Cashion.

Westminster (14-3): McCloud, Werner, Turner, Hull, Mitchell, Carter, Zimmerman, Jones, Calvert, Alexander, Goss.

Lydia (14-6): Jamison, Barrett, George Wilson, Franks, Mosely, Bobo.

Valley Falls (9-5): A. Thomas, Floyd, Smith, White, Cook, Collier, Noland, Raven, Holland, Edgins,

Keller, Edgins, Henderson, C.
Thomas.

Ware Shoals (8-7): McCloskey, McIntyre, Barrett, Henry, Galloway,
McGlaughlin, Holt, Godfrey,
Roush, Livingston, Hawthorne,
Kider, Counts, O. Carter, Couch,
Langston, Grier, Wolfe, Bosley.

Newberry (7-0): Luther, Cromer.

Camperdown (7-3): Jenkins, Gosnell,
Bullard, Pittman, Marchbanks.

Simpsonville (7-6): Stuckey,
Marchbanks, Barrett, Ballew, Cox,
Wilson, Stewart, Moore, Jones,
Jim Yeargin, Tally, Stoddard.

Beaumont (6-2): Millwood, C.
Edgins, A. Pack, Fowler, Young,
Easterly, Powell, Rinehart, R.C.
Park, N. Edgins, Lawrence, Cannon, Sullivan, Tindall, Smith,
Ballard, Cline, Howell.

Walhalla (5-4): Jamison, Poe, Fox,
Fayonsky, Betsill, Rice, Goss, L.
Brown, McCluskey, Alexander,
Calvert.

Clinton (4-0): B. Buchanan, Cunningham, Eubanks, Smith, Young,
Mosely, Betsil.

Fairmont (4-1): Gibson, Cartee, Clayton, Warden, Smith, Nanney, Fortner, McAbee, Cannon, Riddle,
Foster, Bryant.

Watts (4-4): Bobo, Sam Hill, Templeton, Wilson, Cox, Shirley,
Stone, Owens, Thompson.

Mills Mill of Greenville (4-4): Smith,
Shaver, Patterson, Grindstaff,
Shaffer.

Piedmont Lyceum Sluggers (4-4):
Thompson, Sexton, Evans,
Vaughn, Thomas, Westmoreland,
Bryson, Carnes, Fisher, Fowler,
Gresham.

Cowpens (3-0): R. Mabry, Mosely,
Martin, Arnold, Fowler, Tyler.

Pelzer 2nd Team (3-4): Arnold, Hopkins, Otto Cox, Greer, Kay,
Fennell, Crymes, Owens, Crymes,
Harris, Dickerson, Davis, Galliard,

McCullough, McConnell, Barnett.

Poe (3-4): Thackston, McAbee,
Bridwell, Bridwell, Patterson, Riddle, Osteen, Ward.

Union (2-0): Cooper, Sullett, Osteen,
Sullivan.

Poe 2nd Team (2-1): Wallace,
Bridwell, Bridwell, Thornton.

Newry (2-2): Gilliard, Carver, Elrod,
Kirby, Alexander.

Sampson (2-2): Patterson, Bridwell,
Blake, Robertson, Langley, Asbury, Timms.

Inman (2-3): Martin, West, Joe
Messer, Wall, Wood Halford,
Lavender, Stone, Monroe Teague,
Holt, Felix Gregory, Bradley,
Towers, Laughton, Hunter,
Halford, Holden, Vaughn, Stepp,
Byrd, McBee, Bass Waters, Connie
Warren, Max Ross, Ira Gowans,
Pink Pack (manager), Jennings
Waldrop.

Judson (2-17): Wilson, Cook, Bell,
Leach, Landis, Stone, Mullinax,
Landers, McClure, Belcher,
Graves, Washburn, Boswell,
McCullough, Wyatt, Cothran, Putnam, White, Hall, Tallant, Moreland, Padgett, Shanghang, Leach,
Lipton.

Woodside 2nd Team (1-0)

Camperdown 2nd Team (1-0): Chandler, Smith, Fisher.

Fountain Inn 2nd Team (1-0):
Brewington, Farrow.

Pelham (1-1): Gotshaw, Yeargin.

Orr (1-1): McAllister, Donald, Hume,
Fisher, Al Granger, McDonald.

Conestee (1-2): Forrester, Shaver,
Tucker, Tucker.

Mollohon (1-2): Derrick, Neales,
O'Neill.

Anderson (1-2): Smith, Evans,
McCleskey, Watson, Fisher.

Franklin (0-1): Lindsay, Styles.

Judson 2nd Team (0-1): Wilcox.

Abbeville (0-1): Malone, Shealy.

Panola (0-1): Granger, Elledge, Gregory.

Toxaway (0-1): Henson, Fisher.

Vardry (0-1): Barley, Brown, Garrow.

Dunean 2nd Team (0-1): Landers, McCauley.

Arkwright (0-1): Varner, Rangen, B. Holt, Wofford, Meaders, Wood, Beam, C. Holt, Henderson.

Fairview (0-1): Leake, Knight.

Mauldin (0-1): Whatley, Garrett.

Poinsett (0-1): Pittman, Osborne.

Oakland (0-1): Walt Bodie, Willie Bodie, Walt Barber.

Crescent (0-1): Phillips, Garrett, M. Phillips, Fowler.

Chiquola (0-1): J. Calvert, McGaha.

Joanna (0-1): Dean, Prince.

Brandon of Greenville 2nd Team (0-1)

Laurens (0-2): Bobo, Culbertson.

Buffalo (0-2): Gilliam, A. Smith, Allen, Owens, Smith, Quinn, Lamb, Liner, Inman, Allen, Malone, Smith.

Greenwood (0-2): Vines, Long, Pinson, Monroe.

Seneca (0-2): Dalton, Marrett, Harper, Gilliard.

Grendel (0-4): Thompson, Mann, Vines, Mosely, Johnson, Guthrie.

1922

Piedmont Textile League

Dunean, champions (18-3): Granger, Landers, McDonald, Kay Cashion, Bob Putnam, Allen, Floyd, Langston, Jones, Olin Springfield, Wood, Badger, Waldrop, Cothran, Rawlings, Badger, Jamison.

Monaghan of Greenville (12-9): Tipton, Waldrop, Heath, H. Henderson, Whitener, Odom, C. Henson, McCartney, Bagwell, Ellis, Reed, Bowen, McAfee, Roland.

Greer (12-10): Woodward, Putnam, Davis, Miller, Timmons, Leatherwood, Glasgow, Dobbins, Greer, Smith, Glasgow, Jones, Miller, Angel, Green, Smalley, Center, Massey, Stone.

Brandon of Greenville (11-11): Jerry Jackson, Emerson Cashion, Pop Friar, Mutt Rollins, Barre, Murphy Grumbles, Goodenough, E. Rollins, Thackston, Morrow, Bates, Otto Cashion, Porter, Bates, Baker, Tutner, Poe, McCollum.

Victor of Greer (8-12): Jones, Smith, Childers, Hutchinson, R. Brady, Thompson, Poole, Garrett, Patrick, Hooper, Gordon, Wood, Hudson, Clark, E. Brady.

Union Bleachery (3-16): Jack Monroe, Robertson, Turner, Cox, M. Belcher, Bishop, Jacobs, Jenkins, Owens, Evington, Stevenson, Davis, Buington, Nesbitt.

Western Carolina League

Mills Mill of Greenville, champions (14-6): Ram Smith, C. Tinsley, Davis, Revis, Epstein, J. Young, Grindstaff, Jule Smith, Epting, Ballew, Putnam, D. Young, Alvin Tinsley.

Fountain Inn (22-18): Brewington, Williams, Woods, Matt Crawford, Ezell, Marvin Gault, Dooley Nelson, Ed Maroney, Jackson, Drummond, Sam Kellett, Wham, Landreth, Gault, Bannister, Don Parsons, Cooper, DeBoyd, Guy Nelson.

Watts (15-7): Bobo, Barrett, Sam Hill, Parham, Walker, Waldrop, Henry, Wilson, Crawley, Parrish, Spoon, Hembree, Kelly, Owens, Wham, Drummond, Garrett, Nelson, Corley.

Judson (10-13): Landers, Leach, Mullinax, Dickerson, Paul Troutman, McClure, Kelly, Fryar, Jones, Bishop, Trammell, Moreland, Shaver, Bird Wyatt, Jones, Sanders, White, Mauldin, Abercrombie, Munn, McCollum, Poe, Goodencife, McClellan.

Simpsonville (7-15): McElrath, W. Lynch, M. Cox, Cashion, Jones,

Green, Jordan, Richardson, Stewart, Farrow, Blakely, White, Cannon, Lynch, Moss.

Camperdown (6-12): Marchbanks, Pittman, Wilson, Gosnell, Ballard, Yeargin, Hall, Tidwell, Huff, Blakely.

Saluda Textile League

Pelzer (10-5): Haney, Moore, Jordan, Burns, Bennett, George Belk, Mac Bannister, Lester Hooper, Dutch Vaughn, Davis, Cannon, Golden, Fisher, Simpson.

Belton (7-3): Ward, E. Bannister, B. Bannister, Duncan, Blackwell, Landers, Rollins, Clement, G. Orr, Stevens, Fisher, B. Orr, Thomas, Bailey, R. Bannister, Jenkins.

Williamston (6-5): Harper, Worthy, Fisher, Duncan, Breazeale, Gotshaw, Hooper, F. Simpson, Jenkins, Alexander, Taylor, Smith, Paul McCloud, Rogers, Browning, Scott, Andrews, Jamison, Holliday.

Piedmont (4-4): Charlie Verner, Duncan, Lester Fisher, Taylor, Browning, Worthy, Hooper, Poole, Cargill, Breazeale, Gaines, Padgett, Bryson, Padgett, Osteen, Smith, Evans, Fletcher, Henson, Roland, Bannister, Hollingsworth, Bailey.

Anderson (2-5): Watson, F. Simpson, Allen, Taylor, Jones, Keel, Lee, Sweetenburg, R. Simpson, Kennedy, Stevenson.

Orr (1-5): McAllister, Fisher, Steadly, Wiles, Beard, Evans, Freeman, Weaver, McDonald.

Pickens County League

Alice (9-4): Bryce, Loume Patterson, Cashion, Elrod, Kirby, Alexander, Dillard Hendricks, Rison, Sanders, Kelly, Elrod, Campbell, Bowen, Garrett, Domer Reeves, Jack Adkins, Harvey Ellison, Fletcher Skelton, Endle Lee Norris, Alonzo

Pittman, Bob Marchbanks, Ad King, Roy Smith.

Liberty (9-6): Crane, G. Medlock, Richards, Scott, Rube Medlock, E. Osteen, Barrett, Vaughn, Ode Medlock, Dodgins, Cisson, Slayton, Stewart, Clark, Woodward, Bryson, Patterson, Hendricks, Grant, Spake, Scott.

Glenwood (6-5): Taylor, Lawrence, Christopher, Stancil, Spearman, Charlie Alexander, Tatham, Reese, Williams, B. Alexander, Chapman, Jamison, L. Alexander, Carver, Dunn.

Easley (4-7): B. Alexander, Osteen, Tatham, Reese, A. Alexander, Pitts, Duncan, Smith, Dunn, Bryson, Patterson, Stancil, Crawford, Tilson, Spake, Epstein, Spencer.

Central (2-4): Vaughn, Mayfield, Wilson, Bridgman, Herman Werner, Gibson, Poe.

Pickens (1-7): Howell, Hawkins, Sweeney, Wood, Holcombe, Noland, Pace.

Victor-Monaghan League

Victor Boy Scouts, champions (11-2): Brown, Waters.

Apalache (0-1): Stevenson, Tillotson, Smith, Davidson.

Monaghan of Greer (0-1): Anderson, Campbell

Oconee County League

Newry, champions (7-5): Sweentenburg, Carver, Simpson, McGuffey, Carver, Kirby, Alexander, Gibson, Petit, Nelson, Betsill, Duncan, Gillard, A. Duncan, Keel.

Westminster (5-3): Wolfe, Keel, Flint Rhem, H. Werner, Jenkins, Bryson.

Seneca Boll Weevils (4-5): Alexander, Harper, Davis, Medlock, Strickland, Ballenger, Finley, Merritt, Dalton, Lowery, Hughes, Jamison, Brock, Benson, Whitlock, Moore.

Walhalla (1-1): Stewart, Atkinson, Landreth, Brown.

Greenville Textile League: T.M. Bennett (president), Brown Mahon (vice president), Lee Smith (secretary/treasurer)

Brandon Tigers, champions (16-4): C. Floyd, Dill, G. Floyd, Turner, Sexton, Bates, Saxon.

Woodside Boll Weevils (12-6): Dill, Woody, Brookshire, Clifford, McAbee, Sizemore, Smith, Whittle, Brown, Mullinax, Clippard, Fowler, Campbell.

Poe (11-8): Lowery, Ernest, Moore, Osteen, Bridwell, McBee, Woody, Ballew.

Judson Comers (6-4): Landers, Dixon, Dickerson, Mann, Wilson, Emmett Tidwell, Westmoreland, Whitt Crymes, Bell, Chandler, Osteen, McManaway, Christman, White.

Poinsett Skippers (5-13): Bowman, Gray, Pittman, Johnson, Henry, Clifford, King, Turner, Center, Marlowe, Settles, Carrigan, Greer.

Dunean Red Sox (3-14): Landers, McCauley, Langston, Caldwell.

Spartanburg Textile League: F.R. Corwin (president), R.F. Bagwell (vice president), C.F. Patrick (secretary/treasurer)

Pacolet, champions (10-1): George Kirby, T.J. Jett, Lewis Petty, Gossett, Mott, James Kirby, C.F. Lowery (manager), Monroe Teaster, E.E. Vassey, Thomas Holt, Roy Harold, W.J. Harold, Edwin Gardner, Oliver Teaster, Clarence Guyton, T.G. Pearson, Will Worthy, C.F. Patrick, Morgan, Pearson, Harrill, Hooper Fleming, Littlejohn, Mabry.

Glendale (6-6): Fleming, Ray Hunter, Oscar Suttles, T.R. Hooper (manager), Dick Vernon, E.O. Ammons, Pierce Davis, Mack Reaves, Edwin Allen, Homer Nichols, Paul Rogers, Weldon Bagwell, Walter Messer, Boyd Blackwell, W.L. Gossett, Reese, James Harvey, Bradley, Holt.

Tucapau (5-7): Andrew West, M. Sanders (manager), V. Barrett, Love, A.J. Jackson, J.L. Jordan, L.R. Boiter, C. Sanders, Ed Jackson, Bruce Bridges, Roy Willis, Joe Jackson, L.T. Southern, C.A. Cunningham, W.R. White, C.L. Smith, Robert Southern, Blackwell, Ezell.

Arcadia (2-9): Gwinn (manager), B. Mabry, E.B. Barbery, R.D. Corn, Otto Clark, Lee Pitts, J.L. Pettus, G.W. Brooks, William Hunnicutt, Fleming, I.W. Bridgman, H. Rinehart, L.F. Crocker, S.B. Belcher, A. Mabry.

Spartanburg Independent League

Clifton, champions (15-3): Henry Calvert, Joe McDowell, Peterson, Vassey, Bryant McClure, Boyd Hughes, William Dearyberry, Lawrence Vaughn, Oeland, Harris, Boland, Frey, Benton, Charles Martin, C. Lockman, Tindall, Mabry, V. Martin, Gaines Dixon, Paul Calvert, Ed Waters, Henry Savage (manager), Boyce Crocker.

Valley Falls (9-9): Henderson, Lockman, Cook, C. Thomas, White, Holland, Collier, Noten, Powell, Fowler, Ellington, Rogers, C. Bagwell, Rollins, E. Bagwell, Wilson, Parish, A. Thomas, Prince, Rollins, Smith, C. Edgins, Roland, H. Edgins, Allen.

Whitney (8-10): D. Thomas, Hughes, Sumter, Young, C. Thomas, Norris, Searcy, Waddell, Turner, Dixon, Moore, Osteen, Lawrence, Morris, Wall, Burnett.

Converse (4-14): Rickey, Powell, Case, Fowler, H. Cooksey, Martin, E. Cooksey, W. Tillotson, Davis, L. Tillotson, Waters, Holland, Stepp, Pearson, Marshall, Ward,

Fleming, Cooper, Whetsteine, Hooper.

Spartanburg 2nd Teams Textile League

Arkwright (7-6): Buren West, Hardy Fleming, Howard Fleming, Jess Lynch, Guy Miller, Miller West, Ray Benson, Fred Gosnell, Jack Woody, Everett Johnson, Charlie Johnson, Graham, S. Fleming, Belcher, Cothran, Gibson, Pettus, Marshall, Bishop, Henderson.

Spartan (7-7): Ralph Boland, Mitchell Allen, John Pettit, Will Gregory, Alton Banks, Lewie Lockman, Jess Fowler, Lee Hensley, Eugene Wood, Ernest Hensley, Turner, James Brown, Ed Henderson, Holland, Brown, Stuart, Voiselle.

Clifton (6-3): Boyd Hughes, Paul Groce, Barry Groce, Defoix Calvert, Palmer Calvert, Frank Whitlock, Dupree Vaughn, Fred Bridges, Ebb Jolly, Jess Tinsley, Devard Weatherly, Herman Barber, H. Groce, A. Sprinkles.

Drayton (6-3): Will Carter, Felix Gossett, Carl Lane, Edwin Thomas, Claude Snyder, Jess Garrison, Hubert Lytle, George Allen, Marion Langston, John Gossett, Clyde Seay, James Finch, Arnie Lawrence, J. Gardo.

Beaumont (4-3): Lawrence, Millwood, Varley Eison, Bruner Cline, P.D. Eubanks, Fred Waters, Robert Green, Dewey Powell, Clifford Petty, Reuben Nabors, Andrew Sprinkle, Halley Rogers, Frank Nabors, Dewey Eubanks, Wenvel Corn, Pearson, Boyce Powell.

Saxon (3-5): Solesbee, Chapman, Prince, Andy Champion, Thornwell Cate, Walter Smith, Floyd Bennett, Floyd Turner, Grady Connor, Tom Cogdill, Ralph Vaughn, Preston Bishop, Waldo Robertson, Benson, Bager

Phillips, Frank Walden, Tom Cook, Tom Satterfield, Ralph Hawkins.

Whitney (2-3): Roy McAllister, Fred Tennyson, Arthur Reed, Arthur Waddell, Harvey Carmen, Thomas Gossett, Leonard Huskey, R.E. Willis, Doyle Caldwell, Willie Green, Horace Willis, West.

Independent Teams

Newberry (37-14): Bowen, Thomas, Luther, Cromer, Johnny Wertz, Hardeman, Gwilliam, Holbrook, Oliver, Crooks, Boozer, Smith, Howard, Shealy, Mills.

Smyth Sluggers (16-0): Crymes, McDonald, T. Crymes, Greer, R. Bell, D. Crymes, Reeves, Owens, Dickerson, Reed, Bishop, Burnett, Watkins, Hodges, Cox, Brown, Wooten, McConnell, Davis, Kay, Bell.

Ware Shoals (10-5): Watson, Livingstone, Walker, Wolfe, Garrett, Sweetenburg, Mitchell, Chick, Wilson, Bradburn, Mosely, Evans.

Spartan (8-2): C. Taylor, McMillan, R. Taylor, Evans, Fine, Mason, McAbee, B. Taylor, C. Bain, Brown, Fowler, Roland, Swain, Mooneyham, Clippard, Arrington, Burrell, Bain, Gregg, Bright, Davis, Voiselle, Ballard, Morrison, R. Ballard, Coon, Cooley, Bailey, Atkins, Sitton, F. Atkins, C. Atkins, Mabry, Steadings, Layeff, Loyless.

Buffalo (7-1): Dagenhart, Inman, Mosely, Burns, Scott, West, Malone, Sullivan, A. Smith, Allen, P. Smith, Gilliam, Sumner, Liner, Cash, Bridgman.

Beaumont (6-2): Gregg, Harris, C. Edgins, Mahaffey, D. Parnell, McDonald, Cline, P. Edgins, Park, Brooks, Snell, Collins, McDaniel, H. Edgins, Powell, Case, P. Haines, P. Smith, Lynch, Taylor, Turner, Sumter, Kirby, Parham,

Hunt, Tillinghast, Solesbee,
Paxton.

Whitmire (6-3-1): Hamilton, Gilliam,
Linwood, Jenkins, Millwood,
Rhinehardt, W.S. Howard Sr.,
Davis, J. Aughtry, Singleton,
Lominick, C. Aughtry, Milan,
W.S. Howard Jr., Shannon,
Gotshaw, Sanders.

Woodruff (5-9): Betsil, Rogers, Mat-
thews, Ezell, H. Swink, Gowan,
Wofford, Grubbs, Owens, Mathis,
Senn, Cash, Drummond, Parrish,
W. Swink, Fowler, M. Swink,
Gwinn, Gunter, Bolt, Brewington,
Clem, Corn, Wilson.

Union (4-0): Jamison, Sullivan,
Fowler, Mosely, Singleton, Hamilton, Rhinehardt, Betsil, Aughtry,
Thompson, Aughtry, Jenkins, Sullivan, Hilton.

Beattie Sluggers (4-3): Anderson, Bryson, Knight, Smith, Evans,
Gilreath, Thompson, Roland, Garrett, Harrison, Reeves, Breazeale,
Fowler, Dill.

Lydia (4-3): Mosely, Fuller, Mann,
Jenkins, Holliday, Eichelberger,
Garrett, Crowe, Kay Cashion.

Inman (4-4): Stone, Gregory, Teague,
Waldrop, Messer, Towery, Brad-
ley, Stepp, Holden, Cox, Halford,
Warren, Nix, Burns, Walcott,
Brown, Turner, Mull, Evanston.

Franklin (3-1): Lamb, Moore, Lind-
say, Watson, Watkins, Rhymer,
Starnes, H. Gowan, Ballew, P.
Gowan, W. Roddy, E. Roddy, Dill,
Green, Norris, Few.

Mollohon (3-6): Williams, Cone,
Boozer, Hawkins, Frank Shealy,
Burrell, Al Shealy, Boozer, Scurry,
Paysinger, Boozer, Paysinger,
Hawkins.

Eureka (2-0): Yarborough, Murr,
Barr, Grindstaff.

Gray Mill (2-1): Herman Swink, Phillips, Lanford, Aiken, Garner,
Hufstetler, Parish, B. Rogers.

Enoree (2-1): Parham, Westmoreland,
Hooper, Mosely, Ezell, Wilson.

Saxon (2-2): Ballenger, Corn, Bishop,
Solesbee, Champion, Hoy, Smith,
Prince, Hall, Hawkins, Huff, Les-
ter, Bride.

Clinton (2-4): Wellborn, Evans, Riddle, Buchanan.

Fairforest (1-0): Frey, Taylor.

Arkwright (1-1): Rhames, Holt,
Thomas, Varner, Meadow,
Wofford, Godfrey, Henderson,
Crowe, Brown, Fowler, Shook.

Independents (1-1): Austell, Lindsay,
Hunt, Hagood, West, Foster,
Habel, Turnipseed, Drayton.

Poe 3rd Team (1-1): Osteen, Holland,
Christopher, Welch.

Cherokee Falls (1-1): Williams, Oliver, Setzler, O. Sullivan, Young,
Ward, Blackwell, Tabors, Tate.

Duncan (1-2): Bass, Lavender,
Fowler, Ballenger, Jackson, Black-
well, Sims, Hadden, B. Blackwell,
Smith.

Landrum (1-2): Dobbins, Phillips,
Capp, Fox, Gaines, Nevils, Hendricks, Lee, Erwin, Raymond, Edwards, Culbreth.

Chesnee (1-2): Poteat, Walker, L.
Walls, McIntyre, Cudd, C. Walls,
Rowe, W. Martin, Ward, Ham-
mett, Ruppe, McAtir, Young,
Elder, T. Martin, D. Martin, Sim-
mons, Jones, Lancaster, Goode,
Lockman.

Conestee (1-4): M. Tucker, Tucker,
M. Wilson.

Fairmont (1-6): C. Gibson, Clayton,
Fortner, McAbee, Duncan, Riddle,
Nanney, Mason, Cannon, F. Til-
son, Voiselle, Blackwell, Camp.

Laurens (1-7): Doc Hill, Bobo,
Culbertson, Frady, Barrett, Charlie
Wilson, Hembree, Swink, Lanford,
Moody, Bass, Kirby.

Sampson (0-1): Reese, Rhett.

Toxaway (0-1): Evans, Chasteen, Bannister.

Arcade (0-1): Hovis, G. Richards, Baker, Martin, Richardson.

Crescent (0-1): Wilson, Jones, Parsons, F. Fowler, N. Phillips, Fowler, B. Phillips, Cooper, Stevens, Satterfield, Westmoreland.

Greenwood (0-1): Calvert, Price.

Old Mill (0-1): Allen, Fisher.

Fountain Inn (0-1): Phillips, Jackson.

Lockhart (0-1): Gotshaw, Boling.

Limestone (0-1): White, Swaggart.

Pacolet (0-1): Henderson, Morgan, Fleming, Kirby, L. Worthy, Mabry, B. Worthy, Petty, Gary, Teaster, Seay.

Drayton (0-1): Taylor, Kirby, Paxton, Case, Marchant, Cannon, Cook, Clippard, Gosnell.

Blair (0-1)

Valley Falls (0-1)

Oakland (0-1)

Monarch (0-1): Eldridge, Owens.

Joanna (0-2): J. Dean, C. Dean, O'shields.

Johnston (0-2): Deal, Minnick, Herlong, Coleman, Johnston.

Abbeville (0-3): Milam, Galloway, Greer.

Grendel (0-4): Johnson, Lumley, Calvert, Morris, Pinson, Monroe, Bines.

Anderson 2nd Team (no records): Daniels, Edwards.

Camperdown 2nd Team (no records): Hood, Brown.

Gossett Athletes (no records): Alexander, Browning, Scott.

Graniteville (no records): Corley, Padgett, Wise.

Equinox Hornets (no records): Thrasher, White.

1923

Laurens County Textile League: I.E. Bridges (president), C.K. Templeton (secretary/treasurer)

Laurens, champions (12-3): Jack Wilson, Barrett, R. Cox, Bagwell,

Ward, Frady, Cove, Waldrop, Sabie, Gentry.

Lydia (7-7): Smith, Moon, Dudley, Dooley, Morris, Dooley, George Wilson, Patterson, Deaton, Davis.

Watts (6-4): Owens, Dooley, Thomas, Calvert, O. Bobo, Morris, Brewington.

Clinton (1-8): Bodie, Land, Young, Dean, Jones, Bright, Boney, Livingstone, Howard, Norman, Brady, Smith, Clark, Johnny Riddle, Cooper, Bean, Givings.

Piedmont Textile League

Brandon of Greenville, champions (15-4): Mason, Bates, O. Cashion, Floyd, Calvert, Denton, Cross, Goodenough, McCall, Emerson Cashion, Rollins, Morrow, Barr, Arnold, Sentell, Cross.

Dunean (16-3): Springfield, Landers, Granger, Badger, Pittman, Langston, M. Floyd, Waldrop, Henson, Landreth, Wood, H. Badger, Bishop, C.A. Granger, Putman, Sewell.

Monaghan of Greenville (7-12): J. Barbare, O. Jones, G. Barbare, Campbell, R. Jones, Noland, Pitney, Tucker, Robertson, Anderson, McCartney, Simmons, Coleman, Bowen, Christopher, Waldrop, Simmons, Carlisle, Bagwell, McIntyre.

Victor of Greer (6-11): R. Brady, B. Brady, Clark, Childers, Campbell, Pittman, Cooper, Norman, Wood, Campbell, Lefty Gordon, Brooks, Hudson, Hutchinson, Chester, Brown, Camp, Vick, Smith.

Union Bleachery (5-10): G. Turner, B. Turner, A. Turner, Evington, Belcher, Ballard, Nelson, Jenkins, Nesbitt, Hughes, Harrison, Bishop, Keeler, Hester, Dix.

Greer (4-13): Moore, Davis, Dobbins, Leatherwood, Gordon, Timmons, Glasgow, Smith, Miller,

Westmoreland, Center, Jones,
W.D. Lee, Mode.

Central Carolina League

Camperdown, champions (10-3): Sur-
ratt, Arnold, G. Yeargin, C. Huff,
Cisson, Jenkins, Splawn, Craw-
ford, R. Goode, Long, Campbell,
Forrester, A. Yeargin, Hall, Pruitt.
Mills Mill of Greenville (7-6): Walter
Smith, Ram Smith, Wiggins, Ept-
ing, Grindstaff, Revis, Lewis Ab-
bott, Gilliard, Long, Hostetler,
Wilson, Belton, Goss, J. Smith,
Putnam, Saxton, Ballew, Mace.
Judson (4-7): Sanders, McCullough,
McMillan, McClelland, Hudson,
Breazeale, Watson, Chandler,
Crymes, Wyatt, Cothran, More-
land, Waldrop, Hodgson, Lewis,
McCallum, Dill, Trammell,
Bishop, Fryar.
Williamston Spinners (4-10): Worthy,
Breazeale, Gotshaw, R. Browning,
Holliday, Boykin, Smith, Morgan,
Hudgens, McClendon, Morgan,
Whitmire, Scott, J. Davenport, W.
Davenport, Pearson, Wilson,
Long, Fortner.

Eastern Carolina League

Beattie Sluggers, champions (12-1): B.
Smith, Clifford, McAbee, Watson,
Leland, Powell, Roland, Knight,
Evans, Breazeale.
Pelzer Blue Hose (10-7): Suttles,
Golden, Vaughn, Simpson, Cox,
Barnett, Rose, Greer, K. Watson,
Workman, T. Crymes, Westmore-
land, Hopkins, Whitmire.
Conestee (1-8): Cook, Wilson, B.
Shaver, D. Tucker, M. Tucker,
Robertson, B. Tucker, Cox, Lynch,
Tolbert, Huff, Crawford.
Simpsonville (0-2): Lynch, M. Cox,
Cashion, Jim Yeargin.

Greenville Textile League

Poinsett, champions (8-4): Pittman,

Williams, Cooley, Pendleton,
Landers, Hughes, Wood, Vick,
Fisher, Didley, Bailey, Smith,
Oglesby, Gray, Jenkins, Neely,
Thornton.
Judson Comers (7-6): Powell, Bow-
man, Bowen, Wyatt, Franks, Law-
son, Ivory, Whitney, Woody, D.
Crymes, D. Trammell, Landers,
Wilson, Ivester, Tidwell, McClure,
Nash, Chandler, Timms, Kluttz.
Woodside (6-2): Brookshire, Dover,
Bowen, Moody, Clifford, Bolt.
Brandon Tygers of Greenville (6-4):
Hudson, Floyd, Denton, E. Dill, C.
Dill, Ford, Gilliam, Hughes, Mere-
dith.
Poe Ravens (5-4): Ernest, McCauley,
Bates, Dill, Boyce, Edwards, Chris-
topher, Knight, Duffet, Brewster,
Cleveland, Center, McAbee, Pitt-
man, Black.
Dunean (5-5): Landreth, C. Wood,
Pendleton, Williams, Cooley,
Lance, Cook, Hodges, Smith, H.
Wood, Floyd, McCauley, Penland.
Norris Shuttle Factory (4-6):
Woodall, Long, Woodall, Arnold,
Mahaffey, Nesbitt, Pittman, Ballen-
ger, Merritt.
Monaghan of Greenville (3-7): Olson,
Heath, Kelly, McIntyre, Anderson,
Walker, Coleman, Morgan, Elli-
son, Wallace, Timmons, Osteen,
Chandler, Ralph Holden, Will Sim-
mons, Frank Barton, Fleming, Hen-
son.

Saluda Textile League

Ware Shoals, champions (13-4):
Holbrook, Johnny Wertz, Oliver,
Watson, Gresham, Werner,
Walker, Walker, McCaskey,
Barbare, Bowen.
Belton (9-7): Tollison, R. Bannister,
Leroy Mahaffey, McGaha, Flint
Rhem, Strickland, Cobb, Fallow,
Lyle, Owens, Scott, Boland.
Easley (7-8): Dunn, Poe, Kirkland,

Whitener, Alexander, West, Claral Gillenwater, Boland, Sigmon, Simpson, McGee, Duncan.

Alice (7-10): Campbell, McAllister, Patterson, Elrod, Alexander, Gibson, Hendrix, Atkins, Kelly.

Pelzer (5-4): George Belk, Ben Lark, Holden, Dutch Vaughn, Suttles, Mac Bannister, Groce, Hooper, Jordan, Barbare, Gibson, Jenkins.

Glenwood (4-9): Lawrence, Tatham, Parham, L. Alexander, Cogswell, Carver, Cater, Stewart, Stancill, Spearman, Fisher.

Pickens County League

Alice (4-0): Roper, Carter, Hendrix, Cooper, Kelly, Marchbanks.

Pickens (3-0): Hawkins, Pace.

Glenwood (1-1): Wood, Golightly, Wood.

Beverly (0-1): McCallum, Young.

Easley (0-2): Epps, Harris, Tilson, Smith.

Three & Twenty (0-3):

Greenwood League

Grendel (1-0)

Chiquola (0-1): Jones, Hudson, Cox.

Calhoun Falls (no records)

Abbeville (no records)

Ninety Six (no records)

Greenwood (no records)

Central Textile League

Fairmont (5-2): Gibson, Hendrix, Hipp, Leonard, Riddle, J. Gibson, Oneill.

Fairforest (3-2): Martin, W. Taylor, Frey, Frey.

Tucapau (2-2): Ezell, Bridges, Burnett, Mason.

Apalache (0-2): Stevenson, Jolt, Manley, Tillotson, Smith.

Upper Carolina League

Pacolet, champions (7-3): Petty, Kirk, Teaster, Mott, Littlejohn, Sullivan,

Coleman, Gossett, Haynes, Bryant, Flemming, Patrick, Brown, Kirby, Gooden, Worley, Gibson, Jett, Gibson.

Arcadia (1-2): Bridgman, Lavender, Lynch, Petit, West, Hunnicutt.

Limestone (0-4): White, Blank, Gunn, Hensley, Byrum.

Independent Teams

Mollohon (12-6): Frank Shealy, Harry Hedgepath, Ed Corley, Everett Corley, Dan Shealy, Sieby, Wilson, Cromer, Moyer, Hanson, Holmes, Mills, Holbrook, Lominack, Swink, Jones, Al Shealy, S. Shealy, Bodie, Barnwell.

Cohannet (6-3): McIntyre, Hardin, Porter, Barnes, Urickett, Wharton, Martin, Goings, Warden, Martin, Henderson, Trifte, Waldrop, Collier, Burns, Prince, E. Prince.

Inman (5-1): Scott, Warren, Holden, Bradley, Harvey, Hustle, Gregory, Teague, Halford.

Spartan (5-3): Bright, Ford, Bain, Fine, Caldwell, Reid, Roland, C. Taylor, R. Taylor, McAbee.

Clifton (4-1): Calvert, Mabry, Calvert, Martin, Barnett, Hughes, McDougin, Oeland, Waters, Vaughn, J. Martin.

Spartan 2nd Team (4-2): Koon, Caldwell, McAbee, Stewart, Boyd, Foster, Bishop, Gregg, Roland.

Arkwright (4-3): Fleming, Shook, Krester, Kirby, Wofford, Henderson, Pope, Culbreth, Raines, Gibson, Worley, Meadors, Ridder, McAbee, Holcombe, Hughes.

Mills Mill of Woodruff (3-1): Brice, Carter, Taylor, Gwinn, Tucker, Hufstetler, Hufstetler.

Buffalo (2-0): Worley, Crocker, Linhardt.

Saxon (2-0): Hoy, Hall, Campbell, Mitchell.

Glendale (2-1): Hunter, Nichols, Poteat, Moss, Gossett, Nichols.

Beaumont 2nd Team (2-2): Castil, Riddle, Biggs, Thompson, Cogsdill, Mabry, G. Powell, Putnam, Powell.

Woodruff (2-3): Rogers, Mathis, Paris, Guin.

Whitney (2-4): Koon, Thomas, McAbee, Shelton, Petty, Turner, Defor, Blanton, Dickson, Morris, Bullington.

Cowpens (2-4): Whetsteine, Swofford, Crowe, Vassey, Tillotson, Lane, Martin.

Drayton (2-5): Carter, Allen, Davis, Hill, Martin, Powell, Maynard, Buchanan, Kirby, Turner, Gil.

Brandon Wildcats of Greenville (1-0): Bates, Dill.

Landrum (1-1): Fox, Phillips, Allen, Hendrix, Porter, Lambright, Culbreth.

Fountain Inn (1-2): Brewington, Parsons, Kellett, Wells, Ezell, J. Drummond, Brown.

Winnsboro (1-2): Ratcliff, Hipp, Duckett, Pearson, Lowe, Weeks, Lominack, Johnson.

Whitney 2nd Team (1-2): Caldwell, Reid, Gregory, Wood, Huskey, Cook, Holt, Holt.

Enoree (1-2): Cooper, Thornton, Betsill, Parham, McGee, Mosely, Westmoreland.

Valley Falls (1-2): Henderson, Lockman, Holland, Noland, Pipp.

Graniteville (1-3): Deas, Escoe, Padgett, Whitney, Eskew, Corley.

Beaumont (1-4): Edgins, Edgins, Hughes, Lynch, Powell, Ward, Eison, Rogers, Harris.

Chesnee (1-6): Wall, Walker, Young, Martin, Ezell, Scruggs, Scruggs, Blank, Pridmore, Martin, Maynor.

Gray Mill (0-1): Cox, Hostetler.

Oakland (0-2): Longshaw, Sanders.

Saxon 2nd Team (0-2): Mitchell, Kimbrell.

Glendale 2nd Team (0-1): Henson, Suttles.

Clifton 2nd Team (0-1)

Newberry (no records): Lawrence Henderson, Lefty Holbrook, Hughey Crooks, Andy Bowen, Hop Franklin, Buck Corley, Heiny Guilliam, Hipocket Smith, Johnny Wertz, Jim Taylor, Tige Oliver, Tub Cromer, Sam Mills, Andy Thomas, Edgar Hiller.

1924

Saluda Textile League

Pelzer, champions (9-7): Wooten, Cobb, Crymes, Westmoreland, Whitten, Burns, Ross, Hawkins, Easter, Laird, Hopkins, Heath, Hines, D. Moore.

Piedmont (9-6): Fowler, Cargill, Fisher, Smith, Lee, Breazeale, Hopkins, Mahaffey, Clifford, E. Evans, Verner, Ballard, Justus, M. Evans, Poole.

Glenwood (7-5): Lawrence, Alexander, Owens, Spearman, Mullinax, Tatham, Stancil, West, Williams, Mace, C. Alexander, Rose, Fortner, Chapman.

Alice (5-5): Hendrix, Turner, Tatham, Burdette, Alexander, W. Leslie, Epps, Smith, Green, Kelly.

Easley (4-11): Patterson, Simpson, O. Hendricks, Elrod, Dunn, O. Medlock, Burdette, Alexander, Durham, Tilson, Harris, Galloway, Humphries, B. Hendricks, Duncan, Putnam, Looper, Tinsley, Spearman.

Piedmont Textile League

Brandon of Greenville, champions (13-7): Goodenough, Floyd, Calvert, Wiggins, Rollins, Turner, Bouie, Oliver, Cashion, Adams, Hughes, Laird, Knode, B. Bannister, Medlock, Campbell, Roland, Sullivan, H. Bannister, Morrow, Benson, Sentell, Flint Rhem, Pel Ballenger.

Judson (17-6): Landers, Chandler, Tatham, McClure, Cashion, Wyatt, Harvel, Hodgson, Huntington, Patrick, Jackson, Watson, Toler, Ballew, Rogers, Wolfe, Hughes, Kelly, P. Barbare, J. Barbare, Livingston, Burley, Sheppard, Walt Barbare, Emerson Cashion.

Camperdown (13-5): Dyer, Henry Huff, Breazeale, Jenkins, Walker, Crawford, Denton, Young, Cisson, Cato, Badger, Bryson, Dizzy McLeod, Reese, Pruitt, Pace, Dudley.

Dunean (13-5): Springfield, Gus Barbare, Bowman, Waldrop, Sanders, Granger, Paul Barbare, Landreth, Henson, Putnam, Floyd, Jim Barbare, Smith, Carter, McCall, Norman, Holbrook, Cothran, Finney, Galloway, Landers, Weirman, Heck, Radcliffe, Donnelly, Williams, Hunnicutt, Stewart, Phillips, Medlock.

Victor of Greer (9-12): Brady, Brown, Clark, Childers, Putnam, Stevenson, W. Miller, Campbell, Norman, Hooper, Hooper, Pack, Tipton, Jones, Gotshaw, McElrath, Gordon, Granger.

Union Bleachery (5-8): Jenkins, Belcher, Turner, Hughes, Jennings, Harrison, Verner, Burdette, Center, Neely, Bridwell, Wiggins.

Monaghan of Greenville (2-13): Nolan, McCartney, Heath, Abercrombie, Henderson, Coleman, Greer, Antoller, Bramlett, Simmons, Odom, Bagwell, Jones, Knight, Jackson, Goodenough.

Greer (1-15): Davis, Center, Adams, Miller, Moore, Timmons, Cox, Mode, Glasgow, Brooks, Watson, Mahaffey, Fisher, Dobbins.

Anderson County League

Belton (3-0): Knox, Cox, Lyle, Rowland, Smith, Prymus Strickland, John Thomas, Mayfield Taylor, G.R. Bannister, James Clement, Gene Snipes, John Snipes, Clyde Snipes, John Campbell, George Orr, Bill Stephens.

Brogan (0-1): Daniel, English.

Equinox (0-2): Smith, Powell, Earl Mullinax, Cleo Watson, Prue Woolens, Ed Stephens, Ray Taylor, Hovey Watson, Roy Davis, J.T. Dickerson, Plug Parnell, Furman Beck, R.B. Speares.

Greenville Textile League: J.A. Davis (president), George Fryfogle (vice president), Harold Mahon (secretary/treasurer)

Woodside, champions (15-3): G. Brookshire, O. Brookshire, Bowen, Henson, Sizemore, Love, Huff, Crawford.

Poe (8-4): Mooney, McGee, Welch, Majors, Ingle, Smith, Manning, Williams.

Norris Shuttle Factory (7-2): J. Woodall, Barbare, Woodall, Nesbitt, Brewington, Williams, England, Chalmers, Long.

Dunean (5-4): Woodall, Harris, Hodge, McCauley, Hughes, Bishop, Wood, Howard.

Brandon of Greenville (5-6): Hudson, Dill, Williams, Woodson, Godfrey, Smith, Ivester, Denton, Young.

Mills Mill of Greenville (3-3): Belue, Revis, Smith, Brown, Pugh, Mahon, Westmoreland, Berry.

Judson (2-6): Wyatt, Belk, Lewis, White, Bell, Powell, Trammell, Wilson, Crooks, Kluttz, Ivester, Rogers, Hendrix, Moreland, Hill, Sanders, J. Barbare, McClure.

Monaghan of Greenville (0-7): Walker, Olson, Fleming, Scruggs, Osteen, Heath, Heath, Coleman, Gregory, Henson, Christopher.

Spartanburg/Laurens County League

Enoree (8-2): Patterson, McLeod, Kennedy, Cox, Signdale, Betsil, Thornton.

Lydia (4-0): Hurl, Cannon, Bodie,
Patterson, Flowers, Hilton, Mosely.
Laurens (0-1): Frady, Cooper.
Woodruff (0-5): Kohn, Westmore-
land, Mathis, Rogers, Edgins, Par-
rish, Halford.

Eastern Carolina League

Mills Mill of Woodruff, champions
(7-2): Workman, Phillips, Aber-
crombie, H. Swink, Henson.
Simpsonville (7-1): Cox, Cooper,
Parrish, B. Lynch, Ballew, Porter,
Huff, Rogers.
Fountain Inn (2-3): Brewington,
Jones, Owens, Edens.
Conestee (1-8): A. Tucker, Wilson,
Jones, Colbert, Cooper, Hawkins,
Blakely, Cashion, B. Tucker,
Eison, Rogers.

Palmetto League

Ware Shoals (7-3): Kate, Davis, Gra-
ham, Gresham, Walker, Medlock,
Lyle.
Pelzer (1-2): Whitmire, Wooten, Ash-
ley, Barrett.
Belton (1-4): Willingham, Lyle,
Smith, Hopkins, Carlisle, Strick-
land.

Spartanburg County League

Buffalo, 2nd half champions; re-
placed Saxon (10-1): A. Smith,
O'Sullivan, Malone, Crocker,
Inman, Gilliam, Schultz, Allen,
Summer, Liner, S. Smith, Arthur,
Crocker.
Spartan, 1st half champions (10-6):
Taylor, Eison, Mason, N. Clip-
pard, Timmons, Hoke Fine, W.
Clippard, Mooneyham, Allen, Put-
nam, Roland, Woodward, Baines,
Posey, Godfrey, Gregory, Brady.
Arcadia (8-6): Clark, Harris, Corn,
Hunnicutt, West, Curry, Bridg-
man, Mabry, Petty, Perry, Gosnell,
Bennett, Woody, Hoye, Johnson,
Farrow.

Inman (6-6): Bradley, Harvey, J.
Stone, Holden, Gregory, Scott,
Warren, Messer, Tinsley, Parris,
Petit, Halford, Easler, Sizemore,
Collins, Driggers, Teague, Alver-
son, Stepp, Vernon, Holt, O. Stone.
Saxon (5-1): Rushton, Pitts, Revis,
Bishop, Brooks, Champion, Paris,
Corn, Posey, Messer, Lassiter,
Hall, Elledge, Gault, Smith, John-
son.
Whitney (4-10): Turner, Norris,
Hughes, Barrett, Woodall,
Thomas, Rogers, McAllister,
Huskey, Searcy, D. Thomason, C.
Thomason, Moore, Caldwell, Reid,
Gossett, Tennyson, Hammett,
Walters.
Glendale (2-12): Hunter, W. Gossett,
Nicholls, Bagwell, Bradley, C. Gos-
sett, Reese, Allen, Ammons,
Pruitt, Russ, Ogles, Sentell,
Rogers, Easler, Crocker, Suttles,
Easler.

Independent Teams

Fairforest (17-0): J.E. Martin, John
Martin, Doc Taylor, Frey, W.R.
Taylor, Jess Taylor, Joe Benson,
W. Martin, Carver.
Pacolet (7-3): White, Harold, Patrick,
Teaster, Petty, Kirby, Morgan,
Littlejohn, Jett, Harrison, Pear-
son, Lester, Mabry, Vassey, Seay.
Liberty (4-7): Scott, R. Medlock,
Crane, Dunn, Werner, Fairley,
Riggins, Partee.
Williamston (2-0): W. Smith.
Piedmont Champions (2-0)
Belton Blue Stockings (2-0): Thomas,
Fletcher.
Westminster (2-1): Minick, Powell,
Edwards.
Chiquola (2-1): Calvert, McGaha,
Armstrong, Hughes.
Southern Worsted (2-2): Cothran,
Snipes, Clement, McCauley,
Osteen.
Newry (2-3): Carver, Gilliard.

Valley Falls (1-0): Henderson, Fowler.

Beaumont (1-0): West, Abbott, Bennett, Pack, Cooksey, Meadows, Nabors, Pearson, Holt, Carter.

Camperdown 2nd Team (1-0): Gosnell.

Tucapau (1-2): Petit, Smith, Bridges, West, Southern, Jackson, Meadows, Brown, Barrett, Kirby.

Lyman (1-2): Gossett, Tinsley, Aughtry, Hoy, Guthrie, Sims, Guthrie, Vaughn, Crossland, Brown.

Monarch (1-3): Thompson, Gilliam, Smith, Malone, E. Allen, G. Owens, Liner, Fowler, Adams, Howell, Godshell, Sparks, Fleming, R. Owens, Range, Allison, Cabiness.

Clifton (1-4): Crocker, Higgins, Tindall, Oeland, Calvert, Bennett, McClure, Groce, Calvert, Mahaffey, Stapleton, Rinehart, Jolly, Giles, Hughes.

Pelzer Mudcats (0-1): Eaton, McConnell.

Jackson of Wellford (0-1): Carter, McMillan.

Central (0-1): Gaines, Landers.

Walhalla (0-1): Studemeyer, Davis, Burdette.

Pelham (0-1): Gotshaw, Jones.

Jackson of Iva (0-1): Robertson, Hall, Purcell.

Mary Louise (0-1): Gilbert, Scruggs.

Limestone (0-1): McGreer.

Victor of Greer (0-1): Smith, Hudson, Waters, Wilson, Taylor, B. Brown, Stevens, H. Brown, Simmons.

Jonesville (0-1): Addis, Gallman, Holt, Gossett, Mason.

Piedmont (0-1)

Belton Tigers (0-1)

Chiquola (0-1)

Gaffney (0-1)

Orr (0-2): Ruller, Hart, Head, Claud Whitten, Bolding.

Lancaster (no records): M.L. Beckham, Grady Bolin, Chiny McDonald, Harvey Barfield, Dick Richards, Tom Stewart, Thurlow Pittman, Turner Morton (manager)

1925

Spartanburg Textile League: L.G. Osborne (president)

Pacolet, champions (14-5): Mabry, Patrick, M. Teaster, Petty, Kirby, Jett, Searcy, Fleming, L. Teaster, Howell, Newton, Seay, Guyton, Ellison, White, Murphy, Holt, Vassey, B. Littlejohn, A. Littlejohn, Woods, Lee, Barnett.

Inman (12-9): Haney, Parris, Shehan, E. Bradley, Gregory, Patton, J. Stone, Holden, Garner, McAbee, Messer, Pack, Matthews, Garrett, Teague, Bonham, Harvey, O. Stone, R. Bradley, Revis.

Spartan (11-9): Taylor, Mooneyham, Mason, Timmons, Fine, McAbee, Allen, Eison, Bright, W. Roland, Arnold, G. Roland, Tuttle, Woods, Gregory, Posey, Epps, Lockman.

Arcadia (9-7): Perry, Parrott, Scott, Clark, W. Scott, D. Corn, Gosnell, West, Bridgman, Bennett, Hunnicutt, Gordon, Johnson.

Whitney (5-14): C. Thompson, Hughes, Inman, Searcy, Gosnell, Hammett, Rogers, Tennyson, Turner, Reid, Gossett, Norris, D. Thompson, Huskey, Moore.

Valley Falls (2-5); withdrew. L. Collier, Waldrop, R. Collier, Towery, Nolan, Wall, Edwards, Bright, Henderson, Holland, C. Bagwell, Towney, Lockman, Ware.

Franklin (6-11); replaced Valley Falls. Morrow, Porter, Guthrie, Goings, Earl Prince, Burns, Prince, Goss, Cothran, Ridings, Smith, Cook, Hamrick, Ammons, Greenway, Gossett.

Interurban League

Lyman (15-1): Crossland, Rogers, Millwood, Cunningham, Winter,

Norman, Bowen, Sims, Lindsay, Aughtry, Allen, Elwood, Hoy, Gossett, McMakin, Sims, Bones, Thomas, Jordan, Poole, Crawford, Gotshaw, Miller.

Tucapau (10-6): L. Southern, Smith, Mason, West, Barrett, R. Southern, Sigler, Johnson, Warden, D. Southern, Fisher, Brown, Jackson, Williams, Jordan, Bishop, Lemaster, Collins, Gordon, Fredrick, Martin, Crawford, Dixon, Lavender, Bailey, Dixon, Henson.

Victor of Greer (1-2): E. Poole, P. Poole, Brady, Smith, Clark, Gordon, Cooper, Campbell, Hutchinson, Henson, Wilson.

Greer (1-3): Jones, Greer, Glasgow, Davis, Miller, Allen, Center, Timmons, Mode, Watson, Westmoreland, Taylor, Pressley.

Apalache (0-2): R. Stevenson, Kirk, Winter, Jones, Tapp, Davis, Pitt, Smith, Leopard, M. Stevenson, Stevenson.

Pelham (0-4): Arnold, Gotshaw, Barnes, S. Jones, Vaughn, M. Jones, Yeargin, Hendricks, McKinney, Hawkins, Brannon.

Tri-County League

Mills Mill of Woodruff (6-1): F. Bragg, Phillips, Henson, Cogsdill, H. Swink, Guinn, Surratt, Bagwell.

Watts (1-1): Bobo, Brewington, Rogers.

Laurens (0-1): Abercrombie.

Simpsonville (0-3): Stallings, Brewington, Smith, Barbare, Godfrey, Benton, Snipe, Bobo, Owens, Garrett.

Independent League

Southern Railway (13-3)

Beaumont (9-7): E. Edgins, Hammett, Bennett, Smith, Sanders, Powell, H. Edgins, Pearson, Chapman, C. Willis, Ellis, P. Fowler,

Mahaffey, E. Fowler, Cooksey, McGee, D. Taylor, Collier, L. Taylor, Westmoreland, A. Fowler, Phillips, Callahan, E. Willis, Nabors, Prince, Abbott, Tillitson, Whetsteine.

Drayton (4-9): D. Kirby, Carter, S. Hill, Wilson, Walker, McGee, Campbell, Dean, Powell, Byrd, W. McGee, Garrison, D. Hill, Willis, Sexton, Perry, Crocker, C. Kirby, Reagan, Brown, Lawrence.

Arkwright (3-8): Hughes, Henderson, Shook, Culbreth, Pettigrew, Metters, Holt, Taylor, Varner, Kinard, Thomas, Meadows, Hunt, Walden, Thompson, Tiddy, Brooks, P. Brown, Eubanks, Fowler, Powell, Martin, Sullivan, Skates, Prince.

Piedmont Textile League: Harry Jones (president), L.P. Lollis (vice president).

Brandon of Greenville, champions (no records): Lawrence, Oliver, Calvert, Duncan.

Monaghan of Greenville (no records): Reagan, Owens, Patterson, Alexander, Brookshire, Bowen.

Woodside (no records): Belcher, Harrison, Nolan, Campbell, Hurst, McGill.

Southern Worsted (no records): Brookshire, Hendricks, Bowen, Greer, Major, Owens.

Union Bleachery (no records): Ralph O'Connor, Hughes, Ashbury, C. Alexander, Dixon.

Southern Bleachery (no records): Smith, R. Belcher, Cox, Sullivan, McKinney, Campbell.

Glenwood (no records): Green, Calvert, Duncan, C. Pitts, Duncan, Bowie, McCartney, Shakin, Surratt, Belcher, Turner.

Alice (no records): Patterson, Dickson, Humphries, Tillotson, Everett, Greer, McGill, Olson.

Carolina Textile League

Judson (no records): Holliday, Putman, Guthrie, Toler, Reese, Hawkins, Granger, Thurmond.

Dunean (no records): Lyles, Tatham, Granger, Godfrey, Alexander, Guthrie.

Piedmont Mudcats (no records): Looper, Smith, Alexander, Moore, Eaton, McConnell, Fowler, Godfrey, Werner, Brady, Smith.

Pelzer (no records): P. Crymes, Wooten, Rogers, Williams, Hunnicutt, Coleman, Westmoreland, Barnett, Dutch Vaughn, Holliday, Hall.

Waycross GA (no records)

Laurens (no records): Barnes, Yeargin, Smith, Riggs, O'Connor, Gibson, Pezting, McNit, McMillan, Bagwell, Sullivan, Bobo.

Ware Shoals (no records): Smith, Hawkins, Strickland, Miles, Walker, Parrish, Ellis.

Belton (no records): Ellis, Parrish, Guthrie, Tatham, Boylston, Minnick, Walker.

Parker League

Monaghan of Greenville (no records): Lee, Brewington, Neely, Major.

Poe (no records): T. Ingle, McCauley.

Brandon of Greenville (no records): Alexander, Dixon.

Sampson (no records): Reeves, Roberts, Hawkins, Farrow.

Woodside (no records): Thomas, Flemings.

Norris Shuttle Factory (no records): C. Woodall, Long.

Union Bleachery (no records): Lawrence, Medlock.

Dunean (no records): Hughes, Winslow.

Independent Teams

Eureka (10-0): Patrick, Kirkpatrick, Sealey.

Jackson of Wellford (5-0): Bunk, Dobbins, Clark, Huntsinger, Morrell.

Clifton (5-7): Calvert, Hunter, Tindall, Hughes, Groce, Vaughn, D. Calvert, Mahaffey, Jolly, Tate, Griggs, Giles, Robinson, Crocker, Bridges, Orr, Oeland, Mann, Dearyberry, McClure, Stapleton, Sizemore.

Glendale (4-3): Bradley, Suttle, Coggins, Reese, Nichols, W. Gossett, Allen, Ogle, Bush, Messer, C. Gossett, Corn, Fleming, Rush, Bridges, Crocker, Ammons, Reid.

Spartan 2nd Team (3-2): Bishop, Henderson, Carter, Hunnicutt, Guthrie, Posey, Blanton, Arnold.

Chesnee (3-3): Ezell, Nolan, Wall, Ross, W. Martin, Cudd, Elder, McClure, Lockman, Ward, Mosely, Mabry, McCraw, Rupp, Simmons, Walters.

Buffalo (2-4): Ladd, Arrowood, Crocker, Powell, Lanhart, Hightower, Brown, Strakey, Garner, McPherson, Stepple, Smith, O'Sullivan, Gilliam, Waldrop, Allen, Malone, Owens, Liner, A. Smith.

Lockhart (2-0): Vaughn, Odell, Parks, Wilson, Murphy, Epps, Gotshaw, White, Vandeford.

Boiling Springs SC(1-0)

Arkwright 2nd Team (1-0): Meadows, Blackwell.

Enoree (1-0): Brodie, Dillard.

Arcadia 2nd Team (1-1)

Fairforest (1-1): Martin, J. Martin, Gray, C. Taylor, J. Taylor, Benson, W. Taylor, L. Taylor, Brannon.

Landrum (1-2): Foster, Fox, W. Capps, Forrester, R. Capps, Shehan, Culbreth, Edwards, Laughter, Phillips.

Beaumont 2nd Team (1-3): H. Willis, Powell, F. Fowler, Prince.

Lydia (0-1): W. Bodie, White, Riddle, Ballew, P. Bodie.

Woodruff (0-1): Drummonds, Bragg,
W. Swink, Taylor, H. Swink,
McGill, McAllister, Cogdill, Work-
man.

Tucapau 2nd Team (0-1)

Fairmont (0-2): Rhymer, Linder, Gibson, Cannon.

Mary Louise (0-2): Young, Wall,
Elder, Tabors, Williams, Mathis,
F. Henderson, Gilbert, Sullivan,
Thrift, Turner, Goings.

Hawthorne (0-2): Smith, Petty.

Inman 2nd Team (0-3): Wofford,
Smith, Evington, Pridmore.

1926

Parker League

Dunean, champions (14-1): Wood,
Walker, Henson, McMillan,
Hughes, Scott, Turner, Davis,
Tatham, Floyd.

Woodside (10-7): Sturkey, Vehorn,
Ellenburg, Sterling, Dover, Bell,
Stanley, Herbert, Clippard.

Judson (7-4): Tatham, Ivester, Luther, Hendrix, Calfass, Bell, West,
McClure.

Brandon of Greenville (7-5): Couch,
Bannister, Granger, Hudson, Dill.

Southern Franklin (7-9): Brewington,
Butler, Whelchel, Murray, Saxon,
Mahaffey.

Monaghan of Greenville (5-6):
Holder, Hudgens, Ballenger, Fleming, Henson, Kelly, Heath.

Union Bleachery (2-9): Smith,
Bridwell, Cantrell, Hicks, Ellison,
Dixon, Surratt, Batson, Cook.

Poe (1-12): Turnbull, Bishop, Boggs,
Landreth, Stacey, Dill, Harrison,
Thornton, Brewington, Neely.

Piedmont League

Union Bleachery (15-2): G. Turner,
Batson, Smith, Cantrell, Bridwell,
G. Belcher, Dobbins, Dalton, Har-
rison, Floyd, Marchant, Fanning,

Hawkins, Coker, P. Turner,
T. Turner, Childers.

Sampson (10-4): Neely, Major, Smith,
Byars, Heath, Cooper, Center.

Southern Bleachery (8-8): O'Connell,
Gay, Black, Coker, Hughes,
McElrath, Heath, Childers, McKin-
ney, Foster, Bridwell.

Poe (7-10): Tom Ingle, L. Ingle,
Welch, Christopher, Crawford,
Cleveland, C. Coggins, Thornton,
Davis, J. Smith, Revis, Hamlin,
Ragston, Teague.

Camperdown (6-5): J. Breazeale,
Pace, Jenkins, Gosnell, Crawford,
Huff, Crymes, Young, Arnold,
Medlock, McManaway.

Woodside (6-7): Medlock, Brookshire, Shirley, Bowen, Barrett, Simmons, Heaton, Clippard.

Mills Mill of Greenville (5-11): Joel
Smith, W. Smith, Ram Smith,
Grindstaff, Fews, Bridges, Spake,
Revis, Goss, C. Smith, Davis.

Greer (1-13): Poole, Carter, Waters,
Miller, Hood, Center, Eaton, West-
moreland, Green, Kirby, Davis,
Timmons, Glasgow.

Carolina League

Ware Shoals, champions (7-5):
Walker, Kirkland, J. Werner, Wig-
gins, Chalmers, Troutman, Ellison,
Davis, Manley.

Laurens (7-4): O'Connell, Riddle,
Bagwell, Patton, Barrett, Bobo,
Collins, Owens.

Watts (5-6): Edgins, Owens, Betsill,
M. Bagwell, W. Cox, Riddle,
Thornton, Brewington, Tidwell, R.
Swink.

Belton (1-7): Knox, Brooks, Burgess,
Calvert, Beard, Gibson, Owens.

Western Carolina League

Brandon of Greenville (15-6):
Granger, Bannister, Barnes, Oliver,
Lawrence, Sentell, Benton, Huff,
Hall, Medlock, Rogers.

Dunean (9-9): Alexander, Greer, Owens, Patterson, Rogers, Wood, Tatham, Floyd, Harvill, McClure, Taylor, Davis.

Glenwood (7-7): Alexander, Chapman, Courtney, Green, Owens, Stancil, Patterson.

Pelzer (6-7): Wooten, Bolton, Mullinax, Vaughn, Smith, B. Wood, Crymes, Haney, Sargent, C. Wood, Hudgens, Campbell, McCombs.

Alice (6-10): Hendrix, Carter, McCauley, Calvert, McCain, Burdette, McCrory, McManaway, Duncan, C. Pitts, Clippard, Leslie, L. Pitts.

Judson (5-12): Benton, Fox, Hudson, Moreland, D. Landreth, English, Hall, L. Landreth, Hendrix, Chandler, B. Wyatt, V. Landreth, W. Wood, Langston, Hughes, Blackwell, L. Wood, Floyd, Robins, Mullinax, Campbell, Davis, May, Moreland.

Independent League

Lyman, champions (6-3): Walt Barbare, Smith, Millwood, Rogers, Query, Morrill, Carlson, Holcombe, Aughtry, Martin, Bryson, H.J. Lindsay, Norman, J.O. Lindsay, Millwood, Sims, Millwood.

Victor of Greer (3-2): Brady, Waters, Thomas, Poole.

Tucapau (1-3): Fisher, Enlow, Mason, Bridges, Roberts, H. Smith, Nixon, Southern, Williams, West, Fredrick, Barnett, Ward, Paxton, Berry, C. Smith.

Simpsonville (1-4): Gaffney, Cox, Godfrey, Lynch, Mathis, Barbery, Vaughn, Crane, Goodenough, Ballew, Jamison, Bridges, Hughes, Tolbert, Bragg, Taylor, Crane, B. Mathis.

Saluda League

Piedmont, champions (9-3): League,

Patterson, Fowler, McAbee, Pickleseimer, Cargill, Smith, Morehead.

Chiquola (7-4): A. Calvert, Bowie, Moore, P. Calvert, Tice.

Williamston (7-5): Scott, Hudgens, Hopkins, Manley, Stepp, Holliday, Worthy.

Pelzer (2-9): Vaughn, Wooten, Smith, Whitmire, Hopkins, Earl, Bennett, Dowis, Russell.

Big Four League

York (1-0): Smith, McDowell, Campbell.

Chester (0-1): Kirkpatrick, Durham, Laurens.

Spartanburg County League

Clifton (2-0): Tindall, Oeland, H. Calvert, Groce, D. Calvert, Hughes, C. Mahaffey, Vaughn, Stapleton, Jones, Pierson, Bugen, Tate, Coggins, Jolly, R. Mahaffey.

Arcadia (1-0): Perry, Clark, Lavender, Burnett, Byrd, McGee, West, Warden, Corn.

Pacolet (1-0): White, M. Teaster, Kirby, Foy Patrick, Hall, Jett, Harold, Petty, L. Teaster, Mabry, Holt, Guyton.

Inman (1-1): Bradley, Cook, Harvey, Waldrop, J. Stone, Shehan, Prince, O. Stone, Pack, Lawton, Scott, Parris.

Whitney (0-1): Searcy, Arnold, Brooks, Scott, Rogers, Huskey, Hughes, Reid, Caldwell, Hammett, Turner, Pruitt.

Spartan (0-2): McAbee, Mooneyham, Allen, Timmons, Fine, W. Roland, Shelton, Wood, Gregory, Mason, Teddy, Shippey, Eison, Roland.

Independent Teams

Seneca (2-0): Patterson, Henderson, Hoyle.

Poinsett (1-0): Kindrough, Johnson.

Watts 2nd Team (1-0): Grubbs, McGee.

Newberry (1-0): Bouknight, Bouknight.

Mills Mill of Woodruff (0-1):
Thackston, Colblack.
Baldwin (1-0): McDaniel, Durham, E.
Knox.
Poe 3rd Team (1-0)
Apalache (1-1): Stevenson, Hawkins,
Harris, Cripp.
Chesnee (0-1): Newberry, Small.
Joanna (0-1): Flow, McCall, Abrams,
Bedenbaugh.
Lancaster (0-1): Threatt, McDonald.
Sampson 3rd Team (0-1)
Mollohon (no records): Rob Bartley,
Richard Lominack Sr., Bus
Golden, Monk Shell, Colie Jones,
Johnny Bedenbaugh, Earl Hud-
gens, Fred Darby, Roy Hudgens,
Leland Wood, Ralph Setzler, Oscar
Jones.
Ottaray (no records): Bill Queen, Sam
Bagwell, Manning Bagwell.
Brandon of Woodruff (no records):
Cameron, Medlock, Osteen, Bur-
ton, Heath, Huggins, Laurens, Sen-
tell, Oliver.
Drayton (no records): Kirby, Moore,
Federline, Powell, Snyder, Sulli-
van, Rook, Stancell, R. Prince.
Andrews Reed & Harness Shop (no
records): O. Adkins, H. King, F.
Adkins, J. Solesbee, D. Adkins,
Hunsucker, E. Worley, McCarter,
Wooten.
Enoree (no records): R. Waddle,
Mabry, Thackston, O. Gentry, C.
Waldrop, Nelson, Waldrop, F.
Gentry.

1927

Piedmont Textile League

Southern Bleachery, champions
(14-2): Avery Yeargin, Surratt,
O'Connell, Roy Coker, Foster,
Hawkins, Green, Pace, McElrath,
Ralph Coker, Guy, Robinson,
Pack, Yeargin, Jack Black.
Camperdown (11-4): Ward, J. Brea-
zeale, Hall, Huff, W. Breazeale,
Smith, Crawford, Graham, McDow-
ell, Williams, Jenkins, Grant, Wil-
liams, Edwards, Foster, Knight,
Cureton, Gosnell, Young, Graham,
McManaway.
Union Bleachery (8-8): Smith,
G. Belcher, P. Turner, Bridwell,
J.D. Childers, Dalton, M. Floyd,
G. Turner, P. Turner, Brooks, Har-
rison, Greer, Joe Childers.
Woodside (6-10): Coggins, J. Brook-
shire, Jamison, Bowen, Ramey,
Brown, Medlock, O.B. Brookshire,
Harding, Porter, Waldrop, Dill,
Trammell, Campbell, Clippard,
Dover, Paxton.
Sampson (4-8): G. Neely, Majors,
Porter, Hollingsworth, Smith,
Bridwell, P. Neely, Cooper, Gib-
son.
Southern Franklin (2-10): Brewing-
ton, Revis, McCollum, Mahaffey,
Collins, Saxton, Murray, Floyd,
Jones, Davis, Hendricks, Murphy,
Woods.

Western Carolina League

Brandon of Greenville, champions
(17-2): Ball, Heath, Lawrence,
Oliver, Denton, Medlock, McCall,
Osteen, Pratt, Roberts, Sentell,
Denton, Roberts, Morris, Rollins,
G.A. Floyd (manager), Chand-
ler.
Dunean (11-5): Bagwell, Henry,
Tatham, Cashion, Harvel, Sanders,
Barbare, Robins, Walker,
Springfield, Mullinax, Duncan,
Christopher, Gibson, McCauley,
Jamison, Greer, Floyd.
Glenwood (9-5): Mullinax, F. Owens,
Greer, Spearman, Lee Alexander,
C. Alexander, Williams, Fortner,
Patterson, Chapman.
Alice (9-9): Galloway, L. Patterson,
Moore, McCauley, Hendrix,
Green, Owens, Pitts, Mabry, Day,
Cooper, Epps, Lesley, Nabors,

Carter, Pitts, D. Patterson,
Hunter, Tinsley, Chapman, Kirby,
Calvert.
Judson (2-12): Wyatt, C. Moreland,
Landers, Hall, Trammell, V.
Landreth, West, Wood, Chandler,
L. Landreth, Bryant, Crawford,
McClure.
Simpsonville (1-14): Godfrey, D.
Lynch, Williams, Childers, Ballew,
Tolbert, Barbery, Coleman, Jami-
son, Worthy, Bunting, Barbare,
Benton.

Tri-County League

Pelzer Red Birds, champions (13-3):
A. Campbell, Ef Sargent, Crymes,
Dutch Vaughn, Walter Campbell,
Wooten, Oscar McCombs, John
Earl Cannon, Cecil Woods, Wright
Woods, Jim Westmoreland, Ban-
nister, Nig Haney, Holmes, C. Hen-
son, Jess Rogers, Red Woods.
Gluck (1-1): Dick Sweetenburg, Beck,
Tom Kay, Runt Heron, Campbell,
Ham Hamilton, Snake McAllister,
Allen, Allen, Pearman.
Belton (1-5): O. Owens, S. Owens,
Cannon, Knox, Brooks, Bannister,
Moore.
Piedmont (1-7): Fowler, Mitchell, T.
League, Patterson, L. Anderson,
Fisher, Roberts, Rogers, Leverett,
F. Anderson, Leathers.

Saluda Textile League

Pelzer (4-0): Davenport, Edens, Hop-
kins, Alexander, Ellis, Allison,
Edgins, Westner, Parson.
Easley (3-0): Galloway, Morgan,
Hampton, Coody, McJunkin,
Turpin.
Cateechee (1-0): Owens, Bagwell.
Liberty (0-2): Stevenson, Campbell,
Bush, Rogers.
Belton (0-2): Fisher, Thompson, Kay,
Darnell, Owens.
Piedmont (0-2): Wynn, Kings, Evans,
Pack, Morehead.

Parker League

Dunean (9-3): Hudson, L. Wood, Rol-
ing, McClure, Christopher, Harvel,
Hughes, Kelly, Coleman, Huff.
Woodside (8-2): Hubert, Summey,
Wellborn, Carter, Bunton, Martin,
D. Horn.
Southern Worsted (7-4): Smith,
Snipes, Knight, Clements, Green,
Jackson, Brown, Davis.
Poe (7-5): McKnight, Felsch, Christo-
pher, L. Ingle, T. Ingle, Welch,
Cleveland, Neely, Turnbull, Har-
rington, Howell, Cyclone Smith,
Black.
Brandon of Greenville (4-4): Granger,
Bannister, Couch, Dill, F. Wil-
liams, T. Williams, Sullivan,
Lynch.
Monaghan of Greenville (4-5): Hen-
son, Greer, Pittman, Hudgens,
Hendrix, Coleman, Simmons.
Mills Mill of Greenville (3-6): Few,
Fulbright, J. Smith, Davis, Turner,
Fulbright, R. Smith, J. Sexton,
Hardin, Coggins, Burnett, Walker,
Johnson, Mills.
Judson (0-12): Evans, Landrum,
Fleming, Wyatt, Phillips, Bell,
Stepp, Bridwell, R. McClure.

Independent Mill League

Lyman (4-1): McAbee, Smith, Bry-
son, Norman, Fisher, Query, Har-
ris, Martin, Goodenough, Martin,
Smokey Barbare, Robinson, Mill-
wood.
Inman (4-2): Taylor, Vardry, O.
Stone, Prince, Timmons, Waldrop,
Pack, Shehan, Parris, Jones, J.
Stone, Lawter.
Greer (3-2): McElrath, Gordon,
Miller, Allen, Timmons, Glasgow,
Waters.
Tucapau (3-2): McGehan, Wall,
West, Southern, Sims, McAbee,
Fisher, Mason, Jackson, G.
Mason, Gordon.

Arcadia (1-4)
Victor of Greer (1-5): Kohn, Heath, Brady, Clarkson, Gurley.

Oconee County League

Lonsdale (14-1): Stevenson, McDonald, Alexander, R. Stevenson, Cargill, Mason, Madden, Green, Ivester, Graham.
Newry (2-3): Hawkins, Carver, Mulkey, Ellis, Kirby, Curley.
Walhalla (1-4): Massey, Buchanan, Hoot Gibson, Dunlap, Adbady, Davis, Moore.
Westminster (1-4): Reed, Powell, Willis, Mahaffey, Smalley.

Big Four League

Laurens, champions (12-6): P. Campbell, M. Bagwell, Barrett, Cox, Walker, McGee, Frady, Brady, Johnny Riddle, Elgins, Carter, Powers, Bobo, Cox, S. Bagwell.
Joanna (10-5): Young, Willingham, Mosely, Slow, Strickland, Willingham, McCall, Bobo, Betsil, Sweat, Brewington, Hamilton.
Lydia (5-8): King, Ruff, Drummonds, Bennett, Gowans, Frank, Fuller, Betsil, McGowan, Fowler, Taylor, Gowan, Paris, Culbertson.
Enoree (3-11): Gentry, Thornton, Nabors, Justus, Nelson, Cooper, Taylor, Waldrop, Hill.

Reedy River League

Poinsett (9-3): Campbell, Childers, Walton, Gregory, Johnson, McGregor, Robertson, Galloway, Shickes, Snipes.
Vardry (5-2): Smith, Crymes, Kelly, Nabors, Morgan, Brown.
Conestee (3-2): Wilson, Surratt, Stewart.
Gantt (3-9): Myers, Fulbright, Carson, Eskew, Lark, Mitchell, Anders, Brown, Clark.

Spartanburg County League

Clifton, champions (18-5): Johnny Vassey, Emeuel Vassey, Pierce, Owens, Calvert, Mahaffey, Groce, Dixon, Fowler, Tindall, Pearson, Jim Oeland, Taylor.
Southern Railway (14-5)
Pacolet (8-4): Monroe Teaster, Tom Holt, Walt White, Patrick, Pug Guyton, Mabry, Bill Harold, Tobe Campbell, Jim Rice, Lawrence Fleming, L. Teaster, Will Worthy, Fat Morgan, Howell, Parnell, Cook.
Spartan (5-11): Hawkins, Fine, Taylor, Calvert, Loyless, Timmons, Buncombe, Shippey, Isom, G. Roland, W. Roland, Wood, Mason, Lawter, Allen.
Beaumont (4-11): R. Prince, H. Prince, Ellis, Nabors, Wilder, Fowler, G. Green, Holt, Burke, McClure, Shook, R. Green.
Whitney (1-12): Caldwell, Harvey, Hughes, Searcy, Scott, Motes, Hammett, Rogers, Tillotson, Turner, Brooks, Huskey, Nash, Cotner.

Independent Teams

Laurens 2nd Team (2-0): Gosnell, Simmons, Bolt, Cox.
Watts (2-0): Craig, Poole.
Gray Mill (1-0): Bagwell, Green, Barbee.
Lockhart (1-0): Lemaster, Garner, Seale, Blackwell, Burns, Barnes, Allison, W. O'Dell, C. Blackwell, E. O'Dell, VanderHorn.
Central (1-0): Madden, Duncan, Lydia.
Oakland (1-0): Manning Bagwell, Dennis, Andy Bowen.
Camperdown 2nd Team (1-0): Wilson, Wilson.
Fountain Inn (1-1): Mathis, Matthews.
Anderson (0-1): Evans, Henson.
Sampson 2nd Team (0-1)

Baldwin (0-1): Bridges, Durham, Morris.

Newberry (0-2): Jones, I. Bouknight, E. Bouknight.

Mauldin (0-2): Ellis Forrester, Surratt.

Woodruff (0-2): Littlefield, Westmoreland, Hill.

Mills Mill of Greenville 2nd Team (no records): Childs, Abbott.

Cowpens (no records): Waters, Mosely, Varney, Mabry, Mahaffey, Moore, Calvert, Taylor, Martin.

Drayton (no records): R. Moore, West, McGee, S. Moore, Furch, Bennett, Rook, Fowler.

Powell Knitting (no records): Connors, Fisher, Godfrey, D. Gault, C. Gault, Wyatt, Owens, Distaffino.

1928

Piedmont Textile League — A Section

Southern Bleachery, champions (18-1): A. McElrath, Ralph Coker, Smith, Smith, Hughes, L. McElrath, Childers, Pace, Gay, O'Connell, J.D. Childers, Roy Coker.

Union Bleachery (14-4): P. Turner, T. Turner, Revis, Breazeale, Bridwell, Smith, Hawkins, Brooks, Floyd, G. Turner, Belcher, Harrison, Parkins.

Woodside (7-8): Carter, O. Brookshire, Bowen, Hardin, Burton, Herbert, Byars, Byrd, Ramey, Hendrix, Owen, Alexander, Campbell, Aiken, Clippard.

Sampson Spinners (6-10): Davis, G. Neely, Bratton Williams, Roberts, Smith, Hollingsworth, Badger, C. Neely, Mauldin, Williams, Porter, Majors.

Poe (3-11): Harrison, Turnbull, Hall, T. Ingle, Howell, Welch, L. Ingle, Heath, Cooper, Duncan, Fuller, Rice, Hughes, Smith, Collins.

Jackson of Wellford (3-12): D. Williams, Barnett, L. Landreth, B. Landreth, Sanders, Sanders, Cashion, T. Wyatt, B. Wyatt, White, Wilson, Trammell, Hall, Door.

Alice (2-15): Day, Ferguson, Kilby, Campbell, Masters, Spearman, Roper, Tilson, Rambo, Howell, Turpin, Stewart, Humphries, Carter.

Piedmont Textile League — B Section

Southern Franklin, champions (14-3): Lee, Hendrix, Revis, Murray, R. Jones, S. Jones, Tallant, Lemmond, Wilson, Hunter, Mahaffey.

Brandon (10-6): Granger, Floyd, Roberts, Lynch, Williams, Sentell, Couch, Foster, Simmons, Herbert.

Greer (9-8): Fowler, Barbare, Hood, Kirby, Green, Hunt, Flynn, Miller, Hugh, Glasgow, Greer.

Mills Mill of Greenville (8-10): Edmundson, Groce, Turner, Fulbright, R. Smith, McCauley, J. Smith, Revis, Few, Sexton, Campbell.

Poinsett (6-3): Campbell, Robertson, Morgan, McElrath, Emory, Godfrey, Childs.

Southern Worsted (1-4); withdrew. Luther, Jones, Smith, Snipes, Hart, Knox.

Big Six League: S.G. Bishop, president.

Laurens, champions (15-2): Bobo, McGee, Brady, Weisner, W. Cox, Simmons, Jackson, Barrett, Frady, Patton, Littlefield, McMillan, Bagwell.

Newberry (9-8): Mosely, I. Singley, Bouknight, E. Bouknight, Lindsay, Taylor, Adams.

Joanna (6-8): Young, Slow, Abrams, Woodlock, Barrett, Mosely, Fuller, Howell, Wooten, Floe, Ward, Simmons, Parish, R. Clark, Bouknight.

Clinton (6-8): Charlie Wilson, Fuller, Knight, Ward, Farrow, Mosely, Copeland, Kearns, Evans, Trammell, Dickey, Little, Howard, O. Howard, Bailey, Campbell, McCullough.

Woodruff (2-7): Workman, Mathis, Gentry, Matthews, Surratt, Waddell, Westmoreland, Hendrix.

Enoree (1-9): Littlefield, Nelson, Nabors, Gentry, Hilton, Thornton, Edgins, Woods, Rhodes, McGee, Wilson.

Western Carolina League

Pelzer, champions (18-4): Campbell, Dutch Vaughn, C. Woods, John Earl Cannon, Ef Sargent, D. Crymes, Jess Rogers, P. Woods, Red Woods, Lewis Moore, Wright, Jim Westmoreland, Nig Haney, Thompson, Brannon, P. Crymes, Long, Truman Crymes, Haley Davenport, Charles Henson (manager)

Brandon of Greenville (13-8): Lawrence, Oliver, Walt Barbare, Lynch, Heath, Medlock, Denton, Granger, Osteen, Sentell, Fox, Floyd, Foster.

Glenwood (8-7): Green, F. Owens, Alexander, Mullinax, Tatham, Chapman, Patterson.

Alice (8-10): Howell, H. Hendrix, Hughes, Owens, Galloway, Blackwell, West, Granger, J. Pitts, Mathis, Valley, Leslie, O. Hendrix, Bagwell, Carter, Alexander.

Dunean (2-3): Davis, Campbell, Hudson, Duncan, Benson.

Chiquola (2-13): Roberts, Rob Calvert, R. Moore, Davis, Pug Calvert, Coleman, Moreland, Haney, Werner, Holman, Brock, Duckett, Tice, Wood, Sullivan, Bill Calvert, Jim Calvert.

Spartanburg Independent League

Tucapau, champions (1-0): H. Smith, Fisher, Southern, Nixon, Williams, Moorehead, Berry, Lavender, Petty.

Lyman (2-1): Smith, Rogers, Parrish, Bryson, Sims, Martin, Tyson, Query, Millwood, Norman, Barber, McAbee, Cameron, Aughtry.

Southern Railway (0-1)

Mills Mill of Woodruff (0-2): Bobo, Brewington, S. Bagwell, Garrett, Tipton, Taylor, Betsill, Thornton, Sogie, Phillips, Godfrey.

Georgia-Carolina League

Lonsdale (10-4): H. Stevenson, McDonald, Ivester, Watson, C. Heath, Jim Blackwell, Justus, Mason, Davis, C. Alexander, H. Heath, R. Leatherwood.

Westminster (5-1): Alvin Gilreath, Gilbert McManaway, Henry Huff, Reed, Powell, Mahaffey, Watson, Porter, Brigham, Williams.

Walhalla (2-3): Beatty, Shirley, Davis, Elrod, Massey, Winkler.

Lavonia GA (2-4)

Newry (1-1); withdrew. McClelland, Murray.

Liberty (1-3): Heigs, Carson, Waldrop, Medlock.

Toccoa GA (0-2)

Eastern Carolina League

Fountain Inn, champions (13-9): Weisner, Cooper, Scott, Spoon, Lydia, McGee, R. Mathis, B. Lynch, McCauley, Gault, Kelly, Wood.

Pelham (14-5): Arnold, Roddy, Westmoreland, Gotshaw, Yeargin, Vaughn, O. Howard, Campbell, McCullough, R. Poole.

Simpsonville (13-9): Ballew, Bunton, Childress, Calvert, Barbare, Godfrey, Marchbanks, Murphy, Tolbert, Barbery, White, Jim Yeargin, Black, M. Crawford, Simmons, Spoon, T. Ingle, Thornton.

Laurens (3-2): Campbell, Bobo, Patton, Spoon, White, Marchbanks, Yeargin.

Conestee (3-12): A. Wilson, L. Wilson, Adams, Allen, Vaughn, Vaughn, Tyree.

Clinton (0-2): Whitlock, McCullough, Fuller, Mosely, Chick Galloway.

Palmetto Textile League

Ware Shoals, champions (14-4): George Werner, Wright, Graham, Ellis, Gregory, Fletcher, Gilreath, Brown, Bagwell, Bill Werner, Harold Clark, Paul Troutman, Jenkins, Williams, L. Werner, Chalmers, Collins, Davis.

Greenwood (10-3): Walker, Arnold, Joe Allen, Bolton, C. Fowler, Hinton.

Grendel #1 (6-4): Pack, Greer, Nally, Woods, Morehead, Duff, Carithers.

Ninety Six (5-9): Fain, Sanders, Abbott, Fisklor, Attaway, McManaway.

Grendel #2 (3-9): Thompson, Davis, Lyle, Rogers, Hinton, Arnold, Milford, Weathers.

Abbeville (2-12): Milford, Busby, Stalnaker, Burgess, Williams, Long, Dudley, Newt.

Saluda Textile League

Belton (10-0): Willingham, Grubbs, Burgess, Owens, Bannister, Escoe, Thomas.

Piedmont (4-1): Anderson, Thackston, League, Patterson, Pickleseimer, Evans, Lee, Smith, Fowler, Johnson, Poole.

Chiquola (0-5): Vaughn, McGaha, Parks, Calvert, Smith, Johnson, Sullivan, Campbell, Sargent.

Williamston (0-6): Browning, Edgins, Elledge, Kelly, Hudgens, Worthy, Hutchinson, Black, Anderson.

Paris Mountain League

Little Texas (8-2): Barton, Harrison, Smith, Crymes, Stepp.

Camperdown (5-1): Gosnell, Hall, Smith, Breazeale, McDowell, Lackey, Gosnell, Kelly.

Traveler's Rest (2-2): Kay, Cunningham, A. Robertson, C. Robertson, League, Knox.

Mills Mill of Greenville (1-1): B. Wilson, J. Wilson, Hill, Crossland, J. Mills.

Central Textile League

Drayton, champions (no records): Powell, McGee, S. Moore, A. O'Sullivan, Carter, Finch, Wright, B. Moore, Fleming, Barnett, Bennett, Reece, Landers.

Glendale (0-1): Gossett, Ammons, Corn, Hunter, Allen, Ogle, Bates, Rhinehart, Quinn, I. Bradley.

Spartanburg County League

Pacolet (10-1): M. Teaster, Holt, White, Patrick, Guyton, Mabry, Harrold, Campbell, Rice, L. Fleming, L. Teaster, Jett, Kirby, Morgan.

Spartan (7-3): Wood, Calvert, Fine, Loyless, Holcombe, Timmons, Lancaster, Shippy, Gowans.

Beaumont (6-4): Fowler, Wilder, R. Prince, Nabors, Green, Bruce, Shook, Holt.

Whitney (6-6): Harvey, Calvert, McAbee, Scruggs, Huskey, Brooks, Hughes, Turner, Rogers, Searcy.

Clifton (5-6): B. Bridges, Oeland, E. Vassey, Mahaffey, J. Vassey, Groce, Willis, Taylor, F. Bridges.

Martel (4-5): Cook, White, Scott, Nolan, C. Bagwell, E. Bagwell, Johnson, Ezell, Parks, I. Henderson.

Inman (3-6): O. Stone, Shehan, Bradley, Prince, J. Stone, Waldrop, Pack, Davis, Laughter.

Arkwright (1-8): A. Varner, Shook, Jennings, Culbreth, Meadows, Dale, Durham, L. Varner, Mabry.

Independent Teams

Oakland (8-2), Drummond, Harry
  Hedgepath, Mims, Donaldson,
  Mims.
Watts (3-3): Clem, Daniel, Bobo, Bar-
  ber, McMillan, Mosely.
Lockhart (2-0): Rines, Allgood, Gar-
  ner, Ellison, Blackwood.
Clinton 2nd Team (2-0): Whitlock,
  Fuller, Vickery.
Mollohon (1-0): Bus Golden,
  Vaughn, Pig Culclasure, Runt
  Hudgins, Earl Hudgins, Leland
  Wood.
Panola (0-1): Cothran, Owens,
  Weathers, McMillan.
Monaghan of Greenville (0-1): Duffy,
  James.
Orr (0-1): Sanders, Ralph Powell,
  Pete Head, Claude Anderson,
  Charlie Hart, Charlie Massey,
  Wallace Deanhart, Will Massey,
  Willie Pilgrim (manager), Clarence
  Buchanan, James Buchanan,
  Mason Evans, Claud Whitten.
Great Falls (0-1): Cooper, Holmes,
  Stewart.
Whitmire (0-1): Yarborough, Wat-
  kins.
Chester (0-1)
Anderson (no records): Bill Tidwell,
  Henry Lee Fillard, Frankie Clark
  Jr., J.T. Brock, Paul Fredericks,
  Monk Honea, Walt Carter, George
  Orr, Duke Honea, Roy Brown,
  McDuffie Ervin.
Valley Falls (0-1)

1929

*Piedmont Textile League — A Sec-
tion:* Henry B. Jones (president)

Brandon of Greenville, champions
  (17-2): Granger, Oliver, Campbell,
  Williams, Roberts, Wilson, Graham,
  Cameron, Foster, Fox, Pitts, Rollins, Owens, Morrow, Osteen, Medlock, Alexander, McGee, Jackson.

Woodside (13-4): O.B. Brookshire,
  Summey, Bowen, Ramey, Carter,
  Owens, Hubert, Elledge, Paxton,
  Horton, J.D. Brookshire.
Judson (11-9): Dodgens, T. Wyatt,
  Smith, Hooper, Barnett, Major,
  Woods, Jones, Hooper, Howell,
  Hall, Elrod, Landers, Tidwell, Bar-
  nett.
Pelham (9-8): Yeargin, Gotshaw, Ar-
  nold.
Monaghan of Greenville (9-8): Hen-
  drix, Landers, Pittman, Tatham,
  Latham, F. League, Herring, Bag-
  well, Roper, Lambright, Christo-
  pher, Hudgens, Fleming, Smith.
Mills Mill of Greenville (7-9): Ingle,
  G. Revis, McCauley, Turner,
  Revis, O. Goss, Massey.
Dunean (6-10): Hudson, Batson,
  Campbell, J. Kelly, Footsie
  Davis.
Renfrew Bleachery (5-9): Batson,
  Breazeale, McMillan, Dan Law-
  rence, Floyd.
Victor of Greer (4-10): Homer,
  F. Heath, Christopher, C. Heath,
  Greer.
Union Bleachery (2-16): Bridwell,
  Brooks, Locker, Smith, Parkins.

Piedmont Textile League — B Section

Southern Power, champions (14-5)
Slater (12-5): Duncan, Ty Cobb,
  Ford, Bailey, B. Lynch, Lybrand,
  M. Lynch, Gilliard, Sizemore,
  Landreth, Abbott, McMillan.
Conestee (10-10): Adams, L. Wilson,
  A. Wilson, Towery, Woodruff.
Poinsett (8-11): Moore, Morgan, Rob-
  inson, Campbell, Smith, Turner,
  McGregory, Dorr, Hancock, Wil-
  liams, Lavender, Harrison.
Sampson (7-8): Crawford, Burgess,
  Cooper, Bowers, Badger, Neely,
  Barton, Lydia, Bridwell, Batson.
Greer (4-14): Kirby, Green, Cox,
  Woodward, F. Green, Harding,
  Timmons, Clayton.

Western Carolina League: Charles Garrison (president), Carl Weimar (vice president), John Garaux (secretary/treasurer)

Tucapau, champions (15-4): Sam Williams, Hugh Smith, Fisher, Mason, Johnson, McAbee, Nixon, Ingle, Taylor, Lavender, Petty.

Lyman (12-7): Bryson, D.K. Smith, Parrish, Smith, Millwood, Query, Tipton, McElrath, Norman, Martin, Ward, Patterson, Aughtry.

Southern Bleachery (11-7): Robinson, Gay, Ray Coker, Joe Childress, Ralph Coker, McElrath, Belcher, Brooks, Hughes, Gay, Pace.

Piedmont (6-11): League, Pack, Patterson, McElrath, Anderson, Allen, George Bartell, Pickleseimer, Phillips.

Pelzer (5-12): D. Crymes, Rogers, Vaughn, Cooper, Westmoreland, B. Crymes, Kelly, Rippy, Moore, Wooten.

Glenwood (0-6): Hudson, F. Owens, Mullinax.

Mid State League

Laurens, champions (15-4): Bud Gettys, Clyde Surratt, Martin, Burgess, Cox, Sam Bagwell, Dave Gettys, Russell, Huff, Barbare, McManaway, P. Barbare, Patton, Kennedy.

Newberry (12-7): Kennedy, Adams, Bouknight, Singley, J. Taylor, G. Taylor, Dennis, Parkinson, Bowman, Billy Rhiel.

Mollohon (11-9): Setzler, Oscar Jones, Hightower, Mims, Stokes, Hudgens, Franklin, Lefty Smith, Dennis, Wood, Howard, Leonhart, Charlie Golden, Donaldson, Adams, Coley Jones.

Clinton (10-11): Trammell, Thornton, Mitchell, Griffin, Campbell, A. Howard, Swink, Caldwell, Bird, O. Howard, Fuller, Hall.

Monarch (9-7): Howell, G. Owens, Shirley, Middlebrook, Morris, Timmons, Hines, Thompson, Adams.

Lydia (8-12): Paul Mosely, Drummond, Fuller, Mosely, Donaldson, Kinard, Burnett, Wheeler, Silvey, Donahue, Bolston, Cox.

Joanna (8-13): Bouknight, Smith, Fuller, Mosely, Flow, Ward, Walker, Sweat, Clark, Ford.

Watts (4-15): Bobo, Barrett, Sealey, Robbins, O. Bobo, Cargill, Sealey, Blanton, Prince, Garrett, Nabors, Large.

Palmetto Textile League

Grendel, champions (15-9): Obannion, Thomas, Cameron, Corley, Padgett, Livingstone, Watkins, Grier, Doolittle, Donahue, Henderson, Betsill, Barnwell, Feaster, Logan, Carpenter, Justus, Burrell, Mosely, Wheeler.

Greenwood (13-8): Drummond, Nally, P. Patterson, Walker, D. Patterson, Hare, Owens, Carson, Morehead, Carithers, Spears, Boswell, Burgess, Stokes, Frye, Johnson, Pack, Barrett.

Ware Shoals (10-14): Ellis, Graham, Gregory, Wright, B. Werner, Jenkins, Clark, George Werner, Lewis Werner, Godfrey, Davis, Chalmers, Dowis.

Ninety Six (6-15): Tice, Attaway, Sanders, Cashion, McGee, Parkinson, Holliday, Fair, Padgett, Clark, W. Bowie, Cannon, Dowis, McAllister, Crymes, Godfrey, Gambrell.

Blue Ridge League

Lonsdale, champions (15-2): Ivester, McDonald, H. Heath, Stevenson, Alexander, Justus, Mason, Leatherwood, Davis, Watson, Cromer, Blackwell, O. Heath.

Alice (5-8): Hendrix, Duncan,

Lemasters, Millwood, Miller, Mullinax, Owens, Snipes, Ferguson.

Autun (4-8): Garrison, Henry Williams, Burdette, Smith, Hopkins, Brooks, Smith, Whitten, Brady, Miles.

Westminster (4-8): Hoot Gibson, Clary, Alvin Gilreath, Davis, Henry Huff, Clark, McManaway, Cashion.

Oconee-Pickens Textile League

Liberty, champions (15-6): Trotter, Hughes, Bagwell, Summey, Smith, Medlock, Chapman, Mullinax.

Walhalla (12-9): Stoddard, Lee, Blackwell, Winkler, Hardin.

Newry (9-11): Walls, Cater, Pater, Harbin, Alexander, Tollison, Carver, Mulkey.

Central (6-15): J.P. Gaines, Lydia, Joe Jones, Ed Wilson, Stancil.

Dixie Textile League: P.C. Hundley (president), Palmer Drummond (secretary/treasurer)

Mills Mill of Woodruff, champions (11-15): A.M. Taylor, Baxter, Harrison, Watson, Childers, Nelson, Westmoreland, Page, Fowler, Brady, Godfrey, Hostetler, Batson, Brewington, Swink, Phillips, Cooper, Frady, Thomas, Wilder, Benton, Crymes, Ingle, Craig.

Simpsonville (12-9): Childers, Bunton, Jones, Boatwright, Tolbert, Ingram, Ingles, Thomas, McManaway, Smith, Marchbanks, E. Barbare, Westmoreland, Mason.

Brandon of Woodruff, (10-10): F.G. McAbee, Craig, Brewington, Thornton, Crim, Swink, Nelson, Roebuck, Giles, Hill, Blackwell, Gibson, Westmoreland, Rogers, Hawkins, Angel, Sealey, Smith.

Enoree (10-10): Rhodes, Westmoreland, Wolfe, Davenport, Swink, Gentry, Nabors, McGee, Watson, Nelson.

Central League

Drayton, champions (no records): Howell, Cox, Cutter, Hill, Cameron, B. Moore, Prince, S. Moore, Bennett, Finley, Nash, Carter, Byrd, R. Moore, Ray.

Spartanburg County League

Pacolet, champions (12-1): Harrold, Jett, Mabry, T. Holt, Morgan, Rice, White, Teaster, Fleming, Campbell, Patrick, Petty, Cook.

Arcadia (8-4): Ellis Forrester, Jay Blacksville, Coot Gilbert, Clark, M. West, B. West, Rowe, Kirby, Cothran, Bailey, Parrott, Turner, Bridgeman, O. West, Cauthen, Garner.

Inman (8-4): O. Stone, Prince, Pack, Thompson, J. Stone, Waldrop, Pike, Parris, Lauter.

Whitney (8-4): Gunter, Turner, Barnett, Eubanks, Holt, Gossett, R. Reed, Thompson, Morgan, Wright, Massey, Pruitt, Cowell, Henderson, Padgett, Hughes, Huskey, Searcy, Hammett, Vaughn.

Beaumont (5-9): R. Prince, Fowler, Bruce, Green, West, Wilder, H. Powell, Shook, H. Prince, R. Powell, Parton, Splawn, Waters, Kirby, Lawrence.

Clifton (4-8): E. Vassey, Mahaffey, Oeland, Groce, Calvert, Dearyberry, Bridges, Brown, Dorn.

Arkwright (4-10): Parks, Shook, Pearson, Kelly, Godfrey, Jennings, Dale, V. Trail, Walden, Meadows, A. Varner, L. Chapman, J. Mabry, Quinn, C. Poteat, H. Poteat, P. Cooper.

Spartan (1-11): Shipley, Fine, Bullington, Fowler, Gowan, Steadings, Posey, Bright, Burrell, Ross, Worley, Henson, Sawyer, Green, Wood, Taylor, Timmons, Roland, Loyless.

Anderson County League

Orr, champions (17-6): Lee Whitten, Hart, Revels, Powell, Hart, McAllister, Jerry Whitten, Dumb Price, Kirby, Buchanan, Mulkey, Tommy Lyons, McLeskey, L. Powell, McAllister.

Gluck (12-8): R. Allen, H. Allen, F. Tabors, C. Ripley, Reid Blackstone, Dick Sweetenburg, Dawson, Dean, H. Davis, Mosely, Weathers, Hughes, Tillotson.

Gossett (12-8): S. Orr, G. Orr, Fuller, Pearson, Ivester, Chandler, Wilson, Alewine, Spear, English, Bradley, Chamblee, D. Pearson, Putman, Chapman, F. Pearman.

Belton (9-8): Stephens, Fisher, Orr, Bannister, Thompson, Madden, R. Owens, Vance Escoe, Shockley, O. Owens, Kay, Willingham, C. Owens.

Anderson (5-13): Williams, Clark, Dillard, Simpson, M. Honea, Erwin, Kelly, D. Honea, D. Fredricks, Meeks, B. Fredricks, Fretwell, Owens, Brock, Brown, Bone, Wise, Jones, Keaton, Daniel, Tidwell, Spear, Ramsey, Yarborough.

Equinox (2-15): Davis, Smith, Taylor, Foster, Beck, Stewart, Mullinax, Edwards, Watson, Applehite, Gillespie, Boyd, Fredricks, Simpson, McAllister, Harbin, Cooley.

Central Carolina League

Grendel #2, champions (no records): Pearl Austin, Babe Betsil, Dog Obannion, Kay Burrell, Tobe Livingston, Shine Carpenter, Duncan, Paul Mosely, Clyde Cameron, Eb Corley, Feaster, Red Watkins, Jim Young.

Independent Teams

Jackson of Iva (15-2): Jordan, Hamilton, Pitts, Jordan, Davis, Jordan, Baskin, Millwood, Jordan, Hamby, McCoy, Burdette.

Orr 2nd Team (4-1)

Orr 3rd Team (3-0)

Anderson 2nd Team (2-2)

Appleton 3rd Team (2-2)

Lockhart (1-0): Cudd, Vandeford, Cabiness, Mathes, Farr, Gunn.

Equinox 2nd Team (1-0)

Belton 2nd Team (1-0)

Equinox 3rd Team (1-1)

Baldwin (0-1): Bailey, Richardson.

Arial (0-1)

Riverside 3rd Team (0-2)

Riverside 2nd Team (0-2)

Appleton 2nd Team (0-3)

Southern Weaving (no records): Tom Armstrong, H.H. McCall, Haselwood McCall, James Carson, Darwin Carson, Toy Wright, Herman Garrett, Will Gardner, R.W. Sports, A.L. Storey, W.L. Jefferson, T.C. Powell, Jack Fureron, William Rollins, James Gregory.

1930

Piedmont Textile League — A Section: Harry B. Jones (president)

Dunean, champions (16-6): Kelly, Kay Cashion, Henderson, Emerson Cashion, L. Wood, Campbell, Huff, Howell, Smith, Christopher, Jones.

Slater (12-8): Bailey, McMakin, Lance, Fortner, Root, Duncan, Lynch, Phillips, Moody, Bradley.

Southern Power (12-8): Not a South Carolina mill.

Union Bleachery (11-8): Marchbanks, Turner, Hawkins, Harrison, Ivey, Brooks, G. Turner, Bridwell, Brooks, Parkins, Coggins, Belcher.

Woodside (8-10): J. Brookshire, Bowen, Herbert, Carter, Ellenburg, O. Brookshire, Brown, Rainey.

Mills Mill of Greenville (7-11): Ingle, Britten, Revis, Few, Abbott,

R. Smith, Rogers, J. Smith, Coggins, McCauley, E. Smith.

Monaghan of Greenville (7-13): Bagwell, Waldrop, Pittman, Hendrix, Henson, Coleman, Christopher, F. Smith, Roper.

Judson (5-14): Wyatt, Williams, Lander, Hall, Hooper, Dorn, Oliver, Campbell, Kelly, Trammell, Bowen, Gotshaw.

Piedmont Textile League — B Section

Sampson, champions (15-5): Duncan, Bridwell, Badger, R. Morgan, Mauldin, Carter, Harp, Crawford, Neely, F. Morgan, Major.

Renfrew Bleachery (14-7): Batson, Robertson, Roberts, Robinson, Fox, Strawn, Floyd.

Poinsett (14-7): Campbell, Moore, Floyd, Williams, Gamble, Lavender, Robertson, Robinson, Morgan, Cole, Roberts.

Williamston (7-12): Kelly, Hudgens, Black, Miller, Ripply, Anderson, Worthy, Campbell.

Poe (6-10): Sides, Cooper, Brookshire, Roper, Christopher, Waldrop, Huggins, League, Brookshire, Harrison, Lee, Hairston.

Southern Worsted (2-15): Knox, Clement, Waldrop, Snipes, Gallagher, Snyder, Walton, Vess.

Pelham (1-1): Poole, Mason.

Western Carolina League

Tucapau, champions (19-4): Brannon, Fisher, Pace, Johnson, H. Smith, B. Ingle, West, Brown, McAbee.

Southern Bleachery (12-9): Roy Coker, Childers, Robertson, Belcher, Robinson, Yeargin, Coker, Hughes, McElrath.

Pelzer (12-11): Woods, Vaughn, L. Crymes, Holliday, Westmoreland, Escoe, P. Crymes, Roberts, McConnell, Ross, Bobo, Eden, Wooten.

Piedmont (11-14): Dill, McElrath, Henry, Bartell, Hooper, Crowley, Anderson, Fowler, Strand, Leverette, Belcher, Addison, Bennett, Patterson, Patterson, Poole, Prince.

Lonsdale (8-12): Stevenson, W. Heath, Ivester, Watson, Leopard, Golightly, Jackson, Brookshire, H. Heath, Mize, C. Heath.

Liberty (3-16): Clark, Hooper, Bagwell, Chapman, Hughes, Barnett, Burdette, Medlock, Revis, Leopard, Smith, Lowell, Reeves, Thrasher, Rogers, Alexander, Johnson, Frederick, Gaines, Keaton, Hester, Victor.

Brandon of Greenville (1-1): Clay, Lynch.

Easley Textile League: G.L. Alston (president), Johnson Sims (vice president), M.L. Lesley (secretary)

Glenwood (10-2): Lee, Alexander, Owens, League, Spearman.

Arial (8-3): Lawrence, Masters, Roper, Matthews, Massarus, Stokes, Rampey, Thompson, Turpin, Turner.

Alice (7-7): Dodgens, Ferguson, Duncan, Hendrix, Reid, Breazeale, Rice, Reese.

Easley (1-11): Waldrop, Campbell, Waldrop, Hester, Owens, McWhorter, Patterson, Trammell.

Palmetto Textile League

Ninety Six, champions (11-8): Surratt, Sanders, Hartley, Godfrey, Gambrell, Pace, Padgett, Smith, Yeargin, Attaway, Shores.

Greenwood (12-6): Carithers, Morehead, Arnold, Smith, Byrd, Bolton, Burgess, Monroe, Mooneyham, Nally, Walker, Boyd, Davenport, Hinton.

Grendel (7-10): Corley, Livingston, Anderson, Singleton, Thomas, Carter, Jenkins, Wright, Graham,

Bigham, Henderson, Jordan, Mosely, Gaines, Cameron, Lyles, Bowie, Hancock.

Ware Shoals (6-13): Attaway, Elledge, Graham, Sanders, Weaver, Clark, Cudd, Wilson, Stafford, Bartell, Corley, Gregory, Newberry, Hanna, Wright, Williams, Jenkins, B. Werner, George Werner, Chalmers, Stewart.

Palmetto B Textile League

Ware Shoals (no records)
Abbeville (no records)
Chiquola (no records)
Ninety Six (no records)

Mid State League

Oakland, champions (18-5): Manning Bagwell, Harry Hedgepath, Doolittle, Caldwell, Lumon, Stokes, Bowers, Pee Wee Franklin, Bodie, Smith, Hines, Lowman, W. Heavener, Drummond, S. Bagwell, Thomas, C. Dennis, Andy Bowen (manager), Timmerman, Bouknight.

Whitmire (14-7): Patterson, Andy Peterson, Jett, Lewis, Ruff, Donaldson, Howard, Smith, Hightower, Culclasure, Yarborough, Raines.

Joanna (11-10): Bouknight, Ward, Homer, Howard, Rolfe, Clark, Dickey, Barnett, Holloway, Holliday, Farr, Vaughn, Langley, Brunton, Gotshaw, Marshall, Donaldson, Bolton.

Mollohon (10-9): Pee Wee Franklin, Coley Jones, Proctor, Doolittle, Oscar Jones, Setzler, Martin, Epting, Charlie Golden, Jimmy Sowell, Grove.

Newberry (8-10): Dunk Singley, Dave Bouknight, Patterson, Adams.

Monarch (8-11): Hines, Morris, Middlebrook, Blakely, Keteal, Howell, Cogdill, Smith, Knox, Lawrence,

McClain, Gotshaw, Adams, Middlebrook.

Clinton (8-13): Trammell, Silvey, Thornton, Swink, Franklin, Brown, McKinney, Fuller, Cashion, Whitlock, Smith.

Laurens (3-15): Sanders, Martin, Adkins, Townsend, Epting, Cox, Adams, Simmons, Crumley, Razor, Wolfe, Coleman, Culbertson, Johns, Johnston, Walters, Caldwell, Owens, Bunton, Thackston, Prince, Nabors.

East Greenville League

Piedmont (1-0)
Dunean (1-0)
Pelzer (1-1): Edens, McConnell.
Fork Shoals (1-2): Meeks, Thompson, Ward.

Blue Ridge League

Newry (13-1): Cater, Lindsay, Waids, Volke, Carver, McIntyre, McClelland, Alexander, Garner.

Westminster (5-8): C. Crump, Reid, Camp, Lee, Powell, S. Crump, Willis, McGuffey.

Walhalla (4-9): Williams, Hunnicutt, Campbell, Garrett, Smith, Epps, Elliott, Cantrell, Gilliard, Blackwell.

Central (3-8): Cox, James, Wilson, Lyda, Littleton, Burnette, Cothran.

Anderson County League

LaFrance, champions (9-4): Holcombe, Darby, F. Hopkins, D. Hopkins, R. Smith, Garrett, Lattimer, Simpson, J. Smith, Williams, McAbee, Campbell, Haskin, Garrison, Poore.

Belton (7-6): Stephens, Fisher, Bannister, R. Owens, Shirley, S. Owens, Thompson, Shockley, O. Owens, R. Madden, L. Madden, Jones, Shirley.

Jackson of Iva (6-5); withdrew. C. Jordan, Rogers, Hamilton,

S. Jordan, G. Jordan, Baskin,
Davis, Burdette, R. Jordan.
Chiquola (3-8); withdrew. Tice,
Moore, Bowie, Davis, Lollis,
R. Calvert, G. Calvert, Moore,
Duckett, Beacham, Ferguson,
J. Coleman.

Anderson City League

Gossett, champions (15-8): Bradley,
S. Orr, Pearson, G. Orr, Tinsley,
Ivester, Bobo, Chandler, Chap-
man, L. Smith, Summey, Powell,
Smith.
Appleton (13-8): Williams, Moore, A.
Hall, Cargill, C. Hall, Tidwell, T.
Daniel, McCann, C. Daniel,
Ramsey, Freeman, McElrath,
Barnett.
Gluck (12-9): Coot Allen, McLeskey,
Dick Sweetenburg, Withers, Tillot-
son, Dobson, Tabors, Reid Black-
stone, Walker, Manley, Williams,
Ripley, Hughes.
Orr (8-9): Hart, Jerry Whitten, Lee
Whitten, Dumb Price, McAllister,
Buchanan, Mulkey, Powell, Bevel,
Thomas, Ashworth, Mosely, Claud
Whitten, Massey, Barnes, Troy
Kirby, Frith, McClain, Thomason,
Roy Coffee, Claude Anderson,
Ayers, Doutt, Buck.
Anderson (8-11): Saxon, Dinah Simp-
son, Dillard, Bone, Erwin, Wil-
liams, Frank Keaton, Duke Honea,
Fredricks, George Jeffcoat, Sam
Kidd, George Ivester, Thomas Car-
ter, Mack Kidd, Carl Ripley, J.B.
Spearman, George Derrinbacker,
Barney Smith, Milt Cooper, Kirby
Higbe, K.K. Outzs, Ed Carter, Jim
Cathcart, George Carter.
Equinox (5-14): Browning, Gillespie,
Beck, Thrasher, Davis, Taylor,
Watson, Cooley, Mullinax, N.
Cooley, Bishop.

Spartanburg County League

Lockhart, champions (14-2): M. Black-

wood, Burns, Allison, C. Lank-
ford, Crocker, Gunn, W. O'Dell,
E. O'Dell, Smith, Lambright,
C. Blackwood, Allgood, R. Blair,
H. Blair, Woodall.
Whitney (11-6): Scruggs, Padgett,
Hughes, McAbee, Burnett, Har-
vey, Searcy, J. Morgan, Huskey,
J. Holt, Gossett, Rogers, Caldwell,
Reid.
Pacolet (9-6): Jett, Petty, Fulmer,
Mabry, Harrold, Campbell, L. Mor-
gan, Fleming, L. Teaster, White,
Patrick, M. Teaster.
Clifton (8-5): Hughes, E. Vassey, Jim
Vassey, B. Bridges, McCarley, Cal-
vert, Mahaffey, Giles, F. Bridges,
Orr, Taylor.
Arcadia (8-6): Sedberry, Corn, Clark,
Cothran, Johnson, B. West, M. West,
Bennett, Cannon, Turner, Bridge-
man, Hilton, Bogan, Gossett, Upton,
Waters, Franklin.
Arkwright (5-10): Parks, Shook, Jen-
nings, Pearson, Godfrey, Mead-
ows, Fowler, Brown, Kelly, Smith,
Pless, Sparks, Brewington, E. King,
C. King, Cooper, Barber, Knox,
McAbee.
Spartan (3-11): Wood, Henson, God-
frey, Allen, Petty, Timmons,
Gunter, Chapman, Lands, Mooney-
ham, Lynch.
Beaumont (2-12): Parton, Powell,
Shook, Nabors, Cline, Holt,
Green, Fowler, Smith, Ruth, Rush,
Kirby, Splawn, West, Prince.

Independent Teams

Belton (5-1): Madden, Owens, Shock-
ley, Burgess.
Lydia (2-0): Cato, Martin, Burnette.
Simpsonville (2-0): Cooper.
Orr 2nd Team (2-0): Williams,
Moore, A. Hall, Cargill, C. Hall,
Tidwell, T. Daniel, McCann,
C. Daniel, Ramey, Freeman.
Conestee (2-1): A. Wilson, Adams,
Hawkins.

Piedmont Plush (1-0): Vickery, Morgan.

Mills Mill of Woodruff (1-1): Few, Tucker, Chandler.

Orr 3rd Team (1-1)

Appleton 3rd Team (1-1)

Watts (0-1): Smith, Prince.

Brandon of Greenville (0-1): Foster, Whitmire.

Cowpens (0-1)

Fairmont (0-1)

Appleton 2nd Team (0-2): Spake, Daniels, H. White, Landis, C. Hall, Dooley, B. Spake, Hendrix, Spears, Edwards, Duncan.

Limestone (no records): Harlow, Ramsey, Sullivan, Eubanks, Seates, Martin, Huey, Phillips.

Drayton (no records): Cameron, Nash, Carter, Hill, S. Moore, Johnson, B. Moore, Ray, Finley.

1931

Easley Textile League

Arial, champions (11-4): Masters, F. Turpin, Paul Rampey, J. Leslie, Pitts, B. Leslie, Pace, Porter, Chapman, Masters, Perry Rampey.

Pickens (11-4): Roper, Pace, Pace, Howell, Adams, Dillard, Riggins.

Glenwood (10-1): League, Snag Owens, Sam Owens, Hester, L. Alexander, J.B. Spearman, Williams, Pridmore, B. Chapman, C. Alexander, G. Hudson, D. Fortner.

Easley (7-5): Campbell, Waldrop, Gillespie, Ledford, Galloway.

Brandon (4-6): Couch, Von Halen, Lynch, Foster, Giles, Roberts.

Liberty (3-9): Garrison, Hughes, Bagwell, Stevenson, Medlock.

Alice (2-10): Duncan, Dodgens, Williams, Lawrence, Austin, Day, Hendrix, Reese, Breazeale, Walker, Holcombe, Holden, Davis.

Poe (1-10): Hairston, Roper, Sides, Juber Hairston, Hensley, Cooper,

Hammett, Hudgens, Dixon, Brookshire, Gibson, Gibson.

Mid State League

Monarch, champions (16-5): Knox, Howell, Morris, Adams, Owens, Middlebrooks, Moore, Littlejohn, Hines.

Joanna (12-7): Bouknight, Benton, Girk, Prince, Godfrey.

Whitmire (10-8): Yarborough, Thompson, Ruff, Raines, Durham, Lewis, Matthews, Hare, Ward, Stevenson.

Mollohon (9-10): Pee Wee Franklin, Dennis, Drummond, Twin, Bagwell, Lowman, Hare, Morris, Doolittle, Martin, Bishop, McClary.

Watts (8-10): Prince, Knight, Nabors, Gosnell, Culbertson, French, Spoon, Shirley, Robbins, Soggie, W. Cox, B. Cox, Surratt.

Newberry (2-16): Dunk Singley, Brennan, Ward, Tobe Livingston, Hamilton, Dave Bouknight, Shirley.

Central Carolina League

Clinton, champions (11-4): Claude Trammell, Emerson Cashion, Arthur Howard (manager), Red Watkins, Hill, Wyatt, Mosely, Harvell, P.S. Bailey, Gene Richburg, Dean, Paul Martin, Webb Cashion, Beck Fuller, Casper Hallman, Bone.

Enoree (8-7): Rhodes, Watson, Benson, Betsil, Wilson, Thornton, Doyle, Owens, Smith, Rainey, Shippey, Waddell, Phillips, McGee, Blanton, Williams, Gentry.

Laurens (7-7): Waldrop, Chumley, Chesney, Snyder, Godshaw, Bagwell, Cox, Carlton, Surratt, Hedgepath, Smith.

Lydia (3-11): Cato, Burdette, Emery, Masters, Silvey, Godfrey, Abrams, Sealy, Fuller, Giles.

Southern Textile League

Poinsett, champions (16-4): Campbell, Morgan, Robinson, Crisp, Hendrix, Nabors.

Pelham (14-7): Arnold, Tillison, Duncan, Poole, Cox, Satterfield.

Monaghan of Greenville (12-6): B. Smith, Hendrix, Bagwell, Smith, Wiggins, Waldrop.

Southern Worsted (10-10): S. Knox, F. Knox, Lackey, Waldrop, Snipes, DeShields, Blakely.

Renfrew Bleachery (9-10): Dobson, Robertson, Batson, Fox, Morris.

Union Bleachery (6-4): Ivey, Marchbanks, Brooks, Hawkins, Bridwell, Gaffney.

Simpsonville (6-13): Childers, Calvert, Barbery, Wilson, Barbare, Jones.

Southern Print (5-12): Kirby, Keeler, Fowler, Vardry, Meisenheimer, Christopher, Hughes.

Blue Ridge League

Lonsdale (3-0): Stoddard, Blackwell, Alexander, C. Heath.

Westminster (2-1): Cashion, Revis, McGuffin, Crump, Dickerson.

Newry (1-2): Burdette, Carver, Tollison, Schaeffer.

Walhalla (0-3): Watson, Alexander, Stevenson, Hanes, Stoddard, Blackwell, Campbell, Bagwell.

Sampson (5-13): Lynch, Morgan, Mauldin, Major, Crawford, Smith, Belts, Batson, Black, Bean, Tabors, Badger, Crymes, Williams, Osteen, Heaton, Foster, Sexton, McCauley, Harbin, Quinn.

Easley (no records): Humphries, Merck, Campbell, J. Waldrop, L. King, H. Waldrop, Gillespie, O. Waldrop, J. Owens, L. Waldrop, Galloway, McCoy, Cody.

Western Carolina League

Duke Power, champions (14-6)

Southern Bleachery (16-4): Brown, Roy Coker, J.D. Childers, H. Heath, Hughes, Gay, J. Childers, Robinson, Yeargin, C. Heath, Pace, Ralph Coker.

Mills Mill of Greenville (12-18): Hines, Silvey, Ingle, Abbott, Patterson, Craig, Smith, Revis, Jett, Few, Godfrey, Brewington, Littlejohn.

Tucapau (8-9): Fred McAbee, Odell Mason, Slim Smith, Babe Fisher, Jordan, Granger, Allen West, Swift Allen, Sam Williams, Joe Lavender, Tweddie Hill, Pat Ingle, Carol Smith (manager), D.M. Nixon, Doc Taylor, Tack Johnson.

Pelzer (8-9): Holliday, Lefty Crymes, Rogers, Vaughn, Moore, Ellison, Humphries, Jett, Escoe, Sargent, McCombs, Cannon, Johnson, Southern, Westmoreland.

Piedmont (3-13): League, Patterson, Bennett, McElrath, Lee, Tice, D.K. Smith, Anderson, McAbee, Allen, Poole, Bryson, Fowler.

Piedmont Textile League

Slater, champions (9-3): J.M. Bailey, A.B. McMakin, D.W. Wilson, J.A. Lybrand, Charles Henson, E.B. Osteen, C.C. Vaughn, Broadus Abbott, C.B. Vaughn, C.R. Barton.

Judson (6-4): Godshaw, Trammell, Oliver, Jim Hall, Dunn, Dodd, Mahon.

Dunean (5-6): Kelly, Wood, Hudson, Grubbs, Christopher, Howell, Floyd, Campbell.

Woodside (3-9): Whitmire, Whitmire, Morris, Brookshire, Hubbard, Moore, Elledge, Herbert.

Williamston (2-9): Ripley, Kelly, Black, Miller, Hudgens, Burns, Holliday.

Palmetto League

Greenwood (13-7): Frye, Corley, Byrd, Couch, Arnold, Shippey, Walker.

Grendel (7-7): Doolittle, Livingston, Brigham, Timmerman, Passety, Willingham, Mosely, Dixon, Outzs, Hedgepath, Busbee, Granger.

Ninety Six (7-10): Shores, Godfrey, Sanders, Smith, Attaway.

Ware Shoals (6-9): Spires, Graham, Stewart, Newberry, Outzs, Jenkins, Wright, Simmons.

Greenville County League

Dunean (11-4)
Piedmont Plush (8-7)
Fork Shoals (8-7)
Gantt (8-7)
Slater (6-8)
Judson (3-11)

Spartanburg County League

Pacolet, champions (12-3): Holt, Campbell, Harrold, White, Petty, Goforth, Ellison, L. Teaster, Harrell, Fulmer, Jett, Mabry, Morgan, Fleming.

Drayton (11-4): McIntyre, Cameron, Johnson, Mosely, Cothran, Carter, Finley, Taylor, Ray, Reese, Burgess, S. Moore, Arnold, McGee, B. Moore.

Inman (8-5): Justus, Nash, Pack, Prince, Davis, Parker, Lawter, Johnson, Parris, Thompson, Cothran.

Whitney (6-6): Scruggs, Huskey, J. Holt, Hughes, McAbee, O. Holt, J. Morgan, D. Morgan, Pearson, Reese, Padgett.

Arkwright (6-6): Parks, Allen, Godfrey, Kelly, Varner, Brown, Meadows, Walden, Watson, F. Fowler.

Spartan (5-8): Mooneyham, Steadings, Taylor, Fine, Loyless, Angel, Timmons, Wood, Lancaster, McAbee, Roland, Henson, Fowler.

Clifton (4-9): J. Vassey, Giles, Mahaffey, Groce, E. Vassey, McCarley, Hughes, Albright, Barber.

Beaumont (1-12): Rush, Kirby, Green, West, Fowler, Sanders, Guy, Waters, Powell.

Spartanburg Mid-County League

Arcadia, champions (no records): M. West, Cohen, Cothran, R. West, Veal, Rowe, Cannon, Clark, Turner, O. West.

Anderson County League

Appleton, champions (17-2): Al Williams, Clay Moore, Bill Tidwell, Snag McAllister, Shike Cargill, A. Hall, Guy Willie Powell, J.A. McElrath, R.B. Speares, Coffice Hall, Orr, Irvin Sexton, McMaster, Cooley, Garnett Dooley, Coffee Hall.

Anderson (11-8): Alexander, Tinsley, Pitts, Dillard, Owens, Keaton, Fredricks, Spearman, Ivester, Simpson, Yarborough, Thompson, Ripley, Eaton, S. Orr, Hendrix, Brown.

Gluck (10-11): McLeskey, Allen, Weathers, Ripley, Reid Blackstone, Dick Sweetenburg, Walker, Smith, Tabors, N. Sweetenburg, Mosely, Wood, Moore, Dawson, Sam Jordan, R. Jordan, Price.

Orr (7-12): Dude Buchanan, Jerry Whitten, Dumb Price, Burch, Lee Whitten, L. Hart, Thomason, Anderson, Cooper, Chapman, McAllister, Revel, Ashworth, Thrift.

Gossett (6-11): S. Orr, Pearson, G. Orr, Putnam, Ivester, Crymes, Davenport, D. Smith, Chandler, E. Smith, Ripley, Ayers, Sexton, Mosely, Hunnicutt, Saxon, D. Fortner, Alewine, C. Fortner, Shirley.

Belton (6-13): S. Owens, McCoy, Thompson, R. Owens, Escoe, Deanhart, O. Owens, Smith, Shockley, Bannister, Stevens, Burgess, Hanna, Myers.

Catawba Textile League

Lockhart (no records): Burns, Gunn,
O'Dell, C. Blackwood, H. Blair,
R. Blair, M. Blackwood, Hill,
Smith, Farr.
Clover (no records): Carver, McCall,
S. Hammett, R. Hammett, Wilson,
Ryan, Moore, Bell, Kirk.

Independent Teams

Mollohon 2nd Team (no records):
Sam Mills, Cal Duncan, Giles
Kirby.
York (no records): Taft Wright.

1932

Anderson County League

Anderson, champions (14-8): J.B.
Spearman, Sam Kidd, Carl Ripley,
Hancock, Hendrix, Morgan, Dinah
Simpson, Dillard, Mack Kidd,
Evans, Duke Honea, Cole, Ellison
Ivester, Frank Keaton, Jordan,
Jack Derrinbacker, Barney Smith,
Kirby Higbe, Kenneth Outzs, W.E.
Carter (manager), George Jeffcoat,
Roy Cooper.
Orr (13-7): L. Hart, Lyons, Lee Whit-
ten, Heath, Sanders, Thomason,
Barnes, Ashworth, Smith, Frith,
Jerry Whitten, Dude Buchanan,
Croxton.
LaFrance (13-9): Darby, Allen,
Simmons, F. Hopkins, D. Hop-
kins, Lattimer, Williams, A. Gar-
rison, W. Garrison, J. Smith,
Johnson, Medlock, Simpson,
Jason.
Appleton (13-9): Moore, Fisher,
Tidwell, Sexton, Williams, C. Hall,
A. Hall, McElrath, Spear, Spake,
Powell, Fredrick, McAllister, Bai-
ley, Saxon.
Gluck (11-9): Buchanan, McLeskey,
Allen, Reid Blackstone, Manley,
N. Sweetenburg, Tabors, Moore,
Walker, Dick Sweetenburg,

Barnes, Early Hanna, Nally,
Hughes, Weathers, Perry.
Gossett (9-9): S. Orr, Tinsley, Daw-
son, Chapman, Ivester, G. Orr,
Pearson, Smith, Chamblee,
Shirley, Ingle, Werner, Sexton.
Equinox (4-9): R. Davis, McAllister,
E. Mullinax, Beck, Harbin, Jeanes,
Pelfrey, Watson, Craft, Taylor,
O. Mullinax.
Belton (1-17): Smith, Thompson,
Patterson, R. Owens, Deanhart,
Escoe, S. Owens, O. Owens, Shock-
ley, Bannister, Nelson, Stevens,
Burgess.
Jackson of Iva (1-0); withdrew.
C. Jordan, G. Jordan, Sam Jordan,
Price, McCoy, Powell, R. Jordan,
Baskin, Helms, Whitten,
Hartgrove.

Spartanburg County League

Drayton, champions (15-3): Burgess,
Inman, Carter, Bagwell, Bragg,
Benson, Moore, Johnson, Hines,
Ray, Parks, Nash, Cox, Landers.
Pacolet (11-7): Teaster, Morris, Jett,
Long, Harrold, Campbell, Parks,
Petty, Fleming, Fulmer, Mabry,
Lee, Scott, Goforth, A. Littlejohn,
Hodge, J. Littlejohn, Cogdill, Mor-
gan, Ellison, White, Osment.
Lyman (11-7): Cannon, Barbare, Au-
ghtry, Bryson, Smith, Crook, Par-
ris, Sargent, Yeargin, Gibson,
Johnson, Parks, Burgess, Hines,
West, Howard.
Beaumont (9-9): Veal, M. West,
Moore, H. West, Johnson, Fowler,
McIntyre, Poteat, A. West, Wil-
liams, Aughtry, Bryson, Cannon,
Barbare, Cotner, B. West, Drake.
Whitney (8-10): Thackston, Scruggs,
Ridgeway, Holt, Owens, McAbee,
Arnold, Boland, Kelly, Shippey.
Inman (5-13): Epply, Inman, O. Par-
ris, Hawkins, Justus, Mason,
Davis, Pack, Crocker, Ramsey,
Lawter, Seay, Cothran.

Fairmont (no records): Farmer, Gibson, Morrow, Blackwell, Cannon, Belcher, Fortenberry, Turner, Branch, Cothran, Painter.

Crescent (no records): Mabry, Little, Jennings, Kelly, Mahaffey, Griffin, Potts, Poteat, McCullough, Bean, Smith, Lussardt, Allen, McCraw.

Glendale (no records): Harris, Porter, Allen, Wood, Littlejohn, Corn, Allen, Suttles, Rhinehart.

Saluda Textile League

Chiquola, champions (11-3): Werner, Beacham, Shaw, Calvert, Harvey, Campbell, Virgil Stallcup, Keisler, Davis, Blackmon, Ferguson, Ashley, Simmons, Davis.

Pelzer #1 (2-2): Holliday, Sims, Alverson, Byars, Ellison, Emery, Ross, Long, Vickery, Davis, Land, Frier, DeShard, Brown, Smith, Ellison.

Pelzer #4 (no records): Sargent, Wooten, Wilson, Alexander, Lefty Crymes, Galloway, Davis, Humphries.

Conestee (1-2): A. Tucker, Evette, B. Vaughn, L. Wilson, A. Wilson, L. Lowery, W. Vaughn, Ducher, J. Tucker, F. Tucker, G. Tucker, S. Tucker, Shaver.

Williamston (0-3): Holcombe, Anderson, Cannon, Black, Hayes, Kelly, Coffey, Stone, Ripley, Burns, Miller.

Piedmont (0-3): Martin, H. Dill, Bolding, R. Dill, Underwood, Fleming, Barnett, Werner, Rampey, Collins, Gilreath, F. Bolding.

Palmetto League

Ware Shoals, champions (8-6): Werner, Clark, Wright, Proctor, Graham, Eubanks, Sanders, Newberry, Gould, Spires, Williams.

Greenwood (5-4): Hare, Ellis, Bolton, Arnold, Lyles, Lines, Helms, Dennis.

Mathews (4-5): Stokes, Hedgepath, Jordan, Pitts, Doolittle, Gaines, Yeargin, Boyd, Shippey.

Ninety Six (4-7): Garrison, Creekmore, Davis, Sanders, Riley, Surratt, Wooten, Attaway, Bannister, Boyd, Hedgepath, Helms, Burns.

Clinton (1-0): Whitlock, Wilbanks.

Grendel (0-1): Shirley, Wilson.

Mid State League

Joanna, champions (no records): Gus Barrett, Charlie Girk, Olga Hair, Bruce Galloway, Gene Abrams, Clarence Godfrey, Charlie Coleman, Harry Barrett, Hunk Bouknight, Ernest Sweatt, Raymond Abrams, Rolfe Clark.

Monarch (1-0): J. Phillips, R. Phillips, Owens, Littlejohn, Cotner, Timmons, Gallman, Middlebrooks, Shirley, Cogdill, Sims, Nabors, Knox, Morris.

Lockhart (1-1): Burns, O'dell, M. Blackwell, R. Blackwell, C. Blackwell, H. Blair, Fair, Vandeford, Hill, Lemaster, Allgood, Osmint, Highsmith.

Buffalo (no records)

Eureka (no records)

Piedmont Textile League

Renfrew Bleachery, champions (15-3): Johnny Foxx, Claude Batson, Fred Foster, Fletcher Heath, Chick Heath, Lefty Brown, Sam Knox, Ode Medlock, Ted Cabiness, Shag Knox, George Lindsay, Chester Eddy, Roy Foster, Roy Hogg, Ray Humphries, James Bishop, Suddeth.

Mills Mill of Greenville (13-7): Lynch, G. Revis, O. Revis.

Monaghan of Greenville (12-8): Herring, Waldrop, Sanders.

Judson (12-8): P. Wyatt.

Dunean (11-9): Hinson, Floyd, Campbell.

Slater (8-11): Jim Bailey, C. Vaughn, Duncan.

Union Bleachery (3-15): Hawkins, Smith, Brooks.

Sampson (3-17): Crymes, Morgan, Major, Fowler.

Catawba League

Lancaster, champions (no records): Bobby Leonard, Gabby West, Ralph Williams (manager), Holt Lamb, John Bumgardner, Tyler Dewar, Ikie Reeder, Shorty Brian, Al Veach, M.J. Wright, Maxey Welch, Henry Clough, Taft Wright, Gene Belue.

Rock Hill Bleachery (no records)

Aragon (no records)

Great Falls (no records)

Baldwin (no records)

Winnsboro Royal Cords (no records)

Mills Mill of Woodruff (no records): Jack Taylor, Talmadge Craig, Tommy Thomas, Earl Timmons, Walker Campbell, Furman Bragg, Herbert Garrett, Clyde Frady, Eric Craig, Lee Ormand, Odell Stone, Red Swink.

Big Six League

Joanna, champions (13-8): Bouknight, Girk, Coleman, Godfrey.

Mollohon (13-7): Franklin, McIntyre, Ward, Sowell, Setzler, Jones, Golden.

Watts (11-8): Prince, Knight, Byrd, Surratt, Cox.

Newberry (8-12): Jones, Bouknight, Hamilton, Stokes, Singley.

Lydia (7-13): Cato, Giles, Fuller, Girk, Lowd, Emory, Burnette, Abrams, Jones, Alexander, Drummond, Bridwell.

Enoree (6-11): Dixon, Dixon, Trammell, Cox, Thornton, Rhodes, Nelson.

Western Carolina League

Pelzer, champions (13-10): Fayonsky, Crymes, Escoe, Vaughn, Buntin, Pitts, Woods, Heath, Westmore-

land, Jenkins, Heath, Price, Ratensky.

Southern Bleachery (12-8): Hughes, Pack, Yeargin, J.D. Childress, Jones, Meisenheimer, Coker, Hudgens, Jackson, Brown, Childers, Burton, Cashion.

Mills Mill #2 (11-10): Garrett, Westmoreland, Swink, Stone, Ormand, Littlejohn, Frye, Gallman, Craig, Gregg, Bragg, Thomas, Yeargin, Timmons, Taylor, Campbell, Frady.

Piedmont (10-13): Pickleseimer, Berry McElrath, Pack, Tice, Anderson, Bennett, Jones, Bolden.

Duke Power (9-11)

Tucapau (8-12): Moore, Smith, Fisher, West, Ellison, Granger, Austin, Cotney.

Oconee County League

Newry, champions (4-1): Cater, Alexander, Sluder, Kirby, Rampey, Alexander.

Walhalla (2-0): Stoddard, Blackwell.

Westminster (1-4): Reed, Powell, Crump, Lindsay, McGuffin.

Lonsdale (0-2): Watson, Gastley, Alexander, Davis.

Greenville Textile League

Judson, champions (18-14): Godshaw, Wood, Hendrix, Duffey, Kirby, Morgan, Wyatt, Hall, Crawford, Smith, Rook, Ford Garrison, L. Vickery, E. Vickery, McDaniel, Hill.

Dunean (15-13): Stewart, Hailey, Henson, Cashion, Wilson, Carroll, Ashley, Cothran, Ellenburg, Henderson, Wood, Floyd, Hall, Batson, Kelly, Campbell, Smith, Campbell, Badger,

Mills Mill of Greenville (13-6): Revis, Revis, Lynch, Ingle, Abbott, Porter.

Monaghan of Greenville (11-7): Herring, Bagwell, Hunnicutt,

Waldrop, Belcher, Hudgens, Errin, Elder, Christopher.

Slater (7-7): Bailey, Price, Fortner, Vaughn, Liebrandt, Duncan.

Sampson (7-20): Sexton, Belk, Dill, Major, Morgan, Mauldin, Bridwell, Badger, Duncan, Crymes, Moore, Fowler, Roberts, Ferguson.

Gantt (5-5): Morgan, Wood, Stewart, Mahaffey, Murray, Holbrook.

Fork Shoals (1-1): Meeks, Woods, Pitts, Thompson, Arnold.

Piedmont Plush (1-4): Verdin, G. Forrester, Adams, White, Jones, Baldwin, Smith, Shaver, Sheffield, D. Forrester, F. Forrester, J. Forrester.

Central Carolina League

Mills Mill of Woodruff (no records)
Fairmont (no records)
Arkwright (no records)
Woodruff (no records)

Blue Ridge League

Alice, champions (12-6): L. Alexander, Holden, Owens, Dodgens, Roper, Breazeale, Templeton, Hendrix, Robertson, Ward, Ferguson, C. Adams, Osteen, Galloway, Williams, Lesley.

Arial (10-5): Turpin, Rampey, Masters, Perkins, Porter, Ingle, Batson.

Pickens (8-7): Rampey, E. Pace, G. Holland, Hester, Thrasher, Riggins, Brookshire, C. Adams, Dillard, H. Adams, Ligon, G. Adams, O. Adams, J. Holland.

Glenwood (7-8): Spearman, Owens, Fredrick, Hopkins.

Easley (6-9): Hester, Galloway, Waldrop, Welborn, Campbell, Cody.

Liberty (4-11): R. Garrison, Thrasher, Wooten, Rogers, Bagwell, Nettles, McCravey, Medlock.

Southern Textile League

Woodside, champions (13-7): Herbert, Moore, Elder, Brookshire, Eldridge, Helton, Bowen, Owens, Clinton.

Poinsett (15-5): Robinson, Taylor, Crawford, Brown, Gilliard, Campbell, Spencer, Morgan.

Pelham (9-7): Poole, Satterfield, Lott, Arnold.

Poe (6-10): Roper, Andrews, Nau, Sanders, Brookshire, Crossland, Crawford, Raines, Hudgins.

Southern Worsted (5-11): Lee, Best, Suddeth, West, Hogg, Lackey, Waldrop, McGill, Snipes, Broome, Waters, Newman, DeShields.

Simpsonville (4-12): Williams, Calvert, Hamby, Giles, Goodman, Garrett, White, Cooper.

Mid County League

Arcadia (3-4): Cannon, Poteat, D. West, Rowe.

Spartan (2-5): Steadings.

Independent Teams

Jackson of Iva 2nd Team (1-0): Ham, Wilson, Burdette, Pearson, Baskin, S. Burdette, H. Dixon, Davis, H. Davis, Bannister.

Calhoun Falls (0-1): Dixon, Pearson, Barnes, Hilley, Helms, Crowder, Lewis, Cheatham, Hancock, Smith.

Liberty (no records): Easler, J. Holt, O. Holt, C. Chapman, Reid, Williams, Hunt, Green, Caldwell, B. Chapman.

1933

Anderson County League

Appleton, champions (11-1): Allen, Moore, J. McElrath, B. McElrath, Honea, R. Powell, Bill Tidwell, G. Powell, R.B. Speares, Leroy Mahaffey, Keaton.

Orr (8-3): Hart, Beville, Dude
Buchanan, Dumb Price, Tommy
Lyons, Ashworth, Barnes, Kay,
Jerry Whitten, Frith, Croxton, Lee
Whitten.

Gluck (7-4): McLeskey, Tabors,
Vaughn, Herndon, Helms, Early
Hanna, McAllister, Moore, Hughes,
Manley, Weathers, M. Sweeten-
burg, Dick Sweetenburg, Wood.

Belton (5-4): Smith, Deanhardt,
Thompson, Willingham, R.
Owens, O. Owens, S. Owens, Vest,
Stanton, Reid.

Anderson (5-7): Hancock, Hamilton,
Ripley, Pearman, Kelly, Smith,
Dillard, Scott, Blackstone, Ivester,
Yarborough, Simpson, Chamblee.

Gossett (3-6): Inman, Floyd, Chap-
man, Heath, R. Smith, Campbell,
Simpson, D. Smith, Moore,
Hendrix.

Equinox (3-8): Taylor, Thrasher,
Harbin, Cargill, Beck, Dooley,
Davis, Mullinax, Watson, Ivester,
Craft.

Chiquola (1-11): Harvey, Williams,
Alvin Davis, Shaw, Beacham,
Wallace Campbell, Maxie Peter-
son, Moore, Keasler, Thompson,
Sims.

Greenwood League

Ninety Six (5-0): Free, Wilson,
Hunnicutt, Coleman, Harrison,
Willingham, Staggs, Ivester,
Clem.

Mathews (4-1): Andrews, Bowie,
Gilmer, Cromer, Palmer, Barfield, Etheredge, Snipes, Medlock.

Greenwood (4-2): Duff, Aldia, Dominick, Bolton, Shaw, Arnold, Fortson, Thompson, Pickens, Pruitt,
Rice.

Panola (2-3): Rivers, Griffin,
Bratham, Harrison, Proctor, Hen-
derson, Dean, Rhodes, Rougan,
Kay.

Grendel (1-4): Shirley, Cox, Walker,
H. Spriney, Cooper, Burton,
R. Spriney, B. Jordan, R. Jordan,
Anderson.

Connie Maxwell Orphanage (0-6)

Dixie League

LaFrance (4-1): Darby, D. Hopkins,
F. Smith, Craft, F. Hopkins, Wil-
liams, Gaines, Medlock, Simpson,
Smith.

Jackson of Iva (3-2): Hamm, Evans,
McCoy, Jordan, Baskin, Jackson,
Burdette, Gailey, Belcher, D. Jor-
dan, Taylor.

Pelzer (2-2): Rikard, Nelson,
Wooten, Trammell, Alexander,
Emory, Almons, Cannon, Ross,
Littlejohn.

Central (0-4): Thomas, Simmons,
Summey, Gastley, Snipes, Dillard,
Lyda, Doyle, Wooten, Roland,
Frank Howard, Joe Sherman.

Palmetto League

Ninety Six, champions (2-1): Moore,
Sanders, Shuler, Ingle, Owens.

Greenwood (1-0): Couch, Byrd.

Ware Shoals (1-2): Whitten, Werner,
Wright, Winkler, Sanders,
Gambrell, Newberry, Wood,
Simon, Lemon, Jones, Watts,
Spires, Graham, Hines.

Mathews (0-1): Smith, Mann, Dorn,
Henner, Gaines, D. Doolittle,
R. Doolittle, Symmes, Owens.

Grendel (0-1): Dixon, Livingstone.

Piedmont Textile League

Victor of Greer, champions (12-8):
Roper, Lee, Suddeth, King, Gilles-
pie, Esco, V. Tipton, Cabiness,
Cohen, Waters, Westmoreland,
J. Tipton, Green.

Renfrew Bleachery (17-4): Shag
Knox, Granger, Morgan, F. Foster,
Fox, Ravich, Medlock, Heath,
Tollison, Tice, R. Foster, C. Fos-
ter, Morris, Ridgeway.

Slater (9-7): Bailey, Cashion, Vaughn, McMakin, Garrett, Croxton.

Mills Mill of Greenville (9-9): Ingle, Abbott, Revis, McCauley, Porter, Gray, Smith, Chandler, Massey, Osteen, Porter, Goss, Lavender, Smith, Coggins, Fayonsky, Lominack, Swink, Taylor, Barrett, Campbell, Thomas, Watson, Ormand.

Sampson (9-12): Richardson, Major, Mauldin, Duncan, Bridwell, Crymes, Firpo, Fredrick, Pike, Bolt, Wolfe, Spearman, Humphries, Chapman, Buck, Laney, Bowers.

Dunean (8-16): McMillan, Foster, Batson, Kelly, J. Campbell, Belcher, Carroll, Turner, Hudson, Riddle, Christopher, Hendrix, Stewart, Holbrook, Barnes, Wood, Watty, Martin, Putnam, Bailey, Christopher.

Union Bleachery (7-11): Hawkins, Berry, Brooks, Parkins, Belcher, Heaton, Harrison.

Judson (4-1): Duffy, Morgan, Trammell, McGraw, Godshaw.

Monaghan of Greenville (3-14): Herring, Brandon, Waldrop, Henson, Blackwell, Elder, Bagwell, Heath, Robinson, Hooper, Stephenson, Nicholson, Wiggins, Christopher, Smith, Hudgens.

Central Carolina League

Laurens, champions (8-3): Kirby Higbe, Nettles, Cox, Powers, Adams, Gosnell, Surratt, Wood, R. Higbe, Howard, Chumley, Waldrop, Burgess, Keeble, Patton, Whitten.

Brandon of Woodruff (7-3): Betsill, Jackson, Wilson, Sorgee, Nabors, Cashion, W. Lawson, N. Lawson, Grubbs, Simmons, Thornton, Jenkins, Wood, Howard, Taylor, Evans, McAbee, Spoon.

Enoree (3-4): Chumley, Fuller, Blanton, Ivey, Thornton, Emory, Watson, Waddle, McGee, M. Gentry, Gentry, B. Betsil, C. Betsil, Bishop.

Lydia (0-7): Patterson, Tate, Burnett, Abrams, Parrish, Copeland, Bridwell, Brown, Hill, H. Emory, Crocker, Giles, Stroud, Lawson, Land.

Mid State League

Monarch, champions (12-7): Center, Woodall, Reid, Shippey, Morris, Willis, Abernathey, Ellis, Abbott, Fleming, Walker, Bouknight, Carter, Barbare, West, McAbee, Rhinehart, Engle, Morris, Timmons, Walker, Phillips, Powell, Long, Shirley, Knox, Cotner, Cogdill.

Clinton (15-4): Trammell, Goslin, Wellborn, Prince, Weldon, B. Weldon, Leamon, Wertz, Byrd, Jett, Watkins, Bagwell, Brannon, Yeargin, Lyles, Crook, Blackwood, Hallman, Howard, Lee, Bolick, O'diorne.

Joanna (12-6): Bouknight, Girk, Bunton, Godfrey, Helms, R. Clark, E. Abrams, H. Barrett, B. Galloway, Coleman, R. Abrams, G. Barrett, S. Galloway, Sweat, Turner.

Watts (9-8): Prince, J. Byrd, Cox, Knight, Gosnell, Barbery, Stallings, Burgess, Bissett, Bagwell, Sorgee, Taylor, Fowler, Shirley, C. Byrd, Godfrey, Thornton, Money.

Newberry (7-10): Jones, Hamilton, E. Bouknight, Johnny Wertz, Livingston, J. Singley, G. Taylor, Caldwell, B. Bouknight, Cook, Shealy, Ward.

Whitmire (6-10): Williams, Brown, Ward, Yarborough, Ruff, Raines, Ayoub, Surratt, Webb, Busbee, Dennis.

Mollohon (6-12): Sowell, Pig Culclasure, Jones, Burgess, Golden, Coleman, Jackson, Franklin, Martin.

Ottaray (2-13): Gallman, Hines, Smith, Dixon, Shippley, Godshall, Allison, Littlejohn, Mooneyham, Clark, Murrow, Hightower, Callahan, Johnson, Brown, Bailey, E. Lenhardt, J. Lenhardt.

Blue Ridge League

Glenwood, champions (8-4): Benson, Owens, Spearman, Lee, Hopkins, League.

Alice (8-7): Holden, Hendrix, Davis, Laurens, Alexander.

Liberty (7-6): Carter, Gillespie, Daniel, Burnette, Barrett, James.

Easley (6-6): Galloway, Morgan, White, Alexander, Waldrop, Daniels.

Arial (5-6): Rampey, Masters, Turpin, Greene.

Pickens (3-9): Pace, Adams, Holloway, Metz, Rampey, Howell, Bailey, Baker, Adams.

Western Carolina League

Southern Bleachery, champions (11-8): Tice, Joe Benson, Drummond, Al Yeargin, Coker, Wilson, Strbbling, Hughes, Angus McElrath, Snyder, Robinson, Joe Childers, J.D. Childers, Gay, Luke McElrath, Bragg, Joe Davis, P. Yeargin.

Tucapau (10-6): Granger, Macy, West, Carter, Fisher, Smith, Mason, Lankford, Brannon, Hines, Sullivan.

Pelzer (10-7): Escoe, Lefty Crymes, Benton, Red Woods, Bobo, Helms.

Mills Mill of Woodruff (10-10): Ormand, Poteat, Glenn, Thomas, Barrett, Frady, Bagwell, Crossland, Swink, Taylor, Campbell, Fayonsky, Watson, Craig, Timmons, Lominack.

Lyman (7-10): Query, Jett, Ward, Gibson, Smith, Burgess.

Piedmont (6-14): Nau, Covington, League, Anderson, Meisenheimer, Barton, Westmoreland, Hare,

Vaughn, Phillips, Williams, Bennett, Collins, Toney, Fleming, Dill, Henderson, Bennett, Underwood, Duffie, Bolden, Bowie, Pack, Fowler, Allen, Anderson, Patterson, Ramsey.

Oconee County League

Newry, champions (1-1): Tollison, Cater, Alexander.

Lonsdale (0-1)

Westminster (1-0): McGuffin, Lee, Crump.

Greenville Textile League

Brandon of Greenville, champions (7-3): Couch, Hairston, Harrison, C. Williams, Spencer, Von Hallen, Gilstrap, Morrow, Carnes, Campbell, Denton, Smith, Anders.

Woodside (7-5): Hilton, Moore, O. Herbert, Elledge, O. Brookshire, Mason, Jackson, Suddeth, Ellison, T. Herbert, Couch, Ramey, Carter.

Conestee (5-4): Wilson, Wilson, Vaughn, Wright, Evatt.

Piedmont Print (4-4): Forrester, Baldwin, Robertson, Jones, Adams.

Poe (2-8): Crawford, Brookshire, Addis, Sides, Boggs, Anders, Abernathey, Pryor, Adkins, Hairston, Moore.

Catawba League

Lockhart (1-0): Gibson, O'Dell, H. Blair, G. Blackwood, Burns, M. Blackwood, Sullivan, Durham.

Eureka (0-1): Sullivan, Brown, Lightner, Martin, Gunn, Oldham, Melton.

Greenville County League

Fork Shoals, champions (8-2): Wright, Woods.

Judson (6-2)

Dunean (5-3)

Piedmont (4-5)

Southern Worsted (3-6): Hogg, Bass.

Greer (3-7): Pruitt, Chesnee, Todd, Thorne, Roper.

Simpsonville (1-7)

Twilight League

Fairforest (2-1): Williams, Fowler, Traynham, B. Wilder, Ed Wilder, Ridgeway, E. Reeder, J. Mabry, Bridges, Connors, Dobson, Reynolds.

Spartan (2-1): R. Lands, Hollis, J. Lands, Greer, Brown, Painter, C. Fowler, W. Lands, Guy, Gibbs, Blanton, Mooneyham, Brooks, P. Fowler, Henderson, Lowe, J. Dodd, Brown, Dodd.

Valley Falls (2-1): N. Rollins, Nolan, Corn, E. Rollins, Garrett, Glenn, Wilson, Wilson.

Crescent (2-1): McCullough, Beam, Corn, Bouknight, Allen, Jennings, McCreadle, Johnson, Poteat, Porter, Chapman, Edge, Taylor, Peak, Griffin.

Herald-Journal (1-0)

Hub City Lunch Club (1-1)

Saxon (1-1): A. Stepp, Calvert, Eydle, Copia, Solsebee, Rhymer, Cooper, Beam, Wood, P. Stepp, Elledge, Willis, Hendrix, Gosnell, Strange, Lancaster, Watkins.

Inman (1-2): W. Gowan, High, Davis, Rollins, Vaughn, Pack, Martin, Robinson, N. Gowan, Jackson, Jones.

Beaumont (1-2): Waters, P. Green, Wright, O. Green, Splawn, Lindsay, Shook, Sanders, Ward, Park, Prince, Earl, Gibson.

Cleveland Playground (0-1)

Mid-County League

Lyman (6-2): Reid, Sexton, High, Durham, McMakin, Garrett, Reeves, Pettigrew, Alexander, O'Dell, Rogers, Edwards, High, Harvey.

Converse (5-2): Thomas, Mathis, Byars, J. Vassey, Giles, J. Mill-

wood, Wooten, Holland, Quinn, Greer, C. Millwood, E. Vassey, Holland.

Spartan (5-5): Wood, Taylor, Timmons, Steadings, Gunter, Lancaster, Henderson, Fowler, O'Shields, Brooks, Dodd.

Arkwright (4-4): Allen, Bagwell, Meadows, Jackson, Godfrey, Gault, Watson, Sawyer, Brown, Quinn, Varner, Holt.

Fairmont (4-5): Farmer, Gibson, George Blackwell, Vaughn, Arnold, Morrow, Fortenberry, Belcher, Branch, Heatherly, Genobles, Crouch.

Clifton (3-4): McCarty, B. Hatchette, McHughes, Giles, Calvert, Albright, F. Mabry, Vaughn, G. Hatchette, K. McClary, P. Mabry, J. McClary, D. Hatchette, K. Bridges.

Inman (2-2): B. Parris, Bebber, Cashion, Pike, B. Shehan, Crocker, Pruitt, R. Parris, Hudgens, Justice, Pridmore, Shelton.

Jackson of Wellford (2-4): Taylor, Gosnell, Anders, Hawkins, Thompson, Jordan, R. Wilson, Blackwell, Painter, P. Wilson.

Tucapau (2-4): G. Mason, C. Jackson, J. Mason, Hodge, Henderson, Austin, West, B. Jackson, T. Mason, Warden, Smith, Shehan, Blackwell, Cook.

Whitney (0-4): Scruggs, Harvey, Pearson, Poteat, C. Chapman, O. Holt, Sullivan, J. Holt, Caldwell, W. Reese, Chapman, F. Reese.

Spartanburg County League

Drayton (14-5): Burgess, C. Inman, Carter, Johnson, S. Moore, B. Moore, Hughey, O'Sullivan, Ray, Jones, Finley, M. Inman, Shippey, Cothran, Cameron, E. Moore, Kilpatrick, Parks, Manning Bagwell.

Beaumont (11-8): Lambright, McIntyre, Fowler, Thompson, Taylor,

A. West, Garrett, Lowery, Carter,
Powell, Metcalf, Callahan, Austin,
Rush, Soards, Gunn, Murph, Med-
ley, Turner, Glenn.

Inman (10-8): D. Shehan, O. Parris,
Prince, Ingle, Clark, Davis,
Eppley, Pack, Hawkins, Cashion,
Lawter, Bradley, H. Shehan, Har-
ris, Padgett, Cothran, Davis,
McKeithan.

Pacolet (9-11): Tee Fleming, Petty,
White, Campbell, Goforth,
Harrold, Pace, Holt, Red Ellison,
Teaster, Patrick, Robinson, Lee,
Mabry, Tate, Burgess, Osment.

Whitney (8-12): Owens, Little, Kelly,
Scruggs, Huskey, Arnold, Thomp-
son, O. Hyatt, McAbee,
Thackston, Poteat, J.C. Morgan,
J.D. Morgan, L. Drake, Holt,
R. Drake.

Arcadia (5-11): M. West, Veal, B. West,
Ridings, Perkins, Cannon, Rowe,
Dixon, Gowan, Holt, Sims, Coth-
ran, Liske, Wofford, Spencer,
Byars, Stanfield, Chumley.

Independent Teams

Tucapau (44-4): Doolie Southern,
Fred McAbee, Babe Fisher, Jones,
Roy Brannon, Tuck McConnell,
Sam Williams, O'dell Mason,
Hines, Allen West, Hugh Smith,
Big Pack, Swift Allen, Joe Laven-
der, Tweddie Hill, Pat Ingle, Carol
Smith (manager), D.M. Nixon,
Doc Taylor, Tack Johnson.

Gantt (0-2): Stewart, Granger.

York (no records): Taft Wright.

Powell (0-1): Hayes, Ballard, Jolly,
Stepp, Watkins, Mason, Workman.

1934

King Cotton League

Judson White Sox, champions (16-1):
Rampey, Boggs, Golightly, Jay
Groce, Cashion, Vaughn, Jim Hall,

Howell, Price, Lewis, Gotshaw,
Escoe, Wood, Duffie, Woodruff,
Covington, Campbell, Groce,
Rucker.

Glenwood (7-6): Fortner, Hopkins,
Mace, Robinson, Owens, E. Stew-
art, E. Chapman, R. Stewart,
Huffstetler, B. Chapman, Rice,
League, Fortune.

Arial (6-8): Rampey, Masters,
Vaughn, Chapman, Green, Gibson, McCrary.

Alice (6-8): McCravey, Hendrix, Duncan, Davis, Leslie, Bagwell, Durham, Littleton, Breazeale.

Poe (6-9): Prince, Lee, Kernode,
Littlejohn, Werner, Gilreath,
Bean, Alexander, Cammitz, Bar-
bery, Pack, Hawkins, Mad-
den, Collins, Anderson, Roper,
Fowler, Heath, Alexander,
Price.

Poinsett (4-11): Robinson, Cole,
Brady, Daniel, Roberts, Yeargin,
C. Gilstrap, Bridwell.

Blue Ridge League

Pickens, champions (9-2): H. Adams,
C. Pitts, Dillard, Kirby, Cater,
Pace, Ligon, J. Pitts, Roper,
Rampey, Hayes, Reeves,
McNeeley, Tate.

Newry (8-7): Taylor, Alexander, Lindsay, McIntyre, Cater, Hardy,
Kirby, McClelland, Gilden, Williams.

Easley (6-1): L. Waldrop, Hix,
Hendrix, Jamison, Galloway,
C. Alexander, B. Alexander,
R. Waldrop, King, Spearman,
H. Alexander, H. Waldrop, King.

Westminster (2-6): McGuffin, Lee,
Powell, Crump.

Walhalla (1-4): Blackwell, Gilliard,
Reid, Stoudmire, Turpin, Williams, Smith, Epps.

Lonsdale (1-6): Jordan, Weathers,
Lee, Baskin, Watson, Batson,
Gilliard, Owens, Martin.

Pickens County League

Pickens, champions (1-2): Pace, Welborn, Freeman, Chiles, Baker, Holcombe, Bryant.

Liberty #3 (3-0): Stancil, Harrison, Wright, Dodgens, Stewart, Rice.

Alice (1-1): Spearman, Smith, Mauldin, Dill, Cody.

Liberty #2 (0-1): Trotter, Yates.

Western Carolina League

Pelzer, champions (15-6): Ross, Emery, Dickert, Lefty Helms, Burton, Woods, Cannon, Crymes, Benton, Westmoreland, Allen, Peace, Pickleseimer, Harley Heath (manager).

Dunean (14-4): Lord, Owens, McManaway, Bennett, Lee, Suddeth, Wyatt, Alexander, Harvell, Kelly, Bailey, Raby, Phillips, Greene (manager).

Renfrew Bleachery (10-7): Collins, Lea, Hawkins, Fred Knox, Robinson, Batson, Jenkins, Granger, Charlie Foster, Medlock, Ridgeway, Tollison, R. Foster.

Southern Bleachery (7-7): R. Coker, J.D. Childers, Hughes, Stewart, Stewart, P. Yeargin, Stribbling, Jim Gay, Angus McElrath, Robinson.

Brandon of Greenville (6-9): James, Batson, Campbell, Spoon, Mace, Smith, Pitts, Wilson, Crossland, Fisher, Heath, Spencer, Welsh, Fox, Lavender, Bland, Foster, Thornton, Millwood, Granger, Coteen, Sentell.

Slater (6-10): Brigham, Bailey, McMakin, Cashion, Vaughn, Willis, Turner, Wilson, Porter, Sizemore, Wilson, Hembree.

Dixie Stores (4-4): Wiggins, Barbare, Henderson, Smith, Montieth, Reid, Ford Garrison, Wilson, Nabors.

Liberty (2-12): Burdette, Wooten, Dodgens, Thrasher, Coffman, Cothran, Mayhew, Morgan, Gillespie, Gilstrap.

Palmetto Textile League

Ninety Six, champions (18-2): Corley, Lyles, Gaines, Simmons, Sanders, Walker, Attaway, Doolittle, Lowery.

Greenwood (8-3): Williams, Bannister, Bolton, Doolittle.

Mathews (3-3): Simmons, Sanders, Gaines, Whitehead, Lyle, Ridlehoover, Hall, Owens, Jordan, Mosely, Howard, James.

Abbeville (2-3): Welch, New, Stalnaker, Agnew.

Chappells (2-1)

Calhoun Falls (1-4): Patterson, Pearson, Rice, Hancock, Cheatham, Carrithers, Crouch, Cox, Hilley, Chrisley, Fowler, Helms, Cooley, Nally, Clark, Reynolds.

Piedmont Textile League

Camperdown, champions (16-3): Carson, Moore, Maxwell, Nau, McWaters, Henry Huff, Breazeale, Parkins, Jenkins, McDowell, Paul Brown, Hunter, Stewart, Sam Fayonsky, Foster, Wilson.

Woodside (11-7): Helton, Hunter, Wilson, Jackson, F. Smith, Giles, Harrison, Suddeth, Lee, Carter, Payne.

Sampson (9-7): Byers, Holt, Major, Morgan, Bowers, Waldrop, Mason, Mace, Harbin, Bowers.

Victor of Greer (8-5): Pittilo, Spencer, Tipton, Waters, Horn, Suddeth, Lee, Johnson, Crouch, Wilson, Hunter, Broome, Bennett, D. Smith, Harvey, Henderson.

Monaghan of Greer (8-9): L. Smith, Berry, Perrin, Nichols, Henson, Curry, Stevens, Waldrop, Crossland, Speigler, Elder, Christopher, Elder, Wiggins, Godfrey, M. Smith.

Union Bleachery (7-11): Hoot Gibson, Yeargin, Brooks, Ivey,

Parkins, Sikes, Robertson,
D. Smith.

Mills Mill of Greenville (5-12): Ingle,
Revis, Abbott, Gray, McCauley,
Turner, McAllister, Coby, Porter,
Massey, Smith.

Greer (4-14): Chesnee, Montieth, Jarvis, Thorne, Henderson, Reid,
Roper.

Central Carolina League

Laurens, champions (19-4): R. Higbe,
Clark, Wells, Cox, Brady, Bagwell,
Outzs, Shehan, Gross, Lee, Shorty
Horne, Bragg, Patton, Craig, Kee-
ble, C. Horne, Mahaffey, K. Higbe,
Burgess, Watson, Clayton, Adams,
Wells, Kay.

Clinton (15-8): Claude Trammell,
Sanders, Davenport, Poteat,
H. Bailey, Bolick, Fisher, Willis,
Graham, Abrams, Whitten, Rice,
Howard, J. Odiorne, J. Bailey,
Crawford, Reid, Wood, Holliday,
Morgan, Cabiness, O'Diorne,
Smythe, Watkins, Hallman, Byrd,
Greene.

Joanna (14-10): Miller, Dunn, Seltz,
Irby Bouknight, Charlie Girk,
Webb, Ward, Walker, Croxton,
Bruce Galloway, Clark, Harry
Whitten, Smith, E. Abrams,
S. Galloway, Swails, Simpson, Gar-
rison, R. Abrams, E. Girk, Fergu-
son, Coleman, Henson, Robert-
son.

Ware Shoals (12-12): Sloan, New-
berry, Graham, Willis, Werner, Ele-
azer, Wright, Wrinkle, Buddy
Lewis, Outzs, Girk, Sanders, Tom
Ingle, Davis, Davis, Wyatt, Ned
Moore (manager), Sanders, Stone,
Horn.

Watts (10-14): Foster, Byrd, Knight,
Stallings, Rasor, Lynch, Cashion,
Patterson, Huff, Fisher, Bingham,
J. Bumgardner, Hawkins, Jones,
Sedberry, Ledford, McAbee,
Waddell, Taylor, Powell,

Kammetz, Bailey, Putman,
Trammell, Tillman.

Brandon of Woodruff (2-22): Ship-
pey, Swink, Fuller, Henderson,
Langford, Wolfe, Willard, Jones,
Campbell, Callison, Gunn, Huff,
Callison, Langston, Hawkins,
Patterson, R. Betsil, Livingston,
Lavender, Leopard, Fletcher, Jack-
son, Nabors, Scruggs, W. Lawson,
N. Lawson, Watson, Taylor,
Wooten, S. Galloway, Thornton,
Tedesco, Davis, Giles, Radcliffe,
Wilder, Benson.

Mid State League

Whitmire, champions (21-7): Query,
Barker, Dennis, Gillespie, Ward,
Lowman, Rhem, Yarborough,
Raines, McAbee, Matthews, Dud-
ley, Ramsey, Dickert, Livingston,
Bridges, Dickert, Ayoub, Leamon,
Bryson.

Monarch (19-8): Johnny Walker,
Morris, Dixon, Littlejohn, Phillips,
Tutor, Lamb, Murrow, Cogdill, Al-
lison, Middlebrooks, Callahan,
Nabors, Clark, Waters, Wellman,
Mooneyham, Putnam.

Mollohon (14-14): Howell, Pig
Culclasure, Doodie Franklin, Coley
Jones, Outzs, Webb, Harry
Hedgepath, Jackson, Harkrader,
Ingram, Moore, Drummond, Char-
lie Golden, Bus Golden, Martin,
Burgin, Clary, Pee Wee Franklin,
Thompson, C. Jones, McNeil.

Newberry (12-16): J. Singley, Hamil-
ton, Tobe Livingston, Johnny
Wertz, E. Bouknight, Lindsay, Bob
Creekmore, Caldwell, Thompson,
Cook, Al Shealy, E. Singley, Ken-
nedy, Charlie Golden, Taylor,
Stowe, Corley, Stovall, Bishop, Sin-
gleton.

Lockhart (11-17): Allgood, Hill,
Burns, Brown, Clark, Clary, Kat-
zen, Allen, Lemaster, Yonce,
Vaughn, M. Blackwood, O'dell,

R. Blair, C. Blackwood, Gibson,
Williams, Crocker, Franklin,
H. Blair.
Buffalo (7-20): Knowles, Yarborough,
Gold, D. Allen, Singley, Crocker,
Inman, Bolton, Putnam, Watson,
Boozer, Hughey, J. Allen, Lawson,
Timmons, Ezell, Allen, Godshall,
Padgett, Howell, Bridges, Abrams,
Hunt, Simmons, Dixon, Lynch,
Mayhew, Powell, McIntyre,
Gilliam.
Winnsboro (1-0): Hindon, Wells,
Bolden, Joe Jackson, Ingram,
Burrell, Bone, Greer, Pete Frye,
Leroy Morehead.

West State B League

Pelzer, champions (7-2): Pearson,
Galloway, Jordan, Woodcock,
Ross, Cannon, Williams, Emery,
Littlejohn.
Judson (8-2): Chapman, Jordan,
Godshaw, Fisher, McDaniel,
Bishop.
Brandon of Greenville (6-3): Denton,
Smith, Limbaugh, Ramey, Couch.
Poe (2-1): Williams, E. Sides, Boggs,
Brookshire, Averson, C. Sides.
Piedmont (2-9): Sides, Anderson,
Boggs, Tice, Jones, Bennett,
Coker, Smith, Drummond, Reeves,
Mitchell, O. Patterson.
Brooks Brothers (0-1)
Williamston (0-1): Davenport, Holli-
day, Black, Stone, Miller.
Renfrew Bleachery (0-2): Coleman,
Robertson.

Eastern Carolina League

Lyman, champions (28-8): Fisher,
Yancey Senn, Rush Yeargin, Hor-
ace Long, Bill Snyder, Benson, Wil-
son, Jett, Query, Giles, Morgan,
Snake Ward, W.F. Howard (man-
ager), Smokie Barbare.
Mills Mill of Woodruff (24-10): Snag
Ormond, Page, Proctor, Stokes,
Thomas, Timmons, Taylor, Camp-

bell, Lominack, Christopher, Gallo-
way, Barrett, Maxwell.
Drayton (23-11): Shuf Finley, Bill Car-
ter, Davis, Ralph Cothran, M. In-
man, Claude Inman, Manning
Bagwell, S. Moore, Elsie Moore,
Stowe Ray, Houston Hines, Sam
Glenn, Alley, Riptide Tice, Roy
Brannon, Jay Gross, Raymond
Kelly.
Tucapau (17-18): West, Ben Shields,
Mason, Southern, Frew, McAbee,
Brannon, Ingle, Williams,
McConnell, Sullivan.
Converse (14-20): Shehan, Calvert,
Vassey, Gowan, Pete Fowler, Clar-
ence Millwood, Kirkley, Byars,
Giles, Hopper, Mabry, Holland,
Green, Johnson, Mahaffey, Moon-
eyham, Nick Altrock, Mayhew,
Waters.
Inman (14-20): Clay Mahaffey, Dil-
lard, Abernathy, Blackwell, Pack,
Underwood, Floyd, Owens,
Dotherow, Clark, Rhymer.
Pacolet (11-24): Tee Fleming, Arnold,
Bill Harrold, Ernie White, Ellison,
Campbell, Petty, Goforth, Harri-
son, Pace, Vaughn.
Beaumont (8-18): Ralph Prince,
Gunn, Turner, Blanton, Rush,
Monk Thackston, John Pitts,
Jimmy Callahan, Gene Brooks,
Nick Warren, Medley, Parks,
Kelly, Mooneyham, Garrett,
Thomas, Paschall, Murphy.

Dixie Textile League

Pelham, champions (7-3): Clifford
Cox, Frank Pittman, John Cox,
Earl Poole, Dan Greer, Ed Vaughn,
Harold Satterfield, George Black-
well, Parrot Arnold, Fred Steadings,
Claude Pittman, Gene Bridwell.
Simpsonville (4-1): Ballew, Bagwell,
Barbare, Smith, Kirby.
Fountain Inn (2-1): Louie Woods,
McGee, Mathis, C. Woods, W.
Woods, Elledge, Childers.

Piedmont Print (1-3): Hughes, Smith, Roy Coker, J.D. Childers, Joe Childers, Meisenheimer, Forrester, Keeler, Drummond, Phillips, Hendrix, Ralph Coker.

Conestee (0-1): Tucker, Wilson.

Apalache (0-1): Leopard, Bishop, Dorn, Newman.

Spartanburg County League

Inman (17-3): Parris, B. Shehan, Cashion, Pike, Prince, Crocker, Bebber, Abernathey, Gowan, Martin, Pridmore, H. Shehan, Cothran, Hudgens, Eppley, Evington.

Arcadia (11-8): Rowe, Justus, M. West, B. West, Veal, Sims, Cannon, Moon, Jones, Parrott, Calvert, Chumley, Jones, Littlejohn, Lavender, Poteat.

Clifton (11-8): D. Hatchett, Barbare, Waters, M. Mabry, Moore, J. McCorley, Bridges, Vaughn, Groce, Holt, G. Hatchett, Blanton, Calvert, Quinn, Evans.

Gaffney (11-9): Jones, W. Guthrie, Harlow, Fox, B. Clary, Hensley, Turner, Branch, Irke Sprouse, P. Guthrie, Humphries, Davis, Justus, Harris, Hughes.

Arkwright (10-8): Allen, Varner, Wofford, Jennings, Sitton, Gregory, May, Brown, Leek, Holt, Quinn, Ermine, Watson, Shook, McCullough, Ernest Hawkins, Baldwin.

Whitney (10-8): Thompson, D. Morgan, C. Morgan, A. Holt, Chapman, D. Holt, Poteat, P. Holt, Huskey, Pearson, Hughes, Scruggs, Williams, Little, Sullivan.

Valley Falls (5-16): P. Hammett, Little, P. Garrett, Arnold, Powell, A. Nolan, P. Nolan, Bagwell, P. Huggins, Lockman, Hughes, B. Nolan, West, Angle, Clark, Blackwell, Anders, Wilson, Cox, Green, Helderman, Jordan, Brooks.

Fairmont (3-18): Jackson, Gosnell, Fortenberry, Farmer, Shehan, Gibson, Crouch, Belcher, Mayfield, Blackwell, Genobles, Corn, Morrow, McAbee, Duncan, Speaks, Grady.

Mid-County League

Fairforest, champions (11-4): G. Traynham, Hill, L. Taylor, Mabry, D. Traynham, Ridgeway, Lecky, Swink, Dobson, Shores, Wilder, Manley, Dill, M. Taylor, Gilder.

Lyman (10-4): Pettigrew, Alexander, R. Reeves, High, Edwards, C. Reeves, Sheriff, Thorne, S. Morgan, Reid, L. Morgan.

Spartan (10-5): West, Biershenk, Holderman, Mahaffey, Taylor, Howell, Hendrix, Ervin Cribb, Griffin, Wood, Fowler, Steadings, Godfrey, Henson, Lancaster, Lando, Baker, Candler, Gunter, McKee, Timmons, McAbee, Roland.

Glendale (7-7): Harris, Allen, Gossett, Reese, Blanton, Moss, Gosnell, Bush, Bishop, Cudd, Cooksey, Hutchins, Alley, Rinehart, Ogle, Holt, Porter, Thomas, Green, Burnett, Bates.

Pacolet (6-6): W. Mason, Emory, Smith, T. Mason, Green, Scott, Berry, Henderson, Bryant, Banks, Petty, Fowler, Lemons, Pace, Worthy.

Tucapau (6-9): Jackson, Hodge, J. Mason, Glasson, Tapp, Henderson, Lavender, Smith, T. Mason, E. Austin, R. Austin, West, W. Mason, L. Mason.

Saxon (6-9): Bookout, Lining, C. Holmes, Tucker, Cooper, Solesbee, A. Stepp, Lytles, D. Holmes, Jewels, P. Stepp, Chapman, Thomas, Jennings, Corn, Gault, Hall, Millwood, Gallman, Griffin, White.

Clifton (2-12): Calvert, Carver, Massey, Vernon, Willis, J. Coggins,

B. Coggins, G. Coggins, L. Hughes, Jolly, Wright, Albright, B. Hughes.

Catawba League

Baldwin, champions (1-0): Clyde Shoun, Ben Pascal (manager), Farmer, Whitey Heavener.

Lancaster Red Roses (0-1): Upchurch, Williams, Parrish.

Aragon Bleachery (no records): Brown, Arnette, Rhinehardt, Reynolds, Bell, Cox, Luce, Murray, Lankford, Connor, Cotner.

Chester (no records): Sullivan, Brown, Weir, Durham, Holland, Lee, Sullivan, Thompson, Lertner,

Anderson County League

Gluck, champions (11-4): Buck Moore, C. Jordan, McLeskey, Herndon, B. Smith, Sam Jordan, Reid Blackstone, Tabors, Dick Sweetenburg, Walker, Weathers, Posey, Hughes, Woods, Manley.

Chiquola (15-5): Tony Leonard, Husky, O. Anderson, Simmons, R. Leonard, Cunningham, B. Anderson, Beacham, Bearden, Cranford, Young, Jean Belue, Clifford Keasler, Harvey, S. Werner, Moore, Watson, Kettles.

Gossett (12-6): Cannon, Ben Pearson, Sexton, Simmons, Sherman, Floyd, Godfrey, Summey, Chapman, Wood, Dick Smith, Elrod, Leonard, Darby.

Appleton (10-8): Henry Allen, Herron, Ferguson, Berry McElrath, Pearman, Anderson, Ed Tillison, F. Powell, Guy Powell, Hanna, R.B. Speares, Clay Mahaffey, Williams, Tidwell, Keaton, Gunter.

Orr (8-2): Hart, Dude Buchanan, Chavous, Dumb Price, J.H. Barnes, Jerry Whitten, Joe Ashworth, Davis, Lee Whitten, Tommy Lyons, Nicholson, Walters, Claud Whitten.

Belton (4-12): Minyard, Ira Thompson,

McAllister, R. Owens, S. Owens, O. Owens, Deanhardt, Vest, Shockley, Major, Elledge, Nelson, Smith, Bannister, Willingham, Bisset, Hogg.

Anderson (4-15): Salley, Simpson, Moore, Ripley, Jackson, Malone, Turner, Hancock, J.B. Kelly, Scott, Yarborough, C.R. Williams, E. Doolittle, Cooley, Blackston, Norton, Gant, Honea.

Equinox (4-15): Webb, Clay Moore, Croxton, Larry Harbin, Shirley, Beck, Taylor, Davis, J. Craft, Mullinax, J.N. McAllister, Watson, A. Craft, Sewell, Sims, Powell, Stone.

Calhoun League

Chiquola, champions (4-1): J. Shaw, Davis, Thompson, Bell, Dorn, Harvey, Keasler, L. Moore, Gordon Ferguson, Fisher, L. Shaw, Branyon, E. Moore.

Jackson of Iva (3-2): Evans, McCoy, Hartgrove Baskin, Burdette, Dickson, M. Hamm, Belcher, J.L. Green, H. Hanna, Rice, Taylor, Jordan, McAllister.

Equinox (0-2): Stewart, Simmons, Carlton.

Pendleton (0-2): Hanna, D. Williams, Flemming, Clement Duncan, Griffin.

Anderson County Textile Girls Baseball League

Appleton (6-0): Margaret Humphries, Maggie Whitworth, Ruth Watkins, Vickery, Hawkins, Powell.

Anderson (0-1): Honea, Fredricks.

Gossett (no records): Owens, Singer.

Twilight League

Drayton, champions (15-3): Bennett, B. Hughes, Lancaster, G. O'Sullivan, Wilson, Campbell, Pete Laurens, J. Hudgens, Ward, J. O'Sullivan, J. Hughes,

Hub City (12-6)

Valley Falls (11-6): Edwards, Henderson, Wilson, Rollings, Ward, White, Bishop, Pack, Henderson, Garrett.

Crescent (7-9): Davis, Little, Smith, Allen, Taylor, P. Markey, McGraw, B. Mabry, Miller, Poteat.

Carolina Foundry (0-1)

Arcadia (0-1)

Beaumont (0-2): Green, Pack, Wright, Lindsay, Fowler, Prince, Cannon, Floyd, Ward, Wilson.

Saxon (0-15)

Union County League

Ottaray, champions (10-6): Allison, Brown, Lenhardt, Littlejohn, Dixon, Nabors, Shetley, Smith, Lenhardt.

Union (15-2): Blackwell, Gossett, Fowler, Lawson, Sullivan, Murphy, Whitener, Allen, Mathews, Willard.

Whitmire (9-6)

Jonesville (6-10)

Buffalo (5-11)

Excelsior (3-12)

Spartanburg County Colored League

Lyman, champions (10-3): Smith, Garner.

Converse (10-3): Rhinehart, Davis.

Drayton (7-3)

Pacolet (5-6)

Whitney (5-9)

Spartan (3-9)

Big Four League

Lydia (5-3)

Joanna (4-4)

Ware Shoals (4-4)

Clinton (3-5)

Mid Carolina League

Fingerville (15-1)

Powell (8-8)

Converse (8-8)

Cowpens (0-16)

Independent Teams

Williamston (2-1): Black, Stone, Raymond Garner, Thomas, Anderson, Glasby, West, Davenport.

Poe Mill Red Pants (1-0): Hutchinson, Cleveland.

Lydia Big Aces (1-1): Floyd Emory, Herbert Brown, Joe Ben Burnett, Wister Owens, Carl Johnson, Mansell Bridwell, Guy Parrish, Woodrow Jones, A.C. Caldwell, James Hairston, James Bailey, J.B. Patterson, Ray Fuller, R.H. Cobb, Rufus Mills, A.E. Lawson, Bill Crocker.

Central (no records): Frank Howard, Joe Sherman.

York (no records): Taft Wright.

1935

King Cotton League

Brandon Braves of Greenville, champions (16-6): C. Foster, F. Foster, Lyle, Heath, Owens, R. Foster, Christopher, Wilson, Craig, Jenkins, Spencer, Hines, Turbeville, Kinlaw, King, Al Veach, Owens, Snyder, Suggs, Bland, Maxwell, Campbell, Ballenger, Glynn.

Poe Panthers (15-7): Stewart, Price, Fowler, Kernode, Mack, McGaha, Cantrell, Sides, Williams, Ingle, Gillespie, Alexander, McAbee, C. Heath, Cabiness, Eddie Levy, F. Heath, Huff, Grice, Johnson, Barbare, Cashion, Fox, Werner, Sider.

Dunean Dynamos (14-7): King, Gotshaw, Albritton, Suddeth, Scruggs, Settlemire, Harbin, Farmer, Smith, Horne, Cambria, Wyatt, Langston, Phillips, Mason, Luck, Smokey Barbare, Powell, Suggs, Settlemire, Riddle, Putnam, Bell.

Lyman Pacifics (13-8): Petty, Southern, Senn, McConnell, Wilson,

Yeargin, Ingles, Long, Query, Jett, Ward, Burgess, Wahonic, Fowler, Benson, Snyder.

Mills Mill Millers of Woodruff (9-11): Ormond, Stokes, Proctor, Barrett, Campbell, Coker, Craig, Sam Page, Dominick, Christopher, Maxwell, Jeff Bolden, Taylor, Timmons, White.

Judson Red Coats (6-12): Suttlemire, Jim Hall, Furman, Jay Gross, Rucker, Collins, Boggs, Albritton, Carver, Evans, Bolick, Glenn, Rushing, Escoe, L. Maxwell, Kiser, Pack, Dudley, Williams, Alexander, Tiston, Jones, Foster.

Victor Pirates of Greer (6-13): Hawkins, Thackston, West, Miller, Mason, Millwood, Edwards, Crump, Lee, Myers, Bolick, Evans, Greer, Craft, Cline, Poteat, Walters, Gillespie, Inman, Brannon, Ovesty, Lumpkin, Smith, Wood, Braggs, Hipp.

Piedmont Blue Devils (2-17): Tice, Cannon, Waldrop, League, Golden, Patterson, McManaway, Emory, Cooper, Jones, Fayonsky, Goode, Allison, Maxwell, Watson, Rampey, Rogers, Darnell.

Western Carolina League

Sampson Spinners, champions (13-7): Garrison, Harbin, Spake, Dillard, Chapman, Hunt, Deanhardt, Wilbanks, Bowers, Mauldin, Myers, Morgan, Satterfield, Dill, Morgan, Langston, McDaniel, Major.

Pelzer Bears (15-5): Moore, Pickleseimer, Crymes, Heath, Wood, Allen, Westmoreland, Bunton, Bobo, Ross, Helms, Littlejohn, Dillard.

Southern Bleachery Red Flames (10-5): Stribbling, Hudgins, Stewart, West, J. Childers, Langston, Coker, Robertson.

Slater (7-12): Bailey, Willis, Lynch, Charlie Vaughn, Cashion, Hopkins, Major, Childers, Stewart,

Hudgins, Landreth, Price, Wilson, Abbott.

Woodside (6-12): Hunter, Moore, Herbert, Hairston, Jackson, Helton, Wilson, Hall, Smith, Bowen, Gillespie, Ramsey, Lavender, Lister, Suddeth, Tucker, Harbin.

Renfrew Bleachery (3-12): Granger, Lee, Coleman, Knox, Fox, Mason, Johnson, Medlock.

Piedmont Textile League

Union Bleachery, champions (13-4): Gibson, Heaton, Brooks, Marchbanks, Smith, Turner, Ivey, Harrison, Robertson, Epson, Eddie Levy.

Monaghan of Greenville (11-5): Nichols, Waldrop, Hinson, Herring, Wiggins, Smith, Christopher, Porter.

Camperdown (10-7): Brown, Williams, Huff, McDowell, Foster, Harrison, Wilson, Bridwell, Brissey, Childers.

Poinsett (7-6): Turner, Cole, Robertson, Gilstrap, Hyder, Hall, Arnold, Brown, Millwood.

Pelham (2-4): Arnold, Cox, Brown.

Greer (2-5): Brannon, Hamby, Brewington, Bowen, Godfrey, Harvey, McCarter, Giles, Smith.

Dunean (1-13): League, Wood, Thomas, Dominick, Kelly, Bailey, Hardin, Holbrook, Cox, Hancock, Riddle, Bragg, Little, Duncan, Christopher, Lindsay, Jones, Turner.

Central Carolina League

Joanna, champions (19-6): Bill Outzs, Charlie Girk, Irby Bouknight, Lefty Corley, Lee Gunn, Allen Barron, Gus Barrett, Snow Prater, Charlie Coleman, Bruce Galloway, Joe Whitlock, Cocky Blair, Harry Whitten, Robert Higbe, Raymond Abrams, Skeet Galloway, Shorty

Horne, Walker Yonce, Thomas, Addy, High, Bill Ouzts, E. Abrams.

Ninety Six (15-9): Kiser, Sanders, Marchant, Bennett, Hanson, Brady, Wood, Dowis, Glenn, Garrison, Wiley, Granny Hightower, Burris, Lowrey, Walker, Crouch, Burns, Knox, Leonard, Raines, Ramsey, Anderson, Landrum, Davis.

Watts (15-11): Mac McAbee, Tommy Thomas, Forrest O'Bannion, Galloway, Moore, Wright, Nub Smythe, Charlie Byrd, Palmer Knight, Lefty Howard, Buster Hair, D.W. Duncan, Bobo, Copeland, Ben Sprouse, Ben Bingham, Bruce Sedberry, Jack Farr, Jim Bailey, Paul Crane, John Rook, Oscar Haynes, Lyle, Padgett, Burton.

Ware Shoals (14-11): Ingle, Wrinkle, Graham, Bray, Newberry, Sanders, Werner, Davis, Ned Moore, Wright, Eleazer, Buddy Lewis, Holloway, Smith, Graham, Bruce, Chapman, Mabry.

Mathews (10-13): Corley, Sadler, Hanson, Doolittle, Williams, Lyle, Rhodes, Anson, Gaines, Brady, Hogg, Sizemore, Smith, Beale, Whaley, Pratt, Bearden, Smith, Cannon, Brogdon.

Greenwood (9-15): Strickland, H. Bailey, Weathers, Williams, Oelrich, Al Veach, Jordan, Kirby, Rook, Franklin, Rice, Threatt, Norrell, Murrow, Kirkland, Elrod, Shaw, Fowler, Bowie, Lyter, Buck, Chalmers, Reeder, Fortson, Golden, Phillips, J. Bailey, Johnny Walker.

Clinton (7-17): L. Howard, Keeble, McCarter, Trammell, Bolick, Hare, Duncan, Stowe, Thackston, Duncan, Crawford, Hill, Suggs, Watkins, Attaway, Smyth, Dominick, J. Odiorne, A. Howard, G. Odiorne, Whaley, H. Smith, McCall, Leamon, Gillespie, Wood.

Laurens (4-9); withdrew. Hanes,

Rook, Bradley, Watkins, Lefty Surratt, Mills, Stepp, Burgess, Keeble, Bagwell, Cox, Trent, Gosnell, Holcombe, Bragg, Hawkins, Evans, Rook, Brady, Ledford, Thompson, Dixon, Thornton, Hare, Traynham.

Mid State League

Buffalo Bisons, champions (17-4): Gillespie, Short, Fowler, George Rhinehart, Hughes, M. Putnam, Morris, Ezell, Eubanks, Timmons, Cox, Hull, Crocker, Abrams, Ramsey, J. Putnam.

Newberry (13-8): Johnny Wertz, Mickey Livingston, Lowman, Moore, Hugh Stoddard, Irby Bouknight, Reginald Bouknight, Ed Thompson, Roy Caldwell, Bob Creekmore, Derrill Bouknight, Doodie Franklin, Bubba Whittle, Jeff Singley, Garvice Taylor, Walter Hiller, Paul Troutman (manager), Robert Kennedy, Charlie Girk, Charlie Golden, Cortez Ward, Dan Shealy, Leon Eddy, Jimmy Lindsay, Pee Wee Franklin, Morgan.

Whitmire (7-9): Glenn, Yarborough, Connor, Davis, Rhem, Dennis, Ward, Gray, Coward, Callahan, Hopper, Raines, Ingram, W. Ramsey, Dickert, Bob Cotner, R. Ramsey, Lawson, Matthews, Kirkland.

Monarch (5-11): Walker, Morris, Busbee, Putman, Eargle, Shetley, Hendrix, Duncan, Nabors, Phillips, Bryson, Callahan, Cogdill, Allison, Thomason, Middlebrooks, Ledford.

Great Falls (4-4): Wilson, Tarlton, Ross, Hansman, J. Isenberg, R. Isenberg, J. Locklear, Yonce, Funderburk, Wright, E. Locklear.

Lockhart (4-11): Shirley, W. Burns, Deal, Allgood, Cabiness, Hunt, Walker, Clary, O'dell, C. Blackwood, Blair, Vaughn, Broome,

Farr, Crocker, Katzen, Allison,
F. Burns.

Mollohon (2-4); withdrew. Pee Wee
Franklin, Oscar Jones, Pig Culclas-
ure, Charlie Golden, Howell, Coley
Jones, Bus Golden, Martin, Smith,
Jackson, Moore, Bedenbaugh,
Clary, Abrams, Derrick, Sorrell.

Watts (no records): Ben Sprouse, Ben
Bingham, Nub Smythe, Charlie
Byrd, Bruce Sedberry, Jack Farr,
Lefty Howard, Jim Bailey, Tommy
Thomas, Paul Crane, D.W. Dun-
can, Forrest O'Bannion, Palmer
Knight, John Rook, Mac McAfee,
Oscar Haynes.

Blue Ridge League

Glenwood, champions (16-5):
Rampey, E. Stewart, R. Stewart,
F. Owens, B. Chapman, Huffstet-
ler, E. Chapman, W. Owens, Doo-
ley, Spearman, Wilson, Robertson,
Corley, Perry, Hopkins, Corley,
Fortner, Foster.

Arial (11-6): Paul Rampey, Russell
Masters, Chapman, Wilson,
McCravey, Perry, Owens, Willard
Brewer, Charlie Stevens, Tom Day,
Harold Turpin, Chick Crowe,
Blythe McCall, Rackley, Wardlaw
Stevens, Jim Wiggins, McNeeley,
Perry Rampey (manager), Sam
Boggs, Rufus Porter, Guy Grant,
Sam Day.

Easley (11-7): Campbell, Hicks,
E. Merck, Cody, McCauley, Pitts,
King, Garrick, Harbin, Smith,
P. Merck, Galloway, Waldrop.

Westminster (9-4): Jacob, Powell,
McGuffin, McDuffie, Lee, Rooker,
Hawkins.

Lonsdale (7-5): Dooley, Martin,
Waldrop, Gilliard, Owens, Watt.

Alice (7-7): Davis, Hendrix, Smith,
Holcombe, Bagwell, Cater, Chap-
man, McDonald, Duncan, McCoy,
Reeves, Gillespie, Leslie.

Liberty (7-10): Burdette, Wooten,

Thrasher, Carter, Bagwell, Garri-
son, Medlock, Dodgens, Owens,
Lovell, Trotter, Duncan, Baines,
Waldrop, Dooley, J.B. Gilstrap,
Gillespie, Bryson.

Newry (5-9): Cater, Alexander, Tollison, Sluder.

Pickens (5-15): Roper, M. Pace,
Rampey, Ballard, B. Pace, Haw-
kins, McNeely, Wellborn, Adams,
Dillard, McAllister.

Walhalla (0-12): Turpin, Blackwell,
Garrett, Smith, Holcombe,
Gilliard, Gambrell, Rutledge.

Pickens County League

Glenwood, champions (2-0): Corley,
Mull, H.J. Lark, Dodgens, Wilson,
Hopkins.

Liberty (0-2): Grevely, Bagwell,
M. Merck, T. Merck, Smith, Cody.

Dixie Textile League

Brandon of Woodruff, champions
(12-2): Nabors, Knox, Loftis, Barbery, Wilson, Lawson, Littlejohn,
Brewington, Blackwell, Shehan,
Weaver, Ivey, Leopard, Betsil, Taylor, Patterson, Elrod, Page, Jackson.

Simpsonville (8-4): Blackwell, Gray,
Tucker, Adams, Jim Yeargin, D.K.
Smith, Satterfield, Foster, Poole,
Goodenough, Bagwell, Sheffield,
Tinsley, Waters, Hendrix, Coker,
Fowler.

Fountain Inn (6-3): Godfrey,
L. Woods, Childers, Drummond,
Nelson, Giles, Hunter, Shaver,
Gault, Bonner, Williams,
W. Wood, Ryder, Elwood, Fox,
Mathis.

Enoree (3-2): Cooper, Blanton, Sam
Page, Thornton, Craig, Emory,
Williams, Patterson, Ramsey,
Waddell, Rhodes, Betsill.

Greer (2-6): Harvey, Tipton, D. Smith,
E. Smith, McCarter, F. Smith,
Giles, Brewton.

Conestee (2-7): Gray, Wilson, Harrison, Everett, Adams, Tucker, Williams, Hendrix, Allen, Foster, Burton, Gray.

Southern Worsted (1-9): Smith, Ford, Brandon, Hudson, Shipp, Foster, Williams, Newman, Fowler, Pollard, Blease, Power, Sheffield.

West State League

Brandon of Greenville, champions (5-3): Corbin, Beeks, Smith, Von Hollen. Denton, Freeman, Limbaugh, Ramey, Anders.

Williamston (7-2): Thompson, Black, Miller, Burns, King, Browning, Sargent, Holliday, Davenport, Cannon.

Brooks Brothers (3-1)

Poe Panthers (3-5): Side, Brookshire, Cantrell, Lister, Boggs, Williams, Harrison, Ferguson, Childs, Brookshire.

Piedmont (2-3): Cooley, Henderson, Terry, Reeves, McCall, Fleming, Pack, Dill.

Mills Mill Millers of Greenville(2-4): Revis, Chandler, G. Davis, Smith, Revis, Abbott, Henry, Henderson.

Pelzer (2-4): Galloway, Williams, Woodcock, Holliday, Brown, Revel, Ellenburg, Jordan, Pearson, McCall, Littlejohn.

Judson (2-5): Baker, Lewis, McDaniel, Williams, Cobb, Wyatt, Chapman, McDonald, Bishop, McDuffie, Forrest, Vaughn, Morgan, Vickery.

Parker League

Brandon of Greenville, champions (4-3): Batson, Spearman, Spencer, Galloway, Reid, Blackwell, Fricks, Tollison.

Poe (5-1): Cantrell, Sides, Williams, Mack Berry, Alexander, Huggins, Williams.

Monaghan of Greenville (2-1): Hartsell, Bowen, Jones, Kitchen, Wiggins, Thompson, Hopkins.

Camperdown (2-3): Knight, Wilson, Brown, Cooksey, Boling, Gosnell, Erwin.

Beaver Duck (1-2): Turner, Breazeale, Payne, Corbin, Carson.

Woodside (1-4): Alexander, Reid, Hall, Couch, Smith, Bowen, Ramey, Campbell, Clifford, King.

Eastern Carolina League

Arcadia, champions, (26-13): Jones, English, B. Rowe, H. Rowe, Campbell, West, Veal, J. Cannon, Cabiness, Cooper, Monk Thackston, R. Cannon.

Drayton (24-16): Finley, R. Prince, Owens, C. Inman, Bagwell, Claude Center, Stephens, Hill, Ray, Kelly, Carter, Southern, Cothran, Tice.

Gaffney (21-13): Red Shehan, Allison, A. Phillips, E. Phillips, Gold Ferguson, Hensley, Clary, A. Humphries, D. Humphries, Basington, E. Clary, W. Clary, Sprouse.

Inman (19-16): Raymond, Benton, Underwood, Davis, Clark, Bo Dotherow, Allen, Cashion, Prince, Abernathy, Pack.

Converse (15-13): Lark, Mooneyham, Byers, Powers, Lambright, Hall, Mosely, Evans, Fowler, Gentry, Vassey, Sipes, Cosley.

Pacolet (12-16): L. Petty, Goforth, R. Ellison, Harrold, A. Petty, Campbell, A. Pace, Arnold, L. Pace, H. Ellison.

Beaumont (7-20): Gault, Fowler, Garrett, Lowery, Prince, Medley, Dillingham, Millwood, Turner, Pointer.

Clifton (5-23): Mahaffey, C. Inman, Calvert, Vassey, Mabry, D. Hatchett, Dixon, Bridges, Hughes, Barber.

Spartanburg County League

Spartan, champions (14-7): Ralph Steadings, Harold Foster,

Tarbucket Lancaster, Fat Timmons, Dub O'shields, Slim Mooneyham, Suvern Wright, Hobe Fine, Whif Roland, Gene Wood, Tuck McConnell, Blackie Fowler, Bill Wingo, Slim Jackson, Fat Mossebeau, Jack Cothran, Biershenks, Jack Henson, Horace Sitton, Hendrix, Harold Sullivan (manager), Gunter, Rollings, Chandler, Ralph Dodd, Godfrey, Lancaster, Blanton, Frank Helderman.

Arkwright (11-10): Frank McCullough, Lynch, Joe Ashmore, Lowery, Ernest Hawkins, Griffin, Goforth, Sunny Moore, Hellman, Troy Taylor, Owens, Snooks Allen, Louis Watkins, Varner, Jordan, Jennings, Holt, Quinn, Randall, Mahaffey.

Fairforest (14-7): L. Taylor, Mabry, Hill, Ridgeway, Traynham, M. Taylor, Lindley, Shore, Wilder, Dobson, Griffin, Chumley, Dobson.

Inman (9-11): Pridmore, H. Crocker, Cothran, Belcher, Steadman, Pike, Parris, Gowan, Hudgens, Robbins, Crooks, Gorman, Bebber, C. Crocker, Mahaffey, Turner.

Saxon (8-10): Trammell, Bookout, Thomas, Mullinax, Watkins, Jennings, Clark, Gallman, Griffin, Hall, Hendricks, Calvert, Quinn, Jess Littlejohn, Corn, Howell, Green.

Union (7-9): Blackwell, Jolly, Lawson, Byrd, Fowler, Holt, Hicks, Sullivan, White, Fox, Byars, Whitener, Willard, Cothran, Farr, Leonhart, Jeter.

Glendale (7-11): Harris, Holt, Blanton, Bennett, Porter, Bates, Gosnell, Rhinehart, Morgan, Cooksey, I. Gossett, Hutchins, Rush, Bagwell, Linder, Hovis, Reeves, West, Alexander.

Whitney (6-11): Thompson, D. Morgan, J. Holt, J. Morgan, O. Holt, E. Sullivan, T. Holt, Hammett, Huskey, A. Holt, Pearson, Chapman, C. Morgan, Holderman, Hughes, Rhinehart.

Mid-County League

Fairmont, champions (13-3): Farmer, S. Morrow, Fortenberry, B. Gibson, R. Morrow, McAbee, Belcher, Genoble, Black, C. Gibson.

Drayton (12-7): Carter, Lancaster, Bennett, Lander, G. O'Sullivan, J. O'Sullivan, Wilson, Hughes, Moore, Smith, Ward, Collins, Wood.

Fingerville (10-6): Pruitt, Turner, Ridings, Lowe, Ezell, Adkins, Rochester, Earley, Bulman, Durham.

Buffalo (8-2): Eubanks, L. Gillespie, Rhinehart, Hughey, Ramsey, Ezell, Lawson, Inman, Putnam, Gillespie.

Cherokee Falls (5-7): T. Maynor, C. Dillingham, B. Ramsey, C. Ramsey, White, W. Dillingham, Broome, L. Ramsey, H. Earles.

Pacolet (4-9): L. Banks, Green, Pitts, Sutton, Bryant, Williams, Fowler, Hodge, M. Banks.

Clifton (4-10): J. Coggins, Calvert, Barber, McAbee, Allbright, Black, B. Coggins, Massey, G. Coggins, Jolly.

Converse (3-10): Vernon, B. Brown, Mathis, R. Brown, Vaughn, Morgan, Frady, Henderson, Lee.

Big Six League

Lydia (9-2): Kirby, Brown, Crocker, Jones, Patterson, Johnson, Lawson, Pressley, Stroud, Emory, R. Kirby, W. Abrams, Mills, Foster.

Joanna (7-6): R. Abrams, Deese, Earl Morse, E. Turner, Weathers, J. Morse, Hunnicutt, Brown, Farmer, Case, Ross, Rhodes, Kay, G. Turner.

Mollohon (7-7): L. Martin, B. Shealy, Moates, E. Smith, Rhinehart, Mills, Rollins, R. Shealy,

Hufstetler, Cromer, Miller, McCarty, Bouknight, Jackson, C. Smith, T. Shealy, Cromer, Franklin.

Newberry (7-8): Brennan, D. Bouknight, Templeton, J. Shealy, Hamilton, D. Hiller, George Hiller, Darby, Nicholson, Franklin, Lindley, J. Taylor, Singley, G. Taylor, Livingston, E. Shealy, E. Hiller, Cook.

Laurens (5-4): Chumley, Taylor, Good, W. Cline, Walker.

Watts (1-9): Byrd, Burns, Brownlee, McGowan, Copeland, McGraw, Bible, Owens, Craig, Brown, Ward, Brooks.

Textile Four League (Second Teams)

Ware Shoals, champions (1-0): Davis, Wallace.

Panola (0-1): Brandon, Harris, Leek.

Mathews (no records)

Greenville County League

Apalache, champions (12-4): Ruff, E. Belue, Crain, Dobbins, J.W. McCarter, Bishop, B. Leopard, Ballenger, C. Belue, H.T. Lunny, H.C. Cleveland, Newman, Leopard, G.W. Weathers, Robertson, George Blackwell.

Fork Shoals (5-4): Pitts, Williams, Link, Meeks, Campbell, Trammell, Adair, Thompson, Brown.

Simpsonville (4-6): O. Alexander, R. Medlock, Motley, Dillard, Razor, W. Alexander, West, Thackston, Carlton.

Fountain Inn (2-6): R. Meeks, Pitts.

Anderson County League

Chiquola, champions (26-5): Tice, Hines, O. Anderson, Huskey, June Werner, Vickers, Holsonbake, Simmons, Jean Belue, Keasler, Beacham, Cunningham, Thompson, Pigott.

Appleton (18-7): J. McElrath, Allen, Bailey, Berry McElrath, Tillison,

Frank Keaton, F. Powell, G. Powell, Phillips, R.B. Speares, McCann, Salisbury, Harold, Robinson, Gunter, Harrell, Dawson, Honea.

Equinox White Sox (15-15): Shetley, Moore, B. Powell, Harbin, Humphries, Bill Webb, R. Allen, Spearman, Kelly, Shirley, Humphries, Craft, Beck, Davis.

Gluck (12-14): Moore, C. Jordan, Evans, Stovall, Sam Jordan, McAllister, Tabor, Hanna, R. Doolittle, Ballenger, Hamm, Stovall, Sweetenburg, Moon, Perry, Leonard, E. Doolittle, Manley, Blackston.

Orr (12-15): Kerr, McLeskey, Anderson, Hart, Miller, Tommy Lyons, C. Buchanan, Davis, Lee Whitten, Cox, Dumb Price, Dude Buchanan, Croxton, Frith, Johnny Ashworth, Jerry Whitten, Crate Herring (manager), Cotton Herring.

Gossett (10-16): Summey, Jim Blackwell, D. Smith, Pearson, Simpson, Wood, Ervin Sexton, Dockins, Simmons, Watson, Chapman, R. Smith, Chavous, McAllister, Werner, Harrell.

Anderson (6-15): Embler, Simpson, Harry Laval, Ripley, Dillard, Barney Smith, Holbrook, Heaton, Joe Haynes, Honea, Blackston, D. Smith.

Belton (6-17): Nelson, Minyard, McAllister, Bannister, Deanhardt, S. Owens, Warnock, Mace, R. Owens, Vest, King, O. Owens, Cummings, Shockley, Shirley.

Georgia-Carolina League

Hartwell GA (3-0)

Central (3-1): Simms, Frank Howard, Cox, Duncan, Dillard, Kelly.

Calhoun Falls (3-2): Carrithers, Pearson, B. Helms, Hilley.

LaFrance (3-3): Chandler Southerland, Ab Garrison, Frank Hopkins,

Joe Smith, Dewey Hopkins, Williams, Ralph Simpson, Jack Talley, James Craft, Ray Chitwood, Frank Smith, E.O. Okes, Bob Massey, Henry Williams, Oscar Ferguson (manager).
Abbeville (2-4): Boyd, New, McCuen, Welch, Wilson.
Toccoa GA (1-0)
Lavonia GA (1-2)
Appleton (0-4): Dooley, Hendrix, Stewart, Sanders, Ertzberger, Daniels, Gunter, Wells, Spake.

Union County League

West Springs (5-2)
Excelsior (3-2): McDonald, Byrd, Addison, Howell, B. Summer, T. Summer, Estes, Bedenbaugh.
Ottaray (3-3): Eller, Davis, Berry, Vinson, West, Brown, J. Coward, Smith, Willis, A. Coward, W. Leonhart, Cook.
Sedalia (1-5)

Spartanburg County Colored League

Pacolet (10-2)
Lyman (9-3)
Converse (8-4)
Drayton (5-5)
Arcadia (5-8)
Tucapau (4-9)
Spartan (3-8)
Whitney (3-8)

Independent Teams

Newberry 2nd Team (no records): J.B. Livingston, George Hiller, James, Rister, Frank Shealy, Henry Merchant, Irvin Attaway (manager), Virgil Whittle, Marion Franklin, Jimmy Boland, Fred Cook, Ben Nicholson, Carl Taylor, Cortez Ward, Bachmann Stockman.
Mollohon 2nd Team (no records): Cal Duncan (manager), James McCarty, Jay Martin, Winfred Cromer, Paul Smith, Irvin Edwards,

Eugene Harmon, Heyward Mills, T.D. Shealy, Pickens Rinehart, Ray Shealy, Buck Rollins, Wilbur Huffstetler, Hugh Masters, Collie Miller.

1936

Mid State League

Winnsboro, champions (18-3): Carey, Green, Baker, Ward, Gray, Smith, Frye, Bonas, Wells, Rhinehardt, Shealy, Owens, Frew.
Newberry (18-3): Johnny Wertz, Livingstone, Al Shealy, Derrell Bouknight, Pee Wee Franklin, Bubba Whittle, Jeff Singley, Garvice Taylor, Walter Hiller, Irby Bouknight, Reginald Bouknight, Ed Thompson, Roy Caldwell, Bob Creekmore.
Buffalo (8-7): Putman, Perkins, Inman, Duncan, Hyatt, Gowan.
Lockhart (7-9): Deal, O'dell, Steel, Cabiness, Vaughn, Clary.
Joanna (7-10): Smith, Coleman, Farmer, Koon, Wolfe.
Excelsior (6-9): Kirby, Howell, Byrd, Nabors, Walker.
Great Falls (6-10): Ellison, Grant, Wilson, Graham, Carlton.
Whitmire (3-15): Ward, Yarborough, Barker, Lawson, Gaffney, Breazeale.

Central Carolina League

Laurens, champions (18-8): Glenn, Brady, Shehan, Carr, Mills, Putnam, J. Kneece, H. Lee, L. Cicerle, J. Haines, Y. Senn, R. Martinelle, H. Laval, J. Burgess, F. Bragg, R. Abrams, H. Taylor, P. Barbare, J. Hall, A. Kinson, B.J. Cox (manager)
Ware Shoals Riegels (19-5): Howard, L.K. Proctor, Lee, J.C. Davis, James Graham, W.S. Horne, Robert Higbe, Grier Wright,

Jimmie Sanders, J.N. Moore, Leith
Willis, W.T. Howard, H. New-
bury, W.J. Werner, Cleve Cooper,
Eel Weir.

Ninety Six (16-8): Rivers, Buena
Wells, Brice Bennett, Hugh Stod-
dard, Baxter Sanders, Cecil Wood,
R. Doolittle, Barry, C. Carithers,
Duncan, Mel Lindley, Fred Wiley,
Granny Hightower, Ralph Simp-
son, Bill Knox, Dill, Claude Garri-
son, Fred Dowis, H. McAbee,
H. Pletersek, T. Voiselle, K. Smith.

Mathews (15-9): J. Suggs, Younce,
Charlie Jeffcoat, Moore, J. Whit-
lock, Gaines, D. Southern, Gilles-
pie, C. Girk, Weir, Corley,
C. Kettles, Berry, W. Outzs, Girk,
Holliday, Robert Kennedy,
H. Adair, G. Rinehart, J. Hull,
M. Putman, F. Owens, O. Boyd.

Watts (11-13): P. Knight, Kirby,
W.G. Duncan, Paul Turner,
Charlie Byrd, Ladd Maxwell, P.K.
Thomas, B.S. Carpenter, M.E.
Smythe, Bruce Sudberry, A.R.
Bingham, Carl Dickert, Ralph
Mathews, Lefty Corley, Troy
Ward, Frank Lloyd (manager)

Graniteville Rocks (9-15): C. Smith,
D. Smith, H. Hansman, G. Smith,
S. Hopper, W. Whaley, R. Frank-
lin, S. Wells, J. Hays, F. Holland,
J. Marvin, V. Walton, Holson-
back, J. Cooper, H. Franklin.

Riverdale (6-18): Hair, Tice, Gunn,
Davis, Rook, Perkins, Queen,
O. Mason, Duck Wells, Lefty Tice,
L. Berry, P. Abercrombie, E. Ramey,
J. Odiorne, H. Knox, H. Lamb,
J. Farr, F. Mabry, E. Obannion
(manager), Pug Ezell, C. Cooper.

Greenwood (5-19): Doolittle, Elton
Marchant, J.R. Duncan, Murphy,
Jim Bailey, Turner, Boyd, Davis,
Escoe, Herbert Bailey, Doodie
Franklin, Boozer Gallahair,
Sparks, Bolton, Vaughn, Putman,
Shaw, Alton Weathers, Irby

Raines, Hull, Banes, R.L. Norrell,
Charlie Golden, Ora Woods, Tom
Getty, Raymond Hughes, Ted Chal-
mers, Lynn Murrow, Jordan,
Adair.

King Cotton League

Brandon of Greenville, champions
(8-8): Harry Bland, Pel Ballenger,
Bert Wilson, Guy Hawkins, Fred
McAbee, Alvin Jenkins, Ralph
Morgan, Bill Limbaugh, Roy Fos-
ter, Larry Campbell, Joe Spencer,
Charles Foster, Joe Reid, Marshall
Lyle, Manning Bolt, Morgan,
Suggs.

Mills Mill of Greenville (13-5):
Timmons, Christopher, Taylor,
Barrett, Morris, Maxwell,
Brewington, Page, Craig, Shoaf,
Hostetler, Page, Petty.

Pelzer (12-4): Ross, Buntin, Helms,
Cannon, Woods, Pickelseimer,
Harley Heath, Moore, F. Heath,
Emery, Lefty Crymes, Westmore-
land, Galloway.

Lyman (11-8): Senn, Jacobs, Benson,
Rushing, Ward, Burgess, Query,
Jett, Suttlemier.

Piedmont (9-7): Cooper, Lee,
McCall, Wyatt, McPherson.

Judson (6-10): Stokes, Gross, Price,
Hicks, Cicerill, Crymes, Escoe, Collins, Pack.

Southern Bleachery (5-12): Query,
Burgess, Ward, Jett, J. Childers,
Stribbling, Rushing, Stewart, J.D.
Childers, McElrath.

Central YMCA (2-14): Godshaw,
Beck, B. Duffie, Heath, Griffin,
Hunt, Gault, Lee, Aycock,
Hartzell, Hiott.

Blue Ridge League

Easley, champions (14-6): Shaver,
C. Alexander, L. Waldrop, Jame-
son, H. Waldrop, L. Alexander,
Garrett, Hendrix, Dooley, King,
Cox, Dillard, Hudson, Campbell,

Merck, Cody, Pitts, Spearman, McCall.

Liberty (13-6): Morgan, Thrasher, Powell, Owens, Wooten, Lovell, Garrison, Medlock, Gravely, Smith, Pitts.

Lonsdale (6-3): Dooley, Watson, Owens, Gilliard.

Newry (6-3): King, Cater, Alexander, Sluder, Manley, McClellan.

Alice (4-7): Leslie, Bagwell, Williams, Stewart, Cater, Holcombe.

Central (0-14): Pitts, Kendrick, Cox, Thomas, Elliott, Simmons, Cox, Fletcher, Waters, Riggins, Park, Lydia.

Western Carolina League

Woodside, champions (29-13): McCravey, Masters, Hairston, Jackson, Helton, Tucker, Harbin, Suddeth, Virgil Lavender, Chandler, Hall, Ramsey, Wilson, Moore, Gillespie, Heath, Hunter, Brookshire.

Glenwood (10-10): Spearman, Hopkins, Wilson, Mull, Boyd, Foster, Fortner, Owens, Corley, Robinson.

Pickens (7-4): Roper, Daniels, Dillard, O. Adams, Evans, Nichols, Turpin, Stewart, R. Haynes, Gilstrap, C. Hayes, H. Adams.

Sampson (7-5): Weaver, Harvel, Belt, Mauldin, Fowler, Spake, Sterling, Major, Ormond, Crawford, Hunter, Bowers, Gunn.

Arial (7-12): Hunter, Helton, Moss, Boggs, Wilson, Paul Rampey, Masters, McCall, Day, S. Rampey, McCravey, Pitts, Miller, Bagwell, Stokes.

Williamston (4-9): Cannon, Sargent, Miller, Holliday, Mauldin, Chapman, Crawford, Fowler, Dickert, Cooper, Carson.

West State League

Poe, champions (0-1): Sloan, Boggs, Brookshire, Childs, Alexander, Al-

verson, Lister, Williams, Landreth, Ferguson, C. Sides, Steadings, Grastie, Shehan.

Southern Worsted (1-0): Marshall, Brannon, Bess.

Pelzer (0-1): McCall, Galloway.

Piedmont Textile League

Slater, champions (19-3): Brown, Gillespie, Bill Lynch, Jim Bailey, Marvin Hembree, Owen Price, Emerson Cashion, Keaton, Colie Vaughn, Broadus Abbott, Aubrey Ledford, Hopkins, Furman Pinson, Marion Dudley, Charlie Vaughn, Buster Starnes, Harold Taylor, Ansil McMakin, J.D. Putman.

Monaghan of Greenville (11-4): Hopkins, Waldrop, Herring, Nichols, Clark.

Renfrew Bleachery (7-6): Tollison, Coleman, Granger, Wilson.

Union Bleachery (4-7): Ivey, C. Brooks, Robertson, Brooks, Harrison, Rhodes, Turner.

Dunean (3-8): League, Riddle, Floyd, Cox, Holbrook, Foster, Bailey.

Camperdown (1-10): Bailey, Hembree, Browning, Brissey, Howard, McDowell, Bell, Bridwell.

Dixie Textile League

Mills Mill of Greenville, champions (0-1): Revis, Smith, Abbott.

Fountain Inn (1-0): Marshall, Wood, Nelson, McGee, Pratt, Wilson, Smith, Godfrey, Williams, Bond, Carson, Adair.

Simpsonville (no records): Alexander, Garrison, Hendrix.

Fork Shoals (no records): Kellett, Bull, Pitts.

Pacolet (no records): Oneil Landrum, Horace Henderson, Edd Clary, Tommy Jett, Lawrence Fleming, A.C. Phillips, Ernie White, Arthur Goforth, Lynwood McMakin, Red Ellison, Leroy Pace, Claude

Arnold (manager), Tee Fleming, Wilson Lee, Tobe Campbell, Rattler Pace, Cooter Scott, William Clary.

Pickens County League

Pickens, champions (no records)
Arial (no records)

Parker League

Brandon of Greenville (no records)
Dunean (no records)

Big Six League

Ware Shoals (no records)
Enoree (no records)
Mills Mill of Woodruff (no records)
Brandon of Woodruff (no records)
Clinton (no records)
Laurens (no records)

Anderson County League

Chiquola Chicks, champions (16-5): Ned Harris, Hinkie Allen, Cecil Tyson, Charlie Golden, Shag Knox, Crick McCarter, Tack Clark, Al Evans, Bud Voight, Husky, Holsenbake, Davis, B. Anderson, Ollie Anderson, Jim Mobley, Ellis Levicki, Bill Womack, Ramsey, Pop Werner (manager), Paul Paite, Eddie Clement, Leonard Berry, Forrest Keasler, George Lollis, Gallahair, Jean Belue, Lee, Kiser, Bland.
Orr Red Sox (12-3): Alf Anderson, Dumb Price, Mutt Williams, Wagnon, Dude Buchanan, Burrell, Luther Hart, Mike Blazo, Ramon Voight, Harry Davis, Charlie Matthews, Lee Whitten, Joe Ashworth, Harley, Spencer, Treadway, Evans.
Equinox White Sox (9-7): B. Moore, C. Moore, Paul Troutman, Larry Harbin, Bill Webb, Harper, Shirley, G. Spearman, L. Webb, Beck, Allen, J.B. Spearman, Mince, Humphries.
Anderson (9-7): Sneed, Craft, Laval,

Fred Powell, J.B. Kelly, Lonnie Holbrook, Barney Smith (manager), Weir, Tough Embler, Simpson, Heaton, Bob Gettys, Bessinger, Raymond Weathers, Lefty Moore, Glenn Smith, Talmadge Embler, Harris, Blackston, Cargill, Gaines, Daniels, Christman.
Gossett (8-8): Chavous, Vickers, J. Werner, Leonard, Sexton, Cunningham, Summey, E. Werner, Ingle, Wilbanks, Jean Belue, Wood, Porterfield, Pigott, Atkins.
Belton Athletics (5-9): Bumgardner, Minyard, Willingham, McAllister, Deanhardt, Gunn, R. Owens, Nelson, Glenn, D. Owens, Shirley, Hogg, Vost, Cummings, Shockley, Best, Carlton, Warnock, Haynie, Ellison, Hopper, Shirley.
Appleton (5-11): Blackwell, Allen, Bailey, Gettys, McElrath, Robinson, Keaton, Guy Powell, Clint Cason, DuPont Smith, R.B. Speares, Warren, Stewart, Gunter, Britt, Howell, Leroy Mahaffey, Rhinehardt.
Gluck (3-13): C. Jordan, Perry, Sam Jordan, Hamm, Hanna, Bloodworth, H. Allen, Ivester, Linden, Weathers, Sweetenburg, Walker, McLeskey, C. Allen, Black, Bray, C. Moore.

Georgia-Carolina League

Hartwell GA, champions (14-5)
Lavonia GA (10-8)
Appleton (9-7): Harry Stewart, T. Gunter, Jake Britt, C. Hall, B. Wells, M. Cargill, R.B. Speares, Monk Spake, S. Smith, L. Smith.
Calhoun Falls (6-3): Rucker Pearson, Lefty Carrithers, Buck Helms, Neil Chrisley, Bob Overby, John Helms, Al Brown, Barry Burdette, Charlie Rudder, Webb Hilley, Mathews, W.M. Burton, John Nally.

Abbeville (6-11): Whitten, New, Tarre, Welch, Satterfield, Ferguson, L. Wilson, Sealy.

LaFrance (2-15): Chitwood, Jones, S. Smith, J. Smith, Massey, Oakes, Simpson, B. Smith, Massey, Harrison.

Mid Week League

Chiquola (6-2)
Orr (4-2)
Gossett (3-4)
Gluck (1-6)

Greenville Textile League

Mills Mill of Greenville, champions (no records)

Eastern Carolina League

Pacolet, champions (no records): L. Petty, Goforth, Red Ellison, Harrold, A. Petty, Campbell, A. Pace, Arnold, L. Pace, H. Ellison.

Drayton (no records): Durham, Finley, R. Prince, Owens, C. Inman, Bagwell, Claude Center, Stephens, Ray, Hill, Kelly, Carter, Cothran, Southern, Tice.

Inman (no records): Raymond, Benton, Underwood, Davis, Clark, Bo Dotherow, Allen, Cashion, Prince, Abernathy, Pack.

Converse (no records): Lark, Mooneyham, Byers, Powers, Lambright, Hall, Mosley, Evans, Pete Fowler, Gentry, Vassey, Sipes, Cosley.

Brandon of Woodruff (no records)

Arcadia (no records): Jones, English, B. Rowe, H. Rowe, Campbell, West, Veal, J. Cannon, Cabiness, Cooper, Monk Thackston, R. Cannon.

Beaumont (no records): Gault, Fowler, Garrett, Lowery, Prince, Medley, Dillingham, Millwood, Turner, Pointer.

Whitney (no records): O. Holt, A. Holt, Hendricks, Scruggs, Huskey, Wall, Hammett, Hughes, Walker, Thompson, D. Morgan, C. Morgan, Moore, Thomas.

Spartanburg County League

Glendale, champions (15-5): Harris, Allen, Blanton, Anders, Porter, Bennett, Reed, Reeves, Millford, Cooksey, Hutchinson, Gosnell.

Union (14-7): Jeter, Jolly, T. Wilson, Hicks, Fowler, Lawson, Sullivan, Cohen, J. Willard, Fox, Whitener.

Arkwright (13-7): Trammell, Howell, Hendrix, L. Taylor, Hawkins, Jordan, Bagwell, M. Taylor, Weaver, Quinn, H. Taylor, Watson, Nolan.

Spartan (11-10): Tarbucket Lancaster, Fat Timmons, Dub O'Shields, Slim Mooneyham, Suvern Wright, Hobe Fine, Whif Roland, Gene Wood, Tuck McConnell, Blackie Fowler, Bill Wingo, Slim Jackson, Fat Massebeau, Jack Cothran, Biershenks, Sitton, Dodd, Helderman, Henson, Foster, C. Fowler, Steadings.

Clifton (10-10): Massey, Barber, Posey, Calvert, Elders, Mabry, Green, Bell, Coggins, Waters, Pulley.

Fingerville (10-11): Kay, Ezell, Ridings, Lowe, Davis, Adkins, Ramsey, Turner, Durham, Earley.

Drayton (6-13): Moore, Seay, Smith, Haney, O'Sullivan, Wilson, Carter, Finch, Hughes, Ward, Reese, D. Bennett, C. Bennett, S. Ray.

Inman (2-18): Shehan, Crocker, Pike, Gowan, Maxwell, Bagwell, Hudgens, Cline, Abernathey, Fox, Bebber, Steadman.

Mid-County League

Buffalo (15-3): Wright, Walker, O'Shields, Watson, H. Kingsmore, Frost, Gowan, Smith, R. Millwood, J. Haney, Vessey, L. Kingsmore, H. Fisher, C. Fisher, Millwood.

Gaffney (13-6): O. Medley, Guthrie,

W. Medley, Fox, White, Pruitt,
Smith, Jenkins, A. Medley, Mar-
tin, A. Bolton, F. Bolton.
Converse (13-10): Frady, Fowler,
Cudd, R. Mathis, Vernon, F.
Mathis, Brown, Reid, Croxdale,
Henderson, Stepp.
Fairmont (11-7): P. Farmer, B. Mor-
row, R. Morrow, Gibson,
D. McAbee, D. Farmer, Belcher,
C. Belcher, Bradley, Clayton,
S. Morrow, Genoble, O. Farmer.
Monarch (11-9): G. Coward, E. Lenh-
art, W. Sanders, S. Sanders, Wool-
ens, Smith, D. Berry, Garner,
A. Coward, Benson, Ella.
Arcadia (10-8): Gossett, Ballard, Hen-
derson, West, Jones, McIntyre,
Bridgeman, Walker, Bebber, Gibbs.
Glendale (3-14): Gosnell, Rush,
R. Murray, Reese, Thompson,
Bookout, H. Millwood, Warren,
Bishop, Blackwell.
Clifton (2-14): Calvert, Prince, Bar-
ber, Jolly, Thornton, Black, Bag-
well, McAbee, Coggins, Mallory,
McCarthy, Mallory, J. Coggins.

Victor-Monaghan League

Greer (no records)
Apalache (no records)
Walhalla (no records)
Victor of Greer (no records)

Spartanburg County Colored League

Arcadia (no records)
Tucapau (no records)
Pacolet (no records)
Lyman (no records)
Southern Bleachery (no records)
Converse (no records)
Drayton (no records)
Clifton (no records)

Independent Teams

Greer (no records): Cabiness, Gibbs,
Greer, D. Smith, E. Smith,
Brewington, E. McCarter, Harvey,
Brannon, T. Smith.

1937

Piedmont Textile League

Slater, champions (12-4): Croxton,
Lynch, Hembree, Price, Varner,
Emerson Cashion, Coster, Bailey,
Ansel McMakin, Dee Wilson, Felix
Duncan, E.R. Abbott, James
Lybrand, Neal Landreth, Colie
Vaughn, Charles Vaughn.
Balfour NC (5-8)
Monaghan of Greenville (5-4): Her-
ring, Major, Floyd, Kirby, Nichols,
Alexander, Hinson, Stephens,
Suttles.
Renfrew Bleachery (5-4): Tollison,
Wilson, Granger, Williams, Knox.
Union Bleachery (4-4): Robinson,
Harrison, Worrell, Rhodes,
Brooks, Turner, Aycock, Patter-
son, Ivey.
Dunean (2-7): Stewart, Ford, Put-
man, Hamrick, Sankford, Bailey,
Floyd, Riddle, Lindsay, Bragg,
Moore.

Central Carolina League

Mathews, champions (16-5): Corley,
Hall, Smith, Gaines, Davis, Weir,
Matthews, Suggs, Kennedy,
Abrams, Southern, George
Jeffcoat, Lyles, Garrison, Christo-
pher, Suggs, Abrams.
Riverdale (17-9): Turner, English,
Hamilton, Abercrombie, Thorn-
ton, Gantt, Fletcher Chaffin,
Thomas, Lamb, Farr, Dog Obann-
ion, Ramey, Martinell, Odiorne,
D. Wells, Mabry, Christian, Wood,
Sipes.
Chiquola (9-6): Long, Limbaugh,
Maxwell, Bill Womack, Jean Belue,
Kettles, Evans, Warner, Mobley,
Greer, Clement, Foster, Clark,
Shag Knox, Golden, Barbare,
Keisler, Bradley, Leonard, McCar-
ter, Cason, Deanhart, Therfold,
Kettles, Huskey, Harvey, Ned
Harris.

Ninety Six (10-8): Bennett, Bill Voiselle, Norman, Stoddard, Wells, Davis, Sanders, Woods, Smith, Darwin, Hightower, Wiley, Kirkland, Werner, Lowman, Strickland, Miller, Clayton, Corvin, Keen, Wilson, Dowis, Thompson, C. Drummond, A. Drummond.

Ware Shoals (4-11): Smith, Weir, Foster, Proctor, Howard, Davis, Newberry, Stoddard, Wells, Postal, Horne, Edwards, Jordan, Wright, Powell, Evans, Cooper, Bachelor, Werner, Campbell, Davis, Ware, Hancock, Gambrell.

Greenwood (4-11): Jones, Glenn, Escoe, Weathers, Ward, Whitlock, Marchant, Raines, Wrinkle, Kirkland, Furlow, Brady, Doodie Franklin, Eleazer, Dickert, Nub Smythe, Hull, Werner, Gillespie, Justice, Dunkle, Ouzts, Gliney, White, Prater.

Palmetto League

Joanna (2-2): Cooley, Farmer, Prater, Owens, A. Hunnicutt, Case, Abrams, Hawkins, Moore, J. Weathers, Harrison, G. Hunnicutt, Hayes, Taylor, Loftis.

Greenwood (1-0): James, Glenn, Arnold, Fowler, Bolton, Pickens, A. Weathers, Sparks, Higgenbotham.

Lydia (1-1): Miller, Johnson, Brown, Fuller, Burnett, Parker, Emory, Lawson, Patterson, Craig, Castleberry, Claude Crocker.

Ninety Six (0-1): C. Dunwood, McKinney, Morris, B. Dunwood, Bennett, Campbell, Boozer, Ivester, Hunnicutt, Hughes, Voiselle.

Mid State League

Monarch, champions (18-9): Walker, Littlejohn, Middlebrooks, Smith, Sanders, Phillips, Timmons, Nabors, W. Lawson, N. Lawson, Knox, Berry, Denton, Turner,

Farmer, E. Lawson, Sanders, M. Smith, Long, Cabiness, Houston Hines.

Newberry (18-6): Johnny Wertz, Shorty Bouknight, Earl Singley, Jackson, Jones, Bob Creekmore, Bud Whittle, Ed Thompson, Leon Addy, Roy Caldwell, Franklin, Walter Hiller, Alley, Caldwell, Jeff Singley, Taylor, I. Bouknight.

Joanna (15-6): Reid Gowan, Morse, Rudolph Prater, Adams, Galloway, Farmer, Coleman, Clark, E. Abrams, Turner, Galloway, R. Abrams, Ross, Morris, Brown, Ralph Prater.

Winnsboro (14-12): Lewis Gray, Greer, Cline, Gettys, Ward, Frew, Bill Wells, Shealy, Roy Brannon, Greer, Joe Owens, Cook, J. Herndon, Spires, Sargent, Barfield, G. Herndon, Stevenson, Robinson, Bruner, J. Smith, B. Smith, Rinehart, Wages, Troyans, Geddings, Gray, Shealy, Wilson.

Mollohon (10-11): Jackson, Sewell, Cromer, J. Martin, C. Jones, Moates, Kirkland, P. Golden, Wood, R. Martin, Smith, Mills, Jackson, J. Thornton, R. Golden, Rollins, McCarter, Word, Cortland, Bedenbaugh.

Lockhart (8-10): Deal, Odell, Allgood, Broome, A. Cabiness, W. Burns, Veal, Clary, Bryant, Crocker, R. Gibson, Smith, Watts, Whay, Blackwood, Carter, Smith, Byrd, B. Cabiness, B. Gibson, Stalnaker, C. Gibson.

Buffalo (3-15): Watson, Inman, Wright, Putman, Revels, Millwood, Lawson, Sullivan, Burgess, Worthy, Price, Prince, Adams, H. Kingsmore, Frost, J. Kingsmore, Abrams, Haynes, Morse, Haney.

Whitmire (2-16): Ward, Crosby, Watkins, Yarborough, Stone, Tart, M. Reed, Troyans, White, Beck, Rinehart, Painter, Dean, Smith,

Prince, Trofano, O'shields, Tate,
Gaffney, Prather, Stone, Crow,
Erskine, Coon, Derrick, Norte,
P. Brands, B. Reed.

King Cotton League

Judson, champions (17-3): Dobson,
Sides, Stowe, Duffy, Johnny
Stokes, Rushing, Collins, Country
Kneece, League, Fowler, Bland,
Jay Gross, Jim Hall, Stoner, Earl
Stewart, Pack, Ralph Stewart,
Hugh Smith, Tabor, O.V. Lee,
Granger, Dobbins, Fowler, Moore,
Pack.
Brandon of Greenville (14-6): Spen-
cer, Hawkins, Thackston, Wilson,
Morgan, Humphries, Cox, Hall,
Hopkins, Campbell, Jenkins,
Limbaugh, Berry, C. Foster,
R. Foster, Alexander, McAbee,
Burrell, Cason, Tollison, Trokie,
Hawkins, Humphries, Jenkins.
Piedmont (13-11): Underwood, Lee,
McCall, John Emery, Cooper,
Jenkins, McAbee, Carlisle, Flem-
ing, Rampey, Campbell, Ross,
Sneed, Darnell, Henderson, Tom
Pack.
Woodside (9-9): Hunter, Wilson,
Jerry Jackson, Smith, Harbin,
Wood, Moore, McCravey, Garrett,
Gillespie, Couch, Heath, Giles,
Tucker, Mills, Burke, Union,
Lavender, Suddeth, Ramsey, John-
son, Foster, Holcombe.
Sampson (7-9): Kiser, McDaniel,
Nichols, Bowers, King, Fowler,
Spake, McDaniel, Dunn, Glenn,
Lester, Hunt, McCraw, Hart,
Harbin, Garrison, Chapman,
Huskey, Gunn.
Southern Bleachery (7-13): Stibbling,
Nau, C. Childers, Stewart,
Suddeth, Strickland, Hudgens,
Brooks, Weaver, Blackwell, Steele,
L. McElrath, Barbery, A. McCar-
ter, Coker, Bearden, Yeargin,
Gay, Mann, Smith, Joe Childers,

Thrasher, J.D. Childers, Warner,
Dennis, Rollins, A. McElrath.
Greer (6-13): Drake, Brannon,
Watkins, Myers, Ed Smith, Bur-
nette, Hunt, Warner, Pitts, Thorn-
burg, Wynn, Kirby, Abernathey,
D. Smith, Clyde, Giles, Brew-
ington, Pruitt, McCarter, Earl,
Greer, Ramsey, Phillips, Bumgard-
ner, Smythe, Cannon, Waters,
Crook, Drake, Johnson, Hamrick,
Hoke, Spires, Collins, Cabiness.
Pelzer (4-15): Helms, Martin, Gallo-
way, L. Moore, Buntin, Wood,
Ross, Holliday, Walker, King,
Allen, Crymes, Pickleseimer,
M. Moore, Maynard, Heath, Wood-
cock, Rippley, Nimpond, Jordan,
Minyard, Cannon, Helms, Virgil
Lavender.

Blue Ridge League

Arial, champions (13-11): Blyth
McCall, Wiggins, McNeely, Ram-
pey, Boggs, Brown, Masters, Por-
ter, Perry, Williams.
Easley (13-8): Helton, Berry,
Hendrix, Galloway, Gilliam,
Waldrop, Gamble, Juber Hairston,
Alexander, Putman, King, Jami-
son, Hunt, Cooper, Gilliam.
Liberty (12-9): Smith, Wooten, Pitts,
Thrasher, Stewart, Medlock, Garri-
son, Owens, Powell, Turner, Ben-
nett.
Glenwood (11-10): Wilson, Fortner,
Spearman, Corley, Foster, Wil-
liams, Reid, Mull, Owens, Brook-
shire, Forrester, Rankin.
Alice (7-13): Davis, Leslie, Cater, Fer-
guson, Berry, Lynch, Hayes,
Bagwell, Nix, Stewart, Wilson,
Pace, Holcombe.
Pickens (6-10): Roper, Pace, Bolding,
Nichols, Bryant, Jones, Adams,
Hayes.

Palmetto League: Weldon Bagwell
(president), J.E. Stevens (vice

president), P.M. Powell (secretary/treasurer), J.C. Daniels (assistant secretary/treasurer)

Brandon of Greenville, champions (17-3): Ivey, Taylor, West, Lawrence, Roper, Page, Craig, Tiller, McGill, Hendrix, Jamison, Bettis, Cooper, Johnson, Rainwater, Rucy, Harvey, Criard, Laurens.

Lyman (10-8): R. Gowan, Carlisle, W. Gowan, Davis, Smith, White, Ross, Hadden, Briggs, F. Gowan, R. Fowler, Renes, Bridges, Davis, Fowler, High, Mullinax, Vaughn, Young, Griggs, Odell.

Monarch (10-9): Sanders, Berry, C. Calvert, Willis, O. Calvert, W. Linhart, E. Calvert, Moore, B. Calvert, J. Linhart, C. Crocker, D. Coward, A. Coward, S. Samley, G. Coward, Garner, Hawkins, Brannon, B. Coward, O. Crocker, C. Coward, Woolen, E. Coward, Berry, Mitchell, N. Linhart, E. Leonard, S. Linhart, S. Coward, Jamison, B. Coward, B. Crocker.

Cherokee Falls (8-4): A. Patterson, Beatty, L. Ramsey, C. Broome, Holmes, Dillingham, Boheler, Hampton, Bailey, Liner, C. Ramsey, Phillips, Maynor, Earle, Brown, Taylor, B. Ramsey, L. Broome, Riley, Lanier, W. Dillingham, C. Patterson.

Jonesville (7-7): H. Gregory, A. Spencer, D. Spencer, J.B. Holt, McKinney, Osment, J. Hawkins, Hill, H. Spencer, Hyatt, McKnight, Addis, Mabry, Kenny, Allen, Harvey, B. Gregory, Pulmey, Fowler, Allen, Worthy, P. Hawkins, H. Spencer, Worley.

Tucapau (5-6): J. Cook, Sevier, Hendrix, Lavender, Henderson, Childers, Powell, T. Cook, Cox, Tapp, Williams, Rollins, Cooper, Cothran, Austin, Jackson, Glasson, Sherbert, McBride.

Clifton (3-11): Cudd, Frady, H. Willis, Thornton, Black, Mallory, B. Coggins, Vernon, Worley, Henderson, Calvert, Mathis, G. Coggins, Mabry, Bagwell, Matthews, Reed, Bridges, J. Coggins, Powell, McCorley, B. Willis, Blackwell, Blanton, Woolen, D. Calvert.

Chesnee (0-11): Clayton, Stevens, Maynor, Jenkins, C. Jolly, Ramsey, R. Jolly, Dedmon, C. Haynes, Addington, Lockman, Humphries, Moore, Wilkins, Suttles, Cabiness, Durham, Smith, Steadman, Gregory, Wright, Mabry, L. Mabry, Baker, Cook, Collins.

Spartanburg County League

Fairmont, champions (15-13): Farmer, H. McAbee, R. Morrow, Gibson, Poteat, Bradley, Childers, Grenoble, C. Belcher, S. Belcher, Sexton, Dillingham, Barber, Ward, Jenkins, McIntyre, S. Morrow, Davis, B. Belcher, Duncan, Wilder, W. McAbee, Spelce, Ballard.

Jackson of Wellford (16-6): Blackwell, R. Wilson, Jordan, L. Taylor, Dobbins, J. Acton, M. Taylor, Murphy, Jackson, Earl Veal, Cox, R. Acton, Austin, Murphy, Shehan, E. Acton, D. Wilson, Oscar, D. Williams, Dobson, R. Williams.

Valley Falls (14-7): J. Lynch, Guy Hughes, Ernest Powell, Holt, R. Ward, Turner, Garrett, S. Rollins, Henderson, Good, Toddy Hammett, Edwards, E. Rollins, Boyd Hughes, Early, Wilson, Page, Garrett, Rose, Pack, Heldman, Taylor, Clause, Mason, Allen, Shook.

American Legion (13-10)

Inman (11-11): Paris, Gowan, Steadman, Waldrop, Pike, Parker, J. Ramsey, M. High, Abernathy, Howard Crocker, Dobbins, C. High, Doris Mabry, Vaughn, Pridmore, Miller, Pack, Davis, Evington, Gregg, Yomans.

Pacolet (7-11): Curt Randall, Ellison,
Kimberlain, Landrum, Parker,
G. Phillips, Mathis, Petty, Hogan,
Lemmonds, Banks, Loftis, Fowler,
Atchins, Olin Hodge, Kitchens,
Courtney, Lamb, C. Petit, Preacher
Lee, Timmons, Arnold, Greene,
B. Phillips, Whitlock, Gardin,
Tate.

Arcadia (5-15): Henderson, Reid,
D. Gossett, Bing Ballard, Bridg-
man, Cox, Erskine, O. West,
Gibbs, Veal, Sims, Wood, Jones,
Wynn, Lawrence, B. Gossett,
G. Medlock, Powell, McIntyre,
C. Medlock, Gardo, Good, Mann,
Gosnell, Laurens, Honey, Lesley,
M. West, McCombs, Parks,
Shook, Allen.

Hub City (5-15)

Tri-County League

Arkwright, champions (22-6): Walt
Trammell, "Country" Hendricks,
"Cotton" Bagwell, Ed Hawkins,
N. Bagwell, Louis Watkins, Denny
Hendrix, Ballard, Quinn, Mathis,
Dunlap, Shook, Varnes, Preston
Giles, Tuck McConnell, Lowe,
Gunlap, Hinson.

Gaffney (17-13): Britt, N. Clary,
Dewey, Scales, Harlow, F. Clary,
Johnston, Beam, Hughey, Ingle,
Ramsey, Allison, Branch, R. Clary,
Fox, L. Clary, Reece Hensley, Pru-
itt, P. Blackwell, Fleming, Pace,
Hodge, Eubanks, Mathis, Sullivan,
Sprouse, Harmon, White, Harris,
Jenkins.

Glendale (14-9): Rhymer, Cooksey,
Hughes, Rush, Haven Clause,
Smith, Harris, Allen, Ralph Gos-
nell, Buster Hair, Blanton, Thomas,
Herbert Taylor, Linder, Blackwell,
Jennings, Fowler, Scott, Paul How-
ell, Bush, Porter, Anders, A. Pace,
Anderson, Wall, Ashmore, Hairs-
ton, L. Pace, Turner.

Spartan (11-9): Davis, Dub O'shields,

Sitton, Dodd, Foster, Steadings,
Heatherly, Heidlemann, Posey,
Wood, Mahaffey, Fat Timmons,
B. Fowler, Walters, Hellman, Stow
Ray, Suvern Wright, Barbare, Tom
Holt, Weanns, Harry Deal, Pace.

Tucapau (11-9): Jackson, Allen, Bru
Anderson, Hodge, Jim Mason,
Guthrie, Fisher, O. Mason, Glas-
son, Smith, John Justus, Austin,
Hill, Shehan, Arnold, Phillips,
Bell, Robertson, Childers, Lewis.

Clifton (7-12): Reid, Prince, Pat
Elders, Thomas, Furman Mabry,
Mathis, Hughes, Don Hatchette,
Coggins, C. Reid, Lefty Borders,
Evans, Joker Bennett, M. Mabry,
P. Mabry, E. Johnson, Barbery,
Tip Massey, Thornton, Bridges,
Quinn.

Union (6-13): S. Jolly, Whitener,
Hicks, E. Blackwell, Howell,
Fowler, Lawson, Willard, C. Black-
well, B. Jolly, Cohen, Fox, Mitch-
ell, Vinson, Corn, Kirby, Knox,
Harris, Lybrand, Benson, Gossett,
Harrison, Whitmire.

Franklin Spinners (withdrew): Haynes,
Early, Les Davis, Lowe, Kay, Jones,
Ridings, V. McDowell, Hopper,
Reid, D. McDowell, Burns, Lan-
ford, Vernon, Erskine, Humphries,
Cook, Laurens, Adkins, Greno-
bles, Edkins, Calvert, Trammell.

Eastern Carolina League

Pacolet Trojans, champions (38-17):
Wilson Lee, Tommy Jett, Allen,
Spec Barbery, Raymond Ellison,
Lynwood McMakin, A. Pace,
Stribbling, Dover, Arthur Goforth,
Leroy Pace, Tee Fleming, Lewis
Petty, Lefty Wilson, George Black-
well, Ernie White, A.C. Phillips,
Yancey Senn, Lewis Fleming, Wil-
bur Clary, Roy Jones, A. Black-
well, Fanning, Claud Arnold.

Mills Mill Millers of Woodruff (33-24):
Timmons, Red Christopher, Albert

Petty, Ox Taylor, Summey Moore, Maxwell, Raymond Kelly, Morris, Craig, Henry Shoaf, E. Page, Harry Barrett, Campbell, Sam Page, Thomas, Thrasher, Cheatham, Garrett, Moore.

Whitney Elis (29-21): Mud Owens, Kelly Smith, Pug Ezell, Bus Hufstetler, Charlie Bennett, Earl Osteen, Leonard Huskey, Bob Brady, Peterson, Dave Robinson, J.C. Morgan, Oren Holt, Mark Thackston, Clause, Al Ferguson, Moon, Ike Pearson, Barber, Parris, Price Ferguson, Culbreth, Ledbetter, Bob Davis, Hughey, Fowler.

Lyman Pacifics (26-23): Cabiness, Benson, Vaughn, Powell, Russ Yeargin, Harbert Lee, Bill Snyder, R. Morris, Horace Long, Blackwell, Southern, Brown, Harry Kelly, Howard, Williams, Lefty Kalfass, Trelfaull, Dudley, Lominack, King, Ward, Query, Edwards, Wyatt Burgess, Hugh Smith, Lefty Morgan, Rogers, Howard, Cook.

Arcadia (23-22): Lavaino, Don Humphries, J. Cannon, Gene Parks, Roy Hughey, John Rhymer, Jones, Harold West, Wynn, J.E. Blackwell, Kay Burrell, Cooper, Eubanks, D. West, Summey Moore, Louis Veal, Sam Fowler, E. Veal, Lawrence, Hendrix, Slim Mooneyham, Butte, Laurens, Parris, N. West, Reynolds, Slim Cress.

Drayton Weavers (22-22): Rook, Cook, Manning Bagwell, Johnny Johnson, Crick McCarter, B.T. McCraw, Bill Carter, J. Morgan, Clayton, Bennett, Shuford Finley, Smart, S. Morgan, Giles, Dick Cabiness, Mabry, Robinson, Bill Broome, Davis, Brooks, Lewis Moore, Country Kneece, Macey, Storey, Miller, Williams, Wall,

Forrest, Stanton, Brown, Dunlap, Yarborough, Hines, Robinson.

Brandon of Woodruff (18-26): Nobles, Speedy Brewington, Gunn, Weathers, Nabors, Putnam, Kirby, Loftis, Jim Callahan, Red Blanton, Oliphant, Edgerton, Knight, Christopher, Bouknight, Jim Wilson, Page, Red Gillespie, Avant, George Rhinehart, Duncan, Allan, West.

Beaumont (18-27): Gallahair, Oscar Medley, Holsenback, Clarence Millwood, Holt, Prince, E. Moore, O'Sullivan, Lefty Tice, Turner, Foreman, Bradley, McConnell, John Lowery, Ted Garrett, Callahan, Fowler, Starnes, Lee, Shehan, Callison, Farmer.

Converse (17-28): Tip Massey, W. Fowler, Byars, Hicks, Powers, Wallace Thompson, Allen, Vassey, Yonnie Green, J. Fowler, Pete Fowler, Hopper, Evans, Mitchem, Sipes, Bryant, Bridges, Lark, Murrow, Rymer, McSwain, Mosley.

Inman (15-29): Cashion, Otis Parris, Strickland, Clark, Bo Dotherow, Madden, H. Vanesky, Berry, Natcher, S. Vanesky, W. Vaneiewsky, Prince, Guy, Mabry, Abernathy, Paul Edwards, Clay Mahaffey, Price, P. Fox, Garrison, Thrift, Gresham, Jolly, Halsen, Lacy, Gholson.

Catawba League

Great Falls, champions (10-0): Wilson, Tarlton.

Lancaster (8-3): Griffith.

Rock Hill Bleachery Cubs(5-6): Sanders, Gaston, Estridge, Smith, Pittman, Bursel, Free, Hodis, Stroud, Miller, Stover.

Winnsboro (5-6)

Chester Cardinals (3-7): Thompson, Littlejohn, Finley, Comer, Sullivan, Ed Durham, Adams, Knox, Cooper, Robinson, Simpson.

Hermitage (1-10): Denning, Sweet.

Victor-Monaghan League

Victor of Greer, champions (no records): Tipton, Collins, Sipes, Millwood, Bennett, Maness, Watson, Painter, C. Myers, Waters, Hudson, Ballenger, Drake, E. Myers.

Greer (no records): H. Harvey, Smith, Lee, Taylor, Hardin, Burnett, Belcher, M. Harvey, R. Taylor, Westmoreland, Phillips, Cox, Earl, Timmons, Burgin.

Apalache (no records): McCarter, Rector, Blackwell, Wilson, McCarter, Rogan, Lunny, Hopkins, Pruitt, Ashmore.

Anderson County League: Dan Brown, president.

Orr Rifles, champions (24-7): Luther Hart, McCraw, Dumb Price, Matthews, Dude Buchanan, Mutt Williams, Mac McKinney, Ralph Morris, Gene Hollifield, Mahaffey, Ike Pearson, Edgerton, Bob Bowman, Jones, Clayton, Lee Whitten, Bill Webb, Joe Ashworth, Huffstetler, Hughey, Guy Miller, Crate Herring (manager), Atkins, Werner, Alf Anderson.

Gossett (17-10): Evans, Bud Vickers, John Cunningham, Rhinehart, Jim Parker, Irvin Sexton, Bud Voight, Farmer, Willie Wilbanks, Whitfield, Shetley, Buck Leonard, Chris Suber, Chavous.

Appleton Apples (17-11): Green, R.B. Speares, Punchy Williams (manager), Hyder, Fisher, Jones, Robinson, Sanders, Long, King, Weathers, Kane, Jim Blackwell, Clint Cason, Powell, Sid Bailey, Leroy Mahaffey, Girk, McElrath, Gunter, Stewart, Heyward, P.D. Eubanks, Jess Wrinkle, Kirby Higbe, Berry McElrath, Red Miller.

Equinox White Sox (13-19): Hinkie Allen, Jack Harper, Russell Stockman, Larry Harbin, Shag Craft, Frank Keaton, Clay Moore, J.B. Spearman, Bill Webb, Stockman, Stewart, Furman Beck, Henry Moore, Reese Allen, Shag Knox, Arnold Carlton (manager), Clint Cason, J.M. McAllister, J.B. Kelly, Humphries, Mule Shirley, Dusty Holbrook, Al Evans, Bailey, Sprouse.

Lonsdale (12-15): Wilton Shaver, Etheredge, Cater, F. Weathers, Carey, Ernest Dooley, James, Gailliard, Harbin, Sluder, Cargill, Gilden, Hawkins, Williams, Owen, Roy Leatherwood, Joe Mason (manager), Jake Campbell.

Anderson (11-8): Pearman, Rickman, Barney Smith, Gettys, Lonnie Holbrook, Laval, L. Moore, W. Embler, R. Weathers, Werner, Gaines, Castleberry, G. Smith, Bessinger, J. Embler, Goldings, Tough Embler, Fred Powell, Gettys, Clark, J.B. Kelly.

Belton Athletics (5-14): Cotton Nelson, Hoyt Deanhardt, Mule Lollis, McAllister, Roy Owens, Guy Shirley, Reid, Shockley, O. Owens, Haynie, Daughty, Campbell, Stephens, R. Owens, Fortner, Ellison, J.T. King, W. Nelson.

Gluck (4-22): Garrison, Collins, Allen, Wilton Hanna, Barnett, Sam Jordan, McLeskey, Linder, Perry, Rathey, Dick Sweetenburg, Rubin, Tabors, Lefty Bray, Carson, Bob Strickland, Roy Jordan, Gene Manley, Bill Moore, Carlton Miller, Hyder, Wakeland.

Tuesday Textile League

Orr (4-0): Hart, McCraw, Price, Matthews, Buchanan, Williams, McKinney, Morris, Hollifield, Mahaffey, Pearson, Edgerton, Bowman, Jones, Clayton, Whitten, Webb, Ashworth, Huffstetler, Hughey.

Pelzer (4-2): Allen, Crymes, Pickleseimer, Heath, Minyard, Jordan, Clements, Cannon, Helms, Woodcock, Buntin, Taylor.

Chiquola (2-2): Harris, Foster, Clark, Knox, Golden, H. Long, Barbare, Lanford, Limbaugh, Belue, Threlfall, J. Husky, Martin, Leonard, C. Jeffcoat, Williams, Belue, Clements, Kettles, Evans, Greer, Hancock, Carr, Maxwell, Womack, T. Long.

Appleton (2-3): Green, R.B. Speares, Williams, Hyder, Fisher, Jones, Robinson, Sanders, Long, King, Weathers, Kane, Blackwell, Cason, Powell, Bailey, Mahaffey, Girk, McElrath, Gunter, Stewart, Heyward.

Gossett (1-3): Evans, Vickers, Cunningham, Rhinehart, Parker, Sexton, Voight, Farmer, Wilbanks, Whitfield, Shetley.

Piedmont (1-3): Darnell, Dill, Watson, Emory, Underwood, Pack, McCall, Fleming, Werner, Terry, Poole, Crump, Turner, Morgan.

Big Four Textile League: M. Bridwell (president).

Enoree (no records): Betsil, Waddell, Bridges, Simmons, Rhodes, Gilliam, Martin, Nelson, Christian, Sumner, Ivy, Campbell, Query, Golden, Rowe, Abercrombie, Guinn, Murphy, Bearden, Phillips.

Watts (no records): M. Ward, B. Jennings, Bobo, C. Broome, C. Sherer, Warren, S. Broome, A. Wood, C. Brown, P. Jennings, E. Jennings, G. Ward, O. Jennings, F. Brown, Workman, Shaver, Epting, F. Broome, Brewington, Metts, R. Bobo, Brownlee, Sevier.

Lydia (no records): L. Wood, Sanders, Trammell, B. Crawford, Fuller, J. Crawford, Sweat, Anderson, R. Wood, Snelgrove, Hunt, Barbery, Miller, Whitman, Hill,

Fuller, Williams, Morris, Harris, Patterson, Eskew, Kirby, Harrison, Johnson, Lanford, Putman.

Joanna (no records): Rowe, Harrison, Hunnicutt, Myers, Brown, Case, Baylor, Abrams, Turner, Allison, Snelgrove, Sanders, L. Wood, Fuller, R. Wood, Bradford, Henderson, Wells, Campbell.

Georgia-Carolina League

Hartwell GA, champions (10-2)

Calhoun Falls (7-6): Carrithers, Welch, Burris, Hilley, Massey, Overby, Atkins, Tanton, Rinehardt.

Williamston (7-6): Cannon, Stone, Sargent, D. McClellion, Ellison, Miller, Black, Glasby, Dickard, Thompson, Ellison, Campbell,

Abbeville (6-6): R. Doolittle, Eddie Doolittle, Kirby, Simms, Wilson, Boyd, Powell.

Lavonia GA (6-7)

Central (0-12): Riggins, Dodgens, Bell, Simms, Stone, Crawford, Elliott, Frank Howard.

Independent Teams

Mills Mill of Woodruff (15-2): Ingle, Smith, Abbott, McCall, Turner, McAllister.

Poe (9-6): Garrett, Evatt, Brookshire, Brown, Morgan, Brannon, Anders, Thompson, Christopher, Landreth.

Simpsonville (6-10): Hamby, E. Barbery, Medlock, Brasher, O'dell Barbery, Smith, Hall, Hamilton.

Fountain Inn (4-6): Moore, Woods, Weaver, Smith, Nelson, Godfrey, Todd, Chasteen.

Poinsett (3-9): Wood, Brissey, Alexander, Hodges, Brown, Turner, Arnold, Thompson, Gilstrap, Gregory, Bridwell, Smith, Hammett.

Fort Mill (0-1): Archie, Ferguson, Patterson, A. Epps, Harkey, Massey, Whiteside, S. Carrouth, J. Epps, Stallings, Q. Carrouth, Snyder.

1938

Piedmont Textile League

Union Bleachery, champions (8-6): Ivey, Roy Brooks, Rhodes, Robertson, Turner, Gibson, Miller, Charles Brooks, Marchbanks, Cecil Brooks, Bridwell, Heaton, Bishop, Patterson.

Slater (9-8): Croxton, S. Lynch, Hembree, Vaughn, Taylor, Price, McMakin, McDuffie, Putman, Lyle, Ledford, Gosnell, Wilson, Puckett, Pinson, Julian.

Sampson (5-7): Putman, Bagwell, Littlejohn, Mauldin, McDaniel, Sosebee, Fowler, Kneece, McCullough, Bridwell, Roberts, Chapman, Summey, Hembree, Bowes.

Monaghan of Greenville (5-9): Dudley, Alexander, Kitchen, Scott, Sides, Gilstrap, Jones, Elders, Griffith, Hines, Herring, Henson, Heaton, Stevens, Thompson, Waldrop, Godfrey, Stewart.

Renfrew Bleachery (4-4): Knox, Wilson, Medlock, Tollison, Fox, Johnson, Clark, Belcher, Granger, Brown, Turner, Quinn, Edwards, Ridley.

Williamston (4-5): Sargent, Cannon, Casey, Holcombe, Stone, Feller, Dickert, Hood, McClellan, McClellan, Scott, Wilson, Black, Garner.

Southern Worsted (4-6): Brannon, Dill, Mitchell, Alverson, L. Montgomery, Childers, Smith, R. Montgomery, Fowler, Steadings, Vess, McCauley, Ford, Flynn.

Mills Mill of Greenville (no records); withdrew.

Western Carolina League

Lyman Pacifics, champions (30-12): Fowler, Hob Lee, Ward, Goss, Briggs, McCall, Ross, Henderson, Ernest Query, Dudley, Hawkins, Bearden, Roy Hughey, Larry Crawford, Cabiness, Vaughn, Snyder, Yeargin, Horace Long, Bill Carter, Potter, Cook, Fisher, King, Burgess, E. Long, Howard.

Pelzer Bears (21-18): Woods, Lefty Crymes, Lollis, Bobo, Cannon, Norrell, Buntin, Carlick, Carey, Morgan, Pearson, Woodcock, Bannister, George Jeffcoat, Campbell, Foster, Virgil Lavender, Jordan, Minyard, Pickleseimer, Carlisle, Wallace, Heath, Lonnie Holbrook.

Mills Mill of Woodruff (20-20): Craig, Strickland, Abernathy, Morris, Hendrix, Ivey, Bearden, Shoaf, Hopkins, Sam Page, Mud Owens, Ox Taylor, Barrett, Suddeth, Underwood, Campbell, Timmons, Higbe, Watson, Petty, Maxwell, Blackwell.

Appleton Apples, (20-18): Robinson, Ramon Weathers, Berry McElrath, Leroy Mahaffey, Sid Bailey, Hoke Long, June Werner, Fred Powell, Henry Buchanan, Clay Moore, Hinkie Allen, Larry Harbin, Sanders, Jim Blackwell, Ernest Robertson, Raymond Weathers, Varner, Claude Spake, T.L. Crymes, George Cargill.

Southern Bleachery Red Flames (18-20): George Blackwell, McCarter, Stribbling, J.D. Childers, Nau, Bradshaw, Dennis, Steele, Barbare, Lominack, Joe Childers, Lister, McCravey, Gay, R. Barbery, Rags Suddeth, S. Barbery, Swindle, Hill, Hudgens, Lyles Alley, Huggins, Lockaby.

Piedmont (11-27): John Emery, J.F. Fleming, Tom Pack, Earl Cooper, Jerry Underwood, Wilson, League, Roy Darnell, Ernest Henderson, J.W. Rampey, McAbee, Ben Reeves, Snead, Ned Moore, Green, Leroy Anderson (manager), McCall, Sloan Terry, Peek, David Galloway, Ross.

Central Carolina League

Greenwood, champions (21-21): Gillespie, King, Girk, Mule Escoe, Nub Smythe, Gowan, Wood, Edgerton, Howard, Burke, Boyd, Watson, Dickert, McAllister, Morse, Petty, Barker, Thompson, Doodie Franklin, Watson, McAbee, Joe Whitlock, Putnam, Christopher, Smith, Embler.

Riverdale (31-16): Kennedy, Lonnie English, Chaffin, Brannon, Paul Turner, Dog Obannion, Rymer, Minyard, Brewington, Farr, Martinell, Cashion, Scroggins, Thomas, Stevens, Causey, Waldrop, Spragins, Hopper, Newton, Barrett, Taylor.

Mathews (24-11): Corley, Matthews, Godfrey, J. Hall, Mobley, Suggs, Wilson, McCravey, E. Hall, Kennedy, Lyles, Bland, Southern, Abrams, Morgan, Gaines, Nabors, Sullivan, Massey, Rourk, Wright, Burns.

Ware Shoals Riegels (22-17): L. Moore, Ouzts, Davis, J. Moore, Lefty Howard, Smith, Leo Tober, Horne, Wright, Gross, Fowler, Powell, Pack, Ezell, Howell, Hall, Sanders, Owens, Lou Brissie, Virgil Stallcup.

Ninety Six Indians (15-20): Ross, Hopkins, Peace, Beard, Kirby, Sanders, Stoddard, Rook, Ruark, Dougherty, Wells, Mozelle, Bennett, Guerry, Gillespie, Bone, Dowis, Tice, Thompson, Granny Hightower, Howell, Craft, Millwood, Garrison, Girk, Craig, Williams, Ross.

Chiquola Chicks (4-32): Jean Belue, Young, Purkey, Greer, Bill Womack, Beacham, Talley, Lollis, Golden, Martin, Shag Knox, G. Deanhardt, M. Deanhardt, Queen, Nelson, Anderson, Sullivan, Fisher, Luther Rentz, Keasler, McDavid Carr.

Blue Ridge League

Liberty, champions (21-9): Pitts, Owens, Smith, Thrasher, Burnett, G. Gilstrap, Orr, King, Dover, Cooper, G.L. Rutledge (manager), Russell, Gillespie, Bolding, Powell, Hawkins, Alexander, J. Gilstrap, Burdette, Medlock.

Pickens (15-9): R. Adams, Heath, Gillespie, Roper, Nichols, E. Rampey, Folger, Hunter, Hendrix, Gilstrap, Bryant, Rampey, English, O. Adams, H. Adams, C. Adams, Pace, Grant.

Glenwood (13-15): Owens, Foster, J. Wilson, Spearman, Mull, Fox, E. Stewart, Fortner, Gilliard, E. Chapman, Corley, R. Stewart, W. Wilson, B. Chapman, Gilliam.

Arial (11-14): Green, Wiggins, Blyth McCall, P. Rampey, Williams, McNeely, Hendrix, Turpin, Grant, Garrett, Boggs, Juber Hairston, Porter, S. Rampey, Stevens, Day, Fox.

Easley (9-10): Gilliam, Hunter, Hendrix, Hawkins, Jamison, Campbell, Waldrop, Ragsdale, Foster, Garrett, Juber Hairston, Alexander, Galloway, Cleveland, Owens.

Alice (9-20): Williams, Stewart, Christopher, Cater, Thompson, Limbaugh, Riddle, Moore, Ivey, Mayes, Davis, Gillespie, Adams, Heath, Alexander, Landreth, Gilden, McGaha, Bailey, Cleveland, Cox, Ferguson, Riggs.

Greenville Textile League

Brandon of Greenville, champions (14-1): Hendrix, Lawrence, Thackston, Humphries, Acuff, Reid, Joe Anders, Blackwell, Thomas, Foster, N. Anders, C. Foster, Hall, Ingle, Limbaugh, Baldwin, Huff, Foster, Morgan, Loftis, Jennings, R. Foster, Campbell, Sayers, Fowler.

Woodside (9-6): O. Herbert, Hines, Ramsey, Wilson, Pitts, Bowen, Hall, Byrd, Smith, Landreth, Hunter, Justus, J. Pruitt, Tucker, Bomar, A. Pruitt, Bomar, Waldrop, Jasper.

Judson (7-2): Gotshaw, J. Duffie, Bradshaw, C. Cobb, Bussie, Sheck, Trammell, Hazel, Williams, Tidwell, Tallant, McCullough, A. Cobb.

Poinsett (6-6): Turner, Bridwell, Townsend, Gilstrap, Woods, Thompson, H. Fair, Taylor, Crymes, Millwood, Hodge, P. Fair.

American Legion (2-7)

Camperdown (1-6): Dill, H. Burnett, Knight, Cain, Lee, Goodwin, L. McDowell, B. McDowell, J. Huff, R. Huff, Scott, A. Burnett, Brown.

Monaghan of Greenville (0-4): Alexander, Foster, Major, Galloway, Heaton, Jones, Barnette, Fuller, Dudley, Kitchen.

Mid State League

Winnsboro, champions (21-7): H. Smith, Gray, Rushton, Knox, Hamilton, Shealy, R. Smith, Rushing, Greer, Wilson, Wilmont Spires, Barfield, Edwards, Maurice Frew, Brenemer, Wells, Ward, Haney, Sumner, Henderson, Brannon, Wright, Wages, E. Smith, Sipes.

Monarch (18-9): Johnny Walker, Austin Littlejohn, Ralph Phillips, Luther Middlebrooks, Otis Sanders, Hunter, Frank Nabors, Jete Long (manager), Newell Lawson, Willie Lawson, Sam Turner, Alvin Cabiness, Houston Hines, Timmons, Manners, Joe Willard, Simp Sanders, Sidney Sanders.

Lockhart (15-7): B. Cabiness, Vandeford, O'dell, Bill Broome, Selby, W. Burns, C. Gibson, Crocker, Stalnaker, Blackwood, J. Burns, B. Gibson, R. Cabiness, Watts, Tucker, G. Gibson, Shealy, Blackwell, Dell.

Joanna (12-9): M. Hair, B. Brown, Castleberry, Moore, Rudy Prater, L. Farmer, Moser, R. Abrams, Clark, E. Abrams, Blackwell, Clark, Galloway, M. Brown, P. Brown, M. Prater, Earl Morse, T. Brown, Harrelson, Belue, H. Abrams, O. Farmer.

Newberry (11-8): J. Singley, Johnny Wertz, Lowman, Clark, Walter Hiller, Mickey Livingston, Lindsay, Taylor, Fulmer, Irby Bouknight, Whittle, Caldwell, Doodie Franklin, Bob Creekmore, George Hiller, E. Singley, Cromer, Jones, Fuller, Derrell Bouknight.

Mollohon (7-12): Jackson, Bedenbaugh, Cromer, Moates, R. Martin, Mills, Ingram, Bowers, Wood, Golden, Smith, J. Martin, Wallace, Rollins, McCarty, Wooden, Fowler.

Union (2-17): Tice, Blackwood, Randall, Dickson, Williams, Harris, Fowler, Lawson, Hicks, Dick Bell, Long, Willard, Jolly, Whitener, Sanders, Addison, Sullivan, Hill, Cohen, Mabry, Blackwell, Harris, Watson, Lockhart, Brown, Foster, Lybrand, Foster, Campbell, Callahan, Lewis, Anderson, Knox, Stuckie, Lee, Fisher, Crocker, Nabors.

Buffalo (1-17): Putman, Walker, F. Lawson, Cato, Land, Wright, Claus, Abrams, Howard, Frost, C. Millwood, R. Millwood, Price, Clardy, Haney, Revels, Ingle, F. Millwood, E. Millwood, Nelson, Crocker, Allen, Ross, Mayes, Ainsmore, Mann, Gault.

Palmetto Textile League

Clinton, champions (12-3): Trammell, Sanders, L. Woods, B. Crawford, Foster, Butler, Hunt, A. Davis, J. Crawford, C. Crawford, R. King, A. Kirby, R. Woods, Hill, Haines, Attaway, Davenport, Webb, Snelgrove, Glenn, Center.

Greenwood (8-3): Higgenbotham,
Gleason, Morris, Fowler, Jones,
Bolden, Stone, Bush, Pickens,
Haines, Morley, Parks, Glenn,
Weathers, Sparks, Ray, Arnold,
Shaw, Sizemore, L. Howard,
H. Howard, Marchant, Hayes,
James, Farr.

Lydia (5-8): Patterson, Carl Johnson,
Miller, Fuller, Emory, Burnett,
Claude Crocker, Whitman, Lamar
Castleberry, Pressley, McCravey,
Morris, Phillips, McWhite, Brown,
Sanders, Galloway, Perry,
Waddell, Bill Embler, Parris,
Farmer.

Joanna (4-5): Cooley, Hunnicutt,
Farmer, Owens, Rudolph Prater,
Case, Taylor, Abrams, John
Hunnicutt, Hawkins, Pace, Weath-
ers, Moore, Brown, Ross.

Ninety Six (3-6): C. Drummond, Mc-
Kinney, Morris, V. Drummond,
Bennett, Campbell, Boozer, Ivester, Hunnicutt, R. Drummond,
A. Drummond, Boland, Thompson, Bartell, Ruark, Voiselle, Morton, Bailey, Werner, B. Drummond, Carlisle, Griffin.

Ware Shoals (3-6): A. Hill, B. Hill,
J. Sanders, Bailey, Riley, McClure,
H. Cobb, Shaver, Gresham, New-
berry, B. Davis, Ashley, Nabors,
Bolt, Golden, J. Hill, Prickland,
J. Davis, C. Cobb, C. Hill, O. Davis,
Boles.

The Textile League

Arkwright, champions (11-7): J. Bal-
lard, P. Cooper, Layton, E. Bal-
lard, W. Cooper, W. Lynch, Smith,
Roberts, Watson, Pennington,
Brown, Poteat, McAbee, Roach,
Roach, Howell, Waldon, Wood,
Louis Watkins.

Beaumont (12-9): W. Lindsay,
G. Petty, O. Willard, A. Lindsay,
H. Harris, C. Harris, M. Lindsay,
B. Cudd, R. Taylor, D. Lynch,

Charles Thomas, D. Prince, C. West,
Burgess, D. Harris, J. Belcher,
W. Harris, Walker.

Draper (8-7): Smith, E. Carter, Hun-
sucker, R. McBride, W. Carter, An-
derson, B. McBride, Metz, Cook-
sey, Lee Carter, Gravely, Cutts,
May, Belue, O. Mabry, F. McBride,
A. White, Morgan, J. McBride,
E. McBride, Moore, J. Bagwell,
Zimmerman.

Glendale (3-11): M. Mittag, Warren,
Anders, R. Mittag, Simmons,
Thomas, Mabry, R. Murray,
Quinn, P. Murray, Taylor, H. Murray, Puckett, Bishop, E. Blackwell,
Justice, Hutchins, Mason, C. Gilmer, Morris, Reece, Linder, Harris, Blanton, A. Warren, R. Bagwell, L. Gilmer.

Spartanburg County League

Brandon of Woodruff, champions (18-
9): Ivey, E. Loftis, Brandon, Ike
West, Lewis Cooper, Dewey Law-
rence, Roper, Raymond Craig,
Hendrix, McGill, H. Sprouse,
Tiller, Satterfield, Luker, Furman
Page, Clyde McGill, Garrett, Wolf,
Walker, Betsill, Thornton, Fuller,
James, Harold Taylor.

Jackson of Wellford (20-8): Murphy,
Ballard, H. Jordan, Dobson,
R. Wilson, O. Wilson, B. Jordan,
Jackson, Dobbins, J. Acton,
O. Shehan, D. Wilson, Plemmons,
R. Acton, Lefty Cox, Casey Jones,
Myers, Blackwell, Belcher, D. Jor-
dan.

Jonesville (11-10): Gregory, L. Erskine, Henry Spencer, J. Holt,
E. Holt, Clyde McKinney, Hawkins, Fowler, Farr, Nelson, R. Erskine, B. Holt, Hyatt, J. Spencer,
Powell, D. Sprouse, J. Ward, Howell, Carl Farmer, R. Ward, Ellison,
B. Wilson.

Tucapau (9-7): Sevier, J. Cook, Powell, Henderson, Sapp, Dillingham,

Austin, Kitchens, Caldwell, Linder,
T. Cook, T. Cox, D. Cox, Tapp,
Cothran, Williams, Phillips, Jack-
son, Taylor, Hendrix, Page,
G. Mason, O. Mason.
Union (8-13): Prentiss, Lybrand,
F. Leonhart, Mitchell, Campbell,
J. Gregory, Eubanks, Farr, Nelson,
Malpass, W. Leonhart, Gowan,
E. Gregory, Greer, Gallman,
Hughey, Hyder, Sanders, Willard,
C. Blackwell, Crocker, Ed Harris,
E. Blackwell, Morris, Harris, Jolly.
Pacolet (6-13): Osborn, Loftis,
Mathis, Sutton, James Lee, Arthur
Goforth, Tessenear, Harrison,
Courtney, Valentine, Worthy, Os-
ment, Parker, Goforth, Sprouse,
Garner, Whitlock, Tate, Thomp-
son, Ballentine, Petty, John Lee,
Green, Banks, Gaines.
Lyman (6-13): Briggs, D. Gowan,
Smith, C. High, Jenkins, A. High,
Henderson, F. Gowan, Ross,
Fowler, White, Satterfield, Alexan-
der, Pettigrew, W. Gowan, Had-
den, P. Mullinax, Hoag, Silvey,
Boling, Bridges, Bolden, Pruitt,
Burgess, H. Mullinax, Bruce, Ed-
wards, Lowin.
Valley Falls (no records): E. Rollins,
Page, S. Rollins, Wilson, R. Ward,
Stepp, Garrett, Henderson, Clary,
Hughes.

Tri-County League

Inman, champions (19-17): Skinny
Gowan, Otis Parris, Ted Garrett,
Ralph Prince, Roy Turner, Wade
Abernathy, R. Waldrop, E. Parris,
Hilton Culbreth, Mabry, Ink High,
Tucker, J. Waldrop, A. Waldrop,
Bo Dotherow, Ed Parris, Crawford
Grissom, Ragan Fox, Gleason,
Brownie Pack, Gossett, John Bell,
Gowan, J. Ramsey.
Arkwright (25-14): Burns, N. Bag-
well, C. Bagwell, John Lowery,
Perry, Giles, Slim Mooneyham,

Roy Lowe, Ernest Hawkins, Tice,
Chapman, Quinn, Basnight, Curt
Randall, Watkins, Hall, Addison,
Williams.
Spartan (24-10): Dub O'shields,
Sitton, Mud Owens, Ralph Stead-
ings, Dodd, Johnson, Tuck McCon-
nell, Ralph Foster, Shuf Finley,
Pedro Mahaffey, Walt Trammell,
Suvern Wright, Heatherly, Deal,
Horace Shehan, Hughey, Haven
Clause, Harold Foster.
Clifton (15-19): Tip Massey, Ralph
Prince, M. Mabry, Furman Mabry,
Roy Elders, Coggins, Allison,
McCauley, Hughes, John Fowler,
Barber, O'Sullivan, Rook,
Hatchett, Sanders, Bagwell, Roy
Fox, Yonnie Green, McCarter,
Hensley, Pat Elders, Boose Holt.
Tucapau (12-17): Justus, Allen,
J. Mason, Bru Anderson, Hill,
Austin, Lavender, Fisher, Glasson,
Childers, Roy Robertson, Smith,
High, Phillips, T. Mason, Howard,
Jackson.
Glendale (7-25): Hughey, Scott,
Ralph Gosnell, Hensley, Fox,
Haven Clause, Porter, Anders,
Blanton, Riddle, Rush, J. Linder,
Husky, Ramsey, Roy Prince, Har-
ris, Osteen, B. Linder, R. Linder,
Boyd Cooksey, Hendrix, A. Lin-
der, Taylor, Cook.

Eastern Carolina League

Converse, champions (24-12): Thomp-
son, W. Fowler, Vance Powers,
Hicks, Dick Evans, Quay Byars,
Mosely, Croxdale, Pete Fowler,
Yonnie Green, Hugh Lark, Floyd
Sipes, Reid, Bridges, John Vassey,
Lloyd Sipes, Cooksey.
Drayton (15-21): McCraw, Manning
Bagwell, Caton, F. Moore, Sims,
Jones, Morgan, Nabors, Hines,
Wilson, Davis, Country Kneece,
L. Moore, Snow Kirby, Cothran,
Martin, Stowe.

Arcadia (14-17): Earl Veal, Cooper, Hunt, Louis Veal, A. Cannon, Gossett, Henderson, Lavender, McIntyre, Blackwell, Darrell Laurens, West, Bridgman, Sam Fowler, R. Jones, L. Cannon, J. Cannon.

Pacolet (14-17): Lee, Tommy Jett, Murrow, Ellison, Arthur Goforth, L. Pace, Hodge, Hogan, Tee Fleming, Gardin, Lynwood McMakin, K. Goforth, L. Fleming, W. Clary, E. Clary, Garner, A. Pace.

Saluda Valley League

Newberry (2-1): Davis, Shealy, Hiller.
Mathews (0-2)
Mollohon (0-3): Harmon, Franklin, Boozer.
Saluda (no records): Smith, Denning.
Jolly Street (no records)

West State League

Greer (3-0): Hamby, R. Taylor, P. Hardin, Brewington, Bennett, Tipton, A. Hardin, S. Taylor, Haney, Gilliard, Fowler, Greer, McCarter, Don Jackson, Smith, Dobbins.

Piedmont (0-2): Perry, J. Hunnicutt, Evans, Clark, Poole, Mulligan, Alley, Bass, May, Patterson, Jennings, Cooper, Howard, L. Hunnicutt, Taylor.
Duke Power (no records)
Pelzer (no records)

Bi-County League

Fingerville (6-0): Kay, Humphries, Ridings, Culbreth, Calvert, Ramsey, Cartee, Pruitt, Steadman, Turner, Hall, Cook, Atkins, Bullman, Scruggs.

Campobello (0-2): Hawkins, J. Nix, T. Mabry, Smith, B. Nix, Gosnell, Hinson, Evington, Tucker, Epps, D. Mabry, Casey.

Catawba League

Great Falls (3-1)

Rock Hill Bleachery (2-0): Sanders, Estridge.

Lancaster Red Roses (2-0): Wilson, Warren, Williams, Callahan.

Chester (2-7): Davis, Mace, Hendrix, T. Overby, J. Cooper, Wall, Langley, Pearson.

Union County League

Monarch (3-0): Hawkins, J. Coward, Garner, Moore, C. Berry, G. Coward, Turner, Morris, Woolen, D. Berry.

West Springs (0-1): W. Hyatt, Hawkins, O'shields, Crouch, Gowan, Hyatt, J. Hyatt, West, Milford, Lawson.

Excelsior (0-2): Jolly, Addison, R. Hill, A. Hill, Howell, Morris, Kirby, Vaughn, Blackburn.

Landrum (0-3): Senior, Howard, Edwards, Gilbert, T. Bridgman, W. Bridgman, Christopher, Ellis Forrester, Smith, Bolt, Brice, Smith.

Northwestern League

Oconee, champions (18-4): Simpson, E. Hawkins, G. Hawkins, Golden, Robertson, W. Hawkins, Medlock, E. Cobb, Smith, Crump, Cain, McGuffin, B. Cobb, McClain, Batson, Robinson, Cheatham, Wilson.

LaFrance (10-6): Massey, Gaines, Craft, Moore, B. Harrison, Cargill, A. Moore, Jones, C. Harrison, English, Clark, Southerland, Chitwood, Bickley, Medlock, Garrison.

Newry (8-8): Williams, Alexander, Crenshaw, McClellan, Sluder, Rogers, O. Kelly, Hawkins, Cater, Connery, Peebles, Kirby, Gilden, Mannerly.

Walhalla (6-7): Gilliard, Marvin Rackley, Garrett, Jamison, Rutledge, Reid, Tuck, Mauldin, Bentley, Williams, Reaves.

Central (5-8): M. Oates, B. Oates, Thomas, Crawford, Bell, Elliott,

Lyda, Loggins, Spearman,
Fletcher, Evatt, J. Lyda, Poole,
Cox.
Cateechee (3-12): Pilgrim, Fowler,
Reese, McWhorter, J. Stancil, Bald-
win, Owens, Bagwell, Gilstrap, Gil-
lespie, R. Stancil, James, Roper,
Bolden, J. Brown, Boyd, Garrett,
B. Brown, McCall, Pate.

Georgia-Carolina League

Hartwell GA, champions (12-3)
Elberton GA (7-7)
Calhoun Falls (7-8): Welch, Rufus
Pearson, Al Jenkins, Adkins,
Weaver Hilley, Cheatham, Neil
Chrisley, Rucker Pearson, Allen
Reynolds, Rudder, Charlie Car-
rithers, Ed McCaslan, Earl Cooper,
Bill Stevens, Perry Bolding, Dean
Thomas, Henry Bland, Louie Fer-
guson, Jack Hilley, Charles Verner
(manager).
Jackson of Iva (7-14): Owens, Year-
gin, Dickson, Hamm, B. Green,
McCoy, Taylor, Burdette, Lee
Whitten, R. Pryor, J. Green, Law-
ton, M. Green, Price, S. Pryor,
Roy Jordan, Hanna, H. Jordan,
Queens, Yeargin.
Abbeville (6-5): Barton, Wilson,
R. Doolittle, New, Foster, Williams,
R. Powell, G. Powell, E. Doolittle,
Martin, Whitten.
Appleton (5-9): Spake, Wells, Poole,
Gunter, Smith, Watkins, Daniels,
Morrison, Kelly, McGuire, Larry
Harbin.

Anderson County League

Gossett, champions (2-1): Sexton,
Parker, Cunningham, Wilbanks,
Ivester, Smith, Simmons, Moon,
Gilreath, Smith, Abrams, Simms,
Simms, Parker, Evans, Vickers,
Shetley, Whitfield, Cress, Farmer.
Lonsdale (2-1): Shaver, Gilliard,
Thompson, Harbin, Cooper,
Dooley, R. James, Watson,

Campbell, King, C. Watson,
Owens, Edgar, James, Weathers,
Maybin.
Gluck (1-2): Tabor, Wilton Hanna,
Jerome Ripley, Lester Hughes,
Boots Perry, Bray, Sam Jordan,
Moore, Ray Perry, Funny Woods,
Harold Harbuck, Roy Peace,
George Weathers, W.L. Ivester,
R. Jordan, Harbourgh.
Equinox (0-2): Smith, Spearman,
Harper, Larry Harbin, Vickery,
F. Harbin, Beck, Gibbs, Ivester,
McAllister, Davis, Craft, Allen,
Scarborough.

Dixie League

Pelham, champions (no records):
Clifford Cox, Frank Pittman (man-
ager), John Cox, Earl Poole, Dan
Greer, Ed Vaughn, Harold Sat-
terfield, George Blackwell, Parrot
Arnold, Fred Steadings, Claude
Pittman, Gene Bridwell.
Mills Mill of Woodruff (no records):
A. Abbott, H. Abbott, B. McAllis-
ter, Tom Ingle, C. Porter, Cal
McCauley, A. McAllister, C. Gar-
rett, D. Larry, C. Bridges, O. Revis
(manager), Larry Moon.

1939

Mid Carolina League

Joanna, champions (14-10): Harri-
son, Gene Abrams, Rolfe Clark,
Mack Brown, Bruce Galloway,
Snow Prater, Fred Ross, Rudolph
Prater, Algie Abrams, Claude
Cooley, Carl Farmer, Wheeze
Farmer, Tannery, Rhett Abrams,
Elwin Abrams, Bumps Harrelson.
Newberry (14-9): Walter Hiller, J.B.
Livingston, Corley, Fulmer, Clark,
Caldwell, Frank Shealy, James Ris-
ter, Hamilton, Miller, Ragsdale,
Dunk Singley, Bob Creekmore,
Whittle, Carl Taylor, Doodie
Franklin, George Hiller, Merchant,

Lefty Holsenback, J.C. Brooks, Harrison Warren, Fred Cook, Guy Danielson, Roy Ballard, Joe Bedenbaugh, Furman Warren.

Clinton (14-9): Charles Trammell, Rudder, Bowie, Davenport, Tough Embler, Bob Cranford, Henry King, Hunt, John Cranford, Sanders, Lamar Castleberry, Darnell, Riddle, Lankford, Webb, W. Cranford, Bartell, Emory, Davis, Foster, Hampton (manager), Norris.

Mollohon (13-9): Jackson, Cromer, J. Martin, Smith, Lefty Harmon, Charlie Golden, Moates, Gilbreath, Lindler, B. Mills, Wood, McCarty, R. Martin, Tobe Livingston, R. Rollins, B. Rollins.

Lydia (5-12): Emory, Ridgewell, Church, Fuller, Kirk, Morris, Butler, Moore, Roper, Bolick, Rogers, Knox, Foley, Galloway, Harris, Miller, Patterson, Eskew, Wells, Johnson, McCravey.

Whitmire (0-10); withdrew. Thomas, Black, J. Crosby, Wilson, J. Zeigler, Epps, Reid, Yarborough, Crow, Frank, Todd, H. Crosby, Blalock, Brown, Ruskin, Frank, Crater, Tarte, Gaffney.

Blue Ridge League

Easley, champions (16-15): McMahan, Garrett, Juber Hairston, J. Hendrix, F. Waldrop, L. Waldrop, Galloway, McCoy, Owens, McGaha, C. Dunn, Campbell, Skinner, Cleveland, Gilliam, Smith, Jamison, B. McCabe, McCoy, Garrett.

Pickens Pirates (16-15): Gilstrap, D. Adams, C. Adams, Dillard, Rampey, Pace, H. Adams, Childs, Slayton, Stevens, R. Pace, Finley, Cole, Hendrix, Roper, Henderson, Alexander.

Alice (15-12): R. Stewart, C. McGaha, Leslie, B. Williams, R. Williams, Bagwell, I. Stewart, Mulkey, Davis,

Laurence, Pearson, Cater, Chapman, McNeely, Masters, D. Williams, G. Williams, Turner.

Glenwood (15-14): W. Wilson, Fortner, Corley, J. Wilson, Sumter, Tatham, F. Mull, Spearman, Owens, Williams, Foster, Epps, Alexander, Pitts, Gilstrap, Turpin, Rankin, Bolt, Vaughn, Sumter, Simpson, W. Mull, L. Mull.

Liberty (14-15): Dover, James, Thrasher, Mauldin, Owens, Medlock, Underwood, Alexander, Powell, Gillespie, G. Gilstrap, J. Gilstrap, Orr, Watson, Burdette, Smith, Garrison.

Arial (11-18): Foster Vaughn, Masters, McNeely, Wilson, Rampey, Chapman, Boggs, Wiggins, Porter, Pitts, Brewer, Crum, Marchbanks, Roach, Charles Vaughn.

Western Carolina League

Lyman Pacifics, champions (33-19): Morgan, Roy Weathers, Hob Lee, Kenny Chitwood, Ted Cabiness, Bill Vaughn, Snyder, Horace Long, Yeargin, H. Dudley, Fred Powell, Danny Smith, Hart, Hawkins, Finley, Fisher, Will Howard, C. Dudley, Emory.

Mills Mill Millers of Greenville (27-19): Shaver, Craig, Charlie Page, Woodrow Abernathy, Hart, Mud Owens, Timmons, Putman, Brown, Campbell, Pace, Cabiness, Raymond Kelly, Garrett, Raymond Hunt, Bob Wright, Henry Shoaf, Taylor, Fletcher Chaffin, Hollifield, Garrett, Roy Brannon, Maxwell, Riley, Barbery.

Pelzer Bears (25-20): McCall, Ellenburg, Galloway, Cannon, Buntin, Wood, Grant, Virgil Lavender, Campbell, E. Stewart, Heath, Turpin, Woodcock, Jordan, Pitts, Bobo, Bagwell, DeBruhl, Holbrook, Doc Fisher, R. Stewart.

Southern Bleachery Red Flames (21-25): Barry, George Blackwell, Hub McCarter, McCravy, Childers, Wilbanks, Barbery, Lominack, Lister, Hudgens, Buddy Nau, Rags Suddeth, Steele, Brown, Stribbling, McElrath, Dennis, McCoy.

Piedmont (19-22): Hunter, Heath, Morris, Carlisle, Henderson, Rampey, Cooper, Pack, Reeves, Howard, Evans, Parker, Moore, Fleming, Owens, Johnson, Emory, Darnell, Johnson, R. Hunter, Ward.

Appleton (9-32): Bailey, Hawkins, Robertson, Gunter, Morrison, Sparks, H. Long, Dooley, N. Smith, Poole, McGuire, L. Smith, Hopkins, Crymes, Tollison, Taylor, Berry McElrath, Jim Blackwell, Craft, Monk Spake, H. Spake, Marshall, Robinson, Williams, Gaines, Cason, Hall, Morland, Harbin, Early, Ervin Sexton.

Central Carolina League

Ware Shoals, champions (22-17): Howard, Moore, J. Williams, Collins, Horne, Leo Tober, Boozer, J. Long, Ojeda, Ross, Steele, Sanders, Greene, Buchanan, Howell, Stover, Reid, Veal, Wright, Calvin Cooper.

Greenwood (30-15): Mule Escoe, Girk, Edgerton, Dickert, Hall, Webb, Wilson, Joe Whitlock, Jim Mobley, Lefty Kennedy, M. Williams, Watson, Nub Smythe, Jack McAllister, Morse, Moore, Doodie Franklin, Rick Gillespie, Joe Justice, Harvey Kirkland, Irvey Raines.

Ninety Six (26-10): Jean Belue, Morris, Ross, Knox, Voiselle, Veale, Smith, Page, Minyard, Tice, Granny Hightower, Fred Dowis, Lyles, Garrison, Buna Wells, Cox.

Mathews (22-21): Whitfield, McCall, Corley, Eddie Hall, Jeffcoat, Sipes, Bobo, Christopher, Sam Lankford,

James, Taylor, Phillips, Holbrook, Abrams, Southern, Beam, Patterson, Myers, Horn, J. Hall, Giles, Fisher, Martin.

Laurens Admirals (12-17): Mahaffey, Kirby, Finley, Darnell, Embler, Werner, Corley, Page, Pepper Martin, Burgess, Bailey, Strickland, Bagwell, Petty, Henry Allen, Bragg, Cannon, Barrett, Corley, Smith.

Riverdale (10-31): Abercrombie, Turner, Lonnie English, Obannion, Brewington, Cashion, Farr, Waddell, Higbe, W. Sanders, Waldrop, Abercrombie, Craig, Kennedy, Shetley, Billington, Foster, Spraggins, Talley.

Piedmont Textile League

Union Bleachery (13-3): Robertson, C. Surratt, Heaton, Bridwell, Roy Brooks, Bishop, Bell, Ivey, Patterson, Charles Brooks, Neely, W. Surratt.

Brandon of Greenville (8-2): Joe Anders, C. Foster, Humphries, McAbee, Reed, N. Anders, Thomas, Gilstrap, Morgan, Wilson, Foster, Jennings.

Judson (7-5): Trammell, Stokes, Pack, Cobb, Folger, Forrest, Hembree, Ellenburg, Hazel, Bailey, Gotshaw, Duffie, Thomas, Durham.

Southern Worsted (7-9): Brannon, Alverson, Ford, Mitchell, Addison, Steadings, Childers, Dill, Smith, Grastie, Christopher, Fowler, Vest, McCauley.

Monaghan of Greenville (6-8): Blackwell, Thompson, Griffith, Stevens, McAvoy, Waldrop, Elders, Nichols, Godfrey, McCauley.

Renfrew Bleachery (4-6): Knox, Wilson, Burns, Tollison, Brown, Fox, Clark, Revis, Belcher, Johnson, King, Quinn.

Slater (4-7): Dudley, Tucker,

Ledford, King, Boggs, Hornsby,
Price, Taylor, Sizemore, Toby,
Crocker, Croxton, Byars, Bible,
Wilson, Riley, Gosnell, Vaughn,
Forman, Puckett, Vaughn, Veal.
Dunean (3-11): Moore, Riddle, Campbell, Martin, Thomas, Bridges,
Bailey, R. Putnam, Giradeau,
S. Putnam, Burgess, Moore, Morris, Case, Southerland, League,
Lankford, Nabors, Floyd.

Greenville Textile League

Poinsett (2-0): P. Fair, Hodge, H. Fair,
Taylor, Campbell, Wood, Bridwell, Crymes, Turner, Townsend,
Nabors.
Pelzer (0-1): J. Hopkins, Dixon, Nix,
Haney, McClain, Davenport, Hopkins, Stewart, T. Harris, Coker, Connie Mack, Byers, Splawn, B. Harris,
Ross, Bagwell, Ellenburg.
Woodside (0-1): Rampey, Tucker,
Suddeth, Justus, Smith, Wilson,
Waldrop, Bomar, Bowers, Hines,
Landreth.
Indiana Queens (no records): Appleby, A. Pruitt, J. Pruitt, McCall,
Smith, Gordon, Alexander, Miller,
S. Robertson, J. Robertson.
Bahan (no records): Barrett, Hamilton, Harrison, O. Bramlett, Smith,
C. Hill, E. Crymes, Davis,
Bramlett.
Camperdown (no records): L. McDowell, B. McDowell, Jenkins, Griffith,
H. Burnett, Dill, Goodwin, A. Burnett, Brown, Coin, M. McDowell,
Gosnell, Thompson.
Southern Franklin (no records):
H. Abbott, W.E. Hunt, Porter,
W. Hunt, S. Jones, Murray,
A. Abbott, G. Jones, McNeely.
Greer (no records)

Eastern Carolina League

Drayton, champions (32-10): Pete
Laurens, Caton, Moore, B.T.
McCraw, Stowe, Ralph Prince,
Jones, Sap Morgan, Country
Kneece, J. Holt, Turner, Earl
McCraw, Haven Clause, Dodd,
Linder, Dick Carlin.
Pacolet (29-8): Lee, Lynwood McMakin, Red Ellison, Billy Hogan,
L. Fleming, Jett, Hodge, Arthur
Goforth (manager), Joe Cordell,
Spencer, W. Goforth, Gardin,
Gardner, Leroy Pace, K. Goforth,
Tee Fleming.
Converse (25-10): Wally Thompson,
Walter Fowler, Pat Elders, Powers,
Quay Byars, Croxdale, Reid, Lark,
Pete Fowler, Massey, Evans,
J. Fowler, Mosley, Greene, Vassey.
Inman Peaches (20-21): Otis Parris,
Eddie Smith, Ed Hawkins, Eddie
Clark, Bo Dotherow, Ed Parris,
Abernathy, High, Clyde Dobson,
Davis, Roy Lowe, Pack, Curt Randall, Charlie Quinn, Arthur
Waldrop, George Parris, John Bell
(manager).
Tucapau (14-21): Hodge, Anderson,
O. Mason, Smith, Hendrix,
J. Mason, Hill, Phillips, Glasson,
Allen, Hensley, Ramsey, Lavender,
Fox, Tapp, Nick.
Arcadia Reds (13-21): Henderson,
Gossett, McIntyre, Addison,
Parks, Calvert, Cannon, Ballard,
S. Fowler, J. Jones, V. Jones,
Cooper, Blackwell.
Beaumont (7-28): Sanders, Charlie
Cudd, Lewis, Mike O'Sullivan,
Maness, Thomas, Boose Holt,
Seay, Roy Turner, Mahaffey,
Cooksey, C. Holt, Willard, Shirley,
Painter, Harris, Garrett.

Mid State League

Rock Hill Bleachery Cubs, champions
(20-19): Wilson, Alman, Armstrong, Busby, Morgan, Belk,
Truesdale, K. Sanders, D. Sanders,
Dunlap, Knox, Cox, Lynch, Moon,
Edwards, Jordan, Huey, Perkins,
Fowler.

Highland Park (21-11): Perkins, Snipes, Watson, Glunt, Williams, Reeves, Harkey, Ramsey, Estridge, Smith, Reed, Thomas, Brant.

Great Falls (21-15): Wilson, Tarlton, Dawkins, Ellison, Grant, Justus, Funderburk, Baker, Eisenburg, Cooper, Roddy, Lynch.

Monarch (15-21): Phillips, Nabors, Long, N. Lawson, W. Lawson, Berry, Turner, Cabiness, Dudley, Willard, Sanders, Houston Hines, Trammell, Middleton.

Lockhart (15-32): B. Cabiness, W. Burns, Stalnaker, Odell, Gibson, Bill Broome, Laval, Blackwood, Watts, Hill, Crocker, Gibson, R. Cabiness, J. Burns, Warren.

Winnsboro (13-17): Northrup, Rushing, Gray, Weir, Ward, C. Blackwell, Frew, Rhinehart, Shealy, Thompson, N. Bagwell.

Union County League

Buffalo, champions (10-2): R. Millwood, Abrams, Lawson, Wright, Putman, H. Kingsmore, C. Millwood, Price, Frost, Revels, Vess, L. Kingsmore, Walker, Gillman.

Jonesville (10-5): Gregory, Wilson, Jess Holt, Buddy Holt, Self, Nelson, Hill, Morgan, Brown, McKinney, Smith, Farmer, Spencer, Banks, Worthy, Fowler.

West Springs (7-7)

Monarch (4-6): R. Coward, G. Coward, Lenhardt, Sanders, Turner, Morris, A. Coward, Davis, Gaden, Hyder, Phillips, Owens, Proctor.

Lockhart (3-6): Deal, Vandeford, Smith, Farr, T. Deal, Southerland, Warren, Gregory, Lemaster, M. Gibson, Eubanks, Harris.

Santuc (1-6)

Ottaray (no records)

American Legion (no records)

Spartanburg County League

Lyman, champions (17-6): Briggs,

Smith, Sid Dobson, H. Brown, Pruitt, Gowan, Furman Taylor, Hadden, Greer, Furman Dobson, Harrison, Ross, Holden, Ward, Gordon, Mullinax.

Jackson of Wellford (14-7): Murphy, J. Acton, H. Jordan, Shehan, B. Jordan, Belcher, B. Wilson, Dobbins, Myers, Cox, R. Acton, West, Hawkins, Murray, M. Taylor, D. Wilson, Deal.

Union (13-6): Lybrand, Sullivan, Foster, Bill Mitchell, Morris, Harris, B. Jolly, Gregory, Cohen, S. Jolly, Whitener, Willard, Blackwell.

Mills Mill of Woodruff (11-10): Walker, Phillips, Frady, Pop Davis, Brown, Jake Page, W. Page, Godfrey, McGathey, Wampus Bearden, Sam Page, Cox, Miller, Godfrey, Gaffney, Thomas, F. Page, J. Davis.

Apalache (6-11): L. Lunny, L. Pruitt, R. Blackwell, W. Blackwell, L. Rector, R. Bogan, D. Lunny, George Blackwell, Wilson, Rodgers, Tillotson, Hopkins, Bishop, Pettit.

Pacolet (5-6): Allen, C. Parker, Harrison, Hyatt, Green, Kimbrell, G. Parker, Valentine, Goforth, Sprouse, Mathis, T. Parker, Simmons, Tessnair, Messer, Banks.

Glendale (5-10): Mittag, Blanton, Warren, Anders, Thomas, Simmons, Mabry, Quinn, Rush, Linder, Gosnell, Blackwell, Rush, Murray, Puckett.

Riverdale (3-14): Murphy, Lynch, Bolden, Rhodes, Guinn, Gilliam, Jones, Martin, Emery, Wiggins, Nabors, Watson, O'Shields.

Spartanburg County Colored League

Converse, champions (11-3): Joe Tracy, Gray, Rhinehart.

Lyman (10-2)

Arcadia (6-7): Evans, Garner.

Clifton (3-7)

Pacolet (3-7)

Drayton (1-8)

Mid-County League

Fairmont, champions (4-0): Cobb, Duncan, Johnson, A. Boling, McAbee, Wood, Gibson, Switzer, Johnson, James, Owens, Duncan, N. Boling, Bruce.

Tucapau (1-0)

Jackson of Wellford (1-1): B. Blackwell, Nell, T. Blackwell, Stokely, Bright, Cothran, E. Acton, Murphy, R. Acton.

Spartan (1-3): Condrey, C. Heatherly, Brown, Mace, Earnhart, Shook, Taylor.

Valley Falls (0-1)

Converse (0-2)

Camden (0-2)

Cannon's Campground (no records)

Adams-Millis NC (no records)

Anderson County League

Oconee, champions (14-3): Red Simpson, G. Hawkins, Foots Gilden, Ed Hawkins, Milton Cobb, McGuffin, Mel Cobb, Two Simpson, W. Hawkins, D. Cobb, Bill Robinson, Marvin Rackley, Bob Gettys, Ben Sharp, J. Smith, M.D. Ford, W.C. Clearmont, W. Cain, Seymour.

Williamston (8-3): Dockery, Carey, Kimbo, Sargent, Black, Ragsdale, Miller, Garner, Pitts, Glasby, Dickard, McClain, Cannon, McClellan, Scott.

Calhoun Falls (7-8): Stevens, Jenkins, Mauldin, R. Pearson, Hilley, Ferguson, R.F. Pearson, Cooper, Verner, Thomas, Bolding, Reynolds, Welch, Bland, Lefty Carrithers.

Lonsdale (5-5): Shaver, Dooley, Sluder, Cater, Thompson, Harbin, R. James, Martin, J. James, Gillard, Weathers, Smith, Owens.

Gluck (5-6): Boots Perry, Wells, Ivester, Moore, Early Hanna, Carl Ripley, B. Jordan, Hughes, Dick Sweetenburg, Bray, R. Jordan, Harbuck, Tabor, Ray Perry,

Howard, Dick Perry, Sam Jordan, R. Allen, Peace.

Gossett (5-7): Gilreath, Smith, Simmons, Cunningham, Taylor, Ivester, Campbell, Daniel, King, Pigott, Acker, Sexton, Bannister, Simms.

Equinox (4-7): Smith, Spearman, Allen, L. Harbin, Harper, F. Harbin, H. Vickery, Chastain, McAllister, Davis, Moore, Shirley.

Orr Rifles (0-8): Day, Davis, Tommy Lyons, Barnes, Perrin, Dumb Price, C. Ashworth, John Ashworth, Lee Whitten, Joe Ashworth, Gunnells, Chatham, Morris, Crate Herring, Sanders.

Northwestern League

LaFrance, champions (10-4): Bo Cargill, Charles Bickley, Bob Massey, Carmon Harrison, Hoke Long, Buck Crenshaw, Ralph Clark, Chitwood, Boyd Harrison, Luther Rentz, Lindsay, Jones, Nod Moore, Slim Southerland, Frank Hopkins, Olin Boggs, Mutt Mauldin, J.L. Scott, Suddeth, Steve Eakes (manager), Hopkins, Clyde Owens, John Emery, Ronnie Gilstrap, Medlock, Ferguson, Jake Campbell, Frank Smith.

Cateechee (9-4): Bolding, Pilgrim, Reese, Garrett, Gilstrap, Alexander, J. Stancil, McWhorter, Powell, C. Stancil, James, Fowler.

Jackson of Iva (8-4): R. Pryor, Lawton, Hamm, H. Pryor, Baskin, J. Green, Dixon, M. Green, McAllister, Wilson, Burdette, Yeargin, Rutledge, Boyce, Haynes, Simpson.

Central (5-8): Canup, Berry, Carver, Thomas, Sanders, Duncan, Spearman, Cox, M. Oates, Lyda, Elliott, B. Oates, Scoggins, Saddle, Rutledge, Craig, Crawford.

Walhalla (1-7): Gilliard, Hunnicutt, Reid, Jamison, Williams, Benton, Littleton, Stegall, Lee, Garrett.

Georgia-Carolina League

Hartwell GA (no records)
Elberton GA (no records)
Anderson (no records): Ezra Embler,
  Dixon, Stallcup, Jordan, Herring,
  Cleveland, Meeks, McClain, Craft,
  Owens, Werner, McCombs, Ham-
  monds, William Embler, Raford
  Clark, L. D. Brown (manager),
  Roy Bridges, Reed White, Roy Dil-
  lard, Hailey Heaton, Jimmy
  Embler, Duke Honea, Waymon
  Moore, Bill Spencer, Jerome Rip-
  ley, James Daniel.
Jackson of Iva (no records)

Cross County League

Pelham (no records): Byars, Duncan,
  Owens, J. Smith, Hughes, M. Pitt-
  man, C. Smith, Emery, Bridwell.
Mills Mill of Woodruff (no records):
  McAllister, Alexander, O. John-
  son, Childs, Cox, Lindley, Collins,
  Bishop, Robinson, P.L. Johnson.
YMCA (no records)
Gantt (no records)

Independent Teams

Pelzer 2nd Team (no records):
  Gosnell, Taylor, Burton, Stevens,
  Austin, Quinn, King, Smith, Gallo-
  way, J. Ragsdale, B. Ragsdale.

1940

Piedmont Textile League

Brandon of Greenville, champions
  (12-8): Morgan, Surratt, Cox,
  Limbaugh, Humphries, C. Foster,
  Campbell, Joe Anders, Reid,
  N. Anders, Gilstrap, Sanders, Bald-
  win.
Monaghan of Greenville (14-3):
  Elder, Griffith, Smith, McGinnis,
  Thompson, Worthy, Blackwell,
  Stewart, Stevens, Waldrop, Elder,
  Sumter, McAvoy, McCravey. Nich-
  ols.

Slater (10-5): McCall, Wiggins, Tay-
  lor, Rampey, Cashion, Price, Ed-
  wards, Turpin, Watts, W. Wilson,
  Tucker, Dudley, Brewer, A. Led-
  ford, P. Ledford, J. Wilson.
Piedmont (9-8): Norris, Flemming,
  Stewart, Harris, Anderson, Evans,
  Cooper, Reeves, Pack, McAdams,
  Terry, Hooper, Terry.
Union Bleachery (8-8): Neely, Rhodes,
  Ivey, Patterson, C. Brooks,
  Surratt, Heaton, Bridwell,
  R. Brooks, Bishop, Bell, Turner,
  Hawkins.
Southern Worsted (7-8): Brannon, Al-
  verson, Childers, Smith, Dill, Chris-
  topher, Steadings, McCauley,
  Fowler, Vess, Grastie, Ford, Simp-
  son, Mull.
Judson (3-12): Mitchell, Covington,
  Tallant, Holcombe, C. Cobb, For-
  rest, Folger, R. Duffie, Hazel, Dur-
  ham, Pack, Trammell, James,
  Ellenburg, J. Duffie, Wyatt, Isman,
  Wilson.
Dunean (2-13): Riddle, Snoddy,
  Toby, Bailey, Parks, Hardin,
  Thomas, Cox, Putman, Floyd, Cal-
  lahan, McGinnis, Johnson, Cox.

Mid Carolina League

Laurens Admirals, champions (22-5):
  Woodrow Abercrombie, Joe
  Darnell, English, Leonard Hill, Ab
  Petty, Ed Strickland, Furman
  Bragg, June Werner, Mickey
  Stalcup, Gosnell, Allen, Barrett,
  Gosnell, Waldrop, Milton Monroe,
  Bagwell, King, Kirby Higbe.
Joanna (17-11): Smith, S. Prater,
  Farmer, Rudolph Prater, R. Abrams,
  C. Farmer, Mack Brown, Ross,
  E. Abrams, Nabors, R. Clark,
  A. Abrams, B. Galloway, L. Farmer,
  Case, Harrison, Anderson, Pat-
  terson, Addison, G. Prater,
  Clark.
Newberry (10-13): George Hiller,
  Rister, Walter Hiller, Alexander,

Corley, Bob Creekmore, Shealy, J.B. Livingston, Fulmer, Ralph Rowe, Golden, Taylor, Whittle, Caldwell, Pee Wee Franklin, Foy, E. Hiller, Hamblin.

Mollohon (9-13): J. Martin, Pint Harmon, Cromer, Goofey Smith, Grant, Jimmy Sowell, Rinehart, Heyward Mills, J. Jackson, Rudolph Martin, McCarter, Harry Yochem, L. Mills, Golden, Lindler, A. Jackson, Moates, E. Mills, Gilreath, Craft, Day, Irby Bouknight, H. Mills, G. Mills, Lindler.

Lydia (6-13): Fuller, Burnett, Will Rogers, Johnny Eskew, Lamar Castleberry, Patterson, Spearman, Trammell, Harris, Sanders, Galloway, Jones, Miller, Lanford, Johnson, Barrett, Bridwell, Rogers, Dearman.

Clinton (5-11): Farmer, Spider Webb, Moore, Conley Alexander, Robertson, Norris, Snelgrove, Sanders, Hunt, Buddy Crawford, Joe Davenport, H. King, John Crawford, Thompson, E. Crawford, Thornton, T. Cranford, Robinson, Al Butler, Gregory, R. King, Shaw, Center, W. Cranford.

Mid State League

Rock Hill Bleachery Cubs, champions (25-12): Cromer, Lefty Wilson, Fowler, H. Estridge, Allman, B. Campbell, G. Campbell, Roy Hughey, Busby, Huskey, Thornburg, Knox, Moon, F. Campbell, Williams, Templeton, O. Campbell, Key, Allman, Lyle, T. Campbell, Sanders.

Highland Park (21-14): Thomas, Harkey, Hull, Morse, Watson, Duncan, Ramsey, Smith, Ferguson, Reid, Estridge, Moss, Snipes, Cooper.

Winnsboro Royal Cords (20-15): T. Shealy, Harkrader, Banks, Brenemer, Bull Rushing, Thompson,

Ward, Addis, Bone, Barfield, Spires, H. Shealy, A. Shealy, Addy, Heath, Lingle, Rinehart, Byars, Floyd, Abrams, B. Spires, Waters.

Great Falls (18-17): Moore, Roddy, Tarlton, Ralph Ellison, Baker, Dawkins, Funderburk, Mendenhall, Gray, Gibson, Locklair, Justus, Brown, Cooper, Rhodes, DeLoach.

Monarch (13-22): Willard, Shorty Grant, Jete Long, Simp Sanders, E. Phillips, Ralph Phillips, Sam Turner, Newell Lawson, Trammell, A. Cabiness, Houston Hines, Justus, Lefty Carlisle, Elvin Woolen, Owen Woolen, Jim Gregory, Carl Berry, Lefty Matheny.

Lockhart (11-24): Buford Cabiness, O'Dell, Stalnaker, Burns, C. Gibson, Buddy Laval, Opia Watts, Gregory, R.Cabiness, Farr, Hill, Broome, Lemaster, Putnam, Watts, Deal, Farmer, Jenkins, Putnam, Farmer.

West Central Carolina League

Ninety Six Indians, champions (34-16): Pete Fox, Fred Ross, Morris, Leonard, Buna Wells, Jean Belue, Tice, Granny Hightower, Lyles, Foster, Gracie Allen, Beam, Bolding, Glenn Forrester, Smythe, Bahn, Diz Voiselle, Elias, Davis.

Ware Shoals Riegels (29-23): Leo Tober, Moore, Dixie Howell, Collins, Holt, Sam Fowler, Henderson, Shorty Horne, Earl Veal, J. Williams, Knapp, Pepper Martin, Cooper, Sanders, Reid, Moore, Lefty Howard, Cheek, Buchanan, Cannon, Lou Brissie.

Lyman Pacifics (27-19): Rube Morgan, Chitwood, Hob Lee, Gaffney, Bill Yeargin, John Wahonic, Clise Dudley, Danny Smith, Bill Vaughn, Rags Suddeth, Bill Snyder, Spec Barbary, Powell, Watson, Murphy,

C. Yeargin, Horace Long, Reid, Hawkins, Smith.

Mathews Wildcats (27-22): Kennedy, Snipes, J. Hall, Smith, Dog Obannion, Bill Jeffcoat, Ted Cabiness, Melton, Heath, Charlie Jeffcoat, Holbrook, Southern, E. Hall, Abrams, Minyard, Don Helms, Smith, Zempell, Mobley, Hawkins, Wingard, Ken Holcombe, Williams, Sanders.

Greenwood Warriors (24-19): Buster Hare, Girk, Mule Escoe, Hunt, Mutt Williams, Edison, Webb, Lefty Kennedy, Doodie Franklin, Abrams, Dickert, Whitlock, Booth, McAllister, Nub Smythe, King, Earl Morse, Rube Melton, Berry, Jones.

Mills Mill Millers of Woodruff (24-20): Fletcher Chaffin, Gene Hollifield, Henry Shoaf, Wright, Craig, Mud Owens, Bearden, Red Christopher, M. Williams, Ox Taylor, Mills Putnam, Raymond Kelly, Timmons, Gaines, Walker Campbell (manager), E. Page, Jordan, Woodrow Abernathy, Johnson Moore, Fletcher Heath, Harbin, Riley, Sam Page.

Southern Bleachery Red Flames (10-32): McCravey, Hudgins, George Blackwell, Joe Childers, Robinson, Steele, Buddy Nau, O'dell Barbery, Lominack, Dillard, Leister, Hughes, Wilbanks, Robertson, Denny Hendrix, Steele, Smith, Maness, Devine, Meisenheimer, Lyles Alley (manager)

Pelzer Bears (8-32): Lefty Crymes, Swan, D. Helms, Harris, Wood, Epps, DeBruhl, John Helms, Haney, Grant, Virgil Lavender, Stewart, Henderson, Woodcock, Jordan, Bridges, Harley Heath, Parris, McBride, Grant.

Eastern Carolina League

Drayton Dragons, champions (30-15): Country Kneece, Burnett, Haven Clause, Raymond Linder, J.D. Morgan, Biershenk, Hill, Ralph Dodd, Scrappy Moore, Stowe, B.T. McCraw, Virgil Caton, O'shields, Dick Corbin, Pete Laurens, Bennett, Shirley, E. McCraw, Charlie Seay, Ed Hawkins, Art Smith, Shuf Finley, Pedro Mahaffey.

Pacolet White Trojans (27-18): Lynn Morrow, Lynwood McMakin, Raymond Ellison, Bill Broome, Billy Hogan, Tee Felming, Tommy Jett, Lancaster, Edgerton, Arthur Goforth, Olin Hodge, Willie Goforth, L. Pace, Flash Gardin, Curt Randall, Greene, Peaches Lee.

Converse Bluejays (23-16): Walter Fowler, Bill Cooksey, Bill Croxdale, Tip Massey, Clarence Millwood, Vance Powers, Dick Evans, Quay Byers, Thomas, Charlie Reid, Pete Fowler, Hugh Lark, Stan Mosely, Pat Elders, Yonnie Green, Thompson, McSwain.

Inman Bells (23-16): Blackberry Thomas, Otis Parris, Roy Lowe, Hayes Clark, E. Parris, J. Waldrop, George Parris, Casey, Bad Eye Turner, Isaac Helms, Bill Zempell, Wade Abernathy, Colbert, John Bell, E. Abernathy, C. Abernathy, Painter, Gray, E. Thomas, Culbreth.

Avondale NC (18-17)

Arcadia Reds (16-19): Red Lewis, Cooper, A. Cannon, Boose Holt, Claude McIntyre, J. Cannon, Gossett, Calvert, Paul Henderson, J.E. Blackwell, Louis Veal, Harrell, Hughes, Slim Crawford, C. Jones, Gossett, Henderson, Jimmy Carey, J. Jones, J. McIntyre, Medlock, Martin, Seay, R. Jones.

Riverdale (12-23): Granny Craig, Casey Thornton, Paul Turner, Waldrop, Cecil Brewington, Jack Farr, West, Cannon, Betsill, N. Bagwell, C. Bagwell, Hubert Cashion, Weathers, Gwinn, Rocco Montano, Simmons, Robinson, Strickland, King, Nabors, Robertson, Ferguson, Allen, Cheek, Jones, Pitt, Martin.

Gaffney Red Sox (5-30): Branch, White, O. Medley, Harry Sullivan, Tough Embler, Bolick, A. Medley, Whitefield, Camp, Ramsey, Hensley, Fox, Cobb, Brown, Vaughn, Pruitt, Bolick, A. Pace, Curt Randall, Lou Mandell, McAbee, Moore, Lavender, Bridges, Pridmore, McGraw, Jones, Mathis, Hughes.

Blue Ridge League

Easley, champions (16-2): H. Dunn, Hendrix, Spearman, Campbell, Juber Hairston, L. Waldrop, McGaha, C. Garrett, J. Owens, McCoy, Henson, F. Waldrop, C. Dunn, M. Garrett.

Liberty (9-6): Dover, Thrasher, Smith, Watson, Mauldin, Underwood, Morgan, Gillespie, Orr, Powell, G. Gilstrap, J. Gilstrap, Garrison.

Alice (6-5): Turner, McGaha, Bagwell, Davis, Stevens, H. Stewart, R. Stewart, B. Williams, Harbin, L. Harbin, G. Williams, C. Bagwell, Alexander, R. Williams.

Glenwood (6-9): Wilson, Mull, Owens, Leslie, Pitts, Rankin, Corley, Gosnell, Tucker, Mason, Putman, Browning, Reeves, Tatham, Stewart, G. Spearman, C. Spearman, Simpson, Reeves, McHugh, L. Spearman.

Pickens (5-7): Gibson, Adams, Finley, Gibson, Rampey, Roper, Stewart, Page, Gilstrap, Trotter, Childs, Slatten, Brown, Hendrix, Adams.

Arial (3-7): Crum, McNeely, Masters, Anderson, H. Wilson, Brewer, Stevenson, Pitts, R. Wilson, James, Foster Vaughn, Boggs, Charlie Vaughn, Roach.

Newry (1-8): Sluder, Hawkins, Lytle, Taylor, Smith, Tanner, Williams, Black, Howard, O'Kelly, Putnam, Taylor.

Central (1-8): Barry, Craig, Cox, Crane, B. Oates, Thomas, Duncan, Lyda, M. Oates, Carver, Elliott, Logenins, Sanders, Williams, Spearman, Elrod, Hawkins.

Spartanburg County League

Union, champions (23-6): Goo Lybrand, Scuppy Foster, Ben Jolly, Bill Mitchell, Harris, Oscar Sullivan, R. Crocker, Gregory, Crosby, Cohen, Carlos Blackwell, Bill Kirby, Corn, Virgil Morris, Willard, Eland, E. Balckwell, J. Sullivan, Wilson Leonhardt, T. Sullivan, Wilbur Hodge, Hall, Shep Whitener, Woody Cohen.

Lyman (17-11): Briggs, Doyle Smith, Bradley, Gowan, Brown, Mullinax, Hadden, Switzer, Harrison, Pearson, Furman Taylor, Connie Myers, Murphy, Ed Smith, Linder, Gowan, Deal, A. Smith, Mullinax, Veal, Norris, Jenkins.

Mills Mill of Woodruff (14-9): Walker, J. Page, Frady, Phillips, Paul Davis, W. Page, J. Davis, Cox, Charlie Brown, Huckaby, Barrett, F. Page, Dewey Lawrence, Thomas, Atley Cook, Timmons, Jameson, Blanton, Garrett, Brown, Newton, Charlie Page, Snag Calvert, Lanford.

Pacolet (11-12): Allen, Bowen, Courtney, Whitlock, Hogan, Loving, Harrison, Jim Lee, Jim Green, Kansas Goforth, John Lee, Goforth, Tessenair, Dupree, Osment, C. Parker, Teasler, Spencer, Hill, Doc Lemmons, Guy Parker, J. Parker, Phillips, Carter, Flash Gardin.

Tucapau (8-11): Swift Allen, Bru Anderson, Pedro Mahaffey, Hodge, Hill, Pat Elders, Jim Lavender,

Hendrix, Powell, Sandlin, Glasson, Phillips, Hunt, Fisher, West, Poole, Capp, Massey, Evans, Poore.

Jackson of Wellford (8-12): Jim Acton, Dobbins, R. Acton, D. Shehan, Jordan, T. Blackwell, Belcher, Murray, Hopper, Murphy, Stokely, Cox, Ernest Acton, R. Wilson, Dobson, H. Shehan, Pat Hawkins, P. Acton, Bruce, Elders, R. Thilson, Wilson.

Apalache (6-14): Pruitt, Haney, McCarter, Leopard, Bishop, Rector, R. Blackwell, Belue, L. Lunny, George Blackwell, Bogan, Wilson, Odam, D. Lunny, H. Blackwell, Giles, B. Lunny, W. Blackwell, Moss, Papp, Ballenger, West, Pettit, Harvey, Reddin.

Glendale (4-16): Ralph Gosnell, W. Gosnell, James Pruitt, Puckett, Mittag, Simmons, Jug Linder, Wheeler, Warren, Melvin Anders, Hawkins, Warner, Arthur Blackwell, Dunnigan, Deal, Worley, Ward, Blanton, Bagwell, Harris.

Union County League

West Springs, champions (12-4)

Buffalo (8-7): Price, R. Millwood, Abrams, R. Lawson, Revels, Kingsmore, F. Lawson, Vess, Frost, Haney, Putman, Wright, C. Millwood, West, Lands.

Jonesville (5-3): Morgan, Self, Gregory, Buddy Holt, Wilson, Reynolds, Fowler, H. Nelson, Smith, B. Nelson, C. Holt, J. Nelson, Shelton, Addis, J. Holt, Blackwell, Hyatt.

Whitmire (5-4): Blalock, Crow, Weaver, Brown, Black, Tarte, Erskine, Wilson, Garrett, Stone, Thomas, L. Fowler, Hall, J. Fowler, H. Fowler, Livingston, Alexander, Bumgardner, Lee, H. Crosby, Wilbanks, B. Crosby, Collier, F. Crosby, Prince, Finney.

Monarch (3-7): Middlebrooks, Phillips, Turner, Davis, O. Sanders, Nichols, Garner, Gadden, Morris, Hines, Vaughn, Sims, S. Sanders, F. Sanders, C. Berry, Moore, Brown, Gooden, Voiselle, Moore.

Lockhart (1-9): Farr, Revels, C. Deal, M. Gibson, J. Good, J. Gibson, T. Deal, Riddle, Branks, Harris, Burgess, Branch, Cogdill, Gregory, Taylor, Crenshaw, Cabiness, James Deal, Eubanks, Crocker, Jess Deal, G. Gibson.

Palmetto League

Chesnee, champions (16-8): Clayton, Ramsey, Suttles, Ezell, Les Davis, Steadman, Haynes, L. White, H. White, Robins, C. Hopper, E. Hopper, Southern, B. Robins, Splawn, H. Robins, Nolan, B. Hopper, M. Hopper, Duncan, Stevens, Blackwood, Edgerton, Lee Hopper, W. Davis, Allen.

Clifton (14-6): Barbery, Coggins, Worley, F. Mabry, Fowler, Mathis, Cudd, J. Bagwell, Chapman, Burch, P. Mabry, H. Bagwell, T. Mabry, Hammond, Barber, Calvert, McCarley, Tindall, John Mostiller, Morley, Burns.

Broad River (12-9): C. Dillingham, N. Hampton, John Hampton, C. Patterson, H. White, B. Moore, Morehead, Sanders, Moss, Gaffney, B. Broome, W. Dillingham, S. Hampton, Nichols, Ramsey, Earle.

Jackson of Wellford (11-11): C. Jordan, Neill, Sam Bright, Key, Dick Bruce, Bishop, Poole, Jess Cothran, Hooper, Dobbins, McCarter, Byers, Hayes, Hendrix, Erskine, Glasson, Murray, Myers, E. Bright, B. Jordan.

Fairmont (8-11): Wood, Johnson, Owens, Gibson, Belcher, McAbee, Boling, Bruce, Jones, R. Morrow, Clayton, Duncan, Gilliam,

T. Mabry, Bohn, Petit, Black, Morrow, Gibson, Jimmy York, John Earnhart, Ballard, Heatherly, James.

Cannon's Creek (2-17)

Catawba League

Lando (18-12): Tom Overby, Adams, Stephenson, Hough, McCorkle, Rivers, Muncher, Dixon.

Lancaster (17-12): Northrup, Rogers, Warren, Lynch, Smith, Norfolk.

Eureka (14-15): Smith, Starnes, Hood, Thompson, Hunt, Weir, Hunt.

Fort Mill (10-20): Sanders, Erwin, Carrouth, Hamrick.

Spartanburg County Colored League

Converse (5-1): Gray, Rhinehart, Stewart, Ray.

Pacolet (5-2): Robertson, Smith, Johnson, Humphries.

Arcadia (4-2): Evans, Garner, Brasson, Means, Garner.

Lyman Black Cats, 1st half champions (2-2): Green, Young, Swift, Foster, Barton, Bennett.

Tucapau (2-3): Mills, Woodruff, Jones, Glenn.

Drayton (1-2): Rice, Mack, Tucker, Smith, Littlejohn.

Clifton (1-3): A.W. Alexander, J. Alexander, Slimer, Walker.

Woodruff (1-4): W. Casey, Cornell.

Chester County League

Lando (no records): Vinson, Scott.

Chester (no records): McWaters, Langley.

Eureka (no records): Walter Thompson, R. Dabbs.

Greenwood-Laurens County League

Ware Shoals (1-0): Bolt, Brissie, Davis.

Rogers Hosiery (0-1): Worth, Bible, Bobo.

Mathews (no records)

Grendel (no records)

Ninety Six (no records)

Greenwood (no records)

Anderson County League

Calhoun Falls, champions (22-11): Ferguson, Darnell, Bland, Brown, Pearson, Verner (manager), Hilley, Wood, Craft, Darnell, Johnson, Thackston, Martin, Southern, Girk, Verner, Barnett, Reynolds, Jenkins, Lyons, Neil Chrisley, Holbrook, Heath.

Williamston (22-12): Luther Wood (manager), Densel Dockery, Ed Dickard, Quay Miller, John Emory, Ralph Cannon, Broadus Kimbo, Bill Jordan, Raymond Garner, Scott, Dick McLellan, Walker Bagwell, John Pitts, Tollison, Lollis, Howard Cannon, Burr McLellan, Elmo Moody, Grant, Lavender.

Oconee Mountaineers (20-12): Marvin Rackley, Seymour, G. Hawkins, Gilden, Ed Hawkins, Robinson, Milton Cobb, Simpson, Melvin Cobb, Harrison, Gettys, Carrithers, W. Hawkins, Carpenter, Massey, Smith, Cater, McGuffin, Moore, Williams, Ford, Sharp (manager), McGuffin, Jeffcoat, Corbin, McMullen, Byers.

Gossett (20-12): Campbell, C. Hamm, McElrath, Ivester, Sexton, Simmons (manager), Mahaffey, Smith, Acker, Sullivan, Pigott, Cunningham, Allen, Bannister, Edgerton, Fisher, Wofford, Johnson, McCollum.

Orr (11-18): Day, Meeks, Cleveland, Perrin, Barnes, Joe Ashworth, Powers, Carrithers, Wells, Doolittle, Lee Whitten, Flannigan, Bickley, Dude Buchanan, Gunnells, Booth, Williams, Belk, Hare, Vaughn, Johnny Ashworth, Minyard, Price, Sipe, King, R. Ashworth.

Gluck (11-20): Ray Perry, Jordan, Long, G. Bailey, Hanna, Ivester, Tabor, Moore, Weathers, Bray, Blackwell, Harbuck, L.R. Manley (manager), Blackstone, McClesky, Howard, Dick Perry, Hester, S. Bailey, Boots Perry, Smith, Peace, Ripley.

Equinox (4-13): C. Moore, Pearman, S. Moore, L. Harbin, Harper, F. Harbin, Allen, Morrison, Robinson, Stewart, H. Moore, Smith, Richardson, Sullivan, Spearman, Snipes, Bill Womack, Southerland.

Lonsdale (6-10): Joe Mason (manager), Whitt, Powell, Owens, H. James, Snag Owens, Cater, J. James, Thompson, Harbin, Edgar, Stevens, R. James, Dooley, Shaver, Galliard, Rampey, Hopkins.

Georgia-Carolina League

LaFrance, champions (12-7): John Gilliard, Bob Massey, Boyd Harrison, Buck Crenshaw, King, Heaton, Ralph Clark, Olin Boggs, Mutt Mauldin, Sullivan, John Medlock, Henry Moore, Minyard, C. Harrison, Alfus Moore, Charlie Southerland, Cargill, Duckworth, Bridges, Charles Carrithers, J.D. Kelly, Haford, Cooley Garrett, Campbell, J. Craft, Frank Boggs, Larry Harbin, B. Harbin, A.V. Seymour, Dooley, Steve Eakes (manager), Melton Cromer, John Pitts, H. Chitwood, M.W. Mauldin, Raford Clark, Charles Bickley, Clay Moore, Buford Clark.

Anderson (11-7): J. Embler, Spake, Burris, J. Daniels, Bailey, T. Embler, Scott, W. Daniels, Bridges, Littlefield, Clark, Smith, King, Fletcher, Sanders, Carlton, Moore, Perrin, Meeks, Scott, Heaton.

Elberton GA (11-8)

Jackson of Iva (10-7): H. Pryor, Boyce, Hamm, Lawton, Dixon, Latham, Jordan, R. Pryor, D. Green, McAllister, M. Green, B. Green, Hall, Yeargin, Baskin, Clark, M. Pryor.

Belton (8-9): C. Nelson, H. Deanhardt, C. McAllister, Verner, L. Deanhardt, Shaw, Shirley, W. Nelson, Carlton, Willingham, Warnock, Owens, Ellison, Carlton, Campbell.

Lavonia GA (4-14)

Greenville County League

Fork Shoals, champions (5-3): Trammell, Smith, Nelson, Adair, Moore, Farrow, Campbell, E. Williams, L. Pitts, Tumbling.

Pelzer (5-4): Lindley, Lindley, Davis, Austin, Ellenburg, Fowler, Greer, King, Harris, Wooten, McClain, Hopkins.

Piedmont (4-7): Lavender, Bray, White, Allen, Harris, Evans, Fowler, Lindley, Bates, Williams, Stone, Bass, Jones, Taylor, Harrison, Cooper, Brown.

Ridgeway (3-0)

Glenwood (2-0): Cope, Sumter, J. Garrett, Spearman, E. Garrett, Alexander, Trotter.

Greenville Textile League

Simpsonville, champions (12-1): W. Cox, O'dell Barbery, J. Smith, Stutts, B. Cox, Hensley, P. Turner, Bagwell, O. Barbery.

Poinsett (4-1): Gilstrap, B. Turner, Townsend, Alexander, P. Fair, H. Fair, A. Pruitt, J. Pruitt, Taylors, Wood, Appleby.

Bahan (4-2): L.J. Long (manager), Ramsey, E. Crymes, Durham, Reid, Neil, Griffith, McCall, Wilson, Bramlett, Bowen, Hall, F. Bedenbaugh, Jack Bedenbaugh.

Mills Mill of Greenville (0-1): Pace, Cox, A. McAllister, H. Abbott, Netterville, Williams, Massey, Trammell, B. McAllister, McNeely, Garrett, Carson, Brock, Childs, A. Abbott, McJunkin, Smith.

Brandon of Greenville (0-4): J. Stewart, Breazeale, Duncan, Orr, D. Hall, Masters, Taylor, Vickery, Austin, W. Hall, B. Hall, F. Stewart, Howie, Clary, Donahue, McCoy, Mahon, Rodgers.
Kentucky Queens (0-1)

Pickens County League

Pickens (1-0): McGaha, Bolding, Breazeale, D. McNeely, Smith, Brown, Holder, Paces, C. McNeely.
Cateechee (0-1): Pilgrim, Alexander, Fowler, Reese, Parker, Holder, Bagwell, Norris, Chapman.

Independent Teams

Travelers Rest (1-0): Edwards.

1941

Western Carolina League

Pelzer Bears, champions (27-16): Woodcock, Virgil Lavender, Lonnie Holbrook, Charlie Jeffcoat, Stewart, Obannion, Bridges, Cannon, Harris, Woods, Jordan, Densel Dockery, Smith, Hall, Earl Wooten, Kunk, Wood, Lefty Crymes, Parris, Abrams, Minyard, Wahonic, Davis.
Mills Mill Millers of Woodruff (30-16): Petty, Clyde Frady, Christopher, Ox Taylor, Southerland, Putman, Everett Page, Kelly, Fletcher Chaffin, Woodrow Abernathy, Timmons, Ed Strickland, Barrett, Yeargin, Maxwell, Bearden, English, Craig, Sam Page, C. Page, Brady, J. Page, Kirkman, F. Page, Campbell.
Southern Bleachery Red Flames (24-18): Snow Kirby, O'dell Barbery, Lominack, George Blackwell, Robbie Robinson, Dillard, Parker, Steele, Furman Taylor, Hudgens, Charlie Childers, Joe Robertson, Pitts, Andy Hawthorne, K. Owens,

Red Owens, Furman Dobson, Millwood, Meisenheimer.
Lyman Pacifics (21-21): Denny Smith, Ted Cabiness, Gene Hollifield, Rags Suddeth, Vance Powers, Bill Snyder, Bumgardner, George Coan, Paul DeBruhl, Red Murphy, Gibbs, Reid, Snyder, John Wahonic, Horace Long, Giles, G. West, Dudley, Elders, Bearden, Yeargin, Joe Childers, Powell, Christopher, Mendenhall, Smith, Harris, Leroy Mahaffey.
Drayton Dragons (19-23): Campbell, Brownie Newton, Forrest Hunt, Dick Corbin, Bedenbaugh, Leonard Hill, Sap Morgan, Virgil Caton, Hart, Country Kneece, Earl McCraw, McCown, Pete Laurens, Carlton, Earnhart, Taylor, Ralph Dodd, Mills, Boose Holt, Lowe, Haven Clause, D. McCraw, Manning Bagwell, Smart, Sullivan, Cantrell, Waldrop, Ross, Randall, Moody, Seay, Evans, Finley, F. McCraw, Mud Owens, Dizzy Whitfield, John Earnhardt.
Piedmont Rangers (5-32): Patterson, Bradley, Cooper, Reeves, Walters, Evans, Fleming, Abercrombie, M. Adams, Rampey, Pack, Edwards, Fowler, D. Anderson, L. Anderson, Jones, Leroy Mahaffey, Norris, Ivester, White.

Greenville County League

Hickory Tavern, champions (4-5)
Ridgeway (6-1)
Fork Shoals (4-2): L. Pitts, B. Farrow, Moore, W. Farrow, Meeks, Nelson, Bagwell, D. Davenport, J. Davenport, Smith, Kellett.
Piedmont (3-10): Brown, F. Cooper, Cox, Stone, C. Allen, Rogers, Garrison, Williams, Shackleford, J.Allen, Lindley, White, Jones, Dill, Shockley, J. Cooper, B. Allen, Barwick.
Cheddar (2-3)

Southern Bleachery (2-5): Kellett, Bishop, Meisenheimer, Kelly, Owens, Martin, Brown, Neal, Shockley, Trammell, Seminer, Quitton.

York-Chester-Lancaster County League

Clover, champions (1-0): B. Harvey.

Lancaster Red Roses (6-5): Howell, Smith, Jackson, Roberts, Lyons, Robertson, Griffin, Griffin, Rogers.

Great Falls Reds (4-3): Wilson, Orr, J. Gardner, Welch, Henson, Knight, Vinson, Drawdy.

Eureka Blue Birds (3-0): Brooks, Starnes, Hart, Proctor, McWatters, Jackson, Fleming, Cook, Langley.

Gayle Tigers (1-2): Beckham, Taylor, Greene.

Lando Cardinals (0-4): Stevenson, Blanks, Dennison, Scott, Huff, Miller.

Anderson County League

Calhoun Falls, champions (15-8): Reynolds, Darnell, Barrett, Smith, Baskin, McCaslin, Thomas, Hilley, Thackston, Bland, Pearson, Sullivan, Masters, Bickley, Aiken, Stokely, Dockery, Justus, Stevens, McKinney, Christian, Glenn, Barnett.

Oconee (15-8): Simpson, Bagwell, E. Hawkins, Cater, Garrett, G. Hawkins, Smith, Williams, McGuffin, Robinson, R. King, Harris, Gettys, L. King.

LaFrance (10-8): Massey, Medlock, Harbin, C. Harrison, H. Long, Gilliard, B. Harrison, O. Boggs, Mauldin, Ferguson, Campbell, Crenshaw, Webb, Harbison, Mussey, Sutherland, Smith, Emery.

Belton (10-10): Minyard, Epson, C. Fisher, Werner, L. Deanhardt, Campbell, H. Deanhardt, Williams, Carlton, C. Nelson, Womack, Fuller, McAllister, Warnock, W. Nelson, Stone, L. Fisher, Alred.

Gossett (9-9): Cunningham, Wofford, Smith, Ivester, Cleveland, Sullivan, English, Simmons, Burton, Day, Allen, Campbell, Chavous, Burgess, Buffington, Sexton, Mahaffey.

Appleton (8-10): Meeks, Cooley, Sid Bailey, Gaines, Berry McElrath, Jim Blackwell, G. Bailey, Gunter, Weathers, Spake, Morrison, Robinson, White, Perrin, Carithers.

Lonsdale (7-10): Dooley, Shaver, Harbin, Jackson, Hopkins, Shirley, H. James, Edgars, Carrithers, Latham, R. James, Whitt, Ferguson, T. James, M. James.

Williamston (4-13): Hopkins, Ervin, Miller, Emery, Kimbo, Garner, McClelland, Ragsdale, Hampton, Dockery, Dickert, Sutt, Cannon, Burdette, McCollum, Browning, Scott.

Northwestern League

Clemson CCC (11-1)

Cateechee (5-3): R. Stancill, J. Stancill, Mann, Reese, Holden, Gilstrap, Alexander, Pilgrim, Norris, Parker, Garrett, Merck, Livingston, Mitchell, Bolding, Alsep, Langston.

Newry (1-1): D. Taylor, Sluder, T. Crenshaw, Howard, Hawkins, O'Kelly, Russell, P. Putnam, Keaton, Bagwell, C. Crenshaw, Smith, Peebles, Carver, C. Putnam, L. Taylor, Carvin.

Mountain Rest (0-1)

Georgia-Carolina League

Anderson, champions (25-3): H. Hairston, Jim Embler, D. Daniels, B. Daniel, Kelly, Clark, Roy Bridges, W. Moore, E. Embler, H. Heaton, Bill Spencer, Lee Scott, W. Daniels, Dude Scott, Jones, Honea,

A. Heaton, Belue, T. Embler, C. Moore, Dillard.

Orr (20-8): A. Ashworth, Herring, J.R. Ashworth, Howard, Gunnells, Pearce, Powers, Vernon, Holme, Lee Whitten, Carrithers, Powers, Joe Ashworth, Perrin, Vaughn, Sanders, Fred Whitten, Hulme, Day, Hooper.

Pelzer (14-11): Davenport, Haney, Bill Hopkins, Harris, Floyd, Ross, Pridmore, Galloway, Byars, Earl Wooten, Southern, Jordan, McClain, Hall, Kellett, Smith, Dickerson, Carpenter, McKee, Taylor, Center, Alexander, Suddeth, Davis, Sail, Tate.

Jackson of Iva (13-10): H. Pryor, F. Latham, Yeargin, Boyce, Lawton, R. Pryor, Dixon, Hall, Alexander, Green, Owen, D. Lattimore, P. Lattimore, D. Latham.

Arial (9-9): Anderson, Masters, James, Pitts, Turpin, Stewart, C. Stephens, B. Stephens, R. Wilson, Marchbanks, Boggs, Williams, Starnes, Stokes, C. Starnes, McNeely, A. Williamson, F. Vaughn, Carmen, A. Wilson.

Glenwood (4-9): N. Mull, F. Mull, Owens, M. Turpin, Cope, G. Spearman, Reeves, Simpson, C. Spearman, Miller, Chapman, L. Mull, McQuinn, Pitts, McCue.

Central (3-16): Mauldin, Elliott, Craig, Crane, Elrod, Sanders, Moore, Suttles, Hawkins, Lydie, Elrod, Carver, Berry, Green, Lawson, Marchbanks, Lyda, Swiney, James, Gilreath.

Equinox (2-16): Smith, J. Craft, Ivester, Stevens, Allen, Harper, E. Craft, Simpson, Dalton, Harbin, Shirley, Vickery, Moore, Morgan, Eberhart.

Walhalla (0-4); withdrew. Reid, Hunnicutt, Mills, Williams, Beardon, Smith, Bridges, Stegall, Lee.

Mid Carolina League

Joanna, champions (13-6): R. Abrams, Case, C. Farmer, Mack Brown, Bolding, Rollins, L. Farmer, A. Abrams, Tom Clyde, Guy Prater, Galloway, J. Brown, Martin, Rudy Prater, Clark, Earl Morse, Brown, Charlie Girk, Willingham, D. Prater, S. Abrams.

Newberry (10-8): Taylor, Rowe, Walter Hiller, J. Livingston, C. Livingston, Bowers, Whitten, Rister, Shealy, Caldwell, Boland, Brooks, Miller, B. Livingston, George Hiller, Bob Creekmore, Power, Pridmore, Singley.

Watts (8-9): Kirby, Riddle, Werner, Bobo, Dawson, Patterson, Woods, E. Jennings, Fowler, Brownlee, O. Jennings, Bird, Thompson, Waldrop, Darnell, Watkins, Hunt, Butler, Rogers, Williams, Gregory, Lyle.

Clinton (4-13): Burnett, E. Sanders, Alexander, Charles Trammell, H. King, O. Sanders, Davis, Davenport, Darnell, A. King, Crawford, Bible, Webb, Jackson, Shaw, Warren, G. Sanders, Huntington, Center, Foster, Johnson, Huntsinger, Moore.

Piedmont Textile League

Slater Bisons, champions (16-5): Tucker, Gilstrap, A. Ledford, Puckett, Price, Cashion, McCall, Drewery, P. Brown, Dudley, Wilson, McMakin, P. Ledford, Paul Rampey, Rogers, Perry Rampey, Taylor.

Brandon Braves of Greenville (16-3): Blackwell, Humphries, Campbell, Joe Anders, C. Foster, N. Anders, Surratt, Lyles, H. Foster, Limbaugh, Reid, Wynn, Nabors, Morgan, Stewart, McAvoy, Rollins, Frye.

Easley (12-7): McGaha, Jess Henson,

Jamison, Juber Hairston, Hendrix, Owens, Garrett, McCoy, H. Dunn, F. Waldrop, Smith, C. Dunn, Goins, Harris, Herman, Skinner, L. Waldrop, Carvin Medlock, Bill Stevens, Charlie Gaffney, Joe Anders, Paul Mason, James Campbell, Cotton Thomas, Guy Prater, Paul Rampey, Roy Whitaker.

Dunean (6-11): Durham, Bailey, J. Cox, Campbell, Hardin, Giradeau, Stone, Terry, Lankford, P. Cox, Riddle, H. Holbrook, Lister, Surratt, Lindsay, Riley, Toby, Quinton, Byers, Cantrell.

Monaghan of Greenville (6-12): Blackstone, Stewart, Thompson, Elder, Griffith, McAvoy, Owens, Waldrop, Dudley, McCall, Herring, T. Berg, Stevens, Hardin, Queens, Foster, Metz, Hendley, Crawford, Ellis, Myers, Hunt, Smith, Christopher.

Union Bleachery (4-9): Heaton, Bridwell, Patterson, Ivey, C. Brooks, Bell, Hawkins, C.L. Brooks, Neely, Hunt, Marchbanks, Appleby, Surratt, Hester, Turner, Rhodes, Belcher, Burns.

Southern Worsted (3-11): Christopher, Wood, McCauley, Alverson, Hardin, J. Vess, D. Vess, Grant, Brannon, Fowler, Ford, Simpson, Clark, Harvey, McClesky, Simpson, Sloan, Davis, Dill, Clary, B. Dill, McCall, Long.

Renfrew Bleachery (2-9): Brown, Clark, Wilson, Foster, Dell, Tollison, Granger, Belcher, Johnson, Knox, Fox, Thomason, Wood, Tillotson, Greer, Tribble.

Mid State League

Pacolet Trojans, champions. (24-12): Red Ellison, Lynwood McMakin, Tough Embler, Arthur Goforth, Parker, Tommy Jett, Billy Hogan, Bill Broome, Tee Fleming, Olin Hodge, Randall, Lynn Murrow,

Pace, Mathis, Mabry, Martin, Matthews, Country Kneece, Ramsey, McSwain.

Monarch (24-14): Jay Gregory, Lefty Wilson, Jimmy Callahan, Peewee Grant, Jete Long, Charlie Cabiness, Alvin Cabiness, Walt Trammell, Simp Sanders, Carl Berry, Newell Lawson, Sam Turner, Connor, Emery, Mitchell, Ralph Garner, Houston Hines, Wilbur Hodge.

Lando Blanketeers (22-10): McCorkle, Atkins, Muncher, Rivers, Owens, Overby, Hough, Heafner, Biggs, Dixon, Leonard, Robinson, Williams, King, Northrup, Crocker, Bolton, Miller.

Highland Park (16-11): Ruark, Lyles, Snipes, Fowler, Thomas, Smith, Roberts, Estridge, Rinehart, McGee, Watson, Wall, Knox, Harkey, Robinson, Hull, Small, Busby, Brissey, Partlow, Douglas, J. Callahan, Justus, Sanders.

Great Falls Republics (6-24): Ellisor, G. Justus, Mendenhall, Dawkins, Beckham, Roddy, Sealy, Barker, Locklair, Funderburk, Privett, Cooper, A. Justus, Jester, Sumner, Seay, Hodge, Tatum, Hopper, Gibson, Blackmon, Hawkins, Lynch, Vinson, Jones, Grange.

Winnsboro Royal Cords (2-20): Douglas, Banks, C. Rushing, Willard, Wilmont, Spires, Watson, Ward, Shealy, Eskew, Eargle, Gray, Harley, Berry, Corley, Alexander, Warner, Randall, A. Rushing, Grace, Byers, Wages, Jelks, Gunter, Walter, McDonald, Osborn, Waters, Sarge.

Greenville Textile League

Woodside Wolves, champions (11-9): W. Ramsey, Justus, Pruitt, R. Ramsey, Hunter, Tucker, Green, Manley, Bowen, Griffin, Herbert, Waldrop, Foster, Miller, Phillips,

Herbert, Eldridge, Beasley, Hall, Whitmire.

Mills Mill of Greenville (12-8): A. McAllister, McJunkin, Childs, Massey, Giles, Abbott, McCauley, R. McAllister, Grant, H. Smith, Henry, Gaines, White, Phillips, Cox, Terry, Leister, King, Darnell, Kellett.

Bahan (11-4): Thomas, Reid, E. Crymes, Taylor, Lavender, Alexander, T. Crymes, Bramlett, Bedenbaugh, Neal, Gillespie, Dill, Earl Wooten, Hall, Quinn, Harris, Cannon, Ellenburg, Brannon.

Gantt Kentucky Queens (8-8): Riley, Alexander, Lindsay, C. Holbrook, Perry, Blakely, H. Holbrook, Hutchinson, Ellenburg, Burns, Stewart, Hudgens, King, Holliday, Haney, Dickerson, Walls, Millwood, Kellett, Bright.

Simpsonville (6-9): W. Cox, B. Cox, J. Smith, Stuttz, Goodenough, Hensley, H. Barbery, Tucker, McElrath, C. Barbery, L. Henderson, Ballew, Barnes, Montgomery, Mabry, Carley, J. Henderson, Neely.

Poinsett Pounders (6-10): E. Fair, H. Fair, Bridwell, Millwood, Crymes, McClain, Hodge, Townsend, Turner, Hammett, Nabors, Brannon, W. Gilstrap, McCraw, C. Gilstrap, Gillespie, McCall, Gilliard, Phillips, King, Leister, Williams.

Central Carolina League

Mathews Wildcats, champions (25-16): Stancil, Powell, Abrams, Vaughn, Henderson, Kirby, Sanders, Evans, Sipes, Golden, McKinney, Heath, Wall, Beam, Morgan, Lyles, Gaffney, Hall, Lefty Kennedy.

Ware Shoals Riegels (26-19): Jordan, Hill, Williams, O'dell Barbery, Virgil Stallcup, Dodd, Lou Brissie,

Moore, Howard, Sanders, Cooper, Gaffney, Collins, Lollis, Patterson, Howell, Veal, Dickert, Corley.

Ninety Six Indians (24-19): Allen, Granny Hightower, Lyles, Fred Dowis, Grant, Buna Wells, Morris, Corley, Ross, Glenn Forrester, Chasteen, Jean Belue, Fox, Whitaker, Crisp, Bill Voiselle, Loftis.

Greenwood Warriors (4-32): Earl Morse, Doodie Franklin, Patterson, Rushing, Long, McAllister, Bean, Saxon, Mule Escoe, Hunt, Dickert, Fowler, Chasteen, Pete Laurens, Nub Smythe, Corley, Bickley, Davis, Trammell, Johnson, Muncher.

Spartanburg County League

Jackson of Wellford, champions (23-5): Murphy, Myers, R. Acton, Elders, Belcher, J. Acton, Wilson, E. Acton, Dobbins, E. Hawkins, Cox, Neal, Stockley, Smith, Poole, Pat Hawkins.

Brandon of Woodruff (12-10): Foster, R. Craig, G. Roper, West, Lawrence, Loftin, Stroud, Tillers, Waters, Sprouse, Cooper, Littlefield, Garrett, Owens, Murphy, Hendrix, Dewitt Bright, Keller, Turner, Kendrick.

Converse (12-11): Lewis, Croxdale, Dick Evans, Fowler, Millwood, Shehan, Reid, Mathis, Cooksey, Thomas, Fletcher, John Earnhardt, Byars, Greene, Wood, Massey, Hopper, Arthur, Vernon, Whitfield.

Clifton (11-9): Herman Bagwell, Joe Barber, Elmer Burch, Furman Mabry, Joe Coggins, Art Fowler, Lawrence Hughes, Potter, John Mosteller, John McCarley, Dupree McAbee, Tober Ransome, Barney Hawkins, King, Tindall, McDowell, Tip Massey, Willie Coggins (manager).

Lockhart (10-9): Everett Burgess,

F. Goode, R. Cabiness, Farr, C. Deal, Buddy Laval, Watts, A. Goode, Gibson, R. Farmer, Eaves, Taylor, Harris, Belue, Veal, F. Cabiness, C. Farmer, T. Deal, Stalnaker, S. Cabiness, B. Cabiness, Putnam.

Mills Mill of Woodruff (6-10): Walker, Garrett, Thomas, K. Phillips, J. Davis, P. Cox, C. Huckaby, J. Page, W. Page, M. Page, H. Green, Brown, Blanton, Mathis, W. Jones, T. Craig, F. Page, H. Phillips, H. Blackwell, Harold Taylor, C. Page, Fox, J. Craig.

Jonesville (6-13): R. Gregory, Nelson, Smith, Sullivan, Harris, Kirby, Farmer, Addis, Fowler, Holt, Cohen, Shelton, Phillips, Kenny, Johnson, Jones, McKinney, Middlebrooks, Gregory, Gary, Williams, B. Shelton, M. Hyatt, O'shields, J. Hyatt.

Palmetto League

Hayne, champions (16-4): Westbrooks, Mud Owens, Ridgeway, Hendrix, Miller, Brannon, H. Cheatwood, Mink, Bishop, Seay, Frazier, Taylor, M. Cheatwood, Hartsell, Golenhart, McCall, Calvert, Shehan, John Earnhardt, Corbin.

Fairmont (11-7): Johnson, Farmer, James, E. Belcher, Gilliam, Mabry, E. Belcher, Black, Bruce, Gibson, Gregory, Ballard, Wood, Chance, Hayes, Garner, Boling, Genobel, Jones, C. Belcher, Clark, McIntyre, Gilman, Burns.

Cannon's Campground (8-9)

Dunagin (8-9): R. Puckett, Dunagin, Stephens, C. Seay, Simmons, Bagwell, Pruitt, Smith, Joe Seay, Benedict, Narup, Johnson, Deal, Cunningham, Caton, Smart, Middleton, Collins, Murphy, Warren, Burnam, Small, Harris, Partlow, Dayton, Mahaffey.

Chesnee (6-8): Jones, Duncan,

Suttles, Weathers, L. White, Haynes, Davis, Nolan, Steadman, H. White, Clayton, Steames, White, Dillingham, J. Hampton, S. Hampton, Babb, P. Hampton, Brooks, Anderson.

Beaumont (2-14): McCraw, Burnett, Elledge, Turner, Shirley, Painter, West, H. Harris, Cannon, Prince, Willard, Austin, W. Lindsay, Rustin, Shipley, Pack, Maddox, A. Lindsay, Lane, Kennedy, Cooper, Durham, Hall, C. Harris, Clayton.

Spartanburg County Colored League

Arcadia, 1st half champions (1-1): Russell Evans.

Pacolet, 2nd half champions (6-2)

Fairforest (5-1)

Converse (5-3)

Inman (5-4)

Spartan (3-4)

Beaumont (0-8)

Independent Teams

Limestone Athletics (2-1): J. Ramsey, Sullivan, Fox.

Gaffney (1-0): Fox, M. Ramsey, G. Ramsey, Sullivan.

1942

Western Carolina League

Lyman, champions (35-13): Tollison, Bruce, Yeargin, Elder, Stowe, Martin, Cabiness, Smith, Snyder, Krivick, Hawkins, Steadings, Kneece, Murphy, Heath, Morgan, Whitten, Mendenhall, Harbin, Long, Muncher, Woodall, Wahonick, Sanders, Berry, Medlock, Stone.

Mills Mill of Woodruff (29-18): Sanders, Strickland, Putnam, Berry, Petty, Taylor, Kelly, English, Abercrombie, Frady, C. Page, G. Page, Beattie, Chaffin, E. Page, Brady, W. Page, Powell, Howell, Brissie, Craig.

Pelzer (27-15): Earl Wooten, Lonnie Holbrook, H. Jordan, Virgil Lavender, Kellett, Jeffcoat, O'donnell, Dickerson, Haney, Wood, Obannion, Gordon, Brannon, Schyler, Harris, Dewey Quinn, Lefty Crymes, Smith, Minyard, Byrd, R. Jordan.

Southern Bleachery (24-20): George Blackwell, Millwood, Anderson, O'dell Barbery, Lominack, Steele, Bagwell, Owens, McAvoy, Childers, Meisenheimer, R. Stewart, Bishop, Gay, Hughes, Griffith, Parker, H. Stewart.

Mills Mill of Greenville (22-20): Crout, Mitchell, Giles, Harris, Campbell, Limbaugh, Raines, Werner, King, Leister, Cannon, Phillips, Smith, Ratenski, Watson, McJunkin, White, Thackston, Trammell, Morales, Ranton, Byers.

Piedmont (18-23): John Emery, Mobley, Darnell, Hawkins, Patterson, McAdams, Cooper, Pack, Reeves, Evans, Punky Norris, L. Anderson, C. Anderson, Reid.

Easley (12-27): M. Harris, Juber Hairston, McCall, Hendrix, McGaha, Garrett, Wilson, Paul Rampey, Jamison, Jesse Henson, McCall, E. Harris, Owens, Limbaugh, Garrick, Robertson, Harrison, Paul Mason, Bill Stevens, Waldrop, James Campbell, Lefty Whitaker, Charlie Gaffney, Guy Prater, Cotton Thomas, Carvin Medlock, Joe Anders.

Dunean (5-37): F. Cox, Griffith, Bowers, Byars, M. Ledford, Bailey, Thompson, Durham, J. Cox, Metts, Riddle, Moon, Joe Dill, Gonzales, Brannon, Langford, Shuyler, Proctor, Shetley.

Greenville Textile League

Simpsonville, champions (10-6): Cox, Hill, Smith, O'dell Barbery, Goodenough, Burns, Bridges, Tucker, E. Barbery, Bell, Ballew, Sprouse, Paxton.

Sampson (9-7): McDaniel, Sizemore, Tate, McCullough, Duncan, Turner, W. Fowler, Belcher, Harbin, Daniely, Chapman, Bost, J. Fowler, Guest, Hester.

Woodside (7-5): Foster, Bowen, Hines, Justice, Miller, Tucker, Chapman, Boling, Tollison, Whitmire, McCall, Byers, Green, Hunter.

Poe (5-6): Phillips, Ferguson, Landreth, Alexander, Williams, W. Davis, Guest, Pittman, Morgan, Christopher, F. Davis, Templeton, Mosteller.

Poinsett (4-7): Alexander, Scott, P. Fair, H. Fair, Bridwell, Townsend, Earl Fair, Hammett, Lyle Landers, Collins, Elder, Robert Lavender, Jones, Hodge, Anderson.

Camperdown (3-7): McNeely, Huff, Davis, Lollis, Copeland, Dill, Ragsdale, Scott, Davis, Whitaker, Marchbanks, Huff, Goodwin, Loftis, Neal, Foster, Goodwin, Hilliard, Whitaker.

Mid Carolina League

Clinton, champions (6-0): Lyles, Center, Alexander, S. Sanders, Snelgrove, King, O. Sanders, Burnett, Davis, Crawford, Shaw, Shumate.

Joanna (4-4): Trotter, Lefty Farmer, Guy Prater, Rudolph Prater, Harrison, Mack Brown, Williams, Swift, Algie Abrams, Wheeze Farmer, Norman Case, Martin, Tinsley, Bragg, Perry Bolding, Bruce Galloway, Earl Morse, Rhett Abrams, Carl Stroud, Emory Moore, James Brown, Hack Prater.

Buffalo (1-4): Wright, Gilliam, Sanders, Kingsmore, Putnam.

Riverdale (0-2): Nabors, Casey, Winn.

Central Carolina League

Mathews (30-22): Wahonick, Rube
Morgan, Dan Kirby, Beam, Ken-
nedy, Snipes, Fred Powell, Gaff-
ney, McCorkle, Woodcock,
Vaughn, Dixon, Snow Kirby,
Heath, F. Taylor.

Greenwood (29-23): Cecil Muncher,
Clyde Muncher, Al Rushing, Carl
Dickert, Tom Overby, Jim Chal-
mers (manager), Shag Hunt, Mule
Escoe, Gene Mayes, Jack McAllis-
ter, Herbert Riley, Tom Clyde,
Doodie Franklin, Earl Morse, Carl
Adams, Pete Laurens.

Ninety Six (28-23): Jean Belue, Fred
Ross, Glenn Forrester, Calvin
Cooper, Donald Gold, Granny
Hightower, Spec Barbery, Buna
Wells, Bill Corley, J.B. Chastain,
Morris, Fred Dowis, Guy Grant,
Hal Dedmon, Poole, Diz Voiselle,
Gracie Allen.

Ware Shoals (15-34): McSwain,
Moore, Lollis, Collins, Brissie,
McDuffie, Chasteen, Padgett,
Bridges.

Catawba League

Chester Cardinals, champions (8-3):
Ed Durham, J. Fleming, J. Hart,
Gregory, Cooper, McWaters,
Erwin, Murrow, James.

Great Falls Republics (4-4): Vinson,
Drawdy, Wilson, Roddy, Knight,
Smith, Duckey.

Gayle Tigers (2-3): Beckham, Green,
Attaway, Taylor, Cooper, Gaby.

Lancaster Red Roses (1-4): Griffin,
Jackson, Bowers, Smith, Johnson,
Threatt.

Northwestern League

Central, champions (12-7): Crane,
Duncan, Elliott, Craig, Moore,
D. Elrod, Lyda, Berry, R. Elrod,
Mauldin.

Newry (14-7): Taylor, Sluder, War-
ren, Howard, H. Hawkins, Shirley,
D. Hawkins, O. Kelly, H. Taylor,
Smith, Russell, D. Taylor, Salters,
B. Hawkins, C. O'Kelly, Putnam.

Walhalla (8-9): Lee, Stegall, Burgess,
Hunnicutt, Mills, Garrett, Reeves,
Gilden, Stevens.

Cateechee (7-7): R. Stancil, Alexander, Holden, Reese, Campbell,
Gilstrap, Garrett, Chapman,
Alsap, Glasby, Langston, J. Stancil, Prince, Gasley, Pilgrim, Norris.

Clemson CCC (0-1)

Anderson County League

Appleton, champions (17-8): Spake,
Gaines, Long, Ivester, Gunter,
Cooley, Bailey, Morrison, Robert-
son, Sid Bailey, G. Bailey,
Mayfield, Weathers, Bannister,
McGuire.

Orr (20-6): Carrithers, Meeks, Perrin,
Powers, Cleveland, Pierce, Whitten, Vernon, Bridges, Ivester, Herring, Gunnells, White, Good,
Jason, Jensen, Yeargin.

Anderson (13-9): Garrett, Ezra
Embler, Farmer, Dawson, Clark,
Tough Embler, Hancock, Spencer,
White, Moore, Allen, Howard,
Owens, Jimmy Embler, Pierce,
Mahaffey.

Oconee (11-8): Simpson, Jackson,
Smith, Gilden, Cobb, Lindsey,
Harbin, Canup, Gettys, McGuffin,
Robinson, Taylor, Harvey, Haw-
kins, Cater, Carithers, Cannon.

Belton (11-9): Campbell, Minyard,
D. Fisher, McAllister, Deanhardt,
Carson, Nelson, Leo Fisher, Ash-
worth, Cason, Allred, Holbrooks,
Shirley, Carlton, Willingham.

LaFrance (7-11): Long, B. Harrison,
Gilstrap, C. Harrison, Martin,
B. Crenshaw, Massey, T. Cren-
shaw, Southerland, Ferguson,
Long, Boggs, C. Crenshaw, Wright,
Cargill.

Jackson of Iva (3-15): R. Pryor, Baskin, Alexander, H. Pryor, D. Latham, Dixon, Moore, F. Latham, Owens, Boyce, Hall, Jones, McCoy, Fernandez.

Equinox (1-17): Shirley, Harper, Allen, Harbin, G. Stephens, Ivester, Craft, Thrasher, B. Stephens, Simpson, Dalton, Vickery, Stevenson, White, Smith.

Spartanburg County League

Union, champions (25-9): Blackwell, Ben Jolly, Sullivan, Bill Mitchell, Cohen, Earl Phillips, Ballentine, Gregory, Ralph Fox, J.P. Gossett, Fowler, Bud Wright, Wilbur Hodge, Sumner, Bill Kirby, Berry, Gossett, Walt Trammell, Charlie Cabiness, Foster, Hiott, Country Lawson, Cal Callahan, Bill Curry, Fay Chalk (manager), Carlos Blackwell.

Limestone (22-10): M. Hughey, Camp, H. Hughey, Hensley, M. Ramsey, Medley, White, Guyton, Pridmore, Harry Sullivan, J. Ramsey, Clary, McCraw, Gentry, Kennedy, Patterson.

Hayne (19-12): Westbrook, Owens, Stephens, Shehan, Ridgeway, Foreman, Mink, Clayton, Earnhart, B. Cooksey, Deal, Hendricks, McCraw, Cheatwood, Clark, Calvert, Linder, Heatherly, Blackwell.

Pacolet (16-17): B. Brown, Parker, Murrow, Red Ellison, Tee Fleming, A. Goforth, Pace, P. Brown, Mathis, Gate, K. Goforth, Guthrie, Morgan, Arnold, Ballentine, Tommy Jett, Art Fowler, Harris, Hanes, Lee, McSwain, Broome, Harrison.

Jackson of Wellford (13-16): Stokely, Myers, R. Acton, Shehan, J. Acton, Belcher, Dobbins, P. Hawkins, Bright, Jackson, Haney, Stokely, McCarter, Cox, Wilson, E. Acton, Ballenger.

Drayton (12-15): Pete Laurens, Loftis, Hill, B. McCraw, Krivick, Linder, Manning Bagwell, J. McCraw, Moore, Wilson, Stivers, Tindall, Taylor, Porter, Shuf Finley, Clause, Ray, Johnson.

Converse (9-18): Reid, Croxdale, Mathis, Evans, Green, Gossett, Vernon, Art Fowler, Frady, Fletcher, Millwood, King, Pete Fowler, Thomas, McMillan, Burns.

Clifton (3-21): H. Bagwell, Johnson, J. Coggins, Mosteller, Hawkins, Wheeler, Vassey, V. Bagwell, T. Coggins, Tip Massey, D. Bagwell, F. Mabry, McCarley, P. Mabry, D. Coggins, Sprouse.

Palmetto League

Saxon, champions (9-1): Ed Evans, Dillingham, D. Howell, Beatty, Shropshire, Caldwell, D. Horton, L. Horton, E. Reid, Chapman, D. Gregg, White, Hazel, Thornton, M. Blanton, McIntyre, Byce.

Cannon's Campground (4-3)

Fairmont (2-3): Johnson, Wood, A. Boling, Gibson, Bruce, McIntyre, Painter, Green, Gilliam, M. Boling, Farmer, Belcher, McAbee.

American Legion (2-3)

Powell (2-5): Hudson, W. Willard, Tapp, Profitt, J. Lamb, B. Willard, Lambright, Noland, Bright, T. Willard, M. Willard, Stepp, E. Parris, O. Parris, S. Harrill, M. Paul, D. Wilson, C. Willard.

Beaumont (2-6): W. Lindsay, C. McCraw, Prince, Elledge, Blanton, Scruggs, Shirley, Harris, Starnes, Holt, A. Lindsay, Francis, Stoddard, Painter, Ward, J. Blanton, Stutts, Hamrick, Newton.

Spartanburg County Colored League

Pacolet, champions (5-1): R. Johnson, S. Shippey, W.J. Bailey, W. Humphries, D. Gist, W. Littlejohn, J. Rice, R. Smith, J. Johnson.

Fairforest (3-0)
Converse (2-1)
Draper (2-3)
Hayne (1-3)
Mills Mill of Woodruff (1-4)

Independent Teams

Depot Dudes (0-1)
Pelzer 2nd Team (0-1): Hall, Alexan-
der, Galloway, Bray, Davis, Quinn,
Holliday, Maness, Davenport.
Highland Park (0-1)
Williamston (no records)
Belton (no records)

1943

Spartanburg County League

Pacolet Trojans, champions (20-15):
Lee, B. Brown, Fleming, Red Elli-
son, Martin, Pace, Harold, Jett,
Goforth, Pearson, Hyatt, P. Brown,
Garner, High, Valentine, Smith,
Broome, Art Fowler, Murphy,
Berry, Cooksey.
Gaffney Indians (22-12): A. Phillips,
G. Phillips, Hughey, Mendel Ram-
sey, Hensley, Guyton, Clary, Camp,
J. Ramsey, Shehan, Gentry, Hank
Sullivan, Hutchins, Ponder, D.B.
Phillips, Ellis, Hampton, Hutchin-
son, Beale, Alt, Fox, Marzarri,
Schantzman, Mitchell, Scism.
Drayton Dragons (20-10): Wood,
J. Bagwell, M. Bagwell, Hill,
R. Acton, Loftis, Stevens, Finley,
Kneece, Linder, Wall, Petoskey,
Millwood, Moore, O'Shields,
J. Acton, McCraw, Owens, Earl
Wooten, Holbrook, Smith.
Mills Mill of Woodruff (18-12): Petty,
Strickland, Putman, Taylor, Bar-
rett, Timmons, E. Page, Raymond
Kelly, Glanton, Smith, Phillips,
Fletcher Chaffin, Wahonic, T. Cabi-
ness, Campbell, Abercrombie,
Dunn, Craig.
Union Aces (11-18): S. Sanders, Bill

Mitchell, Berry, Fox, Bill Broome,
Jolly, Cohen, D. Sanders, Gregory,
Valentine, Wicks, Hines, Abrams,
Farmer, Atkinson, Fowler, Law-
son, Cabiness, Wilson, Addison.
Clifton Rocks (3-26): Mathis, Art
Fowler, Greene, Gosnell, Bridges,
Chapman, B. Cooksey, Sprouse,
T. Coggins, P. Mabry, B. Coggins,
Adair, Collins, Martin, Massey,
Evans, F. Mabry, Vernon, Jolly,
Bullton, Pick, Pete Fowler, Birch,
Burns.

Greenville Textile League

Monaghan Eagles of Greenville,
champions (21-15): Stewart,
Waldrop, Thompson, Griffith,
McCall, McAvoy, Stevens,
Bagwell, George Blackwell,
Brannon, Ace McDaniel, Charlie
Childers, Elder.
Dunean Dynamos (24-10): Durham,
McJunkin, Willie Wilbanks, Kirby,
Turner, Williams, Cox, Riddle,
Anderson, Stowe, Templeton, Gil-
strap, P. Thomas, Fred Snoddy,
Barbery, Ellenburg, Bishop, Alex-
ander.
Simpsonville (22-15): Stuttz, O'dell
Barbery, Cooper, Emery, Bagwell,
Smith, Nelson, Sprouse,
Goodenough, Burns, Workman,
Cox, Coker, McAllister, S. Bar-
bery, Barnes.
Mills Mill of Greenville (16-18): Har-
ris, Trammell, Smith, Ratenski,
Lister, Haney, McAllister, Werner,
Mitchell, Wooten, Alexander, Mill-
wood, Giles, Sizemore, Darnell,
Dunn, Holbrook, Lavender,
Tyson, Kellett, Phillips.
Woodside Wolves (10-13): Bowen,
Justus, Foster, Pruitt, Tucker,
Byers, Landreth, Bealsey, McCon-
nell, Ellis, R. Herbert, T. Herbert,
Pitts, Wakefield, Hunter, Morgan,
Campbell, Ramsey, O. Herbert.
25th Service Group (2-23); withdrew.

Central Carolina League

Ware Shoals (6-1): Collins, Williams, Earl Wooten, Cooper, Pitts, Patterson, Virgil Lavender, Holbrook, Calvin Cooper, Sanders, Ashley, Earl Morse, Morgan.

Mathews (2-3): Morgan, Hall, Heath, Powell.

Greenwood (1-3): Morgan, Hunt, Farmer, Tipton, Kirby, Sparks, Boswell, Bannister, Earl Morse, Doodie Franklin, Dickert, McAllister, James, Burden.

Ninety Six (no records): Tobe Porter, Frank Edwards, Fred Ross, Bill Corley, Fred Dowis, Jean Belue, Claude Voiselle, Frank Robertson, Buna Wells, Gracie Allen, George Metros, Hank Price, Granny Hightower, Guy Grant, Jim Voiselle, Carl Alexander, Glenn Forrester, Ralph Spires.

Blue Ridge League

Easley (6-1): Robert Campbell, Lefty Harris, Fletcher, Lloyd McGaha, Jones, Paul Rampey, Garrett, Robinson, Vernon McIntyre, Juber Hairston, Ted Ratenski, Mann, Gilstrap, Dunn, Robertson, Thomas, Thrasher, Jesse Henson, Paul Mason, Bill Stevens, J.B. Owens, Carl Jamison.

Liberty (1-3): Dover, Smith, Thrasher, Garrison.

Cateechee (0-2): Stancill, Allsep.

Central (0-2): Summey, Elliott, Berry, Manley.

Anderson County League

Appleton, champions (6-2): Henry Spake, T. Gunter, Hoke Long, Lefty Robertson, Sid Bailey, D.A. Poole, R.B. Speares, Koon Morrison, Leroy Mahaffey, Louie Mayfield, Jim Bolt, Williams.

Orr (6-1): Lodi Carrithers, Reed White, Delbert Pierce, J.T. Perrin,

Mack Gunnells (manager), Thomason, Sammy Meeks, Hart, Billy Buchanan, James, Joe Ashworth, Everett Powell, Roy Barnes, Billy Hawkins, Buck Addison, Roy Bridges, Mutt Sanders, Fred Whitten, Crate Herring, Bannister.

Equinox (3-4): Allen, Stephens, Harbin, Davis, Thrasher, Yates, Vickery, White, J. Davis, Mangrum, Craft, S. Simpson.

Gluck (3-4): Dick Perry, Hanna, C. Jordan, T. Allen, Ivester, Bray, P. Whitlock, R. Allen, J. Whitlock, Tabors, M. Allen, H. Whitlock, A. Allen, Howard.

Gossett (2-5): Simpson, Sullivan, Williams, Ivester, Elrod, P. Ivester, Bannister, R. Williams, Gilreath, J. Patterson, P. Patterson, Barnes, Smith, Black, Chapman, Blair.

Anderson (1-6): Honea, Hancock, Wynn, Embler, Moore, C. Honea, Bridges, Rumsey, McCombs, Dillard, Pierce, Whitworth, Thompson, Dillard, Slaney, Moore, English, Pierce, Burris, Spake, Jones, Seymore.

Independent Teams

Pelzer (1-1): Earl Wooten, W. Quinn, Virgil Lavender, Holbrook, Mullin, Wooford, Taylor, Lefty Crymes, Byrd, Winston, Mullinax, Maness.

1944

Anderson County League

Appleton, champions (6-3): Leroy Mahaffey, Paul Gambrell, Berry McElrath, T. Gunter, Kay, Marshall Elrod, Lefty Robinson, Coon Morrison, Freck Morrison.

Equinox (4-5): Larry Harbin, Wingo Mangrum, Jimmy Davis, Clay Moore, Hubert Vickery, Furman White, Larry Yates, Roy Davis, Reece Allen.

Anderson (3-2): Owens, Honea, Hancock, Moore, Spake, Jones, Pierce, Bridges, Scott.

Gossett (1-4): Minyard, Simpson, Bannister, Simmons, Wofford, Ivester, Simms, Manley, Williams, Shirley.

Greenville Textile League

Dunean, champions (34-15): Willie Wilbanks (manager), Billy Wakefield, Paul Turner, Snow Kirby, Chuck Tuzzeo, Howard Moody, Billy Moody, Frank Ragsdale, Paul Turner, Willie Riddle, Arthur Alexander, Tony Passerelli, Charles Cobb, Valdee Lankford, J.H. Duffie, McGaha, Mosely, Hightower, Smith, Corley, Phillips, Paulos, Ross, Dill, Morris, W. Cox, F. Cox.

Monaghan of Greenville (33-18): George Blackwell (manager), Bud Stevens, Carlos Thompson, Charles Childers, O'dell Barbery, Jay Werner, Roy Steele, Elmo Moody, Buck Waldrop, Charles Hooper, Palmer McAvoy, Mac Stewart, Roy Wilson, Buddy McAvoy, Roy Scott, Yeargin, Smith, McCall, Campbell, Lou Brissie.

Mills Mill of Woodruff (25-17): Ode Revis (manager), Fletcher Chaffin, Jay Abercrombie, Jean Belue, Fred Ross, Everett Page, Roy Childs, Larry Campbell, Strickland, Bolt McAllister, Cuddy Cox, Ralph Bell, Sherrill Barnes, Curtis Power, Ansel McAllister, Petty, Foster, Kirby, Craig.

Pelzer (20-25): Lefty Crymes, Lonnie Holbrook, Al Rushing, Bob Watson, Earl Watson, Littlejohn, Virgil Lavender, Allen, Jordan, Taylor, Stewart, O'Bannion, Galloway,

Easley (12-24): Juber Hairston (manager), Paul Rampey, Charlie Garrett, Lyge Thrasher, Rudolph Jones, Earl Pitts, Orr Watson, Emery, James Henson, Alvin Simpson, J.B. Gilstrap, G.W. Turner, Ed Garrick, Sam Day, Harold Dunn, Medlock, Robinson, Eaves, Johnson.

San Souci (5-30): Wilson, Alexander, Fair, Gresphy, Fowler, Hester, Landers, Masullo, Sizemore, Henderson, J. Alexander.

Independent Teams

Beaumont (31-6): A. Kirby, H. Hatchett, R. Kirby, Pack, R. Walters, F. Ross, Rogers, Taylor, B. Hatchett, Goodlett, Franklin, McSwain, Green, Rush, Parks.

Watts (4-0): Meyers, Hudson, David Templeton, Satterfield, G. Lyles, Taylor, James.

Glenwood (4-0): Weaver, Epps, Pitts, Chapman, Turner, Mull, Gordon, Hendrix, Rhodes.

Clinton (2-1): Jackson, Bull, Satterfield, Rhames, Prater, Trammell, King, Griffith.

Jonesville (1-0): Gregory, Morgan, Smith, Holt, Fowler, McKinney, Blackwell, Owens, Addis.

Arial (1-0): Hughey, Gilstrap, Gillespie, Pressley.

Winnsboro (1-0): Spires, Mosely, Buice.

Williamston (1-0): Singleton, Saxon.

Simpsonville (1-0): F. Barbare, Brookshire, Williams.

Eureka (1-1): McWatters, Ed Durham, Langley, Diggs, Raines, Hart.

Buffalo (0-1): Ray, Wright, Owens, Gilliam, Lawson, G. Gilliam, F. Lancaster, Hamrick, Crist, Riddle.

Spartan (0-1): P. Hall, Dodd, Putman, Mahaffey, Riddle, Taylor, Senn, Stone, Williams.

Union (0-1): Smith, Wicks, Gilliam, Sumner, Bill Mitchell, Bobo, Gregory, Owens, Holt.

Enoree (0-1): Casey, Lamb.

Alice (0-1): Kay, Turner.
Belton (0-1): Greer, Taylor, Bannister.
Mollohon (0-1): Cook, Smith, Rollins, Black.
Lydia (0-4): Hall, R. Harris, Moore, Dunaway, Smith, Fuller, Satterfield, Thompson, Parrish.
Liberty (0-4): Preston, Garrett, Harrison, Garrison, Pressley.

1945

Spartanburg County League

Pacolet White Trojans, regular season champions (15-1): Wilson Lee, Garner, Seay, F. Wilson, Green, Tee Fleming, Tate, Millard Mabry, Valentine, Martin, Toney, Red Ellison, Lynwood McMakin, Horton.
Drayton Dragons (12-3): Pete Laurens, Loftis, Caton, Bullington, P. Arthur, L. Hill, Lambert, Hulan Fagan, Howard Harvey, Rogers, M. Blackwell, Jervis, Manning Bagwell, Country Kneece, Petosky, O'Shields, Hilton.
Union Devils (10-4): Goo Lybrand, Sumner, Bill Mitchell, C. Berry, Allison, Bobo, Gilliam, Hodge, Bucky Valentine, Cabiness, Palmer, Coward, Lynhardt, Lefty Wilson, Hyder.
Glendale Giants (6-12): Harris, Bagwell, Colarick, Jett, Hatchett, Warren, Justice, Ballard, Broome, Burns, Jackie Lahafer, Anders, Holt, Shehan, Deal, Sams, Crosley, Owens, Hillman, Tabor, Tetterhorn, Burgess, Tabor, Clayton.
Converse Cardinals (4-9): Chapman, Groce, Messer, Blake, Vernon, Reid, Wyatt, Taylor, Mathis, Stone, Tip Massey, F. Mabry, Christie, Johnson, Reid, Sprouse, Art Fowler.
Jonesville Blue Jays (4-11): R. Gregory, C. McKinney, T. Morgan, J. Holt, Marvin Hyatt, Blackwell,

Addis, Craig, T. Holt, F. Morgan, Rector, Moss, Blum, Tessenear.
Arkwright Athletics (2-11): Dodd, McKenna, Marrone, Marijan Fuja, Ballard, Wofford, Monroe, Meadows, George, Davis, Maturia, Solesbee, Cooper, Johnson, Travis.

Laurens County League

Clinton Red Devils, champions (11-3): Joe McGee, Griffin, Copeland, Fields, Davis, Mark Raines, Williams, Baker, Norris, Knight.
Hickory Tavern (8-7)
Lydia (2-1): Patterson, Knight, Fuller, Massey, Thompson, Shumate, Harris, Dean.
Watts (2-3): Nabors, Jennings, Templeton, Wood, Wyatt, Carlton, Jean Belue, Nelson.
Joanna (1-2): Charlie Girk, Frady, Rudy Prater, K. Abrams, Abrams.

Greenville Textile League

Monaghan Eagles of Greenville, champions (32-14): Garvin Suttles (manager), Ralph Morgan, Charlie Childers, George Blackwell, Carlos Thompson, Red Barbery, Jack Mintz, Joe Smith, Bud Stephens, Ragsdale, Palmer McAvoy, Roy Brooks, Bert Wyatt, Hoot Major, Buck Waldrop, Wakefield, Paul Rampey, Werner, Ambrose.
Dunean Dynamos (36-13): Willie Wilbanks (manager), Albert Kennedy, Paul Turner, Willie Riddle, Dan Kirby, Bill Corley, Boyd Campbell, Grady Hightower, Paul Thomas, Jimmy Dill, Arthur Alexander, Barnes, Carmen Harrison, J.B. McAllister, Ed Phillips, Barbery, Allen, Rose.
Poinsett Lions (16-27): Claude Gilstrap (manager), Harold Dunn, John Pitts, Cotton Ivey, Robert Alexander, James Alexander, Bill Limbaugh, Homer Riddley, Horace Fair, Paul Fair, Luke Landers,

Ray Hodge, Frank Millwood, Earl Pitts, Robert Lavender, James Crymes.

Pelzer Bears (9-27): Lefty Crymes (manager), David Galloway, Hullon Ford, C.M. Ledford, Hansel Brady, J.L. Goldsmith, Leonard Williams, J.C. Allen, Virgil Lavender, Ray Wooten, J.W. Heatherly, Tommy Looper, Harold Morgan, D.L. Clardy, Robert Davis, L.J. West, D. Williams, Nelson.

Cateechee (1-4); withdrew. Lyda, Allsep, Pilgrim, Stancil, Alexander, Marchbanks, Nicholson, Garrett, King, Shaver, Reese, Saluda, Harbin, Hairston.

San Souci Hustlers (0-5); withdrew. Lynn Goodenough (manager), Lefty Barbare, Bill Moody, Floyd Bramlett, Walter Pinson, Billy Fair, Pete Waldrop, Jim Barrett, Willie Cox, Mike Henderson, Albert Landers, James Stroud, Frank Southern, Roy Wilson, Harry McClure, D. Wilson, Lim Crawford, Temple.

Independent Teams

Gaffney Cherokees (1-0): Clay, N. Ramsey, Allison, Easley, McCraw, A. Phillips, E. Phillips, Kite, J. Phillips, Hamilton, Branch, Hunnicutt, Horton, Spence, J. Ramsey.

Arcadia (0-1): Howie, Guinn, Jackson, Miller, Faulkner, McIntyre, Boyce, Bartlett, Thompson, Hodge, Matthews, Dill, Willis.

1946

Spartanburg County League: Irvin Cribb (pres), Fred Nash (sec)

Jackson of Wellford, champions (33-6): Connie Myers, Pat Hawkins, J. Acton, Pat Elders, Paul Murphy,

Dee Bright, B. Ballenger, Earl Acton, Bud Blackwell, Wilson, Jack Belcher, Lowe, Medlock, Rob Stokely, Charles Jordan, Dobbins, Lefty Cox, Brice, Leslie Williams, Burrell Acton.

Southern Shops Railroaders (28-10): Buddy Westbrooks, Heatherly, Clark, Earnhardt, Ralph Clayton, Powell, Earl Harmon, Mud Owens, Earl McCraw, Henry Deal, Miller, Wofford Shehan, Loftin, Cook, Stephens, Foster, John McIntyre, Hendrix, C. McIntyre, Vance Powers, Clary, Willowbrook.

Jonesville (19-18): Nelson, Morgan, J. Holt, B. Holt, R. Gregory, Self, Smith, Moss, McKinney, C. Holt, Tobe Addis, E. Addis, H. Gregory, Spencer, Gilliam, Rochester, Shelton, Rector, Deal, G. Addis, Warren Addis, Ellis, R. Craig, Melton.

Converse (15-21): Croxdale, J. Gossett, Charles Reid, Y. Greene, Mathis, R. Arthur, Lee Greene, C. Fletcher, R. Gossett, Vernon, W. Greene, Reuben Reid, B. Gossett, King, Millwood, Pete Fowler, J. Fletcher, Stone, Collins, Hopper, Scott, White, Cooksey, Prathin.

Clifton (13-22): H. Bagwell, Barber, Collins, Worley, V. Bagwell, Chapman, Tip Massey, Murph, Clyde Hawkins, Thornton, T. Coggins, Joe Coggins, Mabry, John Mosteller, Edsel Sprouse, Eaves, Scotty Addison, B. Blackwell, Patterson, Cantrell, E. Hawkins, Padgett, Shropshire, Worthy, Groce.

Glendale (10-23): Mittag, Sams, Gosnell, McCraw, Toney, Luke Warren, Howell, Justice, C. Warren, Ralph Bagwell, Blanton, A. Blackwell, Corbin, Harris, Elledge, Tessenair, Berry, Addison, J. Greene, McTeer, Epps, Law, P. Blackwell, Hawkins, Long, Haynes, Thomas, R. Blackwell, Crosley, Elmore, Culbreth.

American Legion (3-8)

Arkwright (2-10): Dodd, Jett, Mason,
George Addison, Wofford,
McMahon, Ballard, Bishop, Ernest
Hawkins, Rinehart, Meadows,
Padgett, Wofford, Hyatt, McMillan, Watson, Addington, Bradley.

Mid State League: James D. Hairston
(sec)

Laurens (19-10): Brown, Skinny
Moore, Charles Gaffney, Mendenhall, Bragg, Pruitt, S. Kirby,
J. Werner, Simmons, Harold
Dunn, Campbell, E. Kirby, Bowie,
Hill, Dobson, Darnell, Wilson,
B. Pane, Myers, Ross, Word,
Z. Bagwell, Spencer, Gilliard,
Dunn, Harrison, Gaylord, Havird,
McJunkins, Mauldin, H. Werner,
George Blackwell, Dan Kirby,
Howard, Landrum, Prater.

Watts (18-11): Bob Hazel, George
Watts, Christopher, Waldrop,
J. Bobo, B. Waddell, Stewart,
H. Waddell, Herb Hutchinson,
Cavender, Rhoten Shetley, R. Bobo,
Gray, Inman, Lyles, Davis, McDuffie,
Pete Laurens, Gregory, McDaniel,
Ashworth, Chastain, Marsh, Nelson, Wilson.

Joanna (17-11): Snow Prater, Guy
Prater, R. Abrams, Farmer,
Brown, Rudy Prater (manager),
Bertram, A. Abrams, Frady,
McCall, Garrett, Galloway, Claude
Voiselle, Whitworth, Hightower,
Logan, F. Prater, E. Prater, Kirkland, Allred, Morrow, O'Shields,
Willingham, Lyles, Fowler, Ruden,
Whittle, Rollins.

Clinton (17-11): Lewis, Davis, Norris,
Cushman, Webb, M. Fallow,
P. Fowler, Woodward, Burnett,
M. Runyan, S. Runyan, Ralph Rowe,
Wilson, Huffstetler, McGee, Snelling, Joe Landrum, Shumate,
Griffin, T. Fallow, Lyle, Marker,
Golden, Moore.

Whitmire (17-11): P. Fowler,
D. Crosby, Miller, Collier, C. Wilbanks, McCall, J. Cabiness, Frier,
Arrowood, L. Fowler, Irby English,
Dixon, Harry Crosby, F. Crosby,
Alexander, Blalock, Dubose,
T. Fowler, Woodcock, Rain,
Rollins, Hardin, F. Wilbanks,
Wilson, Corley, Erskine,
B. Crosby.

Mollohon (12-16): Bus Golden,
M. Jackson, Dave Jackson, H. Mills,
Day, Huffstetler, Bailey, Coward,
L. Mills, J. Mills, Foy, C. Bartley,
Yochem, Kerr, Gay, Charlie
Golden, Boozer, Jarrett, J. Martin,
R. Martin, Kennedy, Whatley.

Lydia (10-18): Grant, Shumate, English, Allen, Mort Cooper, Corley,
Hunter, Wells, Harmon, Evvie
Miller, Kansas Goforth, L. Fuller,
Harris, Kirkland, Bob Fuller, Rogers, Satterfield, Massey, J. Lanford, Thompson, Elders, Sanders,
Parris, Foster, Waddell, T. Fuller,
Knight, Bailey, Fraser, Allison,
Patterson.

Hickory Tavern (4-24)

Western Carolina League: Charles H.
Garrison (pres), I.P. Fair (v. pres),
Dave Tillinghast (sec), Frank
Ballenger (treas)

Mills Mill of Woodruff, champions
(25-17): Bearden, Claude Smith,
Christopher, Waldrop, Runt
Frady, Everett Page, C. Page, Cox,
Jack McAllister, Eric Craig, Raymond Kelly, Ox Taylor, Putman,
F. Page, Joe Hazel, Strickland,
Bordie Waddell, W. Page, Jamison.

Piedmont (30-12): Pat Patterson,
Darnell, Cooper, Pack, Emery,
Starnes, Evans, McAdams, Reeves,
Norris, Rampey, Brock, Sneed, Stevens, Gentry, Mathis, M. Reid,
Fowler, Johnny Copple.

Pelzer (25-17): Turpin, Lavender,
Sanders, Morgan, H. Jordan,

J. Jordan, Hall, Cannon, Haney,
Edwards, Lefty Crymes, Holbrook,
Rampey, Bailey, Quinn, Reynolds,
Holt, Earl Wooten, Jamison,
Waldrop, Ross.

Easley (22-19): McGaha, Garrett,
Henson, Paul Rampey, Owens,
Juber Hairston, Stevens, McCoy,
Mason, W. Harris, Williams,
McLake, Epps, M. Harris, Dunn,
Waldrop, Hendrix, McCoy.

Mills Mill of Greenville (20-22):
Crout, Foster, King, Abbott,
Ratenski, Jett, Tony Smith, Ham-
mond, Giles, Kelly, Mitchell, Cro-
mer, Howard, West, Bell,
Trammell, Kellett, Goodenough,
Cox, Trout, M. Jenkins, Riddle,
Inmell, Wilkerson, M. Jackson,
Norris, Emery, Darnell, McJunkin,
Bishop.

Southern Bleachery (18-24): George
Blackwell, Robertson, E. Smith,
Bishop, Bennett, Parker, Jones,
Yeargin, Gettys, C. Smith, Stroud,
K. Owens, J. Smith, Pruitt, Shock-
ley, T. Owens, O'dell Barbery,
S. Smith, Jenkins, Anderson, Gaddis.

Lyman (15-27): Brown, Woodford
Beasley, Swann, Giles, Farmer, Pinson, E. Medlock, Horace Mullinax,
John Wahonic, Snag Calvert, Everett Hendrix, J. Pruitt, D. Medlock,
Owens, Yeargin, Don Smith, Mul-
lins, B. Pruitt, Tollison, Red Ellison, James Greer, Bill Allen,
Martin, Stroud, P. Fowler, W.
Fowler, Farrow, Mendenhall, Aughtry, Few, Claude Center, Porter.

Dunean (10-23): Durham, Turner,
Phillips, McCoy, Lankford, Metz,
J. Cox, Hester, McCullough, F. Cox,
Lindsay, Willard, Williams, King,
Wilbanks, Wyatt, Templeton,
Lister, Willie Riddle.

Eastern Carolina League: Irvin Cribb
(pres), Clay Williamson (sec)

Pacolet, champions (21-13): Mauldin

Pearson, Smoky Mathis, Tee Flem-
ing, Red Ellison, Olin Hodge, Bill
Allen, Kay Goforth, Harrison, Carl
McSwain, Garner, Guinea Har-
mon, Lee McSwain, Fulton Tate,
Ty Wood, Elders, Arthur Goforth,
Lynwood McMakin, Red Seay, Vi-
tamin Trent, Bill Hogan, Gregg
Scott, James Greene, Tommy Jett,
Jim Lee, Ping Toney.

Drayton (23-8): Pete Laurens,
McCraw, Caton, Loftis, Lonnie En-
glish, Stanley Lancaster, J. Bag-
well, Manning Bagwell, Leonard
Hill, McCall, Kneece, Charlie Seay,
Wilson, Guinea Harmon, Stevens,
Haynes, Petosky, T. Bagwell,
F. Lancaster, Casey, Laughlin,
Arthur.

Union (18-15): Goo Lybrand, Soup
Foster, Ralph Butler, Ralph Fox,
Don Revels, Luther, Bill Mitchell,
Charlie Hodge, Wilbur Hodge,
Bud Wright, Bill Kirby, Lucas,
Miller, Harris, Bannie Valentine,
Hyder, Ben Jolly, Bright, Houston
Hines, Bughen, Fay Chalk, Harrill,
Goode, Ed Harris, Carl Hicks, Wil-
liam Lawson, Farr, Veston Sprouse.

Lockhart (17-16): Stalnaker,
W. Burns, Fletcher Cabiness,
Jones, Moss, L. Burns, Robert
Cabiness, Tipson, Fred Belue, Bill
Broome, Watts, Walter O'dell,
Woodrow Harris, Carl Farr, Gib-
son, B. Cabiness, Vance, Heafner,
Taylor, Warren, H. Burns, Lewis
Crocker, Kitzak, Fowler, Murray,
Lawson, Barron.

Monarch (10-22): Murrow, Bobo,
Crocker, Jete Long, Jolly, Millwood,
Gregory, Sid Sanders, A. Cabiness,
Wilson, Middlebrooks, Woolen,
Voiselle, Watson, Charlie Cabi-
ness, Lenhart, Bobby Edwards,
Coward, Dodson, Bradford, Nor-
ris Dockins, Turner, Lucas,
B. Cabiness, Woods, Padgett,
W. Sanders.

Gaffney Cherokees (8-22): A.C. Phillips, M. Hughey, Mendel Ramsey, R. Hughey, L. Clary, Billy Camp, Hensley, Brown, Shell Pridmore, Hamrick, Gaffney, Earl Gentry, Johnson, Guyton, Harrison, Tom Cheatwood, Jett, Parris, Medlock, Greene, Kite, N. Ramsey, Hunnicutt, Porter, Marlow, Spencer, B. Clary, Stone, R. White, Medley, Christopher.

Anderson City League

Anderson (10-3): Morris Embler, Ezra Embler, Jimmy Embler, Wyatt Embler, Moore, Clark, Spencer, Hill, Dillard, Brooks, Pierce.

Appleton (8-4): Spake, Morrison, Cooley, Gaines, Gunter, Poole, Smith, Morrison, Bailey, Robertson, Berry McElrath, Stewart.

Gluck (6-6): Woods, Ivester, T. Allen, Hanna, Elrod, Fletcher, Whitlock, Hayes, Ashworth, Whitlock, McCombs, Boots Perry, Jordan, Dick Perry, Ripley, Hughes, Heaton, Ray Perry.

Equinox (6-7): Carlton, Stephens, Ivester, Harbin, Thrasher, E.C. White, Yates, Dalton, Craft, Voyles, Smith, F. White, Hilliard.

Gossett (4-8): Simpson, B. Ivester, Simmons, I. Williams, P. Ivester, Gunter, Dockins, T. Williams, Whitlock, Acker, English, L. Ivester, Chance, Hawkins, Smith, Callahan, Fleming.

Orr (3-9): Vernon, Sanders, Day, Perrin, Gunnells, Cleveland, Powers, Cleveland, Ashworth, Sammy Meeks, Fred Whitten, Addison, Mauldin, Barnes, R. White, Smith.

Anderson County League

Williamston (8-3): Cochran, Hampton, A. Gilstrap, Erwin, Ragsdale, McKee, Canup, Bearden, Saxon, D. Gilstrap, McClellan, Cogburn,

Garner, W. Quinn, Miller, Werner, Quinn, Scott.

LaFrance (7-4): Simpson, T. Crenshaw, Nunnally, Hawkins, C. Harrison, Chitwood, B. Harrison, Wright, C. Crenshaw, Williamson, B. Crenshaw.

Belton (7-6): L. Deanhardt, J. Jones, Willingham, Luke Deanhardt, Warnock, H. Deanhardt, B. Nelson, W. Nelson, Allen, Sullivan, Minyard, Fisher, Sherard.

Central (7-6): Mauldin, Sanders, Duncan, Moore, Oates, Elrod, Campbell, Herron, Craine, Berris, Gillespie, Luther Rentz, Poole, Cantrell.

Calhoun Falls (3-9): Chrisley, Manley, Staten, Godfrey, Lawson, Pearson, Erwin, Carithers, Sutherland.

Jackson of Iva (3-9): Jordan, D. Latham, Boyce, Tryon, Baskin, F. Latham, Fields, Green, Yeargin, T. Jordan, Miriam, Jackson, Jones, Carithers.

Martell League

Valley Falls (1-0): B. Pack, Henderson, Powell, Gowan, R. Ward, Hammett, T. Ward, Corn, Laross, Cox, E. Rollins, Whitlock.

Cherokee Falls (0-1): Bailey, Moss, B. Ramsey, J. Hampton, Patterson, B. Hampton, L. Ramsey, M. Hampton, Earle, Cobb.

Central Carolina League: Cy Gordon (pres), Dr. R.H. Park (sec)

Ninety Six Indians, champions (37-24): Buna Wells, Fred Ross, Guy Grant, Frank Edwards, Blackie Drummond, Gracie Allen, Glenn Forrester, Bill Corley, Bill Sherrard, Fred Dowis, Granny Hightower, Jean Belue (manager), Calvin Cooper, Robert Leonard, Bliss McCall, Claude Voiselle, Ralph Spires, Tobe Porter, Frank

Robertson, George Metros, Hank
Price, Jim Voiselle, Carl Alexan-
der, Frank Edwards.
Ware Shoals Riegels (33-28): Lou
Brissie, Abrams, O'dell Barbery,
Ashworth, O. Barbare, Cooper,
Lindstrom, Davis, Andy Haw-
thorne, McDuffie, Williams,
Gambrell, Howard, Pitts, Cooper,
McCoy, Chaffin, Helms, Welborn,
Hoots, Brasher, DeLough, Lynch,
S. Barbery, Howell.
Greenwood Warriors (27-29): Jack
Clifton, Waldrop, Bender, Russ
Lyon, Lefty Kennedy, Lawrence,
Bill Leach, Perry Moss, Barry
Rowe, Willard Sanders, Ackworth,
Cal Drummond, Earl Morse, Carl
Adams, Wayne McDuffie, Bud
Couch, Bolding, Blackwell, Hen-
derson, Stewart, Franklin.
Mathews (19-34): Abercrombie,
Corley, Mendenhall, Grant, Mor-
gan, Sipes, Lynch, Williams, Ash-
worth, Lyles, Vaughn, Gaffney,
Evans, Wells, Bowie.

Piedmont Textile League: E.S.
Tillinghast (pres)

Union Bleachery, champions (6-2):
Heaton, Turner, Bishop, Cecil
Brooks, Bell, Charles Brooks, Ay-
cock, Belcher, Neely, Roy Brooks,
Patterson, Evington, Neely, Miller,
Epps, Rhodes, Nelson.
Brandon of Greenville (6-3): McAbee,
Reid, Campbell, Morgan, Foster,
Humphries, Limbaugh, Wynn, Rol-
lins, Waters, Holcombe, Byrd,
Arnold, Wood, Landreth.
Renfrew Bleachery (1-9): Brown,
Knox, Ivey, Foster, Anderson,
Wood, Edwards, Cunningham,
Lockaby, Granger, Fox, Tollison,
Abbott.
Judson (4-1): Sparks, Porter, Fowler,
Owens, Campbell, Miller, McGill,
Barnett, Griffin, Duffie, Landreth,
Knight, Farrell.

Slater (6-1): Dudley, Puckett, Taylor,
Ellenburg, W. Cashion, F. Cash-
ion, Drury, Wilson, Toby, Hall,
McCall, P. Ledford, Moore,
McMakin, E. Ledford, Rampey,
A. Ledford, E. Cashion, Blyth
McCall.
Camperdown (2-5): Erwin, Dill,
McDowell, Brazeale, Bridwell,
J. Whitaker, Thompson, Coin,
White, Mintz, Burnett, Davis,
Marchbanks, D. Whitaker, Guest,
Burrell.

Greenville County League: Roy
Meeks (pres)

Piedmont (12-2): Brown, Trammell,
Bull Allen, Stone, Rogers,
H. Jones, Williams, J. Allen, Craw-
ford, B. Jones, Shackleford,
Cooper, Davis, S. Allen, Ed Pear-
son, M. Jones, Bolden.
Ridgeway (5-1)
Pelzer (5-2): Middleton, Brown,
R. Wooten, C. Davis, C. Wooten,
J. Davis, Knight, Hopkins,
Davenport, Clardy, Williams,
Taylor, Jordan, Looper, Hodge,
Tripp.
Mills Mill #1 of Greenville (5-7):
C. Smith, Sizemore, Patterson,
McAllister, Brock, Bishop, Low-
ery, Powell, Ball, B. Smith,
Dittmar, Christopher, Abbott,
Watson.
Fork Shoals (3-6): Pitts, Weathers,
Nelson, Williams, Kellett, Smith,
Meeks, Davenport, R. Wilson,
C. Storey, P. Storey, Cooley,
Moore, Gambrell, Weaver, Can-
non, Webb, Baker, Griffin, Smith,
J. Wilson.
Cheddar (1-4)
Pelham (1-7): Moore, Gordon,
C. Pittman, Carl Pittman, Satter-
field, F. Smith, Byers, Leonard,
Emery, Hembree, Cox, Thurston,
Lanster, Ashmore.
West Gantt (3-3)

Greenville Textile League

Monaghan Eagles of Greenville, champions (37-7): Thompson, Fair, McCall, Griffith, Stephens, Vaughn, Childers, Waldrop, Brannon, Stewart, Hardin, McAvoy, Snoddy, Moody, Godfrey, Powers.

Woodside Wolves (21-20): R. Ramsey, Tucker, M. Ramsey, Pruitt, Wilson, Miller, Beasley, Tollison, Brown, Gillespie, W. Hunter, Hines, Manley, Durham, Landreth, Fowler, Hammett, Farrow, Moody.

Poinsett Pounders (22-24): Jack Osteen, Bert Tate, Cooter Crump, Leroy Phillips, Bill Taylor, Buck Gilstrap, Robert Lavender, Earl Fair, Jack Long, Luke Landers, Jack Vaughn, Sparky Hardin, Charles Vaughn, Gilliam, Thomason, Hammett, Mathis, Millwood, Thompson, Christopher, McCullough, Gilliard, Guest, Hodge, Bramlett.

Simpsonville Little Yankees (17-23): Cox, Belue, Tucker, E. Barbare, Bagwell, Terry, Hensley, Lollis, Goodenough, P. Barbare, Stutts, Watson, Lindsay, C. Barbery, Brashler, S. Barbare, G. Henderson, J. Henderson, Nelson, Miles.

Liberty (16-23): Smith, Garrison, Murphy, H. Pace, Crowe, Scott, Pitts, Campbell, J. Gilstrap, G. Gilstrap, Thrasher, Stancell, Mahaffey, O. Pace, Owens, R. Garrison, Wilson, Powell, Dover.

Greenville Air Base (11-27)

Dutch Fork League

Newberry (13-6): Ralph Rowe, Guy Danielson, J.B. Livingston, Walter Hiller, Bowers, Crowe, Joe Bedenbaugh, Horace Warren, Bob Creekmore, J.C. Brooks, Carl Taylor, Gene Holsenback, C. Livingston, James Rister, Furman Warren, Bubba Hiller, Fred Cook, Roy Ballard, Frank Shealy (manager)

Batesburg (11-3): M. Boozer, Miller, F. Boozer, L. Johnson.

Chapin (7-9)

Peak (7-10)

Jolly Street (5-9)

Stoney Hill (4-10)

Central Catawba League

Chester Blue Devils (2-1): Avant, Rock, Darby, Cranford, Mace, J. Hart, Rook, Raines, Phillips.

Fort Mill (no records)

Kershaw (no records)

Lancaster Red Roses (1-2): Griffin, Hardin, Griffin, J. Moore, Whitworth, Thomas.

Independent Teams

Oconee Mountaineers (no records): Willie Hawkins, Jake Campbell, Buck Cater, A.V. Seymour, Clarence Hawkins, Bob Grogan, Rookie Harbin, O.E. Smith Jr., Cecil Chrisley, Bill Saloka, Leslie Wilson, G.L. Ivester, Vernon McCrary, Granny Hawkins, Footsie Gilden, Elliott Sprouse, Bill Robinson, Doc Mitchell.

1947

Mid State League

Watts Warriors, champions (35-20): Bo Gregory, Berry, Mitchell, Ray Bobo, Waldrop, Mills, J. Bobo, Wells, Rhoten Shetley, Dan Kirby (manager), Chastain, Dobson, Lefty Hutchinson, Fowler, Bob Stewart, Lawrence, Nelson, Pete Laurens, Blackwood, Carlos Thompson, McCurry, Shuford, Green, Ralph Harbin, Johnny Stutts, Runt Frady, Charlie Childers, Arkansas Thomas, June Werner, Bobby Hazle, Roy

Brooks, Paul Rampey, Harold Metz, Craig.

Riverdale (38-18): Brewington, Jamison, Smith, Robert Page, Simmons, Watts, Nabors, Williams, Sam Page, O'neil Casey, Hughes, Waddell, Kneece, Ed Stickland, Allen, Snyder, Hazle, Petosky, Broome, Stephens.

Laurens (31-19): Bowie, H. Werner, Todd, West, J. Werner, Brannon, Simmons, Harold Dunn, Smith, Campbell, George Blackwell, Bragg, Mason, Moore, Turk, B. Phillips, A.C. Phillips.

Joanna Sluggers (29-23): Rudolph Prater, Red Christopher, Cecil Farmer, Mack Brown, S. Prater, Vance Logan, Ira Whittle, George Frady, Algie Abrams, Bill Tinsley, Rolfe Clark (manager), Tommy Lasorda, Brown, Embler, Elliott, Greene, Snow Prater, Rhett Abrams, Wheeze Farmer, Harrison, Drummond, Delury, McCarthy, Ralph Prater.

Whitmire (27-20): Red Fowler, Crawford, Chuck Bowers, McCorkle, Frier, Smith, Blalock, Woodcock, H. Crosby, Hootch, Rube Wilson, T. Crosby, Monk Raines, English, Hoss Nesbitt, T. Fowler, D. Crosby, Boots.

Newberry (18-29): Bedenbaugh, J. Livingston, Taylor, Foy, C. Livingston, Pridmore, Cook, Ballew, Rister, Franklin, Brooks, Suitt, Caldwell, Bob Creekmore, Singley, Whitworth, Scarborough, Shealy, Woodcock.

Mollohon (15-33): Smith, Harry Mills, Huffstetler, Charles Bartley, Buddy Golden, Lee Boozer, Jay Martin, Stribble, Holsenback, Harmon, Porter Jackson, Corley, Leland Mills, Frazier, Lynch, Sanders, Maxwell, Durham, Bailey, J. Mills, Redden, Roy Stutts, Skeet Franklin, Jiggs

Woodcock, Cotton Lawson, Fat Livingston, Fred Darby, Tommy Buzhardt, Heyward Mills, H.C. Day, Rudolph Martin, Davis, Adams.

Clinton (8-40): Griffin, H. King, Harris, Sanders, J. Boyd, B. Fuller, Ballew, Davis, Shumate, Darnell, Mitchell, Wilson, Roberts, Boyce, B. Payne, Rich, Norris, F. Payne, Reames, Turner, Tinsley, Crawford, Burnett, McGee, Martin.

Western Carolina League

Lyman, champions (22-8): Darrell Medlock, Harry Thompson, Horace Brown, Rush Yeargin, June Pruitt, Everett Hendrix, Vernon Medlock, Claude Center, John Wahonic, Jack Anderson, B. Medlock, Horace Mullinax, Dudley Tollison, Carlos Thompson, Ralph Huntsinger.

Pelzer (20-8): Ross, Lefty Crymes, Lonnie Holbrook, Cyril Haney, Charles Hall, Virgil Lavender, John Rampey, J.W. Jordan, Hal Morgan, Ralph Cannon, Lefty Dean, H. Johnson, Lindley, Woodford Quinn, Virgil Crymes, Paul Edwards.

Southern Bleachery (19-13): George Blackwell, Wilson, Redden, Sealey, Bishop, E. Smith, Bennett, S. Kirby, J. Smith, Steele, C. Smith, Gibson, Owens, D. Kirby.

Brandon of Greenville (16-16): Reeves, Pete McAbee, Alfred McCoy, Ralph Harbin, James Hester, Lister, Ray Wynn, Arnold, Lowe Landreth, Joe Reid, Lefty Howard, Harry Foster, Ralph Morgan, Larry Campbell, Joe Anders, Luther Barnett, Edgar Harbin, Curt Beasley, Bill Moody, Jack Schuyler, Harold West, Charles Foster, Corbin Landreth, Fred Byrd, Fred McAbee (manager).

Piedmont (13-12): Emery, Evans,

Norris, Cooper, Darnell, Patterson, Pack, Starnes, Brock, Jones, Brown, Fowler.

Mills Mill of Greenville (12-13): Harry Smith, John King, A. Phillips, Carthel Crout, Abbott, Ted Ratenski, Bell, Brock, Dittmar, Hodge, Floyd, Trammell, L. Phillips, Kerr, Metz, Kellett, Kimball, Bishop, Gray, McAllister.

Mills Mill of Woodruff (10-15): Abbie Frady, McAllister, C. Frady, Ed Strickland, Hazel, Raymond Kelly, Turnley, Wampus Bearden, Petty, Phillips, Everett Page, Chaffin, Taylor, W. Page, E. Frady, R. Page, C. Page.

Easley (8-16): Harris, Paul Rampey, Taylor, Juber Hairston, Owens, Stevens, Turpin, Hensley, Gillespie, Simpson, McGaha, Dalton, Bolick, Garrett, B. Campbell, R. Campbell, Galloway, Turner, Henson, Dover, Middleton, McIntyre.

Dunean (7-12): Durham, Wyatt, Wilbanks (manager), Alexander, Harvey, Turner, Barnette, Miller, Willie Riddle, Bobby Stowe, Hendley, J. Cox, Harbin, F. Cox, Stroud, Manley, Langston.

Monaghan of Greenville (7-17): Elders, Nichols, Ellis, Hair, Fuller, Jack McCall, Marshall, McIntyre, Buck Waldrop, Brooks, Coker, Palmer McAvoy (manager), Stewart, Fair, Burdette, Stephens, Brannon, McIntosh, Bagwell, Pittman, Farrow, Craig, Joy, Kidder, Powers, Keller, Blackston.

Tri-County League

Excelsior (12-3): Treadway, Skates Gregory, Alvin Blackwood, Evans, Ben Jolly, Laws, Greer, Sumner, Fowler, Vaughn, R. Jolly, Howell, D. Jolly, Cudd, Virgil Morris, Tom Eaves, Kirby, Smith, Haney.

Fairmont (10-5): Gale Owens, Seay,

E. Belcher, Johnson, Wood, McAbee, C. Hudson, F. Hudson, Bradley, B. Belcher, Bridwell, Burnett, Black, Boling, F. Belcher, Bennett, Floyd, Gibson.

Saxon (10-8): Weese, Gilliam, Shropshire, M. Norton, J. Norton, Byce, Caldwell, Garrett, Sisk, Gregg, Roberts, R.E. Brown, Blanton, J. Martin, Bud Reid, N. Norton, Tapp, Smith.

Arkwright (8-5): Thomas, Arthur Meadows, Monroe, Scott Addison, Bogan, Ballard, Wofford, J. Taylor, Hawkins, Bishop, McMahan, McTeer, Cary, Blalock, Hoochie Deal, H. Taylor, Bullington.

Cherokee Falls (6-5): L. Ramsey, Jack Hampton, M. Bailey, B. Earls, Patterson, T. Hampton, Cobb, M. Hampton, Broome, Dillingham, Hardin, J. Hampton, B. Ramsey, Blackwell, P. Hampton.

Arcadia (6-9): Williams, Jackson, Craig, Lloyd, Turner, Howe, Mahaffey, Childers, Clayton, Lanford, Langston, Thompson, McIntyre, Calvert, Derrick, Durham, Blackwell, Gwynn.

Fairforest (6-11): Buddy Newman, Lancaster, Miller, Ridgeway, Babb, Wilder, Wofford, D.R. Leslie, Bright, Kirby, Sid Dobson, Spitzer, Tony, Smith, West, Poteat, Mosley, Traynham, Johnson, Wood, Seay, F. Belcher, Owens, Bradley, McAbee, B. Belcher, F. Hudson, Rogers, Mabry, Roy Brannon, Martin.

Enoree (1-3): Hanna, Williams, Sumner, Nelson, Burch, Jones, Waddell, Byars, Holmes, W. Hughes, Taylor, H. Hughes, Cherry, B. Lynch.

Drayton Veterans (1-11); withdrew. Hill, Ken Fleming, Williams, Seay, Petit, C. Harvey, Cannon, Marcengill, Arthur, Farmer, Barnwell, Morris, B. Harvey, Morgan, Manning,

Dean, Stevens, Corbin, Weaver, Holt, O. George.

Spartanburg County League

Clifton (13-6): H. Bagwell, Chapman, Tip Massey, Stowe, Mabry, C. Hawkins, V. Bagwell, Sprouse, Worley, T. Coggins, J. Coggins, Tindall, McClure, Clark, Bobby Cannon, Maney, Fortune, Farmer.
Inman Peaches (11-7): Dee Campbell, Otis Parris, George Parris, Waldrop, Jim Everhart, M.B. High, Davis, Rhodes, Rock Campbell, Helms, Otis Mabry, C. Parris, B. Parris, Gaffney, Camp, Brentlow Pack, Donahue, Calvert, J. Warner, Nobles.
Glendale (11-9): Charles Warren, Mahaffey, Haynes, Howard Harvey, Pruitt, White, Arthur Blackwell, F. Blackwell, J. Gosnell, Justice, Linder, L. Warren, Fowler, Mittag, Sams, Jett, Leonard Hill, R. English, C. Blackwell, Lonnie English.
Jonesville (9-8): Nelson, Fate Morgan, James Holt, B. Holt, Derrill Self, Spencer, Junior Shelton, Albert Smith, W. Addis, B. Blackwell, McKinney, McMillan, Moss, Erwin Fowler, Francis, Hilton, Self, Dean.
Jackson of Wellford (9-9): Kitchen, P. Hawkins, Myers, Bright, Belcher, Poole, Murray, Claude McIntyre, Cox, Earl Acton, Murphy, Jordan, J. Acton, Blackwell, Lowe, Burlak, Wright.
Converse (7-9): Croxdale, Charles Reid, Bill Scott, R. Fowler, R. Reid, Christie, Wright, B. Gosnell, Y. Green, Collins, Fletcher, W. Greene, J. Gossett, Crocker, B. Gossett, Lonnie Green, Wyatt, King, Lark, Hudson, Mathis, Blake.
Tucapau (7-13): E. Cook, F. Mason, F. Cook, Elders, Bob Lavender,

J. Mason, Red Pridmore, Strong, Thompson, Shehan, Austin, Bruce, O. Mason, Medlock, Farmer, Hendrix, Fleming, Phillips, J. Blackwell, Anderson.
Southern Shops (5-11): Harmon, Henderson, R. Ward, Shehan, Westbrooks, Cooksey, Franklin, McCraw, Pennington, Henry Deal, John Everhart, Malone, Woody Lynch, Dunn, T. Ward, Thomas, Mintz, Tommy Hammett, Owens, Clayton, Powell.

Eastern Carolina League

Pacolet White Trojans (16-6): Chester Stevens, Smoky Mathis, Red Ellison, Bill Allen, D. Hodge, Tee Fleming, Pearson, Brown, Carl McSwain, Seay, Tate, Lambert, Vitamin Trent, Lynwood McMakin, Sam Hogan, Kay Goforth, Olin Hodge.
Union (15-7): Goo Lybrand, Edward West, Hyatt, Ralph Fox, Bill Kirby, Scrappy Foster, Jett, Charlie Hodge, Wilbur Hodge, Pridmore, Valentine, Harris, Monroe, Brown, Keith, McBrady, Murrow, Kerr, Phillips.
Lockhart (11-10): Stalnaker, Gregory, R. Cabiness, Fletcher Cabiness, J. Gibson, H. Burns, G. Gibson, Freddie Good, Vance Gentry, Sanders, Farr, Moss, Taylor, Harris, Warren, Deal, M. Gentry, Bill Broome, Shearer, Heafner.
Monarch (8-11): Berry, Fred Duckett, O'dell, B. Sanders, Palmer, Smith, Gaden, Cordell, Woolens, Bobo, Knox, Dawkins, Taylor, Nichols, Lenhart, Jake Cantrell, Mitchell, Lefty Wilson, Henderson, S. Sanders, Crocker, Earle, Duncan.
Buffalo (6-15): Grover Gilliam, Jeff Abrams, Ralph Butler, Revis, Millwood, L. Kingsmore, Walker, Lancaster, Owens, F. Lawson, Putman, R. Lawson, Mack Frazier,

Hull, Hughey, Gene Gosey, Knox, H. Kingsmore, Hicks, Ferguson, English.

Drayton Dragons (6-16): Pete Laurens, Acton, Hill, J.D. Loftis, McCraw, Seay, Lambert, Fagan, Country Kneece, Murphy, Manning Bagwell, Virgil Caton, Loftis, English, Haven Clause, Arthur, Bullington, Hall, J. Bagwell, Clark, Carey, O'Shields, Murray.

Twilight League

Cowpens (4-0): Bishop, J. Quinn, Davis, T. Quinn, L. Petit, Ellison, Kirby, Robbins, Linder, Lattimore, Stone, Blake, C. Mathis, T. Mathis, Thornton, Addington, Parris, Lawson.

Beaumont (3-1): C. Pack, Ross, Carl Petty, Ken Harmon, E. Morgan, G. Pack, Turner, Parks, Henderson, Gaffney, Skates, W. Morgan, Moore, Morgan, Tucker, Willis, Green, Nabors, McGraw, W. Petty, G. Petty, Lyles.

Reidville (1-1)

Flatwood (1-1)

Lenoir (1-1)

Crescent (0-3): H. Carlton, E. Brady, G. Carlton, R. Brady, R. Cox, Lowe, Perry, M. Bennett, McAbee, Easter, Fortenberry, J. Bentley, S. Carlton, E. Cox, J.D. Waddell, L. Brady.

Valley Falls (0-4): Martin, Messer, Hill, Corn, Turner, Whitlock, Laws, U. Stepp, Mintz, J. Stepp, Moore, T. Ward, Cox, R. Ward, Mason, Rollins, Garrett, Marlowe, Hammett.

Spartanburg County Colored League

Pacolet (3-0): Johnny Rice, David Bailey, Robert Johnson, A. Curry, W. Humphries, W. Bailey, S. Shippey, R. Hardy, C. Norris, T. Johnson, Wannamaker, McBeth, J. Johnson.

Woodruff (1-0): Sims, Alexander,

Thompson, Woodruff, F. Watson, Watson, Bennett, Green, Bobo, Ford Green.

Gaffney (1-1): Pearson, Goodbolt, McHare, Tear, Smith, J.D. Hoey, J. Smith, Benny, Brown, P. Tear, C. Hoey, Camp, Allen, Guest.

Drayton (1-2): Earl, Miller, Alexander, Tucker, Wilborn, Black, Ray, Martin, McHare, G. Wilborn, McMahon.

Hayne Shops (0-3): C. Foster, Goodman, W. Foster, Jones, J. Burton, L. Burton, Coleman, McMahan, Grover, N. Foster, Jason, Bomar.

Palmetto League

Landrum (7-0): Forrester, Gosnell, Southers, Edwards, Wright, J.M. Wolfe, Morrow, Bridges, Martin, Childress, Fowler, Smith, Aiken, Fox, Kelly, Ray Foster.

Powell (7-1): Lambright, Gaffney, T. Willard, Junior Proffitt, Grimsley, C. Willard, W. Mabry, Smith, Cherry, Harrill, Splawn, Parks, E. Mabry, Calvert, Morrow.

Apalache (5-3): W. Blackwell, Belue, B. Pruitt, Bob Blackwell, Rector, C. Blackwell, R. Ashmore, Vick, Hester, E. Ashmore, Lunney, J. Pruitt, Cox, Leopard, Wilson.

Roebuck (3-1)

Holly Springs (2-0)

Cross Roads (2-2)

Watts (1-0): G. Lyles, Shealy, Hudson, Ward, Waddell, D. Lyles, Bailey, Cavender, Crain, Craig.

Chesnee (1-3): Benham, Patterson, Ezell, Hines, W. Stephens, Humphries, Steadman, P. Stephens, Rodford, B. Stephens, Finley.

Pacolet (1-5): Howell, Whitlock, Hogan, Arnold, Thompson, Nicholson, Harold, Hodge, Fowler, C. Martin, Wells, Fleming, Hodge, Teaster, Hill, Phillips, Ellison.

Dixie Shirt (1-6): Hodge, Tuck, Easler, Royster, Stephens, H. Bray, Millwood, Wood, Lindsay, Houston, Kelly, Edwards, Sexton, Lee, Cook, Suttle, Cox, Blanken, Leslie.

Simpsonville (0-1): J. Thackston, Paxton, Runyan, Tucker, Craft, Woods, Barbery, Thackston, Nelson, J. Landers, Smith, P. Landers, Dillard.

Campobello (0-1): Johnson, Gosnell, Culbreth, Jones, Patterson, Taylor, Castle, Clayton, Patterson.

Fingerville (0-4): Mahaffey, Bullman, Hawkins, Brown, Shehan, Culbreth, C. Atkins, Steadman, Calvert, H. Atkins, Matthews, Blackwell, M. Willard.

Palmetto Textile B League

Ridgeway, champions (18-13): Woods, Clardy, Davis, Hellams, Seawright, Ross, Traynham, C. Wooten, R. Wooten, Davis, McClure, E. Ridgeway, Coleman, Chastain, W. Ridgeway.

Hickory Tavern (18-13)

Fountain Inn (14-7): B. Farrow, Henson, Junior Smith, W. Farrow, Nelson, Plumley, Gault, Surratt, Burgess, Knight, Napier, Culbertson, Barbery, Nelson, Henderson.

Watts (8-5): G. Lyles, E. Shealy, Word, Hudgens, H. Waddell, D. Lyles, Babb, J. Darrell, Cavender, Craine, R. Hudson, Crowe, Hayes, Quinn, Taylor.

Ware Shoals (8-8): Skinner, Dixon, Hill, H. Davis, Cobb, Bunton, Godfrey, Hudson, Shaw, Hancock, Dickerson, D. Davis, Butler, Barbery, Bull, O. Lyles.

Fork Shoals (8-10): Pitts, Cooley, Wilson, S. Williams, Moore, King, McCullough, Storey, Davenport, Surratt, R. Williams, Cothran, Kellett, McClure, Durham, Smith, Brannon, Cox, Kimbrell, Meeks, Suttles.

Simpsonville (6-13): Cannady, J. Thackston, Paxton, Runyan, Tucker, Clark, Dillard, Wood, J. Smith, O'dell Barbery, Cox, Sprouse, Chandler, G. Thackston, Craft, Hammond, T. Smith, J. Landers, Lynn Goodenough, Griffith, Poteat, Tadlock, Moody.

Laurens (3-10): Marion, Spoon, Weathers, Maxwell, Stephens, Russell, Cox, Moore, Roberts, Rowland.

West State League

Pelham (13-0): Clift Cox, Hembree, Pittman.

Lebanon (3-7)

Augusta Road (2-5)

Conestee (2-6): Hendrix, Fowler, Brady, Hester.

Reedy River (1-2)

Pliney (0-1)

Central Catawba League

Lancaster (1-0): Angley, Freeman, Louder, Erwin.

Springsteen (1-0): Stroud, Holt, M. Dover.

Fort Mill (0-1): Mullinax, Griffith, Roberts.

Gayle (0-1): Benson, Melton, R. Byars.

Cherokee County League

Corinth (5-1)

State Line (5-2)

Limestone (4-3): Richmond, Cobb, Hunnicutt, Guyton, H. Hughey, E. Gentry, Hensley, M. Ramsey, Johnson, Gibbons, R. White, H. Ramsey, Phillips, Kite.

Broad River (4-3): Moss, Martin, Green, Shuford, C. Dillingham, Moore, S. Sanders, Chitwood, Adimy, H. Sanders, F. Smith, Teatwood, White.

Hamrick (3-4): Bright, Ruppe, Littleton, Curtis Garner, Broome, Allen, L. Clary, Bolin.

#1 School (3-4)
Alma (1-5): Queen, Mathis.
Draytonville SC (1-4): V. Parris,
A. Parris, K. Parris, Garrison,
Leager, Barnhill, H. Parris, G. Parris, Gordon, J. Parris.

Union County League

Black Rock (10-5)
Liberty Ridge (10-8)
Buffalo (9-6): Kingsmore, Lawson,
J. Raynes, Haney, Duncan, B. Ray,
Vess, Crisp, Wright, Ken Price,
Owens.
Sedalia (9-7)
Monarch (9-8): H. Nichols, Crocker,
Knox, Morris, Woolen, O'dell,
Mabry, Davis, Arthur, Ivey, Eubanks, Alexander, Moore,
T. Nichols, Wright, Wood, Forest.
Whitmire (7-9): B. Elrod, McCall,
Maness, Gorman, Erskine, Nantz,
F. Wilbanks, H. Elrod, P. Wilbanks, Cater, R. Erskine, Finney,
Crosby, Reid, Wilson, Blalock,
S. Wilbanks, Cabiness, McCarthy,
DuBose.
Dutchman (5-9)
Enoree (5-11): Clark, Byers, Waddell,
Summer, Taylor, Holmes, Emory,
Harmon, Martin, Waldrop,
Hughes, Cannon, Frier, Nelson.

Anderson County League

Belton, champions (11-7): T. Deanhardt, H. Deanhardt, Meeks,
L. Deanhardt, Sullivan, C. Nelson,
Jones, Allen, Shearer, Warnock,
Woods, W. Nelson, Fisher, Luther
Rentz, Strickland.
Chiquola (23-8): McDavid Carr, Day,
Campbell, Shag Knox, Bowie,
Deanhardt, Owens, McWhorter,
Bill Womack, Lollis, Bannister,
Ashley, Lee Whitten, Coleman,
Young, Whitman, Stone, Atkins,
McGaha, Ur.
Williamston (14-6): Quinn, R. Gilstrap, Hampton, McClellan,

Saxon, Shiflett, Hensley, R. Cox,
Henderson, Belue, Goodenough,
Redden, Davis, Rogers, Wilson,
Erwin.
Calhoun Falls (12-9): Oates,
R. Chrisley, C. Chrisley, Hoyt
Tilley, Duncan, Tuzzeo, C. Rudder,
Sutherland, Heafner, Pearson, Neil
Chrisley, Rudder, McCaslin,
Carithers, McCarson, Bo Clifton,
McCaskill, Dockins, Sullivan,
Swann.
Jackson of Iva (2-16): Lahair, Jordan, Baskin, Lathan, Jones, Fields,
Higgenbotham, Allen, Smith,
Fryer, Fleming, Stovall, McCombs,
Jackson, Burdette, Ginn, Whitlock.
LaFrance (1-18): Meeks, Moore,
B. Crenshaw, Massey, T. Crenshaw, Kytle, B. Harrison, C. Harrison, Williamson, C. Crenshaw.

Anderson City League

Anderson, champions (13-6): Hill,
Burris, J. Embler, Clark,
T. Embler, Cox Spencer, Burris,
Fouche, Allen, Embler,
Whitworth, Bridges, Ballard.
Gluck (9-10): Minyard, Dick Perry,
T. Allen, Pierce, Heaton, Howard,
Hughes, D. Allen, Whitlock, Ripley, Cooley, Hanna, Fletcher,
McCombs.
Equinox (8-7): Voyles, Yates, Ivester,
Larry Harbin, Craft, Mangrum,
Dalton, Davis, Moore, A. Craft,
Thrasher, Stewart.
Appleton (7-8): Speares, F. Morrison,
Poole, Gaines, Ivester, Gunter,
C. Morrison, P. Smith, Bailey,
Hawkins, E. Smith.
Gossett/Textron (6-9): Burgess,
Buchanan, Hawkins, Ivester,
R. Williams, J. Williams, Mills,
Simpson, Hilliard.
Orr (6-9): Wooten, Ivester, Vernon,
Perrin, Holcombe, Charping,
Barnes, Rhodes, Snipes, Powers,
Cleveland, Stamps.

Greenville Textile League

Woodside Wolves, champions (41-10): Beasley, Ramsey, Fred Foster, Wakefield, Tollison, Gillespie, James Tucker, Hines, Limbaugh, Weaver Hunter, Bert Wilson, Chapman, Farrow, Miller, Gaddy, Fred Cox, Melvin Gailliard, Hendrix, John Lindstrom.

Poinsett Pounders (36-20): Jack Vaughn, Charlie Vaughn, Leroy Phillips, Sparky Hardin, Horace Fair, Jack Osteen, Robert Lavender, Earl Fair, Crump, Bill Taylor, Buck Gilstrap (manager), Burt Tate, Simpson, Jack Long, Luke Landers, Campbell, Briggs, Bill Turner, P. Fair, Coker, Turner, Gailliard, Elmore Lavender, Art Hammett.

Liberty (23-18): J.B. Gilstrap, Mahaffey, Gaines, Owens, R. Gillespie, R. Gilstrap, Fleming, Crowe, Thrasher, Dooley, Dover, Brown, Hentz, B. Hawkins, Johnson.

Simpsonville Little Yankees (22-18): John Stutts, Willie Cox, Earl Bagwell, Earl Brashler, Champ Hensley, R. Terry, Milton Word, R. Cox, Gary Lee Henderson, Jack Goodenough, T. Cox, Hamby, Spec Barbery, Harry Burgess, Lewis Redden, Barnes, Joe Smith, C. Cox, Ballew, W.I. Jones (manager).

Pickens (10-31): McNeely, Brown, Bolding, J. Roper, Green, Johnston, Gilstrap, Roper, Pace, Cater, Bagwell, Slatton, Breazeale, Childs, Hiott.

Victor Pirates of Greer (8-35): Brannon, Pearson, T. Miller, K. Vaughn, Tidwell, Leonard, R. Vaughn, Davis, R. Farmer, Pinson, J. Miller, Ballenger, Childers, Brown, Morrow, McElrath, Pruitt, E. Vaughn, Hughes, Tipton, Myers.

Central Carolina League

Ware Shoals, champions (14-13): Pitts, Joe Williams, Jim Hendrix, Ray Goolsby, Petoskey, Calvin Cooper, Stewart, O'dell Barbery, Andy Hawthorne, Johnny Lindstrom, Collontino, Lefty Howard, Abrams, Louis Lyles.

Mathews (14-10): Ashworth, Helms, Charlie Gaffney, Emory, Rube Morgan, Linder, Abercrombie, Frank Mendenhall, Fred Powell.

Greenwood (13-11): Bill Leach, Perry Bolding, Lefty Kennedy, Mack Couch, Whitey Rowe, Willie Sanders, Russ Lyon, Johnny Ashworth, Cal Drummond, Earl Morse, Coot Adams, Jack Clifton, Jim McDuffie, Lynch, Haulbrook.

Ninety Six (11-19): Sam Corley, John Dowis, Milton Harter, Gracie Allen, Carl Alexander, Bill Corley, Blackie Drummond, Frank Edwards, Willie Sanders, Ralph Spires, Hoss McBride, Buna Wells, Granny Hightower, Jim Voiselle, Glenn Forrester, Fred Dowis, Shorty Harris, Hale Sherrard, Rudy Crump, Roy Phillips, Guy Grant.

Georgia-Carolina League

Oconee (19-5): Jackson, Simpson, G. Hawkins, Gilden, Buchanan, Smith, Harbin, Grogan, Robinson, Seaborne.

New Holland GA (16-8)

Clarksville GA (12-12)

Chicopee GA (11-13): McMillan, Moore.

Habersham GA (11-13)

Gainsville GA (9-15)

Jefferson GA (6-18)

Blue Ridge League

Alice (14-5): W. Stewart, T. Stewart, Bagwell, McGaha, Riggins, McNeely, McJunkin, Reese,

Stephenson, McCollum, Calvin
Kay, McCullough, D. Kay, Hall.
Central (10-2): Berry, Craig, Herron,
Lydie, Fowler, Kelly, O. Sanders,
Elrod, H. Sanders, Hawkins,
P. Sanders, Moore, Phillips.
Walhalla (7-6): Stegall, Gilden, R. Wil-
liams, C. Garrett, Sloan Reeves,
Hunnicutt, Harvey, Z. Garrett,
G. Garrett, Garrett, C. Williams,
Sosebee, Stephens, Jameson.
Glenwood (6-7): J. Chapman,
G. Chapman, Turner, Tatham,
I. Epps, Cope, Mull, Hendrix,
Alexander, Reeves, McCue, Stan-
cell, Hudson, Mull, C. Epps.
Newry (6-8): Howard, Dalton, H. Hawk-
ins, Sluder, O'Kelly, B. Peebles,
Smith, P. Putnam, Chambers,
Carver, Taylor, Greene, Hughes,
Hunnicutt, V. Pace, T. Putnam.
Liberty (5-6): Chapman, Buggs,
Smith, Medlock, Pressley, Bryant,
Crowe, Robertson, Owens,
O. Crowe, Mahaffey, Gaines.
Easley (2-7): Waldrop, Putman,
Hood, Brackett, Newsom, Owens,
Dunn, Waldrop, Galloway,
Hendrix, Spearman, Evett, McIn-
tyre, Hughes, Smith, Pruitt, Tay-
lor, Campbell.
Cateechee (1-11): Pilgrim, King,
Perry, M. Cheek, Tap, McGuire,
Wilhoit, Cheek, Stancell, Allsep,
Langston, Leatherwood, Reece Gil-
lespie.

Piedmont Textile League

Union Bleachery, champions (14-3):
Heaton, Bishop, Turner, Bell,
Patterson, Epps, Belcher, C. Brooks,
R. Brooks, Neely, Robertson,
Bell.
Slater (10-9): McMakin, Christopher,
A. Ledford, Wilson, Rampey,
Cashion, P. Ledford, McCall,
Lybrand, Cox, Dudley, Taylor,
Hall.
Arial (7-6): Pitts, Painter, Crum,

McNeely, Wilson, Stevens, Roach,
Cobb, Houston, James, Vaughn,
Rice, Bagwell.
Judson (4-7): Red Taylor, Batson,
Petty, Monk Lankford, R.C.
Campbell, Red Owens, Walt Hamil-
ton, Kid Duffie, John Holliday,
Bob Porter, Pettit, Fred McGill,
Jack McGill, Bill Massey, Lollis,
Dewey Foster, Dusty Rhodes.
Renfrew Bleachery (3-6): Brown,
Knox, Wood, Foster, Edwards,
Coleman, Ivey, L. Lockaby,
M. Poole, A. Poole, B. Granger,
A. Granger, Turner, Cunningham,
Greer, R. Lockaby.
Camperdown (0-8): McDowell,
D. Whitaker, Cooksey, J. Whita-
ker, Guest, Gunter, Davis, Coin,
Bridwell, Williams, Mintz, Erwin,
Burnette, Breazeale.

Greenville County League

Piedmont, champions (4-5): Patter-
son, Jones, Brown.
West Gantt (13-2)
Cheddar (7-4)
Pelzer (5-4): Alexander, Winston
Quinn, Wooten, Middleton,
Maness, Prince, Hopkins, B. Brown,
Robertson, Earl Brown, Knight,
C. Wooten.
Mills Mill of Greenville (4-4): Bishop,
Toby, Powell, McAllister, Bell,
Watson.
Brandon of Greenville (1-4): William-
son, Duncan, Barnett.
Welcome SC (0-3)
Dunean (0-4): LaBoone, Roddy.

1948

Spartanburg County League

Chesnee, champions (30-13): Bill
Jones, Hoyt McIntyre, J.Y.
Hamrick, Jim Wolfe, Jack
Bagwell, John Brock, Britt Hop-
per, Roy Lowe, Ozark Martin,

Lamb, Sayles Edwards, Humphries, Bonham.

Clifton (24-15): Ken Stowe, Paul
Groce, Tip Massey, Edsel Sprouse,
Mabry, Amos Worthy, W. Coggins, T. Groce, Joe Coggins, Taylor, T. Coggins, G. Sprouse, Tillman Chapman, M. Groce, Barber.

Arkwright (22-22): Ernest Hawkins,
Charlie Bullington, Leonard Hill,
Mack Hill, Scotty Addison, Sam
Foster, Jim Hilton, Ralph Bogan,
Doodie Thomas, John Casey, Fat
Meadows, Wofford, Fred Moss.

Jonesville (19-21): Al Smith, J.B. Nelson, Chuck McMillan, Charles
Holt, Addis, James Holt, Fate Morgan, Thomas Holt, Carl Robertson, Spencer, Shorty Blackwell,
Fate Smith, G. Nelson, B. Holt,
Shehan, Fowler.

Jackson of Wellford (17-18): Lefty
Cox, Pat Elders, Pat Hawkins,
B. Jett, T. Jett, Myers, Harrill,
Barbery, Cox, J. Acton, C. Dob-
bins, K. Dobbins, Harold, Ike Mur-
ray, Dewitt Bright.

Converse (17-18): Fletcher, Bill Scott,
Wyatt, James Blake, C. Mathis,
W. Green, Croxdale, Charles Reid,
Adair, L. Green, F. Mathis.

Drayton (13-21): John Martin, Country Kneece, Jimmy Tollison, Wilbur Stephens, Manning Bagwell.

Glendale (11-21): Mickey Cook,
White, Tommy Jett, Clyde Haw-
kins, Chapman, Chink Warren,
J. Acton, Myers, P. Hawkins, Jim
Lavender, Shehan.

Spartanburg Textile Industrial League

Linda, champions (18-13): Carl
Brown, Robbins, Robert Latti-
more, Arthur, Robert Bishop, Hill,
J. Quinn, Crump, Staten, Mathis,
Addington, Shropshire, J. Petit.

Southern Shops (16-6): Pennington,
Westbrooks, Fromplin, Tommy
Vineyard, Roland, R. Canipe,

Woody Lynch, B. Reid, Clayton,
Lewis, Franklin, Laflin, Malone, E.
Canipe.

Powell (13-8): Junior Proffitt, Country Hendrix, Frank Mason, Red
Pridmore, Walter Mabry, Bill Morrow, Early, Lambright, Godfrey,
Brown, Splawn, Ballard.

Pacolet (13-15): Cotton Whitlock,
Skinny Thompson, Harmon, Hill,
Tate, Rob Phillips, Seay, Howell,
A. Martin, Hodge, Lowery, Lem-
mons, Harold, Teaster, C. Mar-
tin.

Brandon of Woodruff (11-9):
Bearden, Cheek, Howard, O'neil
Wood, C. Taylor, Paul Cox, Ike
West, Jamison, Charles Woody,
Gibbs, Caldwell.

Apalache (10-10): Doc Gibson,
Ruddy Ashmore, D. Lunney, Cox,
Cotton Whitlock, Watson.

Chesnee (5-14): Vaughn, Hayes, Henderson, Martin, Buchanan.

Fingerville (5-16): Shook, Brown,
Mahaffey, Cooksey, Hammett,
Price, Culbreth, Poteat.

Tri-County League

Fairmont, champions (20-21):
O'Shields, Carey, Doc Johnson,
Belcher, Hardwood, Ed Dixon,
James Owens, Albert Wood, Mel-
vin Wham, Stone, Bowen, Burnett,
Blackwell, Boling, Don Leslie,
Cook.

Fairforest (28-10): C.B. Grimsley,
Martin Graham, Paul Craig, Ray-
mond Turner, Bill Blanton, Charlie
Rogers, Judson Seay, Bobby
Miller, Don Leslie, Roy Thomp-
son, Hansil Brady, Abner
Burchfield, J. Thompson.

Saxon (26-13): Bud Reid, Arthur Tay-
lor, George Petty, Skinny McGraw,
Denver Gregg, McClellan, Troy
Norton, Roberts, Grimsley, Queen,
Bud Norton, Erskine, Tapp, Cald-
well.

Arcadia (25-15): Buford Williams, Charles Clayton, Fred Dent, Ward, G.B. Lloyd, Henry Calvert, Ralph Mahaffey, Spook Lanford, Paul Henderson, Ballard, J. McIntyre, Cooper, Claude McIntyre, Jack Brock, Sonny Blackwood.

VFW (11-21)

Valley Falls (no records)

Palmetto League

Landrum, champions (18-8): Foster, Kelly, Gib Gosnell, G. Gosnell, Wright, H. Gosnell, Johnson, Woodrow Bridges, Shehan, B. Gosnell, Dempsey, McIntyre, Southern.

Saluda NC (17-7)

Boiling Springs (10-12): Garland Bagwell, John Fagan, Calvert, Lester Haynes, Hawkins, Brown, Lyda, B. Stepp, Blackwell, Pack, R. Stepp.

Holly Springs NC (8-11)

Tryon NC (7-12)

Cross Roads (5-15)

Palmetto League

Lydia, champions (26-9): Hampton, Fallow, Dees, Roberts, Harris, Crawford, L. Fuller, G. Satterfield, Rowland, B. Fuller, Copeland, King, Lyles, P. Satterfield, Harrison, Hairston, Boland, Townsend, Martin.

Ridgeway (1-1)

Hickory Tavern (no records)

Fountain Inn (0-2): Runyon, Cannady, Henderson, Barbery, Smith, Thackston, Plumbley, Culbertson, Farrow, Alexander, Word, Mimms.

Ware Shoals (1-1): Dickerson, Hill, Skinner, Sanders, Elrod, Ballentine, Malone, Davis, Corn, Butler, Taylor.

Mid-County League

Jonesville, champions (24-11): Theron Morgan, Ceid Addis, Holt, Horne, Carl Robertson, Grady Addis, McKinney, Bill Craig, B. Hodge, Moss, D. Hodge, J. Addis, Harvey, Babe Morgan.

Inman (25-12): Wimpy Raines, Buzzie Shelton, Jack Donahoo, Ralph Cogsdill, Groce, Shockley, Joe Everhart, Rollins, Stephenson, Wilson, Pack, Rhodes, Peace.

Riverdale (18-14): Buck Nabors, Junior Gwinn, Jimmy Hicks, Bud Cherry, Ray Sumner, Billy Byars, Carey Burch, Mitchell Langford, Junior Lawson, Eugene Dunaway, Frank Waddell, Hicks, Bobby Sargent, Bonnie Rhodes, Billy Tucker.

Glendale (13-11): Buddy Blackwell, Jett, Bishop, F. Blackwell, Jerome Millwood, Luke Warren, R. Ogle, Reeves, Carter, Wheeler, Mabry, Fisher, T. Ogle.

Clifton (10-16): Elmer Johnson, Chance, G. Johnson.

Eastern Carolina League

Inman, champions (36-6): Earl McCraw, Belton Parris, Otis Mabry, Alverson, Ike Helms, Allen Clark, Joel Robertson, Reg Campbell, Perrin Waldrop, George Parris, Jake Cantrell, Otis Parris, Rip Collins, Jim Everhart, Earl Prince (manager), E. Parris.

Pacolet Trojans (29-12): Red Ellison, Lynwood McMakin, Carl McSwain, Vitamin Trent, Pee Wee Lambert, Olin Hodge, Frank McMakin, Kansas Goforth, Smoky Mathis, Tee Fleming, Hall, Bill Allen, Chester Stephens, Motts, Hogan, Kerr, Prater.

Excelsior (28-15): Edwards, Cannon, Slug Campbell, Billings, Brown, Wes Howard, Ben Jolly, Carl Berry, Bill Kirby, Bob Phillips, Smith, Brogan, Cabiness, Howell, Belue, Treadway.

Union (19-29): Green, Curveball Blackwood, English, Bennie Valentine,

Fig Newton, Train Harris, Black-
well, Doc Lemon, Scup Foster, Bill
Broome, Ralph Fox, West,
Lybrand, Hodge, Warren.

Monarch (13-21): Little, Grant,
Buddy Berry, Burt Sumner,
Turner, Rogers, Sanders, Voiselle,
Lewis Woolens, Ken Davis.

Buffalo (11-24): Ed West, Bill
Broome, Blackwell, English, Doug
Kingsmore, O'Shields, Seay, Gar-
ner.

Lockhart (7-27): Bill Broome, Goode,
Vance, Fowler, Moss, Red Lynch,
Deal, Gentry.

Gaffney (6-29): Cates, Hansley,
Pridmore, Vassey.

Dixie League

Pelzer, champions (no records)
Southern Bleachery (no records)

Western Carolina League

Lyman Pacifics, champions (40-25):
Everett Hendrix, John Wahonick,
Carvin Medlock, Horace Mullinax,
Jim Aughtry, Vernon Medlock,
Dudley, Perry, Tollison, Rush
Yeargin, Jack Anderson, Horace
Brown, Dick Terry, Leroy Phillips,
Darrell Medlock, Woodford
Beasley, Eurell Eubanks, Earl
Hayes, Claude Center, Pruitt.

Brandon Braves of Greenville (36-21):
Curt Beasley, Larry Campbell, Joe
Anders, Ralph Harbin, Thompson,
Reid, James Hester, Forrester,
Scott, Fuzz Foster, Ruddy Jones,
James Coker, Fred Byrd, Ray
Wynn, Luther Barnett, Harold
West, Carvin Landreth, Ed
Harbin, Taylor.

Woodside Wolves (36-22): Pitts,
Lindstrom, Brannon, Ramsey,
Gilliard, Wakefield, Tollison, Wil-
son, Grenoski, Hendricks, Tucker,
Vaughn, Farrel, Farrow, Arro-
wood, Foster, Howard, Limbaugh,
Fraser.

Southern Bleachery Red Flames
(30-24): George Blackwell, Kirby,
Wilson, E. Smith, W. Bishop, Steele,
Phillips, C. Smith, Owens, Gibson,
K. Smith, Bennett, O'dell Barbery,
Robertson, Gaddis, McAbee.

Monaghan Eagles of Greenville
(30-24): McCullough, B. Bishop,
Brooks, McAvoy, Stephens, Bur-
nett, Fair, Waldrop, B. Phillips,
Hunt, Thompson, A. Phillips,
B. Phillips, Pittman, McKinney,
Bagwell.

Piedmont Rangers (30-26): John
Emory, Medlock, Evans, Norris,
Copple, Pat Patterson, Darnell,
Starnes, Cooper, Pack, Evans,
Nesbitt, Alexander, Rampey,
Howard, Jones, McAdams, Girk.

Pelzer Bears (24-30): Looper,
W. Quinn, J. Jordan, Holbrook,
Cannon, Lavender, Haney, Tur-
pin, Crymes, A. Quinn, Morgan,
H. Jordan, Edwards, Hall, Sulli-
van, A. Jordan, Middleton, Davis,
Dean, Suddeth.

Dunean Dynamos (20-31): Bob
Stowe, Hendley, Riddle, J. Cox,
A. Floyd, Moody, Daniel, Chas-
tain, Turner, F. Cox, Forrester,
Ragsdale, Fowler, Kerr, Wilbanks,
Joyce, Manley, D. Cox, Gladstone.

Mills Mill Millers of Greenville
(16-37): Craft, King, Trammell,
J. Floyd, Ratenski, Bell, Duncan,
Kellett, Brown, Metz, Dittmer,
C. Bishop, Watson, Neely, Wil-
liams, Clark, Moody, Gaddy.

Easley Panthers (14-35): McGaha,
Jameson, Petit, Paul Rampey,
Juber Hairston, Henson, Owens,
Bagwell, McDaniel, Christopher,
Stephens, Dalton, McIntyre, Pitts,
Harris, Campbell, Mason.

Mid State League

Mills Mill of Woodruff, champions
(34-24): Runt Frady, B.T. McCraw,
John Helms, A.L. Curtis Jr.,

Everett Page, Charles Page, Ed
Strickland, Dixie Howell, Babe
Benning, Woodrow Abernathy,
Slug Pecu, Guy Prater, Benning,
Jimmy Embler, Russ Lyon, James
Gaddy, Whitaker, Arkansas
Thomas, Harry Barrett, McAllis-
ter, Hill, Putman, Brock, W. Page,
Chaffin, Abercrombie, Bearden,
Giles.

Laurens Lions (34-24): D. King,
J. Werner, Bowie, Shelton, H. Wer-
ner, Morrow, Harbin, Moore,
Sykes, Dunn, Bell, J. Simmons,
Rams, Starnes, Stokes, Phillips,
Kirby, Blackwell, Barbery, Calla-
han, Raines, Mauldin, Patton,
O'Shields.

Brandon Bombers of Woodruff
(24-27): John Freeland, Arkansas
Thomas, Howard, Claudell Smith,
Cox, Fred Foster, Cheek, George
Blackwell, Johnny Stutts, Grims-
ley, Wooten, Acton, Thompson,
Rex Benson, Clark, Laurens, Sam
Page, Hazle, Lawrence, Gentry,
West, Frady, Freeland, Craig.

Clinton (23-29): Harris, Mason, John
Hairston, Paul Rampey, Babe
Huffstetler, Harvey, McGee,
Leffler, Tolbert, Mish, Paul Fouts,
Burnett, Mills, Snyder, Abercrom-
bie, Raines, Guy Prater, Rams,
Boyce, Collins, Sanders, Millwood,
Runyan, Gregory, Livingston.

Joanna Hornets (22-25): Slug Socey,
Guy Prater, Whitworth, Farmer,
Slug Kennedy, Geats, Guintana,
Snow Prater, Mitrus, Tinsley,
Willingham, Moore, Runyon,
Griffith, Bolding, Patton, Prater,
Earl Morse, Holsenback, Harris,
B. Willingham, G. Franklin.

Riverdale (20-29): Pete Burch, Rex
Benson, Sam Page, Nelson, Ste-
vens, Abercrombie, Lavender,
Cecil Brewington, Herman Snyder,
Waddell, O'neil Casey, Haynes,
Wiles, Williams, Sam Page, Jame-

son, Nabors, Simmons, Brewington, Wells.

Cherokee County League

Broad River, champions (30-9):
Arnold Sanders, Bob Wells, Billy
Lattimore, Cotton Moss, Harry
Lee, Fuzzy Martin, Don Sheppard,
Buck Shufford, Joe Sanders, Hugh
Sanders, Bill Moore, Pinkney
Cook, Eddie Edeimy, Willard
Dillingham, Clyde Dillingham,
Marvin McAbee (manager), Bud
Gold.

Cherokee Falls (30-13): Jack Hamp-
ton, John Hampton, S. Hampton,
B. Earle, L. Hampton, H. Earle,
Broome, Wilson, Patterson, Cobb.

Alma (27-11): Oscar Sullivan, Ellis,
Bright, Bob Parker, Gene White,
Lefty Bolin, Drayton Queen, Brent
Parris, Bolton.

Draytonville (21-10)

Ashworth (18-20)

Asbury (17-19)

State Line (17-19)

#1 School (17-19)

Musgrove (12-24)

Union Cotton League

Union (16-3): Wright, Paul Caldwell,
Harold Nelson, Revels, Haney,
Buck Gossett, Henderson, Charles
Gaden, Caldwell.

Cross Anchor (11-6)

Young's Store (8-10)

Hobbesville (7-8)

Sedalia (7-8)

Black Rock (5-14)

Dutchman (no records)

Lockhart (no records)

Monarch (no records)

Central Carolina League

Watts Warriors, champions (46-18):
Ed Guinther, Paul Hazle, Lloyd
Moore, Hal Walters, Roy Bobo,
Bob Hazle, Acton, Ike Chastain,
Blackwell, Harry Potts, Jake

Lyerly, Woodrow Davis, Roy
Peeler, Allen Droughton, Peters,
O'shields, Claudell Smith, Rhoten
Shetley, Logan, Dewey Quinn,
Herrington.

Ware Shoals Riegels (40-24): Pitts,
Williams, McDuffie, Ray Goolsby,
Cooper, Sherard, Batts, O'dell Bar-
bery, Andy Hawthorne, George
Abrams, A.C. Phillips, S. Barbery,
Johnny Ashworth, Bowman, Bar-
bery, Tanner, Girk, Burns, Roy
Bridges.

Ninety Six Indians (34-23): Gracie
Allen, Dewey Quinn, McBride, For-
rester, Carl Alexander, Willie San-
ders, Guy Prater, Bill Corley, Claude
Voiselle, Buna Wells, Frank Edwards,
Jim Voiselle, Jean Belue, Hank
Price, V. Voiselle, Blackie Drum-
mond, Coot Henderson, Fred Dowis.

Mathews Wildcats (30-30): Frank
Mendenhall, Louis Lyles, Jack
Barnes, Charlie Gaffney, Fred Pow-
ell, Linder, Stokely, Davenport,
Simpson, Thackston, Morris, As-
hworth, B. Johnson, Rube Mor-
gan, Rowe, McDowell, Earl Morse,
Woodcock, Suvern Wright, Floyd,
Koon, Roy Bridges.

Whitmire (15-39): Cranford, P. Fowler,
Farmer, Bowers, Ratteree, Moore,
Holsonback, Crosby, Frier,
L. Fowler, Patterson, Burton,
Dusenberry, J. Johnson, Sykes,
Bass, Scarborough, Bell, Bates,
Pate, Livingston, Drummond,
Mitchell, Long, Dunham, Petosky,
Couch, Camp, Blalock, John
Bledsoe.

Greenwood Reds (11-42): Rowe,
Perry Bolding, Howell, Russ Lyon,
Earl Morse, Embler, Nelson,
Knight, Howard Culbertson, Lan-
dreth, Hightower, Simpson, J. San-
ders, Hill, Evans, Stephenson,
Davis, Johnson, Drummond, Wil-
liams, Chaffin, Nelson, McCaskill,
Blalock, Mason.

Mid Carolina League

Newberry, champions (11-5): J.B.
Livingston, Roy Caldwell, Harry
Gambrell, Marvin English, Furman
Warren, Pee Wee Franklin, Frank
Looper, Ostell Ballew, Kenneth
Cook, Charles Layton, Horace
Warren, Guy Danielson, Bob
Creekmore, James Rister, Living-
ston, Coleman, Chapman, Scarbor-
ough, Robinson, Holsenback.

Whitmire (19-12)

Joanna (7-9)

Lando (1-1): Blackstone, Armstrong,
J. Watts, Crocker, Simpson,
Padgett, B. Watts, Venson,
Haffner, Brannon, Elliott, Scott,
Lee, Reid.

Mollohon (1-16): Woodcock, R. Mar-
tin, Golden, Day, H. Mills, Bartley,
Buzhardt, L. Mills, Jackson,
Stutts, Grant, Lawson, T. Mills,
J. Martin, Woods, Livingston.

Winnsboro Royal Cords (0-1): Smith,
Sims.

Greenville Textile League

Slater, champions (27-11): McCall,
Cashion, Ledford, Taylor, Turner,
Wilson, Lybrand, Belcher, Rampey,
James, Frady, McMakin, Padgett,
Dudley, B. Cashion.

Poinsett Pounders (28-13): Bill Tay-
lor, Robert Lavender, Leroy Phil-
lips, Jack Vaughn, Tommy Lowe,
Luke Landers, Jack Osteen, Jack
Long, K. Fair, Simpson, Cooter
Crump, Ott Hammett, Earl Fair,
Harbin, Pel Ballenger (manager).

Liberty (19-17): Carvin Medlock,
Dover, Thrasher, J. Gilstrap,
R. Gilstrap, Owens, Hawkins, Cas-
tles, Watson, Gillespie, Brown,
Mahaffey, Fleming, Crowe,
H. Medlock, Frazier, Pressley,
King, Smith, Stroud.

Victor Pirates of Greer (19-20): Jack
Belcher, George Blackwell, Ernie

Vaughn, Claude Center, June
Pruitt, Yeargin, Lee Henderson,
Charlie Childers, Randy Vaughn,
Brannon, Tipton, Myers, Cox,
Leonard, Bright, Cabiness,
Childers, Belcher, Snoddy, Bruce.
Simpsonville Little Yankees (16-19):
Cox, Hines, Hensley, Stutts, Henderson, Cannon, Ellis, Runyon,
Reddin, J. McCall, Brasher, Miller,
Ballew, J. Smith, Goodenough,
J. Farrow, Chonko.
Pickens (3-31): Epps, M. Pace,
McNeely, Slatton, Alexander,
T. Pace, Gilstrap, Mitchell, J. Roper,
Hiott, Day, Turner, Hunt, Finley,
Singleton, Anders, G. Roper, Stancil, Wilson, Simpson, Brown.

Spartanburg County Colored League

Hayne (4-0): Ralph Russell, Lefty
Bomar, Styles, Roundhouse
Brown, Clyde Foster, Clowney.
Pacolet (3-1): Willie George Bailey,
George Wannamaker, Lefty Norris.
Converse (3-2): Joe Tracy, L. Russell,
Mitchell, Gray, Longoody, Jim
Rhinehart, Dick Larey, Horse
Harrett.
Gaffney (2-1): Willie Dawkins, John
Frank, Martin.
Valley Falls (1-0): O'Fennell, Gordon,
Grover Hilton.
Fairforest (1-2): Bailey Peak, Foster,
H. Russell.
Drayton (1-4): Charlie Wilburn,
Hawas, Ray, Smith, Owens.
Jackson of Wellford (0-1)
Woodruff (0-1)
Caroleen NC (0-1)

Anderson City League

Abney of Anderson, champions (28-10):
Louis Whitworth, Ezra Embler,
Tough Embler, Red Ballard, Raford Clark, Heaton, Hill, Owens,
Byce.
Gossett/Textron (21-15): Ralph Williams, Horace Rhodes, Bill Holcombe, Fred Hilliard, Mills, Loftis,
Burgess, Simpson, Gunter.
Equinox (16-16): Furman White,
Larry Harbin, George Hilliard,
Boyles, Davis, J. White, Stewart,
Allen, Yates.
Royston GA (15-16)
Orr (11-18): Tom Cleveland, Sammy
Meeks, Powers, Charping, Owens,
Ashworth, Kay, Snipes, McFarland, Charping.
Appleton (8-19): Coon Morrison,
Chapman, Smith, Poole, Whitfield,
Smith, Bailey, J. Bowen, Daniel,
Bowen, Spake.

Anderson County League

Calhoun Falls Clippers, champions
(27-6): Densel Dockery, Nelson,
Jimmy Embler, Dixie Howell, Russ
Lyons, Neil Chrisley, Bill Swann,
Fields, Rudder, Fred Ross, Hoyt
Tilley, Duncan, Ballard, Shifflet,
Southerland, Sid Bailey.
Chiquola Chicks (21-17): McDavid
Carr, Day, Luther Campbell, Shag
Knox, Lollis, Atkins, Donald Ashley, Whitlock, Bill Womack, Coleman, Spark Bannister, Woods,
McWhorter, Leonard, Dowis,
Betts, Landreth, Bowie, Lollis,
Ralph Fields.
Williamston (18-15): Erwin, Rogers,
Hale Sherrard, McClellan, A. Gilstrap, Hampton, Miller, Ralph
Saxon, R. Gilstrap, Haynie,
Rhodes, Bagwell, T. Chrisley,
Cogburn.
LaFrance (15-17): B. Harrison, T. Williams, G. Harrison, Bill Hawkins,
C. Crenshaw, T. Crenshaw, B. Crenshaw, C. Williamson, Patterson,
Snipes, Parker, R. Williams, Massey, Stroud.
Belton (14-15): Gates, H. Deanhardt,
Davis, Harry Meeks, Willingham,
Stevenson, Williams, Luke Deanhardt, Nelson, Strickland, Ellison,
Oates, Meeks, Jones, Sullivan,

Greer, Stephens, Darnell, T. Deanhardt, Warnock, Luther Rentz.
Jackson of Iva (2-26): Jordan, Howard, Stone, Jones, Fields, Green,
Marion, McCombs, Fleming, Gordon, Stovall, Baskin, Latham, Bruce.

Piedmont Textile League

Renfrew Bleachery Rifles, champions
(25-11): Wood, K. Poole, Southern,
Brown, Clarke, Mathis, Turner,
Cunningham, L. Lockaby, Foster,
McClure, McGraw, Anderson,
Granger, M. Poole, R. Poole,
R. Lockaby, Southern, E. Poole.
Judson Red Coats (25-8): Bridwell,
Porter, Hamilton, F. McGill,
Clark, J. McGill, Holbrook,
Duffie, Russo, Lankford, Taylor,
Patton, Brock, Massey, Campbell,
Webb, Black.
Alice Aces (18-18): R. Stephens,
I. Stewart, B. Stephens, McGaha,
Bagwell, Riggins, McNeely, McJun-
kin, D. Kay, W. Stewart, Bolding,
Ragsdale, Parson, McCollum,
Reeves.
Arial Tigers (15-18): Painter,
C. McNeely, F. Bagwell, W. McNeely,
Stephens, Pitts, Turpin, Souther-
land, Houston, Crum, Cantrell,
Martin, Sullivan.
Camperdown Clippers (10-21): Alex-
ander, McDowell, Whitaker, Bur-
nett, Hudgens, Coleman, Guest,
Gunter, Mintz, Stanton, Huff, E.
Davis, Gosnell, Mathis, Griffith,
Crawford, Carter, Breazeale,
Cobb, Carter, Mintz.
Glenwood (6-23): Tatham, Mull,
G. Chapman, L. Epps, I. Chapman,
Spearman, C. Epps, R. Stewart,
Corley, Stancil, Pitts, Cope, Brow-
ning, Owens, Hudson, Latham,
Pearman, McCue, Hendrix, Reeves.

Blue Ridge League

Utica/Lonsdale Mohawks, champions (25-8): Shirley, Schaffer,

Dooley, P. Edgar, H. James, Bur-
gess, Bates, Alexander, Hughes,
Owens, Hamilton, Sosebee,
Shaver, C. Edgar, A. James,
Willimon, Gibson, Poole.
Central (22-11): Fowler, J. Craig,
Cantrell, Moore, H. Sanders, Allen,
James, H. Craig, Phillips, Berry,
P. Sanders, Crane, McJunkin,
Chapman, Herron, Marchbanks.
Chicopee/Walhalla (17-12): Stegall,
Stephens, Gilden, Sosebee, C. Gar-
rett, S. Reeves, R. Williams, Leop-
ard, J. Garrett, Cobb, Jameson,
Simmons, S. Garrett, M. Reeves.
Newry (11-17): Howard, B. Peebles,
H. Peebles, J. Kelly, Hughes,
R. Taylor, Goss, Kirby, B. Put-
man, Simmons, Sisk, D. Taylor.
Cateechee (10-16): Seaborne, Gilles-
pie, Reese, C. Perry, Cheek, Tapp,
McGuire, Posey, P. Perry, Allsep,
King, Gaines, Barry.
Poinsett Lumber Company (3-25)

Carolina League

Fork Shoals (11-4): R. Wilson,
Woods, R. Williams, Allen, Pitts,
Trammell, Storey, Davenport,
Weaver.
Cheddar (9-6)
West Gantt (8-7)
Mountain View (7-9)
Piedmont Plush (7-9): W. Pressley,
Hunter, Arnold, Christopher,
Jenkins, Marlar, C. Pressley, El-
liott, Vickery, Crawford, More-
land, Jones, Harbin.
McElmoyle (4-10)

Greenville County League

Conestee (2-0): G. Tucker, V. Hen-
drix, D. Hendrix, J. Fowler,
G. Peskpos, J. Hester, O. Bush,
R. Hester, Claton, F. Fowler, Ross.
Pelham (1-2): F. Smith, L. Leonard,
Cox, Byars, M. Smith, M. Pittman,
C.L. Pittman, C.A. Pittman,
F. Hembree, Moore, Satterfield.

Sullivan Hardware (0-1)
Sam Floyd Plumbers (1-0)

Independent Teams

Lowenstein (0-1)

1949

Eastern Carolina League

Pacolet Trojans, champions (26-15): Olin Hodge, Red Ellison, Motts, Smoky Mathis, Bill Allen, Sam Hogan, Lambert, Goforth, Ping Toney, Lynwood McMakin, Cotton Whitlock, Greene, Vitamin Trent, Carl McSwain, Seay.

Excelsior Rams (27-15): Cabiness, D. Smith, Kirby, Bill Broome, Carl Berry, Jolly, Simmons, R. Smith, Jenkins, Sam Page, Sumner, Cabiness, Howard Harvey, Treadway, Billings, Jimmy Brown, King, Belue.

Inman (24-13): O. Parris, Pete Laurens, Belton Parris, Earl McCraw, Perrin Waldrop, Shockley, Jim Everhart, Cogdill, Jake Cantrell, Campbell, O'neil Carey, Allen Clark, Joe Robertson, Gene Kirkpatrick, Bob Withrow, Otis Mabry, Ray Buchanan, T.D. Stilwell, Earl Prince, Bill Kerr, Milton Parris, T. McCraw.

Mills Mill of Woodruff (23-14): Runt Frady, Bearden, Arkansas Thomas, Jack McAllister, Claudell Smith, A. Frady, Ray Kelly, Fletcher Chaffin, Everett Page, H. Page, C. Page, Sammy Taylor, Albert Petty, Benning, Putnam, Roy Page.

Union (17-16): Lum Edwards, Foster, Goo Lybrand, Brown, Pete Fox, Bannie Valentine, Bill Mitchell, Jones, Vaughn, Gregory, Harris, Morrow, Ralph Woodward, Wilbur Hodge, Earl Monroe, Kennedy, Ballentine, C. Hodge, Patterson.

Brandon Bears of Woodruff (10-22): Blackie Page, Woody Woodward, Vance Gentry, Woody, Ray Acton, Barney Haynes, Griffin, Mathis, Jones, Buddy Berry, Caldwell, Daniel Howard, Willard, Johnny Freeland, Landreth, Wooten, Knight, H. Page.

Drayton Dragons (9-25): Mack Hill, Seay, B. Hill, Jim Tollison, Boyd Earl, Thompson, Country Kneece, Leonard Hill, Linder, Jarvis, Bobo, Bud Shehan, Ken Propst, Sam Scott, Snyder, Hoyt Gosnell, Art Taylor, Bill Wallace, O'Shields, B.T. McCraw, Jack Hamby.

Laurens (5-25): Bowie, Gregory, Waldrop, Dunn, Bobo, Clark, David Templeton, Darnell, Dambeck, Moore, Bragg, Cavender, Simmons, Maxwell, Cox, Mauldin, Lyles, Reeves, Roberts, Edwards, Hawkins, Russell, Bishop, Snow, Bagwell, Morrow.

Mid-County League

Converse (9-0): Billy Cole, Clyde Mathis, Howard Emory, Joe Childers, Walt Green, Roy Millwood, Gene Wyatt, E. Millwood.

Pacolet (9-3): Red Harvey, Jimmy Howell, Alfred Martin, Skinny Thompson, Tate, Dennis Hill, John Guyton, Fleming, Tate, Teaster.

Riverdale (9-10): Boyd Nelson, Mitchell Lanford, Boyd Nabors, Ken Woodall, Bill Tucker, Jack Holmes, Wiles Hannah, Eugene Dunaway, Wendell Hughes, Junior Lawson, Ray Sumner, Bob Byers, Bob Sargent, Bill Waddell, Jack Owens, Cecil Brewington.

Inman (7-9): Parris, Shelton, Ballenger, Guyton, Teaster, Ray Wilson, Waldrop, Raines, Loftis, Pack.

Jonesville (5-2): Frank Harvey, Theron Morgan, Horn, Bubber Hodge, Grady Blackwell, Moss, Addis.

Arcadia (3-4): Junior Williams, West-
moreland, Faulkner, Guinea Har-
mon, Blaine, Clayton.
Clifton (3-5): Bob Green, King,
Mathis, Chance, Cole, Thomas,
Childers, Wyatt, Hopper, Mill-
wood, Vernon, Joe McDowell.
Chesnee (3-8): Bobby Haynes,
Wright, Walker, Hines, K. Haynes,
Henderson, Vassey, Martin, Bon-
ner, Vaughn, Pete Harris.
Glendale (1-9): Tom Reaves, Warren,
Key, G. Millwood, Dillard,
Wheeler, Nichols, Mince, Ogle,
Bishop, Thomas, Sizemore.

Mid State League

Lockhart, champions (21-3): Mickey
Gentry, Freddy Good, Bob Bailey,
Sanders, Dean Crocker, LeBron
Burns, Wallace Lynch, Fowler,
Revis, Brooks, Vance, Farr,
J. Steen, L. Steen, Coward,
H. Burns, Branks, Gibson.
Mollohon (19-7): Barbery, Bartley,
Fat Livingston, Burns, Gray,
Franklin, Whitaker, Munday,
Tommy Buzhardt, Gregg, Martin,
Stutts, H. Mills, Day, Jackson,
Golden.
Lydia (18-11): Fred Satterfield, Er-
skine, Robinson, Richard Hamp-
ton, Chick Livingston, Lefty Mills,
Buddy Sanders, Tot Fallow, Bruce
Copeland, William Rowland,
Jimmy Hairston, Pecou, Jesse
Boyce, Ralph Roberts, Allred,
John Hunter, McGee, John Dees.
Whitmire (13-9): Reid, Barnes,
Raines, DuBose, Maness, Fenney,
L. Fowler, H. Crosby, Bowers, Al-
exander, Friar, Blalock, McCall,
Elrod, T. Fowler, S. Crosby, Greg-
ory, Finney.
Jolly Street (13-12)
Monarch (10-11): Middlebrooks, Rog-
ers, Dan Sanders, Roy Jolly, Bill
O'dell, D. Allison, Haynie, Grant,
Hamby, Lewis Wooten, Gilliam,

K. Davis, Turner, Nichols,
B. Davis, Bobo, Smith, J. Allen,
Howell, G. Allen, Duckett.
Newberry (8-14): F. Warren, Singley,
Danielson, Miller, Bob Creekmore,
Corley, Bouknight, Tyler, Bell,
Babb, J. Livingston, Ballew, Con-
nelly, Williams, Chapman, Walter
Hiller, H. Warren, Guy Danielson.
Ottaray (0-3); withdrew. Haney,
Palmer, J. Howell, Jolly, Franklin,
Ballew, Allison, Lenhart, L. Sims,
A. Sims, D. Allison, Linder, Cole-
man, B. Howell, Treadway, Bur-
gess, F. Howell, Nichols,
Littlejohn, D. Littlejohn, Linder.

Central Carolina League

Ware Shoals, champions (37-21):
O'dell Barbery, Abrams, Ray
Goolsby, Andy Hawthorne, Pitts,
Calvin Cooper, McDuffie, Skipper,
McConnell, Dunn, Bowden,
Sherard, Wright, Allen, Roy Brid-
ges, Phillips, Skinner, Barnes, Jim
Voiselle, Gudzan.
Watts (35-24): Jack Lyerly, Ham Wer-
ner, Bob Hazle, Ray Bobo, Paul
Hazle, Quinn, Ed Guinther, Ike
Chastain, Allen Draughn, June
Werner, Lloyd Moore (manager),
Metts, Roy Peeler, Guinther, Mor-
gan, Dewey Quinn, Harry Potts,
Lyles, Thomas Hudson, Fats
Hughes.
Clinton (25-26): Ellis Huffstetler,
Fouts, Ralph Harbin, Socey,
Tucker, Louis Lyles, Blackstock,
Farmer, Moore, Roy Whitaker,
Claude Crocker, Glenn, McWhor-
ter, Fox, Gambrell, Alexander,
Gaffney, Prater, Pecou, Lynn,
Thomas, McWaters, Calvin Coo-
per, Pete Mish, Frankie Arevalo.
Riverdale (13-39): Wooten, Callahan,
Medlock, Waddell, Graham, Sim-
mons, Burch, Kirby, Snyder, Drew,
Benson, Reese, Flynn, Ratenski,
Forrester, Shelton, Johnson,

Harrington, Cherry, Childress, Nabors.

Spartanburg County League

Clifton, champions (20-9): Paul Groce, Lee Green, Charles Mathis, Charles Reid, Howard Croxdale, Tip Massey, Johnson, Steve Sandor, Mancil Adair, T. Coggins, Charles Fletcher, P. Coggins, Till Chapman, Edsel Sprouse, Joe Barber, Dick Evans, Joe Coggins (manager).

Chesnee (28-9): John Brock, J.Y. Hamrick, Dennis Henderson, Bill Jones, Chester Stephens, Pete Harris, Ozark Martin, Jack Bagwell, Burns, Sayles Edwards, Jim Wolfe, Junior Henderson, John Humphries, Howard Bonham, Mollie Gossie, Charlie Cash, Shuf Finley.

Saxon (20-13): Rip Collins, Fagan, Lonnie English, Bobby Cannon, Denver Gregg, Clabo, Snag Calvert, Phil Clark, Scott, Painter, Campbell, Gabby Wiles, Red Early, Runt Norton.

Arkwright (17-13): Skinny McGraw, Buck Reid, Charles Bullington, Ernest Hawkins, Berry, Sam Foster, Otis Parris, Charlie Holt, Fat Meadows, Scott Addison, Ralph Bogan, Ty Wood.

Jonesville (14-10): Gator Smith, Greer Blackwell, Carl Rochester, Billy Hodge, Tommy Jett, Junior Shelton, Irwin Fowler, Fate Morgan, Charlie Holt, Burton.

Fairforest (12-13): Charlie Rogers, Billy Morrow, Grimsley, Seay, J.O. Thompson, Pete Brown, Bill Ridgeway, Hawkins, McElrath, Wood, Wigwam, Berry.

Jackson of Wellford (12-17): J. Acton, D. Blackwell, Murph, Ken Dobbins, Farmer, Mason, Red Pridmore, King, Jack Bagwell, Belcher, Pat Hawkins, Jett, Cason, Henderson.

Glendale (11-21): Bill White, Buck Jett, Clyde Hawkins, Gene Medlock, Paul King, Jimmy Hilton, Martin, Warren, Shehan, Roland, Burnett, Chapman.

Arcadia (6-21): Clayton, C. McIntyre, Henry Calvert, Burchfield, Acton, Tom Ward, McClelland, Gorman, Paul Henderson, Moss, Ralph Mahaffey, Ed Hudson.

Fairmont (4-15): Guy Hughes, G. Stone, N. Boling, Johnson, B. Belcher, Farmer, Albert Wood, Owens, Adair, York.

Peach County League

Powell, champions (4-5): Mann, Cherry, Hendrix, Dunbar, Parks, Mabry, Shirley, Proffitt, Godfrey, T. Willard, Lambright, Smith, Crump, Ballard, Harrill.

Landrum (11-2): Gib Gosnell, Dean Gosnell, Glenn Southers, Otis Parris, Wright, Bill Bridges, Grey Gosnell, Cogdill, Shehan, John Martin, John Kelly, Bill Blackwell, Joe Morrow, R.H. Fox, Parris, Johnson, Campbell.

Boiling Springs (4-3): Simmons, Brown, McDowell, Bagwell, Haynes, Pye, Hill, McIntyre, Stepp, Cannon, Lyda, Malone, Easler, Walls, Fagan.

Southern Shops (3-3): Westbrook, Roland, Pennington.

Linda (1-3): Lloyd Petit, Arthur, Dobson, Pryor.

Fingerville (0-2): Stepp, Brown, Padgett, Mahaffey.

Franklin (0-6): Haynes, Brown, Poteat, Mahaffey.

Carolina Colored League

Valley Falls (4-0): L.B. Beason, L.T. Tanner, Gardner, Miller, Smith, Mills Jeter, Doc Sanders, Jack Lowe, Milton, Guest, Isaac Glenn, Lonnie Earl, Hilton, Johnson.

Arkwright (2-1): Oneill Edwards,
U.M. Steam, Gist.
Gaffney (1-0)
Converse (1-0): Father Time Gray,
Johnny Tracy, Rinehart.
Cherokee Springs (0-1)
Blacksburg (0-1): Robertson, Hamrick.
Chesnee (0-1): Johnson, Hilton, Johnson.
Drayton (0-2): Hall, Rice.
Fairforest (0-2): Sims, Woods,
Littlejohn, Robinson, Miller.

Western Carolina League

Lyman Pacifics, champions (31-15):
Everett Hendrix, Patterson, Horace Brown, Yeargin, Carvin Medlock, Vernon Medlock, Jack
Anderson, Reid, Halford, Beasley,
Eubanks, Aughtry, Parris, Mullinax, Davis, Deanhart, John
Wahonic, Harris, Miller, Taylor.
Piedmont Rangers (30-17): Starnes,
Nesbitt, Jimmy Embler, Tom
Pack, S.T. Cooper, Darnell, Frank
Lombardi, Stuttz, John Emory,
J.W. Rampey, John Coppell,
Trammell, Fields, Punchy Howard,
Norris, Herman Jones.
Woodside Wolves (27-15): Jess
Corley, Phillips, J. Hendrix,
Wakefield, Tollison, Foster,
Brannon, Floyd Giebell, Gilliard,
Castle, Taylor, Limbaugh, Griffin,
Farrow, Dibble, Cumby, Wilson.
Brandon Braves of Greenville (22-19):
Jones, Campbell, Joe Anders, Barnett, Burnett, Ervin, McAbee,
R. Jones, Williams, Taylor, C. Foster, Adkinson, Kirby, J. Jones,
McCoy, H. Foster, Coker, Turner,
Landreth, Andrews, Ward, Williamson.
Easley (19-17): Henson, McGaha, Stevens, Hester, Paul Rampey, Long,
Mason, Campbell, McIntyre, Frazier, Juber Hairston, Harris,
Crump, Evatt, Darnell, Lowe.

Pelzer Bears (17-19): Looper, H. Jordan, Marion Middleton, Morgan,
J. Jordan, C. Wooten, Haney,
R. Wooten, Ross, Virgil Lavender,
Lonnie Holbrook, Davis, M. Jordan, Helms, Scott, Edwards.
Dunean Dynamos (15-20): Joe
Landrum, D. Cox, Moore, Thompson, Floyd, Moody, Chastain,
Hunt, Lindsay, Duncan, Clint
Stowe, Landreth, Lavender,
Fowler, J. Cox, Turner, Holt,
Willander, Manley.
Mills Mill Millers of Greenville
(15-20): Trammell, Watson, Ted
Ratenski, King, Bell, Floyd, Smith,
Metz, Kelly, Gaddy, Ditmar, Williams, Kellett, Powell.
Southern Bleachery Red Flames
(11-25): Bishop, Ridgeway, Pruitt,
Blackwell, Bennett, Wilson,
Painter, J. Smith, Childers,
Waldrop, Steele, Coker, C. Smith,
Brannon, Belue, George Blackwell.
Monaghan Eagles of Greenville (9-27):
McCullough, Fair, Wilson, Stevens,
Newton, McAvoy, Hendley, Hudgens, McKinley, Phillips, Walton,
Waldrop, Bishop, Lindsay, Nichols,
McIntosh.

Greenville Textile League

Victor Pirates of Greer, champions
(21-23): Bill Moody, Claude Center, Connie Myers, Yeargin, Cabiness, Hayes, Bill Brannon, Snoddy,
George Blackwell, Bishop, Hester,
Howard, Porter, Vaughn, Mauldin, Runyon, Miller.
Slater Sluggers (24-18): Kirby,
B. Cashion, Rampey, Ledford,
James, Wilson, Turner, McMakin,
Lybrand, Belcher, Taylor, McCall,
Waldrop, Dudley, H. Taylor, Bennett, Leopard, Lybrand.
Judson Red Coats (21-15): Brooks,
Stroup, Duffy, Evington, Bridwell,
Porter, Bishop, Holbrook, Clark,
Hamilton, Petit, Lankford, Campbell.

Poinsett Pounders (21-15): Taylor, Durham, Stovall, Childers, Lavender, Landers, Riddley, Crump, Fair, Christopher, Osteen, Massey, Freeman, Phillips, Bridwell, Vaughn, B. Taylor, Sanders.

Liberty (16-19): Frazier, Chambers, C. Medlock, Carr, Cartee, R. Gilstrap, Mahaffey, Bailey, B. Medlock, Crowe, Cassells, J. Gilstrap, Scott, Thrasher.

Simpsonville Little Yankees (11-24): Goodenough, Owens, Terry, Reddin, Davis, Henderson, Hensley, McCall, McGill, Runyon, O'dell Barbery, Farrow, Alexander, W. Cox, McElrath, P. Cox, Freeman, Cisson.

Cherokee County League

Alma, champions (4-4): Bolin, Clary, Garrison, J. McGraw, White, Porter, Parris, Baker, Queen, Wood.

Broad River (3-1): Eddie Adelmy, Ben Moore, Hufstetler, Ed Moore, Hugh Sanders, Sheppard, Cheekwood.

Limestone (3-4): Gentry, Camp, Pridmore.

Cherokee Falls (1-3): Earl, B. Cobb, Broome, Vassey, N. Wisher, J. Hampton, Steadman, Broome, Dillingham, D. Wicker.

Victor-Monaghan League

Victor of Greer (1-0): Watson, Taylor. Apalache (0-1)

Anderson City League

Jackson of Iva, champions (6-2): Fleming, Woodcock, Jordan, R. Fields, Alexander, Bruce, Stovall, Baskin, Green, H. Fields, Poole.

Anderson (8-3): Hill, Spencer, Jimmy Embler, Clark, Tough Embler, Bridges, Cox, Ballard, Whitworth.

Appleton (7-4): Spears, F. Morrison, Gaines, Poole, Ivester, Bailey, King, Smith, Hawkins, Morrison, Spake.

Equinox (6-9): Oates, Voyles, Davis, Gunter, Whitlock, White, Dalton, Hilliard, Coile, Allen, Harbin, Thrasher, Craft, Yates.

Orr (6-9): Snipes, Rhodes, Charping, D. Rhodes, Cleveland, Robinson, Minyard, Clark, J. Charping, Owens, Henderson, Johnson, Stamps, Perrin, Vernon, Ashworth, Wooten, Holcombe.

Gluck (5-6): Perry, Heaton, T. Allen, Pierce, Hughes, Howard, D. Allen, Minyard, Whitlock, Cobb, McCombs.

Lavonia GA (4-5)

Textron/Gossett (4-7): Simpson, Acker, J. Williams, R. Williams, Burgess, Mills, Pickens, Campbell, Hilliard.

Anderson County League

Calhoun Falls champions (28-6): Densil Dockery, Chigger Nelson, Ralph Williams, Dixie Howell, Russ Lyon, Neil Chrisley, Ted Hampton, Hoyt Tilley, L.V. Rudder, Fred Ross, Jimmy Embler, Fields, McNair, Ralph Saxon, Pee Wee Reynolds, Ed Dickert.

Westminster (19-15): C. Hawkins, Smith, Halford, G. Hawkins, Gilden, Batson, Grogan, Seymour, Robertson, Buchanan, Shaver, Thompson, Kimsey, Buchanan, Chilton, Robinson, Duvall, Kimsey.

Belton (13-17): Nation, Luke Deanhardt, G. Jones, Jimmy Brooks, A. Jones, Strickland, Williams, Alvin Greer, Meeks, Deanhardt. J. Jones, Earl Stephens, Oates, Wilter Nelson, Rock Nation, Luther Rentz, Sullivan, Southerland, Griffith, Allen, Danny Fisher, George Abrams, Charles Davis, Larry Deanhardt, Jack Whitlock.

Chiquola (13-18): Ben Day, Shag Knox, A. Gilstrap, Luke Campbell, McDavid Carr, Whitfield, Marvin

Bowie, Deer, Don Ashley, Coleman, Curley McWhorter, J. Campbell, Meeks, Pierce, Long, McDuffie, Bill Womack, Lee Whitten, Gillespie, Dowis, Hack Lollis, Rob Atkins, Yanalus, McDuffie, Bole, Edwards, Hughes, Deer, Whiffie Wood, Shorty Leonard, Sparky Bannister, Landreth, Betts, Moore.

Abney of Anderson (9-15): Whitworth, Ezra Embler, Tough Embler, Bridges, Gaines, Haley Heaton, Spencer, Owens, Hill, Rayford Clark, Byce, Bailey, Burris.

LaFrance (3-27): Pete Williams, Boyd Harrison, C. Harrison, Gilstrap, Hawkins, Frank Smith, Brown, Bob Williams, Patterson, Mac Landreth, Massey, Charles Chitwood, Simpson, Stroup, T. Crenshaw, Patterson, C. Crenshaw, Kingsmore, Red Jameson, Marion Meeks, Frank Boggs, Mac Smith, Red Addis, Bill Cheek, Williamson.

Piedmont League

Pickens, champions (18-16): T. Pace, M. Pace, Slatton, Finley, McNeely, Hayes, J. Alexander, Johnson, Mitchell, Derosett, C. Day, Gilstrap, Roper, H. Pack, J. Day, Crumpton, Parker.

Renfrew Bleachery (23-8): C. Wood, Lockaby, Brown, E. Poole, Knox, Clark, M. Poole, Turner, R. Poole, Gibson, Mathis, McClure, Foster.

Alice (20-13): Crowe, N. McJunkin, McNeely, B. Stephens, Stewart, J. McJunkin, Hendricks, Turner, Haynes, Riggins, Bagwell, J. Kay, D. Kay, Williams, Cater, Smith, McGaha.

Arial (12-16): Pitts, Painter, Cassels, C. Stephens, Southerland, Wood, D. Crum, Masters, Houston, R. Crum, Hammond, Hester, Ross, Vaughn, McNeely, Wilson.

Glenwood (11-16): Hudson, Cope, Mull, Epps, Browning, Pitts, Vaughn, League, Nicholson, Alexander, Stancil, Thomas, Pierce, Stokes, Wiggins, Rankin.

Woodside (6-21): Gray, Green, R. Taylor, Wakefield, Wood, T. Taylor, White, Hines, Herbert, Chapman, Nelson, King, Hickam, Harris, Morrow.

Palmetto League

Ware Shoals (22-5), regular season winners. Davis, Malone, Skinner, Martin, Ballentine, Keller, Hancock, Hembry, Hudson, Hill, Elrod, Dickerson, Shaw, Sanders, Gudson.

Hickory Tavern (17-10)

Ridgeway (9-7): Thompson, Hill, West, McClure, Ridgeway, Bannister, Taylor, Mane, Ross, Black.

Fountain Inn (6-16): Gault, Plumby, Canady, Nelson, Surratt, Payne, Lancaster, Thackston, Woodside, Turnley, Runyon, Garrett, Mimms, Barbery, Balcombe.

Fork Shoals (4-9): B. Farrow, W. Farrow, B. Fuller, Harris, S. Williams, Pitts, Wilson, Rowe, C. Wood, Bulls, Weaver, R. Williams, King.

King Cotton League

Ninety Six, champions (6-0): Allen, Alexander, Sanders, Forrester, McBride, Corley, Drummond, Wells, Bill Voiselle, Edwards.

Greenwood (8-5): Rowe, Sanders, Perry Bolding, Quinn, Earl Morse, Collum, Hardin, Riddle, Lefty Kennedy, Sparks, Ponder, Outzs, Harbin, Dukes, Kelly.

Mathews (4-8): Beauford, Lyles, Koone, Proctor, Horne, Gaffney, Queen, Stokley, Anderson, Simpson, Morgan, Woods, Morris.

Joanna (1-7): O'Shields, Whittle, R. Willingham, Tinsley, J. Willingham, McCarthy, Orr, B. Abrams, Moore.

Blue Ridge League

Central, champions (23-6): Cantrell, Craig, Moore, Fowler, Chastain, H. Sanders, Duncan, James, L. Sanders, Porter, McJunkins, Crain.

Utica Mohawk/Lonsdale (17-6): Hamilton, Shaver, Burgess, Sosebee, James, Shirley, Davis, Hughes, Dooley, Edgar, McIntyre.

Cateechee (9-6): Seaborn, R. Tapp, Gillespie, Cheek, L. Tapp, C. Perry, McGuire, Posey, Barnett.

Walhalla (3-5): Gilden, Stephens, Reeves, C. Garrett, Leopard, R. Garrett, Williams, Harvey, Stancil, S. Jamison, Jamison.

Poinsett (2-8): Dodson, E. Holcomb. Atkinson, Stancil, Norris, Durkan, O'Donald, I. Dodson.

Newry (0-11): A. Howard, Peebles, Simpson, O'Kelley, Sisk, Simmons, Putman, Kirby, Taylor, Sluder, Howard.

Carolina League

Apalache, champions (15-12): George Blackwell, R. Ashmore, B. Belue, Stewart, Lunny, G. Ashmore, Tooke, Black, Ellenburg, B. Blackwell, Gibson, W. Blackwell, Belcher.

Camperdown Clippers (19-7): McDowell, Alexander, Crawford, H. Davis, Burnett, Roberts, Whitaker, Guest, Henderson, R. Davis, Brown, E. Davis, Gosnell.

Easley B Team (13-12): Owens, Putman, Dalton, Henson, Evatt, Campbell, Newsome, R. Waldrop, Dunn, Kilby, Harris, Waldrop, Turner.

Poe (11-16): Jones, Ward, Dickert, G. Spake, Williams, W. Davis, F. Davis, E. Spake, Lister, Phillips, Waters, Massey, Alexander, Finley.

Greer (7-18): Stock, Harvey, Hinson, Foster, B. Campbell, Brown, Pitts, Gowan, Dobbin, Wilson, A. Campbell, Moore, Knighton, Bramlett, Steward, Green, Watts.

Greenville County League

Pelham (1-0): Pittman, Smith, Smith, Leonard, Byars, Satterfield, Jones.

Conestee (1-1): Perry, G. Tucker, P. Fowler, Gray, Peskopos, Ross, O. Tucker, Hancock, Bush.

West Gantt (0-1): Browning, Lindsay, Reeves, L. Holbrook, B. Holbrook, Manley, McWhite, King, P. Holbrook, Sewell.

Sam Floyd Plumbing (0-1)

AA Textile Minor League

Williamston (4-0): Truman Knight, Thomas Stone, Jimmie Saxon, Bob Glasby, Bill Singleton, Harold Rhodes, Bill Stone, Cogburn, Ragsdale.

Gluck (4-0): Ragsdale, McCombs.

Jackson of Iva (no records)

Chiquola (no records)

1950

Eastern Carolina League

Mills Mill of Woodruff, champions (27-27): Abby Frady, George Watts, Bill Allen, Jack McAllister, C. Frady, Vance Gentry, E. Page, R. Page, Bise, Sam Page, Kelly, Windy Dimmick, Bert Sumner, Barbery, Taylor, Hugh Page, Ralph Williams.

Riverdale (38-13): Cook, George Abrams, John Simmons, Jim McDuffie, Bordy Waddell, Hut Davis, Pete Burch, Ike Chastain, Lefty Nelson, Herman Snyder, Carl Johnson, Nabors, Cy Faircloth, Corley Marchbanks, Benson, Cooper, Ping Toney.

Abney of Spartanburg (25-22): Wooten, Willie Sanders, H. Werner, McBride, Blackie Page, June Werner, Caldwell, Bowie, Lefty

Callahan, Jones, Morrow, Wayne
Lynch, Spec Barbery, John Free-
land, Chuck Terry, Claudell Smith.
Inman (25-28): Bagwell, O. Parris,
Otis Mabry, Perrin Waldrop, Bill
Moody, Shook, Joel Robertson,
Jim Everhart, Jake Cantrell, Belton
Parris, Clark, A.L. Curtis, Bill
Upton, Earl McCraw, Weldon,
Frank Escoe, Dedmon, McSwain.
Pacolet Trojans (18-28): Motts,
Smoky Mathis, Seay, Red Ellison,
Lynwood McMakin, Bogan,
Thompson, Olin Hodge, Vitamin
Trent, Ping Toney, Ken Propst,
Sam Hogan, Pee Wee Lambert,
Green, Goforth.
Union (14-30): George Lybrand,
Bannie Valentine, Carl Berry, Bill
Kirby, Bill Broome, Burt Sumner,
Bill Mitchell, Bailey, Howard,
B. Jolly, A.L. Curtis, Ralph Fox,
Smith, Morgan, Lum Edwards, Art
Taylor, Mac McWhorter.

Western Carolina League

Woodside Wolves, champions
(42-21): Shelton, Hendrix, Monk
Castles, Cumby, Wakefield, Tolli-
son, Bob Lavender, McDowell,
Rice, Brown, Farrow, Gambrell,
Floyd Giebell (manager), Fred Fos-
ter, Lewis Reddin, Glenn Forrest,
Al Curtis.
Piedmont (40-18): Starnes, Nesbitt,
E. Patterson, Cooper, Howard,
Rampey, Ves Storey, C. Patterson,
Evans, Coppell, Chandler, John
Emory, Darnell, Forrester, Ernie
Chambers, Ballew.
Dunean (37-25): Gilliard,
McCullough, King, Acton, Hunt,
Reeves, Friar, Cox, Pardue, New-
ton, Kerr, Ballenger, Ballentine,
Bob Stowe (manager), Hardy Holt,
Reese, Ward Williams.
Lyman Pacifics, (36-23): George
Parris, Vernon Medlock, Carlos
Thompson, Horace Brown, Woody

Beasley, Carvin Medlock (man-
ager), Everett Hendrix, Russ
Yeargin, Jack Anderson, Davis,
Shehan, Taylor, Hamby, Mullinax,
Henderson, John Wahonic.
Brandon of Greenville (31-23): Fred
McAbee (manager), Long, Camp-
bell, Atkinson, Crump, R. Jones,
J. Jones, Moore, Jim Coker, No-
ble, N. Barrett, Southwick, Hester,
Fuzz Foster, Armstrong, William-
son, McCoy, Burnett, Landreth.
Easley (30-24): Bill Stephens, Cotton
Thomas, Jess Henson, Paul
Rampey, Joe Anders (manager),
James Campbell, James Terry, Mc-
Intosh, Juber Hairston, West, Up-
right, Middleton, Chandler,
Norzinski, Owens, Paul Mason,
Fred Marsh, Bill Hawkins.
Monaghan of Greenville (18-34): Smith,
Wilson, Bishop, Hester, Spake,
McAvoy, Gillespie, Fore, Alva
Phillips, Johnson, Don Orthner.
Southern Bleachery (17-35): Cabi-
ness, Howard, George Blackwell,
Bennett, Coker, B. Waldrop,
C. Pittman, Bishop, June Pruitt
(manager), Bob Ballew, Crump,
Long, Smith, E. Waldrop, A. Pitt-
man, Jones, Massengale, Wilson.
Pelzer (16-38): Burkhalter, Looper,
Quinn, J. Jordan, Marion Middle-
ton, C. Wooten, Lavender, Haney,
Hughes, H. Jordan, Sheridan,
Morgan, Holbrook, Jim Ross,
R. Jordan, Sherrard, Griffith, Earl
Wooten, Mauldin, Clardy, Paul
Edwards (manager).
Mills Mill of Greenville (13-39):
Ulmer, Metz, Ratenski, Bell, Tram-
mell, Allen, Turner, Brock, Fred
Dittmar, Bob Hughes, Lefty But-
calls, Alexander, Emory, Erwin,
Bagwell, Lollis, Floyd, Dodder.

Spartanburg County League

Arkwright, champions (23-16): Jim
Hilton, Leonard Hill, Barney

Hawkins, Gator Smith, Ernest Hawkins, Dude Champion, Fat Meadows, Foster, Morgan, Wofford, Reid, Addison, Thomas, M. Hill, Ty Wood.

Chesnee (24-9): B.T. McGraw, John Brock, Jim Wolfe, Stan Harrill, Bill Jones, Sayles Edwards, Pete Vaughn, J.Y. Hamrick, Hoyt McIntyre, Ozark Martin, Chester Stephens, Grimsley, Johnson, Rowe, Godfrey.

Fairforest Flames (22-18): McElrath, Jim Tollison, Cook, Bishop, Holton Hall, Mancil Adair, Martin Graham, Bill Scott, Judson Seay, Bill Blanton, Wally Page, Tommy Reeves, Ridgeway.

Arcadia (21-15): C.B. Grimsley, Thompson, Jones, Paul Craig, Pete Harris, Ed Hudson, Raymond Turner, Ayers, Ralph Mahaffey, Carey, McIntyre, Painter, Thomas, Dickey Holmes, Bobby Cothran, Westmoreland, Shehan, Moss.

Jonesville (12-14): Buddy Holt, Coggins, Moss, Burton, Charlie Holt, Fowler, Buddy Blackwell, Stutts, Shelton, Horne, Bill Hodge, Carl Rochester, Addis, Dean Spencer.

Saxon (12-15): Red Early, Rip Collins, John Clabo, Lonnie English, Kneece, Jack Bagwell, C.W. Branch, Gabby Wiles, Hairston, Denver Gregg, Babe Early, Gorman, Buford Williams, Cannon, Allen Clark.

Glendale (10-18): Richard Ogle, Poochie Arthur, Charles Chapman, Hall King, Bob Cannon, Tot Fallow, Cotton Whitlock, Richard Hampton, Pete Brown, Buck Jett, Buddy Blackwell.

Jackson of Wellford (7-23): Pat Hawkins, Dobbins, Carl Farmer, Bright, Murphy, Lefty Cox, Paul Henderson, Jack Belcher, Black-well, J. Acton, Tucker, Louie Lunney, Earl Acton.

Peach County League

Boiling Springs, champions (7-3): John Fagan, Dewey Calvert, Ward, Cannon, Skipper, Malone, Easler, John Calvert, Warren, Stepp, Eisner, Brannon, A. Brown, Bagwell, C. Gray, Lyda.

Southern Shops (8-4): Lewis Roland, Malone, Tom Vineyard, Westbrooks, Gilliam, Eston Fortenberry, Jim Goodens, Earl Pennington, Red Loftin, Wofford, George Lewis.

Linda (6-6): Steve Sandor, John Groce, Herman Bagwell, Worley, Lum Staten, Estell Sprouse, Ronnie Groce, Mabry, Hill, Brannon, Cole, Lattimore, Haynes, Gray.

Powell (3-4): Bobby Godfrey, J. Mabry, Proffitt, D. Mabry, Smith, Morrow, Parks, D. Mabry, Mason, P. Mabry.

Landrum (3-6): Glenn Southers, Castle, Clark Bridges, Ace Fowler, John Kelly, John Martin, Humbright, Gibb Gosnell, W. Bridges, Whitesides.

Fingerville (2-6): Clayton, Dorman, Mahaffey, Alverson, Cromer, Durham, Greenway, De Foix Padgett, Gilbert, Petit, Bud Hines, Shields.

Greenville-Spartanburg Industrial League

Pelham (13-3): Carol Leonard, Pittman, Satterfield.

Lyman (12-4): Raymond Miller, Mitchell, Lowery, Mason.

Pliney (12-5): Sam Marchbanks, C. Marchbanks, Cox.

Flatwood (9-7)

Holly Springs NC (8-8)

Fairmont (7-9)

Motlow Creek (4-12)

Tucapau (1-15): Tucker, Hawkins.

Carolina Colored League

Pacolet Black Trojans, champions (no records): Isiah Porter, Tom Reid, Jess Crosby, George Wannamaker, John Shippey, Willie Bailey (manager), David Bailey, Theo Rice, Frank Wannamaker, Robert Johnson, Robert Harvey, Walter Sanders, Tommy Reed.

Gaffney Black Tigers (2-0): Albert Gist, Wayne Goudelock.

Drayton Black Dragons (1-0): J.W. Alexander, Carpenter.

Saxon (1-0): Smith, Chimrey.

Inman (0-1): Staggs, Jest.

Converse (0-2): Gaffney, Dawkins.

Cherokee/Rutherford County League

Alma, champions (13-6): A.T. Newton, Hammett, Hank Blackwood, McGee, Jack McGraw, Tick White, Porter, J.B. Phillips, Wilman, Key, Bob Parker, Wood.

Broad River (8-6): Rose, Sanders, Cheatwood, R. Francis, Vassey, R.J. Moss, Sheppard, R. Pridmore, Camp, Boling, Bob DeBruhl, Clarence Smith, Junior Belton.

Cherokee Falls (6-2): B. Cobb, Clary, Tessenair, Patterson, Cobb, Clyde Dillingham, John Hampton, Teaster, Steadman.

Henrietta NC (4-3)

Shelby NC Business College (4-8)

Ellenboro NC (0-1)

Musgrove (0-1)

Caroleen NC (0-3)

Union County League

Hebron (2-1)

Excelsior (2-2): Bill Vinson, B. Rector, J. Crocker, J. Sumner, Millwood, Moss, Gene Blackwood, Runny, Adams.

Buffalo (1-0): Cotton Lawson, Sammy Boy Wright, Baldwin, Larry Harding.

Union (1-0): Valentine, Palmer, Spoon.

Pea Ridge (0-1)

Watts (0-1): Hudson, Taylor, Lyles, Rhodes.

Monarch (no records)

Greenville Textile League

Liberty, champions (29-12): Hamilton, Stroud, Campbell, Sosebee, Hawkins, Bailey, Mahaffey, Medlock, Crowe, Fraser, Deer, Pressley.

Slater (21-17): McCall, Landreth, Dudley, Taylor, Rampey, Wilson, Cashion, Kirby, James, McMakin.

Victor (19-24): Bob Porter, Jack Pitt, George Blackwell, Bill Moody, Center, Donald, Yeargin, Hazel, English, Myers, Belcher, Mauldin,

Simpsonville (18-20): Goodenough, Terry, Cannady, Runyon, Cumby, Henson, Campbell, Owens, Gregory.

Judson (15-20): Ragsdale, Harbin, Ledford, Hamilton, McGill, Bishop, Holbrook, Lankford, Turner, Bobo, Stroupe, Guyton, Rhodes.

Poinsett (13-22): Vaughn, Long, Crump, Lavender, Childers, Landers, Fair, Fair, Taylors.

Anderson County League

Calhoun Falls Clippers, champions (31-7): Golden, Jimmy Embler, Neil Chrisley, Russ Lyon, Dixie Howell, Ralph Williams, Burdette, Nelson, Reynolds, Densil Dockery, Bolding, Ross,

Chiquola Chicks (23-11): Gilstrap, Carr, Day, Campbell, Coleman, Drummond, Knox, Bowie, Edwards, McWhorter, Pitts, Quintana.

Belton (20-18): E. Stephens, Greer, Jones, Deanhardt, Singleton, Fisher, Thompson, Nelson, Sullivan, D. Stephens, Abrams, Davis, Luther Rentz.

Abney of Anderson (17-17): R. Rhodes, Tough Embler, Clark, H. Rhodes, Whitworth, Ripley, Hill, Bridges, Ezra Embler, Heaton, McAllister, Hillard.

Oconee (8-22): C. Hawkins, Grogan, G. Hawkins, Smith, Gilden, Chrisley, Batson, Jones, Buchanan, Whitfield, Thomason, Cleveland, Meeks, Craft, Duvall.

LaFrance (3-27): P. Williams, M. Smith, Boggs, Landreth, F. Smith, Jameson, Rowland, Addis, Harrison, B. Williams, Taylor.

Anderson City League

Jackson of Iva, champions (29-6): Woodcock, Fleming, Jordan, Baskin, Allen, Snipes, Stovall, Bruce, Loftis.

Orr (25-10): Parnell, Charping, Sammy Meeks, Allen, Cleveland, Thomason, Gunter, Vernon, Owens.

Gluck (13-19): Bubba Sweetenburg, Luther, Funny Woods, Roy Whitlock, Wilton Hanna, Howard, Elrod, Hancock, Allen, Early Hanna, Fletcher.

Appleton (16-17): Grant, Carrithers, Chapman, Ben Speares, Smith, Bailey, R. Speares, Alford, Bowen, C. Speares.

Williamston (8-17): West, Bowis, Rhodes, Gilstrap, Watkins, Glasby, Wilson, Chapman, Brown.

Haynesworth (4-24): Brissey, Leach, Long, Littlefield, Williams, Sanders, McAllister, Ellis, Bannister, Ashworth.

Central Carolina League

Clinton, champions (37-23): Frankie Aravello, Harold Blackstock, Burnett, Charlie Gaffney, Ralph Harbin, Ellis Huffstetler, Frank Lombardi, Louie Lyles, Roy Whitaker, Zeb Eaton, Chock Burdette, Pete Mish, Claude Crocker (manager), Calvin Cooper, Guy Prater,

Darrell Hairston, Bill Rowland, Mickey Livingston, Wayne Johnson, Frank Lombardi, Marcus McWhorter.

Joanna (34-27): Paul Fouts, George Biershenk, Farmer, Hal Walther, Ralph Ellis, Frank Myers, James Tally, Roy Marion, Charlie Cudd, Jake Daniel, Bill Harris, Moore, Tommy Abrams, Tony Mazurek, Ray Suitt, Fred Marsh, Richard Willingham, Bill Tinsley, Johnny Moore, James Gregg, Dan Kirby (manager), Wheeze Farmer, Buddy Lewis, Rube Melton, John Brock, Doyle Nunnerly, Hardee, Joe Pennington, Dewey Quinn.

Ware Shoals (33-25): C.J. Allen, Pete Wright, Ray Goolsby, A.C. Phillips, O'dell Barbery (manager), Ray Bowden, Herbert Pitts, Snyder, Andy Hawthorne, Jim Voiselle, Cleve Cooper, Roy Bridges, J.W. Taylor, Walter Snyder, Joe Krakul, George Abrams, Carl Armstrong, George Martin, Lamar Smith, Joe Hill.

Watts (15-43): Eddie Guinther, Darrell Medlock, Alexander, Ray Bobo, Jim Thomas, Leo Niezgoda, Paul Hazle, Jack Lyerly, Rube Morgan, James Bobo, Roy Peeler, Harry Potts, Lloyd Moore (manager), Ham Werner, Harold Dunn, Bryson, Taylor, Paul Cavender, James Mooney, Leo Thomas.

Piedmont Textile League

Poe, champions (33-1): Bridwell, Waters, Phillips, Spake, Leister, Alexander, Landreth, Anders, Godfrey, Barbery, Chastain, Williams, Evington.

Camperdown (19-12): Whitaker, H. Davis, Alexander, Burnett, Guest, Crawford, Mathis, E. Davis, McDowell, Roberts.

Apalache (15-19): George Blackwell, Blackwell, Lunny, Clark, Bogan,

Ashmore, Ashmore, Bishop, Black-
well, Leopard, Ellenburg.
Fountain Inn (13-17): Goodenough,
Cox, Jones, Payne, Tucker, Turn-
ley, Bridwell, Hensley, Plumbey,
Thackston, Goodenough, Bar-
bery.
Easley (13-18): Newsome, Dalton,
Putnam, Lowens, Henson, Camp-
bell, Evatt, R. Waldrop, Roy
Waldrop, B. Owens, Dunn, Turner.
Renfrew Bleachery (12-18): Brown,
Knox, Woods, Hunt, Toole,
Mathis, Belcher, Belcher,
Holtzclaw, Fox.
Greer (4-23): Stack, Miller, Foster,
Stewart, Campbell, Lindsay,
Bridgermain, Campbell, Knighton,
Watson, Stancil.

Pickens County League

Central, champions (14-11): Cantrell,
Fowler, Chastain, Moore, Sanders,
Duncan, Craig, Jackson, Lydia,
Crane.
Pickens (19-7): Stephens, T. Pace,
Slatten, M. Pace, Finley, Roper,
C. Day, F. Day, Hayes, Mitchell,
Parker.
Arial (10-10): Painter, Stephens,
Southerland, McNeely, Crum,
Pitts, Martin, Dickert, Bagwell.
Alice (10-14): Crowe, Riggins, Bold-
ing, McNeely, Stephens, McJun-
kin, Bagwell, McGaha, Hendrix,
Young, C. Kay.
Glenwood (8-7): Vaughn, Mull,
Stancil, Owens, Cotes, Stewart,
Epps, Pearce, Pitts, Browning,
Stokes.
Cateechee (5-7): Alexander, L. Tapp,
R. Tapp, C. Cheek, Barrett,
McGuire, Posey, M. Cheek, San-
ders, Seaborn.
Poinsett Lumber (4-12)

Bi-State League

Seneca (no records): Elliott, Land,
Hughes, Lynch, Putman, Dalton,
Wilson, Poole, Evatt, Gilliard,
Hughes.
Chicopee GA (no records)
Lavonia GA (no records)
Newry (no records): Williams, Putman,
Howard, Kelly, Sisk, Nimmons,
Parham, Putman, Taylor, Saluda.
Lonsdale (no records)

Greenwood Textile League

Mathews (16-3): James Beauford,
Pete Bowie, Ervin Koone, James
Horne, Howard Proctor, Ralph
Evans, Douglas Sipe, Louis Kelly,
Teeter Woods, Bobby Ives, Charlie
Hall, Harley Heath (manager), An-
derson.
Panola (10-6): Whitlock, Riddle, Mott,
Briggs, Stewart, B. McDowell,
Johnson, R.S. Snelling, R.P. Snell-
ing, Barnes, G. McDowell, Wil-
liams, D. Jones, Culbertson,
Stephenson, Jester, Gossett.
Ware Shoals Riegels (10-6): J. Ma-
lone, Bannister, Ballentine, Skin-
ner, Davis, Cann, Girk, Keller,
Hancock, Buzhardt, Sanders,
Black, H. Malone, Dixon, Hem-
bree, Dickerson, C. Malone,
Ridgeway, Jergin.
Ninety Six (7-9): Land, R. Pruitt, But-
ler, Alexander, Sanders, Vaughn,
Grant, Chastain, Henderson,
Wells, McBride, Watkins, McKin-
ney, Carithers, C. Pruitt, Latham,
Belue, Saylors, Meisenheimer,
Land, Corley, Price, Harter.
Greenwood Reds (5-9): Echols, Harri-
son, Mule Escoe, Gaines, Bolding,
Bailey, Johnson, Smith, Harrilson,
Compton, Dickert, Tolbert, Hilley,
Pitts, Boyter, Brazell, McCollum,
Dukes, R. Shaw, Drummond.
Grendel (1-12): Hinton, B. Spivey,
Clark, J. Spivey, Hollingsworth,
Brooks, Simpson, Landreth,
B. Shaw, Ronelle, Brown, Cheek,
McDowell, Randall, Howell,
Simmons, Arnold, Cantrell.

Independent Teams

Joanna Red Sox (3-4): Tot Sanders,
  Villian Crawfield, Odell Suber,
  Arthur Davis, Odell Wilson, Leroy
  Higgins, Eugene McCracklin,
  Henry Higgins, Colie McCracklin,
  John A. Burton, Eddie Burton
  (manager), J. Davis, L. Higgins,
  J. Miller, W. Copeland.

Lyman Blues (0-1)

1951

Spartanburg County League

Saxon Clippers, champions (30-12):
  Chet Stephens, Jack Bagwell, Lefty
  Callahan, Johnny Calvert, Jim
  Tolleson, Lum Edwards, C.W.
  Branch, Frank Rhodes, Mancil
  Adair, Ted Haynes, Dennis
  Barbery, D.R. Wiles, Newton,
  Red Early, Red Barbery, Jerry
  Donald, Denver Gregg, Walt Gos-
  nell, Terry Norton, Collins, Cor-
  neal.
Jonesville Red Sox (26-11): Don
  Hodge, Dean Spencer, Junior Shel-
  ton, Bill Kirby, Charlie Holt, Bill
  Burton, Morgan, Cooper, B. Hodge,
  Carl Rochester, Bill Allen, Jolly,
  Horne, B. Holt.
Pacolet Trojans (25-15): Jim Motts,
  Smoky Mathis, Sam Hogan, Red
  Ellison, Teaster, McMakin,
  Thompson, Olin Hodge, Ping
  Toney, Treat, J. Hodge, McSwain,
  Packard, Howell, Shepherd.
Mills Mill Millers of Woodruff (22-
  17): Raymond Kelly, Runt Frady,
  Morrow, Sammy Taylor, McAllis-
  ter, A. Frady, George Watts,
  R. Page, Wallace Page, Bill Upton,
  Bearden, A. Frady, Albert Petty,
  Putnam, E. Page, Windy Dimick,
  Sumner, Chaffin.
Chesnee (15-20): McIntyre, Bill
  Jones, Brownie Newton, Grimsley,
  Propst, James Blake, Jim Wolfe,

Martin, Childers, Hamrick,
  Harrill, Bo Bonham, Champion,
  Henderson.
Glendale Browns (12-23): Hammett,
  Phillips, Bill Allen, Dick Ogle,
  Pete, Brown, Page, Chapman, Har-
  vey, Parris, Jett, Harrison, Ralph
  Dillard, Lavender, Dempsey,
  Haynes, White, Harrison, Cook-
  sey, Smith, Hicks.
Arkwright (11-24): Hampton, Allen
  Clark, Meadows, Barney Hawkins,
  Addison, Hudson, Wood, Black-
  well, Hicks, Thomas, Ernest Haw-
  kins, Coffey, Mancil Adair.
Jackson of Wellford (8-27): Harris,
  Blackwell, Jack Belcher, Bright,
  Elders, Pat Hawkins, Murray,
  Cox, Dobbins, Murph, Farmer,
  Dixon, Earl, Acton, Page.

Textile Industrial League

Pequot, champions (22-9): Vernon
  McIntyre, McCarter, Ray Turner,
  C. Burton, Arlen Waldrop, Beatty
  Hayes, Dick Taylor, Marvin Brid-
  well, Buddy Shehan, Ed Lauter,
  Bob Cothran, Max Carter, John
  Tollison, John Fagan, Joe Stepp,
  Carey Burch, Doc Lemmons,
  Raughton, Hardee, Bob Crump.
Inman (20-16): Julian Greene, Pee
  Wee Lambert, Farmer, Cogdill,
  Jackson, Otis Parris, Donahue,
  D. Parris, E. Parris, T. Everhart,
  Wiles, Jim Everhart, Belton Parris,
  Matt Shockley, Waldrop, Helms,
  Dewey Halford.
Lyman (18-15): Dewey Halford,
  Buster Hadden, Cook, Ward,
  Mathis, Southern, Roland, Clay-
  ton, Hensley, Raymond Miller, Joe
  Smith, Beasley, Taylor, Johnson,
  Bill High, Joe Mitchell.
Draper (17-15): Smith, Taylor,
  Arthur Belue, Lancaster, Hayes,
  Owens, Bishop, Ed West, Wade
  Corn, Webber, Easler, Brown,
  Bennett.

Southern Shops (15-15): McPherson, Lewis Roland, Reid, Woody Lynch, Deloach, Earl Pennington, John Earnhardt, Malone, Lee, Hart, Wofford Shehan.

Clifton (13-15): T. Coggins, Clyde Mathis, Lefty Fletcher, McFall, E. Johnson, G. Johnson, Edsel Sprouse, Ted Chapman.

Apalache (12-16): Watson, Lunney, George Blackwell, Ralph Bogan, Henderson, Stewart, L. Blackwell, Foster.

Arcadia (11-17): Thrift, Biggerstaff, Bill Holmes, Junior Williams, Coley McIntyre, Brady, Ralph Mahaffey, Paul Henderson, Billy Morrow.

Western Carolina League (Same Teams Functioned as Mid-Week League)

Easley, champions (25-16): Campbell, Connors, Prater, Gaffney, Andrews, Carvin Medlock, Paul Rampey, Whitey Thomas, Roy Whitaker, Joe Anders, Henson, Mason, Bill Cook, Mike Zozinski.

Woodside (32-10): Shelton, R. Hudgens, Charlie Allen, J. McDuffie, Jess Cumby, B. Wakefield, H. Walters, T. Tollison, Floyd Giebell, J.B. Owens, Effie Mull, Werner, Hutchins, Werner, R. Harbin, W. Rice, Wayne Johnson, N. Caldwell.

Ware Shoals (25-13): Abrams, Blackstock, Wright, Mish, Red Barbery, Pitts, Benson, Bowden, Daniels, Cooper, Peeler, Johnny Moore.

Lyman (25-17): D. Medlock, Mullinax, Aughtry, V. Medlock, Farmer, Center, Newton, Beasley, Anderson, Parris, Lavender, Mathis, Simmons, Frady, Hill, Furman Taylor, Simmons, Frady, Anderson, Hill, Taylor, Parris, Wahonic.

Dunean (22-16): Floyd, Gilliard, Simmons, Acton, Pitts, Kirby, Kerr,

Holt, Turner, Sutton, Hunt, Fowler, Brock, Burch, Kennis, Gray, Fowler, Brock, Burch, Earl Gray, Kennis, Hall.

Brandon of Greenville (22-17): Stutts, Phillips, George Blackwell, Larry Campbell, Jimmy Jones, Fred McAbee, Smith, Buddy Ivester, Jim Coker, Harry Foster, Adkinson, Joe Landrum, Williamson, Bill Upton, Logue Landreth, James Hester.

Piedmont (13-22): Copple, Sherard, Patterson, Darnell, S.T. Cooper, Howard, Starnes, Ves Storey, John Tate, Embler, Brock, Forrester, Nesbitt, John Emery.

Mills Mill of Greenville (12-24): Lyles, Freeman, R. Bell, Ted Ratenski, Fred Dittmer, Watson, Trammell, Emery, Butcalls, D. Bell, Lynch, Metz, Freeland, Brock, Glymph, Putnam, McAllister.

Monaghan of Greenville (9-26): Landreth, Bishop, Brooks, Howell, Wilson, Alva Phillips, Socks, Gowan, Kuykendall, Moore, Farmer, McAvoy, Walthers, Dean, McCullough, Parker, Frady, McAvoy.

Victor of Greer (7-28): Coker, Prater, G. Moody, Rube Wilson, P. Hazle, B. Moody, Yeargin, McKay, Joe Hazle, Griffith, Myers, Porter, Ellis, Clark, Morrow, Werner, Cavender, Cooper, Vaughn, Lenhardt, Fred Snoddy.

Peach County League

Boiling Springs, champions (14-1): Green, Calvert, Fowler, Culbreth, Elener, Brannon, Matthews, Hawkins, Lyda, Bennett.

Landrum (13-6): Doc McGinnis, Ace Fowler, Jones, Durham, Campbell.

Fingerville (6-16): Phillips, Johnson, Brown, Poteat, Wright, Greenway, Durham, Padgett, Hines, Collins.

Columbus NC (0-11)

Mid Carolina League

Buffalo, champions (18-6): Doug
  Kingsmore, Larry Harding, Don
  Crisp, K. Price, Bryce, Lawson,
  Lancaster, John Sumner, Putnam,
  Jerry Harding, J.D. O'Shields,
  Gilliam, Wright, C. Price.
Lockhart (12-6): B. Burns, D. Burns,
  Steen, D. Crocker, B. Bailey,
  Broome, Vandiford, B. Crocker,
  K. Bailey, Fowler, Farr, Johnson,
  D. Vandiford.
Union (7-7): Palmer, Morris,
  Vaughn, Voiselle, Vincent.
Excelsior (5-11): Vinson, Harris,
  F. Blue, Petty, Prince, A. Black-
  well, N. Blackwell, Small, Adams,
  Treadway, Burt Sumner, Davis.
Monarch (6-10): Bert Sumner, Fred
  Duckett.
Pea Ridge (3-10)

Spartanburg County Colored League

Drayton Black Dragons (17-0): John
  Wesley Gossett, Miller, Ed Oneill,
  G.W. Alexander, Raymond
  Grover, Cooper Littlejohn, Rufus
  Ray.
Jonesville Black Tigers (0-1): Liggin
  Morris, Mann.
Draper Red Caps (0-1): Jeep Crosby,
  Buster Glenn, Wesley Brown,
  Wallace Foster.
Lyman Blues (0-1)
Pacolet Black Trojans (1-0): Gene
  Crosby, Clarence Hardy.

Dixie League

Brandon of Greenville, champions
  (24-4)
Piedmont (6-0)
Camperdown (3-1)
Pelzer (3-3)
Slater (3-3)
Mills Mill of Greenville (2-3)
Judson (0-5)
Liberty (0-6)

Pickens County League

Cateechee, champions (8-2): Jerry
  Gunter (manager), Reginald Tapp,
  John Perry, Herschel Leather-
  wood, Jack Craig, Jim Allsep (man-
  ager), Seaborn, Leroy Tapp, Carr,
  Claude Dover, Sanders, Frank Bar-
  rett, George Barrett, Robert
  Gunter, Bill Gunter, Elbert Allsep,
  Jerry Crenshaw, Don Allsep.
Central (6-4): Cantrell, Evatt, Barrett,
  Chastain, Crain, Saunders, Phil-
  lips, Wilson, McJunkin, Lyda.
Glenwood (5-5): B. Rankin, Pitts,
  Browning, Epps, B. Hudson,
  F. Hudson, Reeves, Stokes,
  D. Hudson, J. Rankin, Tatham,
  Mull, Stancil.
Pickens (5-5): H. Pace, Stephens,
  J. Rayson, R. Hayes, Slaten, Alex-
  ander, M. Pace, Sargent, G. Raynor,
  C. Pace, Derossett, Mitchell.
Arial (3-7): Dickard, Bagwell, Dick
  Crum, Wilson, McFadden, Vaughn,
  B. Youngblood, Hammond, Nally,
  C. Youngblood, Martin, Hardin,
  J. Teat, B. Teat, Stokes.
Poinsett (3-7): Holcombe, Gilstrap,
  Mauldin, Atkins, Pilgrim, Rankin,
  Bagwell, Jennings, Dobson, Garri-
  son, O'Donald, Bates, Dickard.

Greenville Textile League

Poe, champions (25-14): Spake, Les-
  ter, Bridwell, Godfrey, Phillips,
  Alexander, Evington, Chastain,
  Roberts, Roy Brooks.
Simpsonville (22-20): Goodenough,
  Cannady, Tucker, Reddin, Hutch-
  ins, Allen, Coleman, Henderson,
  Gregory, Morrow.
Slater (19-19): B. Cashion, Cumby,
  Wilson, Thompson, McMakin,
  W. Cashion, James, McCall.
Judson (17-19): Langford, McCall,
  Hamilton, Holbrook, Sosebee,
  Hall, Stroupe, Cook, O'Shields,
  Cannon.

Liberty (17-19): Watson, Gilstrap, Hawkins, Hazle, Pressley, Butler, Medlock, Crowe, Scott, Billy O'Dell.

Pelzer (16-19): R. Wooten, Hall, Quinn, Jordan, Morgan, C. Wooten, Haynie, Turpin, Taylor.

Southern Bleachery (16-20): Cabiness, Howard, Bishop, George Blackwell, Pittman, Pruitt, Farr, J. Smith, O'dell Barbery, Waldrop, Smith, Buck Gray.

Poinsett (16-20): Wooten, Gowan, Long, Lavender, Wilson, Fair, Landers, Hammett, Campbell, Rains, Bise, Woodall.

Anderson County League

Calhoun Falls Clippers, champions (23-14): Densel Dockery, T. Williams, Bobby Ivey, Howell, Russ Lyon, Ralph Williams, Bo Chrisley, Nelson, Burdette, Ernest O'Bannion, Simmons, Fred Ross, Pick Riser, Corley, L.V. Rudder, Dixie Howell, Pee Wee Reynolds, Bill White, Chigger Nelson, Travis Williams, Tommy Ivey.

Abney of Anderson (19-17): Hill, Ezra Embler, Jimmy Embler, Clark, Tough Embler, Roy Bridges, Whitworth, Pierce, White, Werner.

Belton (17-16): Stephenson, Jesse Boyce, Al Greer, Al Gilstrap, Jimmy Jones, Singleton, Cotton Nelson, Rock Nation, Dusty Rhodes, Hale Sherrard, Luther Rentz, Ray Stephens, John Sullivan, James Allen, J.K. Mackey, Dick Stephens.

Oconee (10-22): Tommy Jackson, Cecil Chrisley, J. Smith, Granny Hawkins, Tom Thompson, Garrison, Shaver, M. Smith, Bob Grogan, Bargers, Randall Broome, Batson, Long, Red Lynch, Jim Scott, I.W. Kay, Junior Deer, Regis Kimsey, Bill Solesbee.

Georgia-Carolina League

Appleton, champions (24-12): C. Speares, B. Speares, Leach, Brissey, Williams, Bowen, Smith, Alford, Bailey, R. Speares.

Jackson of Iva (23-11): Fleming, Woodcock, Butler, Jordan, H. Baskin, Bruce, Stovall, McMahan, Allen, Green, C. Baskin, McCullough, Lynch, Fields.

Orr (19-15): Charping, Vernon, Cleveland, Allen, Chapman, Ripley, Parnell, Gunter, Evatt, Owens.

Gluck (16-14): Sweetenburg, Whitlock, Hanna, Golden, H. Howard, E. Woods, McCombs, Hancock, Allen, B. Howard, C. Wood, Fletcher, Brooks.

Elberton GA (13-17)

Royston GA (3-27)

Piedmont Textile League

Pelham (no records): M. Smith, Duncan, M. Pittman, L. Leonard, C. Pittman, B. Leonard, Jones, C. Leonard, J. Pittman, T. Satterfield, S. Smith.

Southern Bleachery (no records): Anderson, P. Coker, Barbare, Barrett, Pace, Derrick, Gaddis, Jackson, Smith.

Palmetto League

Chandler, champions (no records): Taylor, West, Roberts, Manos, J. Woods, J. Campbell, B. Hamby, R. Campbell, B. Durham.

Fountain Inn (no records): Thackston, Gault, Terry, Williams, Cooper, Nelson, Plumbee, Farrow, Goodenough, Wood, Frazier.

Hickory Tavern (no records)

Dry Oak (no records)

Bi-State League

Walhalla (no records): Gilden, Yarborough, Leopard, C. Garrett, J. Garrett, Williams, McCall, Z. Garrett, E. Jameson.

Utica/Lonsdale (no records): Shirley, Shaver, Bright, Burgess, Davis, Alexander, Sosebee, Poole, Robinson, Hughes.

1952

Textile Industrial League

Draper, champions (18-12): Sprouse, Cothran, Bates, Davis, Gray, Easler, Wright, West, J. Smith, Lancaster, Bishop, Padgett, D. Mathis, Jackson, Aughtry, Taylor, Pusey.

Fairforest (19-12): McElrath, Seay, Lambert, Burch, Clark, Hall, Traynham, Ridgeway, Parris, J. Green, Lankford, Belue, Early, Green.

Abney of Spartanburg (18-8): Fortenberry, Satterfield, Cooksey, W. Blackwell, Wilson, Bogan, Lunny, Ashemore, Watson, Taylor, Belue, E. Blackwell, Broome, Byers, Cox, Callahan, Page, Freland, Wood, Sloan, James, Bobo, Crowder.

Jackson of Wellford (17-15): D. Blackwell, Hawkins, Murph, Beasley, Ballenger, Belcher, McIntyre, Hendrix, Murray, Dixon, Blackwell, High, Acton, Cox, J. Henderson, Mullinax, Clark, Murray, Atchison.

Pequot (14-15): J. Pruitt, Holmes, Hanna, Mahaffey, Ward, Biggerstaff, Green, McAllister, R. Pruitt, Thrift, Cannon, McIntyre, Castor, Tollison, C. McIntyre, Turner, T. Blackwell, Dodd, Taylor, Caldwell.

Clifton (12-14): H. Stapleton, Sprouse, M. Groce, Bradley, Green, C. Mathis, Sandor, Hembree, Chapman, Coggins, Emory, R. Groce, Melton, J. Mathis, Vernon, Phillips, L. Stapleton, Epps, Malone, DeLoach, Roland, Childress, Johnson.

Apalache (11-13): Byers, Cox, Freland, Callahan, Page, Woods, Crowder, Sloan, James, Belue, Fortenberry, E. Blackwell, W. Blackwell, Bogan, Lunny, Wilson, Ashmore, Taylor, Satterfield, Cooksey, Werner, Bobo, Watson, Belcher, Tillison.

Southern Shops (5-19): Faulkner, Loftin, R. Canipe, Lewis, Westbrook, Gowan, Reid, Malone, S. Canipe, Vineyard, Goings, DeLoach, Lynch, Mahaffey, Goings, Lockland, Roland.

Mid Carolina League

Buffalo (23-6): Caldwell, Kingsmore, Doug Kingsmore, Hightower, L. Harding, O'Shields, Lancaster, J. Harding, Tucker, Owens, Crisp, Gist, Sumner, Medford, J. Haney, Seaton, Price, Gault.

Monarch (7-3): DeBruhl, K. Davis, B. Davis, Long, Wright, Morris, G. Vinson, Palmer, D. Vinson, Leonhart, Allison, Farmer, Black, Sumner, Kitchens, Dickens, Lawson.

Union (6-6): Garrett, Caldwell, Carson, J. Gault, J. Voiselle, Austin, Goo Lybrand, Farmer, Caldwell, Harmon, Marsh, J. Lybrand, Gossett, B. Voiselle, DeBruhl, Spoon, Henderson, Crocker, Vandeford, Adams.

National Guard (4-5)

Lockhart (3-1): M. Odell, D. Crocker, Beatty, Bill Broome, B. Vandiford, A. Burns, Goode, Deal, B. Burns, L. Burns, H. Burns, Farmer, D. Vandiford, D. Burns.

Excelsior (0-6): Fisher, Burns, J. Vinson, R. Jolly, Small, Eison, Henderson, McNeese, Prince, Duckett, Ivey, Stepp, Malpass.

Carolina League

Holston Creek (2-0)

Pacolet (2-1): Gentry, Pitts, Thomas, Sheppard, Rice, Campbell, Maness, Worthy, Fleming, Smith.

Motlow Creek (1-1)

Cross Roads (0-1)
Boiling Springs (0-2): Donald,
    Fowler, Wright.
Riverdale (no records): Simmons, Lan-
    ford, Parrish, Nelson, Benson, Lit-
    tlefield, Martin, Waldrop, Baldwin.

Spartanburg County League

Saxon Clippers (8-2): Rhodes, Ste-
    phens, Bagwell, Calvert, Tollison,
    Edwards, Branch, Sumner, Barb-
    ery, McCraw, Haynes, Harrill,
    Donald, Edwards, Harold.
Mills Mill Millers of Woodruff (8-6):
    R. Page, Watt, Morrow, A. Frady,
    McAllister, Caldwell, Werner,
    Quinn, W. Page, R. Frady, Dur-
    ham, Clardy, Lynch, Jackson,
    Bearden, Dodd, E. Page, Lanford,
    Forrester, Finley.
Arkwright Tigers (6-4): G. Parris,
    Smith, E. Hawkins, Meadows,
    Mabry, Addison, B. Parris, Put-
    man, B. Hawkins, Toney, Hudson,
    Hicks, A. Meadows.
Jonesville Red Sox (4-8): Shelton,
    B. Hodge, Kirby, C. Holt, B. Holt,
    Morgan, D. Hodge, Horne,
    Rochester, Trent, Jolly, Benton,
    Spencer, Fowler, Burton, Moss,
    Allen, Hogan.
Chesnee (4-11): H. McIntyre, B. Jones,
    Wolfe, Grimsley, Martin, J. Ham-
    rick, J. Jones, F. Hamrick, Ham-
    mett, Wahonick, Champion,
    T. McIntyre, Farmer, Bonham,
    Hopper.

Hub City League

Fairmont (7-1)
Valley Falls (5-3): Laws, Frye.
Powell (4-3): Stepp, Smith.
Seminoles (4-5)
John City (2-3)
Mayo (2-3)

Twilight League

Flatwood (15-1)
Reidville (9-6)

Cannon's Campground (9-9)
Hayne Yard (7-6)
Stone Station (5-4)
Landrum (3-9): Morrow, Belue, Wright,
    Kelly, Bridges, Hunt, McIntyre,
    McGinnis, Jones, Fowler, Southern,
    J. McIntyre, Johnson, Shehan, Sut-
    tle, Williams.
Andrews (4-9)
Liberty Ridge (3-8)

Western Carolina League

Dunean, champions (20-10): Gilliard,
    Reese, Ritter, Acton, Lavender,
    Hunt, Brown, Spake, Holt, Gray.
Easley (17-14): Campbell, Connors,
    Joe Anders, Paul Rampey, Davis,
    Medlock, Thomas, Bagwell, Hen-
    son, Juber Hairston, McIntyre,
    Reddy, Medlock, Mason, Biggs,
    Hal Sturdivant, Navratil.
Victor of Greer (15-14): Ellis, Moody,
    Brown, Hazle, Leonard, Center,
    Gravely, Bryant, Jack Anderson.
Brandon of Greenville (15-14): Camp-
    bell, Porter, Phillips, Jones, Bur-
    nett, Smith, Greer, Eskew, Foster,
    Landreth, Croker.
Woodside (13-16): F. Foster,
    Wakefield, Cumby, McDuffie,
    Allen, Bell, Hutchins, Brookshire,
    Hord, Pittman.
Piedmont (9-21): Copple, Nesbitt,
    Cooper, Patterson, Chambers, Ives-
    ter, Storey, Trammell, Emory, Sin-
    gleton, Howard, Holliday.

Central Carolina League

Ninety Six, champions (28-32): Sipes,
    Herlong, Alexander, Forrester,
    Hall, Sanders, Coleman, Corley,
    Claude Voiselle, Allen, Jim
    Voiselle, Saylors, Bill Voiselle.
Clinton (31-28): Riddle, Blackstock,
    Ellis Huffstetler, Gaffney, Frank
    Lombardi, Louis Lyles, Mish,
    Harbin, Whitaker, Calvin Cooper,
    Siefert, Rowland, Taylor,
    Draughon.

Joanna (29-28): Eddie Guinther, Wheeze Farmer, Fred Marsh, Roy Peeler, Jake Lyerly, Guy Prater, Coot Martin, Kenneth Cook, Johnny Moore, Dan Kirby (manager), Jimmy Kirby, Richard Price, Melvin Pitts, Jimmy Clark, Bobby Morris, Kenneth Boyce, Bill Tinsley, Don Reeder.

Ware Shoals (28-26): Petty, Bowden, Wright, Howell, McAllister, Bobo, Cooper, Skinner, Earl Gray, Andy Hawthorne, Ringer, Candler.

Greenville Textile League

Liberty, champions (24-15): Fred Powers (manager), Cartee, Stephens, Butler, Medlock, Matthews, Pressley, Garrison, Powers, Griffith, Scott, Billy O'Dell, Morris.

Simpsonville (30-14): O'dell Barbery (manager), Medlock, Cannady, Long, Gregory, Barbery, S. Barbery, Floyd, Henderson, E. Davis, Jack Goodenough.

Slater (26-12): Snow Kirby (manager), Cashion, Dudley, Wilson, Shelton, Hazle, Ledford, Bagwell, James, McCall, Crocker.

Southern Bleachery (19-20): Clannie Smith (manager), Cabiness, Howard, Bennett, Blackwell, Bishop, Pruitt, J. Smith, Massingale, Waldrop, Gay, Belue.

Pelzer (16-19): Dewey Quinn, R. Wooten, Hall, Quinn, Jordan, Roberts, Hill, C. Wooten, West, Haney, Suddeth.

Judson (14-21): Harry Gambrell (manager), Cook, Lankford, Gambrell, Gillespie, Owens, Clark, Davis, Stroup, O'Shields,

Poe (12-23): Ansel Bridwell (manager), Bridwell, Phillips, Wilson, Stockton, Foster, Jones, Chastain, Barbery, Williams, Roberts, Vaughn.

Monaghan of Greenville (10-25): Alva Phillips (manager), Fair, Bishop, Moody, Evington, McAvoy, Gowan, Dean, Brown, Stoval, Holiday.

Georgia-Carolina League

Appleton, champions (24-6): C. Spears, Cargill, Morrison, B. Spears, Burgess, Elrod, Bailey, Spears, Smith, Mills, Davis, Alford, Lynch, Grant.

Gluck (24-5): Dick Perry, Gary Jordan, Jack Whitlock, Curtis Woods, Early Hanna, Charlie Golden, Hodges Howard, Maddox, J.D. McCombs, Rudolph Allen, Ginn, Bubba Sweetenburg, Robert Fletcher, G. Elrod, Rufus Elrod, Harley Heaton, Arthur McCombs, Marshall Elrod, Bill Howard.

Jackson of Iva (11-13): Pryor, Jordan, Marion, Alexander, McMahan, Jones, M. Green, Butler, R. Green.

Fiberglass (11-15): R. Kay, Brown, S. Kay, Higgenbotham, Warlick, Hoyt Tilley, McCullough, McClain, Brooks, Ashworth.

Equinox (4-21): Boyles, Davis, Dalton, Mangrum, Eberhart, Mulligan, Norris, Hillard, McAllister.

Royston GA (1-8): Withdrew.

Anderson County League

Abney of Anderson, champions (22-5): Marshall Hill, Woodcock, Jimmy Embler, Tough Embler, Ezra Embler, Stephens, Whitworth, Roy Bridges, Morris Embler, Handcock, Bobby Fleming.

Belton (16-8): Rock Nation, Alvin Greer, Jimmy Jones, Gilstrap, Stephens, Ray Bowden, James Callahan, Harold Rhodes, Larry Deanhardt, Luther Rentz (manager), John Sullivan, Jack Miller, James Allen, Bill Dillard.

Calhoun Falls (12-9): Brown, Densil Dockery, White, Russ Lyon,

Saxon, Nelson, Mitchell, Powell, Ashley, Reynolds, Burdette, Rudder.

Oconee (9-13): Williams, Grogan, Chrisley, Long, J. Smith, Lynch, Hawkins, Batson, M. Smith, Griffin, T. Smith, Broome, H. Smith.

Orr (5-14): White, Perrin, Vaughn, Parnell, B. Allen, Cleveland, T. Allen, Pierce, D. McLane, Owens, Vernon, R. Allen, Navital, Brissey, R. Allen.

LaFrance (no records): Speares, Meeks, Stevens, Holcombe, Addis, Harrison, Williams, O'Neal, Morgan, Manley, Wardlaw.

Palmetto League

Fork Shoals, champions (no records): King, W. Farrow, B. Smith, S. Williams, B. Farrow, Pitts, H. Farrow, Moore, Ballew, L. Smith, Tumblin.

Fountain Inn (no records): Goodenough, Gault, Terry, Plumblee, Payne, Bowen, Barbery, Culbertson, Abercrombie, Barnett, P. Barbery.

Ridgeway (no records)

Ware Shoals (no records)

Hickory Tavern (no records)

Pickens County League

Pickens (no records): T. Pace, Slatton, M. Pace, Roper, Hayes, Sargent, G. Pace, Alexander, Finley.

Cateechee (no records): Gunter, Tapp, Craig, G. Barrett, Seaborn, Pilgrim, F. Barrett, Dover.

Arial (no records): Bagwell, McFadden, Dickard, Wilson, J. Teat, B. Teat, Vaughn, Youngblood, Nally.

Alice (no records): Crowe, Stewart, McGaha, C. Hunter, Fisher, Gibson, Reese, Stokes, Nabors, Wyatt, Sanders, Kay.

Bi-State League

Lavonia GA (no records)

LaFrance (no records): Meeks, Rowland, Williams, Hawkins, Harrison, McConnell, Morgan, Addis, Clark, Holcombe.

Newry (no records): Williams, Hudgens, Alverson, Peebles, Howard, O'Kelly, C. Chambers, O. Chambers, Hawkins, Keats.

Central (no records): Evatt, Cantrell, Bagwell, Crane, Sanders, Nally, Hunter, McJunkin, Knox, Russo, Lyda.

Utica/Lonsdale (no records): Shaver, Shirley, Sosebee, H. Sosebee, Leopard, Davis, G. Sosebee, Poole, Galliard, Bryant, Gibson, Harrison, Blackwell, Bryant.

Walhalla (no records): Trammell, McCall, Williams, Gilden, Crenshaw, Garrett, Jamison, Rogers, Dunean, Maddox, Jefferson, Garrett, Reid.

Independent Teams

Joanna Sluggers (no records): Verner Scott (assistant manager), Lynn Suber (manager), Willie Earl Cromer, Leroy Higgins, Vivian Cofield, Willie Copeland, Tavis Sanders, Odell Wilson, Vaughn Scott, Louis Stedems, George Williams, Mish Suber, William McCracklin, Junior Summerlin, Arthur Davis, Johnny Davis, Eugene McCracklin, Tot Dawkins, Hayne Bell Kiner.

Panola (no records): Ben Johnson, Bruce Farmer.

1953

Eastern Carolina League

Pacolet Trojans, champions (31-6): Moates, Whitlock, Hogan, Allen, J. Hodge, O. Hodge, Rice, Ellison, Thompson, Lemmon, Toney,

Trent, S. Mathis, Howell, Motts, Whitaker, Goforth, Tate, Martin, J. Mathis.

Draper (21-11): D. Mathis, Cothran, Hilton, Cannon, Branch, Taylor, Bates, Gray, Reeder, McIntyre, Davis, Bishop, Burrell, West, Mabry, Acton, M. Thompson, Easler, Frady.

Inman Peaches (18-18): A. Parris, Collins, Ramos, Johnson, B. Parris, Casey, Lambert, Everhart, Moon, Green, Teague, Greenway, Waldrop, Cogdill, Caldwell, Cox, Campbell, E. Parris, Hobson.

Riverdale Owls (17-19): Parrish, C. Simmons, Benson, J. Simmons, Watson, Brown, Burch, Littlefield, Sumner, Lanford, D. Baldwin, Nelson, B. Baldwin, Miller, Chaney, Cherry, Waddell, D. Simmons, Waldrop.

Buffalo Bisons (15-20): Lancaster, Lawson, F. Caldwell, Medford, J. Sumner, Gist, Hightower, Petty, Haney, Rector, Kingsmore, Putnam, Vinson, Crisp, O'Shields, Sumner, Garrett, C. Price, U. Price, Hardy, Owens, Owens, Ballentine, O. Caldwell.

Lockhart River Rats (12-19): Odell, C. Steen, B. Sumner, L. Burns, L. Steen, Smith, Moss, B. Vandeford, Dill, Goode, T. Crocker, Bill Broome, Lawson, Smith, J. Vandeford, L. Burgess, C. Crocker, B. Bailey, B. Burns, Revis, Dean, Farr, R. Bailey, Sides, Gentry, Vinson, Griffith, Johnson.

Jonesville (11-14): B. Hodge, Spencer, Smith, C. Holt, B. Holt, Mason, C. Burgess, Burton, O. Hodge, Cunningham, Bennett, Addis, Brown, Morgan, J. Hodge, Benson.

Greer (6-27): Crane, Jackson, Hughey, Campbell, Wilson, Burgess, McAbee, Stroud, Groves, Walls, R. Simmons, Grubbs, Ross,

L. Simmons, Jordan, Henson, Henderson, Dobbins, Atkins.

Textile Industrial League

Jackson Blue Jays of Wellford, champions (35-12): Bill High, Blackwell, Pat Hawkins, Jack Belcher, Ralph Mahaffey, Frank Mason, Doyle Ballenger, Dean Earl, Milton Waddell, W. Cox, R.T. Burdette, D. Blackwell, John Proctor, James Acton, Bill Murphy, Ken Dodd, John Clark, E. Acton.

Fairforest Flames (33-14): Bishop, Seay, Edwards, Carey Burch, Clark, Ridgeway, McElrath, Gilliam, Frye, Barbery, Greer, Mosely, Hall, Miller, Biggerstaff, Fisher, Brock, Bryant.

Clifton Cubs (24-20): Chapman, Sandor, Green, Coggins, P. Groce, Millwood, Mathis, R. Groce, Bradley, L. Groce, Wood, Brown, Stapleton, Chance, Johnson, Hembree, A. Groce.

Abney Bears of Spartanburg (23-24): Cox, M. Jones, H. Werner, Wooten, Frady, Callahan, R. Page, Byers, James, W. Page, P. Jones, Sumner, Dodd, F. Jones, S. Werner, Lynch, Parks.

Southern Shops (19-16): White, Westbrook, Henderson, Shehan, Laughlin, Lewis, Vineyard, McIntyre, Lunsford, MacGyver, Harrill, Reid, Crantz, Childers, Wyatt, Bagwell, Rhodes, S. Canipe, McGraw, K. Canipe.

Apalache (4-33): R. Belue, Ashemore, Leopard, Wilson, Halford, Bogan, A. Belue, W. Blackwell, Edge, Tillotson, E. Blackwell, Seay, Mitchell, Watson.

Twilight League

Landrum Peaches (7-3): J. Kelly, Southers, Gib Gosnell, Gray Gosnell, Morton, V. Bridges, Morrow, Britain, Shehan, Sandor,

Langham, Wright, Blackwell, Barton, Settles, Fowler, Dean Gosnell, Hart, Davis.

Flatwood (5-3)

Stone Station (4-2)

Hayne Yard (4-4)

Chesnee (4-4): Walker, Bonham, A. Hamrick, Jones, Haynes, Wolfe, Gosey, F. Hamrick, L. Hamrick, Simmons, Forrester, C. Hendrix, Martin, P. Hendrix.

Reidville (3-4)

Cannon's Campground (3-4)

Liberty Ridge (1-6)

Carolina League

Spartan, champions (10-0): Guy, R. Roberts, G. Roberts, Cooksey, Gwinn, Brewington, Deal, Johnson, Fowler, Jackson, Colerick, Schultz.

Boiling Springs (8-4): N. Culbreth, Latta, Fagan, Brannon, C. Culbreth, Hawkins, Donald, Fisk, Brown, R. Canipe, S. Canipe, Malone, McCarter, Suddeth, McMillen, McAbee.

Cashville (5-7)

Grambling (3-5)

Walnut Grove (2-5)

Motlow Creek (1-2)

Holston Creek (0-1)

Cross Roads (0-5)

Hub City League

Valley Falls (4-3): Fowler, Park.

Mayo (2-1)

Arkwright (2-4): Steadings, Skates, Coffey, Watson, Meadows.

Seminoles (no records)

Western Carolina League

Dunean, champions (18-4): Crump, Mel Galliard, Ritter, Marsh, Bob Lavender, Hardy Holt, Lyerly, Pou, Earl Gray.

Woodside (17-6): Bowden, Wakefield, Hazle, McDuffie, Tollison, Farrow, Shelton, Childs, Butt,

Moore, Cy Faircloth, Ray Suit.

Piedmont (12-11): Morrison, Woodcock, Lynch, Patterson, Ivester, Hooper, Storey, Weisner, Ernie Chambers.

Easley (11-11): Campbell, Connors, Joe Anders, Dalton, Blackwell, Ashworth, Medlock, Rampey, Bagwell, Juber Hairston, Joe Garren.

Brandon of Greenville (5-17): Greer, Campbell, Porter, Phillips, Smith, Jones, Roper, Spake, Foster, Coker, Landreth, Byrd.

Victor of Greer (5-19): Gravely, Parris, Leonard, Bennett, Taylor, Lybrand, Phillips, Yeargin, Howard, Wilder, Snoddy.

Greenville Textile League

Simpsonville, champions (34-7): Henderson, Cabiness, Peeler, W. Davis, E. Davis, O'dell Barbery, Long, Gregory, Jack Goodenough, Buck Gay.

Slater (27-15): Garrett, Bagwell, Wilson, Medlock, Kirby, Dudley, Jones, Bliss McCall, Stephenson, Hazle, Waldrop, Roy Whitaker.

Liberty (22-16): Stephens, Powers, Crouch, Medlock, Pressley, Smith, Garrison, Furman Taylor, Jim Scott, Billy O'Dell.

Utica/Lonsdale (20-18): Shaver, Berry, Shirley, B. Hawkins, Leopard, G. Hawkins, Gilden, Bright, Sosebee, Nig Griffith, J.C. Hicks.

Judson (16-19): McDonald, Lankford, Atkins, Trammell, Cook, O'Shields, Young, Adams, Stroupe, Sheehan.

Pelzer (11-23): Earl Wooten, West, Marion Middleton, Hamby, Morgan, Hall, Roberts, Hill, Martin, Dean, Pruitt, Ross.

Poe (10-25): L. Phillips, Bell, Jones, Wilson, A. Phillips, Foster, Hester, Vaughn, Chastain, Westmoreland, Bridwell, Roberts, Leslie.

Monaghan of Greenville (9-26):
Gowan, Newton, R. Evington,
Dean, Brown, Fair, Cornelius
Evington.

Carolina League

Mathews, champions (14-14): Pete
Bowie, Booty Sipes, Mott, Thorn-
well Briggs, Louie Lyle (manager),
James Beauford, Ervin Koon, Tee-
ter Woods, Allison Gossett,
Tommy Long, Ray Snelling, Ralph
Evans, Charlie Hall, Earl Proctor,
Bags Thackston.
Ninety Six (20-8): Pratt, Sanders,
Alexander, Forrester, McCarthy,
Coursey, Dowis, Black, Frank Ed-
wards, Pace, Jim Voiselle, Bobby
Saylors.
Ware Shoals (16-12): Collins, Setzler,
Abrams, McAllister, Cooper, Bal-
lentine, Elrod, Richey, Andy Haw-
thorne.
Calhoun Falls (15-13): Randy Whaley.
Saluda (9-13): Fox, English, Martin,
Smith, B. Herlong, J. Herlong,
Higgenbotham, N. Pardue, S. Par-
due, Oxner, Padgett.
Greenwood (7-13): Harrison, Riddle,
Gaines, Harbin, J. Spivey, Sanders,
Boggs, B. Spivey, Stewart, Brooks.

Anderson County League

Oconee, champions (25-8): R. Wil-
liams, Grogan, Red Lynch, Bo Bat-
son, J. Smith, Broome, M. Smith,
Pokey Hawkins, Sosebee, Dean
Taylor, Bob Gettys, Thompson,
Ashworth, Gettys, Gerald Dempsey.
Abney of Anderson (23-9): Marshall
Hill, Bobby Fleming, Tough Embler,
Jimmy Embler, Morris Embler,
Rhodes, Hailey Heaton, Tommy
Bridges, Roy Bridges, Howard
Oldershaw, Ezra Embler, Dan Cas-
tles, Jimmy Smith, Junior Bridges.
Calhoun Falls (20-9): Densel Dock-
ery, Arthur Burdette, Dewey Quinn
(manager), Ralph Fields, Bo Chris-

ley, Billy Brown, Chigger Nelson,
Tootsie Henderson, Bo Sammons,
Fred Ross, Billy Cann, Don Ashley,
Jimmy Knox, Lefty Kennedy,
Maxie Putnam, Ansel Bradberry,
Brian Lowe, Woodfield Quinn,
Gene Molnar, Ralph Saxon, Randy
Whaley.
LaFrance (16-13): Bob Speares, Mel-
vin Meeks, James Stephens, Bill
Holcombe, Red Addis, Alvin
Clark, Olin Mullikin, Hudson,
Rowland, Maney, Pete Williams,
Reid White, Neil Hunnicutt, Ken-
neth Smith, Billy Brown, Bill
Griffith.
Belton (15-11): E. Stephens, Greer,
Jones, Clyde McAllister, Dean-
hardt, Boonie Hancock, Culbert-
son, Miller, Coker, Sullivan,
Campbell, Luther Rentz.
Orr (12-15): Parnell, White, McClain,
Owens, R. Allen, King, Johnston,
Addison, C. Parnell, Franks, Ellis
Drew, Snipes.
Jackson of Iva (11-14): Fleming, Jor-
dan, Waters, Stovall, Bruce, Gil-
strap, McMahan, Jones, Brown,
Loftis, McConnell, Jiggs Wood-
cock, Ivester, Green.
Gluck (8-18): Earley Hanna, Davis,
Charlie Golden, Whitlock, Arthur
McCombs, Ginn, Gordon, Slater,
Fletcher, Maddox, Allen, Stancil,
J.D. McCombs, Billy Vaughn,
Bubba Sweetenburg, Howard.
Fiberglass (7-19): Warlick, Seares,
Minyard, Higgenbotham, Hoyt
Tilley, Mitchell, Kay, Brooks,
Cobb.
Appleton (7-20): L. Speares, Frank
Morrison, B. Speares, Gerald
Bailey, Chrisley, Bubba Alford,
Snipes, Poole, Gunter, Simpson,
Smith, Grant.

Pickens County League

Arial, champions (2-0): Dickard,
Bagwell, S. Teat, Wilson, Pitts,

McFadden, J. Teat, Youngblood, Vaughn, B. Nalley, Durham.

Alice (0-2): Seaborn, F. Barrett, Pilgrim, Gunter, G. Barrett, Alsep, Tapp, Crenshaw, S. Lively.

Cateechee (no records): Crowe, McGaha, Hunter, McCue, Parsons, Patterson, Sanders, Young, Durham, Masters.

Newry (no records): W. Albertson, Howard, Chambers, O'Kelly, Nimmons, Keaton, Blackwell, Hudgens, James, G. Albertson.

Pickens (no records): Lockee, J. Singleton, Sargent, Hayes, G. Pace, E. Singleton, Slatten, S. Finley, P. Pace, Dodson.

Central (no records): Cantrell, Skelton, Berry, Clayton, Sanders, Lyda, J. Cantrell, Stancil, Evatt, O'Dell.

Palmetto League

Clinton, champions (12-4): Truman Owens, Tot Fallow, Hamrick, H. Fallow, S. Owens, Braswell, Stratford, Roberts, Rowland, Foster, Will Hampton (manager).

Fountain Inn (no records): Adair, Goodenough, Cannady, Terry, Runyon, Plumby, Jones, Culbertson, E. Goodenough.

Fork Shoals (5-5): Williams, B. Farrow, W. Farrow, S. Williams, Storey, Moore, L. King, Klozar, Donald, Green, J. King.

Watts (0-3): Dixon, Bowie, G. Lyles, Oates, D. Lyles, Waddell, Stokes, Cook, Hudson.

Buncombe County League

Valley Falls (no records): Sevier, Dunn, Miller, Cunningham, Corland, Shope, Lance, F. Lewis, R. Lewis.

1954

Eastern Carolina League

Berkeley NC Spinners, champions (22-5)

Jonesville Red Sox (26-16): B. Hodge, Brown, S. Morgan, Holt, D. Hodge, Addis, Craig, Cunningham, Morgan, Burton, Knox, Mason, Lenhardt, P. Brown, Rochester, Mason, Addis.

Pacolet Trojans (15-13): Mott, Whitlock, J. Hodge, Ping Toney, Wells, Thompson, Green, Tate, Smith, Trent, Allen, Ray Ellison, Mathis, Red Ellison, Bryant, Hogan, Seay, Harper, Pace.

Apalache (1-25): Satterfield, Belue, Leopard, Wilson, Bogan, Tillotson, Blackwell, Mills, Mitchell, Watson, Godfrey, McCoy, Clark, Justice, Crane, Taylor, Willis, Jones, Vogel, E. Blackwell, Campbell.

Mid State League

Lockhart, champions (11-6): B. Burns, D. Vandeford, Vinson, Broome, L. Burns, D. Burns, Odell, Revis, Moss, Benson, Steen, Hyatt, C. Vandeford, Johnson, O'Dell, Crocker, Brenemer, Woodward, Gentry, Groce.

Chester (10-6): Lowery, Watts, McCorkle, Osborne, Belcher, Cabiness, H. Sullivan, Snipes, Mulnair, Cranford, Thompson, W. Sullivan, Tennant, Carter, Lee, Spivey, Crosby, Howe.

Gaffney (7-5): Bradley, Clary, Camp, Petty, Branch, Pendley, Moss, J. Simmons, F. Hammett, A. Hamrick, Phillips, Mayfield, N. Hammett, R. Hammett, McMillan, Henry Wood.

Whitmire (7-5): Caldwell, Raines, Alexander, Elrod, Frier, Brown, English, Brock, Jones, Wilbanks, R. Fowler, Gasque, Blalock, L. Fowler, Silver, Johnson, Warren, Finney.

Buffalo (7-7): J. Crisp, Caldwell, Duncan, Rector, O'Shields, G. Crisp, Putnam, McMillan, Hightower,

R. Putnam, R. Petty, Price, Med-
ford, Sumner, Kingsmore, Harding.
Union (6-8): B. Harris, N. Crocker,
Morris, Duckett, DeBruhl, R. Har-
ris, Wade, Alexander, Berry, Bil-
lingham, Dorman, Odell, Gray,
Gregory, Cook, L. Berry, Lybrand,
Vaughn, Miller, C.B. Jolly, B. Jolly,
D. Valentine, Hodge, B. Sumner,
B. Valentine, L. Crocker.
Blacksburg (5-7): Wilson, D. Moss,
Cobb, Phillips, Broome, Martin,
Parker, Hampton, Sanders, Baker,
Adsbury, Ellis, Parker, Earles,
Brooks, Wallace, Gilliam, Lawson,
Harding, McMillan, R. Moss,
Dillingham, J. Moss, Biggers.
Monarch (0-1); withdrew. Woods,
Bobo, Moore, Morris, C. Duckett,
Vinson, Lenhardt, Wright, Bulling-
ton, Moss, O'Dell, Davis, Knox,
Bell, Smith, DeBruhl, Allison.

Spartanburg County League

Abney of Spartanburg, champions
(20-7): Byers, Wooten, Watson,
Callahan, Watts, J. Simmons,
F. Jones, R. Simmons, Woody,
Lynch, Parris, N. Jones, J. Sim-
mons, James, Page, Hicks.
Fairforest (13-8): Johnson, Bagwell,
Burch, Bishop, Edwards,
Mahaffey, Morrow, Ridgeway,
Seay, Case, Barbery, Mason,
Hyder, Mosely, Culbreth, Cannon,
Reed.
Jackson of Wellford (11-9): Ballen-
ger, Blackwell, Harrill, Acton,
Hawkins, Henson, Cox, Waddell,
Hensley, Wilson, F. Dixon, She-
han, Halford, High, Beasley,
E. Dixon.
Spartan (0-20): Guy, Hudson, Quinn,
F. Fowler, Leverett, Fryar, T. John-
son, E. Fowler, Martin, Hicks,
Godfrey, F. Taylor, Rhodes,
G. Roberts, R. Roberts, Vaughn,
West, Nesbitt, Strange, Shehan,
Dodge.

Carolina Colored League

Pacolet, champions (11-1): Walt
Sanders, Will Bailey, D. Bailey,
Frank Smith, Miller, Hardy, Monk
Humphries, Jay Sanders, Wes
Brown.
Draper Red Sox (5-2): Booker, Alvin
Simpson, Glenn, Morris, Brown,
Talley, Helton, Albert Simpson,
Wiley Sanders, Joe Free, Smith,
Russell.
Lockhart Blues (5-5): Roosevelt
Gilliam, Jeffries, Wilson, Gore.
Fairforest (3-3): Cap Means, J. Wil-
kins, Bonner, Brown, Salters,
Jeter, Suber, Lyles, Foster.
Flatwood (2-5)
Jonesville (1-9): Farmer Jones, Jimbo
Foster.
Chester (0-1): Milner, Miles.

Carolina League

Boiling Springs, champions (14-1):
R. Kanipe, J. Kanipe, R. Brannon,
J. Calvert, Brown, S. Kanipe,
C. Brown, S. Malone, J. Malone,
McAbee, M. Culbreth, C. Cul-
breth, Hawkins, Fagan.
Landrum (1-1): Morrow, B. Bridges,
R. Jones, Kelly, Barton, T. Jones,
R. Bridges, L. Jones, Metcalf, Hunt-
singer.
Walnut Grove (1-1)
Grambling (0-1)
Park Hills (0-1)
Cashville (0-1)
Holston Creek (0-1)

Twilight League

Campobello (1-1): Parris, Morrow,
Gib Gosnell, Gray Gosnell, Wright,
Johnson, Blackwell, Rogers, Reid,
Sandor, Fulbright.

Buncombe County League

Fairview (0-1): Fox, Morrill, G. Carter, Duncan, Hamlin, L. Carter,
Williams, Wall, Gaddy.

Western Carolina League

Easley, champions (23-15): J. Campbell, Hensley, Paul Rampey, Ashworth, Joe Anders, Medlock, Henson, Bagwell, McIntyre, Mulroy, Juber Hairston.

Woodside (30-8): Bowden, Phillips, Hazle, McDuffie, Wright, Smythe, Moody, Wakefield, Shelton, Limbaugh.

Dunean (19-13): Shelton, Ritter, Stowe, Lyerly, Lavender, Gallaird, Marsh, Dellinger, Holt.

Brandon of Greenville (12-20): McAbee, L. Campbell, Conners, Smith, Harbin, Ivester, Spake, Porter, Wiliamson, Coker, Foster, Harvey.

Piedmont (9-20): John Childers, Tom Tober (manager), Pat Patterson, Marion Middleton, Ernie Chambers, S.T. Cooper, Jiggs Woodcock, Jerry Weisner, John Tate, Fate Hill, John Emory, Carroll Emory, Hal Starnes, Truman Hill.

Victor of Greer (6-23): Aughtry, Warren, Howard, Leonard, Blackwell, Vaughn, Frier, Cox, Swanson, Yeargin, Roper, Godfrey, Werner, Adkins.

Greenville Textile League

Utica/Lonsdale, champions (22-19): Williams, King, Hawkins, Pagle, Lynch, Allred, Bright, Griffith, Poole.

Simpsonville (29-11): Henderson, Cabiness, Long, Peeler, Barbery, Clark, Gregory, Morrow, Goodenough.

Liberty (25-12): Powers, Stephens, D. Medlock, H. Medlock, Danielson, Pressley, Hair, Garrison, Scott, Taylor.

Poe (17-22): Fowler, Bridwell, Wilson, Hester, Foster, Vaughn, A. Phillips, L. Phillips, Roberts, Ross.

Monaghan of Greenville (14-18): Gowan, Brookshire, Fair,

Evington, Newton, Farrow, Hudgens, Dean, Pippin, Nash.

Slater (5-14): Waldrop, Bagwell, Hazle, McJunkin, Garrett, James, Martin, McCall, Stephenson, Kirby.

Carolina Textile League

Mathews, champions (30-11): Bowie, Bone, Koone, Lyle, Briggs, Buford, Long, Beasley, Proctor.

Ware Shoals (26-15): Riddle, Abrams, Setzler, McAllister, Cooper, Williams, Ballentine, Malone, VanderMeer.

Clinton (22-16): Truman Owens, Tot Fallow, Ellis Hufstetler, Charlie Gaffney (manager), Ralph Roberts, Calvin Cooper, Jim Braswell, Sam Owens, Rowland, Moe Fallow, Red Mauldin, Leslie Sharpe.

Johnston (19-15): English, Martin, Burkhalter, Herlong, Floyd, Smith, Roger, Davenport, Parrish, Foy, Myer, Connove.

Calhoun Falls (19-17): Densel Dockery, Evans, Nelson, Quinn, Neil Chrisley, Hoyt Tilley, Parnell, Bradberry, Brown, Whaley, Sammons, Waters.

Joanna (17-17): Cook, Hollingsworth, Peeler, Alexander, Prater, Boyce, Johnson, Kirby, Jenkins, Moore, Clark.

Ninety Six (10-24): Pratt, Johnson, Sanders, Landreth, Edwards, Pace, Stephenson, Coursey, Claude Voiselle, Chastain, Bennett, Jim Voiselle, Forrester.

Greenwood (2-30): Owings, Harrison, Brooks, Poole, Hagood, Johnson, Escoe, Pitts, Baxter, King, Cantrell.

Anderson County League

Abney of Anderson (24-11): Hill, Fleming, Jimmy Embler, Tough Embler, Speares, Ezra Embler, R. Bridges, Whitworth, Oldershaw, Byce, McCallum, D. Hopper.

Oconee (21-15): Roussie, Long, Sose-
bee, Batson, Hawkins, B. Smith,
M. Smith, Broome, Dempsey,
McGraw,
Belton (18-14): Greer, Hancock, Ste-
phens, Jones, Leo Fisher, Luther
Rentz, Land, Allred, D. Fisher,
Rock Nation, Davis.
Orr (5-28): Cox, Allen, M. Addison,
Holcombe, Franks, Poore, Parnell,
Aiken, Patterson, D. Addison,
Bubba Sweetenburg, White,
Franks, Smith, Drew.

Palmetto League

Poinsett (no records): Brown, Ran-
kin, Baker, Addis, Coker, Haw-
kins, Sayles, Webb, Hall.
Fiberglass (no records): Warlick,
Sears, Higginbotham, Hoyt Tilley,
Minyard, Mitchell, Loftis, Brooks,
Findley, Saylors, Freeman.
Lee Steam Plant (no records)
Peerless (no records): Lusk, Bell,
Duncan, Taylor, Roger, Campbell,
H. Strickland, M. Strickland,
Brock, Craft, Branyon.
Gossett (no records): Bennett, Fuller,
L. Moore, B. Williams, Deanhardt,
Baxter, Ivester, Reynolds, Vaughn.
Belton (no records): Lowe, Philyow,
Fisher, Land, Hawkins, Lance,
Culbertson, Madden, Allen.
Abney of Anderson (no records):
D. Hooper, C. Smith, Radford,
McCallum, Sanders, Whitfield,
Bridges, J. Smith, Mitchell,
T. Hooper, Vinson, Jones.
Newry (no records): Albertson, Goss,
Gaines, Chambers, Hudgins,
T. Keaton, W. Keaton, Blackwell,
Lee, Thomas, Waters, Parham.

Piedmont League

Union Bleachery, champions (3-0):
H. Turner, Bell, C. Robertson,
Harbin, P. Turner, M. Epps,
R. Bishop, J. Robertson, Evington,
Robertson.

Sampson (0-3): Smith, Neely, Harbin,
Hardin, Burgess, Dudley, Finley,
Holditch, Fowler.
Poinsett (no records): Campbell,
Evatt, Woodall, Cox, Vaughn,
Freeman, Gilstrap, Gilliam, Tay-
lor.
Renfrew Bleachery (no records):
Vernon, Foster, A. Belcher,
O. Belcher, Johnson, Cunningham,
B. Abbott, Stewart, Holtzclaw.

Pickens County League

Alice (no records): Crowe, Parsons,
Youngblood, Durham, Cater,
Hunter, P. McGaha, Masters,
F. McGaha, McCollom.
Pickens (no records): Pace, Simmons,
Singleton, Pace, Hayes, Slatton,
S. Finley, Mann, Day, Stokes, Dod-
son, Johnson, Bryson.
Arial (no records): Waldrop, G. Roper,
Bagwell, McFadden, Wood, Young-
blood, Teat, Nalley, Sweet, Crum.
Liberty (no records): Allgood, Martin,
Carr, Murphy, Mahaffey, Reeves,
B. Crowe, C. Crowe, Pilgrim, Jones,
Pressley.
Cateechee (no records): R. Tapp, Sea-
born, Leatherwood, Mahaffey,
R. Dover, Reeves, Cheek, B. Dover,
Shirley, Tapp, Crenshaw.
Easley (no records): Owens, Putnam,
Pitts, Garrick, Bagwell, Campbell,
Simpson, McCree, Newsome,
Turner.
Central (no records): Cantrell, Skel-
ton, Barry, Crane, Merck, Stancil,
Cantrell, Leslie, Wilson.
Walhalla (no records): Bell, Hughes,
B. Garrett, Reid, Williams, P. Gar-
rett, Medford, Overman.

Georgia-Carolina Negro League

Calhoun Falls (no records)
Anderson VFW (no records)
Belton (no records)
Chiquola (no records)
Fiberglass (no records)

Center Rock (no records)
Flat Rock GA (no records)

1955

Spartanburg County League

Jackson of Wellford, champions (33-9):
Jack Belcher, Felix Dixon, Dee
Blackwell, Ken Dobbins, Mann,
Doyle Ballenger, Frank Mason,
Ken Hensley, Jim Mullinax, Larry
Wilson, Ray Blackwell, Pat Haw-
kins, Lefty Cox, N. Blackwell,
Mason, Price.

Fairforest (24-11): Ray Blank, Claude
Culbreth, Joe Childers, Groce,
Bishop, Jim Blake, Carl Brown,
Casey, LeFoix Padgett, Burch,
Bemond, Mack Culbreth, Bill
Ridgeway, Judd Seay, Roy Beach.

Jonesville Red Sox (18-11): Billy Bur-
ton, Bill Hodge, Charlie Holt,
Floyd Shealy, Brady Morgan,
Bobby Brown, Clyde Addis,
S. Morgan, Lynch, Boot Addis,
Pete Brown.

Inman (11-16): Jim Everhart, O'neil
Casey, Julian Green, Cogdill,
Emory, Belton Parris, Teague,
Greenway, N. Green, Allen, Ham-
mett, E. Parris, O. Parris, Newful,
Vaughn.

Buffalo (7-18): Glenn, Crisp, R. Putnam, Frank Caldwell, J. Putnam,
Jack Fuller, Lawson, Dewey Caldwell, Ray, Medford, Petty.

Apalache (5-16): Godfrey, McCoy,
Ralph Bogan, Bus Belue, Tillotson,
Hensley, Cox, Eston Fortenberry,
Fuller, W. Blackwell, Mitchell.

Carolina League

Landrum (22-2): Ace Fowler, Charlie
Pace, Clark Bridges, Bobby Bridges, McIntyre, Morrow, Kelly,
Morton, Barton, Bridgman, Car-
ruth, Metcalf.

Boiling Springs (21-1): Gerald Malone, Bobby Marlow, Fagan, Robin

Ellenburg, John Calvert, Gene Eisner, Johnson, Horace Agnew, Roy
Brannon, H.C. Hawkins.

Motlow Creek (4-3)
Cross Roads (3-6)
Holston Creek (2-4)
Glenn Springs (0-1)
Grambling (0-1)
Lanham School (0-5)

Twin County League

Pacolet, champions (15-4): Fulton
Tate, Smoky Mathis, Skinny
Thompson, Frank Teaster, Bill
Allen, Smith, Donald Tate, Flem-
ing, Lambert, Whitlock, Motts.

Chesnee (14-7): Tom McIntyre, Jones,
Carol Haynes, R. Hamrick, Dor-
man Henderson, Woodford Quinn,
Martin, F. Hamrick, Brock, Walker,
B. Henderson, E. Hamrick, Vaughn,
Hayes, Lollis.

Henrietta NC (13-7)

Gaffney (11-9): R. Hammett,
Dillingham, Phillips, Bill Smith,
Benson, Petty, Parker, Whitey Vassey, Wood, Vinesett, Gene Crocker, M. Hammett, Spencer, Pendley.

Spartan (3-15): Johnson, G. Roberts,
Putnam, Splawn, McNeely, Sut-
ton, Taylor, Morrow, J. Roberts,
Donald, R. Roberts, Fowler.

Cliffside NC (3-16)

Twilight League

Campobello, champions (7-3): Darrill
Medlock, Beasley, Steve Sandor,
Johnson, Hank Wright, Slim Au-
ghtry, Gray Gosnell, Davis,
McElrath, Cook, Bill Blackwell,
Gib Gosnell, Ward, Morrow, Ful-
bright, Williams.

Draper (7-2): Adair, Gray, Easley.

Liberty Ridge (6-1)

Southern Shops (5-3): Earl McCraw,
Stan Harrill, Doyle Shell, C.B.
Grimsley, J.D. Alexander, Cookie
Collins, Loflin, Shields, Lynch,

Shehan, Graham, Vineyard, Heatherly, Fortner, Dell, S. Kanipe, Devine, Vann, Brooks.

Flatwood (3-4)
Hayne Yard (2-6)
Reidville (2-7)
Cannon's Campground (2-8)

County Colored League

Pacolet Black Trojans (3-0): Wes Brown, Jim Foster, Sam Shippey, Monk Humphries, Frank Smith, Miller, Hardy, Porter, Hardy.
Gaffney Brown Bombers (0-1): Lock, Jeffries, Smith.
Clinton Tigers (0-1): Evans, Sanders, Wilson, Ware, Fleming.
Blacksburg Sluggers (no records): Bradley, White, Russell.
Spartan (no records): Jefferson, Foster, Davis.

Western Carolina League

Berkeley NC, champions (27-5)
Dunean (19-9): Galliard, Brown, Ritter, Stowe, Holt, Gray, Ashley, Cox, Ragsdale.
Brandon of Greenville (15-15): F. McGee, Harbin, Spake, Smith, Dillworth, Williams, Buchanan, Miller, Williamson, Rhodes, Byrd, Hall.
Victor of Greer (14-14): Warren, Bennett, Leonard, Howard, J. Cox, Vaughn, R. Vaughn, Yeargin, Smith.
Poe (12-14): Crump, Wilson, Vaughn, Hester, Marsh, Foster, Alexander, Phillips, Barbery, Huckaby, Ward, Westmoreland.
Monaghan of Greenville (10-18): Pittman, Brookshire, Fowler, Newton, Gowan, Stanton, Wilhoit, Major, Merck.
Piedmont (10-18): Reeves, Weisner, Hiott, Hill, Howard, Davis, Bridges, Hooper, Emery, Tate, Golding, Stewart, Wallace.

Slater (7-21): Martin, Taylor, Payne, Hazle, McGill, Kirby, James, Garrett, Moon, Sprouse.

Cottonwood League

Easley Sluggers, champions (23-10): Campbell, McIntyre, Joe Anders (manager), Paul Rampey, Ashworth, L. Bagwell, Evatt, Juber Hairston, Hal Ensley, Galloway, Suddeth, Newsome, Garrett, Dalton.
Liberty Lions (19-12): Taylor, Stutts, McJunkin, Medlock, Hair, Duncan, Garrison, Cartee, Scott, Powers.
Woodside (16-19): Bowden, Nelson, Shelton, McDuffie, Wright, Limbaugh, Woods, Julian, Kay, Wakefield.
Simpsonville (6-23): Ballew, Henderson, Knox, Gregory, Sloan, Wooten, Terry, Runyan, Buddy Sheehan, Popler.

Pickens County League

Alice, champions (12-2): Crowe, Massengale, Durham, Woods, P. McGaha, Parsons, E. Youngblood, F. McGaha, Cater, Mitchell.
Arial (10-12): Hunter, Teat, McFadden, Masters, Youngblood, Roper, Cantrell, Guinn, McCall.
Pickens (9-4): Pace, Singleton, Simmons, Bivens, Sargent, B. Finley, C. Finley, Hiott, Slatten, Mann, Burgess, Bryson, Patterson.
Cateechee (8-4): Leatherwood, Bagwell, Cashion, C. Cheek, Whitaker, Dover, E. Cheek, J. Reeves, Merck.
Central (8-6)
Liberty (4-9): Seaborn, Martin, Carr, Locker, Reeves, Holiday, Evans, Pilgrim.
Glenwood (4-11): Vaughn, Alexander, Pierce, Epps, Rankin, Chapman, Nicholson, Leslie, Pitts, League, Greer, Brooks, Owens.

Central Carolina League

Joanna, champions (8-10): Truman Owens, Glenn McGee, Kenneth Cook, Jake Lyerly, Martin Gwinn, Darrell Johnson, Jim Clark, Jim Braswell, Johnny Moore, Tommy Foy, Bobby Estes, Jim Kirby, Olin Stewart, Tom Abrams, Dan Kirby (manager), Niven, Billy Cooper, Dan Newman, Wheeze Farmer, Everett Mays, Bob Jenkins, Charles Malpass, Bill Dobbins, Dusty Reaves, Roy Peeler.

Mathews (9-6): Bowie, Beasley, E. Proctor, Briggs, Koone, Lyle, H. Proctor, Beauford, J. Lyle, Craig.

Ninety Six (8-9): Coursey, Owens, Brown, Forrester, Chastain, Hagood, Brooks, Minor, G. Voiselle, Butler, Bennett, J. Voiselle.

Calhoun Falls (7-6): Nelson, Evans, Parnell, Waters, Burdette, Spears, Fields, Ross, Whaley.

Anderson County League

Belton, champions (21-11): Looper, Lowe, Jones, Sosebee, Stephens, Rock Nation, Larry Deanhardt, Mann, Leo Fisher, Nelson, Bridges, Land, Ellison.

Abney of Anderson (23-9): Ezra Embler, Jimmy Embler, Tough Embler, Hill, Russ Byce, Fleming, R. Bridges, Whitworth, Poore, Palmer, Radford, Sanders.

Pelzer (16-14): Earl Wooten, West, Hall, Marion Middleton, Morgan, Muth, Roberts, Watson, Ross, F. Roberts, Harper, Alexander.

Lee Steam Plant (2-25)

Palmetto League (Anderson Loop)

LaFrance Rockets, champions (14-1): Neil Hunnicutt, Pete Williams, C. Garrett, Alvin Clark, Jimmy

Kay, Cleo Martin, Bill Holcomb, Red Addis, Bobby Williams, John Simpson, Oscar Hudgens, Troy Keaton, Jack Byrd, Beans Gentry, Robby Martin, Kenneth Smith, Hook Harrison, Walter Holcombe, Mullikin, Keaton.

Orr (2-3): Saylors, M. Aiken, Parnell, Ashworth, Wellborn, Buchanan, Bannister, English, Addison, Cox, Patterson, Makison, Snipes, Wellborn.

Fiberglass (1-0): Warlick, Parnell, E. Higgenbotham, Lowe, L. Speares, Robinson, B. Higgenbotham, Kinard, Stubblefield, Minyard, J. Smith.

Abney of Anderson (1-1): Hart, Hill, Fleming, McCollum, Moore, O. Davis, R. Bridges, J. Bridges, Smith.

Poinsett (0-1): Spears, Coward, Saylors, Deanhardt, Patterson, Smith, Cox, Sanders, Moore, Coker.

Belton (0-1): Lowe, Thompson, Meeks, Rock Nation, Nelson, Leo Fisher, Culbertson, Bridges, Ellison, Philyaw, Allen.

Gluck (0-3): Earley Hanna, Charlie Golden, McCombs, Fletcher, Allen, Bannister, Bostic, Jordan, Ragsdale, Whitlock.

Peerless (no records)

Palmetto League (Laurens Loop)

Chandler (no records): R. Campbell, J. Campbell, Ward, Donald, Kellett, Monroe, Tumblin, Raines, Jeanes.

Hickory Tavern (no records)

Watts (no records): Putman, K. Cook, Harding, D. Lyles, Waddell, Baldwin, B. Cook, Hazle, Hudson.

Lydia (no records): Owen, Campbell, Satterfield, Oakley, Leatherwood, McElonnon, Vandeford, Fuller, Hampton, Sease.

Piedmont Textile League

Union Bleachery, champions (no records): H. Turner, McClure, Robertson, Bell, P. Turner, Epps, Smith, W. Turner, Sizemore, Jones.

Mills Mill of Greenville (no records): J. Thompson, T. Putman, Gray, B. Putman, D. Thompson, McAllister, Quinn, McCall, Lowery, Patterson, Porter, Raines, Massey.

Sampson (no records): Morehead, Neely, Snider, Finley, Burgess, Dudley, Painter, Franklin, Fowler.

Poinsett (no records): Campbell, Crymes, Martin, Lavender, Sweet, Cox, Powell, Taylor, Floyd.

Cotton Belt League

Lockhart (2-0)
Whitmire (0-1)
Wilkesburg (0-1)

Independent League

Abney/Toxaway, champions (no records)

Cheddar (11-5)

Phalanx (10-6): Metz, Ivester, Anderson, S. King, D. King.

Newry (3-12): L. Thomas, Chambers, Orr, Keaton, Albert, James, Keaton, Shirley, Campbell.

Hammond (0-1)

Jackson of Iva (0-1): Bruce, Brown, Green, Higgenbotham, McConnell, Fields, Hall, A. Fields, Cary.

Independent Teams

Lockhart Blues (1-0): Pete Gaines, Eison, Bradley Gore.

Newberry Black Sluggers (0-1)

Apalache (7-21): Godfrey, McCoy, Ralph Bogan, Bus Belue, Tillotson, Hensley, Eston Fortenberry, Fuller, W. Blackwell, Cox.

Bibliography

Anderson *Independent,* 1929-1955.

Calhoun Falls *News,* May 4th, 1947.

Carlton, David L. *Mill and Town in South Carolina: 1880-1920.* Baton Rouge, LA: Louisiana State University Press, 1982.

Cole, Donald B. *Immigrant City: Lawrence, MA 1845-1921.* Chapel Hill, NC: University of North Carolina Press, 1963.

Dunwell, Steve. *The Run of the Mill.* Boston: David R. Godine, Publishers, 1978.

Ely, Richard T. "An American Industrial Experiment." *Harper's Monthly,* CV, No. 625 (1902), pp. 39-45.

Greenville *Mountaineer and Enterprise,* April 19th, 1889 and September 6th, 1893.

Greenville *News,* 1901-1955.

Hall, Jacquelyn Dowd., et al. *Like a Family: The Making of a Southern Cotton Mill World.* Chapel Hill, NC: University of North Carolina Press, 1987.

Hembree, Michael, and David Moore. *A Place Called Clifton.* Clinton, SC: Jacobs Press, 1987.

_____, and _____. *Clifton: A River of Memories.* Clinton, SC: Jacobs Press, 1988.

Johnston, Olin D., et al. *Anderson County, SC: Economic and Social.* Columbia, SC: University of South Carolina Press, 1923.

Kohn, August. *The Cotton Mills of South Carolina.* Charleston, SC: Daggett Printing Co., 1907.

Lahne, Herbert J. *The Cotton Mill Worker.* New York: Farrar and Rinehart, Inc., 1944.

Newberry *Observer,* 1889-1925.

Potwin, Marjorie. *Cotton Mill People of the Piedmont.* New York: Columbia University Press, 1927.

Robinson, George O. *The Character of Quality: The Story of Greenwood Mills.* Columbia, SC: R. L. Bryan Co., 1964.

Simpson, William Hayes. *Life in Mill Communities.* Clinton, SC: Presbyterian College Press, 1941.

Spartanburg *Herald,* 1906-1955.

Thorpe, Richard. *Cotton Mill Cowboys.* Greenville, SC: Richwood Press, 1984.

Index